Communications
in Computer and Information Science 2130

Rationale

The CCIS series is devoted to the publication of proceedings of computer science conferences. Its aim is to efficiently disseminate original research results in informatics in printed and electronic form. While the focus is on publication of peer-reviewed full papers presenting mature work, inclusion of reviewed short papers reporting on work in progress is welcome, too. Besides globally relevant meetings with internationally representative program committees guaranteeing a strict peer-reviewing and paper selection process, conferences run by societies or of high regional or national relevance are also considered for publication.

Topics

The topical scope of CCIS spans the entire spectrum of informatics ranging from foundational topics in the theory of computing to information and communications science and technology and a broad variety of interdisciplinary application fields.

Information for Volume Editors and Authors

Publication in CCIS is free of charge. No royalties are paid, however, we offer registered conference participants temporary free access to the online version of the conference proceedings on SpringerLink (http://link.springer.com) by means of an http referrer from the conference website and/or a number of complimentary printed copies, as specified in the official acceptance email of the event.

CCIS proceedings can be published in time for distribution at conferences or as post-proceedings, and delivered in the form of printed books and/or electronically as USBs and/or e-content licenses for accessing proceedings at SpringerLink. Furthermore, CCIS proceedings are included in the CCIS electronic book series hosted in the SpringerLink digital library at http://link.springer.com/bookseries/7899. Conferences publishing in CCIS are allowed to use Online Conference Service (OCS) for managing the whole proceedings lifecycle (from submission and reviewing to preparing for publication) free of charge.

Publication process

The language of publication is exclusively English. Authors publishing in CCIS have to sign the Springer CCIS copyright transfer form, however, they are free to use their material published in CCIS for substantially changed, more elaborate subsequent publications elsewhere. For the preparation of the camera-ready papers/files, authors have to strictly adhere to the Springer CCIS Authors' Instructions and are strongly encouraged to use the CCIS LaTeX style files or templates.

Abstracting/Indexing

CCIS is abstracted/indexed in DBLP, Google Scholar, EI-Compendex, Mathematical Reviews, SCImago, Scopus. CCIS volumes are also submitted for the inclusion in ISI Proceedings.

How to start

To start the evaluation of your proposal for inclusion in the CCIS series, please send an e-mail to ccis@springer.com.

The realisation of this big international scientific event would not have been possible without the participation of independent reviewers. Therefore, special thanks go at this point to the more than 70 experts who were actively involved in improving the quality of the reviewed manuscripts. A huge thank you is extended at this time to: Agnieszka Iwanicka, Alena Haskova, Antonio Palacios-Rodríguez, Arif Das, Bård Ketil Engen, Cesar Alberto Collazos, Christopher Walker, Claudia Blanca Gonzales, Cristian Cechinel, Daniel Mara, Dominika Jagielska, Elma Selmanagic Lizde, Emmanouela Seiradaki, Francesco Sulla, Francisco Alcantud, Haris Memisevic, Hasan Saliu, Ismar Frango, Jakub Solecki, Jan Beseda, Jelena Maksimovic, Joanna Wnek-Gozdek, Julio Ruiz-Palmero, Katarzyna Potyrała, Katarzyna Smoter, Kristina Kovaitė, Laslo Horvath, Leen d'Haenens, Lisbet Rønningsbakk, Lucie Rohlikova, Lucie Rotenbornová, Małgorzata Bogunia-Borowska, Małgorzata Krzeczkowska, Małgorzata Michel, Marco di Furia, Maria Dardanou, Maria Faściszewska, Mariana Porta, Marianne Undheim, Melchor Gómez García , Michał Klichowski, Milan Klement, Monika Frania, Mykhailo Boichenko, Natalia Demeshkant, Natalia Walter, Nektarios Moumoutzis, Oleksandr Burov, Panagiota Babatsouli, Paweł Grygiel, Piotr Plichta, Plamena Zlatkova, Polixeni Arapi, Rachid Boudri, Ramune Kasepere, Richard Kabito, Sabina Civila de Dios, Sara Martins, Sedigheh Moghavvemi, Sheila Garcia Martin, Sławomir Trusz, Solfia Poulimenou, Solomon Sunday Oyelere, Sonia Magali Arteaga Sarmiento, Sylwia Galanciak, Sylwia Opozda-Suder, Tonje Hilde Giæver, Valentina Pennazio, Valeria Farinazzo Martins, Vladimir Costas, Yana Topolnyk, and Zsolt Simonka. Thank you for your support of NMP 2023 by participating in the preparation of double-blind reviews, which had a considerable impact on the overall publication.

The NMP 2023 conference was supported substantively by the InnoEduca research group from the University of Malaga (Spain). I would therefore like to express my gratitude to Prof. Julio Ruiz-Palmero, for the fruitful cooperation with Andalusian experts in media pedagogy. International collaboration is a defining feature of the NMP conference series, fitting in with the need for a global transfer of knowledge and skills in the digitalisation of education. Such an assumption was evident in the previous edition of NMP 2022 (Tomczyk, 2023), and has been further developed in the current one. Further events in the New Media Pedagogy series are also planned with the participation of prominent research centres carrying out implementations and diagnoses in the innovative use of ICT in education. More details about the new NMP are available at www.ict-education.pl.

Finally, I would like to express my special thanks to the National Agency for Academic Exchange (NAWA), which, within the framework of the Mieczysław Bekker grant (BPN/BKK/2022/1/00007/DEC/1), significantly supported the realisation of the international conference New Media Pedagogy 23.

March 2024   Łukasz Tomczyk

Reference

Tomczyk, Ł. (2023). New Media Pedagogy: Research Trends, Methodological Challenges and Successful Implementations. Communications in Computer and Information Science, vol. 1916. Springer Nature Switzerland. https://doi.org/10.1007/978-3-031-445 81-1

Łukasz Tomczyk

Editor

New Media Pedagogy

Research Trends, Methodological Challenges, and Successful Implementations

Second International Conference, NMP 2023
Cracow, Poland, November 21–23, 2023
Revised Selected Papers

 Springer

Organization

Chair of the Conference Board

Łukasz Tomczyk   Jagiellonian University, Poland

Scientific Conference Board

Hasan Arslan	Çanakkale Onsekiz Mart University, Turkey
Yuriy Bilan	Rzeszów University of Technology, Poland
Małgorzata Bogunia-Borowska	Jagiellonian University, Poland
Ludvik Eger	University of West Bohemia, Czech Republic
Maria Amelia Eliseo	Universidade Presbiteriana Mackenzie, Brazil
Francisco David Guillen-Gamez	University of Málaga, Spain
Nataliia Demeshkant	Pedagogical University of Cracow, Poland
Laura Fedeli	University of Macerata, Italy
Paul Flynn	University of Galway, Ireland
Judit García-Martín	Salamanca University, Spain
Anna Gaweł	Jagiellonian University, Poland
Ileana Maria Greca	Burgos University, Spain
Akhmad Habibi	University of Jambi, Indonesia
Leen d'Haenens	KU Leuven, Belgium
Tonje Hilde Giæver	OsloMet, Norway
Tomasz Huk	Silesian University, Poland
Agnieszka Iwanicka	Adam Mickiewicz University, Poland
Vicente J. Llorent	Cordoba University, Spain
Therese Keane	La Trobe University, Australia
Bård Ketil Engen	Oslo Metropolitan University, Norway
Michał Klichowski	Adam Mickiewicz University, Poland
Janina Kostkiewicz	Jagiellonian University, Poland
Jan Kříž	University of Hradec Králové, Czech Republic
Daniel Mara	"Lucian Blaga" University of Sibiu, Romania
Maria Lidia Mascia	University of Cagliari, Italy
Haris Memisevic	Sarajevo University, Bosnia & Herzegovina
Anders D. Olofsson	Umeå University, Sweden
Delfín Ortega-Sánchez	Burgos University, Spain
Julio Ruiz Palmero	University of Málaga, Spain
Maria Pietronilla Penna	University of Cagliari, Italy

Piotr Plichta	University of Wroclaw, Poland
Katarzyna Potyrała	Cracow University of Technology, Poland
Jacek Pyżalski	Adam Mickiewicz University, Poland
Roberta Renati	University of Cagliari, Italy
Natale Salvatore Bonfiglio	University of Cagliari, Italy
Fazilat Siddiq	University of South-Eastern Norway, Norway
Francisco Simões	CIS-IUL - Centro de Investigação e de Intervenção Social (ECSH), Portugal
Piotr Siuda	Kazimierz Wielki University in Bydgoszcz, Poland
Siri Sollied Madsen	Tromso University, Norway
Marek Sokołowski	University of Warmia and Mazury in Olsztyn, Poland
Solomon Sunday Oyelere	Luleå University of Technology, Sweden
Lazar Stošić	FAMNS, Serbia
Magdalena Szpunar	Silesian University, Poland
Arthur Tatnall	Victoria University, Australia
Łukasz Tomczyk (Chair of the Scientific Board)	Jagiellonian University, Poland
Giusi Toto	Foggia University, Italy
Hüseyin Uzunboylu	Near East University, Northern Cyprus
Natalia Walter	Adam Mickiewicz University, Poland
Michał Wierzchoń	Jagiellonian University, Poland
Ewa Ziemba	University of Economics in Katowice, Poland

Technical Program Committee

Łukasz Tomczyk (TPC Chair)	Jagiellonian University, Poland

TPC Members

Karina Blamowska	Jagiellonian University, Poland
Izabela Kielar	Jagiellonian University, Poland
Arif Das	Ataturk University, Turkey
Mariano Núñez-Flores	University of Córdoba, Spain

Contents

Teacher Digital and Media Competence in Cyber Security - A Perspective on Individual Resilience to Online Attacks

Łukasz Tomczyk[1](✉) (iD), Francisco David Guillén-Gámez[2] (iD),
and Vicente J. Llorent[3] (iD)

[1] Jagiellonian University, Stefana Batorego 12, 31-135 Kraków, Poland
lukasz.tomczyk@uj.edu.pl
[2] Malaga University, Blvr. Louis Pasteur, 25, 29071 Málaga, Spain
[3] Univeristy of Cordoba, Cordoba, Spain

Abstract. The aim of this article is to explore the current typology of teachers' digital competences in digital security from the perspective of individual experience. The article is an attempt to highlight the digital and media skills that relate to digital security arising from the profession - a profession of public trust. The subject matter analysed is linked to the need to minimise the scale of cyber-attacks on teachers resulting from the rapid development of various e-services, as well as to gaps in digital and media skills in this professional group. The study is the result of qualitative interviews conducted in the second half of 2023 among Polish in-service teachers. On the basis of the analysis and categorisation of statements proposed by Graneheim and Lundman, 11 components of digital and media competences enabling the improvement of the digital safety of in-service teachers were identified. Among the indications, the surveyed teachers highlighted issues such as: 1) finding and evaluating information, 2) the consideration of one's digital footprint, 3) the skilful use of social networking sites (SNSs), 4) securing access to data, 5) legal knowledge, 6) knowledge of the style of use of new media among young people, 7) implementing a restrictive new media use model, 8) lifelong learning, 9) digital hygiene, 10) outreach, and 11) a set of factors that complement digital competences. This article is part of the project "Digitally Secure Teacher" funded by the National Agency for Academic Exchange NAWA (Poland) within the framework of the M. Bekker national module.

Keywords: Teachers · digital safety · digital skills · cyber aggression · cyber attack · cyber violence · Poland · resilience

1 Introduction

Teacher digital competence has now become a point of interest for many researchers around the world [1, 2]. In the individual dimension, the ability of teachers to make effective use of the potential of information and communication technologies (ICT) is the starting point for understanding the digital transformation stage that Polish schools

Ł. Tomczyk (Ed.): NMP 2023, CCIS 2130, pp. 1–23, 2024.
https://doi.org/10.1007/978-3-031-63235-8_1

require. From the macro-social dimension of the implementation of ICT in schools, the discussion is about the necessity of slowing down the pressure to implement ICT in teaching and learning activities [3]. In recent years, both individual and school system dimensions have been the subject of much discussion among school-related stakeholders. This is due to the fact that we have entered a post-pandemic time in which the perspective of issues relating to how parents, teachers, and students use new media has changed [4].

Within the various discussions that intensified during the period of crisis e-learning, much emphasis was placed on the development of students' digital competences, changes to the core curriculum related to digital competences, ameliorating the issue of digital exclusion, improving the equipment of schools with new media, and in-depth reflection on the real possibilities of digital educational technologies [5, 6]. An important point in the discussions on the current stage of digitalisation is the attempt to constructively transfer the experience of crisis e-learning to the need to modernise teacher education in the wider context of the era of intensive development of the information society [7, 8], or the acceleration of the scale of phenomena assigned to the risk paradigm of media pedagogy [9]. The latter is currently dominated by the topic of young people's risk behaviour in cyberspace [10]. Within the framework of reducing ICT-mediated risk behaviours, the role of teachers is usually reduced to carrying out preventive actions - anticipating or resolving situations in which a young person is a perpetrator or victim of e-risks [11, 12].

In the literature related to the digitalisation of education or the prevention of ICT-mediated risk behaviours, the focus of action and research has shifted to a youngster [13]. Although this approach is important and valuable, it does not provide a holistic view of cyber security in the school setting. One of the many empirical gaps is the fragmented or outdated nature of research on teachers' digital security [14]. Such a state of affairs means that there are currently several gaps in the identification, for example, of the scale of the phenomena related to attacks on teachers in cyberspace [15]. Although there are general theoretical frameworks related to cyber security, e.g. DIGCOMP [16], and the fragmentary reports on attacks on teachers due to their profession, it is hard to find reports in the literature in this area that present an individual perspective of teachers' experiences.

Research that focuses on teachers' digital competences is currently being intensively conducted worldwide [17]. This is due to the fact that the ability to use ICT effectively has a significant impact on the effectiveness of teaching and learning processes in this era of the intense development of the information society [18–20]. Nevertheless, when analysing the components of digital competence, it is important to be aware that the use of hardware and software to achieve teaching objectives does not cover the entire definition of digital competence, which is also understood as the ability to understand how new media change how social groups work. In this last dimension, the whole set of knowledge and skills related to digital security plays a significant role [21].

An interesting example of research on digital competences is offered by the study 'DigComp 2.2: The Digital Competence Framework for Citizens - With new examples of knowledge, skills and attitudes', which clearly assumes that digital security for citizens is related to skills in the areas of: securing IT devices, protecting personal data and privacy, protecting health and well-being, and protecting the environment [22]. These four components related to digital competence can be differentiated by the level of proficiency achieved in any given area. Assumptions in the assessment of this area of digital competence are therefore consistent with the assessment of other digital competences, e.g. foreign language proficiency and mathematical skills. Digital competences, as the team representing the European Commission have pointed out, may vary somewhat from one profession to another, which is why when analysing teachers' digital competences it is worth referring to an additional theoretical framework, the Digital Competence Framework for Educators (DigCompEdu). Although the framework created by the European Commission is one of the most highly respected and favoured frameworks for digital competences, the issue of teachers' digital safety is not sufficiently highlighted and described in it. In DigCompEdu there is Sect. 6.4 Responsible use, where among the many tasks related to the effective use of ICT, the importance of actions to ensure physical, mental, and social well-being when using ICT is emphasised. It is also the teacher's role to assist students in developing their digital competences that enable them to limit their e-risks and therefore use cyberspace safely and responsibly [23]. As mentioned in the introduction, such an assumption is necessary due to the need to ameliorate the various negative phenomena to which students are exposed (e.g. cyberbullying, problematic Internet use, sexting, digital piracy, and identity theft, to name but a few). The aforementioned DigCompEdu framework is therefore clearly student-centric and does not ensure that digital safety is strengthened for the entire school ecosystem. Therefore, within the framework of digital safety-related analyses, there is a need to go beyond the typical perception of the phenomenon of digital safety only in a student-centric context and to pay attention to the safety issues briefly outlined in DigComp 2.2 [24, 25].

The topic of digital security is increasingly becoming the focus of IT experts [26, 27]. Digital security, like security in the offline space, is important due to the natural human need for psychological well-being. Exposure to various types of e-threats, e.g. aggression from other users of online services, identity theft, theft of logins and passwords, and online vilification, leads to a range of negative emotions and to negative psycho-physical consequences in the long term. Therefore, the need to achieve digital security exists in various professional groups and its sufficient level is particularly desirable in professions of public trust, to which the teaching profession belongs [28].

In pedagogy and media psychology, there has been a noticeable increase in research dedicated to the digital safety of young people [29] while ignoring the challenges faced by other elements of the school ecosystem. The lack of sufficient, up-to-date research dedicated to teachers' digital safety in selected countries means that this group is left isolated when faced with an online attack arising or resulting from their profession. The residual and outdated nature of the data relating to the CEE region [14, 15] means that it is currently difficult to state unequivocally what challenges teachers face in the situation of an online attack from students or parents. The lack of up-to-date data also makes it difficult to plan measures to support educators in the context of the various forms of attacks to which teachers are potentially exposed. In turn, the aforementioned theoretical frameworks, e.g. DigComp, do not provide an understanding of the mechanisms of attacks on teachers with respect to the specificities of the school environment. The factors cited therefore necessitate a research effort in which the student-centric perspective is complemented by the perspective of the teacher, who may also be targeted.

The present study is part of the discussion on the digital safety of teachers in Poland with a particular focus on the biographical experiences of educators and the resulting proposals for pedagogical practice. Based on the data collected among in-service teachers, the article categorises the statements as a basis for the development of a typology of digital competences to enhance digital security. The article proposes a direction for the development of teachers' digital competences in the field of cyber security, understood specifically in terms of limiting attacks on representatives of this professional group by students and their parents. The study is also in line with the need to remove the taboo topic that teachers, as representatives of a profession of public trust, are automatically protected on the Internet.

2 Methodology

2.1 Aim and Subject Matter

The aim of the research is to build a typology of digital competences focused on teachers' digital safety. The aim of the research is linked to paying particular attention to teachers' critical experiences of online attack due to their profession. The aim of the research is linked to the redefinition of important areas such as the ability to anticipate and minimise online threats, combined with processes in the school environment. The aim of the research goes beyond a simple diagnosis of digital skills, providing an opportunity to integrate recommendations into the theoretical framework of digital competences skills linked to real situations, the challenges faced by teachers.

The subject of the research in this article are the statements of teachers who agreed to participate in a survey carried out as part of the 'Digitally Secure Teacher' project, supported by the National Academic Exchange Agency under the Mieczysław Bekker grant (national component BPN/BKK/2022/1/00007/DEC/1). The subject of the research concerned the answers to an open question contained in an online questionnaire made available to active teachers from the Śląskie (Silesian) and Małopolskie (Lesser Poland) Voivodeships (Poland).

2.2 Research Procedure

The research was conducted in the second half of 2023. The research was carried out in an online format using an online questionnaire. Teachers participated in the study (N = 733) and provided answers on 1) the extent of attacks against them online due to their profession, 2) support strategies available in the school environment when an attack against a teacher occurs, 3) the types of skills, knowledge, and activities a teacher should have in order to be safe online. Due to the complexity of the questionnaire, as well as the breadth of the data obtained, each area was developed as an individual research report. This article presents the part related to the knowledge, skills, and activities that enhance the teacher's ability to protect themselves from attacks by students and parents.

The study used a qualitative data analysis strategy – the teachers' responses to biographically critical events relating to cyber attacks on themselves, and the fallout to those events. The theoretical basis developed by Graneheim and Lundman [30, 31] was used to analyse the teachers' statements. First, research material was collected from active teachers. Subsequently, the research material that met the criteria for analysis was separated by verifying that the responses obtained were thematically related to the research objective. In the next step, each statement was analysed and labelled according to emerging codes (type of skills, knowledge, and activities related to cyber security). At this point, it should be emphasised that the codes were not imposed top-down, but were constructed during the analysis of the statements. The next step was to group the codes according to consistency derived from similarities. The resulting categories were validated by an external expert (the co-author of the report) to confirm or redefine the resulting categories. The final results of the process were presented in the form of 11 categories, and characterised using teachers' statements. The entire research process is illustrated by Fig. 1.

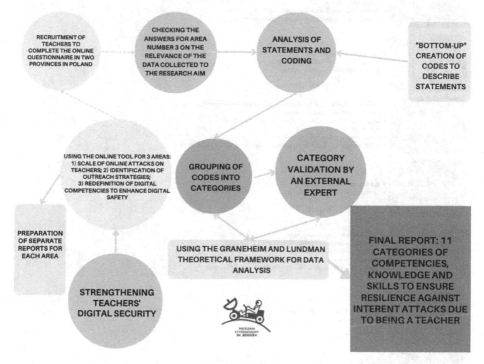

Fig. 1. Research Procedure for a Digitally Secure Teacher.

2.3 Ethics

The research was carried out in accordance with social research ethics with particular attention to the principles concerning the biographical analyses of crisis events [32]. As part of the research procedure, the teachers were informed about the purpose of the research, how the data would be processed, and the agency funding the research, and

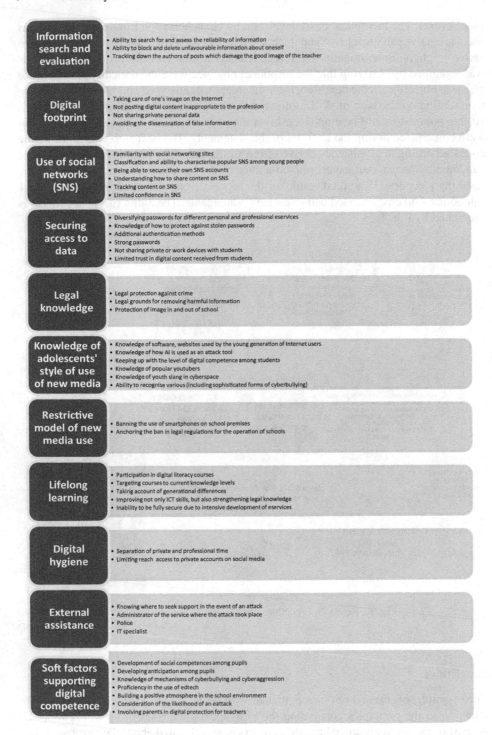

Fig. 2. Research Procedure for a Digitally Secure Teacher.

were given the opportunity to potentially contact the person responsible for designing the research questionnaire. The research tool (an online survey) did not include questions about personal details that would allow the identification of the respondent.

3 Results

The qualitative data collected allowed, through analysis and categorisation, the identification of 11 components of digital and media competences related to cyber security. The respondents referenced dimensions relating to: 1) searching for and evaluating information related to their digital security, 2) the consideration of their own digital footprint, which could become the basis for an attack, 3) the skilful use of SNS, 4) securing access to data both online and offline, 5) legal knowledge related to the protection of oneself in cyberspace due to one's profession, 6) the knowledge of the style of use of new media by young people, 7) the implementation of a restrictive model of use of smartphones and the Internet in the school ecosystem, 8) lifelong learning as a basis for keeping up with the prevention of e-risks; 9) improving one's own digital hygiene, 10) the ability to seek external help in the event of a crisis situation, and 11) understanding and noticing the set of factors that complement digital competences. The eleven categories derived from the respondents experiences of online attacks are illustrated in Fig. 2.

3.1 Searching for and Evaluating Information

The respondents highlighted issues related to information retrieval and the ability to evaluate and use information. Skills of this type are useful in many contemporary professions, accounting for the universality of the selected categories presented in the empirical section of this paper. When analysing statements from this category, attention should be paid not only to those activities that relate to simple information selection, but also to the ability to assess the reliability of information efficiently.

> *Communication and information competence - the ability to search for information on a given topic, select it, evaluate it critically, use it to solve current problems (R140, 41, F)*
>
> *Issues related to the creation, retrieval, processing, verification, selection, and use of information (R195, 44, F)*

Linked to the above indication at a relatively general level is the category of skills relating to finding the authors of false content. This activity is particularly valuable in a situation where a teacher is attacked. Such a critical incident, according to the respondents, should also be supported by the skills of identifying those who interact with defamatory content, as well as blocking and removing offensive posts.

> *Should freely and consciously navigate the internet and have the capacity to investigate who is publishing the content (R222, 44, F)*
>
> *Have the competence to quickly verify who creates messages, offensive texts, who reads and comments on them (R537, 55, F)*

Ability to remove dangerous and damaging passages about yourself (R668, 59, F)

Block such entries, locate whoever posted such an entry (513, 54, F)

Competence related to searching for and processing information is a basic skill to protect oneself in the online space. These skills are also the basis for building further skills to protect against more sophisticated forms of digital attacks.

3.2 Digital Footprint

The digital security of teachers requires the consideration of a number of factors that relate not only to simple forms of digital hardware security, but also to knowledge at the intersection of computer science and the social processes that occur in cyberspace. One such element is the issue relating to what is called one's digital footprint. In analysing the statements, it is clear that the respondents understand that the presence of a teacher in a social space can be observed by both students and their parents. Reflecting on the content that constitutes the teacher's digital footprint online is a protective factor against negative consequences, e.g. attacks from parents or students.

Thinking broadly about the content posted online and, above all, understanding how a teacher should take care of their data and image online (R174, 42, F)

Do not upload inappropriate photos on social media. Be mindful of event descriptions and comments on social media forums (R148, 42, F)

The teacher's digital footprint is also linked to the idea of protecting one's own personal data, or any other type of data that allow one to cause harm to a teacher. The skill associated with managing one's own data in the digital world is particularly important in a context where teacher data is linked to access to various services within the school's facilities.

The teacher should be careful when accessing different websites, not to give out his/her data (R232, 45, F)

Being able to navigate the digital world and knowing that on many portals you 'pay' with your data would be very useful (R284, 46, F)

The digital footprint should also be considered, as suggested by R32, in the context of the important media competence component of being critical of the transmission of unverified or erroneous information. The dissemination of damaging information in cyberspace strikes at the authority of the teacher and at the same time generates an image of a person lacking in elementary competence, one who is susceptible to fake news.

Knowledge of how social media works (avoiding chain letters, passing on unverified information, etc.) (R32, 32, F)

Every online processing activity, even trivial actions such as liking a post on the Internet or passing on information, leaves a digital footprint. Knowledge of how one's digital footprint is generated is not only an indicator of the level of media and digital competence, but an element that avoids many problematic situations in which teachers' online activities (private as well as professional) can be linked to the ethics of their profession.

3.3 Social Networking Sites (SNS)

According to the respondents, the careful use of SNSs is the key to being safe in cyberspace. This state of affairs is due to the fact that, for students, SNSs are their primary communication environment in cyberspace. SNSs are a source of opinions and a kind of place where different kinds of interactions take place. SNSs can therefore be a place for both positive interactions as well as a platform for potential attacks on others, including educators.

Social media literacy, knowledge of popular online portals (R6, 24, F)

Above all, a basic knowledge of social networks (R106, 40, F)

Due to the wide selection of SNSs, in the opinion of the teacher quoted below, it is necessary to have not only knowledge of the existence of such services, but also the ability to characterise individual e-services of this type. The digitally secure teacher in R318's opinion should have detailed knowledge that enables them to understand the specifics of the particular e-space in which students currently operate.

Know and understand how the different SNSs differ (what is the difference between, for example, sending a photo on Snapchat and posting someone's photo to a group on Messenger) (R318, 48, M)

Among the key skills involved in operating an SNS, there is also the issue of how to properly secure access. Regardless of your profession, account takeover through identity theft is a problematic situation.

Ability to secure their SNS accounts and operate these portals (what they share and with whom) (R240, 45, F)

The next two statements quoted below contradict each other, but create an interesting approach among educators to the circulation of digital content on the Internet. R449 points out that educators should keep track of SNS content in the context of possible attacks that may target themselves. R474, on the other hand, emphasises that educators are not able to detect all the negative information about themselves on the SNS due to the specificity of this type of e-service. These mutually exclusive approaches create two types of attitudes towards problematic situations mediated by new media.

The teacher should skillfully follow the SNS (R449, 52, F)

We are unable to keep track of the SNS and the entries of our students-we do not have the time to do so (R474, 53, F)

The issue of minimising potential attacks in the SNS space is outlined by R224, who emphasises the need to limit one's trust in people, content, links, and invitations received in the SNS. This type of approach is not only found in the SNS context, but is also typical in other e-services.

Know and apply the principles of limited trust in SNS (R224, 44, F)

Whether teachers are active users of SNSs or not, knowledge of such e-services appears to be considered an elementary skill. Moreover, in line with the general statements made earlier, a teacher in a profession of public trust is obliged to maintain standards of expression in public places, which is what SNSs are today. Therefore, knowledge of how to function as an SNS user should be combined with the ability to consider one's digital footprint.

3.4 Security of Data and Access to Data

Securing access to data appears to be one of the activities that prevents the occurrence of situations related to unauthorised access to key e-services. Taking care to secure access to private as well as professional e-services avoids situations where a teacher's identity is taken over, which is one form of cyber-attack by students.

Being able to secure their data online when using different types of learning platforms or when sending emails or sharing materials with students (R116, 40, F)

Ability to take care of account passwords (R9, 26, F)

When analysing the statements illustrating the category of securing access to data, it is important to draw attention to the statements of R17 and R379. Both emphasise that attacks on teachers require basic knowledge of how to steal passwords. Such actions rely on both social engineering and the use of specialised software. In addition, it is important to be aware that files sent by students may carry malware aimed at taking over access to the digital devices used by teachers.

Knowledge of the profiles of hacking attacks on a company account (R17, 29, M)

Limited trust in material sent by students in email correspondence or on educational platforms (e.g. TEAMS) (R379, 50, M)

Another type of security measure that is not only typical for teachers is the use of strong or complex passwords. This action should also be reinforced by changing passwords for services that contain sensitive data (e.g. e-journals with school grades). The following responses therefore clearly highlight the importance of basic skills that do not require complex digital competences to effectively protect teachers from digital attacks.

Additional privacy protection passwords (R45, 34, F)

Know the types of security and follow the security rules, e.g. use a strong password, change it (R321, 48, F)

Using strong security passwords or changing them frequently (R331, 48, F)

An important element in minimizing the risk of theft of private and professional data is to secure digital devices against third-party access. This action makes it impossible to simply copy data or install spyware. This action does not require specialised digital skills, but results in an effective physical block against access to sensitive data.

This is not about digital competence just common sense. No prudent person shares their phone number with students or their parents. Similarly with social media (R261, 46, F)

Account hijacking is a major challenge that teachers face, though the same is broadly true across society. However, in the situation of unauthorised access to private accounts, e.g. work email, SNS, or private data (e.g. photos on a computer), the situation causes negative feelings for the teacher. Such a privacy incident not only involves a breach of social rules, but clearly lowers the authority of the teacher as a digitally competent person.

3.5 Knowledge of Legal Aspects

Protecting teachers from online attacks and dealing with problematic situations requires that kind of knowledge that should be classified as legal. Cyber attacks on teachers can take many forms. The ability to link the attack to a consequence for the perpetrator's action appears to be key in resolving the situation and providing a sense of security. The ability to remove content that damages a teacher's image, whether in the form of comments or images (e.g. photomontages, photographs taken without consent), is a basic skill in increasing one's sense of digital safety.

Legislation on online crime and dissemination of images (R12, 28, F)

The ability to report, for example, a post that violates one's good image. But above all, teachers should have a range of non-digital competences, e.g. knowledge of the law (R42, 34, F)

Legally guaranteed - and respected - right to the protection of one's image in the performance of official activities and in private situations (R73, 37, F)

The above responses clearly underline that digital competence is not sufficient to prevent attacks against teachers. Due to the complexity of the phenomena of cyberbullying and cyberaggression, there is a need for specialised knowledge. Legal knowledge makes it possible to accurately determine not only the severity of the incident, but also to take the appropriate steps to remove the threat to the teacher.

3.6 Implementation of Restrictiveness in the School Environment

One way to limit the ability of students to commit cyber attacks against their teachers – certainly during school hours – is to limit their use of smartphones. The introduction of restrictions in this area is a physical element that offsets the potential threat to teachers and other students. This assumption is based on the fact that smartphones offer unlimited possibilities for audio recording and video creation, together with the rapid distribution of such material on the Internet.

Ban on bringing a phone into the premises. I am in favour of restricting the use of smartphones (R23, 31, F)

Total legal prohibition preventing use on educational premises (R182, 42, M)

A ban on phones in school would partially fulfil some of the purpose of this topic (R714, 63, F)

The restrictive approach creates a sense of security against selected forms of attacks (e.g. video recording, image creation, content distribution). However, it does not provide full protection against all the types of attack that may be carried out beyond the school premises. The restrictive model is currently being implemented in many countries as a remedy for some of the negative phenomena mediated by ICT.

3.7 Knowledge of Young People's Style of Use of New Media

According to the respondents, understanding how young people use new media is a protective factor for the digital safety of teachers. Knowledge of the software, websites, and social networks that young people use allows for an understanding of their living environment. Knowing the specifics of the digital environment is an input condition for a full understanding of both positive and negative situations that are mediated by digital information channels, which are one of the main communication tools in this group.

The teacher should have some knowledge of the applications used by the pupils, possess conversation and communication skills, know the dangers of the Internet (R26, 31, F)

He or she should keep up to date with what teenagers are living, keep up with them and take an interest in their lives, including online (R84, 39, F)

Know the apps/portals that young people are using and be aware of what they are watching, listening to-what is current (R89, 38, F)

Teachers now also include issues relating to artificial intelligence (AI) among their basic knowledge of styles of use of new media. The intensive development of AI, which can be a relatively uncomplicated tool for harming a teacher, is forcing this group into completely new areas of cyberspace, which are characterised by great dynamism.

Above all, he should have knowledge of application development, new technologies related to AI (R32, 31, M)

Know the applications students use, have an idea of instant messaging, artificial intelligence and know how to use them. The teacher must keep up with the students and their competences (R54, 34, F)

Knowledge of styles of use refers not only to aspects related to software and hardware use among young people, but also to social aspects. This knowledge can become crucial not only in building authority, but also in knowing about the negative authority figures that may shape risky ICT-mediated behaviour patterns.

Must impress students with greater knowledge of technology and be familiar with current fashion websites (R662, 59, F)

They should know the online personalities important to them, e.g. YouTubers (R687, 61, F)

Knowledge of styles of ICT use also relates to the vocabulary used by today's young people in the context of the activities they undertake in the online world. If a teacher is unaware of the words that young people use to talk about different forms of online attack, they will not suspect the danger in many of the things they hear their students talking about – sometimes quite openly.

They need to know what is meant by cyberbullying; what form it can take. It would be good for the teacher to be familiar with the language used by young people so that he or she can better spot online aggression (R687, 61, F)

Discernment of the type of games and social media used by young people, discernment of contemporary phenomena of aggression and online threats (R662, 59, F)

Cyberspace has become a natural environment for the socialization of young people. In the online space, it is now possible to notice many phenomena objectively assigned to the risk paradigm or the opportunity paradigm. Knowledge of these becomes a starting point not only for understanding today's generation, but also makes it possible to strengthen the overall level of digital safety in the school environment.

3.8 Lifelong Learning

For the respondents, acquiring new skills that are useful in enhancing digital safety is a remedy for problematic situations involving attacks against teachers. Teachers belong to a profession whose members are constantly improving their own skills both in terms of supporting learning and teaching processes and in terms of educational issues. In the context of online attacks, the respondents point out that digital competences are differentiated by metric age and rapid socio-technical transformations.

Knowledge of digital competences should be increased every year through special courses/meetings/presentations as the world is evolving very fast and such refresher courses are needed to keep up with it (R34, 33, F)

Keeping abreast of current information on the current risks associated with children and young people's use of the Internet (R140, 41, F)

The teacher should keep up to date with technology as much as possible, students are always 10 steps ahead anyway, so the teacher should at least keep up with the news (R345, 48, F)

The respondents emphasise that the teaching group is characterised by varying levels of knowledge about digital safety. Generational differences mean that even intensive reinforcement of knowledge and skills cannot bridge generational differences in the style of use of new media. R 170 points out that training programmes should be tailored to the level of digital knowledge and skills of educators.

> *He should take an annual refresher course culminating in an examination. Prior to the course, he should take an entrance test on the extent to which he is unfamiliar with modern technology. At 50, he should be able to retire or get a position that does not require him to be better at these blocks than his students. I think I know close to 300 teachers, and no teacher around 50, not even a computer scientist, can grasp this subject better than the students (R170, 43, F)*

> *I am concerned that students are more competent and proficient in the use of multimedia, the older generation of teachers has a problem with this (R453, 52, F)*

Among the training forms of support, the respondents highlight several possibilities that clarify the general need in this area. R35 points out that training to improve digital skills should be provided by recognised experts who specialise in media pedagogy. In turn, R81 emphasises that teachers need to supplement their knowledge of the legal consequences for perpetrators of cyber attacks.

> *Take part in EduAction training with Prof. [name anonymised] (R35, 33, F)*

> *Undergo appropriate training, know what the legal consequences are for students (R81, 38, F)*

One respondent points out a fact related to the time-consuming nature of activities classified as Lifelong Learning (LLL). As with other dimensions of digital competence, learning about the mechanisms of ICT-mediated attacks requires knowledge of many digital tools, communication platforms, and mechanisms for spreading information, as well as ways to protect oneself. For those with low competence in this area, learning more is seen as a time- and energy-consuming activity.

> *It's hard to say it's all changing so fast it's hard to keep up and consumes too much time (R86, 38, F)*

One teacher denies LLL issues. The intensive development of information society services means that, despite the strengthening of digital competences and knowledge of digital security, the average teacher improving their own skills is not able to fully protect themselves against this phenomenon.

> *I am afraid that, despite the training we have received, we are still exposed to this phenomenon (R503, 54, F)*

LLL is a universal category that, regardless of the area under analysis, is a natural activity for selected professional groups. Given the socio-technical changes taking place, including the rise of various e-threats to which teachers were previously not exposed, the need for LLL is clear as a form of preparation for educators against a potential attack from students or other groups.

3.9 Digital Hygiene

An interesting theme that has not been found very often in the literature so far is the issue of digital hygiene. The ability to take adequate care of one's well-being due to intensive ICT use, according to two respondents, is an issue that strengthens educators' digital security. Digital hygiene, in this case, is the ability to limit screen time, as well as to separate private and professional life in the context of using a variety of e-services, or interacting with students during non-working time.

He should take care of his digital hygiene himself (R95, 39, F)

Be able to separate work from leisure time and limit the reach of their accounts so that students don't find us on FB and write to us using various apps. (R99, 39, F)

Skills related to setting boundaries around the use of ICT are becoming one of the key competences regardless of profession. However, given the specific nature of the teaching profession, as well as the environment in which educators work, it makes sense to pay more and more attention to the issues of teacher-student communication outside the official timeframe set by working hours. Limiting the inclusion of students in private information spaces as also falls under the umbrella term of digital hygiene. It is important to be aware that the issue of digital hygiene among teachers has been little explored to date and is in itself an empirical gap.

3.10 External Assistance

In many crisis situations, irrespective of the distinction between online and offline spheres, external support is one of the elements that enable the problem to be solved. This is due to the fact that crises such as a cyber-attack can be complex, long-lasting, and require specialised knowledge and skills. In the case of the analysed behaviours that educators may experience due to their profession, attacks can be so varied in nature that it is unlikely that any one teacher can protect themselves against everything – and thus it becomes crucial that teachers know they can count on internal support. Therefore, having the knowledge of who can offer such help is the key to solving a problematic situation. Of course, this knowledge, as R137 points out, should be underpinned by the ability to classify attacks due to the aspects set out in the legal framework.

I don't think a teacher needs to have all the competences - they should know who to go to and ask for help (R66, F, 36)

Know where to find support and where to report these violations (R102, 39, F)

Knowing where to seek support, who to report abuse to. Awareness of what is a criminal act when boundaries are crossed. Externally assisted wellbeing - coping with crisis situations becomes key for the teacher here (R137, 41, F)

Should be able to identify violent situations and know where to report them (R8, 26, F)

As one respondent noted, help should be sought at the point of the attack. In the first instance, in the case of a breach of the rules of a particular e-service (e.g. a social network), it is necessary to notify the administrator of the situation. In the event of a breach of legal boundaries or a feeling of insecurity, support can also be mobilised via law enforcement.

Knowledge of how to report and get help in cyberbullying situations from the portal/network administrator and the Police (R191, 42, F)

Another type of support is the guidance obtained from IT specialists. Given that cyber attacks on teachers can be carried out using non-standard techniques and tools and leave a permanent digital footprint, such a situation can present a competence challenge for a teacher with a lack of specialisation in IT. The solution to such a situation is counseling related to solving the problem using the knowledge and skills of school IT specialists or experts from outside the workplace.

The teacher should have contact with a computer professional. A computer professional knows how to deal with dangerous phenomena on the web. Contact with people who are professionally involved in computing provides important information in such a situation (R183, 43, F)

The form of support presented is an example that teachers' competence and knowledge are not always sufficient to solve the problem. In the hypothetical situation of an attack, social, legal, and competence support is available from a number of external actors through both formal and informal counselling routes.

3.11 Soft Factors Complementing Digital Competence

The above-mentioned categories form a closed set of skills related to digital and media competences which can be developed through professional training, pedagogical improvement, or self-education. Digital and media competences are the basis for digital safety, which itself is a boundary condition. Another type of preventive action is to pay attention to the soft factors that shape an appropriate value system that protects teachers. The importance of soft aspects is also highlighted due to the lack of technical and legal protection against all the potential types of attack that teachers may face.

To PREVENT (cyber)violence/aggression you need social competences more than digital competences (R247, 45, F)

We cannot keep up with the popularity of more and more new applications, even specialised law enforcement agencies cannot keep up. Therefore, counteraction should be based on psychological competence, not digital competence (R312, 48, F)

According to R282, the students' disposition to engage in ICT-mediated attacks can be reduced by developing the students' emotional sensitivity. An effective method in this area is to create situations in which students are forced to anticipate certain negative situations by stepping into a role. Among the soft factors related to attacks on teachers, the issue of having knowledge about the mechanisms of violence and aggression including those mediated by ICT also emerges. Such knowledge is crucial to understanding this kind of problematic behaviour.

In my opinion, it is mainly to deflect the situation and show that cyberbullying hurts. Also, learning to let go rather than commenting on everything (R282, 47, F)

Know the sources of cyberbullying: behavioural, social, relevant developmental psychology relating to adolescence (R221, 44, F)

According to R719, teachers who are proficient in the use of digital educational technologies in a variety of professional activities are automatically classified by students as having a high level of digital competence. Proficiency in the use of digital educational technologies may be a protective factor against attacks on the teacher in this case.

Pupils knowing that the teacher is proficient in the use of an electronic diary, digital textbooks, uses computer programmes in the classroom, is aware of the ways to communicate online are certainly more cautious. They feel that such a teacher is not defenseless against their attacks and they are not anonymous (R719, 64, F)

Building prevention ahead of attacks against teachers, according to R290, should involve forming positive relationships with students. A values-based attitude becomes a protective factor in this case, as well as shaping the school climate in a positive way.

Always relationships, honesty, emphasising their dignity and that of their students. No one hates a teacher who is an OK person (R290, 48, F)

Another type of soft area is the consideration of the probability calculus in which teachers are currently under attack on the Internet. Such a phenomenon regardless of different types of conditions can occur in any school environment.

Above all, be aware that such phenomena happen and can happen to anyone. (R144, 42, F)

However, despite the lack of a real impact on minimising the selected types of attacks on teachers, there is a need to consider additional stakeholders who are able to reduce negative phenomena. In the case of responses R198 and R262, the focus here shifts to parents or legal guardians, whose responsibility it is to set boundaries in the way their children use ICT.

Unfortunately, the teacher has no control over the aggressive content that students send each other on social media after lessons. Parents need to control this. Teachers can only organise talks on the subject, inviting specialists in this field to school. Teachers cannot control what students do online. That is what parents are for (R198, 44, F)

Ideally, parents should be in control of their children. Then the focus will be shifted from the teacher to the parent. Why is it again the teacher who has to counteract? (R262, 46, M)

The soft aspects presented are complementary to ICT-related skills and knowledge. Addressing the social aspects of ICT-mediated violence and aggression allows us to go beyond the technocratic model of digital security, in which high digital literacy and e-services play a leading role in minimising negative behaviour..

4 Discussion

The accelerated advance in the use of ICT in all areas of society highlights the imperative need for teachers to acquire strong cybersecurity skills with the purpose of guaranteeing a safe and secure digital environment in the educational process. The purpose of this study was to identify the digital competences that teachers must possess regarding digital security based on personal experiences, in order for this to serve as a help to other teachers, and consequently, minimize possible cyberattacks and also reduce possible gaps in media skills.

From the qualitative review of the interviews carried out with the teachers, it is evident that the first aspect to highlight is the ability to search for and evaluate information critically and reliably online, as Tomczyk [33] also recommends. In this way, it will be possible not only to safeguard the integrity of the information published on the Internet, and consequently to be able to protect oneself against possible online threats through fake news [34], but also be able to block and report those authors who publish negative information that may affect their reputation as a teacher.

The second component is related to the digital security of teachers, their digital footprint on the network, and the protection of personal data to avoid possible negative repercussions. In this sense, good practices must be oriented towards carefully reflecting on the information or personal opinions published on the Internet (for example, forums or social networks) which may be accessible to the rest of the educational community through forums and social networks. Incidentally, and as recommended by Huang et al. [35], "Professionalism is imperative – if you wouldn't say it in a social or work setting, don't say it online, in the most public of forums" (p. 65). In short, what is shared online can have considerable public reach and affect the perception of the teacher as a professional.

The third component highlighted by the teachers focuses on the importance of using social networks from the point of view of online security. Although social networks are fundamental for teachers' communication [36], they can also be platforms for possible attacks since, as Gallego-Arrufat et al. [37] note, there are many teachers who carry out digital practices which entail risk such as sharing information or inappropriate content, or even not using secure passwords on their digital profiles. Therefore, as Buchanan [38] states, it is crucial that teachers know how to ensure secure access, take care of their own digital footprint, and protect their identity in an environment where account theft is a constant concern.

The fourth aspect was related to taking care of data security and secure access to digital services. Kubacka et al. [39] emphasize the importance of protecting yourself from documents which may include all kinds of viruses, trojans, spyware, or ransomware, in our case, coming from students to the teaching community. To combat this type of cybercriminal activity, Pusey & Sadera [40] highlight the need for teachers to acquire skills to manage these situations and protect their data online, both on learning platforms or when interacting with students through email [41]. But in addition to having practical skills in this matter, teachers point out that a strong knowledge of the legislation on online crime and image protection is also necessary (the fifth component in the study). Sometimes it is not enough to only have skills in safeguarding digital integrity; the possession of specialized knowledge in cybersecurity laws [42] is vital, since this can affect the teacher's digital footprint, both in public aspects and private.

The sixth component was the implementation of restrictions in the school environment regarding the use of smartphones with the purpose of mitigating the risk of cyberattack. Faced with this issue, Podila et al. [43] does not suggest such restrictive policies, but rather good practices that educationally promote the safe and ethical use of technology in educational centers.

The seventh aspect was the understanding of the style of use of digital media by young people. Familiarity with the digital platforms, applications, and social networks used by this demographic allows educators to enter their virtual environment, which will facilitate the identification and addressing of possible cyber attacks against themselves. Furthermore, the inclusion of topics related to artificial intelligence (AI) in the repertoire of basic knowledge of teachers shows the need to stay up-to-date in a dynamic cyberspace where students can carry out cyber attacks against teachers with fake images created with AI.

The eighth approach is the need to carry out lifelong learning with the aim of acquiring new skills, especially in the area of digital security, to address the increasing challenges of online attacks. To achieve this, it is necessary to promote a culture of cybersecurity [44] through the many educational contexts in all their forms (formal, non-formal, and informal), as well as through national programs to increase awareness about cybersecurity [45], since in this way, this training will be a beneficial tool aimed at complementing the failure of technical solutions to address all the specific vulnerabilities in cyberspace. However, to integrate this cybernetic culture into the educational organization of the centers, and subsequently developed into training programs, it is necessary that this be previously established by the corresponding administrations in the different cybersecurity curricula [46].

The ninth aspect was digital hygiene, which is a relatively new issue and is still emerging in the scientific literature. However, there are some studies which underline the importance of this concept and its implications for personal and professional well-being [47]. For example, several researchers have examined the impact of excessive screen time on mental and physical health, especially in young people [48], with the need to establish limits on screen time and promote a healthy balance between online and offline activities, as stated by Tamilarasi [49], in our case, with the teaching community.

The last two components are more related to external components than to teachers' digital skills. The first is related to soft skills where social, emotional, and moral skills seem to be able to provide a more effective response than digital skills themselves to the challenge of the proliferation of cyberattacks [50]. Tolga et al. [51] reflect on the development of emotional sensitivity among students as a crucial component to strengthen the ability to protect themselves against various forms of ICT-mediated attacks. However, if these skills are not sufficient to address the problem of cyberattacks on teachers, it is essential to resort to external assistance with specialized knowledge (the last element highlighted by teachers). The idea of seeking external assistance with specialized knowledge when necessary reflects a cautious and collaborative attitude in approaching difficult situations, which could be beneficial in an educational and broader context.

5 Conclusions

The accelerated advance of ICT in society highlights just how critical the need is for teachers to acquire strong cybersecurity skills that ensure safe digital environments in the educational process. The identification of 11 key components of digital security competences, based on teachers' experiences, provides valuable guidance for preventing cyberattacks and reducing gaps in media skills. It is crucial to recognize the importance of the skills to search for and evaluate information online, protect one's digital footprint, operate social networks safely, and protect personal data. In addition, the need to understand and address the use of digital media by young people, promote a culture of cybersecurity in educational environments, and recognize the importance of soft skills in preventing cyberattacks is highlighted. Ultimately, collaboration and continuous learning, along with seeking specialized external assistance when necessary, are essential elements in effectively addressing cybersecurity challenges in education.

Acknowledgments. The study was conducted in accordance with the Declaration of Helsinki, and approved by the NAWA (BPN/BKK/2022/1/00007/DEC/1). The article is a part of the project funded by the National Agency for Academic Exchange (NAWA) under the Bekker programme (country component).

References

1. Tomczyk, Ł, Fedeli, L. (eds.): Digital Literacy for Teachers. Lecture Notes in Educational Technology. Springer, Singapore (2022). https://doi.org/10.1007/978-981-19-1738-7
2. Santos, A.R.P., Pérez-Garcias, A., Mesquida, A.D.: Formación en competencia digital docente: validación funcional del modelo TEP. Innoeduca. Int. J. Technol. Educ. Innov. **9**(1), 39–52 (2023). https://doi.org/10.24310/innoeduca.2023.v9i1.15191
3. Vlachopoulos, D., Thorkelsdóttir, R.B., Schina, D., Jónsdóttir, J.G.: Teachers' experience and perceptions of sustainable digitalization in school education: an existential phenomenological study of teachers in Romania, Greece, Cyprus, Iceland, and The Netherlands. Sustainability **15**(18), 13353 (2023)
4. Walter, N., Pyżalski, J.: Lessons learned from Covid-19 emergency remote education. Adaptation to crisis distance education of teachers by developing new or modified digital competences. In: Tomczyk, Ł, Fedeli, L. (eds.) Digital Literacy for Teachers, pp. 7–23. Springer, Singapore (2022). https://doi.org/10.1007/978-981-19-1738-7_2
5. Long, T.: Smart classroom in the era of education informatization 2.0. Int. J. Educ. Hum. **12**(2), 279–282 (2024). https://doi.org/10.54097/sm67dx71
6. Chauhan, D., Singh, C., Rawat, R., Chouhan, M.: Conversational AI applications in Ed-tech industry: an analysis of its impact and potential in education. In: Conversational Artificial Intelligence, pp. 411–433 (2024)

7. Koutska, I.: Tecnología educativa 'introducida' por la pandemia COVID-19. Innoeduca. Int. J. Technol. Educ. Innov. **9**(2), 115–133 (2023). https://doi.org/10.24310/innoeduca.2023.v9i2. 15481

8. Oguguo, B., Ezechukwu, R., Nannim, F., Offor, K.: Analysis of teachers in the use of digital resources in online teaching and assessment in COVID times. Innoeduca. Int. J. Technol. Educ. Innov. **9**(1), 81–96 (2023). https://doi.org/10.24310/innoeduca.2023.v9i1.15419

9. Łukasz, T.: Research trends in media pedagogy: between the paradigm of risk and the paradigm of opportunity. Int. J. Cogn. Res. Sci. Eng. Educ. (IJCRSEE) **9**(3), 399–406 (2021). https://doi.org/10.23947/2334-8496-2021-9-3-399-406

10. Smahel, D., et al.: EU Kids Online 2020: Survey results from 19 countries. EU Kids Online (2020). http://hdl.handle.net/20.500.12162/5299

11. Güllü, H., Karahan, E., Akçay, A.O.: A comprehensive investigation of cyberbullying and cyber victimization among secondary school students. Educ. Inf. Technol. **28**(10), 12633–12650 (2023). https://doi.org/10.1007/s10639-023-11687-8

12. Llorent, V.J., Díaz-Chaves, A., Zych, I., Twardowska-Staszek, E., Marín-López, I.: Bullying and cyberbullying in Spain and Poland, and their relation to social, emotional and moral competencies. Sch. Ment. Heal. **13**, 535–547 (2021). https://doi.org/10.1007/s12310-021-09473-3

13. Zych, I., Llorent, V.J.: Bias-based cyberbullying in Spanish adolescents and its relation to social and emotional competencies and technology abuse. J. Early Adolesc. **43**(1), 37–58 (2021). https://doi.org/10.1177/02724316211020365

14. Kopecký, K., Szotkowski, R.: Cyberbullying, cyber aggression and their impact on the victim - The teacher. Telematics Inform. **34**(2), 506–517 (2017). https://doi.org/10.1016/j.tele.2016. 08.014

15. Kamil, K., René, S.: Specifics of cyberbullying of teachers in Czech schools - a national research. Inform. Educ. **16**(1), 103–119 (2017). https://doi.org/10.15388/infedu.2017.06

16. Reisoğlu, İ, Çebi, A.: How can the digital competences of pre-service teachers be developed? Examining a case study through the lens of DigComp and DigCompEdu. Comput. Educ. **156**, 103940 (2020)

17. Guillén-Gámez, F.D., Mayorga-Fernández, M.J., Álvarez-García, F.J.: A study on the actual use of digital competence in the practicum of education degree. Technol. Knowl. Learn. **25**, 667–684 (2020)

18. Guillén-Gámez, F.D., Mayorga-Fernández, M.J., Bravo-Agapito, J., Escribano-Ortiz, D.: Analysis of teachers' pedagogical digital competence: identification of factors predicting their acquisition. Technol. Knowl. Learn. **26**, 481–498 (2021)

19. Şimşek, A.S., Ateş, H.: The extended technology acceptance model for Web 2.0 technologies in teaching. Innoeduca. Int. J. Technol. Educ. Innov. **8**(2), 165–183 (2022). https://doi.org/ 10.24310/innoeduca.2022.v8i2.15413

20. Stosic, L., Dermendzhieva, S., Tomczyk, L.: Information and communication technologies as a source of education. World J. Educ. Technol.: Current Issues **12**(2), 128–135 (2020)

21. Tomczyk, Ł: What do teachers know about digital safety? Comput. Sch. **36**(3), 167–187 (2019)

22. Vuorikari, R., Kluzer, S., Punie, Y.: DigComp 2.2: The Digital Competence Framework for Citizens - With new examples of knowledge, skills and attitudes. Publications Office of the European Union, Luxembourg (2022). https://doi.org/10.2760/115376

23. Punie, Y., Redecker, C.: European Framework for the Digital Competence of Educators: DigCompEdu. Publications Office of the European Union, Luxembourg: (2017) https://doi. org/10.2760/178382

24. Svelec-Juricic, D., Bulic, M.: Personal cyber security management: based on the example of masters of education. In: Economic and Social Development: Book of Proceedings, pp. 211–220 (2022)

25. Biškupić, I.O.: Digital strategies in higher education-from digital competences to digital transformation. In: EDULEARN22 Proceedings, pp. 8675–8684. IATED (2022)
26. Dodel, M., Mesch, G.: Inequality in digital skills and the adoption of online safety behaviors. Inf. Commun. Soc. **21**(5), 712–728 (2018)
27. Huda, M., et al.: From digital ethics to digital partnership skills: driving a safety strategy to expand the digital community? In: Digital Transformation for Business and Society, pp. 292–310. Routledge, London (2023)
28. Tomczyk, Ł., Potyrała, K..: Digital safety of children and young people in the perspective of media pedagogy. Wydawnictwo Naukowe Uniwersytetu Pedagogicznego, Kraków (2019)
29. Vandoninck, S., d'Haenens, L.: Children's online coping strategies: rethinking coping typologies in a risk-specific approach. J. Adolesc. **45**, 225–236 (2015)
30. Graneheim, U.H., Lundman, B.: Qualitative content analysis in nursing research: concepts, procedures and measures to achieve trustworthiness. Nurse Educ. Today **24**(2), 105–112 (2004)
31. Graneheim, U.H., Lindgren, B.M., Lundman, B.: Methodological challenges in qualitative content analysis: a discussion paper. Nurse Educ. Today **56**, 29–34 (2017)
32. Dubas, E.: Andragogical biography research-scopes, difficulties, ethics of the researcher (selected aspects). In: Dubas, E., Stelmaszczyk, J. (eds.) Biographies and learning, "Biography and biography research", vol. 4. Wydawnictwo Uniwersytetu Łódzkiego, Łódź (2015)
33. Tomczyk, Ł: Skills in the area of digital safety as a key component of digital literacy among teachers. Educ. Inf. Technol. **25**(1), 471–486 (2020). https://doi.org/10.1007/s10639-019-099 80-6
34. Al Zou'bi, R.M.: The impact of media and information literacy on students' acquisition of the skills needed to detect fake news. J. Media Literacy Educ. **14**(2), 58–71 (2022). https://doi.org/10.23860/JMLE-2022-14-2-5
35. Huang, R.H., et al.: Personal data and privacy protection in online learning: guidance for students, teachers and parents, pp. 1–109. Smart Learning Institute of Beijing Normal University, Beijing (2020)
36. Greenhow, C., Askari, E.: Learning and teaching with social network sites: a decade of research in K-12 related education. Educ. Inf. Technol. **22**, 623–645 (2017). https://doi.org/10.1007/s10639-015-9446-9
37. Gallego-Arrufat, M.J., Torres-Hernández, N., Pessoa, T.: Competencia de futuros docentes en el área de seguridad digital. Comunicar **27**(61), 57–67 (2019). https://doi.org/10.3916/C61-2019-05
38. Buchanan, R.: How to build a positive digital footprint for your school and for your students. The school leadership survival guide: what to do when things go wrong, how to learn from mistakes, and why you should prepare for the worst, pp. 169–186 (2021)
39. Kubacka, A., Biały, D., Gołąb, R.: Perception of information security in the process of distance learning during the COVID-19 pandemic on the example of university teachers' experiences. Int. J. Res. E-learning IJREL **7**(2), 1–18 (2021)
40. Pusey, P., Sadera, W.A.: Cyberethics, cybersafety, and cybersecurity: preservice teacher knowledge, preparedness, and the need for teacher education to make a difference. J. Digit. Learn. Teach. Educ. **28**(2), 82–85 (2011). https://doi.org/10.1080/21532974.2011.10784684
41. Alexei, L.A., Alexei, A.: Cyber security threat analysis in higher education institutions as a result of distance learning. Int. J. Sci. Technol. Res. **3**, 128–133 (2021)
42. Kuzminykh, I., Yevdokymenko, M., Yeremenko, O., Lemeshko, O.: Increasing teacher competence in cybersecurity using the EU security frameworks. Int. J. Mod. Educ. Comput. Sci. **13**(6), 60–68 (2021)
43. Podila, L.M., et al.: Practice-oriented smartphone security exercises for developing cybersecurity mindset in high school students. In: 2020 IEEE International Conference on Teaching, Assessment, and Learning for Engineering (TALE), pp. 303–310. IEEE (2020)

44. Pătrașcu, P.: Promoting cybersecurity culture through education. In: Conference Proceedings of eLearning and Software for Education (eLSE), vol. 15, no. 02, pp. 273–279. Carol I National Defence University Publishing House, Bucharest (2019)
45. Udroiu, A., Vevera, V.: Lifelong learning for raising cybersecurity awareness. In: INTED2018 Proceedings, pp. 5381–5387. IATED (2018). https://doi.org/10.21125/inted.2018.1272
46. Irons, A., Crick, T.: Cybersecurity in the digital classroom: implications for emerging policy, pedagogy and practice. In: The Emerald Handbook of Higher Education in a Post-COVID World: New Approaches and Technologies for Teaching and Learning, pp. 231–244. Emerald Publishing Limited (2022). https://doi.org/10.1108/978-1-80382-193-120221011
47. Sklar, A.: Sound, smart, and safe: a plea for teaching good digital hygiene. LEARNing Landscapes **10**(2), 39–43 (2017). https://doi.org/10.36510/learnland.v10i2.799
48. Akulwar-Tajane, I., Parmar, K.K., Naik, P.H., Shah, A.V.: Rethinking screen time during COVID-19: impact on psychological well-being in physiotherapy students. Int. J. Clin. Exp. Med. Res. **4**(4), 201–216 (2020). https://doi.org/10.26855/ijcemr.2020.10.014
49. Tamilarasi, M.: Mobile empowerment: enhancing education and connectivity for college students. Int. J. Engl. Lit. Soc. Sci. **8**(3), 294–300 (2023). https://doi.org/10.22161/ijels.83.48
50. Marín-López, I., Zych, I.: Bullying, cyberbullying, and social, emotional, and moral competencies. In: Cyber and Face-to-Face Aggression and Bullying among Children and Adolescents, pp. 72–87. Routledge, London (2024)
51. Seki, T., Çimen, F., Dilmaç, B.: The effect of emotional intelligence on cyber security: the mediator role of mindfulness. Bartın Üniversitesi Eğitim Fakültesi Dergisi **12**(1), 190–199 (2023). https://doi.org/10.14686/buefad.1040614

Digital Literacy and Perception of Inclusive Education of Preservice Teachers at Indonesian Universities

Khofidotur Rofiah[1,2](✉) ⓘ, Ransom Tanyu Ngenge[2] ⓘ, Citra Fitri Kholidya[1] ⓘ, and Ima Kurotun Ainin[1] ⓘ

[1] Universitas Negeri Surabaya, Surabaya, Indonesia
khofidoturrofiah@unesa.ac.id
[2] Uniwersyte Komisji Edukacji Narodowej w Krakowie, Kraków, Poland

Abstract. Digital literacy and inclusive education have emerged as new areas of research as a result of advancements in technology and the need for diverse learning environments. In this chapter, we examine the correlation between improved digital literacy skills and inclusive education practices among preservice teachers across Indonesian universities. Adopting a mixed-methods design, we administered an online survey to 604 preservice teachers, assessing their familiarity and knowledge of information and media literacy. This was supplemented by the use of DigComp and SACIE-R as the foundation for and understanding of the perceptions of preservice teachers with regards to inclusive education. The findings show a predictable and positive correlation between improved digital literacy skills and inclusive education practices. New themes, such as hands-on digital literacy experiences in teacher education and the significance of digital competence in enhancing the teaching process, emerged from our study. Despite its narrow geographic scope and demographic scale, the study shows that there is the need for curriculum reforms in teacher education in Indonesia to include digital literacy. This will enable preservice teachers to possess digital competencies, guaranteeing their readiness to address the varied needs of their diverse student populations in an ever more digitised society.

Keywords: Digital literacy · inclusive perception · teacher education · Indonesian universities · teacher candidates

1 Introduction

In our October 2023 article on the perceptions and realities of inclusive education for students with disabilities at Universitas Negeri Surabaya (UNESA) [1], we found out that "despite some improvements, students with special needs at UNESA continue to encounter impediments in pursuing higher education." In spite of this, it is important to acknowledge that the situation at UNESA cannot be used to describe the situation of inclusive education in Indonesia as a whole. Besides, we think that in the present digital age, inclusive education should not only give priority to students, preservice teachers,

Ł. Tomczyk (Ed.): NMP 2023, CCIS 2130, pp. 24–43, 2024.
https://doi.org/10.1007/978-3-031-63235-8_2

and teachers with disabilities, but also consider to those without disabilities, who are lacking in digital skills. The objective, in our age and time, should be to guarantee that all educators, irrespective of their abilities and disabilities, acquire the essential digital competencies requisite for digital literacy and inclusive educational practices.

In this case study, we look at Indonesia as a country that has made tremendous progress in digitalisation over the last decade or so [2]. Partly as a result of the COVID-19 pandemic, not only has the value of Indonesia's digital industry grown financially from US$41 billion (about $130 per person in the US) in 2019 to US$77 billion (about $240 per person in the US) in 2022, but the number of internet users has also skyrocketed, from 150 million users in 2019 to 203 million in 2021, reflecting a considerably high 73.7 percent internet penetration rate for the total population [3]. Regardless of this impressive and visible growth, the macro statistics of Indonesia's digital literacy rates are comparatively low, ranking 61st out of 100 countries in terms of education and readiness to use the internet [4]. As of January 2022, around 73.7 million Indonesians still do not have access to the internet, accounting for 26.3 percent of the entire population. Indonesia now lacks internet connection in around 12,500 communities and 104,000 schools [5]. As we endeavour to grapple with the question of whether an increase in digital literacy among Indonesian preservice teachers as well as their perception of how the utilisation of these skills could potentially contribute to a more inclusive educational system, we see the data above, particularly concerning internet access and number of internet users, as a point of departure.

1.1 Research Objective(s)

The digital literacy skills gap in Indonesia in still wide [6–11]. A March 2022 Diagnostic Report of the SMERU Research Institute on the digital landscape in Indonesia shows that "only 30% of Indonesian students aged 15 years old have a higher than Level 2 proficiency in reading compared to the OECD average of 77%" and "only 30% of students in Indonesia have achieved the minimum level of proficiency (Level 2 or higher) in reading" [12]. Consequently, the implementation of High Order Thinking Skills (HOTS) by the Ministry of Education has not materialized as expected due to limited digital literacy skills of teachers to deliver ICT lessons in subjects not specifically related to ICT [13]. This is further complicated by inequalities based on sex, sector, age group, income levels, region and above all disability status with only 18% of persons with disabilities having access to the internet largely because of the unavailability of user-friendly mobile interfaces. The 2020 Diagnostic Report of the SMERU Research Institute, as indicated in Fig. 1 below, gives a general idea of the digital skills landscape in Indonesia, with education, which is at the center of this study, understood as a critical factor in the acquisition of digital literacy skills.

Although the above figure gives us a general understanding of digital literacy in Indonesia, it does not particularly address the levels of digital literacy among preservice teachers and their perception of its corresponding impact on inclusive education. For example, what specific categories of digital skills do Indonesian preservice teachers have? Are digital skills part of their everyday life? How often and to what extent do they incorporate their digital skills as part of the drive to promote inclusive education? How do they perceive integrating digital skills into their inclusive education practices?

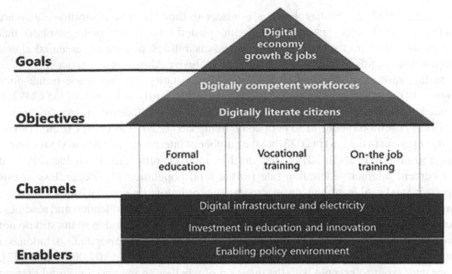

Fig. 1. Framework for digital skills development in Indonesia [12]

These, among others, are some of the questions we attempt in this chapter. By so doing, this study throws more light on the level(s) of digital literacy skills among Indonesian preservice teachers, considering its impact on inclusive education.

1.2 Research Objectives

- Assess the levels of digital literacy among preservice teachers in selected Indonesian universities.
- Examine the preservice teachers' perception of inclusive education practices in selected Indonesian universities.
- Determine the correlation between digital literacy and perception of preservice teachers toward inclusive education.

Based on the research objectives above, digital literacy skills of preservice teachers is our independent variable and the extent to which they use these skills to promote inclusive education is the dependent variable. The digital literacy skills here include knowledge of information and media literacy, the ability to use digital tools and technologies such as laptops and smartphones whereas integrating digital literacy into their work ranging from the ability to create inclusive learning environments, providing differentiated learning, accepting diverse learning styles and ensuring cohesion. This study, therefore, touches on key issues in education technology and inclusion, critical for Indonesia that is experiencing rapid digitalisation. Acknowledging the ways in which digital literacy may enhance inclusive education practices can greatly influence the quality of education, making it more accessible for students with disabilities.

2   Conceptualisation and Literature Review

Borrowing from reputable sources such as the UNESCO Institute for Statistics within a scientific context [14], the European Commission [15], and integrating the inclusive pedagogy frameworks from The Royal [16], we provide a clear definition of the basic principles of digital literacy. This review also explores the incorporation of these ideas in educational settings, with a focus on the importance of digital competency in improving inclusive teaching methods. This provides an overview of the present state of digital literacy among preservice teachers in Indonesia and its influence on inclusive education [17, 18].

2.1   Definitions and Dimensions of Digital Literacy

This study incorporates components of digital literacy as defined by the UNESCO Institute for Statistics [14], the International Telecommunication Union [19], and the European Commission [14]. Digital literacy is the ability to access, manage, understand, integrate, communicate, evaluate and create information safely and appropriately through digital technologies for employment, decent jobs, and entrepreneurship. It includes competences that are variously referred to as computer literacy, ICT literacy, information literacy and media literacy.

Digital literacy, as conceptualised above, enables efficient and secure management, analysis and synthesis of information. Its curriculum may include computer science, information and communication technology (ICT), information literacy, media literacy, data processing, IT use and digital ethics and culture [10, 20–26]. The training may also includes, such as in the case of the United Kingdom, computer literacy, use of office applications, multimedia editing and internet surfing [16]. The idea of digital literacy comprises five essential competency categories: information and data literacy, communication and collaboration, digital content production, safety and problem-solving [18]. Primarily, "information and data literacy" is an essential aspect that encompasses the proficiency to efficiently find, get, assess and use digital information [15, 27–30]. The importance lies not only in the ability to get information but also in the capacity to evaluate its legitimacy and relevance [14]. Communication and collaboration are equally two essential terms for digital literacy. They denote the employment of digital technologies to engage, cooperate, and participate in digital networks or communities [30–32]. This may range from understanding how to interact with others and maintaining a balanced digital persona [18]. Conversely, "digital content creation", with illustrations from Poland [31, 32], includes the fundamental process of creating and altering digital material, which may take the form of text and multimedia For this to work, it is relevant to have a good understanding of basic design principles and intellectual property rights [15]. The concept of "safety" in digital literacy pertains to safeguarding oneself and others against potential hazards linked to digital activity. This component includes understanding of privacy settings, recognition of digital hazards, and display of responsible conduct on the internet [15]. Proficiency in resolving issues within digital environments is crucial. This involves using digital tools to tackle problems, uncover answers, and promote innovation [33]. The ability to understand and use new digital technologies for effective learning and productivity is included within it [34]. Given Indonesia's increasing adoption of digitisation, it is crucial to assess the digital capabilities of preservice teachers. The essential elements of digital literacy include problem solving, safety, information and data, communication and collaboration and digital content production. Every element has a crucial function in obtaining a thorough comprehension of digital literacy, which is necessary for effectively navigating the intricate and ever-changing digital environment in various educational settings [35]. Furthermore, they together empower folks to attain expertise, discrimination, and ethical accountability in using digital technology, showcasing its extensive array of capabilities, and comprehension. The interconnectedness of these aspects highlights that proficiency in one area may enhance and strengthen abilities in another, leading to a well-rounded proficiency in digital literacy.

2.2 Concepts and Frameworks of Inclusive Pedagogy

Inclusive education refers to teaching methods that recognise and adjust to the diverse needs of each student, ensuring equitable and unbiased access to educational opportunities. In other words, "common education makes it possible to create conditions for a "good school for everyone" [36]. This method is based on the notion that education should be customised to each person, rather than if all learners should conform to a pre-established standard [37]. Inclusive education is modifying instructional approaches to accommodate diverse learning styles, talents, and backgrounds. The core of this idea is on the Universal Design for Learning (UDL) paradigm, which "sets a goal to allow all learners to achieve their optimal learning experience that matches inclusive education" [38, 39]. This type of framework prioritises three fundamental principles: facilitating diverse modes of representation to enable learners to acquire information through various channels, facilitating diverse modes of action and expression to allow learners to demonstrate their knowledge in multiple ways, and facilitating diverse modes of engagement to harness learners' interests and motivations. Another crucial element is the implementation of differentiated teaching, in which instructors deliberately design multiple methods "dynamic, individualised instruction" [40] for students to acquire knowledge, comprehend it, and exhibit their understanding, in order to address the heterogeneous requirements within a classroom [41, 42]. This strategy entails adapting content, procedure, product, and learning environment to provide an inclusive and stimulating learning experience for every learner, which is what we equally observe amongst Indonesian student-teachers.

2.3 Intersection of Digital Literacy and Inclusive Pedagogy

While looking at policy and practice of "digital equity and inclusion in education" of Organisation for Economic Co-operation and Development (OECD) countries [43], which is synonymous to what we choose to call digital literacy and inclusive pedagogy, the authors highlight the significance of integrating digital skills into teaching methods to cater to the learning requirements of all students. In other words, teachers must possess digital literacy abilities in order to be able to create and deliver teaching that is both accessible and captivating for a wide range of students [44]. Within this context, digital technologies are utilised to implement the principles of Universal Design for Learning (UDL). This means that technology provides multiple ways of presenting information, such as multimedia, interactive simulations, and digital texts, to cater to different learning preferences [39]. In addition, learning platforms such as Vinesa (Virtual learning Universitas Negeri Surabaya) as the digital learning platform developed by one of universities in Indonesia, WhatsApp, Teams, Zoom, and Blackboard common in Indonesia should assist preservice teachers in determining their level of digital competency and working on improving them [46–48]. The advantage is that it will make them more conscious of the specific needs of students and, by so doing, facilitate personalised learning. The use of these digital platforms also allows for the customisation of teaching materials [43]. An example is an education software like Vinesa that makes life easy for lecturers at Universitas Negeri Surabaya (UNESA) in scheduling lessons and designing tailored learning pathways based on students' progress, abilities, and areas for development. Consequently, present-day teachers with digital literacy skills are more likely to practice inclusive education, and this represents a huge milestone in transforming education in Indonesia. It is a beacon for quality education that accommodates and responds to the needs of students with special needs in the digital age [39, 46].

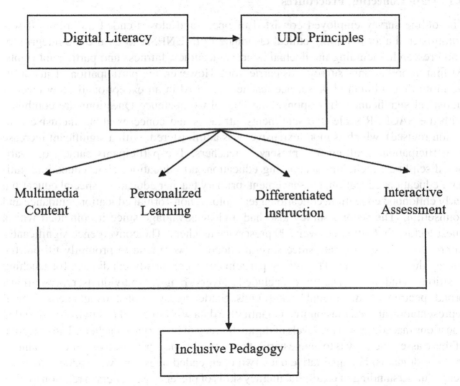

Fig. 2. The connection between digital literacy and inclusive education

Figure 2 above shows the correlation between digital literacy and inclusive education. In essence, preservice teachers with digital literacy skills will have a higher tendency towards inclusive education, and vice versa. In effect, this will lead to more diverse, individualised, and engaging learning environments. This is common with using Universal Design Learning (UDL) principles, differentiated learning, multimedia tools, and collaborative evaluations, thereby making it more streamlined to meet the specific needs of each student, especially those with disabilities.

3 Methods

Our research methodology included both quantitative and qualitative approaches. This not only made the study more credible but also made it easy to examine the competencies of preservice teachers with regard to digital literacy and their perceptions of inclusive education. The cross-sectional methodology employed included an online survey administered through Google Forms during November and December 2023. Administering an online survey made it easy to reach a diverse number of participants from different disciplines across UNESA. Below is a chart flow of our research methodology (Fig. 3).

3.1 Data Collecting Procedures

The online survey employed consisted of open- and closed-ended questions. It was administered after obtaining ethical clearance from UNESA to ensure the integrity of good research, including intellectual honesty, accuracy, fairness and participant rights. At first, a preliminary survey was carried out. However, the participation of just a little more than a hundred preservice teachers resulted in an exceptionally low level of statistical significance. In response, the Digital Competence Questionnaire combined with the SACIE-R scale (the sentiments, attitudes and concerns about inclusive education revised), which is more extensive, was administered, with a significant increase in participation, totalling 604 preservice teachers. The participants came from various disciplines, including accounting education, art education, civic education, culinary education, educational management, primary teacher education, special education, early childhood education, educational technology, non-formal education, guidance and counselling. The second survey also had a clear advantage since it coincided with a guest lecture that attracted over 700 preservice teachers. The convergence significantly improved the response rate since several attendees were able to promptly fill out the survey during the event. The survey participants were mostly candidates for teaching positions in Indonesia. The survey included a diverse range of individuals, representing a broad spectrum of educational backgrounds, gender, age, year of study and geographical representation around the country. Quantitative data was collected through closed-ended questions that addressed the levels of digital literacy of preservice teachers. The objective of these assessments was to gauge participants' proficiency, perspectives, and encounters in these domains. For qualitative data, two open-ended questions were added to gain a deeper understanding of the digital literacy skills of preservice teachers in relation to their perception of inclusive education. The questions related to preservice teachers' opinions on whether Indonesian universities are prepared for digital literacy and inclusive pedagogy competences. Secondary data comprises prior research obtained from many academic sources and electronic databases, such as Springer, Francis & Taylor, ResearchGate, Google Scholar, university online libraries, journal websites and renowned policy groups.

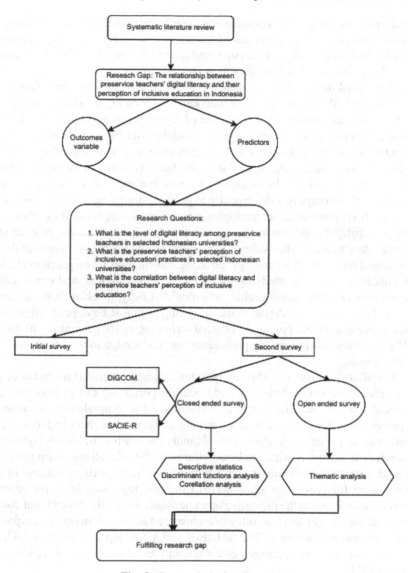

Fig. 3. Research design flow chart

3.2 DigComp and SACIE-R

Digital Competence Questionnaire is a data gathering tool developed by Çebi and Reisoğlu based on the DigComp framework [35]. This questionnaire sought to examine five dimensions of digital competence, including "Information and data literacy," "Communication and collaboration," "Digital content creation," "Safety," and "Problem-solving." The DigComp framework classifies digital skills into five distinct domains: information and data literacy, communication and collaboration, digital content creation, safety, and problem-solving [18, 34]. Within the realm of "information and data literacy," individuals possess a range of skills including identifying information needs, navigating digital platforms, conducting content and data searches, critically evaluating, comparing, interpreting, analysing, storing, organising, and processing digital information, content, and data. "Communication and collaboration" refers to the act of actively engaging with others using digital devices and applications. This extends to exchanging information, data, and content with a diverse group of individuals, embracing the sharing and quoting of resources, and recognising the importance of digital technologies in formal contact with the organisation. This involves navigating social media, digital platforms, and community networks, using collaborative technologies to foster expansion, following ethical principles when sharing information, grasping the benefits of digital identity, and understanding the interdependent relationship between online and offline presence. "Digital content creation" encompasses the capacity to produce digital material in many forms, express oneself via multimedia technologies, alter information provided by others while adhering to copyright regulations, and having expertise in simulations, programming, and software development. The "safety" domain focuses on raising awareness of the hazards associated with digital technology, ensuring information privacy, comprehending privacy concerns, and acknowledging the physical, psychological, and environmental consequences of extensive use of digital technologies. Lastly, "problem-solving" entails addressing difficulties in the digital realm, choosing the most appropriate digital technology, comprehending the potential of digital technologies for generating information and self-expression, and possessing proficiency and knowledge in the key technologies within the domain.

The SACIE revised version [45], incorporates 15 items structured around three principal variables: Sentiments, Attitudes, and Concerns pertaining to Inclusive Education among preservice teachers. This scale is well-suited for a comprehensive examination of the perceptions of inclusive education among preservice teachers in Indonesia. (1) The sentiments of preservice teachers towards individuals with disabilities significantly influence their interactions with disabled children in the educational setting. (2) Positive attitudes towards inclusion correlate with higher likelihoods of success in practical application for preservice teachers. (3) Concerns regarding inclusive education assume significance, given the prevailing apprehensions within the educational community regarding the efficacy and feasibility of inclusive education, with teachers expressing a lack of sufficient preparedness. The SACIE-R yielded an alpha value (α) of .83, with the three subscales demonstrating consistent reliabilities: $\alpha = .86$, $\alpha = .86$, and $\alpha = .70$, respectively [45].

The study activities were done complying with ethical protocols. Participants were provided with information on the research's objective and their consent was gained prior to their involvement. The poll guaranteed both anonymity and secrecy, with participants being reassured that their replies would be only used for research endeavours.

3.3 Data Analysis Method

The quantitative data analysis included using the 27.0 edition of IBM SPSS software to identify and comprehend patterns, trends, and correlations. The qualitative responses were subjected to thematic analysis [46] to identify the dominant themes/subthemes, perspectives, and opinions expressed by the participants. This dual strategy ensured a comprehensive understanding of the information. Table 1 below details the demographics of the participants.

Table 1. Sample characteristics

	f	%
N	604	100
Gender		
Male	80	13.25
Female	524	86.75
Year of study		
1st year	554	91.70
2nd year	17	2.80
3rd year	30	5.00
4th year	3	0.50

As indicated in the table above, the female participants comprised the majority, making up 86.75% of the total, while males composed just 13.25%. The second characteristic of the participants in this study is according to their academic year. The majority of pre-service teachers who participated in this study 91,7% from the first year, and the smallest number was 0,5% in the final years.

4 Results

For the quantitative part, parametric tests are conducted based on the dataset (refer to Table 2) which indicated that our distribution follows a normal pattern, with skewness and kurtosis values falling between -1 and 1 [47].

Table 2. Descriptive statistics for the main variables (N = 604)

Variable	Min	Max	Mean	SD	Skewness	Kurtosis
Perception about inclusion	15	75	43.01	10.217	0.642	0.354
Digital competence	30	155	126.35	18.988	-0.574	0.678

The descriptive statistics reveal that the mean perception about inclusion score is 43.01, signifying the average in the sample, while the standard deviation of 10.217 indicates some variability in scores around the mean. On the other hand, the mean digital competence score is 126.35, with a higher standard deviation of 18.988, suggesting greater variability in scores. This implies that participants, on average, scored around 43.01 on perception about inclusion and 126.35 on digital competence, with digital competence scores exhibiting a more diverse range compared to perception about inclusion scores.

4.1 Correlation Analysis

Here, we present the statistical correlations between digital skills and perception regarding inclusion among the participants. This research used Pearson's correlation coefficient to examine the magnitude and direction of these relationships, offering insights into the interconnectedness of many factors within digital literacy and perception of inclusive education (Table 3).

Table 3. Relationship between digital competence and perceptions of inclusion

Variable	1	2
Digital competence	1	.105**
Perception about inclusion	.105**	1

$^{**} p < 0.001;\ ^{*} p < 0.05.$

The correlation study indicates a statistically significant positive association ($r = 0.105$) between digital competence and sense of inclusion at a significance level of 0.01. As digital proficiency improves, people's opinions regarding inclusion become more promising. The correlation value of 0.105 indicates a slight positive association between perceptions of inclusion and overall digital skills. As the sense of inclusion scores increases, there is a minor correlation with a rise in digital competence scores. The p-value of 0.010, which is statistically significant, suggests that the observed link is very unlikely to have arisen by random chance. There is compelling data indicating a genuine correlation between perceptions about inclusiveness and scores measuring digital ability. The study findings indicated a statistically significant albeit modest positive association between perceptions of inclusion and digital competence ratings in the sample of 604 observations. The data suggest a positive correlation between the two variables, indicating that an increase in one variable is accompanied by a minor increase in the other variable. This provides vital information on the link between these two measurements.

4.2 Regression Analysis

Our regression analysis examines the relationship between several aspects of digital competence and the formation of attitudes of inclusion. This research uses linear regression to examine the influence of each component of digital literacy on inclusive pedagogical practices, providing a more profound understanding of the predictive capability of these abilities (Table 4).

Table 4. Impact of digital competence dimensions on inclusive pedagogy

	Unstandardized Coefficients		Standardized Coefficients	t	Sig.
	B	Std. Error	Beta		
(Constant)	37.425	2.840		13.176	.000
Information and data literacy	−.037	.176	−.015	−.210	.834
Communication and collaboration	−.137	.241	−.043	−.568	.571
Digital content	.116	.219	.034	.530	.596
Safety	−.080	.118	−.056	−.677	.499
Problem solving	.577	.191	.209	3.026	.003

The linear regression model given predicts the preservice teachers' impression regarding inclusion based on many independent factors. The intercept term, also known as the constant, has a value of 37.425. Its standard error is 2.840, and it is deemed statistically significant with a p-value of less than .001. The unstandardised coefficients for the independent variables are as follows: Information and data literacy has a coefficient of −.037, communication and cooperation have a coefficient of −.137, digital content has a coefficient of .116, safety has a value of −.080, and problem solving has a coefficient of .577. The coefficients indicate the alteration in the dependent variable when there is a one-unit modification in the related independent variable. The standardized coefficients (Beta) quantify the extent to which each independent variable contributes to units of standard deviation. The t-values and corresponding p-values provide information about the statistical significance of each coefficient. The coefficient for problem solving is statistically significant (p = .003), indicating that it has a substantial influence on the dependent variable, even when considering other factors.

4.3 Open-Ended Responses

This study incorporates two open-ended questions to supplement the survey results. The initial inquiry pertains to the viewpoints of student teachers regarding the necessary preparations in university concerning the knowledge and proficiency in digital literacy for teacher candidates. Conversely, the subsequent inquiry concerns the necessary preparations in university concerning the knowledge and proficiency for teacher candidates in teaching within inclusive schools. The two responses to this question were qualitatively examined using Braun and Clarke's six thematic stages of analysis. The first stage involved familiarising oneself with the data, which entailed reading and rereading the datasets of the two open-ended questions. (2) In the first phase of code generation, the focus is on identifying and categorising noteworthy characteristics or patterns in the data and assigning codes to corresponding sections. Codes often consist of concise sentences or words that encapsulate the fundamental nature of the information. (3) The act of searching for themes involves identifying bigger patterns or themes by grouping together pertinent codes. Themes are broad and encompassing notions that establish connections between several codes and provide a more thorough intellectual capacity of the data. The last phase, denoted as stage 4, entails the meticulous examination and enhancement of the selected topics. (5) After confirming the themes, they are further specified and called. The last phase is composing the report, whereby the discoveries are shown, using citations or illustrations from the data to substantiate each subject. The interviews were analysed and yielded two primary themes, each consisting of six sub-themes. These are seen in Fig. 4. Data extracts are determined based on the open-ended replies obtained during the survey.

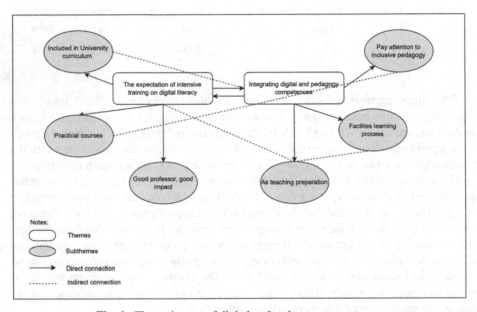

Fig. 4. Thematic map of digital and pedagogy competences

Theme 1. Expectation of intensive training on digital competences
Subtheme 1. Inclusion in university curriculum
The expectation of teacher candidates to understand and have digital competency skills was considered particularly important by participants. The need for universities to prepare student teachers to understand digital literacy and use it wisely by revitalising the curriculum and including digital literacy courses in it. For example, some of the preservice teachers wrote:

> ...the teacher education curriculum should include materials on digital literacy. This could include various aspects of digital literacy, such as knowledge, skills, and the ability to evaluate digital information.' (P12), '...universities need to develop curricula that add digital literacy in education subjects, training on digital behavioral aspects, creating software in education, online safety and training to teach

digital literacy to students.' (P15), 'providing digital literacy courses and giving special training related to digital media to increase student skills in the digital world.' (P19).

Subtheme 2. Practical courses

Respondents consistently highlighted the importance of practical experiences for teacher candidates within digital literacy. Participant P3 stressed the necessity for universities to offer opportunities such as internships or learning projects that involve the application of digital literacy. This hands-on approach was deemed essential for the practical skill development of teacher candidates, enabling them to effectively navigate real-world challenges in their future roles as educators.

'It is also important for universities to provide opportunities for teacher candidates to engage in relevant practical experiences, such as internships or learning projects that involve the use of digital literacy. This will help them develop their skills in a practical way and deal with the challenges they may face in the real world as teachers.' (P3).

Other preservice teachers supported this idea by pushing for the use of hands-on experiences in technology instruction. The objective is to provide teacher candidates with the essential abilities to navigate the intricacies of the modern digital environment. '…to integrate practical experience in technology teaching to prepare them for the challenges of today's digital world.' (P10). Indeed, other participants echoed these sentiments, suggesting an increase in the number of assignments or projects applying digital technology. This approach aims to enhance the capabilities of teacher candidates, ensuring their readiness for the challenges they will encounter in their professional journeys: '…increasing the number of assignments or projects using digital technology so that teacher candidates can be more capable in the future.' (P12).

Subtheme 3. Good professor, good impact

The participants accentuated the critical role of selecting professors based on their competence in digital literacy, aligning with established procedures. One of the participants underscored the importance of adherence to existing criteria for professors, especially in digital competences 'selecting professors who are competent in digital literacy and in accordance with existing procedures' (P5). This statement is also underlined by P2 who really want a good, qualified professor: 'provide professors who are truly qualified, not those who tell stories here and there, are proud of themselves but forget their duties as educators!' (P2). Other participants suggested that universities should enhance their provision of services related to digital literacy by offering structured and easily understandable support. Furthermore, the emphasis was placed on the significance of having qualified professors in the field to guide students effectively, enabling them to enhance their knowledge and skills in addressing digital literacy challenges as the following statement:

'Universities should be able to provide more services to students related to digital literacy in a more structured and easier to understand manner, especially qualified professors in this field. So that students can also increase their knowledge and skills for digital literacy problems.' (P7)

Theme 2. Integrating digital competence with pedagogical competence

Subtheme 4. Digital literacy as teaching preparation for prospective teachers
The emerging subtheme is the critical role of digital literacy as teaching preparation for student-teachers' in the university. Participants agreed that they need to cultivate knowledge and skills in digital literacy to effectively integrate technology into their teaching practices: 'student-teachers need to prepare their knowledge and skills in digital literacy to integrate technology effectively in their teaching practices' (P8). 'In this era, we must always learn about knowledge and how to use technology, such as good utilization of digital media, so that we can provide learning that is appropriate in this era' (P9). The reasons for the importance of digital literacy as teaching preparation were clearly conveyed by participants: 'Teachers need to integrate digital literacy and pedagogy skills, so that they can support successful learning and can develop. It is also important to prepare teachers' digital skills, as student-teachers' digital skills still fall short of students' digital capabilities' (P13), '…. This will help them develop practical skills and deal with the challenges they may face in the real world as teachers (P1).

Subtheme 5. Digital competence facilitates the teaching process
The participants persistently emphasized the pivotal role of digital competence in easing the teaching process. It is crucial for student teachers to be able to use ICT tools and educational software enhancing the teaching process: 'Mastering digital literacy will help teacher candidates understand the various technological tools and software that can be used in the teaching process when I become a teacher in the future' (P11). 'they should be familiar with several types of digital devices and platforms and have a good understanding of how technology can be used to enhance student learning' (P7). Furthermore, participants expressed that digital literacy serves as an effective way to answer contemporary needs in present days: 'Digital literacy is effectively addressing the skill requirements arising from contemporary advancements, and in addition to this, it is essential to equip preservice teachers with diverse learning methods and directions' (P4).

Subtheme 6. Pay attention to inclusive pedagogy
One of the emerging subthemes considered interesting was the relationship between digital literacy competence and inclusive competence. Participants considered that as prospective teachers who will later work with children with special needs in schools, it is necessary to master digital literacy to support the implementation of inclusive education. 'should teach how to use assistive technology such as speech to text in inclusive education.' (P1), 'teacher candidates must be able to access, use (read: digital literacy) interpret and communicate information and ideas through a variety of learner needs.' (P6), 'teaching and imparting knowledge, teaching (read: digital literacy) more about how to deal with and assist students with disabilities in the general community.' (P3), 'They should also be trained to understand the inclusive needs of students with diverse backgrounds and abilities, so as to create a supportive learning environment for all' (P12).

5 Discussion

The technological perspective is commonly prioritised over the pedagogical viewpoint. Consequently, the incorporation of Information and Communication Technology (ICT) in education is frequently portrayed as the central symbol of revolutionary educational change. This representation is intricately connected to the rhetoric that underlies the ideological framework of the so-called "Information or Knowledge Society." It symbolises the primary antidote to the educational challenges posed by the sophisticated technology and intense competition prevalent in contemporary society [48]. However, in today's technological era it is an absolute necessity to engage digital competencies and integrate them with pedagogical competencies.

Nevertheless, our research emphasises the need to combine digital competence with instructional skills. The results replicate the study conducted by Campbell and Kapp (2020), which investigated the digital behaviors and perspectives of English language educators. One important finding is that student-teachers' beliefs about their digital skills do not align with the real skills needed in modern classrooms. These results are in line with the previous research that suggested that digital literacy stands out as a pivotal protective element within the comprehensive framework of digital safety, particularly within educational institutions. Consequently, the identification and promotion of digital literacy have emerged as prominent challenges confronting contemporary schools [49]. This discrepancy underscores the need for curricular overhauls that give priority not just to the attainment of digital competencies but also to their seamless integration with pedagogical approaches to guarantee inclusive and efficient instruction. Although in the Indonesian context, there are still negative experiences felt by Indonesian students regarding online study during the pandemic [17]. However, the Indonesian government continues to endeavor to involve digital literacy and technology in teacher preparation education [39]. This statement pertains to the wider discussion in education on the use of technology in facilitating inclusive education [38]. The results also underline the notable discrepancy in digital literacy skills in Indonesia. The issue of the digital divide is often examined in global educational research, where it is common to address the associated challenges [6, 7]. This study's emphasis on differences related to different demographic characteristics is in keeping with existing worldwide research on gaps in digital literacy [8]. Therefore, it is crucial to integrate digital literacy into the teacher education curriculum, as this study recommends. Previous research confirmed the idea that embedding digital skills into the curriculum is critical to narrowing the digital gap and preparing teachers to cater for the requirements of modern education [30, 31].

Other notable findings were the application of digital resources in inclusive education, in line with the principles of Universal Design for Learning (UDL), which encourages the use of digital technologies to fulfil various learning preferences [41]. The findings of this research support the general opinion that digital resources should be integrated into education to meet the diverse needs of pre-service teachers [46, 47] and to prepare them to be ready as future teachers who can teach better, supporting all students in inclusive settings. This paper suggests that the embedding of digital literacy training into teacher education programmes will have beneficial outcomes, which carry significant implications for both policy and practice. While this research provides significant insights, it also highlights drawbacks and reveals areas that need more investigation. This highlights the need for comprehensive research covering diverse geographical areas and educational experiences. The literature often highlights the need to conduct ongoing research to follow the development of evolving digital technologies [24, 25]:

- Incorporate digital literacy into teacher education programmes, ensuring a harmonious balance of focus on technological and pedagogical competencies.
- Improving teacher training programmes to include courses on inclusive teaching strategies, with a particular emphasis on leveraging digital resources to enhance learning experiences for diverse students.
- Reducing disparities in digital inaccessibility, particularly in remote and poor areas, to provide equitable and uniform availability of digital resources for all prospective teachers.
- Conduct comprehensive research to assess the potential impacts of integrating digital literacy into teacher education on classroom practices and student performance.
- Analysing different digital literacy and inclusive pedagogical methods in various cultural and educational contexts.
- Examining the influence of new technologies on the ability to use digital tools effectively and promote equal access to education, considering the context of technological advances.

This study provides factual information on the existing level of digital literacy among prospective teachers in Indonesia and their perceptions of inclusive education. It also constructs a conceptual framework for better understanding the intersection of digital literacy and inclusive pedagogy. Moreover, it proposes to Indonesian policymakers and educators a detailed plan for creating and implementing digital literacy programmes. However, future research should endeavour to include a broader spectrum of people, including different geographical areas and educational backgrounds. Undertaking an extensive qualitative analysis has the potential to reveal deeper insights into the experiences and difficulties faced by future teachers.

6 Conclusion

The current study shows the importance of enhancing digital literacy competencies in preparing preservice teachers who will work in inclusive education settings. There is a significant correlation between their perception of inclusive education and their digital competencies. The qualitative results also concluded that preservice teachers in Indonesia need to improve their digital competencies by two emerging themes based on thematic analysis for the open-ended questions: (1) expectation of intensive training on digital competencies, and (2) integrating digital competence with pedagogical competence. The limitation of this study, however, is the lack of nationwide participation for universities, which consisted of only UNESA with similar sample characteristics. Future research should consider more universities in different part of Indonesia from public to private, a wider sample size and the diversity of the participants, for example, preservice teachers who have learning difficulties. That being said, our study highlights the need for preservice teachers to improve digital literacy skills to provide a more inclusive education environment in Indonesia. This strategy tackles the changing educational requirements and uses technology to cater to various learning needs, thereby promoting wider academic accessibility and involvement.

References

1. Rrofiah, K., Ngenge, R.T., Sujarwanto, S., Ainin, I.K.: Inclusive education at Universitas Negeri Surabaya: perceptions and realities of students with disabilities. Int. J. Spec. Educ. (IJSE) **38**, 14–25 (2023). https://doi.org/10.52291/ijse.2023.38.18
2. Palaon, H.: Indonesia's digital success deserves more attention. https://www.lowyinstitute.org/the-interpreter/indonesia-s-digital-success-deserves-more-attention
3. Negara, S.D., Meilasari-Sugiana, A.: The State of Indonesia's Digital Economy in 2022 (2023)
4. Amanta, F.: Unpacking Indonesia's digital accessibility. https://www.thejakartapost.com/paper/2022/06/29/unpacking-indonesias-digital-accessibility.html
5. Azzahra, N.F., Amanta, F.: Promoting Digital Literacy Skill for Students through Improved School Curriculum. https://www.cips-indonesia.org/publications/promoting-digital-literacy-skill-for-students-through-improved-school-curriculum
6. Limilia, P., Gelgel, R.A., Rahmiaji, L.R.: Digital Literacy Among Z Generation in Indonesia (2022)
7. Azzahra, N.F., Amanta, F.: Promoting Digital Literacy Skill for Students through Improved School Curriculum (2021)
8. Long, T.Q., Hoang, T.C., Simkins, B.: Gender gap in digital literacy across generations: Evidence from Indonesia. Finan. Res. Lett. **58**, 104588 (2023)
9. Silitonga, M.S.: The public sector's digital skills gap in Indonesia: the challenges and opportunities. J. Good Gov. 70–79 (2023). https://doi.org/10.32834/gg.v19i1.585
10. Reddy, P., Chaudhary, K., Hussein, S.: A digital literacy model to narrow the digital literacy skills gap. Heliyon. **9**, e14878 (2023). https://doi.org/10.1016/j.heliyon.2023.e14878
11. Indah, R.N., Toyyibah, A.S., Budhiningrum, N.A.: The research competence, critical thinking skills and digital literacy of Indonesian EFL students. J. Lang. Teach. Res. **13**(2), 315–324 (2022). https://doi.org/10.17507/jltr.1302.11
12. SMERU Research Institute: Digital skills landscape in Indonesia (2022)
13. Dwi Utami, F., Nurkamto, J., Marmanto, S., Taopan, L.L.: The Implementation of Higher-Order Thinking Skills in EFL Classroom: Teachers' Perceptions (2019). https://doi.org/10.17501/26307413.2019.2107
14. UNESCO Institute for Statistics: A global framework of reference on digital literacy skills for indicator 4.4.2 (2018)
15. Vuorikari, R., Kluzer, S., Punie, Y.: European Commission. Joint Research Centre: DigComp 2.2, The Digital Competence framework for citizens: with new examples of knowledge, skills and attitudes (2022)
16. The Royal Society: Shut down or restart? | Royal Society. https://royalsociety.org/topics-policy/projects/computing-in-schools/report/
17. Sujarwanto, Sheehy, K., Rofiah, K.: Online higher education: the importance of students' epistemological beliefs, well-being, and fun. IAFOR J. Educ. **9**, 9–30 (2021). https://doi.org/10.22492/ije.9.6.01
18. Ferrari, A., Europeiska kommissionen. Gemensamma forskningscentret: DIGCOMP a framework for developing and understanding digital competence in Europe. Publications Office of the European Union (2013)
19. International Telecommunication Union: World Telecommunication/ICT Development Report 2010 - Monitoring the WSIS targets (2010)

20. Tomczyk, Ł., Wnęk-Gozdek, J., Mróz, A., Wojewodzic, K.: ICT, digital literacy, digital inclusion and media education in Poland. In: ICT for Learning and Inclusion in Latin America and Europe Case Study from Countries: Bolivia, Brazil, Cuba, Dominican Republic, Ecuador, Finland, Poland, Turkey, Uruguay, pp. 159–190. Uniwersytet Pedagogiczny w Krakowie (2019)
21. Council of Europe: Media and Information Literacy - Digital Citizenship Education (DCE). https://www.coe.int/en/web/digital-citizenship-education/media-and-information-literacy
22. Park, H., Kim, H.S., Park, H.W.: A scientometric study of digital literacy, ICT literacy, information literacy, and media literacy. J. Data Inf. Sci. **6**, 116–138 (2021). https://doi.org/10.2478/jdis-2021-0001
23. Fisser, P., Strijker, A.: Digital literacy as part of a new curriculum for The Netherlands (2019)
24. Vodă, A.I., Cautisanu, C., Grădinaru, C., Tănăsescu, C., de Moraes, G.H.S.M.: Exploring digital literacy skills in social sciences and humanities students. Sustainability. **14**, 2483 (2022). https://doi.org/10.3390/su14052483
25. Ilomäki, L., et al.: Critical digital literacies at school level: a systematic review. Rev. Educ. **11** (2023). https://doi.org/10.1002/rev3.3425
26. Svendsen, A.M., Svendsen, J.T.: Digital directions: curricular goals relating to digital literacy and digital competences in the Gymnasium (stx) in Denmark. Nord. J. Digit. Literacy **16**(1), 6–20 (2021). https://doi.org/10.18261/issn.1891-943x-2021-01-02
27. Grefen, P.: Digital literacy and electronic business. Encyclopedia **1**, 934–941 (2021). https://doi.org/10.3390/encyclopedia1030071
28. Chetty, K., Qigui, L., Gcora, N., Josie, J., Wenwei, Li., Fang, C.: Bridging the digital divide: measuring digital literacy. Economics **12**(1), 20180023 (2018). https://doi.org/10.5018/economics-ejournal.ja.2018-23
29. Schreiter, S., et al.: Teaching for statistical and data literacy in K-12 STEM education: a systematic review on teacher variables, teacher education, and impacts on classroom practice. ZDM – Math. Educ. **56**, 31–45 (2023). https://doi.org/10.1007/s11858-023-01531-1
30. Reisoğlu, İ, Çebi, A.: How can the digital competences of pre-service teachers be developed? Examining a case study through the lens of DigComp and DigCompEdu. Comput. Educ. **156**, 103940 (2020). https://doi.org/10.1016/j.compedu.2020.103940
31. Earnshaw, R., Vince, J.: Digital Content Creation. Springer, London (2001)
32. Nowak, B.M.: Development of digital competences of students of teacher training studies - Polish casus. Int. J. High. Educ. **8**, 262 (2019). https://doi.org/10.5430/ijhe.v8n6p262
33. Redecker, C.: European Framework for the Digital Competence of Educators: Digcompedu (2017). https://doi.org/10.2760/159770
34. Carretero, S., Vuorikari, R., Punie, Y.: EUR 28558 EN The Digital Competence Framework for Citizens With eight proficiency levels and examples of use (2017)
35. Çebi, A., Reisoğlu, İ: Digital competence: a study from the perspective of pre-service teachers in Turkey. J. New Approaches Educ. Res. **9**, 294 (2020). https://doi.org/10.7821/naer.2020.7.583
36. Głodkowska, J.: Inclusive Education Unity in diversity. Wydawnictwo Akademii Pedagogiki Specjalnej, Warszawa (2020)
37. Florian, L., Black-Hawkins, K.: Exploring inclusive pedagogy. Br. Educ. Res. J. **37**, 813–828 (2011). https://doi.org/10.1080/01411926.2010.501096
38. Navaitienė, J., Stasiūnaitienė, E.: The goal of the universal design for learning: development of all to expert learners (2021)
39. Meyer, A., Rose, D.H., Gordon, D.T.: Universal design for learning: theory and practice. CAST Professional Publishing (2014)
40. Kilbane, C., Milman, N.: Differentiated Learning and Technology: A Powerful Combination, p. 10 (2023)

41. Tomlinson, C.A.: Differentiate Instruction in Mixed-Ability Classrooms 2nd Edition 'Curiosity and inspiration are powerful catalysts for learning' (2001)
42. Losberg, J., Zwozdiak-Myers, P.: Inclusive pedagogy through the lens of primary teachers and teaching assistants in England. Int. J. Inclusive Educ. **28**(4), 402–422 (2021). https://doi.org/10.1080/13603116.2021.1946722
43. Gottschalk, F., Weise, C.: Digital equity and inclusion in education: an overview of practice and policy in OECD countries OECD Education Working Paper No. 299 (2023)
44. Dudeney, G., Hockly, N., Sharma, P., Barrett, B.: How to teach English with technology * blended learning. ELT J. **62**, 422–424 (2007). https://doi.org/10.1093/elt/ccn045
45. Forlin, C., Earle, C., Loreman, T., Sharma, U.: The sentiments, attitudes, and concerns about inclusive education revised (SACIE-R) scale for measuring pre-service teachers' perceptions about inclusion. Exceptionality Educ. Int. **21** (2011). https://doi.org/10.5206/eei.v21i3.7682
46. Braun, V., Clarke, V.: Conceptual and design thinking for thematic analysis. Qual. Psychol. **9**, 3–26 (2022). https://doi.org/10.1037/qup0000196
47. George, D., Mallery, P.: SPSS for Windows Step by Step. A Simple Study Guide and Reference. Allyn & Bacon, Boston (2010)
48. Drenoyianni, H., Stergioulas, L.K., Dagiene, V.: The pedagogical challenge of digital literacy: reconsidering the concept–envisioning the 'curriculum'–reconstructing the school. Int. J. Soc. Hum. Comput. **1**, 53 (2008). https://doi.org/10.1504/IJSHC.2008.020480
49. Tomczyk, Ł: Skills in the area of digital safety as a key component of digital literacy among teachers. Educ. Inf. Technol. (Dordr). **25**, 471–486 (2020). https://doi.org/10.1007/s10639-019-09980-6

Digital Education in German Primary Schools: A Challenge for School Leadership

Andreas Dertinger[(⊠)] and Cindy Bärnreuther

Friedrich-Alexander-University Erlangen-Nuremberg, Regensburger Straße 160,
90478 Nuremberg, Germany
{andreas.dertinger,cindy.baernreuther}@fau.de

Abstract. Digital literacy is an important part of school education. However, its development and curricular implementation in German elementary schools has been slow. This article uses a qualitative study to examine how the curricular implementation of digital education is currently progressing in German primary schools and what influence the Covid-19 pandemic has had on it. In the study, focus group interviews were conducted with different stakeholders in primary education in Germany in order to combine multiple perspectives on this situation.

The results reveal several challenges for German primary schools in implementing digital education. School leadership has an important role to play in addressing these challenges. The development of internal school media concepts proved to be an important tool for promoting digital school development. In contrast, the Covid-19 pandemic had a limited long-term impact on the implementation of digital education in primary schools. More important and sustainable are the digital school development initiatives that the primary school was already pursuing before the pandemic.

Keywords: Digital Education · Primary Schools · Digital School Development

1 Introduction

Digitalization is having an enormous impact on our society [1]. It is changing the way we live, communicate and work. This socio-technological development should be taken into account in schools; therefore, students need to receive a digital education. With the Digital Education Action Plan and the DigComp Framework, the European Commission has developed a strategic plan for digital education and a concrete competence model for its implementation in European schools [2, 3]. In order to ensure that digital education in schools contributes to providing all students with the necessary skills to act as autonomously as possible in a digitalized society throughout their school careers, basic digital competences should be taught as early as primary school [2, 4, 5]. However, the curricular integration of digital education in schools is a complex task influenced by a variety of factors at the level of national school administrations and individual schools. In Germany, the Standing Conference of the Ministers of Education and Cultural Affairs (Kultusministerkonferenz, KMK) serves as the starting point for the implementation of

Ł. Tomczyk (Ed.): NMP 2023, CCIS 2130, pp. 44–58, 2024.
https://doi.org/10.1007/978-3-031-63235-8_3

digital education at primary school. With the strategy "Education in the Digital World" [6] and the recommendations "Teaching and Learning in the Digital World" [7], the KMK sets the framework for digital school development in German schools.

In the course of this ongoing digital school development and the implementation of digital education, the Covid-19 pandemic and the associated worldwide school closures occurred. These disruptions also affect the implementation of digital education in primary schools. Against this background, the DiBiGa project was carried out at the Friedrich-Alexander-University (FAU) Erlangen-Nuremberg and the "JFF - Institute for Media Research and Media Education" from 12.2021 to 12.2023. It investigated the impact of the Covid-19 pandemic on digital education in German primary schools and its current implementation.

This article examines the curricular anchoring of digital education against the backdrop of the possibilities of digital school development. Particular attention is given to the impact of the Covid-19 pandemic on this process.

2 Digitalization and School Development

The social implications of digitalization pose complex challenges for school development [8]. Research on digital school development often emphasizes the establishment and integration of technical infrastructure within educational institutions [9]. In contrast, digital school development is a much more multidimensional process that should not be viewed exclusively from a technology-centered perspective. Therefore, digital school development should primarily focus on issues related to the curricular integration of digital technologies and their pedagogical and didactical use, as the basis for implementing appropriate digital education in the classroom [8]. It is, therefore up to the school leadership to guide the development and curricular implementation of pedagogical approaches that can systematically organize the integration of digital education according to the equipment available, the subject structure and the age-specific development of the children.

However, the options available to school leaders are not only determined by the conditions of the school, but are also shaped by social and institutional contexts and the demands of educational policy. Herzig [10] provides a distinction within Germany among (1) the federal and state levels, (2) the regional and local levels, and (3) the level of the individual school. Thus, school leadership is involved in a complex multi-level system with regard to its options for digital school development. School management in German schools is thus embedded in a complex system which creates a number of bureaucratic hurdles [11].

Given this context, research indicates a pressing need for the advancement of digital technology integration and digital school development within German primary schools. Although, in contrast to the secondary school sector, there is little representative data available for German primary schools, the studies that do exist point to this situation. Existing, older studies show that the implementation of digital education in primary school classes depends primarily on individual teachers [12, 13]. This contradicts the idea that school leaders have a controlling influence on the implementation of digital education. Additionally, data from the context of the Covid-19 pandemic has also high-lighted the various ways in which digital media are used to organize emergency remote teaching [14] and how these methods vary greatly from teacher to teacher [15].

Another important factor influencing the potential for digital education in primary schools is their existing technical infrastructure. Representative studies at the beginning of the Covid-19 pandemic show a lack of appropriate equipment and the necessary infrastructure, especially for primary schools in Germany [16]. Although this situation is improving slightly as the pandemic progresses, it is still insufficient from the point of view of teachers and principals for the appropriate use of digital media in the organization of teaching [17, 18]. The "Progress in International Reading Literacy Study" (PIRLS) also shows that the equipment and use of digital media in German primary schools is significantly below the international average [19]. For example, the study shows that only 16.7% of primary school students in Germany use digital media for at least 30 minutes to search for and read information during a normal school day.

As previously outlined, school leadership is a key element in digital school develop-ment and in improving the described situation in primary schools in Germany. School leadership is responsible for the five dimensions of digital school development: organiza-tional development, curriculum development, personnel development, technology devel-opment and cooperation development [20]. Digital school leadership operates within in a complex relationship between internal school requirements and external actors. It is important to note that school leadership is not provided by a single person who leads the entire school hierarchically. Instead, contemporary concepts of school leadership emphasize the importance of distributed leadership [21]. This makes it clear that school development in general, and digital school development in particular, is a cooperative task for the entire teaching staff, in which school development measures are jointly coordi-nated, documented and implemented in different constellations within the teaching staff [22].

The basis for this school development in Germany is a federally structured education system, in which the federal states are responsible for educational matters. This also applies to digital education. Although national framework guidelines exist, the specific organization and implementation of digital education is the responsibility of the federal states. The "Strategy for Education in the Digital World" of the Standing Conference of the Ministers of Education and Cultural Affairs [6] serves as an important framework for the digital education in the federal states. However, the federal states have the autonomy to integrate these standards into their curricula and to design the corresponding teaching and learning content. What is common throughout Germany is that digital education is not implemented as a separate subject, but rather as an integrated subject. For states and schools, this requires the development of concepts to coordinate and systematically implement subject-specific digital education.

The "Strategy for Education in the Digital World" of the Standing Conference of the Ministers of Education and Cultural Affairs [6] includes a framework for digital competences, based in particular on the European DigComp framework [3]. The KMK framework comprises six competence areas, five of which are directly based on the Dig-Comp model: "Research and storage of data" ("Suchen, Verarbeiten und Aufbewahren"), "communication and collaboration" ("Kommunizieren und Kooperieren"), "producing and presenting" ("Produzieren und Präsentieren"), "protection and safety" ("Schützen und sicher agieren") and "problem solving" ("Problemlösen"). The KMK strategy adds "analysis and reflection" as a sixth competence domain. It is the responsibility of the federal states in Germany to delineate the framework and its six competency areas for school education. As a result some federal states have slightly different models and concepts for the implementation of digital education.

An issue in implementing this framework in schools is that Germany does not yet have a concept for defining different levels of competence within the competence areas. This presents a specific challenge for primary schools due to the fast development of children's learning needs [23]. In digital school development, schools must therefore find solutions to implement the requirements of the KMK competence framework systematically, curricular, subject-related and age-specific in the classroom.

The development of media concepts has proved to be a productive approach in bringing together the complex interplay between available resources, external actors, teachers' starting points and the specificities of pupils and schools, and translating this into a curricular organization of digital education [24]. Media concepts are developed jointly by the staff of the school. On the one hand, they clarify how to use the current possibilities available to organize digital education in different subjects and year groups. On the other hand, the planned steps for the further digital school development are documented in the media concepts. According to Lorenz & Eickelmann in 2021, 67.7% of German secondary schools reported having a media concept [25]. No nationwide data is available for primary schools in Germany. Nevertheless, in Bavaria, 94% of primary school teachers surveyed in a representative study stated that their school had a media concept [26]. In this federal state, though, schools have been obliged to develop such a concept since the end of the 2018/19 school year [6, 27]. Further research is needed on the qualitative design of media plans and the conditions for their successful implementation [24].

The described situation shows that digital school development, and in particular the deliberate and targeted curricular implementation of digital education, is a complex challenge for German primary schools. The approach taken in this article is based on the concept of distributed leadership, where school development is a task managed by a leadership team and implemented collectively by the teaching staff. For German primary schools, the above overview reveals particular challenges with regard to the complex conditions of the (German) school system and the systematic and curricular implementation of digital education in primary school lessons. One established method for systematically integrating digital education into German primary schools based on these conditions involves the development and implementation of school media concepts.

Against this backdrop, the Covid-19 pandemic has posed enormous additional challenges to the global education system. The school closures associated with the pandemic have significantly increased the importance of digital technologies for teaching [14, 28, 29]. German primary schools were also faced with the need to organize their teaching digitally [30]. This increased the importance of digital media in the classroom, and students needed to have basic digital media skills in order to participate. These changes may have contributed to increased efforts to embed digital education in the primary school curriculum. In addition, the importance of clear guidelines, flexible school planning and rapid adaptation to technological developments may have become clearer.

The article focuses on current initiatives to integrate digital education into the German primary school curriculum and the role of the Covid-19 pandemic in this context. It is based on the project "DiBiGa - Future prospects for digital education at primary school age" which investigates the conditions and organization of digital education in German primary schools during and after the pandemic. The findings offer insight into various stakeholder groups' perspectives and assessments regarding the implementation of digital education into the primary school curriculum in Germany, and what challenges and conditions for success they perceive. On the basis of the project, the article examines two research questions:

- How do school stakeholders experience the curricular implementation of digital education in German primary schools and what challenges and conditions for success do they perceive?
- Did the Covid-19 pandemic have an impact on the implementation of digital education in German primary schools from the perspective of the stakeholders surveyed, and how did this impact manifest?

3   Methods

The project "DiBiGa - Future prospects for digital education at primary school age" ran from 12.2021 to 11.2023. It is a joint project of the Friedrich-Alexander-University (FAU) Erlangen-Nuremberg and the "JFF - Institute for Media Research and Media Education". The project consisted of three phases: a systematic literature review [31, 32] (12.2021–03.2022), focus group interviews [33] with different actors of digital education in primary schools [34] (06.2022–03.2023) and a participatory process (08.2023–11.2023). The results of the three project phases were continuously triangulated.

A central aspect of the project was the focus group interviews, which were used to gather the experiences and assessments of different stakeholders in digital education at primary school age. The interviews were conducted online to enable nationwide participation. The JFF conducted a total of ten focus group interviews involving children, parents and educational professionals. FAU interviewed stakeholders in the school context. The article discusses the results of these interviews from the school context. This involved conducting three focus group interviews comprising a total of 14 school principals, four interviews involving a total of 16 representatives from teacher associations, and three interviews including a total of 15 representatives from school administrators. The participants came from 13 of the 16 German federal states (Table 1).

The audio recordings of the focus group interviews were transcribed and analysed with qualitative content analysis [35] using MAXQDA 2022. Deductive and inductive methods were used.

Three heuristic categories were deductively developed to describe the conditions of digital education [36]: "media-related school development", "educational practice," and "individual and family circumstances of the children." These categories were further subdivided into inductive subcategories. Seven subcategories were inductively formed

Table 1. Sample

Focus-Group	Stakeholder	Persons	Federal States	Age	Date
SLGD 01	Headteachers	Five	Bavaria, Rhineland-Palatinate	45–57	14/7/22
SLGD 02	Headteachers	Five	Bavaria, Berlin, Saxony	46–61	19/9/22
SLGD 03	Headteachers	Four	Bavaria, Baden-Wuerttemberg, Hamburg	49–67	2/2/23
LKV GD01	Representatives of teachers' associations	Four	Bavaria, Brandenburg, Rhineland-Palatinate	37–61	11/11/22
LKV GD02	Representatives of teachers' associations	Three	Rhineland-Palatinate, Schleswig-Holstein	30–56	17/11/22
LKV GD03	Representatives of teachers' associations	Five	Bavaria, Baden-Wuerttemberg	36–63	13/2/23
LKV GD04	Representatives of teachers' associations	Four	Bavaria, Baden-Wuerttemberg, Mecklenburg-Western Pomerania	36–55	16/2/23
SAGD 01	Representatives of school administration	Six	Bavaria, Baden-Wuerttemberg, Hamburg, Hesse, North Rhine-Westphalia	42–59	29/11/22
SAGD 02	Representatives of school administration	Five	Bavaria, Baden-Wuerttemberg, Rhineland-Palatinate, Berlin, Brandenburg	31–58	30/11/22
SAGD 03	Representatives of school administration	Four	Bavaria, Lower Saxony, Saarland	40–61	7/12/22

in the category "media-related school development", six subcategories in the category "educational practice", and three subcategories in the category "individual and family circumstances of children". The subcategory "media-related curriculum development" is employed to examine the integration of digital education into the curriculum of German primary schools.

Interview statements in this category describe the way in which digital education is integrated into the school curriculum. This includes the overall development of the curriculum in the context of digital education, as well as school initiatives to establish media concepts that serve as a starting point for the design of a digital education curriculum. The sub-category describes opportunities and challenges in the process of curricular implementation of digital education in German primary schools and includes the perceived impact of the Covid-19 pandemic on this process.

The interviews were coded by four people and intercoder reliability was calculated for each subcode [37]. Intercoder reliability was confirmed for three of the ten interviews by randomly selecting one interview from each stakeholder group. The calculated intercoder reliability for the subcode under consideration is between $x = .91$ and 1.00 (Table 2). Based on this reliability, the developed category system was discussed and revised by the entire research team. The entire data material was coded according to the finalized category system, with continuous exchange and discussion between the researchers.

Table 2. Intercoder reliability

Subcode	School Principles (Interview SLGD03)	Teachers Associations (Interview LKVGD03)	School Administration (Interview SAGD02)
media-related curricula	$x = .91$	$x = 1.00$	$x = 1.00$

4 Results

Based on the first research question, it is initially discussed how the stakeholders interviewed (school principals, representatives of teachers' associations and school administrators) perceive the current conditions of the curricular implementation of digital education in German primary schools (4.1). The second research question will then be examined and the influence of the Covid-19 pandemic on this process will be explained from the interviewees' perspective (4.2).

4.1 Implementation of Digital Education in German Primary Schools

Using the code "media-related curriculum development", the following section describes how the interviewees currently assess the conditions for implementing digital education in German primary schools and what challenges and opportunities they perceive in this context. As a specific tool for this school development process, the assessments of the interviewed stakeholders on the approach of the media concept are then discussed.

With regard to the curricular implementation of digital education in German primary schools, the situation is heterogeneous depending on the federal state. According to the stakeholders interviewed, digital education is taken into account to varying degrees and with different obligations for primary schools in the federal states. However, across the federal states, the interviewees tend to perceive too little obligation from education policy, which means that the successful implementation of digital education depends heavily on the initiatives of particular schools. In this context, many of the interviewees complained about undifferentiated and/or lack of standards and guidelines for schools to implement digital education at the national, state and local levels.

"[...] is simply due to the fact that, um (...) yes, media-related school development has certainly developed individually at individual schools and good concepts have also emerged, but [...] that overall, if we think in terms of Germany as a whole, Germany has simply (...) not really made any progress because everyone has cooked their own little soup, every federal state at least and almost every school in the federal state has done something different and nothing has been learnt from it." (LKVGD01, po.110)

However, in contrast to this overarching trend towards the importance of more stringent government guidelines and regulations for digital education, some stakeholders saw the danger of overly restricting schools' freedom of action.

Another controversial issue was the cross-curricular implementation of digital education in Germany. Some of the interviewees saw the advantage in the fact that the broad and complex subject area of digital education can be addressed in different contexts in a systematic and differentiated way. Other interviewees saw the problem that this would lead to an unclear distribution of responsibilities and make the integration of digital education more difficult and increasingly dependent on single teachers.

"[...] that it is intended as a cross-cutting task. Um, but of course that offers every teacher the excuse of, yes, what else am I supposed to do? And I think that's also a big problem. Erm if/ if it was decidedly said that we now had a subject for digitalization or the digital world, as is now being introduced from the fifth grade in Hesse, at least that, er then/ then the child would at least be called by its name" (SAGD01, pos. 86)

Considering these two main areas of tension, the focus group interviews identified several challenges hindering the curricular implementation of digital education in German primary schools. These challenges exist at three levels: pupil prerequisites, the teaching staff as well as structural and administrative conditions of the schools.

Firstly, the children's personal backgrounds are very different and digital technologies are very present in their everyday lives. The children therefore have different skills and experiences in using digital media. It is a great challenge for teachers to respond to these starting points in a pedagogically appropriate way.

Secondly, the challenges of digital education also extend to the teaching staff. In the focus group interviews, teachers reported very different conditions within the teaching staff in terms of attitude, motivation and willingness to participate in the digital school development. It is considered important to involve teachers fully and systematically in the school development process in order to increase their willingness and motivation.

Thirdly, significant challenges are perceived at the level of education policy and school administration. A fundamental conflict is perceived between rapid technological developments and what are considered to be slow administrative changes. A lack of long-term planning by the school administration is considered. This leads to a lack of or inappropriate technological equipment at school level and to long and difficult bureaucratic processes. There is also a lack of cross-school planning, for example in the form of joint online-courses. The lack of coordination between schools makes it difficult to effectively implement digital education concepts and share best practices.

Interviewees named cooperation and collaboration within the teaching staff and between school leadership and teachers as important conditions conducive to meeting these challenges. One principal chose the image of gears to illustrate the fine tuning of all the stakeholders involved:

"One was this, uh, image with the cog, so to speak, that you/ I am school headmaster and class leader at the [organization] at the same time, that I came, so to speak, uh, with the vision and then, uh, in everyday school management, I've been doing that for three years now and in everyday corona life I actually, uh, have to make sure that these cogs run and interlock for everyday life and that I don't impose myself on my colleagues with my previous knowledge." (SLGD01, pos.25)

It is also considered important to find an appropriate balance between the development of clear conditions by the school administration and education policy and the self-initiated organization of digital education as part of the school's internal development. While respondents do not always agree on how to strike this balance, there is a consensus that it is a key issue for digital school development.

"So, if I want everyone to work with it and make progress, then I have to have a concept, as has already been mentioned a few times. And the state has to have that first. Because what exactly the schools do with it is another story, but I have to have an idea of where I want to go and I can't just hand things out and then see what I can do with them." (LVKGD01, pos. 38)

The interviewees discussed the media curriculum as a crucial tool for managing the relationship between current structural conditions and internal school development. Schools identified the development of a media concept as an important prerequisite for the successful implementation of digital education, provided that it is used to develop a differentiated approach for each subject and year group. A clear definition not only supports teachers, but also creates transparency for pupils and parents. It is important to consider all teachers, their expectations, goals and concerns in this process. The interviews indicated that ongoing development and revision of media concepts are necessary for schools to adjust to evolving conditions and expectations while advancing digital education.

"Well, we have now introduced the Media Compass into primary schools in [town]. It's a, yes, as the name suggests, it's based on the various skills that are developed up to the sixth grade. This ranges from applying and acting to analysing, reflecting, uh problem awareness and acting confidently in the um/ (.) in/ in the digital world. Researching and informing and producing and presenting were also important. Because we cover all of that. And uh we are also required in [location] to use this media compass and also to create a media concept for the schools. We've done that for ourselves too. And there are all these aspects in it, how to/ how to distribute it to the classes, so in/ in a coherent process." (LKVGD02, pos. 33)

Addressing the first research question has shown that the curricular implementation of digital education in German primary schools is based on two intertwined processes that need to be coordinated. On the one hand, there are external - and often challenging - structural conditions due to school administration and education policy, which have an important influence on the implementation of digital education in primary schools. On the other hand, internal school development plays an important role in how these conditions are dealt with and how the curricular development of digital education is implemented on a school-specific basis. In line with existing research [38], it has been shown that joint, cooperative and closely coordinated work within the teaching staff is an important prerequisite for the successful integration of digital education into the curriculum of primary schools. The media concept proves to be an important tool for organizing such joint work, in which the internal and external conditions of digital education can be harmonized. However, the media concept must also be given a high priority in the development of the school and must be developed progressively and cooperatively.

4.2 Impact of the Covid-19 pandemic

The Covid-19 pandemic caused a temporary but profound disruption to schooling around the world. During this time, the use of digital technologies also became a necessary part of teaching in German primary schools. The second research question focuses on whether and to what extent this upheaval has influenced the curricular implementation of digital education in German primary schools.

Overall, the stakeholders interviewed reported a limited impact of the pandemic on the implementation of digital education. Of greater importance was whether schools had been involved in digital school development prior to the pandemic. These schools were able to use their previous experience in the pedagogical use of digital media to cope better with the pandemic and to continue their digital school development during this time.

"[...] the media curriculum itself has remained the same. So before, then the pandemic and now. Um, we just have a/ a/ a/ a/ a mandatory approach to distance learning during the corona period. What is used? How often do the lessons have to be streamed? Erm and so on and so on. So we have that, but ONLY for the time of the pandemic, so for the distance/ where distance or hybrid teaching was running. And since that's over, we've gone back to the normal um/ normal er use of the media in/ was then no/ back in force." (SLGD03, pos. 68)

Schools that were already engaged in digital school development before the Covid-19 pandemic had clear advantages. They could draw on tried-and-tested structures and experience, which allowed them to adapt more flexibly to the challenges posed by the pandemic. Early engagement with digital education thus lays the foundation for sustainable and effective integration into teaching. It is emphasized that media-related pilot projects and similar initiatives before the pandemic had a positive impact on school development during and after it. Media concepts developed before the pandemic were also important, as they could be adapted to the changed situation. The need to switch to digital teaching methods led to adjustments in the media concept in order to meet the requirements of distance learning.

In conclusion, despite the pandemic having a minor impact on digital school development and media concepts, the existence of established structures and obligations ensured a certain degree of stability.

5 Discussion

The curricular implementation of digital education at German primary schools is a complex task in which the interplay between the structural conditions of school administration, education policy and the initiatives of individual schools play a particularly important role for school development. This article looks at this interplay from the perspective of two research questions. Firstly, it delves into how various stakeholders in primary education perceive and assess the integration of digital education into the curriculum. Secondly, it analyses the effects of the Covid-19 pandemic on this implementation. Regarding the integration of digital education into the curriculum of German primary schools, it's evident that pertinent stakeholders still acknowledge several challenges.

Balancing the demands and expectations set by school administration and its bureaucratic processes with the internal development of primary schools proves to be extremely challenging. The resulting challenges are exacerbated by the heterogeneity of the teaching staff in terms of their attitudes and pedagogical use of digital media, as well as the varying abilities of students to use digital technologies. It became clear that intensive cooperation and coordination at the level of the individual schools is required in order to adequately deal with these diverse and complex challenges. In line with the current discourse of school pedagogy, distributed leadership approaches are likely to be suitable for dealing adequately with these requirements [39, 40]. The development of school-specific media concepts proved to be an important tool for advancing digital school development and implementing digital education at primary schools. However, it became clear that this development must be pursued intensively and systematically. Only through the consistent and continuous (further) development of school media concepts with the intensive involvement of the teaching staff will this prove to be a viable tool for the curricular implementation of digital education. Media concepts are therefore an integral part of digital school development.

Overall, the perceived impact of the Covid-19 pandemic on digital school development in German primary schools is limited. While minor impacts are reported, the pandemic has brought about little lasting change due to the pre-existing mandatory nature of the digital school development. Media-related pilot projects and similar initiatives prior to the pandemic had a greater impact on the digital school development and the ability of primary schools to cope with the pandemic.

The results have certain limitations that need consideration. First, due to the qualitative design of the study, the results are not representative of German primary schools. Second, the limited time frame for data collection in the immediate aftermath of the Covid-19 pandemic may have led to the neglect of long-term developments, as short-term adjustments may have been overestimated. Third, due to the lack of national data on school-specific media policies in primary schools, there is a limitation in the comprehensive assessment of these policies. Finally, the study is partly based on self-reporting by teachers, principals and school administrators, which could lead to social desirability bias. Nevertheless, considering these limitations, the project's qualitative and multi-perspective approach enables a nuanced understanding of the curricular integration of digital education in German primary schools. The results of the presented study are also important for considerations of the European and global education system. They provide a differentiated insight into the complex interplay between different institutions and stakeholders in digital school development. This analysis can be compared with approaches in other countries to identify similarities and differences. In this way, conditions for success and challenges of digital school development can be identified on a European or even international level. Different education systems, school types and stakeholder groups can be taken into account. Further international and cross-country research can build on the results presented here, provide new scientific insights and contribute to the development of evidence-based recommendations for policy makers and educational experts.

6 Summary

In the context of the societal changes due to digitalization, there are initiatives at the European level aiming to integrate digital education into school curricula. The implementation of these developments in German schools, especially at the primary level, poses great challenges. Based on a qualitative research project, this article discusses the views of stakeholders of German primary schools on the curricular implementation of digital education and the influence of the Covid-19 pandemic on this process. Through this, the relevance and possibilities of digital school development for dealing with the various challenges of an adequate curricular implementation of digital education became apparent. The school's internal media concept proved to be an important tool for digital school development, provided that it is developed continuously, systematically and with the involvement of the teaching staff. However, it also became clear that digital school development is not only the responsibility of the individual school, but also depends on structural and educational policy conditions.

The results presented expand the state of knowledge by providing a multi-perspective and differentiated insight into the implementation of digital education in German primary schools, taking into account the interplay between different fields of action. In order to gain a more detailed insight into the various interrelationships, the results presented here should be followed by further research. In addition to in-depth qualitative studies, quantitative research projects are also useful in order to relate the findings to larger samples. In addition, it is important that further studies provide an international and cross-country perspective on the results presented in this paper.

References

1. Hepp, A.: Deep Mediatization. Routledge (2019)
2. European Commission. Digital Education Action Plan 2021–2027. Resetting education and training for digital age (2020). https://eur-lex.europa.eu/legal-content/EN/ALL/?uri=CELEX:52020DC0624. Accessed 01 Jan 2024
3. Redecker, C., Yves, P.: European Framework for the Digital Competence of Educators: DigCompEdu. Edited by Europäische Kommission. EUR, Scientific and technical research series 28775. Publications Office of the European Union. Luxembourg (2017). https://doi.org/10.2760/159770. Accessed 10 Jan 2024
4. Pedaste, M., Kallas, K., Baucal, A.: Digital competence test for learning in schools: development of items and scales. Comput. Educ. 203(9), 1–19 (2023). https://doi.org/10.1016/j.compedu.2023.104830. Accessed 10 Jan 2024

5. Huang, C., Wang, J.C.: Effectiveness of a three-dimensional-printing curriculum: developing and evaluating an elementary school design-oriented model course. Comput. Educ. **187**, 1–28 (2022). https://doi.org/10.1016/j.compedu.2022.104553. Accessed 10 Jan 2024
6. Kultusministerkonferenz: Bildung in der digitalen Welt. Strategie der Kultusministerkonferenz (2017). https://www.kmk.org/fileadmin/pdf/PresseUndAktuelles/2018/Digitalstrategie_2017_mit_Weiterbildung.pdf. Accessed 08 Jan 2024
7. Kultusministerkonferenz: Lehren und Lernen in der digitalen Welt. Die ergänzenden Empfehlungen zur Strategie Bildung in der digitalen Welt (2021). https://www.kmk.org/fileadmin/veroeffentlichungen_beschluesse/2021/2021_12_09-Lehren-und-Lernen-Digi.pdf. Accessed 10 Jan 2024
8. Håkansson Lindqvist, M., Pettersson, F.: Digitalization and school leadership: on the complexity of leading for digitalization in school. Int. J. Inf. Learn. Technol. **36**(3), 218–230 (2019) https://doi.org/10.1108/IJILT-11-2018-0126. Accessed 10 Jan 2024
9. Krein, U.: What's your take on school leadership and digitalization? A systematic review of publications from the last 20 years. Int. J. Leadersh. Educ. (2023). https://doi.org/10.1080/13603124.2023.2237939. Accessed 08 Jan 2024
10. Herzig, B.: Institutionen der Medienpädagogik. Schule und Medien. In: Sander, U.F., von Gross, F., Hugger, K.U. (eds.) Handbuch Medienpädagogik, pp. 841–851. Springer, Wiesbaden (2022). https://doi.org/10.1007/978-3-531-91158-8. Accessed 10 Jan 2024
11. Krein, U.: Hätten Wir keinen Digitalpakt, hätten wir eine bessere Ausstattung: Schulische Infrastruktur zwischen politischen Versprechungen Und netzfreier Realität. MedienPädagogik: Zeitschrift für Theorie Und Praxis Der Medienbildung **49**, 185–203 (2022). https://doi.org/10.21240/mpaed/49/2022.06.28.X. Accessed 10 Jan 2024
12. Breiter, A., Aufenanger, S., Averbeck, I., Welling, S., Wedjelek, M.: Medienintegration in Grundschulen. Untersuchung zur Förderung von Medienkompetenz und der unterrichtlichen Mediennutzung in Grundschulen sowie ihrer Rahmenbedingungen in Nordrhein-Westfalen. Vistas, Berlin (2013). https://www.medienanstalt-nrw.de/fileadmin/user_upload/LfM-Band-73.pdf. Accessed 10 Jan 2024
13. Schmid, U., Goertz, L., Behrens, J.: Monitor Digitale Bildung. Die Schulen im digitalen Zeitalter. Bertelsmann, Gütersloh (2017). https://www.bertelsmann-stiftung.de/fileadmin/files/BSt/Publikationen/GrauePublikationen/BSt_MDB3_Schulen_web.pdf. Accessed 08 Jan 2024
14. Bond, M.: Schools and emergency remote education during the COVID-19 pandemic: a living rapid systematic review. Asian J. Distance Educ. **15**(2), 191–247 (2021). https://doi.org/10.5281/zenodo.4425683. Accessed 10 Jan 2024
15. Schneider, R., Sachse, K.A., Schipolowski, S., Enke, F.: Teaching in times of COVID-19. The evaluation of distance teaching in elementary and secondary schools in Germany. Front. Educ. **6**, 1–17 (2021). https://doi.org/10.3389/feduc.2021.702406. Accessed 10 Jan 2024
16. Forsa Politik- und Sozialforschung GmbH: Das Deutsche Schulbarometer Spezial. Corona-Krise: Folgebefragung. Berlin (2020). https://deutsches-schulportal.de/content/uploads/2021/01/Deutsches-Schulbaromater-Folgebefragung.pdf. Accessed 10 Jan 2024
17. Forsa Politik- und Sozialforschung GmbH: Das Deutsche Schulbarometer Spezial: Zweite Folgebefragung. Berlin (2021). https://deutsches-schulportal.de/deutsches-schulbarometer/downloads/Deutsches_Schulbarometer_Lehrkraeftebefragung_September_2021_Final-1.pdf. Accessed 10 Jan 2024
18. Gogolin, I., Köller, O., Hastedt, D.: Kontinuität und Wandel der Schule in Krisenzeiten. Erste Ergebnisse der KWiK-Schulleitungsbefragung im Sommer/Frühherbst 2020 (2021). https://www.leibniz-ipn.de/de/das-ipn/aktuelles/archiv/KWiK_Ergebnisse.pdf. Accessed 10 Jan 2024
19. Lorenz, R., Goldhammer, F., Glondys, M.: Digitalisierung in der Grundschule. In: McElvany, N., et al. (eds.) IGLU 2021. Lesekompetenz von Grundschulkindern im internationalen Vergleich und im Trend über 20 Jahre, pp. 197–214. Waxmann (2023)

20. Gerick, J., Eickelmann, B.: Pädagogisches Leitungshandeln im Kontext der Digitalisierung – Prioritäten und Aufgaben von Schulleitungen in Schulentwicklungsprozessen mit digitalen Medien. In: Huber, S.G. (ed.) Jahrbuch Schulleitung 2019. Befunde und Impulse zu den Handlungsfeldern des Schulmanagements, pp. 259–278. Karl Link Verlag, Köln (2019)
21. Schiefner-Rohs, M.: Schulleitung in der digital geprägten Gesellschaft. In: Buchen, H., Rolff, H. (eds.) Professionswissen Schulleitung, 4th edn., pp. 1402–1419. Beltz.Weinheim, Basel (2016)
22. Muckenthaler, M., et al.: Teacher collaboration as a core objective of school development. Sch. Effectiveness Sch. Improv. Int. J. Res. Policy Pract. 31(3), 486–504 (2020). https://doi.org/10.1080/09243453.2020.1747501. Accessed 08 Jan 2024
23. Kammerl, R., Dertinger, A., Kramer, M.: Wie verändern sich Kindheit und Grundschule in einer durch Digitalität geprägten Welt? Digitale Bildung als Herausforderung für pädagogische Akteur*innen. In: Irion, T., Peschel, M., Schmeinck, D. (eds.) Grundschule und Digitalität. Grundlagen, Herausforderungen, Praxisbeispiele, pp. 54–67. Grundschulverband, Frankfurt am Main (2023)
24. Schulze, J., Drossel, K., Eickelmann, B.: Implementierung schulischer Medienkonzepte als Kooperationsanlass. Eine multiperspektivische Betrachtung zu Kooperationsprozessen zwischen Schulen der Sekundarstufe I und dem Unterstützungssystem der Medienberatung NRW. MedienPädagogik: Zeitschrift für Theorie und Praxis der Medienbildung 49, 115–136 (2022). https://doi.org/10.21240/mpaed/49/2022.06.25.X. Accessed 08 Jan 2024
25. Lorenz, R., Eickelmann, B.: Nutzung digitaler Medien im Unterricht der Sekundarstufe I und Nutzungsbedingungen im Trendvergleich von 2017 und 2021. In: Lorenz, R., Yotyodying, S., Eickelmann, B., Endberg, M. (eds.) Schule digital – der Länderindikator 2021. Lehren und Lernen mit digitalen Medien in der Sekundarstufe I in Deutschland im Bundesländervergleich und im Trend seit 2017, pp. 63–88. Waxmann, Münster (2021)
26. Lohr, et al.: Digitale Bildung an bayerischen Schulen vor und während der Corona-Pandemie. vbw, München (2021). https://www.vbw-bayern.de/Redaktion/Frei-zugaengliche-Medien/Abteilungen-GS/Bildung/2021/Downloads/Bi-0174-001_Digitale-Bildung-an-bayerischen-Schulen-vor-und-w%C3%A4hrend-der-Corona-Pandemie_ohne-Fax.pdf. Accessed 10 Jan 2024
27. Staatsinstitut für Schulqualität und Bildungsforschung München: Medienkonzepte an bayrischen Schulen. Referat Medienbildung (2019). https://mebis.bycs.de/assets/uploads/mig/3_2017_10_ISB_-Medienkonzepte-an-bayerischen-Schulen.pdf. Accessed 10 Jan 2024
28. Al Mazrooei, A.K., Almaki, S.H., Gunda, M., Alnoor, A., Sulaiman, S.M.: A systematic review of K–12 education responses to emergency remote teaching during the COVID-19 pandemic. Int. Rev. Educ. 68, 811–841 (2022). https://doi.org/10.1007/s11159-023-09986-w. Accessed 10 Jan 2024
29. Yi, P.: Teachers' communities of practice in response to the COVID-19 pandemic: will innovation in teaching practices persist and prosper? J. Curriculum Teach. 11(5), 241–251 (2022). https://doi.org/10.5430/jct.v11n5p241. Accessed 10 Jan 2024
30. Porsch, R., Porsch, T.: Homeschooling as an exceptional situation findings from a nationwide survey of parents with primary school children. In: Fickermann, D., Edelstein, B. (eds.) Langsam vermisse ich die Schule. Schule während und nach der Corona-Pandemie, pp. 61–78. Waxmann, Münster (2020)
31. Dertinger, A., Kramer, M., Koschei, F., Schmidt, L., Eggert, S., Kammerl, R.: How has distance schooling during the COVID-19-pandemic affected digital education of elementary school children? A systematic review. J. Elementary Educ. Res. 16(2), 449–464 (2023). https://doi.org/10.1007/s42278-023-00182-1. Accessed 10 Jan 2024
32. Dertinger, A., Kramer, M., Kammerl, R.: Ein Mosaik an Erkenntnissen. Interdisziplinäre Perspektiven auf das Grundschulalter während des pandemiebedingten Distance-Schoolings auf

Grundlage eines systematischen Literaturreviews. MedienPädagogik: Zeitschrift für Theorie und Praxis der Medienbildung **20**, 461–494 (2023). https://doi.org/10.21240/mpaed/jb20/2023.09.18.X. Accessed 10 Jan 2024

33. Merton, R.K., Fiske, M., Kendall, P.L.: The Focused Interview. A Manual of Problems and Procedures. Free Press, New York (1956)

34. Bärnreuther, C., Dertinger, A., Kammerl, R.: Digitale Bildung: (k)ein Schub durch Covid-19? On: Lernen in der digitalen Welt **15**, 30–31 (2023)

35. Kuckartz, U.: Qualitative text analysis: a systematic approach. In: Kaiser, G., Presmeg, N. (eds.) Compendium for Early Career Researchers in Mathematics Education. IM, pp. 181–197. Springer, Cham (2019). https://doi.org/10.1007/978-3-030-15636-7_8 Accessed 10 Jan 2024

36. Bärnreuther, C., Kammerl, R., Stephan, M., Martschinke, S.: Professionalisierung für Digitale Bildung: Ein Rahmenmodell zur Untersuchung der Kompetenzen angehender Lehrpersonen. In: Irion, T., Böttinger, T., Kammerl, R. (eds.) Professionalisierung für Digitale Bildung im Grundschulalter: Ergebnisse des Forschungsprojekts P^{3}DiG, pp. 235–250 (2023). https://doi.org/10.31244/9783830996415. Accessed 10 Jan 2024

37. O'Connor, C., Joffe, H.: Intercoder reliability in qualitative research: debates and practical guidelines. Int. J. Qual. Methods **19** (2020). https://doi.org/10.1177/1609406919899220. Accessed 01 Jan 2024

38. Rolff, H.G.: Schulentwicklung kompakt. Modelle, Instrumente, Perspektiven. Beltz, Weinheim (2023)

39. Brown, B., Jacobsen, M.: Principals' technology leadership: how a conceptual framework shaped a mixed methods study. J. Sch. Leadersh. **26**(5), 811–836 (2016). https://doi.org/10.1177/105268461602600504. Accessed 10 Jan 2024

40. Schiefner-Rohs, M.: Distributed Digital Leadership: Schulleitungshandeln im Wandel. In: Buchen, H., Horster, L., Rolff, H.G. (eds.) Schulleitung und Schulentwicklung: Führen, Managen, Steuern (04/19, F 8.16/1–22). Raabe. Fachverl. für Bildungsmanagement, Zürich (2019)

Pathway Analysis of the Dynamics of Teacher Educators' Professional Digital Competence

Siri Sollied Madsen[1]($\boxtimes$) (iD), Heidi I. Saure[2] (iD), Marit H. Lie[2] (iD), Aleksander Janeš[3] (iD), Andreja Klančar[3] (iD), Rita Brito[4] (iD), and Steinar Thorvaldsen[1] (iD)

[1] UiT The Arctic University of Norway, 9037 Tromsø, Norway
`siri.s.madsen@uit.no`
[2] NLA University College, 5812 Bergen, Norway
[3] University of Primorska, 6000 Koper, Slovenia
[4] ISEC Lisboa, Universidade Católica Portuguesa, 1750-142 Lisbon, Portugal

Abstract. Institutions offering teacher education have generally been criticized for giving pre-service teachers an insufficient education regarding the pedagogical use of digital technology. In this study we investigate the dynamics of professional digital competence (PDC) among teacher educators (in primary, secondary and early childhood teacher education programmes) in Norway, Slovenia, and Portugal. A survey was constructed based on the understanding of digital competence consisting of an individual's knowledge, skills, and attitudes. Three constructed variables from the survey (Attitudes, Knowledge and skills, and Use, regarding digital technology in higher education) were analysed, and we found small differences in mean scores between the three countries. However, a pathway analysis via regressions revealed markedly different dynamics of PDC, and we discuss implications of our findings on teacher educators' use of digital technology.

Keywords: Digital Competence · Attitudes · Skills · Knowledge · Teacher Education · Teacher Educators · Higher Education

1 Introduction

The European Commission defines digital competence as a key competence for lifelong learning [1], but digital competence within teacher education is complex. Teacher educators need sufficient digital competence to teach in a digitized era, whilst at the same time they are to facilitate pre-service teachers' own development of professional digital competence (PDC) [2]. The teacher educators' PDC therefore contains several levels of competencies, including their own didactical understanding of using technology as well as content for facilitating pre-service teachers' development of PDC for other levels of the educational system. Teacher education has across nations been criticized for not preparing pre-service teachers regarding a sufficient level of PDC [3–5]. Our study aims to contribute to knowledge on what factors influence the development of PDC amongst teacher educators. More specifically, we investigate the dynamics of

The original version of this chapter was revised. This chapter was previously published with non-open access. A correction to this chapter can be found at
https://doi.org/10.1007/978-3-031-63235-8_30

digital competence, building on the established understanding of digital competence as consisting of an individual's knowledge, skills, and attitudes [6–9]. Our study is based on survey responses from teacher educators from higher education institutions in Norway, Slovenia, and Portugal.

Research question: What are the dynamics of teacher educators' professional digital competence, and how is this related to their application of digital technology in educational practices?

2   Background

2.1   Conceptual Understanding of PDC

There are several frameworks developed trying to grasp the complexity of PDC, such as the TPACK model [10], the professional digital competence framework for teachers [11] and DigCompEdu [12]. Digital competence has developed into a complex concept, and Erstad et al. [13] discuss how this is related to a lack of conceptual clarity. What is common for the above-mentioned frameworks is that they to some extent build on the notion of competence as consisting of skills, knowledge, and attitudes (Fig. 1). This understanding is also widely used when talking about digital competence. Ferrari [6] did a review of 15 frameworks, and merged and summarized a common definition of digital competence:

> Digital Competence is the set of knowledge, skills, attitudes, abilities, strategies, and awareness that are required when using ICT and digital media to perform tasks; solve problems; communicate; manage information; collaborate; create and share content; and build knowledge effectively, efficiently, appropriately, critically, creatively, autonomously, flexibly, ethically, reflectively for work, leisure, participation, learning, and socialising.

The understanding of knowledge, skills, and attitudes as central for digital competence is also evident in recent studies and newer formal frameworks [1, 7, 8, 12, 14].

2.2   Governmental Approaches to Digital Competence in Education and Lifelong Learning for Norway, Slovenia and Portugal

The European Commission defines digital competence as a key competence for lifelong learning [1]. This understanding of competencies is globally used and is also found in policies for Norway, Slovenia, and Portugal. The same understanding of the concept is for instance described in official Norwegian reports, such as NOU 2014:7 [15] and NOU 2018:2 [16], which are formal policy documents guiding the governing of education. The same notion of digital competence is also found in Slovenian policy and documents [17] and other documents related to education [18]. Slovenia focuses intensively on the digital transformation of society, the state, local communities, and the economy to improve the quality of life of the Slovenian population. The digital transformation of the society is regarded as a key strategy to manage the future in a sustainable way [17].

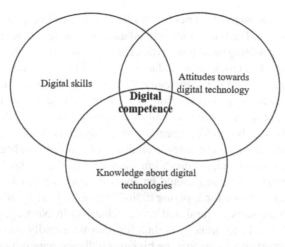

Fig. 1. Digital competence as a combination of knowledge, skills, and attitudes [1, 7].

The establishment of the Slovenian Ministry for Digital Transformation, the adoption of the Digital Slovenia 2030 strategy [17] and sectoral strategies and action plans such as the Slovenian Action Plan for Digital Education [18] have laid the foundations for this process.

The Portuguese Ministry of Education has placed a lot of emphasis on digital skills in education. To this adds the "National Digital Skills Initiative e.2030, Portugal INCoDe.2030" [19]. This is a public policy initiative, launched in 2017, which aims to promote digital skills. For the Portuguese Ministry of Education, digital skills are essential for the full exercise of citizenship, also acting as a facilitator of employability, as they respond to the demands of the growing digitalization of the labor market: a more qualified active population gives rise to new forms of work, new professions, innovative markets and products and, therefore, more robust and competitive economic activities. The Digital Education Action Plan-Portugal (DETP, 2021–2027) [20] was initiated by the European Commission to promote the effective use of digital technologies in schools by supporting innovation in teaching and learning practices.

Even though several European frameworks are building on the same notion of digital competence, there are differences in the educational contexts and cultures in countries across Europe. This is evident when looking at national reports and policies from the three nations included in our study.

2.3 Norwegian Higher Education and Digital Technology

In 2021 the Norwegian ministry of education and research launched a strategy for all higher education institutions in Norway, applicable for 2021–2025 [21]. The strategy builds on the notion that there is a great unused potential regarding the application of digital technology in higher education. This strategy highlights the structure and content of education. Higher education needs to be made available through decentralized and flexible programs, as well as programs that contribute to develop students' need for specific PDC. Policy reviews of teacher programs for early childhood education show that implementation of PDC in local curricula is limited compared to expectations expressed in national frameworks. The level of implementation also varies across institutions [22].

One challenge in meeting these goals is that educators have not developed their digital practices sufficiently. Pedagogical and didactical aspects related to applying technology in education are described to not sufficiently align with the content and the intention to facilitate students' learning processes. Educators need training in how to transform traditional education to education with, as well as through the means of, digital technology [21]. In a national report about pedagogical use of digital technology in higher education, it is clearly stated that digital technology itself does not contribute to higher pedagogical quality [23]. On the other hand, the prevailing discourse in Norwegian higher education is that digital technology can and should be applied in ways that adds value to teaching. Other legitimate reasons for applying digital technology are to offer flexible study programs to reach students in rural and remote districts in Norway. The Norwegian education system's use of technology is therefore not necessarily pedagogically motivated. The same report concludes that the biggest challenge regarding pedagogical use of digital technology in higher education is a lack of relevant and sufficient PDC among educators [23].

2.4 Slovenian Higher Education and Digital Technology

The use of digital technologies in Slovenian higher education is evolving, with a growing emphasis on digital competence among educators. While progress has been made, ongoing efforts are needed to ensure that all educators possess the necessary digital skills and pedagogical knowledge to effectively integrate technology into their teaching practices [24].

The Slovenian National Assembly, in March 2022, adopted a resolution on the national program of higher education until 2030 [25]. This resolution aims to improve the quality, attractiveness, and responsiveness of higher education to society. The document sets out strategic objectives in the following areas: (i) linking the higher education system to social development; (ii) improving legislation and increasing funding; (iii) enhancing quality; (iv) promoting internationalization; and (v) advancing digitalization [26]. The resolution underscores the significance of digital competencies and skills for successful operation in modern society and emphasizes the need to adapt higher education programs and processes to digital trends. It also proposes measures to enhance digital infrastructure, support, and inclusion in higher education. Furthermore, the document highlights the connection between digitalization and the green transition, which are key priorities of the EU and Slovenia. It asserts that higher education must contribute to addressing the challenges posed by digital and green transformations while promoting sustainable development and innovation in these areas. It is predicted in the document that digital internationalization will become an integral part of the higher education system, facilitating increased mobility, collaboration, and knowledge exchange among higher education institutions, students, and employees in Slovenia and abroad [26].

2.5   Portuguese Higher Education and Digital Technology

Higher education in Portugal does not have a specific policy regarding the development of digital skills. However, the European Digital Competence Framework for Educators (DigCompEdu) [12] is launched in Portuguese, a document aimed at teachers, from pre-school education to secondary education and higher education, but also towards adults, including general and professional training, special education, and non-formal learning contexts [27]. The Digital Education Action Plan-Portugal (DETP, 2021–2027) [18] was initiated by the European Commission to promote the effective use of digital technologies in schools by supporting innovation in teaching and learning practices. Based on European Union policy initiatives, the Portuguese Ministry of Education has implemented measures in all education cycles, from pre-school to higher education. To this end, the Ministry of Education has created the Action Plan for Digital Education, transversal to all study cycles in Portugal. It is suggested that teachers carry out an Action Plan for Digital School Development [28]. This Plan aims at the efficient use of digital technologies in teaching and learning and must be implemented by the Digital Development Team of each institution. Through the Digital Education Action Plan, it is intended that educational institutions have a common vision of high-quality, inclusive, and accessible digital education, with the aim of supporting the adaptation of education and training systems to the digital era.

3   Methods

This study is based on a survey conducted at institutions providing teacher education in Norway, Slovenia, and Portugal (Table 1). The target group for the study was teacher educators at teacher programs for early childhood education, and primary and secondary education. The sample from Norway included two institutions: UiT the Arctic University of Norway, with campuses in Tromsø and Alta, and NLA University College, with campuses in Oslo and Bergen. The Slovenian sample was from the University of Primorska, and the Portuguese sample was from the Catholic University of Portugal. These three countries were included in the survey because they differ with regards to context; national strategies, infrastructures, and teacher education systems (see Sect. 2.2–2.5. For more detailed context description, see Janes et al. 2023 [29] and Madsen et al. 2023 [30].

Table 1.   Number of participants.

Nation	Participants (n)	Response rate
Norway	175	76.42%
Slovenia	39	67.24%
Portugal	37	78.72%

An online questionnaire was used, with five-point Likert-type scales (from 1: Strongly disagree, to 5: Strongly agree). Based on the questionnaire three main constructs were established: 1. Attitudes towards digital technology in higher education (8 items), 2. Skills and knowledges regarding digital technology in higher education (8 items), and 3. Use of digital tools when teaching (16 items). For construct details see Appendix. The survey was translated to the different native languages and distributed by email through an online survey tool (Nettskjema) to all teacher educators associated with the range of teacher education at each institution. Data was gathered late 2021 and during the first half of 2022.

3.1 Ethical Considerations

The survey was anonymous, and participation was voluntary. We did not collect personal data or sensitive information; therefore, ethical approval was not formally needed.

3.2 Analysis

A simple pathway modelling and exploration was conducted via regression analysis. The dependent and independent variables were interchanged to find the best model fit. Data were analysed in SPSS (Version 29.0, IBM, Armonk, NY, USA). We calculated mean scores for the different constructs, and report mean scores for each of these. For reliability we calculated Cronbach's alpha for a measure of internal consistency, with satisfying results (Table 2). Following this, multiple linear regression analysis was conducted, and effect sizes were estimated by the standardized beta coefficients, with conventions: 0–0.1 = weak effect, 0.1–0.3 = modest effect, 0.3–0.5 = moderate effect, and >0.5 = strong effect [31, p. 749]. A goodness of fit was determined from the adjusted R-square (i.e. explanatory power): 0–0.1 = poor fit, 0.1–0.3 = modest fit, 0.3–0.5 = moderate fit, and >0.5 = strong fit [31, p. 804]. When presenting the results, explanatory power is shown as percentage based on the adjusted R-square.

The results from the regression analyses are presented in tables based on the different models and individual analyses were conducted for each nation (Table 3, 4 and 5). The statistically significant standardized regression coefficients for each nation in Tables 3, 4 and 5 are further visualized in three models of the dynamics of digital competence (Figs. 2, 3 and 4). As the elements within digital competence are mutually affecting each other we conducted regression analyses without assuming a one-way relationship between attitudes, skills, and knowledges. Neither are we assuming that there is a one-way relationship between competencies and use of technology, as using technology will also affect educators' level of knowledge, skills, and attitudes.

3.3 Limitations

The study has several limitations that could affect the validity of the results and needs to be addressed. The study includes small sample sizes for some of the nations, which makes the results less reliable. Due to the small sample sizes and the fact that data is collected at only one university for some nations, we have no intention of generalizing the finding to a larger national context. Nevertheless, we have no indication that the universities included in the study stand out in comparison to other universities.

Results regarding comparison between nations must be read with reservations, as the survey response scales are constructed with vague quantifiers. For instance, what is understood as "often" in one national context could differ from another national context.

When conducting research within our own workplaces there is always a risk of researcher bias. As this is a quantitative study with limited elements of subjective interpretations, we assess this risk as limited. There is a risk during the discussion that we are affected by preconceptions associated with our positions within the field we are researching.

4   Results

Teacher educators in all three countries showed a similar pattern in their answers (Table 2). The construct "use of digital tools when teaching" indicate that they occasionally utilised digital tools (Table 2). The mean scores for Norway show a tendency towards answering "rarely". On the construct "attitudes toward digital technology" the mean score indicated answers in the range from neutral to "agree", which can be interpreted as relatively positive attitudes, but with some restraints (Table 2). On this construct the variation around the mean (standard deviation) was highest among the constructs for Norway and Slovenia, indicating a higher variation in answers when it came to attitudes than the two other constructs. On the questions about knowledge and skills related to technology, the teacher educators evaluated themselves quite positively (Table 2). The Norwegian and Portuguese teacher educators mostly agreed on statements describing different aspects of their skills and knowledge, whereas the teacher educators from Slovenia scored slightly lower on this variable.

Table 2. Mean scores (SD). 1–5 (See Appendix for details).

Multi item constructs	Norway	Slovenia	Portugal
Use of digital tools when teaching (16 items, alpha = 0,775)	2.89 (0.53)	3.06 (0.65)	3.00 (0.49)
Attitudes towards digital technology in higher education (8 items, alpha = 0,811)	3.21 (0.74)	3.54 (0.73)	3.67 (0.56)
Knowledge and skills related to technology in higher education (8 items, alpha = 0,775)	4.00 (0.57)	3.65 (0.67)	3.99 (0.60)

4.1   Norway

When looking at the pathway-analysis based on the Norwegian sample, there were significant and reciprocal relations between Use and Knowledge & skills, and between Knowledge & skills and Attitude (Fig. 2, Table 3, 4 and 5). The effect sizes of the significant predictors were all within the modest effect interval (for intervals see Sect. 3.2). No significant relations were found between the variables Attitude and Use (Fig. 2, Table 5).

Table 3. Regression analysis with Use as the dependent variable, and Attitude, and Knowledge & skills as predictors.

Nation	Predictors	Beta (standardized)	P-value	R-square
Norway	Knowledge and skills	**.362*****	<.001	.16
	Attitude	.103	.187	
Slovenia	Knowledge and skills	**.591****	.013	.15
	Attitude	−.232	.312	
Portugal	Knowledge and skills	.410	.080	.09
	Attitude	−.365	.117	

Table 4. Regression analysis with Knowledge and skills as the dependent variable, and Use, and Attitude as predictors.

Nation	Predictors	Beta (standardized)	P-value	R-square
Norway	Use	**.308*****	<.001	.29
	Attitude	**.376*****	<.001	
Slovenia	Use	**.270***	.013	.61
	Attitude	**.693*****	<.001	
Portugal	Use	.214	.080	.49
	Attitude	**.711*****	<.001	

Table 5. Regression analysis with Attitude as the dependent variable, and Use, and Knowledge & skills as predictors.

Nation	Predictors	Beta (standardized)	P-value	R-square
Norway	Knowledge and skills	**.419*****	<.001	.21
	Use	.098	.187	
Slovenia	Knowledge and skills	−.122	.312	.55
	Use	**.802*****	<.001	
Portugal	Knowledge and skills	**.724*****	<.001	.49
	Use	−.194	.117	

Attitude was thus not a predictor for teacher educators' use of technology, and neither was their use of technology predicting their attitude. Knowledge and skills on the other hand seemed to be a central element for both use and attitude. However, the variation explained in either of the three regressions were modest (Table 3, 4 and 5, see Sect. 3.2 for intervals of explanatory power).

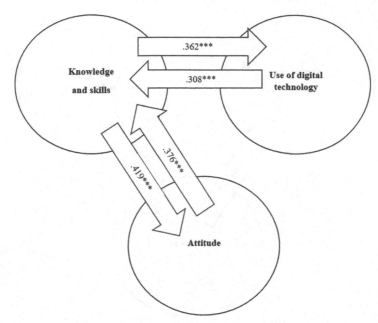

Fig. 2. Dynamics between elements of digital competence and the use of digital technology in Norwegian teacher education (significant standardized coefficients in the arrows). Arrows point from predictors to dependent variables.

4.2 Slovenia

The results from the Slovenian dataset (Fig. 3) showed that the variables Use and Knowledge & skills were mutually affecting each other; Use was a significant predictor of Knowledge & skills and vice versa. The teacher educators' knowledge and skills could be predicted by both Use and Attitude (Table 4). This model had strong explanatory power (0.61 = strong fit, see Sect. 3.2 for intervals of explanatory power). The effect of attitude was more than double the effect of Use on Knowledge & skills. Following the pathway, we see that Attitude influenced Knowledge & skills, Knowledge & skills had an impact on Use, and Use was a significant predictor of Attitude. There was thus a circuit of indirectly related variables.

4.3 Portugal

For the Portuguese sample there was a distinct mutual relationship between Knowledge & skills and Attitude (Fig. 3). The knowledge & skills of the teacher educators in Portugal could explain almost 50% of the variation in their attitudes and vice versa (R^2 in Table 4 and 5). There were no significant relationships between Use and Attitude, or between Use and Knowledge & skills.

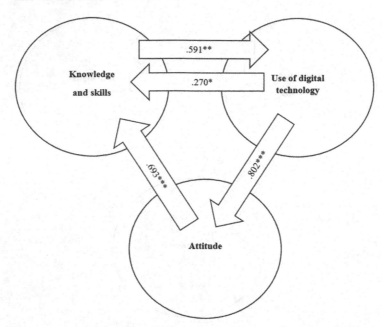

Fig. 3. Dynamics between elements of digital competence and the use of digital technology in Slovenian teacher education (significant standardized coefficients in the arrows). Arrows point from predictors to dependent variables.

5 Discussion

Teacher educators in the three countries included in our study (Norway, Slovenia, and Portugal) had quite similar use of digital technology in pedagogical settings, which was also the case for knowledge and skills, and attitudes towards the use of digital technology. However, the dynamics of the relationships between these factors were distinctly different between the countries. One consistent finding though, was that the use of digital technology could not be predicted by the teacher educators' attitudes in any of the countries.

Provided that the goal of the governmental processes described in the Sects. 2.2 to 2.5, is to improve and increase the use of digital technology in teaching, our results indicate that processes aiming to influence the attitudes of teacher educators will not necessarily lead to success. This contrasts previous studies where attitudes were found to have the strongest effect on technology use [32]. We found, on the other hand, that attitude was a significant predictor for teacher educators' knowledge and skills, and that knowledge and skills could partly explain the use of digital technology in their teaching. Based on our results it may seem like the educational systems are still in their empirical phase, i.e. experience with digital technology is gained prior to established attitudes regarding the matter. Attitude thus seemed to be a factor that indirectly affected teacher educators' use of digital technology, while the actual use of digital technology and gained skills and knowledge seemed to be the basis for developed attitudes in the current phase of the digital transformation of education.

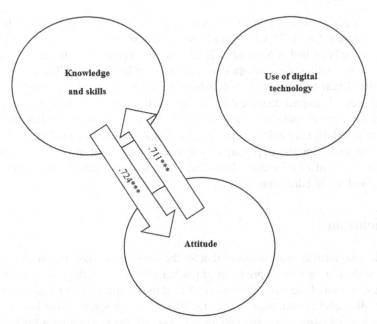

Fig. 4. Dynamics between elements of digital competence and the use of digital technology in Portuguese teacher education (significant standardized coefficients in the arrows). Arrows point from predictors to dependent variables.

The actual use of digital technology in the teacher educators' pedagogical work is likely to be influenced by factors that we have not measured, such as curriculum content, expectations and technical-pedagogical support provided by leaders, structure of the study programmes, responses from students, or access to equipment and software in the lecture rooms [2, 33–36]. These are possible explanations to why we found that knowledge and skills, or attitudes towards digital technology, to a limited extent could explain the teacher educators' use of digital technology in our study. In fact, these constructs could not explain the use of digital technology amongst Portuguese teacher educators at all. Furthermore, we deal with self-reported data, in which there is a risk that they are overrated (see e.g. [7, 37]. This could influence the measured relationship between the extent of teacher educators' use of digital technology, their attitudes and knowledges and skills. In general, conclusions based on our findings should be drawn with some caution. For instance, the results from the Norwegian sample differ from previous results based on the same survey tool conducted prior to the pandemic. A comparative study of teacher educators from Norway and New Zealand concluded that the professional use of digital tools was dominated by professional attitude [38].

The Covid-19 pandemic and the recent introduction of AI could be relevant setbacks or changes in the development of PDC amongst teacher educators. The imposed and extensive use of distant education during Covid-19 changed pre-service teachers' attitudes towards education [39]. Teacher educators are also expressing concerns regarding students' in-depth learning and development of critical thinking skills when learning is influenced by digital technology [40]. Times are challenging for teacher educators as the context is developing fast, and there is an ongoing need to adapt to these challenges [41]. For instance, ChatGPT set a record for the fastest-growing consumer application in history when launched in November 2022. The tool is estimated to have reached 100 million monthly active users within two months after launch [42]. The implication of an educational transformation like this, where we are in the process of finding out artificial intelligence's impact on education, is that teacher educators must proactively seek to educate themselves and their students [43]. Indeed, in our study we have found that knowledge and skills may influence the teacher educators' use of digital technology. Our findings thus underline the importance of teacher educational institutions to facilitate further development of educators' knowledge and skills to achieve competent use of digital technology in education.

6 Conclusion

The conducted pathway analyses show that for the contexts we have investigated, knowledge and skills is a significant predictor of teacher educators' pedagogical use of digital technology for two of the three countries included in our study. Attitude does not significantly predict teacher educators' use of technology when teaching but has an indirect relation to teacher educators' use of technology, as attitude is a predictor for knowledge and skills. What sems to be a disruption within teacher educators' PDC is argued to be related to the ongoing educational transformation, inducing educators to rapidly develop new knowledges and skills.

Acknowledgements. We would like to acknowledge Beate Gjesdal for contributing to collecting data at NLA, this was an important part of the process and contributed to a large Norwegian data set.

Funding. Not applicable.

Availability of Data and Materials. The datasets used and/or analysed during the current study are available from the corresponding author on reasonable request.

Competing Interests. The authors declare that they have no competing interests.

Appendix: DigiCross Survey Items Used in This Study

Use of Technology When Teaching
Which digital tools and work methods have you used in your own teaching in the past year?

The following variables have the alternatives: 1 Never, 2 Rarely, 3 Occasionally, 4 Often, 5 Extensively

1. Digital tools for testing with multiple choice questions
2. Platforms like Moodle or Fronter (Learning management systems).
3. Digital tools for presentations (like Powerpoint or Prezi)

4. Word processor
5. Spreadsheets (like Excel)
6. Use of video
7. Production of film/video/animation
8. Online discussions
9. Online meetings (like Lync, Adobe Connect or Skype)
10. Production of Wiki (website which allows collaborative modification)
11. Screen capture (like Camtasia or Mediasite)
12. Programs for scientific analyses (like SPSS)
13. Student response systems, Online questions answered by phone or computers (like Kahoot og Socrative
14. Tools for collaborative writing (like Google docs)
15. Social media (like Facebook or Twitter)
16. The internet as a source of knowledge

Digital Skills and Knowledge About Technology in Teacher Education

The following variables have the alternatives: 1 Strongly disagree, 2 Disagree, 3 Neutral, 4 Agree and 5 Strongly agree.

1. I am familiar with digital tools that can help diversify teaching.
2. I am, in general, confident when using digital tools.
3. I find it easy to become familiar with new digital tools.
4. I can use digital tools which are appropriate for the subjects I am teaching.
5. It is difficult to use digital tools as an educational resource within my subject (reversed).
6. When I am using digital tools it is difficult to adjust the content to the individual student's needs (reversed).
7. I have no clear idea of learning outcome when using digital tools in my teaching (reversed).
8. I use digital tools when giving feedback to students.

Attitudes Towards Technology in Teacher Education

The following variables have the alternatives: 1 Strongly disagree, 2 Disagree, 3 Neutral, 4 Agree and 5 Strongly agree.

1. When I use digital tools in my teaching, I find it adds value.
2. The use of digital tools is essential for good teaching.
3. Society's expectations of the impact of digital tools are exaggerated (reversed).
4. Expectations related to the use of digital tools in education frustrates me (reversed).
5. In professional debates at my university, the expectations of the impact of digital tools are exaggerated (reversed).
6. The use of digital tools is disruptive for the relationship between student and educator (reversed).
7. Digital tools can make the students more interested in the subject I am teaching.
8. I like testing new digital tools in my teaching.

References

1. European Commission, Directorate-General for Education, Youth, Sport and Culture: Key competences for lifelong learning. Publications Office (2019). https://data.europa.eu/doi/10.2766/569540
2. Nagel, I., Guðmundsdóttir, G.B., Afdal, H.W.: Teacher educators' professional agency in facilitating professional digital competence. Teach. Teach. Educ. **132** (2023). https://doi.org/10.1016/j.tate.2023.104238
3. Gudmundsdottir, G.B., Hatlevik, O.E.: Newly qualified teachers' professional digital competence: implications for teacher education. Eur. J. Teach. Educ. **41**(2), 214–231 (2018). https://doi.org/10.1080/02619768.2017.1416085
4. Napal Fraile, M., Peñalva-Vélez, A., Mendióroz Lacambra, A.M.: Development of digital competence in secondary education teachers' training. Educ. Sci. **8**(3) (2018). https://doi.org/10.3390/educsci8030104
5. Nelson, M.J., Voithofer, R., Cheng, S.-L.: Mediating factors that influence the technology integration practices of teacher educators. Comput. Educ. **128**, 330–344 (2019)
6. Ferrari, A.: Digital Competence in Practice: An Analysis of Frameworks. Publications Office of the European Union, Luxembourg (2012)
7. Hämäläinen, R., Nissinen, K., Mannonen, J., Lämsä, J., Leino, K., Taajamo, M.: Understanding teaching professionals' digital competence: what do PIAAC and TALIS reveal about technology-related skills, attitudes, and knowledge? Comput. Hum. Behav. **117**, 106672 (2021)
8. Spiteri, M., Chang Rundgren, S.-N.: Literature review on the factors affecting primary teachers' use of digital technology. Technol. Knowl. Learn. **25**, 115–128 (2020)
9. Vuorikari, R., Kluzer, S., Punie, Y.: DigComp 2.2: The Digital Competence Framework for Citizens—With New Examples of Knowledge, Skills and Attitudes; Publications Office of the European Union, Luxembourg (2022). https://publications.jrc.ec.europa.eu/repository/handle/JRC128415. Accessed 25 Mar 2024
10. Koehler, M.J., Mishra, P.: What is technological pedagogical content knowledge? Contemp. Issues Technol. Teach. Educ. **9**, 60–70 (2009)
11. Kelentric, M., Helland, K., Arstorp, A.-T.: Professional Digital Competence Framework for Teachers (2017). https://www.udir.no/globalassets/filer/in-english/pfdk_framework_en_low2.pdf. Accessed 25 Mar 2024
12. Redecker, C., Punie, Y.: European Framework for the Digital Competence of Educators: DigCompEdu. Publications Office of the European Union, Luxembourg (2017). https://doi.org/10.2760/178382
13. Erstad, O., Kjällander, S., Järvelä, S.: Facing the challenges of 'digital competence'. Nord. J. Digit. Literacy **16**(2), 77–87 (2021). https://doi.org/10.18261/issn.1891-943x-2021-02-0
14. European Commission: Digital Education Action Plan (2021–2027). Resetting Education and Training for the Digital Age; European Union: Maastricht, The Netherlands (2020). https://ec.europa.eu/education/sites/default/files/document-library-docs/deap-communication-sept2020_en.pdf. Accessed 1 June 2023
15. NOU 2014:7. Elevenes læring i fremtidens skole – Et kunnskapsgrunnlag [Students learning in future schools – a knowledge foundation] (2014). https://www.regjeringen.no/no/dokumenter/NOU-2014-7/id766593/. Accessed 25 Mar 2024
16. NOU 2018:2. Fremtidens kompetansebehov I – Kunnskapsgrunnlaget [Future needs of competencies I – a knowledge foundation] (2018). https://www.regjeringen.no/no/dokumenter/nou-2018-2/id2588070/. Accessed 25 Mar 2024
17. Government of the Republic of Slovenia: Digital Slovenia 2030 – An Overarching Strategy for Slovenia's Digital Transformation by 2030 (DSI 2030). https://nio.gov.si/nio/asset/strategija+digitalna+slovenija+2030?lang=en. Accessed 21 Jan 2024

18. Ministry of Education of the Republic of Slovenia: Digital Education Action Plan (ANDI) 2021–2027. https://www.gov.si/assets/ministrstva/MVI/SDIG/SI-Digital-Education-Action-Plan-EN-web.pdf. Accessed 25 Nov 2023
19. INCoDe, Iniciativa Integrada de política pública dedicada ao reforço de com-petências digitais. https://www.incode2030.gov.pt/incode-2030/. Accessed 02 Jan 2024
20. European Commission, Digital Education Action Plan (2021–2027). https://education.ec.eur opa.eu/focus-topics/digital-education/action-plan. Accessed 02 Jan 2024
21. Norwegian Ministry of education and research: Strategi for digital omstilling i universitets-og høyskolesektoren, 2021–2025 (2021). https://www.regjeringen.no/contentassets/c151af ba427f446b8aa44aa1a673e6d6/no/pdfs/kd-strategi-digital-omstilling.pdf
22. Madsen, S.S., Unstad, T., Tveiterås, N.C., Dardanou, M., Habbestad, H., Kosner, L.: Plan-verkets blindsone? En analyse av profesjonsfaglig digital kompetanse i emneplanbeskrivelser for barnehagelærerutdanning. Nordisk barnehageforskning **20**(4), 103–128 (2023). https://doi.org/10.23865/nbf.v20.531
23. Korsberg, L., Svartefoss, S.M., Bergene, A.C., Hovdhaugen, E.: Pedagogisk bruk av digital teknologi i høyere utdanning. Rapport 2022:1. NIFU (2022)
24. Čampelj, B., Jereb, E.: Report on smart education in the Republic of Slovenia. In: Zhuang, R., et al. (eds.) Smart Education in China and Central & Eastern European Countries. LNCS, pp. 293–319. Springer, Singapore (2023). https://doi.org/10.1007/978-981-19-7319-2_12
25. Resolucija o nacionalnem programu visokega šolstva do 2030 (ReNPVŠ30), Uradni list RS, št. 49/22 (2022). http://www.pisrs.si/Pis.web/pregledPredpisa?id=RESO139
26. European Commission, Directorate-General for Education, Youth, Sport and Culture: Education and Training Monitor 2022 – Country Analysis: Slovenia (2022). https://op.eur opa.eu/webpub/eac/education-and-training-monitor-2022/en/country-reports/slovenia.html#6-higher-education. Accessed 01 June 2023
27. Lucas, M., Moreira, A.: DigCompEdu: quadro europeu de competência digital para educadores. Universidade de Aveiro (2018)
28. SELFIE PTK (N/D). O que é o Plano de Ação para o Desenvolvimento Digital da Escola (PADDE) baseado na SELFIE? [What is the School Digital Development Action Plan (PADDE) based on SELFIE?]. https://education.ec.europa.eu/focus-topics/digital-education/action-plan. Accessed 2 Jan 2024
29. Janeš, A., et al.: Preliminary results from Norway, Slovenia, Portugal, Turkey, Ukraine, and Jordan: investigating pre-service teachers' expected use of digital technology when becoming teachers. Educ. Sci. **13** (2023). https://doi.org/10.3390/educsci13080783
30. Madsen, S.S., et al.: International perspectives on the dynamics of pre-service early childhood teachers' digital competences. Educ. Sci. **13** (2023). https://doi.org/10.3390/educsci13070633
31. Cohen, L., Manion, L., Morrison, K.: Research Methods in Education, 8th edn. Routledge, Washington (2018)
32. Blackwell, C.K., Lauricella, A.R., Wartella, E.: Factors influencing digital technology use in early childhood education. Comput. Educ. **77**, 82–90 (2014). https://doi.org/10.1016/j.com pedu.2014.04.013
33. Røkenes, F.M., et al.: Teacher educators' professional digital competence in primary and lower secondary school teacher education. Nordic J. Digit. Lit. **1**, 46–60 (2022)
34. Lindfors, M., Pettersson, F., Olofsson, A.D.: Conditions for professional digital competence: the teacher educators' view. Educ. Inquiry **12**(4), 390–409 (2021). https://doi.org/10.1080/20004508.2021.1890936
35. Amhag, L., Hellström, L., Stigmar, M.: Teacher educators' use of digital tools and needs for digital competence in higher education. J. Digit. Learn. Teach. Educ. **35**(4), 203–220 (2019). https://doi.org/10.1080/21532974.2019.1646169

36. Carpenter, J.P., Rosenberg, J.M., Kessler, A., Romero-Hall, E., Fischer, C.: The importance of context in teacher educators' professional digital competence. Teach. Teach. (2024). https://doi.org/10.1080/13540602.2024.2320155
37. Merritt, K., Smith, D., Renzo, J.C.D.: An investigation of self-reported computer literacy: is it reliable? Issues Inf. Syst. **6**(1), 289–295 (2005)
38. Madsen, S.S., Thorvaldsen, S., Archard, S.: Teacher educators' perceptions of working with digital technologies. Nord. J. Digit. Literacy **13**(3), 177–196 (2018). https://doi.org/10.18261/issn.1891-943x-2018-03-04
39. Madsen, S.S., Thorvaldsen, S.: Implications of the imposed and extensive use of online education in an early childhood education program. Nordisk barnehageforskning **19**(1) (2022). https://doi.org/10.23865/nbf.v19.258
40. Madsen, S.S., Thorvaldsen, S., Sollied, S.: Are teacher students' deep learning and critical thinking at risk of being limited in digital learning environments? IntechOpen (2021). https://doi.org/10.5772/intechopen.96151
41. Nagel, I.: Digital competence in teacher education curricula: what should teacher educators know, be aware of and prepare students for? Nord. J. Comp. Int. Educ. **5**(4), 104–122 (2021)
42. Hu, K.: CHATGPT sets record for fastest-growing user base - analyst note. Reuters (2023). https://www.reuters.com/technology/chatgpt-sets-record-fastest-growing-user-base-analyst-note-2023-02-01/#:~:text=The%20report%2C%20citing%20data%20from,analysts%20wrote%20in%20the%20note
43. Trust, T., Whalen, J., Mouza, C.: Editorial: ChatGPT: challenges, opportunities, and implications for teacher education. Contemp. Issues Technol. Teach. Educ. **23**(1), 1–23 (2023)

Digital Skills in Contemporary Schools - Where We Are and Where We Should Go

Jacek Pyżalski[✉]

Adam Mickiewicz University, Poznan, Poland
pyzalski@amu.edu.pl

Abstract. Summary: The chapter explores digital skills among the young generation in the context of school education, emphasizing the need for a comprehensive approach beyond the oversimplified views prevalent in educational discourse. It challenges the narrow focus on work-related skills and labor market needs, calling for a broader developmental and socialization perspective that includes well-being aspects related to ICT use. The author critique common misconceptions, such as the assumption of universally high digital skills among young people, highlighting inequalities and the minority experiencing serious online risks. The chapter draws on comparative studies, EU Kids Online and ySkills, to provide insights into the digital skills levels of European adolescents. It discusses the typologies of digital risks and opportunities, advocating for educational efforts that prioritize digital literacy and skills development. The author propose measures to address digital inequalities, involving young people in educational design, and promoting digital skills as life skills integrated into all educational subjects. The conclusion underscores the importance of a holistic approach to digital skills education in the contemporary era.

Keywords: digital skills · schools · media education

1   Introduction

The chapter focuses on digital skills among the younger generation within the framework of school education, examining the future requirements for educational curricula and activities in this domain. These issues are frequently overlooked and predicated upon oversimplified representations within the educational discourse, encompassing both researchers and educational practitioners, as well as the general public. On one hand, discussions often adhere to narrow theoretical constructs, confining the discourse on digital skills among the younger generation solely to issues pertaining to workforce competencies and the demands of the labor market, both current and prospective [1–3]. However, from an educational standpoint, such an approach significantly constrains considerations of developmental and socialization facets, and rigidly aligns educational philosophy with a purely transmissive goal. Furthermore, it partially overlooks crucial concerns, such as the well-being of young individuals in relation to ICT utilization, particularly within the salutogenic dimension that emphasizes the potential benefits of digital engagement [4].

Ł. Tomczyk (Ed.): NMP 2023, CCIS 2130, pp. 75–84, 2024.
https://doi.org/10.1007/978-3-031-63235-8_5

Contributing to potential bias is the prevalent reliance on attitudes, assumptions, and oversimplifications as the basis for educational discourse, which often diverge from accurate research findings that more closely reflect reality. A prominent example is the widespread belief in the "high digital skills" possessed by most of the youth population, presumed to be acquired merely through early and long exposure to technology usage. However, such a perspective largely disregards the substantial diversity and inherent inequalities elucidated by high-quality research data [15]. Similarly, this applies to engagement in online risk behaviors, where research indicates that only a minority of young individuals, particularly in cases of significantly harmful involvement, actually experience such serious risks [4–7].

Overall, it is the vital need to implement theory and empirical knowledge into educational practice in a consistent way. This means practically choosing the priorities for certain digital skills as well as elaborating the educational methodology that is adjusted to the needs of diverse subpopulations of young people.

The depiction of the theoretical and empirical dimensions of digital skills among the younger generation is evidently broad and thus oversimplified. The discourse varies across different countries, professional spheres, stakeholders, and educational systems. There are notable instances where educational programs are informed by the actual state of digital skills as established in research [8]. Indeed, the reality of education concerning digital skills appears to be characterized by a cacophony of diverse actors, assumptions, and goals, sometimes concurrently contradicting each other. Certain educational programs are occasionally driven by moral panic and lack clearly defined long-term objectives [9].

Nevertheless, certain issues seem to be universal, regardless of sociocultural factors, necessitating similar measures and actions to enhance how young people are supported and educated in terms of digital skills.

This chapter endeavors to critically examine key conceptualizations and typologies of digital skills in young people. Additionally, it presents selected findings on the level of digital skills among European adolescents based on two major comparative studies: EU Kids Online and ySkills.

Both projects are comparative in nature and employ a standardized methodology across all participating countries. EU Kids Online is a multinational research network comprising European and other countries' researchers focusing on the digital experiences of the younger generation. It aims to understand children's online opportunities, risks, and safety through various methods, engaging in dialogue with national and European policy institutions (source: https://www.lse.ac.uk/media-and-communications/research/research-projects/eu-kids-online). The cornerstone of this collaboration is the implementation of a large-scale survey on online risks and opportunities, as well as the factors influencing them, in all participating countries. The survey utilizes a stringent and standardized methodology [the common questionnaire] tailored to the specific socio-cultural context of each country [7]. The first large-scale comparative study, encompassing 25 countries with a sample of over 25,000 respondents, was conducted in 2010 [9], while the second study, involving 19 countries, was conducted in 2020 [7].

The ySKILLS Project (ySkills.eu) aims to maximise long-term positive impact of digital environment on various aspects of wellbeing for all children, by stimulating resilience through the enhancement of digital skills. The project, funded within the European Union's Horizon 2020 research and innovation programme, focused on digital skills in the context of both risks and opportunities and rights (participation, information, freedom of expression, education, and play, and to protection from harm). One of the pillars in this project is the longitudinal study (3 waves with the one-year distance) conducted in six countries in the samples of adolescents aged 13–18 (with the sample of approx.. 6000 at each wave). The selected data from the second wave of this research project (gathered in 2022) is analyzed in this chapter.

2 Digital Skills and Young People – Theoretical Framework

The International Telecommunication Union (ITU) defines digital skills as those abilities that facilitate beneficial outcomes for users and their social environment. They are described as "the ability to use ICTs in ways that help individuals to achieve beneficial, high-quality outcomes in everyday life for themselves and others," while also aiming to "reduce potential harm associated with more negative aspects of digital engagement" [10, p. 23]. This definition is also adopted in both EU Kids Online [7] and ySkills [11], the foundational projects for this chapter. This approach integrates both protection from potential harm arising from ICT usage and support for positive utilization, addressing risks and opportunities in psychological and social dimensions, such as cyberbullying or exposure to harmful (e.g., sexual) content. Conversely, the opportunity paradigm is salutogenic and centers on potential benefits, paying more attention to aspects such as learning through technology, online civic engagement, or utilizing technology to support well-being and social connections. Both paradigms are supported by empirical evidence. For instance, data demonstrates that a significant proportion (though certainly a minority) of young people engage in online risk behaviors or encounter online harm in various forms, including passive exposure to inappropriate content or more active participation in harmful activities [7]. Undoubtedly, some of these young people experience serious harm, as documented in cases of cyberbullying, which also encompasses various forms of online hate speech [12, 13].

3 Digital Risks and Opportunities

The EU Kids Online risk typology delineates three roles that young individuals may assume, along with four areas of risk (see Table 2). These roles encompass the recipient of online content, a participant engaged in active interaction with others online, and an active actor who initiates and perpetuates online risk behaviors. Risks may manifest in various forms, including commercial risks associated with marketing activities targeting children, risks of an aggressive or sexual nature, and risks pertaining to values that may contradict commonly accepted norms.

Building upon this typology, we can advocate for the implementation of protective measures at multiple levels, such as internet market regulations and school curricula. Within the scope of this article, an important measure involves the development of digital skills that have the potential to shield young individuals from experiencing online risks, including situations where they are actively involved. Generally, these skills can be employed preventively, prior to encountering the risk. However, they can also be beneficial for individuals directly facing serious risks, such as victims of electronic aggression. In this conceptualization, the objective is safety-oriented and reflects an approach reminiscent of European policies from twenty-five years ago and earlier [9] (Table 1).

Table 1. Digital risks according to the EU Kids Online typology

Risks:	Commercial	Aggressive	Sexual	Values
Child as recipient (content viewer)	advertisements/spam	Violent/hateful content	Pornographic content	Biased/dangerous content (for example unreliable health information, racist content)
Child as participant (involved in contact)	Tracking personal information/data/profiling	Victimization of online hate/aggression/cyberbullying	Being a victim of grooming/sexual exploitation	Receiving self-harm/dangerous persuasion by others online
Child as actor (actively initiating and maintaining action)	Gambling, breaching copyrights	Perpetration of online hate/aggression/cyberbullying	Production or publication of pornographic content	Providing dangerous/harmful advice to others online

Source: adapted from [9]

On the opposite end of the spectrum, we encounter potential digital opportunities (see Table 2). Engagement with these opportunities can also take three different forms, mirroring the structure observed with digital risks. These opportunities span four spheres: education and learning (including within the digital realm), social participation and civic engagement, creativity and self-expression, and identity and social connection. It is evident that all these objectives have historically been significant in education and have now acquired a digital dimension.

It is important to emphasize that while these opportunities are potential, their actual realization is influenced by numerous factors. Research indicates that, like serious risks, the exceptional opportunities are only experienced by a minority of the young population [5, 7]. For example, in the second wave of the ySkills project, only one in nine respondents reported signing online petitions twice or more times in the past year, and only 6% participated twice or more often in online campaigns or protests. One of the most critical factors influencing such involvement is, once again, the level of digital skills, which may either facilitate or hinder the digital opportunities available to individuals [4].

It must be emphasized that despite the inherent connection between digital risks and opportunities, there exists a significant body of research that exclusively focuses on risks and predominantly advocates for educational activities geared towards protection [14].

In summary, safeguarding against digital risks and promoting digital opportunities should be considered fundamental goals of contemporary education. Digital skills serve as the common denominator for both educational objectives. Establishing educational contexts and environments where young people can acquire and apply digital skills in

Table 2. Digital opportunities according to the EU Kids Online Typology

Opportunities	Education, learning and digital literacy	Participation and civic engagement	Creativity and self-expression	Identity and social connection
Child as recipient (content viewer)	Educational resources/materials	Global information	Diversity of resources/models	Receiving /using advice on important issues (e.g. mental health)
Child as participant (involved in contact)	Contact with others with same interests	Exchanging/support among activist groups	Cooperating/being invited to create	Communication, support on online platforms/social networking sites
Child as actor (actively initiating and maintaining action)	Self-initiated or collaborative learning	Implementation of active civic engagement actions	Content creation	Identity expression, online image

Source: adapted from [9]

practice appears to be the most straightforward approach to achieving these goals [15, 16]. All these specific objectives can be categorized under the umbrella term of digital literacy, which is recognized as a crucial aspect of contemporary society. It is important to note that digital literacy encompasses a broader conceptual framework than the concept of skills alone [4].

4   The Level of Digital Skills in Young Population According to EU Kids Online and ySkills Data

Certainly, the concept of digital skills that we adopt, as well as the methodology used for measurement, influences both research outcomes and the practices based on them.

One significant aspect is the delineation of which digital skills are encompassed in a particular conceptualization, as well as how they are operationalized and measured. Assessing digital skills poses a challenge, and researchers have yet to reach a consensus on this issue. It is particularly difficult to develop appropriate indicators for skills that are often defined in broad terms [11].

Furthermore, the operationalization and measurement of certain digital skills are more complex than others. Soft skills, in particular, present challenges in translating them into proper research indicators [17]. Moreover, there is considerable inconsistency observed; various researchers utilize different indicators and criteria for categorizing digital skills or may name similar skills differently, leading to differences in measurement approaches [18, 19]. This discrepancy makes it exceedingly challenging to interpret data and compare results across various research projects.

In light of these challenges, it is beneficial to provide overarching overviews of methodologies used to measure digital skills, particularly among young populations. A significant proportion of research on digital skills relies on self-reports, predominantly through surveys, where respondents evaluate their possession of particular skills. However, this approach introduces methodological dilemmas [20]. For example, questions may be formulated either broadly or narrowly, and surveys may suffer from basic design flaws, as noted by Helsper [11].

Moreover, self-assessment of digital skills inherently has limitations. Young people assessing their digital skills do so based on their opinions rather than objective criteria. This can lead to significant discrepancies, where individuals rating themselves at the same point on a scale may possess vastly different skill levels [21].

Consequently, there is a growing trend towards measuring digital skills using performance tests. In such tests, participants are required to perform concrete tasks that demand a certain level of digital skills, aiming to eliminate the subjective aspect present in self-assessment procedures. This approach seems very accurate but at the same time very costly and difficult to implement on the larger scale [22].

Two projects that have operationalized digital skills based on theoretical assumptions and undergone proper psychometric procedures are EU Kids Online and ySkills, as briefly described in the chapter introduction.

Despite digital skills often being taken for granted among young populations, research data reveals a more nuanced reality. For instance, the EU Kids Online project conducted a large-scale survey across 19 countries, mostly European, involving young people aged 12 to 16 years old. This project identified several categories of digital skills, including operational skills, information and navigation skills, social skills, creative skills, and mobile skills. Gender differences in self-assessed digital skills were negligible, with slight variations observed in certain countries. However, older adolescents generally reported higher digital skills compared to their younger counterparts. Notably, while young people reported high levels of operational and social skills, a significant proportion reported low levels of information and navigation skills, as well as content creation skills—a concerning finding given the prevalence of disinformation and fake news in the digital landscape [23].

Similarly, the ySkills project focused on longitudinal analyses of young people's digital skills across six countries. This project employed a typology known as the Youth Digital Skills Indicator (yDSI), which operationalized four groups of skills, namely:

1. Technical and operational skills that relate to the proficiency in managing and operating ICT, including technical skills of devices, platforms, and applications. It covers the knowledge of using buttons, adjusting settings, and programming (that is separated as a specific technical and operational skill).
2. Navigation and information processing skills that involve the ability to search and select digital sources of information critically. It also refers to evaluation information in a critical manner.
3. Communication and interaction skills include the ability to use various digital media and technological features to interact with others online. It also covers building networks and assessing the influence of communication and interpersonal interactions critically.

4. Content creation and production skills involve the ability to create high-quality digital contents. It also extends to comprehension how it is produced and published, and how it influences others [11].

Some data is presented in the Table 3.

Table 3. Mean proportion of skills at high level in the whole ySkills sample (wave 2)

	Mean proportion of skills at high level (max level 1)
Technological and operational skills	,59
Programming skills	,07
Information navigation and processing skills	,37
Communication and interaction skills	,65
Content creation and production skills	,39
All digital skills	,39

The results from the ySkills project align with those from EU Kids Online as outlined previously. Once again, information, navigation, and processing skills, as well as content creation skills, are reported as lower in comparison to technological and operational skills, as well as communication and interaction skills. Notably, programming skills are generally rarely assessed high. Importantly, the mean for the general proportion of high-level digital skills is also relatively low, standing at 0.39.

Across the entire sample spanning all six countries, boys scored significantly higher in all dimensions, particularly in technological skills, including programming, except for communication and interaction skills, where girls reported higher scores. Additionally, older children scored higher than their younger counterparts. However, it is worth noting that some research suggests that the high confidence exhibited by boys in certain studies may not necessarily reflect their actual digital competences [4]. Moreover, variations among countries regarding these findings have also been observed.

5   The Future: How to Teach Digital Skills Better?

5.1   Breadth of the Digital Skills Conceptualizations

Media education and informatics should endeavor to expand the catalog of digital skills and move beyond the prevailing approach that prioritizes technical and operational skills as the educational core. This sentiment is aptly articulated by the International Telecommunication Union, which advocates for a focus on a broad range of digital skills encompassing "technical operational, information management, social, and content-creation skills" [10, p. 3]. Additionally, the same organization highlights that "algorithms, the proliferation of bots, and a shift to the Internet of Things and Artificial Intelligence, augment the need for critical information and advanced content-creation skills. With the increased complexity of ICT systems, and an exponential increase in the amount of data being collected, transferable digital skills and lifelong learning are indispensable" [10, p. 3].

5.2 Tackling Digital Inequalities

Contrary to common opinions, inequalities do not appear to be solely a generational phenomenon, with newer generations being more competent. Instead, they seem to be linked to traditional disparities associated with socioeconomic background, disability, or vulnerable life conditions [24, 25].

This underscores the necessity of customizing media education to address specific needs in both content and teaching methods and tools. Addressing this issue requires educational research that focuses on the specificities of digital skills and the factors influencing them within certain subpopulations of young people. Based on this understanding, media education curricula should be at least partially tailored to the needs of young people affected by inequalities. A notable example of such tailored resources is the handbook prepared by The School with Class Foundation [26].

5.3 Involving Young People in Design or Media Education and Other Measures Concerning Digital Skills

While proposing measures aimed at supporting and protecting young people in the digital world, it is essential to provide them with opportunities to voice their opinions and assess the proposed ideas [27, 28], in accordance with the Children's Rights Amendment (CRC Committee, 2021). Such an approach mandates that educational and supportive measures designed to protect young people should simultaneously respect their rights and freedoms [29–31].

This also entails involving young people in the research process from planning procedures to interpreting results. A notable example is the project by Dennehy, Cronin, and Arensman [32], which focused on electronic violence. In this project, young people were engaged throughout the research process, providing their perspectives on various measures.

It is important to acknowledge that many young people express doubts about whether their opinions will be considered, as in many cases, such procedures are merely superficial [32]. This underscores the need for genuine involvement of young people in activities where research and educational measures concerning digital skills are developed and implemented.

5.4 Digital Skills Equal Life Skills

In the traditional approach, digital skills have been perceived as specific tools essential for the contemporary and future labor market. While this understanding holds considerable merit, it does not present the complete picture. Digital skills are integral to all aspects of human existence, including social relations, self-development, learning, and other vital spheres. Given that these aspects have traditionally been at the core of education, the necessity of incorporating the development of digital skills into the educational system is evident. However, due to the pervasive nature of digital skills in the everyday lives of the younger generation, they cannot be acquired solely through traditional approaches, such as having a separate school subject. Instead, digital skills should be a significant component of all educational activities, showcasing and reinforcing their digital dimension. This clearly supports the integration of teaching digital skills into the curricula of all school subjects [33] as well as non-formal and informal education.

To conclude, the importance of teaching digital skills (being life skills nowadays) seems to be obvious. However, the concrete content and methodology of such educational activities should be carefully planned based on solid diagnosis as outlined in this chapter.

References

1. Donoso, V., et al.: Report on interviews with experts on digital skills in schools and on the labor market. KU Leuven, Leuven: ySKILLS (2020)
2. Kiss, M.: Digital skills in the EU labor market. European Parliamentary Research Service (2017)
3. Zeidmane, A., Vintere, A.: A case study of students' views on the digital skills needed for the labour market. Int. Assoc. Dev. Inf. Soc. 2(5), 99–110 (2016)
4. Haddon, L., Cino, D., Doyle, M.A., Livingstone, S., Mascheroni, G., Stoilova, M.: Children's and young people's digital skills: a systematic evidence review. Leuven, KU Leuven: ySKILLS (2020)
5. Pyżalski, J. (ed.): Pozytywny internet i jego młodzi twórcy. Dobre i złe wieści z badań jakościowych.: NASK (2019)
6. Pyżalski, J.: Electronic aggression. In: Yan, Z. (ed.) The Cambridge Handbook of Cyber Behavior. Cambridge University Press (2023)
7. Smahel, D., et al.: EU Kids Online 2020: Survey results from 19 countries. EU Kids Online. https://doi.org/10.21953/lse.47fdeqj01ofo
8. Pyżalski, J., Plichta, P., Szuster, A., Barlińska, J.: Cyberbullying characteristics and prevention—what can we learn from narratives provided by adolescents and their teachers? Int. J. Environ. Res. Public Health 19(18), 11589 (2022)
9. Livingstone, S., Mascheroni, G., Staksrud, E.: European research on children's internet use: assessing the past and anticipating the future. New Media Soc. 20(3), 1103–1122 (2018). https://doi.org/10.1177/1461444816685930
10. International Telecommunication Union (ITU): Measuring the Information Society Report, Volume 1. ITU Publications (2018). www.itu.int/en/ITU-D/Statistics/Documents/publicati ons/misr2018/MISR-2018-Vol-1-E.pdf
11. Helsper, E.J., Schneider, L.S., van Deursen, A.J.A.M., van Laar, E.: The youth Digital Skills Indicator: Report on the conceptualization and development of the ySKILLS digital skills measure. KU Leuven, Leuven: ySKILLS (2020)
12. Kwan, I., et al.: Cyberbullying and children and young people's mental health: a systematic map of systematic reviews. Cyberpsychol. Behav. Soc. Netw. 23(2), 72–82 (2020)
13. Pyżalski, J., Smith, P.: Nationality and ethnicity-based (cyber) bullying: how should we tackle this phenomenon in survey studies? Psychol. Soc. Educ. 14(3), 11–17 (2022)
14. Khurana, A., Bleakley, A., Jordan, A.B., Romer, D.: The protective effects of parental monitoring and internet restriction on adolescents' risk of online harassment. J. Youth Adolesc. 44, 1039–1047 (2015)
15. van Deursen, A.J.A.M., Helsper, E.J.: Collateral benefits of internet use: explaining the diverse outcomes of engaging with the Internet. New Media Soc. 20(7), 2333–2351 (2017). https://doi.org/10.1177/1461444817715282

16. van Deursen, A.J.A.M., Helsper, E.J., Eynon, R., van Dijk, J.A.G.M.: The compoundness and sequentiality of digital inequality. Int. J. Commun. **11**, 452–473 (2017). https://ijoc.org/index.php/ijoc

17. Cobo, C.: Mechanisms to identify and study the demand for innovation skills in world-renowned organizations. On Horiz. **21**(2), 96e106 (2013). https://doi.org/10.1108/107481 21311322996

18. Van Laar, E., Van Deursen, A.J., Van Dijk, J.A., De Haan, J.: The relation between 21st-century skills and digital skills: a systematic literature review. Comput. Hum. Behav. **72**, 577–588 (2017)

19. Van Laar, E., Van Deursen, A.J., Van Dijk, J.A., de Haan, J.: Determinants of 21st-century skills and 21st-century digital skills for workers: a systematic literature review. Sage Open **10**(1), 2158244019900176 (2020)

20. Litt, E.: Measuring users' internet skills: a review of past assessments and a look toward the future. New Media Soc. **15**(4), 612–630 (2013)

21. Mahmood, K.: Do people overestimate their information literacy skills? A systematic review of empirical evidence on the Dunning-Kruger effect. Commun. Inf. Lit. **10**(2), 3 (2016)

22. Pagani, L., Argentin, G., Gui, M., Stanca, L.: The impact of digital skills on educational outcomes: evidence from performance tests. Educ. Stud. **42**(2), 137–162 (2016)

23. Herrero-Diz, P., Conde-Jiménez, J., Reyes-de-Cózar, S.: Spanish adolescents and fake news: level of awareness and credibility of information (Los adolescentes españoles frente a las fake news: nivel de conciencia y credibilidad de la información). Cult. Educ. **33**(1), 1–27 (2021)

24. Plichta, P.: Prevalence of cyberbullying and other forms of online aggression among Polish students with mild intellectual disability. e-Methodology **2**, 112–127 (2015). https://doi.org/10.15503/emet2015.112.127

25. Plichta, P., Pyżalski, J., Barlińska, J.: Cyberbullying versus self-image creation on the internet: are the underlying mechanisms different in young adults with disabilities? Interdyscyplinarne Konteksty Pedagogiki Specjalnej **20**, 101–122 (2018). https://doi.org/10.14746/ikps.2018.20.05

26. School with Class Foundation: Be Internet Awesome for All. Developing Digital Citizenship in children with various Educational needs, School with Class Foundation (2023)

27. Livingstone, S., Third, A.: Children and young people's rights in the digital age: an emerging agenda. New Media Soc. **19**(5), 657–670 (2017)

28. Livingstone, S.: Children's rights applying the digital world! LSE Blogs (2021). https://blogs.lse.ac.uk/medialse/2021/02/04/childrens-rights-apply-in-the-digitalworld/

29. Van Royen, K., Poels, K., Vandebosch, H.: Harmonizing freedom and protection: adolescents' voices on automatic monitoring of social networking sites. Child Youth Serv. Rev. **64**, 35–41 (2016)

30. Milosevic, T., et al.: Effectiveness of artificial intelligence–based cyberbullying interventions from youth perspective. Soc. Media Soc. **9**(1), 20563051221147325 (2023)

31. Vandebosch, H., et al.: A scoping review of technological interventions to address ethnicity-related peer aggression. Aggression Violent Behav. 101794 (2022)

32. Dennehy, R., Cronin, M., Arensman, E.: Involving young people in cyberbullying research: the implementation and evaluation of a rights-based approach. Health Expect. **22**(1), 54–64 (2019)

33. Livingstone, S., Mascheroni, G., Stoilova, M.: The outcomes of gaining digital skills for young people's lives and wellbeing: a systematic evidence review. New Media Soc. 14614448211043189 (2021)

Comparing Pre-service Preschool and Primary School Teachers' Views on Their Pedagogical Digital Competencies, Attitudes, and Future Use of Digital Technologies in Teaching

Andreja Klančar[1]([⊠]) [iD] and Aleksander Janeš[2] [iD]

[1] Faculty of Education, University of Primorska, 6000 Koper, Slovenia
andreja.klancar@pef.upr.si
[2] Faculty of Management, University of Primorska, 6000 Koper, Slovenia
aleksander.janes@fm-kp.si

Abstract. This contribution examines and compares the views of pre-service preschool and primary school teachers regarding their pedagogical digital competencies and attitudes towards the integration of digital technologies in the educational setting, and the role these attributes will play in the use of digital technologies in their future teaching practice.

In the survey, 85 pre-service primary school teachers and 170 full-time and part-time undergraduate students, who were pre-service preschool teachers, took part. The research on the students' views reveals that a positive attitude towards integrating digital technologies in educational settings is common among most individuals in both groups. Although students can easily become acquainted with new digital tools, they encounter challenges when using these technologies educationally and strategically to enhance the teaching and learning process.

The findings of the linear regression analysis (with predictors of attitudes and pedagogical digital competence) conducted on pre-service preschool and primary school teachers indicate that attitudes towards integrating digital technologies in the educational setting significantly predict the future integration of digital technologies in their future teaching practices.

Keywords: Digital Technologies · Digital Competencies · Attitude · Future Teaching Practice

1 Introduction

The digital transformation of society is significantly impacting changes in education. The digitization of processes increasingly requires individuals to not only be competent in using digital technologies (DT) but also comprehend their operational principles. This includes a comprehensive understanding of artificial intelligence, a heightened awareness of cybersecurity, and an ethical perspective on technology usage. Therefore, it is important to continually educate teachers and students and develop the competencies that will enable them to successfully operate in an increasingly digitized world [1].

© The Author(s), under exclusive license to Springer Nature Switzerland AG 2024
Ł. Tomczyk (Ed.): NMP 2023, CCIS 2130, pp. 85–104, 2024.
https://doi.org/10.1007/978-3-031-63235-8_6

Teachers' digital competencies play a vital role in fostering the development of students' digital competencies [2, 6]. [7] emphasize that teachers' digital competence should be comprehensive, contextually relevant, systematically structured, trainable, and continuously evolving. Moreover, it should be adaptable to incorporate the necessary skills, attitudes, and knowledge teachers need to facilitate their students' learning and active participation in the digital world [7].

The integration of DT in Slovenia's education system has seen significant advancements since 1994, focusing on infrastructure, teachers' digital competencies, and developmental projects. This progress followed substantial advancements after 1992, with additional progress post-2000 due to the Internet's expansion, leading to a shift towards developing teachers' pedagogical digital competencies and didactics that incorporate digital tools. The period from 2006 to 2015 was marked by the national e-education project, which was crucial for this development. Despite these advancements, a gap persists between the availability and actual use of these technologies in teaching, as indicated by the 2006 s international SITES survey and still evident in the TALIS 2018 study [9], underscoring the need for further teacher training and fostering a positive attitude towards DT. The development of digital competencies among preschool and primary school teachers did not occur simultaneously; initial efforts focused on primary and secondary school teachers, with subsequent expansion to include preschool teachers [3]. The COVID-19 pandemic revealed deficiencies in teachers' digital competencies, which could be partly attributed to the lack of mandatory ICT training for teachers [4]. Under the National Recovery and Resilience Plan (NRRP), Slovenia is enhancing teachers' digital competencies across all educational levels. The government's Digital Education Service, part of the Ministry of Education, Science and Sport, oversees the digitization of education, including implementing the ANDI 2021–2027 Slovenian digital education action plan. This plan, which outlines Slovenia's digital education strategy for the next 7 years, includes establishing a national coordination center for digital education and focuses on the ongoing professional development of teachers' digital competencies [5].

Over the last two decades, teachers' pedagogical digital competencies have garnered significant attention from educational researchers. Various frameworks have been developed to define the competencies needed for teaching in 'digital classrooms[1]'. Notable among these are the Digital Competence Framework for Educators – DigCompEdu [77], the UNESCO's ICT Competency Framework for Teachers [10], and the TPACK framework [11]. Additionally, within the Slovenian National E-education Project (2008–2013) (E-šolstvo (2008–2013), the national framework of teachers' pedagogical e-competences named 'e-competent teacher standard' was developed and piloted. It was composed of six key teachers' competences: 1) knowledge and critical use of ICT; 2) searching, selecting, and critically evaluating information and concepts; 3) remote communication and collaboration; 4) planning, performing, and evaluating the use of ICT in teaching and learning; 5) safe use of e-contents, complying with legal and ethical principles of their using and downloading; 6) designing, creating, updating and publishing of contents on the internet. The implementation of the 'e-competent teacher standard' encountered

---

[1] A digital classroom is a classroom that uses computers and tablets, the internet, and educational software to enhance student learning. The digital classroom can be an extension of the physical classroom that provides additional opportunities for collaboration and research.

difficulties, mainly due to the absence of supportive policies and the lack of financial resources after the end of the project. Following these challenges, the DigCompEdu model [19], developed and scientifically validated under the auspices of the European Commission initiative, has become a widely accepted digital framework for educators in Slovenia.

Findings suggest that, in addition to the development of (pedagogical) digital competencies, attitudes towards the use of DT also play a crucial role in determining the success of future integration of these technologies in teaching [12, 44, 66]. Authors emphasize that openness and positive attitudes towards the use of DT in education are important dimensions of teachers' digital competence [49, 54, 55, 66]. Conversely, teachers' disengaged attitudes can significantly impede the meaningful use of DT in teaching [66]. This limitation not only affects the teaching process but also hinders students' acquisition of knowledge and development of skills necessary for active participation in an increasingly digitalized environment and society.

Research indicates that a gap still exists between access to DT, guidelines for their use, and their actual implementation in teaching and learning [8]. The education of future teachers plays a crucial role in bridging this gap.

This study examines and compares the views of pre-service preschool and primary school teachers regarding their pedagogical digital competencies and attitudes towards the integration of DT in the educational setting, and the role these attributes will play in the use of DT in their future teaching practice.

Research Question: How will the future use of DT in the educational environment be related to the pedagogical competencies and attitudes towards the integration of DT in the educational setting of pre-service primary school teachers compared to pre-service preschool teachers?

2 Literature Review

2.1 Digital Competence

The development and understanding of digital competence, particularly in the context of education, have evolved through various models proposed by authors and institutions (e.g. UNESCO's ICT Competency Framework for Teachers [10], TPACK [11], DigCompEdu [77]). Starkey [31] provides a valuable framework for categorizing digital competence frameworks into three distinct areas: general digital competencies, digital competencies for teaching, and professional digital competencies. The first category, generic digital competence, covers basic digital skills that are applicable in a variety of domains, not exclusively in the field of teaching. The second category, digital teaching competence, is more specialized, focusing on how educators integrate DT into their teaching practices. This includes selecting, (critical) evaluation, and planning the use of DT in educational settings. The third category, professional digital competence, differs in that it refers to environments in which DT is a central component of the teacher's professional role in a digitally oriented-education system [31]. This classification emphasizes the complexity of digital competence in education, highlighting the need for educators not only to possess digital skills but also to integrate these skills effectively into their teaching to enhance the learning experience.

The emergence of the DigComp study in 2013 was an important step towards a better understanding and development of digital competencies in Europe. The DigComp 2.2 [18] framework describes the digital skills that citizens need to have, including information management, content creation, information and content brokering, digital security, and problem-solving skills, which is the basis of the European Framework of Digital Competences for Teachers (DigCompEdu) [19], which focuses not on technical skills but rather presents a pedagogical framework that supports the use of digital tools to enhance innovative teaching and learning.

In 2017, the specific term 'Professional Digital Competence' was defined for educators, introducing a comprehensive framework for understanding teachers' professional digital competencies [25]. The Technological Pedagogical Content Knowledge (TPACK) framework [26, 27, 48] has been instrumental as a referential model, particularly among Norwegian researchers, in conceptualizing and defining technological aspects and DT. This framework encompasses a wide range of challenges and opportunities brought about by the development of digital competencies.

Furthermore, research by Thorvaldsen and Madsen [28], along with other studies [29, 30, 61], have contributed significantly to our understanding of digital competence in education. These studies have identified three key aspects of digital competence: pedagogic and didactic, subject-specific, and technological, all of which align with the TPACK framework [26, 28, 30]. This alignment underscores the necessity for a holistic and integrated approach to digital competence.

Recent studies [17, 22, 23, 55], have focused on developing metrics for assessing the overall professional digital competencies of pre-service teachers. These assessments largely rely on self-reported data encompassing elements such as skills, usage, and attitudes. The Digital Competence in Teacher Education (PEAT) model [73] emphasizes the integration of technical and pedagogical skills, as well as ethical perspectives and attitudes, suggesting that openness and positive attitudes towards the use of digital technology in education are important aspects of teachers' digital competence. Although attitude is not included in the TPACK model, it is understood in the current study as an important consideration in making sense of the dynamics within pre-service and primary teachers' digital competence.

2.2 Attitudes

Allport's (1935) [16] description of attitudes as mental states of readiness established over time, which impact an individual's response to relevant objects and events, models attitudes toward information technology (IT). These can include a feeling of hopefulness, nervousness, curiosity, practical value, equality of opportunity, and conviction that men and women should have equal access to opportunities (Gokhale et al., 2013 [20] as referenced in Blayone et al., 2021, p. 654 [21]).

The importance of attitudes as a core component of digital competence is also highlighted in the European Commission's digital education action plan for 2021–2027. This emphasis follows the Council of the European Union's Recommendation on Key Competences for Lifelong Learning, which provides a comprehensive definition of digital competence. This definition encompasses knowledge, skills, and attitudes as integral components. Knowledge consists of established facts, figures, concepts, ideas, and theories that support understanding in a specific area or subject. Skills are defined as the ability and capacity to carry out processes and use existing knowledge to achieve results. Attitudes refer to the disposition and mindsets toward acting or reacting to ideas, people, or situations.

Professional attitudes towards digital tools are an important factor influencing preservice teachers' use of DT in the classroom, as evidenced in studies [39, 64, 73]. Professional attitudes not only form their preparedness to use digital tools but also the effectiveness of their integration into their teaching practices. Teachers' experience with DT has a significant impact on their attitudes towards the use of DT in education. Those who have positive experiences and high levels of confidence in their computing skills tend to have positive attitudes toward the integration of DT into teaching [37, 38, 47]. This association highlights the importance of providing opportunities for teachers to develop their skills and knowledge of DT, thereby fostering more positive attitudes towards the use of DT in educational settings.

The concept of 'Theory of Action', used as a theoretical framework in various studies [40], facilitates an analytical distinction between 'theory in use' and 'espoused theory'. This differentiation is crucial for comprehending the gap between what educators know and believe about DT and how they apply them in practice [35, 39]. So and Kim [39] found that even if teachers have the knowledge and skills to use technologies (attitudes towards practices, referred to as espoused theory), they are incapable of using them in practice (actions in practice, referred to as theory in use) [68]. Based on these studies, Mou and Kao's study [41], and the study of Bice and Tang [33], we can summarize that there is a probable correlation between teachers' ICT experiences and their beliefs about the integration of DT.

2.3 Initial Teacher Training and Future Use of Digital Technologies in Teaching

The integration of DT into initial teacher education is a key element in the training of future teachers for the changing demands of the education field [34]. With the spread of digital resources in the education space, pre-service and in-service teacher training in the use of DT has become an essential priority, as the wider availability of digital resources opens both a multitude of possibilities and a wide range of challenges [13].

The main barrier to the integration of DT into teaching is limited access to technology, combined with a lack of digital literacy among pre-service teachers, and the unequal availability of infrastructure in educational institutions [13, 14]. Mirzajani et al. [15] point out that factors such as insufficient training, lack of knowledge and skills, and unavailability of the necessary hardware, software, or time are important barriers. To overcome these barriers, the need for leadership support in the field is crucial [13, 14].

Developing digital competencies is a crucial component of pre-service training. Research by Lorenz et al. [13] suggests that the perceived technological pedagogical content knowledge of teachers may be the most important predictor of the actual use of DT and their computational thinking skills. Similarly, the findings of Pozas and Letzel [78] indicate that both attitudes and perceived competency are strong predictors of the use of DT in future teaching practices.

The European Commission's Action Plan 2021–2027 emphasizes the need for all learners to acquire digital competencies, which include skills, knowledge, and attitudes [35]. Attitudes, in particular, are a key component of professional digital competence and are crucial for the successful integration of DT in schools [5, 7, 12, 41]. A gap exists between the stated goals for digital competencies in international and national teacher education curricula, actual school practices, and pre-service teachers' experiences of acquiring digital competencies during their initial training [9].

Initial teacher education programs should prioritize developing digital teaching competencies of pre-service teachers, aligning with (educational) digital competencies frameworks, and also developing positive attitudes toward the use of DT [32].

3 Methodology

To compare groups of students, we used samples of students from Pre-Service Preschool (PSP) Teachers and Pre-Service Primary School (PS) Teachers study programs. The data were processed using IBM SPSS Statistics 28.

3.1 Pre-Service Preschool (PSP) Teachers

The sample consists of 170 full-time and part-time students in the 1st, 2nd, and 3rd year of the higher professional program Early Childhood Education at the University of Primorska, Faculty of Education, of whom 8 were male (5%) and 162 were female (95%). The data was collected between June and December 2021.

3.2 Pre-service Primary School (PS) Teachers

The second sample consists of 85 full-time and part-time preservice teachers of the higher Professional program Primary Education at the University of Primorska, Faculty of Education of whom 9 were male (11%) and 76 were female (89%). The lower response rate is due to the involvement of very young regular students who are not keen on answering online questionnaires. Data was collected in the spring semester of 2021–22.

3.3 Methods

The study used descriptive, Pearson correlation and causal non-experimental methods of pedagogical research. For the research, an online questionnaire was used, which contained open-ended questions, optional questions, and five-point Likert-type scales (from 1: Strongly disagree, to 5: Strongly agree). The questionnaire was developed and tested by [54, 55] at UiT the Arctic University of Norway.

We used closed-ended questions to obtain demographic and computer use frequency data, the question of past digital tools use was an open-ended question, and the remaining questions were answered using a five-point Likert-type scale of views. These issues were thematically divided into three constructs: application of digital tools in future teaching practice (AT), pedagogical digital competencies (PDC), and professional attitude towards DT (ATT). Cronbach's Alpha was used as a measure of internal consistency or validity (Table 1). Cortina [48], p.102 stated that if the number of construct's items is greater than 10, Cronbach's Alpha greater or equal to 0.7 is preferred. If the number of construct items is smaller than 10, Cronbach's Alpha greater than 0.5 is preferred.

Normality tests were performed and most data on variables and constructs are acceptably normally distributed. Furthermore, the variance inflation factor (VIF) was calculated and is 1.845 for both independent variables ATT and PDC. The normality of the distribution of residuals has been tested and represents some slight deviation but residuals follow the line. We have a normal distribution in this case. The Breusch-Pagan statistic was used and indicated that the error term is the same across all values of the independent variables. Cook's distance was calculated which is less than 1 (0.000 for minimum, 0.168 for maximum, and 0.012 for mean).

4 Empirical Findings and Discussion

The data that are presented in this paper are part of an international survey DigiCross involving Norway, Slovenia, Portugal, Turkey, Ukraine, and Jordan. In this paper, only Slovenian data and findings are presented. The data can be accessed on dedicated platforms.

4.1 Cronbach Alpha

Cronbach's Alpha (Table 1) was used as a measure of the internal consistency of the questionnaire. The results were found to be sufficient to conduct further statistical analyses. This is viewed as the most appropriate measure of reliability when applying Likert-scale statements [67].

Table 1. Comparison of the Cronbach Alpha.

Constructs	PSP	PS
PDC (8 var.)	0.69	0.731
ATT (8 var.)	0.64	0.743
USE (16 var.)	0.84	0.857

Note: Acceptable Cronbach Alpha values range from 0.69 to 0.857. A low Cronbach Alpha value may be due to a small number of questions, poor intercorrelations between items, or heterogeneous constructs; Pre-Service Preschool (PSP); Pre-Service Primary School (PS) Teachers.

4.2 Application of Tools in the Future

As shown in Table 2, AT is a better indicator for the respondents' reported future use when compared with the average of the construct reporting on the respondents' expected future use (USE; based on 16 digital tools). Tools are not defined explicitly when the respondent uses the single variable as a measure. This gives the responders the freedom to answer despite any constraints that might arise from using a predetermined set of tools. The correlation and regression analysis of both constructs showed that the AT construct has greater explanatory power.

Table 2. Comparison of the application of tools in the future constructs.

Construct	Average (SD) PSP	Average (SD) PS
AT (Single variable)	3.56 (0.82)	4.00 (0.724)
USE (16 var.)	3.19 (0.53)	3.27 (0.789)

Note: AT-application of tools in the future; USE-use of digital tools in the expected future pedagogical work; Pre-Service Preschool (PSP); Pre-Service Primary School (PS) Teachers.

4.3 Pedagogical Digital Competence Construct

The construct's statements were accepted or rejected by a portion of the preservice teachers while being entirely accepted or rejected by a portion of them (Table 3). Therefore, given that digital competencies are acknowledged as a common element in literature, they may be generated by imposed national education policy. Preservice teachers don't seem certain that using DT results in improved learning and more enthusiasm from pupils in preschool and primary schools [45].

The various teacher preparation programs in Slovenia are designed to get pre-service students ready to work within the rules. Between these programs, there are differences

Table 3. Comparison of Pedagogical Digital Competence Constructs.

Construct variables	Average (SD) PSP	Average (SD) PS
I am familiar with digital tools that can help diversify teaching	3.38 (0.807)	3.48 (0.811)
I am, in general, confident when using digital tools	3.52 (0.851)	3.48 (0.921)
I find it easy to become familiar with new digital tools	3.77 (1.003)	3.62 (0.886)
I can use digital tools which are appropriate for the subjects I am teaching	3.70 (0.678)	3.56 (0.698)
It is difficult to use digital tools as an educational resource within my subject	2.94 (0.885)	3.56 (0.763)
When I am using digital tools, it is difficult to adjust the content to the individual students needs	3.11 (0.836)	3.04 (0.879)
I have no clear idea of the learning outcome when using digital tools in my teaching	2.95 (0.915)	3.35 (0.960)
I use digital tools when giving feedback to students	2.98 (0.903)	3.48 (0.781)

Note: SD-Standard Deviation; Pre-Service Preschool (PSP); Pre-Service Primary School (PS) Teachers.

in how digital competency is approached and where it fits into curricula and educational policy. Slovenia is currently in the process of integrating the development of digital competencies into the curricula at all levels of education (from kindergartens to universities), where pedagogical digital competencies are becoming vital across all programs and all subjects.

In the set of questions about pedagogical digital competencies (Table 3), PSP and PS students chose the highest values for the statement "I find it easy to become familiar with new digital tools", (PSP; 3.77 (1.003) and PS; 3.62 (0.886)). This is encouraging but there can be noticed higher SD.

The lowest score for the PSP students was the agreement with the statement "It is difficult to use digital tools as an educational resource within my subject" (2.94 (0.885)). For the PS students the lowest score (3.04 (0.879)) was in agreement with the statement "When I am using digital tools, it is difficult to adjust the content to the individual student's needs". The data again indicate a lower level of pedagogical digital competencies, namely in the areas of teaching and learning, empowering students, and guiding and supporting students in acquiring subject-specific digital competencies.

The survey's findings are consistent with those of several authors, who have found that teacher education still shows a general lack of knowledge and abilities among pre-service teachers and teacher educators regarding how to use DT in a pedagogical and didactic manner [61], p. 253, [72]. According to the findings, pre-service teachers exhibit a somewhat average degree of digital competence and struggle to align DT and content [50]. Numerous authors have noted that pre-service teachers frequently believe they lack the necessary skills to teach and learn in classrooms using DT [58, 62, 69, as cited in 71]. Preservice teachers and teacher educators should get the skills necessary to select and use the proper digital tools in the classroom, as well as the chance to do so while pursuing their education and receiving in-service training [65].

According to research, using DT does not necessarily result in the development or improvement of advanced digital competencies. As opposed to skills (i.e., quality of use) or competence (i.e., attitudes and use strategies), European assessments currently place a greater emphasis on measuring access and use [42].

DigCompEdu is compatible with the TPACK theory, according to authors [74], and it must be properly incorporated if teachers want to advance their digital professional development. Therefore, combining these two study methodologies is necessary to create a legitimate and trustworthy tool for assessing academic teachers' digital competency.

However, because TPACK is centered on teacher comprehension, it is not possible to evaluate students' technology use in schools or higher education institutions in a quick, straightforward, or comprehensive manner [75]. A fundamental challenge for educators is how to understand and relate to students' varied degrees of digital experiences and skills under various settings (such as internal and external variables) and how to motivate students to develop their lifelong digital competencies on their terms. Students who enroll in undergraduate or continuing education programs in higher education are mostly technologically literate. Current discussions in this sector cannot convincingly resolve when students grasp core digital competencies since numerous complex demographics and other factors play a role. Findings indicate that while pre-service teachers have a positive attitude toward DT and moderate levels of general pedagogical digital competence, they feel additional specific and in-depth preparation is required within their initial training [13]. Including more advanced digital training can promote group learning opportunities. Through virtual communication platforms, aspiring educators can interact with mentors and peers to participate in discussions, exchange instructional strategies, and work together on projects. Through these exchanges, they can hone their technological skills and get ready to effectively manage digital classrooms in the future. DT used in pre-service instruction is also important because it contributes to improving teachers' digital literacy [79 as cited in 13]. Technology integration can be hampered by a variety of factors, including uneven infrastructure availability in educational institutions, a lack of digital literacy among pre-service teachers, and restricted access to technology [14]. Specifically, training and competency in digital resources would appear to be an essential component of pre-service training. Several authors recently found that attitudes and perceived competency are strong predictors of DT's future use [17, 76, 80]. It is generally acknowledged that higher education has not completely embraced digital capabilities as a fundamental, core literacy [56].

4.4 Professional Attitude Construct

According to the results of the measurement of the ATT construct, there were both advantages and disadvantages of using DT in future teaching practice (Table 4).

Table 4. Comparison of Professional Attitude Constructs.

Construct variables	Average (SD) PSP	Average (SD) PS
When I use digital tools in my teaching, I find it adds value	3.61 (0.851)	4.07 (0.651)
The use of digital tools is essential for good teaching	3.07 (0.894)	3.34 (0.867)
Society's expectations of the impact of digital tools are exaggerated	2.55 (0.850)	3.08 (0.759)
Expectations related to the use of digital tools in education frustrate me	3.15 (0.948)	3.32 (0.966)
In professional debates at my university, the expectations of the impact of digital tools are exaggerated	2.75 (0.827)	3.47 (0.749)
The use of digital tools is disruptive to the relationship between student and teacher	3.12 (1.014)	3.53 (0.983)
Digital tools can make the students more interested in the subject I am teaching	3.83 (0.738)	4.14 (0.693)
I like testing new digital tools in my teaching	3.42 (0.965)	3.65 (0.869)

Note: SD-Standard Deviation; Professional Attitude (ATT); Pre-Service Preschool (PSP); Pre-service Primary School (PS) Teachers.

In the set of questions about the professional attitude towards the use of DT in education (Table 4), the PSP (3.83 (0.738)) and PS (4.14 (0.693)) students chose the highest values for the statement "Digital tools can make the students more interested in the subject I am teaching". The lowest score for the PSP (2.55 (0.850)) and PS (3.08 (0.759)) students agreed with the statement "Society's expectations of the impact of digital tools are exaggerated." The statement "The use of digital tools is disruptive to the relationship between student and teacher." has somewhat lower agreement 3.12 (1.014) for PSP and 3.53 (0.983) for PS students but is the one with the highest standard deviation. This implies a large dispersion in the responses. If we review all eight items of the Professional Attitude construct, we can find that students of both groups are in favor of using DT (items with lower SD). Among them, due to some items with greater dispersion of SD, are some students who feel that they need a more substantive and systematic approach to using DT in their studies and professional work with children in the future.

Professional attitude (ATT) towards using DT in education is a factor that influences preservice teachers' use of DT in their classrooms. According to research, preservice teachers' attitudes about technology play a significant role in determining how success-fully they will integrate technology in the future teaching practice [44, 64], and [73, 75, 76].

The results are in line with several studies [51, 70], cited in [53], which assert that attitudes toward teaching and digital literacy are two important factors influencing the digital practices of both in-service and pre-service teachers. There is a likelihood that there is a causal relationship between teachers' views and their level of digital competence. More precisely, as noted in [53], favorable attitudes support increases in teachers' digital competence [63, 64], and [70]. The authors also make note of the fact that teachers' openness and favorable views regarding the use of DT in the classroom seem to be significant aspects of their digital competence [31, 46, 49, 50, 54, 55, 66]. Teachers' beliefs, attitudes, and efficacy, according to Palak and Walls [59], are crucial for the effective integration of DT in education [52]. As a result, studies have generally found that preservice teachers have favorable attitudes toward the use of DT in the classroom [57]. A very favorable attitude toward the use of digital resources is described as very practical and functional for creating students learning tasks. This result is very similar to other studies conducted where the attitude and competence about DT use of students were analyzed [as cited in 84]. Recent studies provide evidence to indicate that teachers perceived technological pedagogical content knowledge may be the most important predictor of the actual use and thinking of DT [81]. The key to higher education reform is a change of mentality. From that, it follows that the general shift from a teaching to a learning paradigm in higher education is possible with a parallel change in the conceptions that university teachers have about teaching and learning [82, 83 p. 331 as cited in 84].

In summary, demonstrating a more proactive attitude toward DT will enable pre-service and in-service teachers to more firmly build pedagogical digital competency, regardless of age [46 as cited in 50]. This suggests that these digital pedagogies—rather than teacher-centered strategies improve student engagement in the learning process [60, 68, 75, 76, 79].

4.5 Correlations Between Constructs

The study employed the Pearson correlation coefficient to investigate potential relationships between the prospective utilization of DT and professional attitudes and pedagogical digital competencies (Table 5). AT to PSP Pearson correlations are above 0.5 in both cases (PDC PSP; 0.526 and ATT PSP; 0.532). The correlation is statistically significant at the 0.01 level. The higher the level of digital competencies developed, the greater is the possibility for future teachers to use DT in their future teaching practice in kindergartens. The same is true for professional attitudes towards the use of DT and the future use of DT in kindergarten teaching.

The AT to PS correlation analysis shows that the professional application of digital tools in the future (AT) correlates relatively low with PDC PS (0.340), and slightly more with professional attitude (ATT PS; 0.363). All correlations are relatively low, positive, and significant at the level of 0.01. In terms of the implementation of DT, a generally low correlation is linked to a very invasive top-down national governance of education. This results in a situation where external factors are governing educators' application of tools. And when use is driven by both external and internal forces, correlation is lower as there are other factors explaining some of the practitioners' use of technology. Bergum Johanson et al. [43] reported that several researchers in Norway have highlighted a lack of connection between what is stated about digital knowledge and skills in international and national plans for teacher education, what is happening in school practice, and the preservice teachers' experiences of their learning of digital knowledge and skills in their teacher education. Similar results are noticed in other research where the attitude, knowledge, and skills of DT used by students were analyzed [84].

Table 5. Correlations between Constructs.

Construct	PDC PSP	PDC PS	ATT PSP	ATT PS
AT	0.526**	0.340**	0.532**	0.363**
PDC PSP	–	–	0.656**	-
PDC PS	–	–	–	0.677**

Note: ** Significant at the 0.01 level (2-tailed). AT-application of tools in the future teaching practice; PDC-Pedagogical digital competence; ATT-Professional attitude (attitude towards DT in education); Pre-Service Preschool (PSP); Pre-service Primary School (PS) Teachers.

Table 5 presents the correlation between PDC PSP and ATT PSP, which is significant, positive, above 0.5, and moderately positive (0.656). Similarly, the correlation between PDC PS and ATT PS is significant, positive, above 0.5, and moderately positive (0.677). Both correlations are significant at the 0.01 level. That shows the importance of both constructs for the future use of DT. Since the correlation is moderate, we can conclude that the relatively small sample of respondents also contributes to this.

Results are consistent with multiple studies suggesting that teachers' attitudes and pedagogical digital competence are two crucial factors influencing both in-service and pre-service teachers' digital practices [51, 70] as cited in [53] and [75, 76, 84].

4.6 Standardized Multiple Linear Regressions Analysis

The results of the linear regression analysis of the two samples (Table 6) indicate that the regression model uses predictors of PDC and ATT to explain 36.3% (PSP) and 12.1% (PS) of the future usage of digital tools in pedagogical activity (AT). The results are statistically significant at the 0.01 level (2-tailed). This fact suggests the conclusion that there must be external factors that are not covered by the model used. External factors could, for instance, be policy, requirements, beliefs, and external expectations. It has been argued that the governance of education must, to some degree, put the use of DT above pedagogical considerations. The individual regression analysis for each sample reveals a slightly more complex picture, suggesting different dynamics among the samples. This could imply the implementation of curriculum changes in study programs as pointed out by previous research [75, 76].

Table 6. Standardized multiple linear regression analysis.

Predictors	S.C.B (p-significance)	Adjusted R-Squared
PDC PSP	0.30 *** (p < 0.01)	36.3%
ATT PSP	0.37 *** (p < 0.01)	
PDC PS	–	12.1%
ATT PS	0.363*** (p < 0.01)	

Note: *** Significant at the 0.01 level (2-tailed). S.C.B. is the standardized coefficient of the variable. Dependent variable: AT—application of digital tools in future teaching practice; predictors: PDC-Pedagogical digital competence; ATT-Professional attitude (attitude towards DT in education); Pre-Service Preschool (PSP); Pre-service Primary School (PS) Teachers.

Regarding the explanatory power of the regression coefficients, we can summarize that in the case of Slovenia, both sample's ATT regressions coefficients are higher (Table 6). So, attitude towards DT in education remains the main construct that influences students' future use of DT in teaching practice. In the case of PDC PS, the standardized coefficient of the variable was excluded from linear regression because of the small sample of respondents. Findings pointed out that digital knowledge, skills, and attitude (supported by values and beliefs) frameworks should be segmented by educational stakeholders (PSP and PS Teachers, teachers' educators, and administrative personnel) and levels (early childhood, primary, secondary, and higher education) with corresponding assessment instruments [85]. Integrating DT in educational settings is essential for PSP and PS Teachers' programs to develop pedagogical digital competence (e.g., through alignment with the DigCompEdu framework), while also developing positive attitudes toward DT use [31].

When integrating competence assessment and development into teaching strategies and preservice teacher training, we must take into account the field-specific digital competence and how we can support the development of such competence cross-curricula to provide high-quality professional development in higher education. Furthermore, comprehension of such competence and related conceptions is necessary to enable the evaluation process of digital competence particular to a given field [86].

5 Conclusion

This study investigates pre-service preschool teachers' and pre-service primary teachers' pedagogical digital competence, use of DT, and attitudes towards technology in the educational setting.

To answer the research question: "How will the future use of DT in the educational environment be related to the pedagogical competencies and attitudes towards the integration of DT in the educational setting of pre-service primary school teachers compared to pre-service preschool teachers?".

From the diverse responses provided, we can infer that there is a relatively very good degree of willingness to learn about and use DT in teaching and learning. Additionally, in terms of training, we can see that there is a concern for a greater level of inclusion of DT and digital-related content during their initial training period, particularly before they enter practical involvement. These recommendations reflect an eagerness to embrace DT in pre-service preschool teachers' and pre-service primary teachers' education and a desire for comprehensive training that prepares future teachers to be effective pedagogical digitally competent educators. This readiness to incorporate technology-based learning resources is seen as a necessary first step toward future use of DT [77, 78].

Therefore, it makes sense to pay special attention to the development of students' pedagogical digital competencies during their studies and to the planning and implementation of didactically meaningful activities for the development of preschool and elementary school children's digital competencies and the acquisition and transfer of knowledge in the field of computing and informatics, which are key to living and working in a digital society. It is important to equip students with knowledge and skills so that they will be able to transfer the acquired knowledge from the mentioned areas into practice, share them with colleagues in kindergarten and elementary schools, and thus help reduce the generational gap regarding the use of DT [13, 77, 78].

The importance of PDC and ATT constructs is demonstrated by the current study as well as studies from other authors. The stated intention to use DT in the future also demonstrates the readiness of compared respondents to integrate technologies into their pedagogical activity. For effective use of DT in pedagogical processes with preschool and primary school students, they also require their own experience in addition to integrating it into study processes.

The research is limited by a single measurement, a small sample size, and the involvement of only one Slovenian faculty of education. Prospects for future research encompass focus groups in the design of the assessment instrument and in the process of developing and validating the pedagogical digital competency model. Limited research has been done on the effects of all significant constructs on students' future efficiency and effectiveness in the classroom and future workplace, including developmental and diagnostic evaluations.

References

1. Brodnik, A., et al.: Okvir računalništva in informatike od vrtca do srednje šole. Poročilo strokovne delovne skupine za analizo prisotnosti vsebin računalništva in informatike v programih osnovnih in srednjih šol ter za pripravo študije o možnih spremembah (RINOS) [A framework for computer and information science from kindergarten to secondary school. Report of the Expert Working Group for the Analysis of the Presence of Computing and Informatics Content in Primary and Secondary School Curricula and for the Preparation of a Study on Possible Changes (RINOS)]. Ministrstvo za izobraževanje, znanost in šport [Ministry of Education, Science and Sport], Ljubljana (2022). https://redmine.lusy.fri.uni-lj.si/att achments/download/3060/Porocilo_RINOS_10_1_22.pdf. Accessed 5 Dec 2023
2. Bećirović, S.: Digital competence of teachers and Students. Digit. Pedag. 39–50 (2023). https://doi.org/10.1007/978-981-99-0444-0_4
3. Čampelj, B., Jereb, E.: Report on ICT in education in the Republic of Slovenia. In: Liu, D., Huang, R., Lalic, B., Zeng, H., Zivlak, N. (eds.) Comparative Analysis of ICT in Education Between China and Central and Eastern European Countries. LNET, pp. 353–370. Springer, Singapore (2020). https://doi.org/10.1007/978-981-15-6879-4_18
4. European Commission. Education and Training Monitor 2020 – Slovenia (2020). https://op.europa.eu/webpub/eac/education-and-training-monitor-2020/countries/slovenia.html. Accessed 5 Dec 2023
5. European Commission. Education and Training Monitor 2022 – Slovenia (2022). https://op.europa.eu/webpub/eac/education-and-training-monitor-2022/en/country-reports/slovenia.html#2-focus-on. Accessed 5 Dec 2023
6. Lin, R., Yang, J., Jiang, F., et al.: Does teacher's data literacy and digital teaching competence influence empowering students in the classroom? Evidence from China. Educ. Inf. Technol. **28**, 2845–2867 (2023). https://doi.org/10.1007/s10639-022-11274-3
7. Basilotta-Gómez-Pablos, V., Matarranz, M., Casado-Aranda, L.A., et al.: Teachers' digital competencies in higher education: a systematic literature review. Int. J. Educ. Technol. High. Educ. **19**, 8 (2022). https://doi.org/10.1186/s41239-021-00312-8
8. Madsen, S.S., Thorvaldsen, S., Archard, S.: Teacher educators' perceptions of working with digital technologies. Nordic J. Digit. Lit. **13**(3), 177–196 (2018). https://doi.org/10.18261/issn.1891-943x-2018-03-04
9. Japelj Pavešić, B., Peršolja, M. Špegel Razbornik, A.: Zaostajanje uporabe IKT za poučevanje v slovenskih osnovnih in srednjih šolah. Sekundarna študija na osnovi podatkov TALIS 2018, razširjena s študijama primerov poučevanja matematike na daljavo v osnovni in srednji šoli [The lagging use of ICT for teaching in Slovenian primary and secondary schools. Secondary study based on TALIS 2018 data, extended with two case studies of distance learning mathematics teaching in primary and secondary school]. Pedagoški inštitut, Ljubljana (2020). https://www.pei.si/wp-content/uploads/2021/01/Zaostajanje-Slovenije-v-uporabi-IKT-za-poucevanje.pdf. Accessed 28 Nov 2023
10. United Nations Educational, Scientific and Cultural Organization: UNESCO's ICT Competency Framework for Teachers. UNESCO, France (2018)
11. Mishra, P., Koehler, M.J.: Technological pedagogical content knowledge: a framework for teacher knowledge. Teach. Coll. Rec. **108**, 1017–1054 (2006). https://doi.org/10.1111/j.1467-9620.2006.00684.x
12. Voogt, J., Fisser, P., Pareja Roblin, N., Tondeur, J., van Braak, J.: Technological pedagogical content knowledge – a review of the literature. J. Comput. Assist. Learn. **29**(2), 109–121 (2012). https://doi.org/10.1111/j.1365-2729.2012.00487.x
13. Hughes, S.P., Corral-Robles, S., Ortega-Martín, J.L.: Let's get digital: ICT training needs in pre-service language teaching. Educ. Sci. **13**(1238), 1–16 (2023). https://doi.org/10.3390/educsci13121238

14. Bozdogan, D., Rasit, O.: Use of ICT technologies and factors affecting pre-service ELT teachers' perceived ICT self-efficacy. Turk. Online J. Educ. Technol. **13**, 186–196 (2014)
15. Mirzajani, H., Mahmud, R., Wong, S.L.: A review of research literature on obstacles that prevent use of ICT in pre-service teachers' educational courses. Int. J. Educ. Lit. Stud. **3**, 25–31 (2015)
16. Allport, G.W.: Attitudes. In: Murchinson, C. (ed.) A Handbook of Social Psychology, pp. 789–844. Clark University Press, Worcester (1935)
17. Janeš, A., et al.: Preliminary results from Norway, Slovenia, Portugal, Turkey, Ukraine, and Jordan: investigating pre-service teachers' expected use of digital technology when becoming teachers. Educ. Sci. **13**, 783 (2023). https://doi.org/10.3390/educsci13080783
18. Vuorikari, R., Kluzer, S., Punie, Y.: DigComp 2.2: the digital competence framework for citizens—with new examples of knowledge, skills and attitudes. Publications Office of the European Union, Luxembourg (2022). https://publications.jrc.ec.europa.eu/repository/handle/JRC128415. Accessed 06 Sept 2022
19. lEuropean Framework for the Digital Competence of Educators: DigCompEdu; Publications Office of the European Union, Luxembourg (2017). https://publications.jrc.ec.europa.eu/repository/bitstream/JRC107466/pdf_digcomedu_a4_final.pdf. Accessed 12 Sept 2023
20. Blayone, T.J.B., Mykhailenko, O., Usca, S., Abuze, A., Romanets, I., Oleksiiv, M.: Exploring technology attitudes and personal–cultural orientations as student readiness factors for digitalised work. High. Educ. Skills Work-Based Learn. **11**(3), 649–671 (2021). https://doi.org/10.1108/HESWBL-03-2020-0041
21. Gokhale, A.A., Brauchle, P.E., Machina, K.F.: Scale to measure attitudes toward information technology. Int. J. Inf. Commun. Technol. Educ. **9**(3), 13–26 (2013)
22. Erstad, O., Kjällander, S., Järvelä, S.: Facing the challenges of 'digital competence' a Nordic agenda for curriculum development for the 21st century. Nordic J. Digit. Lit. **16**(2), 77–87 (2021). https://doi.org/10.18261/issn.1891-943x-2021-02-02
23. European Council. Council Recommendation of 22 May 2018 on Key Competences for Lifelong Learning, 2018/C189/01. European Council, Brussels, Belgium (2018)
24. UNESCO. The ICT Competency Framework for Teachers Harnessing OER Project Digital Skills Development for Teachers. UNESCO (2022). https://www.unesco.org/en/digital-competencies-skills/ict-cft. Accessed 21 Dec 2023
25. Kelentrić, M., Helland, K., Arstorp, A.-T.: Professional digital competence framework for teachers. The Norwegian Centre for ICT in Education, Troms, Norway (2017). https://www.udir.no/contentassets/081d3aef2e4747b096387aba163691e4/pfdk-framework.pdf. Accessed 05 June 2023
26. Koehler, M., Mishra, P.: What is technological pedagogical content knowledge (TPACK)? Contemp. Issues Technol. Teach. Educ. **9**(1), 60–70 (2009)
27. Tveiterås, N.C., Madsen, S.S.: From tools to complexity?—a systematic literature analysis of digital competence among preservice teachers in Norway. In: Tomczyk, Ł., Fedeli, L. (eds.) Digital Literacy for Teachers. Lecture Notes in Educational Technology, pp. 345–389. Springer, Singapore (2022). https://doi.org/10.1007/978-981-19-1738-7_18
28. Thorvaldsen, S., Madsen, S.S.: Perspectives on the tensions in teaching with technology in Norwegian teacher education analysed using Argyris and Schön's theory of action. Educ. Inf. Technol. **25**(6), 5281–5299 (2020). https://doi.org/10.1007/s10639-020-10221-429
29. Instefjord, E.J., Munthe, E.: Educating digitally competent teachers: a study of integration of professional digital competence in teacher education. Teach. Teach. Educ. **67**, 37–45 (2017). https://doi.org/10.1016/j.tate.2017.05.016
30. Gudmundsdottir, G.B., Hatlevik, O.E.: Newly qualified teachers' professional digital competence: implications for teacher education. Eur. J. Teach. Educ. **41**(2), 214–231 (2018). https://doi.org/10.1080/02619768.2017.1416085

31. Moynihan, D., Gorman, A., Leahy, M., Scully, D.: All the world's a stage: examining the actors that influence the development of primary pre-service teacher digital competence in the Republic of Ireland. Educ. Sci. **13**, 1045 (2023). https://doi.org/10.3390/educsci13101045
32. Starkey, L.: A review of research exploring teacher preparation for the digital age. Camb. J. Educ. **50**, 37–56 (2020). https://doi.org/10.1080/0305764X.2019.1625867
33. Bice, H., Tang, H.: Teachers' beliefs and practices of technology integration at a school for students with dyslexia: a mixed methods study. Educ. Inf. Technol. **27**, 10179–10205 (2022). https://doi.org/10.1007/s10639-022-11044-1
34. Pedro, N., Matos, J.F., Pedro, A.: Digital technologies, teachers' competences, students' engagement and future classroom: ITEC project. In: Rensing, C., de Freitas, S., Ley, T., Muñoz-Merino, P.J. (eds.) EC-TEL 2014. LNCS, vol. 8719, pp. 582–583. Springer, Cham (2014). https://doi.org/10.1007/978-3-319-11200-8_80
35. European Commission. Digital Education Action Plan (2021–2027). Resetting Education and Training for the Digital Age. Publications Office of the European Union, Luxembourg (2020). https://education.ec.europa.eu/focus-topics/digital-education/action-plan. Accessed 06 Jan 2024
36. Ertmer, P.A., Ottenbreit-Leftwich, A.T., Sadik, O., Sendurur, E., Sendurur, P.: Teacher beliefs and technology integration practices: a critical relationship. Comput. Educ. **59**, 423–435 (2012)
37. Efe, H.A.: The relation between science student teachers' educational use of web 2.0 technologies and their computer self-efficacy. J. Baltic Sci. Educ. **14**(1), 142–154 (2015)
38. Inan, F.A., Lowther, D.L., Ross, S.M., Strahl, D.: Pattern of classroom activities during students' use of computers: relations between instructional strategies and computer applications. Teach. Teach. Educ. **26**(3), 540–546 (2010)
39. So, H.-J., Kim, B.: Learning about problem-based learning: student teachers integrating technology, pedagogy and content knowledge. Australas. J. Educ. Technol. **25**, 101–116 (2009)
40. Argyris, C., Schön, D.: Theory in Practice Increasing Professional Effectiveness. Jossey-Bass, Hoboken (1974)
41. Mou, T.-Y., Kao, C.-P.: Online academic learning beliefs and strategies: a comparison of preservice and in-service early childhood teachers. Online Inf. Rev. **45**(1), 65–83 (2021). https://doi.org/10.1108/OIR-08-2019-0274
42. Ala-Mutka, K.: Mapping digital competence: towards a conceptual understanding. Publications Office of the European Union, Luxembourg (2011). https://doi.org/10.13140/RG.2.2.18046.00322
43. Bergum Johanson, L., Leming, T., Johannessen, B.-H., Solhaug, T.: Competence in digital interaction and communication—a study of first-year preservice teachers' competence in digital interaction and communication at the start of their teacher education. Teach. Educator (2022). https://doi.org/10.1080/08878730.2022.2122095
44. Blackwell, C.K., Lauricella, A.R., Wartella, E.: Factors influencing digital technology use in early childhood education. Comput. Educ. **77**, 82–90 (2014). https://doi.org/10.1016/j.compedu.2014.04.013
45. Brito, R., Silva, J., Patricia Dias, P.: From perception to action: the adoption and use of digital technologies by pre-school and primary school. Int. J. Innov. Res. Educ. Sci. **10**(2), 2349–5219 (2023)
46. Casillas, S., Cabezas, M., García, F.J.: Digital competence of early childhood education teachers: attitude, knowledge and use of ICT. Eur. J. Teach. Educ. **43**(2), 210–223 (2020)
47. Celik, V., Yesilyurt, E.: Attitudes to technology, perceived computer self-efficacy and computer anxiety as predictors of computer supported education. Comput. Educ. **60**(1), 148–158 (2013)

48. Cortina, J.M.: What is coefficient alpha? An examination of theory and applications. J. Appl. Psychol. **78**(1), 98–104 (1993). https://doi.org/10.1037/0021-9010.78.1.98

49. Dumford, A.D., Miller, A.L.: Online learning in higher education: exploring advantages and disadvantages for engagement. J. Comput. High. Educ. **30**, 452–465 (2018). https://doi.org/10.1007/s12528-018-9179-z

50. Galindo-Domínguez, H., José Bezanilla, M.: Digital competence in the training of pre-service teachers: perceptions of students in the degrees of early childhood education and primary education. J. Digit. Learn. Teach. Educ. **37**(4), 262–278 (2021). https://doi.org/10.1080/21532974.2021.1934757

51. Kucirkova, N., Rowsell, J., Falloon, G. (eds.): The Routledge International Handbook of Learning with Technology in Early Childhood. Routledge, London-New York (2019)

52. Kundu, A., Bej, T., Dey, K.N.: An empirical study on the correlation between teacher efficacy and ICT infrastructure. Int. J. Inf. Learn. Technol. **37**(4), 213–238 (2020). https://doi.org/10.1108/IJILT-04-2020-0050

53. Luo, W., Berson, I.R., Berson, M.J., Li, H.: Are early childhood teachers ready for digital transformation of instruction in Mainland China? Child Youth Serv. Rev. **120**, 105718 (2021). https://doi.org/10.1016/j.childyouth.2020.105718

54. Madsen, S.S., Thorvaldsen, S., Sollied, S.: Are teacher students' deep learning and critical thinking at risk of being limited in digital learning environments? In: Hernandez-Serrano, M.J. (ed.) Teacher Education in the 21st Century – Emerging Skills for a Changing World. IntechOpen (2021)

55. Madsen, S., Thorvaldsen, S.: Implications of the imposed and extensive use of online education in an early childhood education program. Nordisk barnehageforskning **19**(1), 1–20 (2022). https://doi.org/10.23865/nbf.v19.258. Accessed 26 Oct 2023

56. Martzoukou, K., Fulton, C., Kostagiolas, P., Lavranos, C.: A study of higher education students' self-perceived digital competences for learning and everyday life online participation. J. Doc. **76**(6), 1413–1458 (2020). https://doi.org/10.1108/JD-03-2020-0041

57. McGarr, O., McDonagh, A.: Digital competence in teacher education. Output 1 of the Erasmus+ funded developing student teachers' digital competence (DICTE) project (2019). https://dicte.oslomet.no/. Accessed 19 May 2023

58. Ottenbreit-Leftwich, A.T., Glazewski, K.D., Newby, T.J., Ertmer, P.A.: Teacher value beliefs associated with using technology: addressing professional and student needs. Comput. Educ. **55**(3), 1321–1335 (2010). https://doi.org/10.1016/j.compedu.2010.06.002

59. Palak, D., Walls, R.T.: Teachers' beliefs and technology practices: a mixed-methods approach. J. Res. Technol. Educ. **41**, 417–441 (2009). https://doi.org/10.1080/15391523.2009.10782537

60. Prestridge, S.: The beliefs behind the teacher that influences their ICT practices. Comput. Educ. **58**(1), 449–458 (2012)

61. Røkenes, F.M., Krumsvik, R.J.: Prepared to teach ESL with ICT? A study of digital competence in Norwegian teacher education. Comput. Educ. **97**, 1–20 (2016). https://doi.org/10.1016/j.compedu.2016.02.014

62. Sang, G., Valcke, M., Van Braak, J., Tondeur, J.: Student teachers' thinking processes and ICT integration: predictors of prospective teaching behaviours with educational technology. Comput. Educ. **54**(1), 103–112 (2010). https://doi.org/10.1016/j.compedu.2009.07.010

63. Scherer, R., Tondeur, J., Siddiq, F., Baran, E.: The importance of attitudes toward technology for preservice teachers' technological, pedagogical, and content knowledge: comparing structural equation modeling approaches. Comput. Hum. Behav. **80**, 67–80 (2018). https://doi.org/10.1016/j.chb.2017.11.003

64. Sosa Díaz, M.J., Valverde Berrocoso, J.: Perfiles docentes en el contexto de la transformación digital de la escuela. Bordón. Rev. Pedag. **72**(1), 151–173 (2020). https://doi.org/10.13042/Bordon.2020.72965

65. Spante, M., Sofkova, H.S., Lundin, M., Algers, A.: Digital competence and digital literacy in higher education research: systematic review of concept use. Cogent Educ. **5**(1), 1519143 (2018). https://doi.org/10.1080/2331186X.2018.1519143

66. Štemberger, T., Čotar Konrad, S.: Attitudes towards using digital technologies in education as an important factor in developing digital competence: the case of Slovenian student teachers. Int. J. Emerg. Technol. Learn. **16**(14), 83–98 (2021). https://doi.org/10.3991/ijet.v16i14.22649

67. Taherdoost, H.: Validity and reliability of the research instrument: how to test the validation of a questionnaire/survey in a research. Int. J. Acad. Res. Manage. **5**(3), 28–36 (2016). https://doi.org/10.2139/ssrn.3205040

68. Tømte, C., Enochsson, A.-B., Buskqvist, U., Kårstein, A.: Educating online student teachers to master professional digital competence: the TPACK-framework goes online. Comput. Educ. **84**, 26–35 (2015). https://doi.org/10.1016/j.compedu.2015.01.005

69. Tondeur, J., VanBraak, J., Guoyuan, S., Voogt, J., Fisser, P., Ottenbreit-Leftwich, A.S.: Preparing student teachers to integrate ICT in classroom practice: a synthesis of qualitative evidence. Comput. Educ. **59**(1), 134–144 (2012). https://doi.org/10.1016/j.compedu.2011.10.009

70. Tondeur, J., Scherer, R., Siddiq, F., Baran, E.: Enhancing preservice teachers' technological pedagogical content knowledge (TPACK): a mixed-method study. Educ. Tech. Res. Dev. **68**(1), 319–343 (2020). https://doi.org/10.1007/s11423-019-09692-1

71. Uerz, D., Volman, M., Kral, M.: Teacher educators' competences in fostering student teachers' proficiency in teaching and learning with technology: an overview of relevant research literature. Teach. Teach. Educ. **70**, 12–23 (2018). https://doi.org/10.1016/j.tate.2017.11.005

72. Urrea-Solano, M., Hernández-Amorós, M.J., Merma-Molina, G., Baena-Morales, S.: The learning of E- sustainability competences: a comparative study between future early childhood and primary school teachers. Educ. Sci. **11**, 644 (2021). https://doi.org/10.3390/educsci11100644

73. Yusop, F.D.: A dataset of factors that influence preservice teachers' intentions to use web 2.0 technologies in future teaching practices. Br. J. Educ. Technol. **46**(5), 1075–1080 (2015). https://doi.org/10.1111/bjet.12330

74. Demeshkant, N., Trusz, S., Potyrała, K.: Interrelationship between levels of digital competences and technological, pedagogical and content knowledge (TPACK): a preliminary study with Polish academic teachers. Technol. Pedag. Educ. (2022). https://doi.org/10.1080/1475939X.2022.2092547

75. Lai, J.W.M., Bower, M., De Nobile, J., Breyer, Y.: What should we evaluate when we use technology in education? J. Comput. Assist. Learn. **38**(3), 743–757 (2022). https://doi.org/10.1111/jcal.12645

76. Madsen, S.S., et al.: International perspectives on the dynamics of pre-service early childhood teachers' digital competences. Educ. Sci. **13**(633), 1–25 (2023). https://doi.org/10.3390/educsci13070633

77. Ghomi, M., Redecker, C.: Digital competence of educators (DigCompEdu): development and evaluation of a self-assessment instrument for teachers' digital competence. In: Proceedings of the 11th International Conference on Computer Supported Education-CSEDU, pp. 541–548. CSEDU, Heraklion (2019)

78. Marino, O., Gutierrez, J. A., Aguirre, S.: From digital citizen to digital professional. Kybernetes **48**(7), 1463–1477 (2019.). https://doi.org/10.1108/K-07-2018-0390

79. Setyowati, D.: The development of the survey of technology use, teaching, and technology-related learning experiences among pre-service English language teachers in Indonesia. J. Foreign Lang. Teach. Learn. **2**, 11–26 (2017)

80. Pozas, M., Letzel, V.: Do you think you have what it takes?—exploring predictors of pre-service teachers' prospective ICT use. Technol. Knowl. Learn. **28**, 823–841 (2021)

81. Lorenz, R., Heldt, M., Eickelmann, B.: Relevance of pre-service teacher training to use ICT for the actual use in classrooms—focus on German secondary schools. Technol. Pedagog. Educ. **31**, 563–577 (2022)

82. Bolívar, A.: La planificación por competencias en la reforma de Bolonia de la educación superior: un análisis crítico. ET-Educ. Temática Digit. **9**, 68–94 (2007). https://nbn-resolving. org/urn:nbn:de:0168-ssoar-73427. Accessed 24 Sept 2022

83. Marentic-Pozarnik, B.: From green to red tomatoes or is there a shortcut by which to change the conceptions of teaching and learning of college teachers? High. Educ. Eur. **23**, 331–338 (1998)

84. Martínez-Serrano, M.D.C., Ocaña-Moral, M.T., Pérez-Navío, E.: Digital resources and digital competence: a cross-sectional survey of university students of the childhood education degree of the University of Jaén. Educ. Sci. **11**, 452 (2021). https://doi.org/10.3390/educsci11080452

85. Mattar, J., Santos, C.C., Cuque, L.M.: Analysis and comparison of international digital competence frameworks for education. Educ. Sci. **12**, 932 (2022). https://doi.org/10.3390/educsci12120932

86. Sillat, L.H., Tammets, K., Laanpere, M.: Digital competence assessment methods in higher education: a systematic literature review. Educ. Sci. **11**, 402 (2021). https://doi.org/10.3390/educsci11080402

The Dilemma of Teacher Training for the Use of the Metaverse and Other Immersive Technologies in Teaching and Learning Processes: An Integrative Review

Ingrid Weingärtner Reis$^{(\boxtimes)}$ (iD), Melise Peruchini (iD), Vania Ribas Ulbricht (iD), and Julio Monteiro Teixeira (iD)

Universidade Federal de Santa Catarina, Florianópolis, Brazil
iwreis@utpl.edu.ec, {melise.peruchini,julio.teixeira}@ufsc.br

Abstract. The use of virtual environments in educational processes is a reality, and even at different levels, it is present in the daily life of educational institutions. There are many challenges to overcome, and access to technological resources is just one of them. The preparation of individuals for this context is part of the formation of a cyber-citizen, who not only uses technology but also understands the ethical and social implications of its use. From this scenario, we intend to investigate the main strategies used in the training processes of the academic community, especially teachers, regarding immersive technologies, such as AR, VR and the metaverse. The main results indicate that teachers who have undergone training for the use of these technologies understand their importance and impact on the learning processes, they recognize that there are opportunities for students to develop practical knowledge, solve problems more effectively, foster creativity, and more. However, they also acknowledge the limitations of using these technologies properly, such as generational differences and a lack of understanding of how to make sense of them in the teaching and learning process. Moreover, the results shows that teacher training strategies need to be reassessed, as traditional methods continue to be employed, thereby constraining opportunities for practical learning.

Keywords: Metaverse · Teacher training · Virtual Reality

1 Introduction

The term "cybercitizen" or "e-citizen" arises within the context of the discussion about cyberspace, a term introduced in the novel "Neuromancer" by [1], released in the early 1980s. According to [2], cyberspace is a place that encompasses both the physical infrastructure of digital communication and the human interactions that occur in this environment. This concept influenced people's relationship with technology and information, giving rise to new identities such as that of a cybercitizen.

Contemporarily, the term "cybercitizen" refers to an individual - a citizen - active in the digital space. It describes someone who uses information and communication technologies responsibly, ethically, and effectively [3]. The authors [4] expand this discussion to include the relationship between digital citizens or cybercitizens and government aspects, recognizing that the internet has the potential to assist in the social and economic development of nations.

Expanding the interpretation of the cybercitizen condition, it can be inferred that it is related to the need for appropriate technologies to respond to various social demands. Citizens have duties, responsibilities, and rights in this cyberspace, and it is expected that they do not remain on the sidelines of new forms of interaction and knowledge production.

For this present study, the role of the teacher in the process of teaching and learning in this digital and virtualized context of human relations is of direct interest. The teacher is a fundamental actor, and thus is always involved in the pedagogical and educational actions that take place in this new environment. As mentioned earlier, the notion of citizenship is expanded and transformed in some ways in this virtual environment. It is a new way for people to participate in social and political life.

On the other hand, educational institutions have been experiencing a constant evolution in the incorporation of digital technologies into their teaching methods. This trend was accelerated by the COVID-19 pandemic, which brought the need for quick adaptation to social distancing circumstances, highlighting the importance of maintaining the continuity of learning despite physical barriers. The impact that this experience had on humanity is undeniable, accelerating important processes of Digital Transformation.

Technologies are incorporated into people's daily lives in various ways. In education-related processes, this also occurs, and some of these technologies have transformative potential with a significant impact on pedagogical processes. To mention a few, there is an increasing adoption of immersive technologies such as augmented and virtual reality, which provide multidimensional learning experiences that go beyond traditional academic actions. These technologies open doors to a new era of interactive teaching and learning processes, allowing educational institutions to reimagine and revitalize their pedagogical methods.

According to [5], a combination of virtual worlds, augmented reality, and the internet comprises the metaverse. It is not to be confused with the internet itself but relies on it. This author uses four dimensions to configure the metaverse: Augmented Reality - as technologies that add information in layers to the real world; Life-logging - which records people's actions in the metaverse and is important for both trust and the environment as a whole, as it supports transactions, for example; Mirror Worlds - mirrored models of the real world that allow simulations, for instance; and, finally, Virtual Worlds - environments that simulates the economic and social life of the real world.

The concept of the metaverse also originates from the human imagination through the novel called "Snow Crash" [6]. In this work, the author presents the metaverse as a virtual and three-dimensional representation of the world where social interactions among people can be developed through avatars. The virtual world closely resembles the real one, allowing for various types of relationships, including economic, recreational, and educational processes.

According to [7], the metaverse is an "interoperable and large-scale network of virtual worlds" (p. 42) that can be experienced synchronously and persistently by a theoretically unlimited number of people. Due to its constitution and characteristics, this world provides people with a sense of presence and continuity, as mentioned earlier by [5], regarding life-logging in this environment.

The current technological context affects teaching and learning processes, and as a result, it is necessary to rethink all the aspects involved in this process. It is crucial to reflect on the challenges faced by teachers in the use of these immersive technologies, especially in how they are being trained. The importance of adequately equipping teachers, providing them with sufficient resources to fully integrate these technological tools from curriculum development to the moment of delivering lessons should not be overlooked. It is not just about providing access to technologies; rather, it is necessary to provide conditions for teachers to understand the best use of these technologies at different stages of the teaching and learning process.

At the heart of the digital transformation in education lies the competence of educators to critically engage with new technologies. This involves empowering teachers so they can adapt to and adopt innovative resources. Teacher training programs are crucial in this process and should be carefully designed to incorporate elements that meet the contemporary demands of education.

Considering, therefore, the context of new technologies and the need to ensure comprehensive training for teachers, this article aims to conduct an integrative literature review, seeking to compile practical and theoretical results about the strategies used in the training processes of the academic community, especially teachers, regarding immersive technologies. The goal is to organize a systematic and organic knowledge base that allows us to understand how these training process are being implemented and what impacts are observed by teachers. As mentioned earlier, the focus of this research is on the teacher and how this actor fits into this context.

The following section presents the methodological framework of this article. Subsequently, the results of the integrative review are presented, along with the analysis and discussion derived from these results. Finally, the final considerations of the study are presented.

2 Methods and Materials

The present research aims to identify fundamental aspects, such as challenges encountered in teacher education regarding the use of the metaverse and other immersive technologies, through a systematic integrative literature review. This type of review broadens the research perspective as it considers empirical or theoretical, experimental or non-experimental studies to understand a specific phenomenon [8, 9].

In order to provide the necessary rigor for the results of this research to contribute to the development of knowledge on the subject, rigorous steps were applied for the search, selection, and analysis of the found articles, following the guidelines of [10]. These authors propose that integrative reviews in the fields of social and applied sciences should follow the following stages: defining the research topic, establishing inclusion and exclusion criteria, identifying preselected studies, categorizing the studies, analyzing and interpreting the results, and presenting the review and synthesis of knowledge.

The databases used were Web of Science, Science Direct, and Scopus, as they have a multidisciplinary nature, allowing for broader coverage of areas. The ERIC database was also used, considering its focus on education-related research. To identify aspects of teacher education in the metaverse and related technologies, the following search string was applied: ("metaverse" OR "virtual world" OR "virtual reality" OR "augmented reality") AND ("teacher education" OR "teacher training" OR "professional development" OR "pedagogical training").

It is important to note that, although the metaverse is broader than just virtual reality or augmented reality, in this research, they are considered to be components of the metaverse. Therefore, adding them to the search string is a strategy to overcome the limitation of the term "metaverse" itself. In this way, the scope of the review is expanded to include topics directly related to the main focus of this research, which is the metaverse environment.

The inclusion criteria were: open access articles in English, Spanish, and Portuguese. Conference papers and articles without citations were excluded. Applying the research string and inclusion and exclusion criteria, initially, 377 articles were found, with 126 from the ERIC database, 22 from Science Direct, 123 from Scopus, and 106 from Web of Science. The search was conducted during the months of September and November 2023. Out of the 377 articles found, 253 were eliminated due to duplication or, after reading abstracts, were considered outside the main scope of the research. After a full reading of the articles, we arrived at the final number of 112 articles, which were considered for analysis. Figure 1 details the steps applied and the numbers obtained for the integrative review.

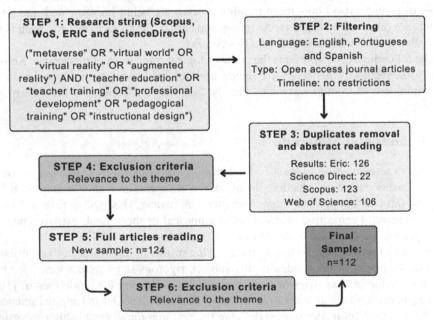

Fig. 1. Representation of the steps performed for the integrative review, as well as the results obtained at each stage.

Regarding the identification of articles, since there was no time restriction, publications were found from 1992 to 2023. Until 2018, publications related to the themes identified by the search descriptor were limited, accounting for less than 20% of the results. From the year 2019 onwards, there is a considerable increase in publications, reaching a peak of 21 publications in the year 2021.

The analysis of the data collected in the integrative review was conducted using thematic analysis [11], a qualitative approach that helps to identify and analyze themes or patterns from a set of data or information. Thematic analysis was carried out in stages, starting with familiarization and immersion in the data, allowing researchers to gain a deep understanding of the content of the articles selected from the initial reading. After thorough reading, the content was categorized, identifying the relevant characteristics in a systematic way. This allowed the data and information to be organized and grouped into themes, reflecting on the level of abstraction and relevance to the research objectives.

In a subsequent stage, the themes identified were reviewed and refined in an iterative process by the researchers. The themes were validated through constant comparison with the data set, ensuring that they were representative of the material collected. This analytical approach enabled not only the identification of existing knowledge and practices related to teacher training in the context of the metaverse, but also an understanding of perceived challenges, strategies and impacts.

3 Results and Discussions

The integrative review provided enlightening insights into the topic of teacher training in the use of immersive technologies, such as the metaverse, Virtual Reality, and Augmented Reality. In this section, we present the results of the review itself, followed by the analysis conducted to understand key elements in achieving the objective of this study.

Next, thematic analyses are presented for the selected articles, as well as the discussions, where an attempt was made to relate data and information obtained from the articles with the fundamental references on the research topics.

3.1 Teacher Training in the Use of Immersive Technologies

Teacher training is a complex challenge faced by educational institutions. Considering the constant change in student generations and the training needs for a world also in transformation, teachers must stay updated and have the competence to engage in dialogue with students.

So, the concerns and challenges in teacher training are related to topics such as access to technology, integrating them into the overall teaching and learning process, providing training that helps bridge the generational gap, and others that will be presented below.

To facilitate the analysis and consequently reading, some analysis themes were established, which are: teacher training strategies; factors impacting teachers' technology adoption; challenges encountered; and the results of the training and studies considered.

Theme 1: Teacher Training Strategies
Teacher training was an essential criterion for considering articles in the studies used.

Thus, even if not in the form of formal courses or clear strategies, teacher training was always present. Considering the studies found in the literature review, the relevant information was grouped together to make sense of the findings and give them greater significance. Table 1 represents the authors identified of each study within this theme.

Table 1. Main training strategies identified and authors

Strategy categories	Types of strategies	Authors
University teacher training	Training offered during university	[12, 13]
	Comprehensive training	[14, 15]
Additional training	Traditional training	[16–25]
Use of technology and practical activities	Online courses, using apps and virtual environments	[26–35]
	Practical activities	[12, 16, 36–38]
	Short course	[39, 40]

Below are the results and discussions specifically on the strategies found.

University Teacher Training

The use of new technologies is nothing new in teacher training. On the contrary, as can be seen from the studies identified, there is a growing concern to update teachers and give them access to resources that can be applied in the classroom. However, it is surprising that, of the studies found, few include experiences or practices used since university training.

Few studies address the topic from the perspective of teachers' initial education [12, 13]. Most studies mainly focus on teachers' additional and supplementary training in technology-related topics. This, in some way, helps to understand some teachers' perception that there is a disconnect between the use of technology and an organic understanding of the teaching and learning processes, starting from curriculum development to student assessment [14, 15].

Additional Training

As mentioned before, most studies refer to complementary training for teachers on the use of technologies in the teaching and learning process.

As for further training, it is interesting to note that the majority of the reports deal with traditional courses, in the model of workshops or formal sessions, where teachers attend presentations or have limited interaction with immersive technology, often addressing topics such as "immersiveness" in a superficial manner [16–25]. As part of the experiences mentioned above, there are also course programs that are applied online or through applications for extensive course offerings.

Use of Technology and Practical Activities

It is worth noting that among the strategies identified are those that use contemporary technology resources as part of the training, including experimentation and practice.

Authors such as [41–44] and [45] analyze teachers' perceptions of the use of specific technologies like Augmented Reality and Virtual Reality. The use of mobile applications is also evident in studies by [26, 27] and [28].

Other strategies that involve the use of virtual environments appear in studies by [29] and [30] who used Second Life; virtual participation in escape rooms [29], and other uses of virtual reality [31, 32].

It is worth noting that even in more traditional courses such as workshops and practical classes, there is a diversity of activities, indicating the efforts made to capture the teachers' attention regarding the use of technology in the teaching and learning process. The author [36] conducts live courses involving a combination of theoretical activities, group work, and role-play. On the other hand, [37] focus on augmented reality applications for solving puzzles and enhancing algorithmic thinking.

Other authors who use workshops and immersive technologies for teacher training include [17, 23, 24] and [25]. It is noteworthy the work of [37], which presented a differentiated strategy by developing a course since the prototyping, with the assistance of experts, for subsequent testing and validation among teachers.

In some cases, teachers took part in the evaluation of Augmented Reality, Virtual Reality and metaverse environments, experiencing students' perspectives on the teaching and learning process. This particular resource highlights the generational difference between teachers and students [12, 16].

Although e-Learning is not a novelty, the evolution of e-Learning platforms presents new interactive, adaptive, and collaborative elements that go beyond traditional methods of distance education, such as simple readings or videos [33–35]. These platforms are often used in the teaching training process as identified in this literature review. Other courses directly encompass Virtual Reality and Augmented Reality [44], as well as other technologies and applications in short-term courses [40].

It can be inferred from the identified strategies that technologies enhance the teacher training process. Although the generational gap is a limiting factor along with the lack of addressing the subject in teachers' initial education, it is possible to see the transitional phase currently being experienced. The prevalence of online training and the use of e-learning platforms reflect an important trend in teacher education, providing flexibility and potentially a level of customization that takes into account the differences in age, university education, and didactic knowledge of each teacher.

Gamification and the use of interactive methods, such as games and simulations, have also been identified as effective strategies in increasing engagement and knowledge retention. It can be inferred that teacher training programs should also incorporate playful resources that are not only informative but also engaging and adaptable to the individual needs of teachers.

Teacher training should be seen as an ongoing process, not an isolated event. This implies the implementation of comprehensive and systemic development programs that address technological aspects as well as pedagogical alignment. It is essential to keep educators updated on new technologies and teaching methodologies. Furthermore, personalized training is crucial to meet the diverse needs and learning styles of teachers.

Another important element is the possibility of coordinating theory and practice through classroom simulations, practical projects, and the development of games that allow teachers to address everyday situations. This is vital for teachers to apply the knowledge they have acquired in real contexts.

Undoubtedly, improving teacher training involves identifying and adopting innovative and interactive strategies, ongoing professional development, personalized learning, and the effective integration of theory and practice.

Theme 2: Factors Influencing Teachers' Adoption of Technologies

In the second theme, we sought to identify factors that influence teachers to use technologies in the classroom, beyond simply knowing or mastering them. These factors can be considered positive or negative, serving as a stimulus or a barrier to the adoption of immersive technologies in the classroom. However, although the studies highlights various points of concern, there is a number of factors that are seen as positive. To give an overview of these factors, they have been grouped together and related to their authors in Table 2.

Table 2. Elements that influence the adoption of technology by teachers and authors

Category of influence factors	Influence factors	Authors
Impact on student performance	Use of immersive technologies stimulates students	[37, 39, 46, 47]
	Possibility of better monitoring students	[12]
Didactic and pedagogical aspects	Increases teachers' confidence in the classroom	[45, 48]
	Possibility of connecting theory to practice	[17, 25, 29, 37, 49–53]
	More effort required from teachers	[14, 15, 17, 26, 55]
Contextual aspects	Post-pandemic context	[39]
	Lack of technology in schools	[45, 49]

Impact on Student Performance

Thus, some studies indicate that teachers believe that immersive technologies can increase students' motivation, interest, and engagement in learning [37, 39, 46, 47]. Similarly, [49] identified benefits of using Virtual Reality technologies, even on desktop computers, since the early 2000 s. This helps us to understand that there is a potential to be explored in the teaching and learning experience in awakening students' curiosity to new ways of creating knowledge.

The possibility of simulation is one of the most important factors in the use of metaverses and immersive technologies in education. Something relevant and timely found in the studies in this review is the fact that, by carrying out these practical activities over and over again, it is possible to gather a lot of information about the performance of students and even teachers. This can be used to improve the content, techniques, methods, approach, design and provide personalized support to the individuals involved [12], helping to improve student performance.

Didactic and Pedagogical Aspects

When considering didactic-pedagogical aspects, we are referring to the components and approaches involved in the teaching and learning process. These aspects cover the strategies, methods and techniques used by teachers to help students develop and ensure the effective creation of knowledge spaces.

In this sense, the first reflection that can be made is in relation to the teachers themselves, how they are impacted by the use of these technologies in the classroom domain. According to [48], incorporating immersive technologies into teacher training programs can help improve teacher performance and confidence in the classroom. The results obtained by these authors show that the experience provided by virtual environments operates at a level beyond involvement, allowing students to enter a state of concentration. Interactivity in the environment facilitates the representation of the knowledge being covered in the lesson content, the sense of presence allows navigation and exploration in a context that seems realistic, possible and, in a way, familiar to students, and the state of flow increases concentration on the stimuli provided [48].

Other aspects mentioned by teachers are related to educational practices as a whole. Research shows that teachers mention learning outside the classroom and long-term memory retention, as well as using technologies to connect theoretical content with practice [29, 49–51]. For example, Augmented Reality can help students visualize concepts that are difficult to understand or observe in reality, such as the systems of the human body [37], or event other concepts related to Science, Technology, Engineering, and Mathematics in general [17, 52, 53], aiding in the comprehension of abstract content due to its visual appeal [25, 54]. Additionally, Virtual Reality in teacher training can provide a realistic and authentic experience, helping them develop their presentation and classroom management skills [45].

Other factors influencing the adoption of these technologies include performance expectations, effort expectations, facilitating conditions, and social influence [26]. Teachers view these technologies as promising but emphasize the need for relevant curriculum-related content [14, 15, 17].

Contextual Aspect

Furthermore, in some cases, the adoption of new technologies appears to be imperative in a post-pandemic scenario that requires blended learning and hybrid teaching methods. The Author [39] argue that teachers are willing to adopt innovative methods that assist them in student-centered strategies. However, other authors highlight the resistance and hesitation that some teachers exhibit when it comes to adopting new technologies, as we will see in the challenges section.

There are also aspects that negatively influence teachers' adoption of technologies. In this sense, [55] identify the complexity of creating effective instructional experiences using Virtual Reality by teachers. Factors such as access to appropriate technology and teachers' knowledge of how to best utilize these resources weigh heavily. Similarly, regarding the use of Virtual Reality, the difficulty and cost of designing these environments are highlighted by [45]. The factors influencing teachers' use of technology in education are multifaceted and interconnected. It would be impossible to evaluate these factors independently or in a unifocal manner. Teachers' technological knowledge and competence play a crucial role in building digital citizenship; those who are familiar with and confident in using technology tend to integrate it more effectively into their pedagogical practices. Additionally, teachers' attitudes and perceptions toward technology are determining factors; if they view it as a valuable tool for teaching, they are more likely to use it, incorporating it in various ways and at different levels in the teaching and learning process. Technical support and available resources are also fundamental, as teachers need access to up-to-date devices, software, and structured support. Furthermore, school infrastructure, including high-speed internet access and modern equipment, is essential to facilitate the use of technology.

Theme 3: Challenges Faced by Teachers

Teachers face the great challenge of integrating innovative technological resources, such as the metaverse, into the teaching and learning process and also of using these resources from the training they do. This requires not only technical skills, but also an understanding of how these technologies can improve educational results, how to use them most appropriately and how to measure their use. The adoption of the metaverse presents an opportunity to create immersive and engaging learning experiences that transcend the traditional boundaries of the classroom. However, this also requires continuous professional development and a willingness to explore new pedagogical approaches. The readings carried out from the review help to identify a number of challenges faced by teachers in their training process and especially in the use of these technologies. These challenges are organized in Table 3.

Procedural or Operational
When analyzing the challenges found in the studies, perhaps the most impactful is related to the pedagogical dimension and the cognitive load on teachers, considering the pressure of learning and incorporating these new technologies into their daily teaching practice. Teachers mention negative aspects related to cognitive overload [37, 56] and the possibility that the use of these technologies may lead to distractions and technological dependence, both on the part of students and teachers [40, 55, 57].

Furthermore, the lack of educational materials, instructional design without clear guidelines, the absence of a theoretical foundation for making decisions about proper integration into the teaching and learning process, the difficulty of interaction in a context formed by the blending of the real and virtual, the lack of educational research, and the lack of institutional support are some of the elements that represent significant challenges for teachers [49, 50, 58].

Some research endorses the need for more teacher training, pointing to a lack of professional development [42], limited familiarity with these immersive technologies [31, 49, 50], little to no practical or theoretical experience [24], deficiencies in the ability to create digital content [41], and a lack of understanding of concepts such as Augmented Reality and Virtual Reality [13, 44]. These are all challenges that teachers must face, with institutional support.

Table 3. Challenges faced by teachers in adopting immersive technologies and authors

Challenge Category	Challenges	Authors
Procedural or operational	Cognitive overload	[10, 37]
	Distraction and technological dependence by students	[40, 55, 57]
	Pedagogical aspects and instructional design - how to integrate technology?	[25, 48, 49, 56, 58]
	Teacher unfamiliarity with technology	[13, 17, 24, 31, 39, 41, 42, 49, 50]
	Teachers' doubts about effectiveness	[17, 50]
	Improved training opportunities for teachers	[45, 48]
Institutional or structural	Cost of using, acquiring and training technologies	[42, 45, 46, 55]
	Adequate physical space	[45]
	Lack of time and institutional support	[17, 29, 44]

Hence, the perception regarding the mentioned challenges is that there is a need to balance pedagogical and technical knowledge to at least create virtual objects or environments, and therein lies an obstacle for teachers [48]. According to [25], there is a need to acquire equipment, understand the technology, create the technological environment, and generate interest and engagement. All of these steps require competencies, time, and support at various levels of knowledge.

There is also a complex element to identify and address, which is the acceptance of technology use by teachers. When considering the significance of teacher training to address the current context in the face of digital transformation, it is understood that teachers' willingness is a crucial factor for the appropriate and timely use of these technologies. Teachers must be prepared and supported by the educational institution to achieve the expected results. We initially discussed digital citizenship or the responsibility of individuals when using technology, aiming to use it effectively in the teaching and learning process. For this reason, it is necessary to understand that cognitive overload, technology dependence, lack of time and support, among other factors mentioned earlier, may be related to teachers' acceptance of these technologies. This research identifies situations where new teachers express stronger convictions about the negative impacts of technology on student learning, which can affect their confidence in using technology in instructional settings [50]. Other studies show hesitation on the part of teachers to allow students to use mobile devices in the classroom [17].

On the other hand, the challenge can be viewed from an encouraging and mature perspective. Incorporating these technologies into the teaching and learning process with new practice-focused approaches contributes to the cutting-edge training of teachers and even other professions [45]. It is also recognized that teachers' confidence in using these tools increases because they have the opportunity to simulate realities very close to their daily lives [45, 48]. Therefore, teachers benefit from personal and professional development that are aligned with the current context of the world.

Institutional or Structural
When the challenges presented above are taken into consideration, it becomes clear that financial aspects represent a significant challenge for teachers in using and applying these technologies in the classroom. These technologies are expensive, both in terms of acquisition and in terms of the training and preparation of those involved [45, 46, 55]. Specifically, the difficulty and cost of designing Virtual Reality environments, acquiring devices or resources for Augmented Reality, accessing wearable devices, and even basic internet connectivity issues are mentioned [42, 45, 46]. In this regard, it appears to exist the concern about potential disadvantages for students in vulnerable situations or with lower socioeconomic conditions.

Technical difficulties are also a challenge. These difficulties arise at different points in the literature review and have an impact on the outcomes of teacher training. They also affect the perception of teachers regarding the benefits of using technologies and on the learning process itself [17, 39]. Complexity in navigation control, inconsistent or uninteresting appearance, and misalignment between the teacher's objectives and the student's focus can pose challenges in the preparation and use of Virtual Reality, for example [49]. According [39], technical difficulties and a high failure rate in completing the experiences impact teacher evaluations, as teachers tend to adopt a neutral or disengaged stance. Furthermore, technical difficulties can include classroom noise, given the inadequacy of spaces for the use of technologies like Virtual Reality [45].

The lack of time is also frequently mentioned in the papers analyzed, presented as a limitation [29, 44], exacerbated when combined with a lack of institutional support [17].

The challenges faced by teachers in the use of technology in the classroom are diverse and impact the decision on the appropriate use of technology in the teaching and learning process. The effective curricular integration of technology requires not only technical skills but also creativity and pedagogical innovation, often without clear guidelines or examples of best practices. Teacher training, in this sense, should be broad and significant, and not limited to the use of technological resources.

Theme 4: Results of Training and Articles
The results of the trainings appear to significantly depend on the overlap of the challenges encountered. Knowing each of the themes presented and discussed above from the studies used helps teachers understand the forces they are up against and potentially improve results. This review allowed the identification and organization of the main results obtained by the teachers and also the results of the researches, which are systematized in Table 4.

Failure to Use Technology Properly
On the financial side, Wyss et al. [24] point out that teachers do not use certain devices with adequate frequency because they cannot afford them. Similarly, the expectation of effort is a dominant factor in determining technology use behavior [26], and this can

Table 4. Grouping of the main results obtained from the selected studies

Grouping the results	Influencing elements two results	Authors
Failure to use technology properly	Lack of resources; lack of time; limited training	[17, 25, 26, 37, 45, 47–49, 51, 58]
Possibility for teachers to develop digital skills	Use of technology in the educational context; development of skills	[17, 28, 36, 38, 40, 41]
Increased student motivation and improved learning outcomes	Better use of teaching resources	[25, 45, 47, 49]
Need to link technology and pedagogical elements	Misalignment	[17, 18]

be linked to the challenge of the lack of time that teachers have due to their duties in schools and educational spaces.

According to Wells and Miller [46], there is a mix of favorable opinions and a considerable degree of uncertainty about the technology, which also appears in other articles. Apparently, teachers believe that these technologies are effective for teaching subjects that require more visual material, but they emphasize the need for infrastructure and well-informed individuals regarding topics of Virtual Reality, Augmented Reality, and the metaverse [25, 45, 47, 49] argue that technology should be used to enhance the learning experience of students, rather than merely following technological trends.

Other science training programs have also shown improved learning outcomes after the use of Augmented Reality materials, along with the development of cognitive skills and student motivation. However, these positive outcomes are mixed with some opposing opinions, such as a desire to stick to traditional teaching methods, a lack of teaching skills, and inadequate infrastructure [37, 48].

Possibility for Teachers to Develop Digital Skills
Some authors have observed positive results from the training in their research, such as [31, 41], who mention that teachers who used augmented reality demonstrated greater digital competence than those who did not use it. In the studies by [40] and [38], participants mostly had positive opinions about the training focused on science education.

While teachers may have some knowledge of immersive technologies to a certain extent [5, 17], there are still numerous doubts about how to apply them in the educational context. Some authors mention that, in addition to limited training opportunities, the available training is, sometimes, inadequate [51, 58]. The demand for more training, or longer training programs, is mentioned in studies by [17, 51], and [24]. However, the need for mastery of both pedagogical and technological knowledge reinforces the dilemma of using these technologies [36].

Increased Student Motivation and Improved Learning Outcomes

Research by [23] also reported positive effects of Augmented Reality on student learning outcomes and motivation with more financially accessible tools. In similar studies, [31] demonstrate that participants who used the virtual classroom environment in their training were better able to reflect and show more empathy towards students, while participants in the control group seemed more undecided. Additionally, [32] indicated significant emotional impacts in the use of virtual reality systems in an analysis using electroencephalogram (EEG) signals, highlighting the extremely realistic aspects of the systems in scenarios that simulate material reality within the safety of the virtual environment.

Need to Link Technology and Pedagogical Elements
As we have seen, technology is an important element in the teaching and learning process, but it must be based on and accompanied by pedagogical logic and intent.

Furthermore, the pace of technological development far exceeds the pace of teacher training, leading to anxiety and insecurity [17]. Therefore, it is essential to reinforce that pedagogical opportunities in virtual worlds entail profound changes in the perspective of teachers themselves [30], and these changes have proven to be challenging. Many teachers hesitate to use immersive technologies due to a lack of confidence, time, or motivation to acquire new skills, along with a discomfort involving new technologies [17].

As seen, studies on teacher training in the use of educational technologies yield a range of significant results. It is evident that while teacher training in educational technologies can bring benefits, it should be accompanied by a concern for pedagogical alignment, including adequate support and resources, and an approach that takes into account the individual needs and challenges of both teachers and students. The need to address the behavioral aspects of the teacher is also evident, ensuring that they have the autonomy to understand where and how to use each technology. The more secure they feel in their technological skills, the more open they will be to experimenting with new methodologies and innovating in their pedagogical practices. This increased confidence may have a direct impact on student engagement and performance.

4 Final Considerations

The present research aimed to investigate the strategies used in the training processes of the academic community, especially teachers, through the use of immersive technologies within educational context. By analyzing the set of information obtained from the literature review on teacher training in the context of educational technologies, it is evident the importance of developing teachers' skills and training them based on the perspective of digital citizenship and digital competencies.

In this sense, we argue that training programs that focus on digital competencies and digital citizenship would not limit teachers to mere technology use but, moreover, would enable them to understand how these technologies influence the interaction in digital educational environments. Therefore, teachers become proficient in technology but, above all, develop critical thinking and act as responsible mediators to guide students in an ethical and safe space of digital navigation.

The integration of technologies such as Virtual Reality, Augmented Reality, meta-verse environments, even e-learning platforms, and mobile applications in education requires teachers to have a broad and systemic understanding that goes beyond the technical dimension. It is necessary to prepare teachers to be aware of the ethical, social, and security implications associated with these technologies. Developing digital citizenship competence in teachers involves preparing them to address issues such as privacy, digital security, online ethics, and digital literacy. This is essential for creating a learning environment that not only uses technology to enhance teaching but also prepares students to be responsible and informed digital citizens.

However, according to the findings from the studies used, there are still challenges to overcome, such as economic and access-related aspects of technology. Both educational institutions, teachers, and students have differences in their capabilities to use technology uniformly. Therefore, digital literacy, ongoing use, familiarity with technology, and technical support are important elements for overcoming challenges in teacher training.

There is also a need to improve the integration between technological tools and pedagogical aspects. According to the results obtained, the integration of technology still appears as a somewhat foreign element in the natural teaching and learning process. There may be various causes for this, ranging from teacher training to the incentives provided by educational institutions.

Finally, despite the many challenges and needs, it is evident that both teachers and students are discovering the benefits of using these technologies. The possibility of acting more practically, understanding concepts more tangibly, and using resources like simulators are undoubtedly strong arguments for adopting these technologies in the teaching and learning process.

Building upon the findings and gaps highlighted in this research, there are some potential avenues for future investigation regarding the identified challenges. Future research should focus on examining in depth the strategies used for teacher training, especially regarding the integration between technological tools and pedagogical approaches in the educational context. Longitudinal studies could also benefit from examining long term impacts of immersive technology integration in education. This could involve tracking digital literacy skills, attitudes towards technology and real-world scenarios related to immersive education over time.

Furthermore, future research efforts should aim to address the identified gaps and challenges in teacher training and technology integration by adopting multifaceted dimensions of digital citizenship, digital competencies, pedagogy, and technology implementation in educational context.

In conclusion, through this literature review, centered on teacher training, we aim to highlight a direction that often remains overlooked in educational strategies, as we endeavor towards creating inclusive, equitable, and effective learning environments in the digital age.

References

1. Gibson, W.: Neuromancer. Aleph (1984)
2. Lévy, P.: Cibercultura. (Trad. Carlos Irineu da Costa). Editora 34, São Paulo (1999)

3. Koch, A.: Cyber citizen or cyborg citizen: baudrillard, political agency, and the com- mons in virtual politics. J. Mass Media Ethics **20**, 159–175 (2005)
4. Zhou, Z., Gao, F.: E-government and knowledge management. Int. J. Comput. Sci. Netw. Secur. **7**(6), 185–189 (2007)
5. Lee, S.G., Trimi, S., Byun, W.K., Kang, M.: Innovation and imitation effects in Meta-verse service adoption. Serv. Bus. **2**(5), 155–172 (2011). https://doi.org/10.1007/s11628-011-0108-8
6. Stephenson, N.: Snow crash (Trad. Fábio Fernandes), 3rd edn. Aleph, São Paulo (2022)
7. Ball, M.: The Metaverse: And How it Will Revolutionize Everything. W. W. Norton & Company Inc, New York (2022)
8. Broome M.E.: Integrative literature reviews for the development of concepts. In: Rodgers B.L., Knafl K.A. (eds.) Concept Development in Nursing, 2nd edn., pp. pp. 231–250. W.B. Saunders Co., Philadelphia (1993)
9. Whittemore, R., Knafl, K.: The integrative review: updated methodology. Methodol. Issues Nurs. Res. **54**(5), 546–553 (2005). https://doi.org/10.1111/j.1365-2648.2005.03621.x
10. Botelho, R.R.L., Cunha, C.C.A., Macedo, M.: O método da revisão integrativa nos estudos organizacionais. Gestão Sociedade **5**(11), 121–136 (2011)
11. Braun, V., Clarke, V.: Thematic analysis. In: Cooper, H., Camic, P.M., Long, D.L., Panter, A.T., Rindskopf, D., Sher, K.J. (eds.) APA Handbook of Research Methods in Psychology. Research Designs: Quantitative, Qualitative, Neuropsychological, and Biological, vol. 2, pp. 57–71. American Psychological Association (2012). https://doi.org/10.1037/13620-004
12. Álvarez, I.M., Manero, B., Morodo, A., Suñé-Soler, N., Henao, C.: Immersive virtual reality to improve competence to manage classroom climate in secondary schools. Educ. XXI **26**(1), 249–272 (2023). https://doi.org/10.5944/educxx1.33418
13. Attwood, A.I., Bruster, B.G., Bruster, B.G.: An exploratory study of preservice teacher per-ception of virtual reality and artificial intelligence for classroom management instruction. SRATE J. **29**(2), 1–9 (2020). https://files.eric.ed.gov/fulltext/EJ1268557.pdf
14. Al-Adwan, S., Li, N., Al-Adwan, A., Abbasi, G.A., Albelbisi, N.A., Habibi, A.: Extending the technology acceptance model (TAM) to predict university students' intentions to use metaverse-based learning platforms. Educ. Inf. Technol. **28**, 15381–15413 (2023). https://doi.org/10.1007/s10639-023-11816-3
15. Alda, R., Boholano, H., Dayagbil, F.: Teacher education institutions in the Philippines towards education 4.0. Int. J. Learn. Teach. Educ. Res. **19**(8), 137–154 (2020). https://doi.org/10.26803/ijlter.19.8.8
16. Aivelo, T., Uitto, A.: Digital gaming for evolutionary biology learning: the case study of parasite race, an augmented reality location-based game. LUMAT **4**(1), 1–26 (2016). https://doi.org/10.31129/LUMAT.4.1.3
17. Lasica, I.E., Meletiou-Mavrotheris, M., Katzis, K.: Augmented reality in lower secondary education: a teacher professional development program in Cyprus and Greece. Educ. Sci. **10**(4), 121 (2020). https://doi.org/10.3390/educsci10040121
18. Marques, M.M., Pombo, L.: The impact of teacher training using mobile augmented reality games on their professional development. Educ. Sci. **11**(8), 1–21 (2021). https://doi.org/10.3390/educsci11080404
19. Peterson, K., Stone, B.A.: From theory to practice: building leadership opportunities through virtual reality science expeditions. Int. J. Whole Child **4**(1), 67–74 (2019). https://files.eric.ed.gov/fulltext/EJ1213644.pdf
20. Pombo, L., Marques, M.M.: Guidelines for teacher training in mobile augmented reality games: hearing the teachers' voices. Educ. Sci. **11**(10), 1–12 (2021). https://doi.org/10.3390/educsci11100597

21. Rowe, S., Riggio, M., Amicis, R., Rowe, S.R.: Teacher perceptions of training and pedagogical value of cross-reality and sensor data from smart buildings. Educ. Sci. **10**(9), 1–18 (2020). https://doi.org/10.3390/educsci10090234
22. Şeyihoglu, A., Kartal, A., Tekbiyik, A. Vekli, G.S., Konur, K.B.: The design and implementation of a teacher training program for improving teachers' disaster literacy: interdisciplinary disaster education program (IDEP). Probl. Educ. 21st Century **79**(5), 1–23 (2021). https://doi.org/10.33225/pec/21.79.781
23. Tzima, S., Styliaras, G., Bassounas, A.: Augmented reality applications in education: teachers' point of view. Educ. Sci. **9**(2), 99 (2019). https://doi.org/10.3390/educsci9020099
24. Wyss, C., Buehrer, W., Furrer, F., Degonda, A., Hiss, J.: Innovative teacher education with the augmented reality device microsoft hololens-results of an exploratory study and pedagogical considerations. Multimodal Technol. Interact. **5**(8), 45 (2021). https://doi.org/10.3390/mti5080045
25. Yilmaz, M., Simsek, M.C.: The use of virtual reality, augmented reality, and the metaverse in education: the views of preservice biology and mathematics teachers. MIER J. Educ. Stud. Trends Pract. **13**(1), 64–80 (2023). https://doi.org/10.52634/mier/2023/v13/i1/2422
26. Nizar, N.N.M., Rahmat, M.K., Maaruf, S.Z., Damio, S.M.: Examining the use behaviour of augmented reality technology through MARLCardio: adapting the UTAUT model. Asian J. Univ. Educ. **15**(3), 198–210 (2019). https://files.eric.ed.gov/fulltext/EJ1238762.pdf
27. Mei, B., Yang, S.: Chinese pre-service music teachers' perceptions of augmented reality-assisted musical instrument learning. Front. Psychol. **12**, 1–7 (2021). https://doi.org/10.3389/fpsyg.2021.609028
28. Sural, I.: Augmented reality experience: initial perceptions of higher education students. Int. J. Instruct. **11**(4), 565–576 (2018). https://doi.org/10.12973/iji.2018.11435a
29. Muir, T., Allen, J.M., Rayner, C.S., Cleland, B.: Preparing pre-service teachers for classroom practice in a virtual world: a pilot study using second life. J. Interact. Media Educ. **1**, 1–17 (2013). https://doi.org/10.5334/2013-03
30. Thomas, M., Schneider, C.: Language teaching in 3D virtual worlds with machinima: reflecting on an online machinima teacher training course. Int. J. Comput.-Assist. Lang. Learn. Teach. **8**(2), 20–38 (2018). https://doi.org/10.4018/IJCALLT.2018040102
31. Stavroulia, K.E., Christofi, M., Baka, E., Michael-Grigoriou, D., Magnenat-Thalmann, N., Lanitis, A.: Assessing the emotional impact of virtual reality-based teacher training. Int. J. Inf. Learn. Technol. **36**(3), 192–217 (2019). https://doi.org/10.1108/IJILT-11-2018-0127
32. Stavroulia, K.E., Lanitis, A.: Enhancing reflection and empathy skills via using a virtual reality based learning framework. Int. J. Emerg. Technol. Learn. **14**(7), 18–36 (2019). https://doi.org/10.3991/ijet.v14i07.9946
33. Istifci, I., Lomidazde, T., Demiray, U.: An effective role of e-learning technology for English language teaching by using meta communication actors. In: 2011 5th International Conference on Application of Information and Communication Technologies (AICT), Baku, Azerbaijan, pp. 1–5 (2011). https://doi.org/10.1109/ICAICT.2011.6110951
34. Nagendran, A., Compton, S., Follette, W.C., Golenchenko, A., Compton, A., Grizou, J.: Avatar led interventions in the Metaverse reveal that interpersonal effectiveness can be measured, predicted, and improved. Sci. Rep. **12**(21892), 1–10 (2022). https://doi.org/10.1038/s41598-022-26326-4
35. Uzule, K.: Teacher training and education programs in Latvia: are e-competences included? Bus. Manage. Econ. Eng. **18**(2), 294–306 (2020). https://doi.org/10.3846/bme.2020.12631
36. Mørch, A.I.: Two 3D virtual worlds as domain-oriented design environments: closing the educational gap with the action-breakdown-repair model. Int. J. Inf. Learn. Technol. **37**(5), 295–307 (2020). https://doi.org/10.1108/IJILT-03-2020-0029

37. Turan-Güntepe, E., Dönmez Usta, N.: Augmented reality application-based teaching material's effect on viscera learning through algorithmic thinking. J. Sci. Learn. **4**(4), 365–374 (2021). https://files.eric.ed.gov/fulltext/EJ1321114.pdf

38. Syawaludin, A., Gunarhadi, Rintayati, P.: Development of augmented reality-based interactive multimedia to improve critical thinking skills in science learning. Int. J. Instruct. **12**(4), 331–344 (2019). https://doi.org/10.29333/iji.2019.12421a

39. Mystakidis, S., Christopoulos, A.: Teacher perceptions on virtual reality escape rooms for STEM education. Information **13**(3), 1–13 (2022). https://doi.org/10.3390/info13030136

40. Seckin-Kapucu, M., Yurtseven-Avci, Z., Sural, I.: Innovative approaches in development of educational materials: a case study of science teachers. Turk. Online J. Dist. Educ. **22**(4), 58–81 (2021). https://doi.org/10.17718/tojde.1002765

41. Moreno-Guerrero, A.J., Rodríguez García, A.M., Navas-Parejo, M.R., Jiménez, C.R.: Digital literacy and the use of augmented reality in teaching science in secondary education. Rev. Fuentes **23**(1), 108–124 (2021). https://doi.org/10.12795/revistafuentes.2021.v23.i1.12050

42. Tan, L., Thomson, R., Koh, J., Chik, A.: Teaching multimodal literacies with digital technologies and augmented reality: a cluster analysis of australian teachers' TPACK. Sustainability **15**(13), 10190 (2023). https://doi.org/10.3390/su151310190

43. Walker, R., et al.: Welcome, how can i help you? Design considerations for a virtual reality environment to support the orientation of online initial teacher education students. Educ. Sci. **13**(5), 1–13 (2023). https://doi.org/10.3390/educsci13050485

44. Mystakidis, S., Fragkaki, M., Filippousis, G.: Ready teacher one: virtual and augmented reality online professional development for K-12 school teachers. Computers **10**(10), 1–16 (2021). https://doi.org/10.3390/computers10100134

45. Atal, D., Kızılışıkoğlu, G.: Comparison of the anxiety levels of teacher candidates during actual and 360° video virtual reality presentations. J. Educ. Technol. Online Learn. **5**(4), 1–19 (2022). https://doi.org/10.31681/jetol.1164117

46. Wells, T., Miller, G.: Teachers' opinions about virtual reality technology in school-based agricultural education. J. Agric. Educ. **61**(1), 92–109 (2020). https://doi.org/10.5032/jae.2020.01092

47. Zhang, Y.: Virtual reality in ESL teacher training: practical ideas. Int. J. Technol. Teach. Learn. Soc. Int. Chin. Educ. Technol. **16**(1), 20–36 (2020). https://doi.org/10.37120/ijttl.2020.16.1.03

48. Badilla-Quintana, M., Sandoval-Henríquez, F.J.: Students' immersive experience in initial teacher training in a virtual world to promote sustainable education: interactivity, presence, and flow. Sustainability **13**(22), 12780 (2021). https://doi.org/10.3390/su132212780

49. Ausburn, L.J., Ausburn, F.B.: Desktop virtual reality: a powerful new technology for teaching and research in industrial teacher education. J. Industr. Teach. Educ. **41**(4), 1–16 (2004). https://files.eric.ed.gov/fulltext/EJ753111.pdf

50. Bahng, E., Lee, M.: Learning experiences and practices of elementary teacher candidates on the use of emerging technology: a grounded theory approach. Int. Electron. J. Elem. Educ. **10**(2), 225–241 (2017). https://doi.org/10.26822/iejee.2017236118

51. Manna, M.: Teachers as augmented reality designers: a study on Italian as a foreign language – teacher perceptions. Int. J. Mob. Blended Learn. (IJMBL) **15**(2), 1–16 (2023). https://doi.org/10.4018/IJMBL.318667

52. Fransson, G., Holmberg, J., Westelius, C.: The challenges of using head mounted virtual reality in K-12 schools from a teacher perspective. Educ. Inf. Technol. **25**, 3383–3404 (2020). https://doi.org/10.1007/s10639-020-10119-1

53. Fuchsova, M., Korenova, L.: Visualisation in basic science and engineering education of future primary school teachers in human biology education using augmented reality. Eur. J. Contemp. Educ. **8**(1), 92–102 (2019). https://doi.org/10.13187/ejced.2019.1.92

54. Aso, B., Navarro-Neri, I., García-Ceballos, S., Rivero, P.: Quality requirements for implementing augmented reality in heritage spaces: teachers' perspective. Educ. Sci. **11**(8), 1–25 (2021). https://doi.org/10.3390/educsci11080405
55. Ausburn, L.J., Ausburn, F.B.: Effects of desktop virtual reality on learner performance and confidence in environment mastery: opening a line of inquiry. J. STEM Teach. Educ. **45**(1), 1–35. https://ir.library.illinoisstate.edu/cgi/viewcontent.cgi?article=1159&context=jste
56. Ausburn, L.J., Ausburn, F.B., Kroutter, P.: An exploration of desktop virtual reality and visual processing skills in a technical training environment. i-manager's J. Educ. Technol. **6**(4), 43–55 (2010). https://files.eric.ed.gov/fulltext/EJ1098351.pdf
57. Aytan, T.: Evaluation of electronic writing experiences of Turkish teacher candidates at WATTPAD environment. High. Educ. Stud. **7**(4), 1–18 (2017). https://doi.org/10.5539/hes.v7n4p1
58. Barroso-Osuna, J., Gutiérrez-Castillo, J.J., Llorente-Cejudo, M.C., Ortiz, R.V.: Difficulties in the incorporation of augmented reality in university education: visions from the experts. J. New Approaches Educ. Res. **8**(2), 126–141 (2019). https://doi.org/10.7821/naer.2019.7.409

Information and Communications Technology Used by Polish Speech-Language Therapists: Research Project Report

Anna Michniuk[1] and Maria Faściszewska[2(✉)]

[1] Adam Mickiewicz University, ul. Międzychodzka 5, 61-712 Poznań, Poland
anna.michniuk@amu.edu.pl
[2] University of Gdańsk, ul. Wita Stwosza 51, 80-308 Gdańsk, Poland
maria.fasciszewska@ug.edu.pl

Abstract. This article presents the findings from the 2023 research project carried out in Poland among Polish speech-language therapists (SLTs). The study was quantitative in its general approach, but it also included some open-ended questions. The online questionnaire, consisting of 47 questions, was shared with the Polish Association of Speech Therapists, the Polish Logopedic Society, various psychological and pedagogical counseling centers, and the universities which offer courses in neurological speech therapy (designed solely for SLTs), as well as publishing it on social media groups for SLT, e.g. *Logopedki bez hejtu!* on Facebook (*Female SLTs without hate*). The research project involved 105 participants (n = 105), most of whom were women (n = 103), one man and one person decided not to declare their gender identity. The aims of the research project were 1) describing how new technologies can support speech therapists in their work; 2) developing new digital media applications in speech therapy; 3) setting out guidelines and recommendations on using new technologies in speech therapy. This article is however to present the replies to the following questions. 1) What kind of devices and applications/software do Polish SLTs use in their practice? 2) How do they use information and communications technology (ICT) in their practice? 3) Do they work online with other specialists, patients, and parents/caregivers? It appears that Polish SLTs often use ICT (usually: a computer with Internet access in their offices) as a way to prepare themselves for work, e.g. making worksheet and flashcard print outs. However, the SLTs work offline (in person) definitely more often than online (remotely).

Keywords: digital media · information and communications technology (ICT) · speech-language therapy

1 Introduction: ICT in Speech-Language Therapy

Information and communications technologies (ICT) have been widely used in health care, including the constantly evolving domain of speech-language therapy. The field includes prevention; diagnostics; synchronous, asynchronous, and hybrid types of

Ł. Tomczyk (Ed.): NMP 2023, CCIS 2130, pp. 124–136, 2024.
https://doi.org/10.1007/978-3-031-63235-8_8

telepractice; electronic consultations with parents and other specialists, as well as educational and training activities [13, 17, 20, 24]. The COVID-19 pandemic situation has significantly changed service delivery across various sectors, including education, medicine, and notably, speech-language therapy. The majority of institutions employing SLTs were compelled to adopt a new mode of service, known as *telepractice*, which involves the use of ICT to deliver services remotely rather than in person [7]. The World Health Organisation (WHO) [28] defines telepractice as the provision of clinical and rehabilitation services via ICTs by means of telephones, mobile apps, and other video conferencing platforms, especially in situations where patients and their clinicians are geographically separated by both short and long distances.

One of the first documents with the guidelines for speech therapists working remotely was published in 2014 in Australia [25]. The American Speech-Language-Hearing Association (ASHA) issued their recommendations in 2016 [2] to subsequently update them in 2021 [3]. According to ASHA, the basic steps for an SLT using telepractice are as follows. 1) Familiarise yourself with ASHA's telepractice guidelines. 2) Select a video conferencing platform. 3) Find or create digital resources. 4) Guide clients through the process [1]. In numerous countries, including Poland, no formal recommendations regarding telepractice as used by SLTs have been established to date. While teleworking can offer substantial benefits, it simultaneously poses unique challenges and require careful consideration, especially as far as safeguarding the interests of both the professional and the client goes. The key aspects here include maintaining confidentiality and privacy, protecting personal data, obtaining informed consent regarding the advantages and limitations of remote services, adhering to ethical guidelines, meticulous record-keeping, providing therapy evaluation, and working with other specialists, among other factors. The aforementioned ASHA recommendations list several programmes that can be used in online therapy. In Poland, similar programmes are available, e.g. *Kokolingo*, the *mTalent* series, or *Afast. Powiedz To!* [16]. However, the range of products available online for SLTs is not extensive, and there is also a lack of training on the use of the products.

During the COVID-19 pandemic, numerous studies have explored the use of ICT in the field of speech therapy, with a particular focus on online practices [6, 11, 22, 23]. The main streams of research focus on comparing the effectiveness of speech language therapy provided by telemedicine with conventional on-site therapy [4, 8]. More and more research is being done on telepractice used in specific groups of patients, e.g. school children [26], children with hearing loss [5, 12, 14], adults with Alzheimer's disease [29], patients with aphasia [10]. The studies with adult subjects have yielded no evidence as to any differences in language between the therapy administered face-to-face and online. There is a study on the use of videoconferencing in early intervention, i.e. conducting home visits with parents and their children under 3 years of age as part of the Virtual Home Visit Project (VHV) [21]. For example, The National Center for the Assessment and Management of Hearing (NCHAM) [19] works to secure access to appropriate early intervention (EI) services for families of children diagnosed as deaf or hard of hearing. They use electronic ICTs in all areas, from diagnosis to therapy and to consultations.

In Germany [13] a research project was conducted on the use and acceptance of digital media technologies among SLTs to determine their users' requirements and concerns regarding the newly introduced technologies. The results show that the use of IT in therapy is accepted, but it is important from both the institutional and the individual perspective to create optimal conditions for the use of the technology, as well as providing training and education, which will increase the willingness to use digital technologies in therapy and the frequency of their application.

2 Methods

The study project was quantitative in its general approach, but it also included some open-ended questions. It was conducted at two Polish universities: Adam Mickiewicz University in Poznań and the University of Gdansk. The questionnaire has 47 questions in total (including demographic questions). The survey employed a variety of question types, such as closed-ended, multiple-choice, rating, checkbox, and ranking questions.

2.1 Research Problems

This research project aims to 1) describe how new technologies support speech therapists; 2) propose innovative ways of using digital media in speech therapy; and 3) provide guidelines and recommendations for the use of advanced technologies in speech-language therapy.

The study investigated the use of ICTs by Polish SLTs in five areas: prevention, diagnosis, therapy, self-education/self-training, and cooperation with others, including specialists, patients and their parents/caregivers. The study aimed also to gather perspectives from the SLTs on the use of ICT in their work. This article also addresses several supporting questions. 1) What kind of devices and applications/software do Polish SLTs use in their practice? 2) How do they use information and communications technology (ICT) in their practice? 3) Do they work online with other specialists, patients, and parents/caregivers?

2.2 The Research Group

The research project involved 105 (n = 105) people. Most of them were women (n = 103), one man (n = 1), one person decided not to declare their gender identity. The mean age of the subjects is 39, the median age – 40, and the mode age – 24. The oldest subject was 65 years old and the youngest – 23. The study found that almost 40% of the participants worked in large cities with populations over 250K (Table 1). Moreover, a considerable 42% of them had over 11 years of experience as SLTs, while only 13% had less than one year of experience (Table 2). The majority of participants (49%) obtained their qualifications through a post-graduate course. State elementary schools (n = 29) and self-employment (n = 23) were the most popular places of employment among the research group (Table 3).

Table 1. Main places of work

Place of work	Frequency (n = 105)	Percentage
country	10	9.52
suburbs	4	3.8
town with population up to 50k	27	25.71
town with population 50–100k	10	9.52
city with population 100–250k	13	12.38
city with population > 250k	41	39.04

Table 2. Professional experience as a speech therapist

Experience (in years)	Frequency (n = 105)	Percentage
<1	14	13.33
1–5	31	29.52
6–10	16	15.23
11–15	20	19.04
>15	24	22.85

Table 3. Source of qualifications

Education	Frequency (n = 105)	Percentage
BA studies (3 years)	9	8.57
MA studies (2 years)	12	11.42
MA studies (5 years)	15	14.28
post-graduation course	52	49.52
other	17	16.19

Data Collection

All the data were collected online (via MS Forms). The request to complete the questionnaire was sent to the Polish Association of Speech Therapists, the Polish Logopedic Society (Polskie Towarzystwo Logopedyczne), various psychological and pedagogical counseling centers, and the universities which offer courses in neurological speech therapy (designed solely for SLTs), as well as publishing it on social media groups, e.g. *Logopedki bez hejtu!* on Facebook (*Female SLTs without hate*).

This questionnaire can serve as a starting point for further research on the use of ICT in speech-language therapy, such as conducting focus groups, although the number of responses received was unsatisfactory, probably due to the complex nature of the questionnaire and the fact that it was only available in digital form.

3 Results

3.1 What Kind of Devices and Applications/Software Do Polish SLTs Use in Their Practice?

The study shows that Polish speech-language therapists possess basic and widely used ICT equipment in their offices. Computers are almost universally available (89% of the participants), as are printers (81% of the participants) and smartphones (69%). Additionally, 72% of the participants indicated that they have a photocopier. Roughly half of the SLTs have: headphones (52%), a microphone (42% of respondents), a voice recorder (48%), a CD/mp3 player (52%). Overall, most SLTs have access to computers, smartphones, and either printers or photocopiers in their offices (Table 4).

Table 4. Office resources of Polish SLTs

Type of resources	Frequency (n = 105)	Percentage
computer/laptop	93	88.57
interactive whiteboard	29	27.62
projector	26	24.77
tablet	33	31.42
smartphone	73	69.52
interactive floor projection	12	11.42
edurobots e.g. Ozobot	9	8.57
VR goggles	4	3.81
video camera	14	13.33
voice recorder	50	47.62
microphone	44	41.9
headphones	55	52.38
3D printer	10	9.52
3D pen	7	6.66
Bluetooth speaker	44	41.90
CD/mp3 player	55	52.38
printer	85	80.95
photocopier	76	72.38
other	5	4.76

It is clear from the study that a significant majority (almost 69%) of Polish SLTs incorporate educational games and online applications into their daily practice. Online communication tools rank second with 56%, followed by the *mTalent* series software with 37%. The *mTalent* series is a computer programme specifically designed to enhance the skills of children and teenagers with special educational needs. It focuses on developing their communication, reading, listening, concentration, writing, speaking, articulation, and numeracy skills [16] (Table 5).

Table 5. Office resources of Polish SLTs – software & applications

Type of resources	Frequency (n = 105)	Percentage
mTalent series	39	37.14
Kokolingo	2	1.90
Afast	7	6.66
Logopedia PRO	18	17.14
Multimedialny Pakiet Logopedyczny	17	16.19
Eduterapeutica Logopedia	16	15.24
Bambik series	1	0.95
Online games (e.g. *Wordwall*)	72	68.57
Toker Professional	0	0
Porusz umysł series	11	10.48
GoSense series	3	2.86
Mówik	24	22.86
Eye trackers (e.g. *Tobii*)	5	4.76
Online communication apps (e.g. MsTeams, Zoom)	59	56.19
Computer software on CDs	24	22.86
other	19	18.09

Speech therapists purchase ICT tools on their own (almost 66% of the participants), they receive them from an employee (50%) or they apply for European Union funds (11%) (Table 6).

Table 6. Sources of ICT tools for Polish SLTs

Source	Frequency (n = 105)	Percentage
self-purchase	69	65.71
UE funds	12	11.43
sponsors	0	0
employer	53	50.48
patients/caregivers	1	0.95
other	9	8.57

3.2 How Do Polish SLTs Use ICT in Their Practice?

During the six months prior to the research, over 60% of the SLTs who completed the questionnaire stated that they used ICT at least once a week during their sessions (Table 7).

Table 7. Using ICT by Polish SLTs during 6 months before the study

Answer	Frequency (n = 105)	Percentage
never	8	7.62
less than once a month	10	9.52
at least once a month	23	21.90
at least once a week	62	59.04
hard to say	2	1.90

Polish SLTs interviewed draw inspiration for their work from a variety of sources, including various teaching and therapeutic resources available on the internet. The most frequently utilized sources of materials are online workshops and seminars (63%), professional groups on Facebook (54%), and forums for speech therapists (48%) (Table 8).

Six months prior to the study, the most common tools used by the participants for prevention strategies were games and auditory exercises (57%), worksheets downloaded from the internet (48%), flashcards (48%), workbook photocopies (42%). For diagnosis, the most popular tools were flashcards (76%), workbook photocopies (50%), worksheet printouts downloaded from the internet (47%) as well as games and auditory exercises (46%). In the case of speech-language therapy, Polish SLTs most frequently use printed materials from the internet (worksheets) and auditory games (Table 9).

Table 8. Sources of inspirations and materials used by Polish SLTs

Answer	Frequency (n = 105)	Percentage
I don't look for inspiration or materials	1	0.95
blogs	22	20.95
YouTube channels	19	18.09
forums for specialists	47	44.76
Facebook groups	57	54.29
Instagram profiles	19	18.09
TikTok profiles	3	2.85
online workshops and seminars	66	62.86
books available online	22	29.95
articles available online	12	11.43
books available in library	14	13.33
articles available in library	6	5.71
suggestions from colleagues	19	18.1
other	3	2.86

Table 9. ICT use 6 months before the study

Answer	Prevention (n = 105)	%	Diagnosis (n = 105)	%	Therapy (n = 105)	%
printed materials from the internet	50	47.62	49	46.67	88	83.81
photocopies from (work)books	44	41.90	52	49.52	78	74.29
multimedia presentations	20	19,04	10	9.52	19	18.1
movies	5	4.76	2	1.90	7	6.66
audiobooks/podcasts	2	1.9	1	0.95	4	3.81
digital cartoons	0	0	0	0	0	0
auditory games and exercises	60	57.14	48	45.71	85	80.95
3D printed therapeutic aids	2	1.90	1	0.95	3	2.86
mobile games	7	6.66	3	2.86	27	25.71

(*continued*)

Table 9. (*continued*)

Answer	Prevention (n = 105)	%	Diagnosis (n = 105)	%	Therapy (n = 105)	%
online communication apps (e.g. MsTeams, Zoom)	12	11.42	6	5.71	9	8.57
flashcards	50	47.62	80	76.19	75	71.43
interactive books	14	13.33	13	12.38	18	17.14
speech therapy software on CDs	20	19.05	19	18.1	33	31.43
other	7	6.66	18	17.14	10	9.52

3.3 Do They Work Online with Others like Specialists, Patients, Parents, or Caregivers of Their Patients?

The research shows that Polish SLTs do not work online very often. While 58 participants did not do it at all, 19 people used online communication to talk to parents or caregivers, 18 people consulted other specialists, 18 participants gave therapy, and 11 subjects shared their knowledge online (e.g. by preparing webinars).

Opinions about working online varied widely among the SLTs interviewed. An SLT from the Silesian voivodeship, with 4 years of professional experience, expressed dissatisfaction with remote work. *Speech therapy with preschool and early school children, especially if the therapy involves articulation or is a myofunctional therapy, must not be conducted remotely. The effectiveness of my therapy was significantly lower in the remote class setting arranged during the pandemic. The children had difficulty concentrating during online sessions when they were home. Due to poor internet connection and inadequate equipment the virtual presentation of exercises was not always sufficient. It is important to note that I could see and hear much less than in real life setting.* An SLT from the Mazovian Voivodeship, with over 15 years of professional experience said, *In my case, remote work entailed sending exercises and their descriptions to patients. I have not used online platforms for teaching – face-to-face contact with patients is better.* An SLT from the Pomeranian Voivodeship, with 2 years of professional experience is quoted as saying, *The patient's performance of a task or an exercise cannot be verified with complete certainty as the microphone may distort the sounds uttered.*

The participants pointed out several advantages of online work, including better contact with parents, greater parental involvement, the ability to reach patients who live far away, and the opportunity to diversify the therapy. An SLT from the Pomeranian Voivodeship, with 1–5 years of professional experience (the participant did not indicate the year in which the qualification was obtained), said, *My therapeutic work proved effective during the epidemic, especially considering the fact that the parents were more involved. At present, my sessions are conducted exclusively in my office. The diagnoses then were based only on the interviews with the parents and the videos recorded by them and sent to me, which I found to be insufficient and unreliable.* An SLT from the Kuyavian-Pomeranian Voivodeship, with 2 years of professional experience, claimed that *sometimes it works, sometimes it doesn't – like everything else in this profession;) Sometimes remote work can be a great option, especially when a child is unable to attend in person (e.g. due to changing plans or an illness). I always make sure to get all of my classes done. Also, I have one young patient who lives so far away this is the only way we can work.* An SLT from the Pomeranian Voivodeship, over 15 years of professional experience, said, *It is good when you can keep the effect of office work (…), additionally, it is ok in controlling the therapeutic process after various treatments and surgeries in the orofacium.*

4 Discussion

It is essential to highlight the diversity in the use of ICT among speech therapists globally. In the US and Australia, teleworking is on the rise, leading to the development of new diagnostic and therapeutic solutions and novel tools that can be used in the online environment [27]. Remote speech-language therapy is a highly sought-after service in the US. It is worth noting that even myotherapy, which addresses a range of concerns such as correct breathing, tongue-thrust, sleep issues, and care, can also be effectively provided online, subject to certain conditions [18]. However, Poland has no regulations and recommendations in place with regard to the use of telepractice by speech-language therapists. Also, remote work is not very common in Poland. Polish SLTs hold differing opinions on this issue – some of them enjoy that type of working arrangement, whereas others deem it painfully ineffective.

An important idea would be to conduct international comparative research on how SLTS from different countries use digital technologies in their work. How they assess the effectiveness of the use of them in the prevention, diagnosis and therapy of various speech disorders and other communication difficulties.

When conducting research on the use of ICT in speech-language therapy, it is important to consider various factors such as cultural differences, healthcare system structure, technology accessibility, internet quality, and the individual preferences of the professionals integrating ICT into their practice. It is imperative to consider local contexts and individual factors when examining the use of technology in speech therapy, as these differences can significantly impact the effectiveness of treatment. Research has unequivocally shown that speech therapy offices lack the appropriate equipment to conduct therapy using ICT. Out of 102 participants, 12 have no basic equipment required for speech therapy sessions, e.g. a computer, and 58 of them do not have a microphone. It is crucial to acknowledge that speech-language therapy requires specialized equipment and skills to make the most of ICT, and this applies to both the therapist and the patient. And it does present a challenge to telework implementation by speech therapists. However, with proper support from parents or educators, children can effectively utilize video conferencing technology [12]. Our research shows that Polish speech-language therapists frequently use ICT for self-preparation. They watch webinars to broaden their knowledge and build their skills, as well as looking for interesting therapeutic and educational materials to print out for their patients. Using ICT during meetings may not be a common practice, but it can be a valuable tool for Polish SLTs. While worksheets, flashcards, and games are frequently used, incorporating online therapy and digital competences can improve therapy sessions in a responsible and meaningful way. It is recommended that training is provided to acquire these skills. It is worth noting that currently the academic curricula in Poland do not address this issue [9]. With the access to the necessary equipment, software, and applications in their offices, as well as fast and reliable internet for both therapists and patients, Polish speech therapists will be more likely to use digital technologies.

Large, well-controlled, randomized clinical trials on the use of telemedicine in speech therapy practice are yet to be seen as pilot studies still dominate the literature [15]. Information and communication technologies are useful tools for speech therapists, especially in the case of combined practices, but they should not be considered a perfect replacement for services delivered face-to-face. This alternative model can assist parents in consulting with a respected specialist who works far from their place of residence, maintain continuity of therapy in the event of illness, and facilitate speech therapist consultations with other specialists. More research is required in this area, particularly on the perceived acceptance of the use of digital technology in speech-language therapy.

References

1. Andricks J., Smith, S.: 5 steps to get started in telepractice (2020). https://leader.pubs.asha.org/do/10.1044/5-few-steps-to-get-started-in-telepractice/full. Accessed 10 Dec 2023
2. ASHA. Special interest group 18: Telepractice survey results. American Speech-Language-Hearing Association (2016). https://www.asha.org/siteassets/practice-portal/telepractice/2016-telepractice-survey.pdf. Accessed 10 Dec 2023
3. ASHA. Telehealth: Advancing health in America. American Hospital Association (2021). https://www.aha.org/telehealth. Accessed 10 Dec 2023
4. Chaudhary, T., Kanodia, A., Verma, H., et al.: A pilot study comparing teletherapy with the conventional face-to-face therapy for speech-language disorders. Indian J. Otolaryngol. Head Neck Surg. **73**, 366–370 (2021). https://doi.org/10.1007/s12070-021-02647-0
5. Constantinescu, G., et al.: A pilot study of telepractice delivery for teaching listening and spoken language to children with hearing loss. J. Telemed. Telecare **20**, 135–140 (2014). https://doi.org/10.1177/1357633X14528443
6. Farren, E., Quigley, D., Lynch, Y.: Telepractice in service delivery: a survey of perspectives and practices of speech and language therapists in Ireland during COVID-19. Adv. Commun. Swallowing **25**(1), 5–16 (2022). https://doi.org/10.3233/ACS-210036
7. Guglani, I., Sanskriti, S., Joshi, S.H., Anjankar, A.: Speech-language therapy through telepractice during COVID-19 and its way forward: a scoping review. Cureus **15**(9), e44808 (2023). https://doi.org/10.7759/cureus.44808
8. Grogan-Johnson, S., Alvares, R., Rowan, L., Creaghead, N.: A pilot study comparing the effectiveness of speech language therapy provided by telemedicine with conventional on-site therapy. J. Telemed. Telecare **16**, 134–139 (2010). https://doi.org/10.1258/jtt.2009.090608
9. Karowicz, A.: Przeszkody i wyzwania w pracy zawodowej logopedy podczas pandemii Covid-19. Logopaedica Lodziensia **5**, 87–104 (2021)
10. Kearns, Á., Kelly, H.: ICT usage in aphasia rehabilitation – beliefs, biases, and influencing factors from the perspectives of speech and language therapists. Aphasiology **37**(3), 456–478 (2023). https://doi.org/10.1080/02687038.2022.2030462

11. Kwok, E.Y.L., Chiu, J., Rosenbaum, P., Cunningham, B.J.: The process of telepractice implementation during the COVID-19 pandemic: a narrative inquiry of preschool speech-language pathologists and assistants from one centre in Canada. BMC Health Serv. Res. **22**, 81 (2022). https://doi.org/10.1186/s12913-021-07454-5
12. Kronenberger, W.G., et al.: Remote assessment of verbal memory in youth with cochlear implants during the COVID-19 pandemic. Am. J. Speech Lang. Pathol. **30**(2), 740–747 (2021). https://doi.org/10.1044/2021_AJSLP-20-00276
13. Leinweber, J., et al.: Technology use in speech and language therapy: digital participation succeeds through acceptance and use of technology. Front. Commun. **8**, 1176827 (2023). https://doi.org/10.3389/fcomm.2023.1176827
14. Lund, E., Werfel, K.L.: The effects of virtual assessment on capturing skill growth in children with hearing loss. Lang. Speech Hear. Serv. Schools **53**(2), 391–403 (2022). https://doi.org/10.1044/2021_LSHSS-21-00074
15. Mashima, P.A., Doarn, C.R.: Overview of telehealth activities in speech-language pathology. Telemed. e-Health **14**, 1101–1117 (2014). https://doi.org/10.1089/tmj.2008.0080
16. Michniuk, A., Faściszewska, M.: Using digital media in speech therapy. In: Tomczyk, Ł (ed.) NMP 2022. CCIS, vol. 1916, pp. 69–82. Springer, Cham. (2023). https://doi.org/10.1007/978-3-031-44581-1_6
17. Molini-Avejonas, D.R., Rondon-Melo, S., de La Higuera Amato, C.A., Samelli, A.G.: A systematic review of the use of telehealth in speech, language and hearing sciences. J. Telemed. Telecare **21**, 367–376 (2015). https://doi.org/10.1177/1357633X15583215
18. Myo-moves. https://www.myo-moves.com. Accessed 10 Dec 2023
19. National Center for Hearing Assessment and Management (NCHAM). A practical guide to the use of teleintervention in providing spoken language services to infants and toddlers who are deaf and hard of hearing (2012). https://www.infanthearing.org/ti-guide. Accessed 10 Dec 2023
20. Olszewski, A., Smith, E., Franklin, A.D.: Speech-language pathologists' feelings and practices regarding technological apps in school service delivery. Lang. Speech Hear Servi. Schools **53**, 1051–1073 (2023). https://doi.org/10.1044/2022_LSHSS-21-00150
21. Olsen, S., Fiechtl, B., Rule, S.: An evaluation of virtual home visits in early intervention: feasibility of "virtual intervention." Volta Rev. **112**(3), 267–281 (2012)
22. Patel, R., Loraine, E., Gréaux, M.: Impact of COVID-19 on digital practice in UK pediatric speech and language therapy and implications for the future: a national survey. Int. J. Lang. Commun. Disord. **57**(5), 1112–1129 (2022). https://doi.org/10.1111/1460-6984.12750
23. Sikka, K.: Parent's perspective on teletherapy of pediatric population with speech and language disorder during Covid-19 lockdown in India. Indian J. Otolaryngol. Head Neck Surg. **75**, 14–20 (2023). https://doi.org/10.1007/s12070-022-03310-y
24. Sutherland, R., Trembath, D., Roberts, J.: Telehealth and autism: a systematic search and review of the literature. Int. J. Speech-Lang. Pathol. **20**, 324–336 (2018). https://doi.org/10.1080/17549507.2018.1465123
25. Speech Pathology Australia [SPA] Telepractice in Speech Pathology [Position Statement] (2014). http://www.speechpathologyaustralia.org.au. Accessed 10 Dec 2023
26. Waite, M., Theodoros, D.G., Russell, T.G., Cahill, L.M.: Assessment of children's literacy via an Internet-based telehealth system. Telemed. e-Health **16**(5), 564–575 (2010). https://doi.org/10.1089/tmj.2009.0161
27. Wales, D., Skinner, L., Hayman, M.: The efficacy of telehealth-delivered speech and language intervention for primary school-age children: a systematic review. Int. J. Telerehabilitat. **9**, 55–70 (2017). https://doi.org/10.5195/ijt.2017.6219

28. WHO, Consolidated telemedicine implementation guide. https://www.who.int/publications/i/item/9789240059184. Accessed 10 Dec 2023
29. Vestal, L., Smith-Olinde, L., Hicks, G., Hutton, T., Hart Jr., J.: Efficacy of language assessment in Alzheimer's disease: comparing in-person examination and telemedicine. Clin. Intervent. Aging 1(4), 467–471 (2006). https://www.ncbi.nlm.nih.gov/pmc/articles/PMC2699639/. Accessed 18 Mar 2024

Designing and Developing Educational Mobile Application Training for Teacher Candidates for Innovative Pathways

Elif Polat[1] , Sinan Hopcan[1](✉) , and Laura Fedeli[2]

[1] Istanbul University-Cerrahpasa, 34320 Istanbul, Turkey
{elif.polat,sinan.hopcan}@iuc.edu.tr
[2] University of Macerata, 62100 Macerata, Italy
laura.fedeli@unimc.it

Abstract. With the widespread use of mobile technologies today, educational mobile applications have become increasingly important not only for general education, but also for special education. Motivated by the imperative to equip future educators with the knowledge to utilise these pivotal tools, qualitative research on prospective teachers/educators enrolled in an Italian university was designed to discern their needs concerning educational mobile application training following an inclusive approach. As an initial step, a needs analysis form was administered to 171 teacher candidates in a pilot study, with any ambiguities in the form subsequently addressed. This was followed by consultations with four special education experts, which informed the development of a provisional training plan and accompanying materials. The refined needs analysis form was later disseminated to a different set of 57 prospective teachers/educators. Drawing on the insights from these data, the conclusive training plan and materials were developed, integrating feedback from two educational technology specialists. The training spanned a cumulative duration of 10 h. At its culmination, feedback was garnered from the participants and assessed to gauge the efficacy and pertinence of the training regimen. The study can contribute in analysing the training needs and students' expectations in terms of curriculum development towards technology-enhanced learning with a focus on mobile applications, special needs, and inclusive approaches.

Keywords: educational mobile applications · special educational needs · teacher training

1 Introduction

In the Italian school system, the teacher training initiatives about the introduction of technology show at least five decades of experience. From the first attempts in the secondary school context, in the computer literacy field with the "National Plan for Informatics" (Piano Nazionale Informatica [PNI], 1985) [1] with a focus on technical/practical skills, the training courses advanced, in the 1990s, with the Development Programme of Digital Technologies (Programma di Sviluppo delle Tecnologie Digitali-PSTD) and the effort

© The Author(s), under exclusive license to Springer Nature Switzerland AG 2024
Ł. Tomczyk (Ed.): NMP 2023, CCIS 2130, pp. 137–155, 2024.
https://doi.org/10.1007/978-3-031-63235-8_9

to equip schools with multimedia classrooms/labs, but also in this further early attempts (1997–2000) it was clear that the professional development of teachers, in terms of technology, should go far beyond the provision of equipment and a mere technical training. Rather, it should embrace a more comprehensive vision where literacies (information literacy, computer literacy, digital literacy, etc.) could intertwine with methodological approaches and pedagogical theories.

In order to gather useful data on the national situation and the digitalisation process, a Technological Observatory was created by the Ministry of Education (2000), and the monitoring process on the territory started to offer a more detailed picture of school readiness. The acquisition of a systemic approach was strengthened in 2007 with the first actions (e.g., cl@ssi 2.0) of the "National Plan for Digital Education", which achieved its final version in 2015 (Piano Nazionale Scuola Digitale [PNSD] - The Ministry of Education, University and Research, 2015) [2]. The plan represents a reference framework in the Italian school context since it aims at setting and promoting key actions (4 macro areas and 35 actions) to enable an innovation strategy process in the school ecosystem. The PNSD, as a milestone of "La Buona Scuola" school reform (Law 107/2015) [3], addresses the role and impact of technology through several dimensions. Among them is a deep interest in training opportunities for teachers that address initial teacher training (actions of refreshing the university curricula), induction courses (actions of support in the first year of employment), continuous in-service training opportunities for school personnel, and the establishment of the profile of "Digital Animator" in each school.

In terms of university curricula and technological competence objectives, the Ministerial Decree n.249 (10 September 2010) [4] establishes that the learning paths aimed at training the professional profile of teachers from pre-school to secondary school needs to take into account the acquisition of digital competences with an inclusive perspective where all students, including those with special needs, should be able to take advantage of technology-integrated didactics. The focus on digital competence and technology-enhanced learning (TEL) is underlined also in post-lauream offers [5], such as the teacher training programme for special needs, an academic learning specialisation path (Ministerial Decree 9 August 2013, n. 706) to train teachers as experts in inclusive approaches, and a professional profile integrated into classrooms where students with disabilities are present.

2 Background

The field of TEL embraces different dimensions of technology design, use, and assessment [6]. These dimensions have attracted interest at the international level in relation to innovation processes that can affect the educational system from pre-school to lifelong learning [7–9]. TEL approaches and theories embrace a variety of delivery models, from face-to face instruction to e-learning and blended solution. In all those teaching/learning settings, mobile devices can be fully integrated and have acquired a major interest due to their wide dissemination as personal portable devices among students of all ages and the richness of functionality they developed thanks to increasingly intense production of applications whose functions include entertainment (e.g., games, music), organisation (e.g., note taking, archive, annotation), production (e.g., photos, videos), communication and social relations (e.g., instant messaging, social networking), and educational aid/support (e.g., connection to LMS, CMS).

In the context of pre-school and primary school, mobile devices and educational apps are successfully used in the perspective of game-based learning, not only for the approach to specific disciplines [10, 11], but to activate collaborative and problem-solving strategies [12]. Besides, mobile applications find a suitable role in embracing educational approaches which foster an inclusive perspective like the Universal Design for Learning (UDL) principles [13, 14] and flexible approaches that can support diverse learning needs and engage students with disabilities in playful and motivating activities [15].

A wide area of international research trajectories and related outputs has focusing on general evaluation criteria (e.g., usability, accessibility, customisation), classroom best practices with students with different disabilities, and their integration with virtual and augmented environments [16–20]. Those findings are of paramount importance as theoretical and practical resources for teaching professional profiles to enable them to select the needed equipment and develop the proper competences to design, create, and apply mobile applications in their educational contexts.

The international landscape of mobile learning and digital education has raised interest also in the Italian educational context in the impact that personal mobile devices can have at school if properly integrated in the teaching/learning process. The PNSD contains a specific action (action #6 "Active Policies for BYOD – Bring Your Own Device") that supports the use of a personal smartphone/tablet in the classroom with a set of guidelines for teachers and headmasters in order to frame the choice of using such devices during the teaching/learning process in a design plan where it is clear for all involved actors at school (teachers, students) and external to it (e.g., family) what the objective and the rationale of such use are.

The current study is in line with the international interest in mobile application use and is contextualised to prospective teachers/educators. The context is thus represented by the students enrolled at the University of Macerata (Italy) in the Department of Education, Cultural Heritage and Tourism, who were involved in a needs analysis step open to all participants without restriction of level of degree (included post-lauream students with teaching experience) or attendance year, but all focussed in the education science field. The training phase in its implementation was, instead, targeted to undergraduate and graduate degree courses. The 10-h hands-on course (one ECTS English-taught optional seminar) took place during the first semester of the 2023–2024 academic year and was aimed at approaching different prospective teaching profiles (teachers, educators, pedagogists) that can interact in the school system, not only in the instructional design step, but also in the teaching process in the classroom. For this reason, the seminar had a cross-curricular connotation and included students of three different degree courses: education science (EQF 6), pedagogy (EQF 7), and pre-primary school teacher training (EQF 7).

3 Current Research

The topic of training teacher candidates on educational mobile applications is considered by the researchers as "a felt need". In this context, an extensive literature review at the international level was conducted [21–26] to determine critical aspects and trajectories of research. Subsequently, research questions were formulated, and the purposive sampling method was chosen due to its accessibility. The qualitative case study [27] thus aims to determine the learning needs of teacher/educator candidates in the field of educational mobile applications and to design and develop a suitable training on the topic by triangulating students' feedback with external experts' opinions. In line with this purpose, the study aims to collect initial inputs about the following research questions: (1) What are the needs of teacher candidates in terms of mobile applications and educational and inclusive use? (2) What are the basic principles a teacher training course should follow to address the design, development, and use of mobile applications?

In order to collect data from both students and external experts, a set of tools was employed: (1) a needs analysis form to identify the needs and current situations of teacher candidates to be used to optimise the design of a training course, (2) a semi-structured interview with experts to acquire proper inputs about content selection and activity design in the training course, and (3) a final semi-structured interview for teacher candidates to assess the efficacy of the training. In terms of a more detailed description of the above mentioned data gathering tools we highlight that (1) the needs analysis form deals with 6 demographic questions and 12 thematic questions (mostly open-ended) aimed at investigating technology usage experiences and information related to educational mobile applications; (2) the semi-structured interview protocol used with expert consists of 5 open questions related to target competence areas (e.g., design; assessment, etc.), strategies and disciplinary content; (3) the semi-structured interview protocol used with teacher candidates aimed at gathering teacher candidates' views about the training, shows 5 open-ended questions related to motivation, engagement and challenges.

After the pilot application of the needs analysis form, the questionnaire (submitted via Google form) was submitted to another group of students, and taking into account the results, the training content was finalised. The training was then provided to 11 students. Afterward, interviews were conducted with the teacher candidates, and their opinions on the training were obtained.

3.1 Needs Analysis

The study consists of 170 teacher candidates as pilot participants and 58 teacher candidates as main study participants. Almost all the participants in the pilot study (90%) are attending the secondary grade course, while 6 of them (4%) are in kindergarten and 8 (5%) are in the primary grade course. In the pilot study, out of 171 participants, 25 were male (15%) and 146 were female (85%); looking at the age distribution of the pilot participants, 72 (42%) were between 26 and 35 years old, 59 (35%) were between 36 and 45 years old, and 40 (23%) were 46 years old and above.

In the main study, of the 58 participants, 7 were male (12%) and 51 were female (88%) with the following age range: 32 (55%) were between 26 and 35 years old, 14

(24%) were between 36 and 45 years old, 7 (12%) were between 36 and 45 years old, and 5 (9%) were 46 years old and above.

Participants were informed about the purpose of the study and the principle of voluntariness. The needs analysis form and semi-structured interview forms were reviewed for face and content validity by two educational technology experts. A total of 171 participants completed the needs analysis form in 10–15 min. This was also considered as a pilot application. They reported one unclear question in the form, which was then revised. Afterward, 58 teacher candidates filled out the form. For the data analysis, descriptive statistics and content analysis methods were used. The group in the pilot study consists primarily of students enrolled in a specialisation course for special needs who may show a varied (in duration and continuity) teaching experience in their field; therefore, due to their status, they are not appropriately compared with individuals in the second group. Pilot participants are enrolled in a specialized university course, serving simultaneously as students and as teachers under temporary contracts. This dual role is designed to integrate practical teaching experience with academic study, providing a comprehensive understanding of their field from both perspectives.

Table 1 presents the technological tools owned by the participants. According to the table, almost all the participants own a smartphone, and many also have a computer and a tablet.

Table 1. Answers to "What technology devices do you normally use for personal and/or professional use (you can indicate multiple options)?"

	Pilot Study		Main Study	
	n	%	n	%
Only computer	11	6.4	7	12.1
Only smartphone	3	1.8	2	3.4
Computer and smartphone	86	50.3	28	48.3
Computer, smartphone, and smart watch	7	4.1	1	1.7
Computer, smartphone, smart watch, and graphics tablet	1	0.6	0	0
Computer and tablet	3	1.8	1	1.7
Computer, tablet, and smartphone	51	29.8	12	20.7
Computer, tablet, smartphone, and audiovisual production media	1	0.6	0	0
Computer, tablet, smartphone, and smart watch	7	4.1	2	3.4
Tablet and smartphone	1	0.6	5	8.6
Total	171	100	58	100

According to Fig. 1, the majority of both groups indicated their technological proficiency as moderate (45% in the pilot group, 36% in the main group) and good (37% in the pilot group, 43% in the main group).

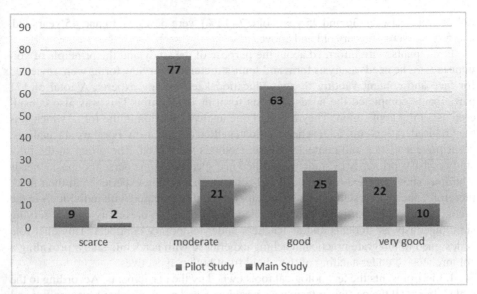

Fig. 1. Answers to "How do you generally assess your competence with respect to the use of technology?"

As seen in Fig. 2, similar to the previous item, participants mostly rated their level of competence in developing technological materials as moderate (47% in the pilot group, 40% in the main group) and good (30% in the pilot group, 38% in the main group).

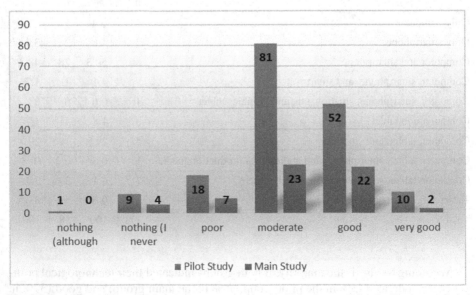

Fig. 2. Answers to "How do you rate your expertise in designing and developing instructional materials through technologies?"

According to Fig. 3, about half of the participants in the pilot group (49%) have previously used mobile applications for teaching purposes, whereas this rate is 35% in the main group. Additionally, those who have never used them constitute 31% in the pilot group, while this rate is 10% in the main group.

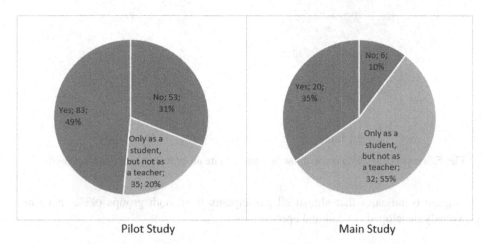

Pilot Study   Main Study

Fig. 3. Answers to "Have you ever used mobile applications for teaching?"

According to Fig. 4, nearly half of both groups (43% in the pilot group and 57% in the main group) are not aware of the features of applications for special education.

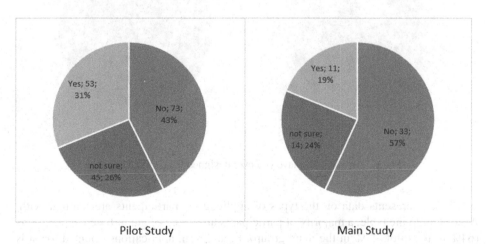

Pilot Study   Main Study

Fig. 4. Answers to "Do you know some features (graphical and functional interface) of apps for students with disabilities?"

Figure 5 shows the distribution of participants' knowledge of app evaluation using a rubric. In the pilot group, 9% responded with "yes", while in the main group, 26% responded with "yes".

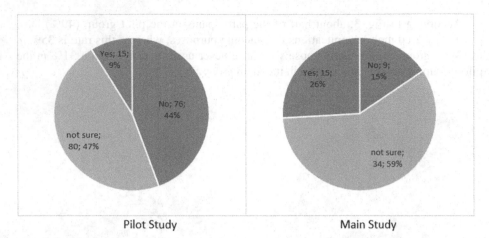

Fig. 5. Answers to "Would you know how to evaluate an educational app using a rubric?"

Figure 6 indicates that almost all participants from both groups (93%) have not previously developed educational applications.

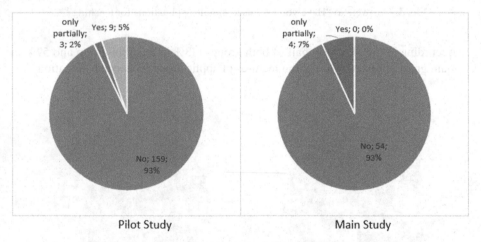

Fig. 6. Answers to "Have you ever designed educational apps?"

Table 2 presents data on the types of applications participants are familiar with. According to the table, a majority of participants are aware of game-based applications (64% in the pilot, 47% in the main group). In addition, applications oriented towards reading (30% in the pilot, 28% in the main group), writing (22% in the pilot), and physical interaction (24% in the main group) are known more than others. A significant portion of participants stated that they were not familiar with any of the types of applications listed in the table (31% in the pilot, 43% in the main group).

In a general, it is indicated that participants perceive they have a moderate level of knowledge about technology use, educational mobile applications, and educational

Table 2. Answers to "I know mobile apps for pupils with disabilities that:"

	Pilot Study		Main Study	
	f	%	f	%
Develop/reinforce reading skills	51	29.8	16	27.6
Develop/reinforce writing skills	37	21.6	7	12.1
Are based on play	110	64.3	27	46.6
Are tangible, i.e., physical and multisensory involvement	15	8.8	14	24.1
They use programming	25	14.6	7	12.1
They use virtual reality	12	7	5	8.6
They use augmented reality	5	2.9	3	5.2
None	53	31	25	43.1

mobile applications for special education, but specifically they point out the need for training on the features, design/development and evaluation of educational mobile applications for special education.

3.2 Experts' View

This part consists of four field experts to acquire proper inputs about content selection and activity design in the training course. The information about the experts interviewed for the needs analysis is as follows: Expert 1 (E1) specialises in special education with 15 years of experience and is affiliated with a university. Expert 2 (E2) has 30 years of experience in educational technology and also works at a university. Expert 3 (E3) is another special education specialist with 5 years of experience at a university. Lastly, Expert 4 (E4) has 6 years of experience in special education and is employed by a university. The interviews lasted about 20 min each. For the data analysis, the content analysis method was used.

Theme 1: Incorporating Mobile Applications for Special Needs Students into Teacher Education Programmes

All experts (n = 4) indicate that the topic of "mobile applications for students with special needs" should be added to the education technology and similar courses that teacher candidates take. One of the experts (n = 1) (E1) expressed this as follows: "I believe that mobile applications currently should be given special attention in order to develop truly inclusive forms of active teaching."

Two of the experts (n = 2) said that even a separate elective course covering this subject could be offered. Looking at the experts' opinions, it is seen that they think teacher candidates should receive training on mobile applications for students with special needs.

When asked about the potential impacts of incorporating education on mobile applications into teacher training programmes, the responses emphasised positive effects. All experts (n = 4) believe that it would be beneficial to include training on mobile applications for students with special needs in teacher education. The experts have various reasons for considering this beneficial. One expert (n = 1) (E4) mentioned that it would be useful because teacher candidates could take on a guiding role in the use of rapidly developing technologies. Another expert (n = 1) (E1) highlighted the benefit of teachers being able to pay more attention to the principles of UDL in materials, which would, in turn, create a more suitable inclusive education environment for students' needs, emphasising: "Surely there would be many more teachers able to structure truly inclusive pathways because they would respond to the three fundamental principles of the UDL, and there would be more students with special educational needs (SEN) put in a position to be able to actively participate in classroom activities by having pathways that are more calibrated to the different needs of each." In conclusion, the expert opinions suggest that this training for teacher candidates could have a positive impact on future inclusive environments and potentially create a multiplier effect.

Theme 2: Essential Topics and Skills in the Training
Experts were asked about the priority topics that need to be taught in this field. Although their views vary, there are converging aspects. Two experts (n = 2) mentioned that accessibility and customisation are essential for more inclusive environments. The importance of how mobile applications should be used for inclusive education can be emphasised by this quote from an expert (E1): "The perspective is inclusive, and therefore everyone must be enabled to participate actively. Teachers often tend to see only the technical aspect of a piece of equipment or application, but later, after understanding how it works, they become aware that although they have acquired the ability to use it, they do not know what to do with it in teaching, i.e., they need to know the inclusive educational paths that can be implemented, their integration in a broader design aimed at all students, including those with SEN".

Both E1 and E2 (n = 2) underlined the importance of selection and evaluation of applications. Furthermore, one expert (n = 1) (E1) suggested that additional topics should also be addressed. The introduction of current mobile applications, their use, and benefits according to types of disabilities are stated to be very important. On the other hand, two other experts (n = 2) (E3, E4) recommended more specific educational topics, such as including mobile applications that simulate real life in teacher training (E3), as well as individualised education programmes, peer bullying prevention, family/teacher information applications, education, and literacy (E4). In summary, looking at the expert opinions, it is evident that there is a focus on including different types of mobile applications in education and on the selection/assessment of target-oriented applications, as well as ensuring accessibility and customisation to create more inclusive environments.

All experts (n = 4) emphasised the need for core skills such as design/development and assessment to be taught in a hands-on manner. The following excerpt is illustrative: "The way to acquire them [design/development competencies] should involve laboratory activities, active strategies where the design of a path with a mobile application, its evaluation from a provided case, is experienced in practice" [E1]. On the other hand, one expert (n = 1) (E2) suggested the introduction of different types of applications in real contexts or by creating simulated environments. One of the experts (n = 1) (E4) highlighted the necessity for apps to be designed according to inclusive environments and in accordance with special education theories. In conclusion, the consensus among the expert opinions is that necessary skills, particularly in designing and developing mobile applications, should be provided in a practical, hands-on manner within educational settings. The course content as a result of the inputs offered by the needs analysis and experts' view is presented in Table 3.

Table 3. Content of the training

Course Topics:	Activities:	Approach

• Introduction
• Conceptual topics
  o Main concepts and definition of educational mobile applications
• Mobile application for children with disabilities
• Types of mobile educational applications
  o Writing applications
  o Reading applications
  o Tangible applications (science, math, language learning, sensory learning, therapy)
  o AR-VR applications
• Design and development of mobile application
  o Techniques for application selection and evaluation
  o Design features of mobile applications
  o Design and develop mobile apps by MIT App Inventor
	• Examining sample apps
	• Designing mobile apps
	• Developing basic apps by MIT App Inventor
	• Designing and developing AR/VR apps
	• Evaluating mobile apps by a rubric
		• Students are required to download 1–2 applications for each type of mobile application, from both iOS and Android, and then examine them based on certain criteria and discuss them in the classroom.
		• Roughly thinking of educational scenarios and designing screen layouts in App Inventor according to design rules
		• Writing codes and running them on mobile devices
		• Designing and developing apps in the CoSpaces programme
		• Evaluating a mobile application with a rubric

3.3 Teacher Candidates' View After Training

This part consists of 11 teacher candidates who participated in the training and whose opinions were obtained after the training. The opinions of teacher candidates on the training reflect the extent to which these needs have been met and the new skills they have acquired. The course was not mandatory, and the sample included Italian students enrolled in an education science degree course (n = 1) and a pre-school and primary teacher training degree course (n = 9) as well as one student from Poland participating in the Erasmus study programme. In the training, 10 individuals were between the ages of 22 and 25, while only one individual was 51 years old. They were asked to fill out this form in writing. These interview forms lasted approximately 20 min. For the data analysis, the content analysis method was used. As a result of the content analysis [28], two themes emerged: benefits of the training and challenges of the training.

Benefits of the Training

All teacher candidates (n = 11) who attended the training stated that it met their expectations. "The course met my expectations because it gave me the opportunity to discover applications I was not previously aware of and to obtain accurate information about them" [S3]. Many of the teacher candidates (n = 9) also mentioned that the training was particularly informative and interesting. "Every topic addressed was really interesting and very helpful for the work to be done. Especially since we move so quickly in the world of technology, these applications will be very beneficial" [S1].

Nearly all teacher candidates (n = 7) stated they will explore various mobile applications in depth for their future students with disabilities. One student expressed this issue as follows: "…To learn new applications and new technological tools that I can use with students with disabilities and thus pave the way for a more conscious future" [S10]. Most of the teacher candidates (n = 9) mentioned that the training was beneficial not only for theoretical knowledge but also for including practical activities. They emphasised the importance of hands-on examination of these applications in the classroom for practical use. One student provided a striking quote on this subject:

> I did not expect so many practical activities before starting this course. I came with expectations to discuss the subject. On the contrary, I had a good surprise because I had the chance to try many different applications, created my own application, saw what it looked like during the process, and learned what is important when working with children with different disabilities and how to choose or create the right application for a specific problem. I usually don't like programming, and it has always been a problem and an unpleasant thing for me. This time, thanks to numerous explanations, patience, and help, I discovered it was not as difficult as I thought. My favourite part was always the practice because it gave me the opportunity to create and discover new possibilities in teaching. [S11]

Some of the teacher candidates (n = 5) indicated that applications could be used not only for students with disabilities, but for all students. For example, one student said: "We saw that these applications could also be beneficial for students without disabilities, for instance, in learning to write or learning a language, or to understand complex concepts" [S7].

Under the theme "The Positive Aspects of the Training," teacher candidates generally noted that the training met their expectations and was interesting and informative, and that the inclusion of practical applications was beneficial. They acknowledged discovering various applications for students with disabilities. Additionally, some candidates expressed that these applications could be utilised not only for students with disabilities but for all students, thereby facilitating the creation of inclusive environments.

All the pre-service teachers (n = 11) stated that thanks to this training, they had the opportunity to get acquainted with many new applications that they did not know before. One of the excerpts illustrates this: "I wasn't familiar with any of the apps that were presented, but I found them very appealing; they are creative, interesting, varied, and more. I hope I can use them with children with disabilities. I know many teachers who work as support teachers for children with disabilities, and I will recommend these apps to them to make their teaching easier as well" [S6].

Furthermore, all the teacher candidates (n = 11) reported that they will definitely use mobile applications for their students in their future teaching careers due to the benefits taught in the class. One excerpt illustrated this: "I am planning to become a teacher, and the thought of how complex the competition can be is worrying me. But knowing that I can rely on technologies reduces my concern and makes my future expectations more hopeful" [S6].

In addition, almost all the pre-service teachers (n = 9) stated that they learned how to use educational mobile applications in their future classrooms. One teacher candidate (S3) emphasised this: "Until now, I have had limited experience in schools with mobile apps for students with disabilities; therefore, almost all the topics of the course have been an important foundation for me to develop future insights…The course has therefore made it clear to me that there are many applications that can be profitably used in cases like this, many of which are easily available online for free or at a low cost".

Approximately half of the pre-service teachers (n = 5) stated that they also learned how to select mobile applications suitable for students' needs. For example, one teacher candidate stated:

Each disability has to be treated differently because of the necessity that it creates. The seminary explained those necessities and the applications and their charac- teristics that can help children affected by them. For example, we saw that a child with visual difficulties could need a bigger text or a different type of font to read better. For each application were explained pros and cons, the problems, and the advantages and disadvantages so that we choose the ones that we think could be better for us to use. I think that I learned a lot of new things that the university courses didn't explain to us. [S9]

Only two pre-service teachers (n = 2) stated that it was useful to develop their own practices. One of the teacher candidates explained this with an example:

The thing which was totally new and undiscovered for me personally was the fact that I can create an app by myself and dedicate it for a special group of children with special needs. In Poland, I'm working with children with Down syndrome, and I found many useful tools to use after I return. In my opinion, integration between children with special needs and without them is crucial in education nowadays. As a future teacher, we should have in our minds that it's very important to create an open environment to let our students work together without notice that some of them have special needs. [S11]

The teacher candidates stated that the training was useful for them in terms of learning applications that can be used for students with disabilities, learning how to use them in their classrooms in the future, learning how to choose and use applications by considering student needs, and learning how to develop their own applications (see Table 4).

Table 4. Theme 1 frequencies

Category	n
Meeting expectations	11
Being informative and interesting	9
Providing practical experiences	9
Offering various applications for students with disabilities	7
Presenting applications for all students	5
Acquiring knowledge about new apps	11
Learning future use of apps	9
Selecting and using apps for students' needs	5
Developing own apps	3
Use in future professional life	11

Challenges of the Training

While only two teacher candidates (n = 2) stated that they did not experience any difficulties, the others (n = 9) indicated that they faced some challenges. These were especially challenges about time limitation (n = 3), challenges while developing apps in CoSpaces and MIT App Inventor (n = 3), challenges in using different applications with unique features (n = 2), challenges in understanding technical terms (n = 3), and some technical problems (Wi-Fi connection, etc.) (n = 1). In addition, teacher candidates who experienced difficulties (n = 6) mentioned that they overcame these challenges with the support of peers.

Especially in relation to the limited time, teacher candidates emphasised the need to extend the duration of education and to definitely include it in the curriculum. For example, one of the teacher candidates (S7) underlined this situation as follows:

> I believe it is important to have an in-depth knowledge of the different applications that can be introduced in schools, especially for children with disabilities. In the various meetings [lessons], I have been able to see how functional these can be for students ... I believe it is important to introduce an expanded version of this course because it would allow everyone to become familiar with and handle numerous useful applications, especially for children with disabilities. It was interesting for me to discover them, and I would have liked to have more hours available to delve deeper but especially to practice with these, asking for further suggestions from professors. [S7]

As can be seen, teacher candidates experienced various difficulties, especially due to time constraints. They expressed the need to extend the duration of this education and to integrate it into the curriculum to solve this problem. Other reasons for their struggles may be due to their unfamiliarity with technical subjects. It is also important that they were able to solve the issues they struggled with with the support of peers and instructors (see Table 5).

Table 5. Theme 2 frequencies

Category	n
Challenges about time limitation	3
Challenges while developing apps in CoSpaces and MIT App Inventor	3
Challenges while using different apps	2
Challenges in understanding technical terms	3
Having no challenges	2
Eliminating challenges with a supportive environment	6
Some technical problems (Wi-Fi connection, etc.)	1

In summary, based on the opinions of teacher candidates, it can be concluded that the needs were accurately identified in the needs analysis and that the content and activities of the training were designed to meet these needs effectively. Teacher candidates express that the training, prepared based on the findings of the needs analysis, had a positive impact on their learning processes. The results of the interviews with teacher candidates indicate how this training enhanced their competencies in using/designing educational mobile applications for students with disabilities and contributed to their teaching practices.

In Table 6, there is a comprehensive alignment of various elements: needs identified through a needs analysis, the sources of these needs (either teacher candidates or experts), specific training topics addressed during the training, and the views expressed by teacher candidates after the training. This triangulation of data effectively demonstrates how the training programme was tailored to address the specific needs identified by teacher candidates and experts. The post-training feedback from the teacher candidates reflects the success of the training in meeting these needs and enhancing their skills, thus validating the effectiveness of the training content and methodology in addressing the initial gaps identified in the needs analysis.

In this study, the data obtained from three sources in the needs analysis and the post-training data triangulate each other. The post-training views of the teacher candidates also indicate that the training was designed in accordance with the needs of the teacher candidates. Table 6 shows needs identified through a needs analysis, the sources of these needs (either teacher candidates or experts), specific training topics addressed during the training, and the views expressed by teacher candidates after the training.

Table 6. Triangulation of the steps

Expressed Need/Issue	Source	Training Topics	Post-Training Views of Teacher Candidates
General & educational technology usage and proficiency laboratory activities and active strategies	Teacher candidates and experts	Usage of technological tools (Different kinds of apps, CoSpaces, MIT App Inventor) with hands-on activities Practical laboratory activities and active learning strategies	Emphasis on practical application
Lack of experience in developing mobile applications	Teacher candidates and experts	Design and development of mobile application	Developing own apps
Awareness of features applications for special education	Teacher candidates and experts	Design features of mobile application	Acquiring knowledge about new apps
Introducing current applications, use and benefits according to disability types, mobile apps simulating real-life scenarios, and use of applications in real contexts or simulated environments	Experts	Mobile application for children with disabilities Types of mobile educational applications	Learning future use of apps Acquiring knowledge about new apps
Accessibility and customisation	Experts	Main concepts and definition of educational mobile applications, mobile application for children with disabilities, and design and development of mobile application	Acquiring knowledge about new apps Learning future use of apps

(*continued*)

Table 6. (*continued*)

Expressed Need/Issue	Source	Training Topics	Post-Training Views of Teacher Candidates
Skills in selection and evaluation of applications	Teacher candidates and experts	Techniques for application selection and evaluation	Selecting and using app for students' needs
Usage of different types of educational mobile applications	Teacher candidates and experts	Mobile application for children with disabilities and types of mobile educational applications	Learning future use of apps Use in future professional life

4 Conclusion

The training course was a 10-h optional learning experience, and no results can be generalised, but a few inputs from the participants can confirm that even a short learning opportunity, if properly designed, can affect prospective teachers' attitudes in terms of motivation towards TEL and the integration of mobile applications in the didactical context. Even though participants were mostly enrolled in the degree course for prospective pre-primary school teachers, their teaching experience varied a lot, since (1) they were in a different course year, (2) not all of them had already started the internship, and (3) some of them were adult students with a full-time position at a school (they got their job before the reform, and they could start their profession with the secondary school diploma for teaching at pre-primary school). This variety was a resource for discussion and viewpoint exchange in a collaborative approach, mainly considering that no participant is a native English speaker and the language barrier could be overcome thanks to mutual support and the hands-on approach of the professors. The course was challenging and motivating since participants were engaged in using applications with their personal mobile devices to design and create simple scenarios according to the principles of a game-based approach to learning, where challenges are targeted to students' skills and problem-solving strategies gratify the effort in the learning process.

Students' final reflections and feedback after the course completion underline that there is a need to either include mobile application in the syllabi of the instructional technology courses and/or select a set of optional courses/seminars to be offered each year in order to integrate the current curriculum and develop students' overall digital competence [29]. The vast majority of participants in the needs analysis step state they are familiar with mobile apps for pupils with disabilities that are based on play, and it seems necessary to plan a multifaceted learning offer about different kinds of applications. This could help obtain a comprehensive vision and develop a rich "tool box" in terms of practices and methodology that enable teachers to select the applications and devices (smartphones/tablets) that best suit the specific needs and situations they experience each day in professional practice.

Students are fully engaged with technology in their daily routine, and the integration of mobile applications and/or use during their learning path at university is just a continuum that needs to be given a specific motivation and rationale to be fully exploited [30]. Thanks to the integration of educational mobile application training, students can learn in first person what they will need to be able to do in their future profession, where children are already familiar with mobile devices but need to be guided through personalised paths and self-regulated learning opportunities, especially in interventions with children with disabilities. Mobile devices and educational applications show a particular "power of action" due to the flexibility of personalisation of the applications.

References

1. Avvisati, F., Hennessy, S., Kozma, R.B., Vincent-Lancrin, S.: Review of the Italian strategy for digital schools. OECD Education Working Papers No. 90. OECD Publishing, Paris (2013). https://doi.org/10.1787/5k487ntdbr44-en
2. MIUR: Piano Nazionale Scuola Digitale (PNSD). https://www.istruzione.it/scuola_digitale/allegati/Materiali/pnsd-layout-30.10-WEB.pdf. Accessed 20 Nov 2023
3. MIUR: La buona Scuola. https://www.istruzione.it/allegati/2017/La_Buona_Scuola_Approfondimenti.pdf. Accessed 20 Nov 2023
4. MIUR: DM 10 September 2010, n. 249. https://www.miur.it/documenti/universita/offerta_formativa/formazione_iniziale_insegnanti_corsi_uni/dm_10_092010_n.249.pdf. Accessed 20 Nov 2023
5. Fedeli, L.: A Multidimensional perspective on digital competence, curriculum and teacher training in Italy. A scoping review on prospective and novice teachers. In: Tomczyk, Ł., Fedeli, L. (eds.) Digital Literacy for Teachers. Lecture Notes in Educational Technology, pp. 261–274. Springer, Singapore (2022). https://doi.org/10.1007/978-981-19-1738-7_14
6. Passey, D.: Technology-enhanced learning: rethinking the term, the concept and its theoretical background. Br. J. Edu. Technol. **50**(3), 972–986 (2019)
7. Laurillard, D.: Technology enhanced learning as a tool for pedagogical innovation. J. Philos. Educ. **42**(3–4), 521–533 (2009)
8. Laurillard, D., Oliver, M., Wasson, B., Hoppe, U.: Implementing technology-enhanced learning. In: Balacheff, N., Ludvigsen, S., de Jong, T., Lazonder, A., Barnes, S. (eds.) Technology-Enhanced Learning, pp. 289–306. Springer, Dordrecht (2009). https://doi.org/10.1007/978-1-4020-9827-7_17
9. Price, S.: Review of the impact of technology-enhanced learning on roles and practices in Higher Education. Report of Kaleidoscope Jointly-Executed Integrative Research Project (2005)
10. Kwok, C., Ng, S., Ho, C., Ip, S., Kui, C.D.: A mobile game-based learning approach for motivating preschoolers and primary students in learning mathematics. In: Lee, L.-K., U, L.H., Wang, F.L., Cheung, S.K.S., Au, O., Li, K.C. (eds.) ICTE 2020. CCIS, vol. 1302, pp. 35–45. Springer, Singapore (2020). https://doi.org/10.1007/978-981-33-4594-2_4
11. Gao, F., Li, L., Sun, Y.: A systematic review of mobile game-based learning in STEM education. Educ. Tech. Res. Dev. **68**, 1791–1827 (2020). https://doi.org/10.1007/s11423-020-09787-0
12. Giannakas, F., Kambourakis, G., Papasalouros, A., et al.: A critical review of 13 years of mobile game-based learning. Educ. Tech. Res. Dev. **66**, 341–384 (2018). https://doi.org/10.1007/s11423-017-9552-z

13. Hall, T.E., Meyer, A., Rose, D.H.: An introduction to universal design for learning. In: Hall, T.E., Meyer, A., Rose, D.H. (eds.) Universal Design for Learning in the Classroom: Practical Applications, pp. 1–8. Guilford Publications, New York (2012)
14. Fedeli, L.: A cross-case analysis of ICT courses in teacher training programmes for special needs: technology affordances and universal design for learning. Educ. Sci. Soc. **2**, 59–71 (2022)
15. Evmenova, A.: Preparing teachers to use universal design for learning to support diverse learners. J. Online Learn. Res. **4**(2), 147–171 (2018)
16. Giasemi, V., Pachler, N., Kukulska-Hulme, A. (eds.): Researching Mobile Learning: Frameworks, Tools and Research Designs. Peter Lang Verlag, Oxford (2009)
17. Radoslava, K., Kralev, V.: An evaluation of the mobile apps for children with special education needs based on the utility function metrics. Int. J. Adv. Sci. Eng. Inf. Technol. **8**(6), 2269–2277 (2018)
18. Eder, M.S., Diaz, J.M.L., Madela, J.R.S., Magusara, M.U., Sabellano, D.D.M.: Fill me app: an interactive mobile game application for children with autism. Int. J. Interact. Mob. Technol. **10**(3), 59–63 (2016)
19. Drigas, A., Angelidakis, P.: Mobile applications within education: an overview of application paradigms in specific categories. Int. J. Interact. Mob. Technol. **11**, 17–29 (2017)
20. Fotaris, P., Pellas, N., Kazanidis, I., Smith, P.: A systematic review of augmented reality game-based applications in primary education. In: Proceedings of the 11th European Conference on Games Based Learning ECGBL 2017, pp. 181–190. Academic Conferences and Publishing International Limited (2017)
21. Hopcan, S., Tokel, S.T.: Exploring the effectiveness of a mobile writing application for supporting handwriting acquisition of students with dysgraphia. Educ. Inf. Technol. **26**, 3967–4002 (2021)
22. Polat, E., Cagiltay, K., Aykut, C., Karasu, N.: Evaluation of a tangible mobile application for students with specific learning disabilities. Aust. J. Learn. Difficulties **24**(1), 95–108 (2019)
23. Bai, H.: Preparing teacher education students to integrate mobile learning into elementary education. TechTrends **63**(6), 723–733 (2019)
24. Burke, D.M., Foulger, T.S.: Mobile learning in teacher education: insight from four programs that embraces change. J. Digit. Learn. Teach. Educ. **30**, 112–120 (2014)
25. Burden, K., Hopkins, P.: Barriers and challenges facing pre-service teachers use of mobile technologies for teaching and learning. Int. J. Mob. Blended Learn. **8**, 1–20 (2016)
26. Soykan, E., Ozdamli, F.: The impact of M-learning activities on the IT success and m-learning capabilities of the special education teacher candidates. World J. Educ. Technol.: Curr. Issues **8**(3), 267–276 (2016)
27. Yin, R.K.: Case Study Research: Design and Methods. Sage Publications, Thousand Oaks (2013)
28. Yıldırım, A., Şimşek, H. (eds.): Sosyal Bilimlerde Nitel Araştırma Yöntemleri [Qualitative Research Methods in the Social Sciences], 9th edn. Seçkin Pub., Ankara (2013)
29. Tomczyk, Ł, Fedeli, L. (eds.): Digital Literacy for Teachers. Springer, Singapore (2022). https://doi.org/10.1007/978-981-19-1738-7
30. Fedeli, L.: School, curriculum and technology: the what and how of their connections. Educ. Sci. Soc. **2**, 42–50 (2017)

NICT Acceptance Among Teachers and Students in the Context of Higher Education Reform in Morocco

Abdelmounim Bouziane[1]([⊠]) [iD] and Karima Bouziane[2,3] [iD]

[1] Interdisciplinary Laboratory for Research on Organizations (LIRO), National School of Commerce and Management, Chouaib Doukkali University, El Jadida, Morocco
bouzianeabdelmounim@gmail.com
[2] Laboratory for Applied Language and Culture Studies (ALCS), Faculty of Letters and Humanities, Chouaib Doukkali University, El Jadida, Morocco
[3] CEOS.PP, ISCAP, Polytechnic of Porto, Porto, Portugal

Abstract. The use of communication technologies during the covid19 crisis has prompted the government of Morocco to consider the use of NICTs as a factor of improvement of education, hence the need to study the interaction of the various actors concerned by this orientation with those technologies.

This study (conducted during 2022) aims to investigate the willingness of teachers and students to embrace NICT as tools for learning. Situated within the context of higher education reform (launched in 2021 and entered into force in 2023), which integrates NICTs as enduring tools for continuous and sustainable learning within universities, this research explores the subject's multifaceted dimensions. The research methodology employs variables derived from TAM. This approach enables an assessment of the degree to which technology-centered teaching methods are embraced and offers insights into the satisfaction levels of various stakeholders regarding the Ministry of Education's innovative policy in Morocco. The sample size consists of 1300 teachers and 11200 students. Data collection was accomplished through questionnaires and then analyzed via SPSS.

The study's outcomes underscore that the students' acceptance of technology hinges on the perceived knowledge growth, remote teaching experience and the satisfaction with distance teaching. While the linear regression model regarding teachers was not significant, this opens up avenues for new studies.

Keywords: ICT · Higher Education · Teachers · Students · Reform · Moroccan Universities

---

NICT—New Information and Communication Technologies.
ICT—Information and Communication Technologies.

© The Author(s), under exclusive license to Springer Nature Switzerland AG 2024
Ł. Tomczyk (Ed.): NMP 2023, CCIS 2130, pp. 156–170, 2024.
https://doi.org/10.1007/978-3-031-63235-8_10

1 Introduction

The landscape of higher education in Morocco is undergoing a transformative shift, driven by the educational reform initiated in 2022, known as the ESRI[1] Pact. This reform includes a multifaceted approach, with a particular focus on promoting language education, expanding teaching staff, and integrating Information and Communication Technology (ICT) into courses. The general goal of this initiative is to establish distance learning as a permanent mode, aligning Moroccan universities with the evolving needs of contemporary education. In this context, understanding the acceptance of ICT as a permanent learning tool becomes primordial. The acceptance of this technology-driven educational approach not only influences the educational experiences of students but also holds implications for the teaching community, the primary stakeholders in this transformative process. The outbreak of the COVID-19 pandemic brought with it a profound shift in the way education is delivered across the globe. Forced to adapt to the constraints of remote learning, many nations, including Morocco, witnessed an accelerated integration of communication technologies into their educational systems. This pivotal moment in history prompted the Moroccan government to recognize the potential of New Information and Communication Technologies (NICTs) as stimulants for enhancing the quality and accessibility of education. Therefore, it became essential to conduct a thorough investigation to comprehend the dynamics of this transition and evaluate the readiness of the primary stakeholders involved. In 2021, Morocco embarked on an ambitious journey of higher education reform, a landmark initiative that came into full force in 2023. Central to this reform was the incorporation of NICTs as integral tools for continuous and sustainable learning within universities. This strategic shift marked a significant exit from traditional educational paradigms and signified a commitment to embrace technology as a conduit for educational progress. This article presents the findings of a study conducted in 2022, designed to delve into the willingness of educators and students to embrace NICTs as essential instruments for learning within the context of these sweeping higher education reforms. The research was conducted to answer a main question which is:

How can we determine if teachers and students in moroccan universities are accepting NICTs as a permanent tool for learning all the time?

2 Literature Review

The significance of higher education reforms in Morocco cannot be underestimated, as they play a crucial role in establishing a robust and modern educational system able of meeting the growing demands of society and the economy. Over the years, the Moroccan government has implemented substantial measures to enhance higher education, with a particular focus on expanding access to higher education and improving the quality of instruction. However, despite the numerous reforms that have been initiated, several challenges persist. Many authors and researchers have addressed topics related to higher education reform, whether they are related to the limitations of the existing system, the potential of the sector, or recommendations for improving and enhancing universities.

---

[1] National Plan for Accelerating the Transformation of the Higher Education, Scientific Research, and Innovation Ecosystem.

The theoretical study by Llorent-Bedmar [9] examined the state of higher education in Morocco after gaining independence in 1956, outlining primary goals, mainly, modernizing higher education to match evolving socioeconomic needs, aligning it with the labor market, improving quality, and integrating the private sector while preserving cultural identity. This study revealed a mismatch between degree programs and job market needs, resource constraints, competition from prestigious institutions, and the necessity for systemic reform. Recommendations highlighted rationalized management, increased university responsibility for knowledge transmission and socioeconomic development, competition and diversification, private sector involvement with adequate funding for state institutions, adoption of a European-style qualification system, enhanced career counseling, cultural preservation within modernization, addressing high dropout rates, and preparing Morocco for global competitiveness through human resources and scientific research. In essence, the study underscored the need for a comprehensive higher education reform to ensure relevance, competitiveness, and alignment with Morocco's socioeconomic progress.

In the same context of assessing the contributions and shortcomings of higher education reforms, Lazrak and Yechouti [8] explored key issues relating to higher education in Morocco. They began by outlining tentative definitions, missions, and functions of universities and higher education institutions. Subsequently, they provided a historical overview of major educational reforms in Morocco and the associated changes. The article also touched on governance in higher education, particularly the concept of cost-sharing. Furthermore, it delved into the history of English Language Teaching (ELT) and outlined characteristics of English Departments in Morocco. They engaged with the debate surrounding private versus public higher education. Lastly, they addressed the critical concern of Brain Drain.

In the same line of analyzing various elements related to education, we can find that several authors have attempted to study the various challenges existing at the level of higher education and universities.

Kabba and Zouhair [7] examined four principal challenges of higher education in Morocco: linguistic dualism, incoherent public policy, massification, and financial dependency on the state. The challenges are as follows: the language divide, particularly the dominance of French, posed significant equity challenges. Reforms lacked coherence and a long-term strategy, often driven by political changes. Massification and strained resources affected the teaching quality. The funding model for higher education was unsustainable in the long run; when compared to the GDP, the level of funding allocated to higher education in Morocco, as well as in other MENA countries, has been already high. To address this issue of limited financial resources and over-reliance on the state, the authors suggested that Moroccan universities should take advantage of the new financial autonomy provided by the law[2]. This move would enable them to access sufficient resources to ensure an acceptable level of performance by giving them the opportunity to seek sources of income independently of the state budget.

---

[2] Law No. 01–00 regarding the organization of higher education.

Also, Mabrouk [10] discussed the challenges and strategies for educational development in Morocco. It emphasized the importance of education for societal and economic progress. While acknowledging the efforts made by the state in terms of budget allocation, infrastructure development, and the generalization of basic education, it also highlighted persistent issues. These included inequalities between urban and rural areas, gender disparities, and a disconnect between economic growth and socio-cultural progress. The article proposed a comprehensive strategy to address these challenges, covering infrastructure improvement, curriculum development, social support, media engagement, and scientific research.

In the same logic of analyzing various policies conducted by the Moroccan ministry of higher education, Dardary, Azar and Belaaouad [4] traced the evolution of Morocco's education system and its reform initiatives since independence in 1956. It emphasized the critical role of education in societal advancement and analyzed various reform efforts, such as the National Charter and the Emergency Program. The article offered a detailed overview of the challenges and achievements, highlighting persistent issues like financial management, governance, and school dropout rates, while also underscoring the strategic importance of ICT integration through the GENIE Program[3]. It provided valuable insights into Morocco's educational reform journey, emphasizing the need for continuous improvement and adaptation to meet the evolving needs of the country's education system.

Through various analyzed and debated works, we can say that the Moroccan government has been able to implement several policies and strategies to ensure a reform of higher education aimed at improving the quality of education, learning, and research within universities. However, several challenges, deficiencies, and issues can be observed. The major problem stands in the shortage of human resources (teachers and administrative staff) and infrastructure (limited capacity) in the face of a significant number of students, in addition to the absence of university institutions in certain regions of Morocco. ICT (Information and Communication Technology) can be considered effective means to address the various existing problems, especially since during the COVID-19 health crisis, they were the only available channels for delivering classes and organizing exams, allowing for the continuity of education. ICT constitute effective means to address several weaknesses within the higher education system, whether they are related to learning, internal management, and/or scientific research. Several studies have been conducted regarding the emphasis on the benefits of ICT in higher education. These studies have also focused on the conditions for integrating ICT within universities, particularly in terms of technology acceptance.

Ben Youssef and Hadhri [2] conducted a study during the 2005/2006 academic year in French universities to assess the adoption and usage intensity of key information and communication technologies (ICT) among higher education teachers. Their research highlighted the rapid adoption of basic ICT tools like word processing and spreadsheets but also revealed structural barriers to advanced technologies such as database software. The results have shown that the factors influencing ICT acceptance, include gender

---

[3] The GENIE program is an operational implementation of the national strategy for the generalization of Information and Communication Technologies in Education (ICT). It is based on several components, such as: infrastructure, teacher training and digital resources.

and seniority. This study is providing a reference for our study on ICT acceptance in education reform. It underscores the importance of targeted training and organizational changes, aligning with our reform goals.

In the same framework of highlighting the factors influencing ICT acceptance, Oulmaati, Ezzahri and Samadi [12] investigated the utilization of ICT among History and Civilization students at Abdelmalek Essaadi University in Morocco, with a focus on accessibility and usage. The analysis revealed a dual digital gap, including unequal ICT access and limited integration into the learning process. While students possessed smartphones and had regular internet access, their primary usage was for communication through social networks and messaging apps, missing out on opportunities for collaboration and knowledge construction. Moreover, many students lacked formal communication channels with their teachers. The study underscored the necessity for establishing formalized communication between students and professors. To facilitate the effective integration of ICT into education, the study recommended the implementation of a national strategy that promotes widespread ICT access and supports pedagogical innovations in higher education.

Also, Neggady Alami and Fahssis [11] assessed the digitalization strategy of Hassan II University in Morocco, highlighting commendable efforts in governance and digitalization. However (according to the authors) the human factor, crucial to this system, lacks the necessary support and training for effective ICT adoption. Consequently, teachers face challenges in incorporating technology into their practices, often resorting to self-training. Collaboration among senior teachers is common. While material resources are essential for a "smart university," developing technological competencies and ensuring ICT adoption by all users are equally vital. Tailored digital training for pedagogy would promote efficient technology integration. Despite progress, significant challenges remain for harmonious and responsible operation, particularly in a competitive environment. Sharing information across institutions and optimizing existing infrastructure are key challenges. These findings can serve as a foundation for our current efforts to emphasize the importance of comprehensive training for both teachers and students. Additionally, it underscores the need for collaborative problem-solving and infrastructure optimization, offering valuable insights for our recommendations in the reform process.

Technology acceptance is a highly essential element to investigate; however, there are situations where the use of ICT presents itself as the only viable alternative. This is the case with distance education, which has forced both teachers and students to suddenly experiment with and use ICT in education. At this stage, several researchers have conducted studies, but this time to assess the experience of using ICT in teaching. In this regard, El Aissaoui [5], have investigated the perspectives of Moroccan university professors concerning the incorporation of information and communication technology (ICT) into their teaching practices. The objectives of this research include understanding the attitudes of respondents towards ICT use in teaching, examining factors that affect the integration of ICT in teaching, and exploring whether there exists a correlation between the attitudes of Moroccan university professors towards ICT and their actual incorporation of technology in their teaching methods. The outcomes of the study demonstrate that Moroccan university professors exhibit favorable attitudes towards the use of ICT in teaching, with no detectable association between age or gender and these attitudes.

Additionally, the study indicates that variations in teaching experience do not significantly influence attitudes. Importantly, the findings reveal a positive connection between the attitudes of respondents and their level of technology integration in teaching.

We can also find the study conducted by Ahandar [1] that aimed to assess the actual use of information and communication technologies (ICT) in university teaching, particularly within the context of distance education due to prevailing unfavorable conditions that restricted traditional classroom instruction. The study's findings revealed that participants had demonstrated an acceptable level of ICT proficiency, albeit with a moderate utilization of ICT programs in their teaching practices. Furthermore, participants encountered challenges when attempting to integrate ICT into higher education. The study concluded by providing recommendations for optimizing the use of ICT in higher education, with the potential to enhance the quality of teaching and learning.

3 Methodology

Data collection was fulfilled through questionnaire (primary data). The questionnaire concerning the student survey was sent to 11200 students from different universities in Morocco. Also, the questionnaire related to the teachers survey, was sent to 1300 teachers from the 12 Moroccan universities. All universities are represented in our sample.

Data analysis will be conducted through linear regression using SPSS software.

To identify the variables to be included in our research, we conducted 2 group interviews involving 10 teachers and 15 students. During those interviews, the interviewees outlined various elements that can be used in our questionnaire and research model. Other variables were added following the analysis of the literature review, and other one related to the perceived usefulness and perceived ease mentioned in the Technology Acceptance Model theory.

The variables introduced in the research model concerning the acceptance of students of ICT were as follows (Table 1):

Table 1. Determination of research variables: Acceptance of students of ICT

Variables	Possible answers
level of familiarity with ICT	The questions regarding these variables were formulated in such a way that respondents had to select one of these five choices:
The perceived ease of ICT	
Perceived Technological Effectiveness	Strongly Disagree
The perceived usefulness	Disagree
	Neutral
	Agree
	Strongly Agree

(*continued*)

Table 1. (*continued*)

Variables	Possible answers
Home Computer Equipment	The questions regarding these variables were formulated in such a way that respondents had to select one of these five choices: 1: Only one device (tablet or smartphone or laptop, desktop), 2: two devices... up to 4 to indicate 4 means
Remote Teaching Experience	The questions regarding these variables were formulated in such a way that respondents had to select one of these two choices:
Pre-Lockdown Distance Learning Offerings	
Perceived Knowledge Growth	Yes
Satisfaction With Distance Teaching	No
Acceptance Of ICT As Permanent Tool	

Also, the variables introduced in the research model concerning the acceptance of teachers of ICT were as follows (Table 2):

Table 2. Determination of research variables: Acceptance of teachers of ICT

Variables	Possible answers
level of familiarity with ICT	The questions regarding these variables were formulated in such a way that respondents had to select one of these five choices:
The perceived ease of ICT	
Perceived Technological Effectiveness	Strongly Disagree
The perceived usefulness	Disagree
	Neutral
	Agree
	Strongly Agree
Home Computer Equipment	The questions regarding these variables were formulated in such a way that respondents had to select one of these five choices: 1: Only one device (tablet or smartphone or laptop...), 2: two devices... up to 4 to indicate 4 means
Remote Teaching Experience	The questions regarding these variables were formulated in such a way that respondents had to select one of these five choices:
Virtual Class Relationship Assessment	
Satisfaction With Distance Teaching	Yes
Acceptance Of ICT As Permanent Tool	No

In summary, this research method involves collecting primary data through questionnaires from a large number of students and teachers in Moroccan universities. The data will be analyzed using linear regression, and the variables to be included in the research were identified through group interviews, a literature review, and the application of the Technology Acceptance Model theory[4]. This approach aims to provide a comprehensive understanding of the factors influencing the adoption or acceptance of technology in the educational context in Morocco.

In our research, we are using various variables to examine the acceptance of information and communication technologies (ICT) in higher education. The same research model will be employed for both students and teachers. Our objective is to thoroughly explore the factors influencing the willingness to permanently use ICT in teaching. Furthermore, the research variables are drawn from previous studies examining both students' and teachers' attitudes and behaviors towards ICT in education. Therefore, these same variables are used to determine the factors impacting the acceptance of ICT as a permanent learning tool for both students and teachers.

4   Results

Two statistical analyses were carried out. A first analysis for the study of students' acceptance of ICT as a permanent tool of education and a second to study the acceptance of teachers. To study the feasibility of the statistical method used (Linear Regression), several tests are extracted and interpreted, namely: The DW test, the R and R2, and the F statistic.

4.1   Students' Acceptance of ICT as a Permanent Learning Tool in Moroccan Universities

The preliminary tests carried out to confirm the method used to analyze the data related to students' acceptance with ICT were as follows (Table 3):

Table 3. Model extracted from SPSS (Linear regression): Acceptance of Students of ICT

	Tests performed	Results
Linear regression	R	0.963
	R^2	0.927
	R^2 adjusted	0.927
	DW	0,437
	Probability of Fisher	0.000

The correlation index $R = 0.9$ close to 1. So, we can conclude that there is a correlation between the level of students' acceptance and the explanatory variables that we have included. The R2 = 0.9, and therefore we can say that the explanatory variables explain about 90% of our variable to be explained. The F-statistic is lower than 5%, we can

---

[4] TAM is a model that explains users' acceptance of new technologies based on perceived usefulness and ease of use. It helps predict user behavior regarding technology adoption.

confirm that our statistical model is valid. In general, despite the DW being less than 1, we can assert that our research model is significant.

After the analysis of the feasibility of the statistical model, it seems necessary to present an extraction of the table of correlations of Pearson in order to visualize the various existing relations between the acceptance of the students of ICT and the various explanatory variables incorporated in this model. The Table 4 gives an idea about the level of correlation existing between each of the explanatory variables and the students' acceptance.

Table 4. Correlation of Pearson: Acceptance of Students of ICT

	Variables	Acceptance Of ICT As Permanent Tool
Pearson Production	level of familiarity with ICT	0,035
	The perceived ease of ICT	0,176
	Perceived Technological Effectiveness	0,107
	The perceived usefulness	0,058
	Home Computer Equipment	0,118
	Remote Teaching Experience	0,884
	Pre-Lockdown Distance Learning Offerings	0,256
	Perceived Knowledge Growth	0,885
	Satisfaction With Distance Teaching	0,885
	Acceptance Of ICT As Permanent Tool	1

Student's acceptance of ICT as a permanent tool of teaching in university depends on several elements. We find as variables with a strong influence:

The Perceived Knowledge Growth
The Perceived knowledge growth is a crucial element for evaluating the learning method. If students feel that their knowledge is improving through online courses, they will accept the implementation of this form of education as permanent.

Remote Teaching Experience
Experience in distance teaching also has a strong correlation with the acceptance of ICT as a means of education. The more experience students have with distance teaching, the more predisposed they will be to accept this method of learning.

Satisfaction with Distance Teaching
Satisfaction with online courses significantly affects students' acceptance of ICT. This

result appears rational. The more satisfied one is with ICT in education, the more inclined they are to accept it as a permanent means of teaching.

The experiences of distance teaching delivered during the lockdown, the computer equipment possessed by students have a weak influence on their acceptance of ICT in education. Other variables such as perceived usefulness, perceived ease have almost no impact.

4.2 Teachers' Acceptance of ICT as a Permanent Learning Tool in Moroccan Universities

The preliminary tests carried out to confirm the method used to analyze the data related to teachers' acceptance with ICT were as follows (Table 5):

Table 5. Model extracted from SPSS (Linear regression): Acceptance of Students of ICT

	Tests performed	Results
Linear regression	R	0.483
	R^2	0.233
	R^2 adjusted	0.229
	DW	0,901
	Probability of Fisher	0.000

The correlation index $R = 0.4$. So, we can conclude that there is almost no correlation between the level of teachers' acceptance and the explanatory variables that we have included. The R2 = 0.2, and therefore we can say that the explanatory variables explain only 20% of our variable to be explained.

After the analysis of the feasibility of the statistical model, we can affirm that the research model is not significant. The independent variables cannot explain the teachers' acceptance of ICT as a permanent tool of education in universities.

5 Discussion

The reform of higher education in Morocco announced in 2022 (ESRI Pact) focused on several elements, including the promotion of language education, the expansion of teaching staff, and the integration of ICT (Information and Communication Technology) in courses. The Ministry of Higher Education aims to establish distance learning as a permanent mode that Moroccan universities can adopt to meet learning needs. In this context, the acceptance of ICT as a permanent learning tool needs to be examined. Our research aims to investigate the factors that can influence the acceptance of students and teachers (the primary stakeholders in this process) regarding the permanent use of ICT in education. Regarding students' acceptance of ICT as a means of education, several variables have been highlighted: Perceived Knowledge Growth, Remote Teaching Experience: and Satisfaction with Distance Teaching.

The study emphasizes that the perceived improvement in knowledge and learning is an important factor in students' acceptance of ICT in education. When students experience, shows intellectual growth through online courses, they are more likely to view this form of education as a permanent and effective method. This finding underscores the importance of the educational outcomes associated with ICT. If students believe that their understanding and knowledge are advancing, they are more inclined to support and embrace online learning. This suggests that educators and institutions should focus on ensuring that online courses effectively enhance students' knowledge and skills.

Another key factor identified in this research as affecting the acceptance of ICT is the level of experience. Students who have had more exposure to online learning are more predisposed to accept ICT as a viable means of education. In essence, familiarity and comfort with the online learning environment play a crucial role in shaping students' attitudes. This implies that universities and instructors should offer opportunities for students to gain experience with online education, as it can lead to greater acceptance and effectiveness of ICT-based teaching methods. Encouraging exposure and engagement with digital learning tools can be an important strategy.

The study also highlights the significance of students' satisfaction with online courses. When students are content and happy with their online learning experiences, they are more likely to accept ICT as a permanent mode of teaching. This is a common-sense finding, as satisfaction often drives acceptance. It emphasizes the need for institutions and educators to continually improve the quality of online courses, ensuring that they meet students' needs and expectations. By enhancing the satisfaction of students in the online learning environment, institutions can further promote its acceptance and adoption.

These results confirm conclusions drawn by previous studies. Bouziane, Tahri and Bouziane [3] have demonstrated in their study exploring the factors influencing technology acceptance in education during the Covid-19 pandemic, that the perceived improvement in skills by students is one of the predominant factors influencing the acceptance of e-learning within Moroccan universities. Another study that can be highlighted to discuss our results is the one conducted by Han and Ellis [6]. This study provides confirmation of the result stating the existence of a correlation between student satisfaction with the improvement of their skills and the acceptance of ICT as a permanent learning tool, and a rejection of the result dictating that the perceived ease of technology has no impact on students' acceptance of ICT.

The impact of perceived knowledge growth on students' acceptance of information and communication technologies (ICT) is undeniable. When students observe an improvement in their knowledge through online courses, it strengthens their belief in the effectiveness of this form of learning and encourages them to accept ICT as a permanent educational tool. Indeed, the perception of an increase in their understanding and knowledge stimulates their interest in online learning and reinforces their confidence in this mode of education. This observation underscores the crucial importance of educational outcomes associated with ICT in fostering their adoption by students. Thus, investing in high-quality online programs that facilitate real knowledge growth can play a decisive role in promoting the acceptance of ICT in higher education.

Regarding the acceptance of ICT by teachers, the statistical model produced non-significant results. This outcome leads us to infer that there may be other variables that hold more relevance than those selected in our study. Notably, it is crucial to acknowledge the diverse perspectives expressed by both teachers' unions and educators at large regarding all facets of the educational reform. While some advocate for structural changes initiated by the ministry, others assert that any change should involve teachers directly and not be imposed solely by governmental bodies. This multifaceted context implies that the acceptance of ICT by teachers could be influenced by factors beyond those included in our model. Therefore, further exploration and consideration of these additional variables are warranted to comprehensively understand the dynamics shaping teachers' attitudes towards ICT integration in education.

6   Recommendations

Many recommendations can be implemented to encourage both the permanent acceptance of ICT as a means of education and the acceleration of the establishment of online courses and classes. Here are some suggestions:

Evaluate the experiences of distance teaching delivered during the COVID-19 crisis, considering elements such as student feedback, teacher feedback, assessment of learning outcomes, and technology assessment.

- Conduct long-term studies to assess the sustained effectiveness and acceptance of ICT in education for both students and teachers. This ongoing evaluation will help adapt strategies as needed. The actions to be implemented are as follows:

  - Establish a research team dedicated to conducting longitudinal studies on the integration of ICT in education;
  - Design research methodologies that capture both short-term and long-term impacts of ICT implementation;
  - Regularly collect data from students, teachers, and other stakeholders to track changes in attitudes, skills, and learning outcomes over time.

- Develop customized strategies for enhancing ICT acceptance among both students and teachers, considering their specific needs, experiences, and levels of satisfaction. The actions to be implemented are as follows:

  - Conduct surveys and interviews to gather insights into the challenges and preferences of students and teachers regarding ICT use;
  - Use the feedback obtained to tailor training programs and support initiatives that address the identified needs and preferences;
  - Collaborate with educational psychologists or specialists in human-computer interaction to design user-friendly ICT tools and resources.

- Provide ongoing professional development for teachers to ensure they are well-prepared to effectively integrate ICT into their teaching methods. The actions to be implemented are as follows:

- Offer regular workshops, seminars, and training sessions focused on ICT integration in education;
- Provide resources such as online courses, tutorials, and guides to support self-directed learning for teachers;
- Encourage peer learning and collaboration by establishing communities of practice where teachers can share experiences and best practices related to ICT integration.

• Prioritize Knowledge Enhancement: Universities should prioritize enhancing students' knowledge and learning outcomes through online courses. This includes ensuring that online education effectively contributes to intellectual growth. The actions to be implemented are as follows:

- Review existing courses to identify areas where online learning can supplement or enhance traditional methods;
- Collaborate with professors to design online courses that align with learning objectives and promote intellectual growth;
- Establish channels for students to provide feedback on online courses, ensuring continuous improvement.

• Create opportunities for students to gain more experience with online learning. Familiarity and comfort with the online learning environment play a crucial role in shaping students' attitudes. Offering more online courses and resources to support digital learning is essential. The actions to be implemented are as follows:

- Increase the variety of online courses available to students, covering a range of subjects and levels;
- Provide training and support.

• Continuously improve the quality of online courses to meet students' needs and expectations. High student satisfaction with online courses is associated with greater acceptance. Institutions should invest in resources, technology, and training to create a positive online learning experience. The actions to be implemented are as follows:

- Conduct regular assessments: Gather feedback from students and instructors to identify areas for improvement in online course design and delivery;
- Invest in professional development: Provide training for faculty on effective online teaching strategies, instructional design principles, and technology usage.

• Explore Additional Variables (teacher acceptance of ICT): Given the limited significance of the model used for analyzing teachers' acceptance of ICT, further research should delve into other variables that might influence teachers' acceptance. Understanding these factors can help tailor strategies to enhance teacher buy-in. The actions to be implemented are as follows:

- Design surveys or interviews: Gather data from teachers to identify additional variables that may impact their acceptance of technology;

- Analyze findings: Interpret the results to understand the most significant factors influencing teacher attitudes toward ICT;
- Develop targeted interventions: Based on the findings, devise strategies to address barriers and promote greater teacher acceptance of technology in the classroom.

- Involve Teachers in Decision-Making: Recognize the diverse opinions among teachers and unions regarding educational reforms. Involving educators in the decision-making process related to the integration of ICT in education can lead to more successful implementation.

Several cases can be enumerated to illustrate the opportunities that the use of ICT in education can provide. Morocco, through a partnership with UNICEF, has established a report studying the experiences observed during the COVID-19 pandemic. The report concluded that most of the steps outlined in the recommendations are essential for improving the education system and ensuring the effectiveness of learning. Similar elements can be observed in the education monitoring reports published by UNESCO, as well as in reports from the World Bank on education and digital development, which visualize concrete examples of experiences from different countries. This highlights the importance of evaluating experiences and learning from them to enhance educational practices, particularly in integrating ICT effectively.

7 Conclusion

The findings of this study provide valuable insights into the acceptance of Information and Communication Technology (ICT) as a permanent learning tool in Moroccan universities, particularly from the perspectives of both students and teachers. The research has identified critical factors that influence this acceptance and sheds light on the challenges and opportunities in integrating ICT into the education system. For students, the research underscores the importance of perceived knowledge growth. When students believe that their understanding and knowledge improve through online courses, they are more likely to embrace ICT as a permanent mode of education. This suggests that educational institutions should prioritize pedagogical approaches that effectively enhance students' knowledge and skills in the digital learning environment. Additionally, students' level of experience with online learning plays a significant role in their acceptance of ICT. The more exposure students have to online education, the more predisposed they are to view it as a viable means of learning. To facilitate this, universities should offer opportunities for students to gain experience with digital learning tools, fostering familiarity and comfort with the online learning environment. Furthermore, the study highlights the importance of students' satisfaction with online courses. Satisfaction is a key driver of acceptance. To encourage ICT adoption, institutions should focus on continuously improving the quality of online courses to meet students' needs and expectations, enhancing their overall satisfaction. However, the research also reveals that the model used to assess teachers' acceptance of ICT was not significant. It is suggested that other variables not considered in this study may influence teachers' acceptance. The diverse opinions within the educational community, with some advocating for structural changes and others emphasizing the importance of teacher involvement in the reform process, underscore the complexity of this issue. This context suggests that teacher acceptance of ICT may depend on factors beyond those explored in the current model. In light of these findings, it is recommended that Moroccan universities take a multi-faceted approach to promote the acceptance of ICT in education. This includes fostering pedagogical innovation, providing training and support for both students and teachers, and ensuring equitable access to technology and digital resources. Continuous assessment and adaptation of strategies, as well as interuniversity collaboration, can further facilitate the integration of ICT into the education system.

Ultimately, the research informs the ongoing efforts to reform higher education in Morocco and emphasizes the need to consider the experiences and perceptions of key stakeholders, both students and teachers, in shaping the future of education in a digital age.

References

1. Ahandar, A.: The reality of using ict in teaching in Moroccan universities from university professors' perspective. Arab J. Qual. Assur. High. Educ. **14**(50), 95–110 (2021)
2. Ben Youssef, A., Hadhri, W.: The dynamics of usage of information and communication technologies by university professors: the case of France. Réseaux **155**, 23–54 (2009)
3. Bouziane, A., Tahri, W., Bouziane, K.: Satisfaction and acceptance of ICT in learning activities during Covid19: the case of Moroccan students. In: Tomczyk, Ł. (ed.) NMP 2022. CCIS, vol. 1916, pp. 254–265. Springer, Cham (2022). https://doi.org/10.1007/978-3-031-44581-1_18
4. Dardary, O., Azar, Z., Tridane, M., Belaaouad, S.: Education reform: a strategy for a school of success. Iraqi J. Sci. Spec. Issue 313–321 (2021)
5. El Aissaoui, A.: Moroccan university professors' attitudes towards the integration of information and communication technology in teaching. Rev. Écon. Gestion Soc. **23**, 1 (2020)
6. Han, F., Ellis, R.A.: Predicting students' academic performance by their online learning patterns in a blended course: to what extent is a theory-driven approach and a data-driven approach consistent? Educ. Technol. Soc. **24**(1), 191–204 (2021)
7. Kabba, F.E., Zouhair, E.: The challenges of higher education in Morocco. Int. J. Sci. Eng. Res. **10**(9), 57 (2019)
8. Lazrak, M., Yechouti, Y.: Issues in Moroccan higher education. Int. J. Engl. Lang. Transl. Stud. **5**(2), 86–93 (2017)
9. Llorent-Bedmar, V.: Educational reforms in morocco: evolution and current status. Int. Educ. Stud. **7**(12), 95 (2014)
10. Mabrouk, E.H.: Problems and strategy of educational development in Morocco. New Trends Issues Proc. Humanit. Soc. Sci. **6**(1), 430–439 (2019)
11. Neggady Alami, T., Fahssis, L.: Intégration des TIC dans l'enseignement supérieur: Cas de l'Université Hassan II. La Revue de Management et Cultures, No. 4 (2019)
12. Oulmaati, K., Ezzahri, S., Samadi, K.: The use of ICT in the learning process among the students of history and civilization at Abdelmalek Essaadi University, Morocco. Int. J. Sci. Eng. Res.t. J. Sci. Eng. Res. **8**(2), 972 (2017)

Current Situation Due to the Persistent Impact of COVID19 Lockdown on Digital Skills

Alberto Díaz-Burgos[1(✉)], Jesús N. García-Sánchez[1],
María-Lourdes Álvarez-Fernández[1], and Sónia Brito-Costa[2,3]

[1] Universidad de León, 24071 León, Spain
adiazb01@estudiantes.unileon.es
[2] Instituto Politécnico de Coímbra, Education School, 3045-093 Coimbra, Portugal
[3] INED - Center for Research and Innovation in Education, Polytechnic Institute of Porto, Porto, Portugal

Abstract. Some of the key factors that have determined the current and persistent effects of the worldwide and massive lockdown during the COVID-19 pandemic on various digital competencies are presented. In recent decades, ICT (Information and Communication Technologies), and more recently, artificial intelligence, have gained importance in education and the family environment, promoting essential skills in Generation Z. Digital competence is now an essential part of the educational curriculum. This article presents a research study aimed at investigating the challenges faced by the educational system and families during the COVID-19 lockdown, particularly in adapting to exclusively online teaching methods. It seeks to assess the impact of this period on the acquisition of digital competence, the role of families in supporting learning, and its effects on satisfaction, well-being, and academic performance. By fostering national and international collaborations with universities and foundations, the study aims to improve digital competence and family literacy, ultimately contributing to the enhancement of quality education and societal inclusion in both social and employment contexts.

Keywords: Digital competence · Education · Family environment · COVID-19 lockdown · Psychology

1 Background

1.1 Justification

Since the last third of the 20th century, there has been a focus on the key role and impact that both ICT and artificial intelligence (AI) have had on all aspects of society. Thus, they were progressively incorporated into different social spheres, creating new opportunities for access to knowledge and communication [1]. Their presence, specifically in educational and family environments, was justified because, in addition to meeting the needs resulting from the current reality of the 21st-century child and adolescent collective, considered digital natives and defined as Generation Z, the benefits arising from

Ł. Tomczyk (Ed.): NMP 2023, CCIS 2130, pp. 171–183, 2024.
https://doi.org/10.1007/978-3-031-63235-8_11

their acquisition and development were multiple [2]. They fostered aspects such as autonomy, efficiency, responsibility, flexibility, critical thinking, and reflection, among others, thus favouring developmental and learning processes and, consequently, well-being and quality of life, preparing this collective for their future professional life [3].

On the other hand, AI has revolutionized education in recent years by enabling the adaptation of content and teaching strategies to individual student needs, enhancing the effectiveness of the educational process. Additionally, it simplified the automation of administrative tasks, such as exam assessment, allowing teachers to focus on direct interaction and student support. AI also fostered gamification and the use of virtual tutorials, making the learning process more engaging and easily. However, addressing ethical and privacy issues associated with data collection and usage was crucial, as well as ensuring equity and accessibility in the utilization of this technology for all students. In summary, AI transformed education, providing promising opportunities but also presenting fundamental challenges that needed to be considered in its implementation [4–6].

At present, the importance of digital proficiency as a foundational aspect of the educational curriculum is detailed in the Common Framework of Digital Competence for Teachers. This framework is integrated into significant international teaching standards, such as those established by organizations like the International Society for Technology in Education [7] and the United Nations Educational, Scientific and Cultural Organization [8]. Digital competence stands out among the essential competencies mandated by current regulations. The Recommendation of the European Parliament and the Council of the European Union [9] characterizes digital literacy, as the capacity to master abilities associated with seeking, acquiring, processing, and communicating information, thereby converting it into knowledge. This competency covers a wide range of skills, from accessing information to conveying it through different formats, leveraging ICT and AI as crucial elements for informing, learning, and communicating. However, for students to acquire and refine this competency, it is imperative that teachers undergo training and possess digital competence [10].

The COVID-19 lockdown catalysed a fundamental change in how students and teachers interacted with technology, generating a significant impetus in the development of their digital competence. The need to adapt to online education led to a deeper immersion in digital tools, from learning platforms to collaborative applications [11]. It seems evident that this transition had an impact on crucial psychoeducational variables; for instance, it challenged motivation by imposing a new learning format, generating both enthusiasm and discouragement, depending on adaptability and prior experience with technology [12].

Moreover, this abrupt change also influenced academic well-being since the ability to effectively manage digital tools could make a difference in the educational experience, affecting self-confidence, sense of achievement, and emotional connection with the learning process [13]. The direct relationship and the extent of development achieved in each variable were questions this study aimed to address, providing that added value.

All this development exposed the need to review studies published in recent years because technological advancements, such as the emergence of artificial intelligence, seemed to indicate differences not only in the way of learning and teaching but also in society. Individuals, due to constant and rapid changes, utilized their adaptability and learning capacity to develop digital skills that enabled autonomous navigation in educational and social spheres. This set of skills was known as digital competence [14].

The review of scientific literature on models of digital competence development had highlighted the predominant focus on teacher training, aiming for the extension and transfer of this digital teaching competence to students [15]. This need emphasized the importance of digital skills in the family context, involving families in this process [16]. Although numerous studies had concentrated on digital competence linked to the family environment, many utilizing data from the latest Programme for International Student Assessment (PISA) study and other international surveys like ICILS or TIMSS, there was recognition of the lack of new studies focusing on specific territories and comparisons, especially considering the pre/post-COVID-19 pandemic situation as well as cultural and geographical factors. Addressing this gap was the primary goal of this study.

Systematic reviews have been conducted on various factors within the PISA 2018 study. Examples include the utilization of digital devices within households and social interactions. However, insufficient attention has been given to the family context [17]. On the other hand, there were studies revealing inequalities in access to new technologies based on geographical location, but these were not contextualized from an educational perspective, nor did they address psychological variables [18]. Therefore, there arose a necessity for a comprehensive systematic review focusing on the acquisition of digital proficiency, the impact of the family environment on its cultivation, disparities among cultural and geographical regions, and their effects on academic performance, enjoyment, and personal fulfilment. Moreover, it was deemed crucial to investigate potential fluctuations in these variables following the COVID-19 situation [19].

Through the study, the aim was to address the following question: How has the persistent impact derived from the COVID-19 confinement affected the progression of digital proficiency and psychoeducational factors based on the outcomes demonstrated in the PISA study and subsequent dataset analyses?

The general objective of this study was to delve into the development achieved concerning digital literacy and key psychological and educational variables in family environments across different cultural and geographical circumstances prior to and following the COVID-19 pandemic.

The following hypothesis was proposed: Significant empirical differences will be displayed pre- and post-pandemic in international studies, exploring psychoeducational patterns shaped by digital literacy and psychological variables across diverse cultures and demographics.

Through all this, the impact of the rapid educational digitalization during the pandemic will be revealed, highlighting the mediating role of psychological factors in academic outcomes. Additionally, it will address gaps in understanding the family impact during COVID-19 confinement and evaluate the influence of problematic internet use on digital competence and learning efficiency [20].

2   Method

The study was designed with the purpose of addressing the knowledge gaps outlined earlier. It aimed not only to respond to previous question based on the review of scientific literature but also to continue previously proposed research. Furthermore, in light of technological advancements, new inquiries were raised that demanded investigation and answers. Therefore, three comparisons were established between the results of the PISA 2018 and 2022 datasets and subsequent studies in different cultural or geographical contexts. Collectively, all this allowed for the continuation of existing research and provided answers to new questions arising regarding the influence of new technologies on digital skills and the psychoeducational variables associated with digital competence.

Consequently, the study was structured as follows, addressing the response to research question, and thus, achieving the objective (see Fig. 1):

Fig. 1. Study division.

The initial approach involved a thorough and detailed examination. A systematic review concentrated on exploring the impact of the family environment, digital skills, and various psychological and educational factors on the academic performance, well-being, and personal contentment of students in compulsory secondary education. This review was rooted in the insights derived from the PISA 2018 datasets and subsequent studies. The process unfolded across four stages, drawing from the methodologies proposed by Miller et al. [21] and Scott et al. [22]. Initially, a diagram outlining pertinent terms and thematic categories was established. Subsequently, an exhaustive search for scholarly literature was conducted utilizing databases such as Web of Science or Scopus.

Stringent criteria for inclusion and exclusion were employed, spanning the timeframe from 2013 to 2023, with requirements including full-text accessibility and publications in either Spanish or English. Furthermore, other criteria were taken into account in line with the contributions made by Cooper et al. [23]. Following this, the analysis focused on methodological rigor and indicators rooted in scientific evidence, drawing from guidelines proposed by Risko et al. [24] and Torgerson [25]. This assessment utilized the MQQn framework, which consists of seven indicators, to evaluate the quality and effectiveness of the studies. Furthermore, evidence-based indicators and effect sizes of the studies were also evaluated.

A detailed qualitative analysis was conducted to identify and compile key arguments and evidence that would address the objective outlined in this review. This entire process was documented and graphically represented following the PRISMA statement [26].

The second approach is based on a comparison between the PISA 2018 dataset and the upcoming PISA 2022 dataset and subsequent studies regarding the impact of the family environment, digital competencies, and other psychological and educational variables on the academic performance, well-being, and personal satisfaction of compulsory secondary education students. This gains particular relevance due to the challenge faced by the educational system and family environment in exclusively transitioning to online teaching during the COVID-19 pandemic-induced lockdown, followed by the concurrent implementation of online and in-person teaching that continues to date. Initially, it involves downloading the Big Data from each dataset and selecting a sample for comparing five cultural, linguistic, and geographic environments (Europe and Asia). Subsequently, conducting Exploratory Factor Analysis (EFA) becomes necessary, focusing on validating and analysing differential patterns. Current statistical packages like SPSSv29, Amos 29, or Mplusv8.10 are utilized for confirmatory and measurement analyses.

A third approach centres on using Structural Equation Modelling (SEM) analyses with data collected from the previous approaches and the aforementioned statistical packages. This entails descriptive frequency analysis, evaluating relationships between variables constituting digital competence, and applying a causal structural equation model. Additionally, it involves analysing data reliability and describing their characteristics, including determining means and standard deviations. Several articles analysing PISA results at national and international levels during the COVID-19 pandemic have been published [27], shedding light on the development of digital literacy during this period, forming the foundation of our research [28].

The final focus specifically targets two European regions. It aims to showcase the differences experienced during the pandemic period between rural and urban areas of these two European regions in educational and psychological keys. Following the download of Big Data from both PISA studies, an analysis and validation of differential patterns occur, following the aforementioned methodological steps and utilizing statistical packages or their updates.

It is noteworthy that although the systematic review has concluded and has yielded significant findings, the comprehensive analyses mentioned earlier are currently underway, as the latest PISA survey has been released [29]. Subsequently, a thorough examination of the data will be conducted, potentially leading to the anticipated outcomes detailed in the subsequent section. This sequential approach ensures a comprehensive and rigorous assessment of the data, maximizing understanding and the validity of the conclusions drawn.

3   Results

The completion of the entire study aims primarily to provide empirical results that address specific research question, validate proposed hypothesis, and achieve the objective. The goal was to bridge the existing gaps in our current understanding, primarily due to the rapid technological advancements people had to adapt to in order to be digitally competent in today's society and educational environment [30].

This study was clearly framed within applied research in the educational field, with a primary focus on enhancing digital competence, strengthening the literacy context within the family environment, and optimizing the educational system as a whole [31]. Its development was geared towards the overall improvement of educational quality, with the ultimate purpose of fostering high-level learning capable of generating positive impacts both economically and socially [32].

Currently, digital literacy, along with psychological and educational variables and the family context, are widely recognized as fundamental elements for effective learning, as well as for the full participation of individuals in society and the economy [33]. They are considered basic requirements for achieving significant social and labour inclusion. In this sense, the study acquired significant social value by addressing these crucial issues that directly impact people's lives [34].

The outcomes of the conducted systematic review not only reveal the escalating concern regarding the development of digital competence, reflected in the increased design and implementation of interventions aimed at competency development in recent years, alongside a rise in the number of systematic reviews. They also highlight a meticulous attention to psychoeducational variables, such as satisfaction, well-being or motivation. This is demonstrated through an escalating control over both variables via feedback meetings and satisfaction surveys within these interventions. (see Fig. 2).

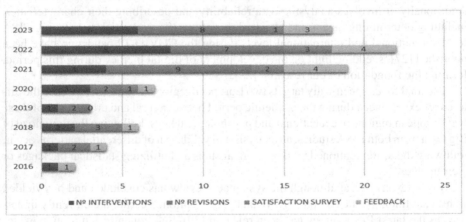

Fig. 2. Presentation of the results of the systematic review. Annual breakdown of interventions targeted at fostering digital competence; quantity of systematic reviews regarding digital competence acquisition; interventions integrating satisfaction surveys; interventions featuring ongoing feedback loops between participants and instructors.

Originally, the objective was to comprehend the involvement of families in fostering digital competence. This inquiry commenced with studies, exemplified by Casillas-Martín et al. [35], which underscored a direct correlation among these variables. The purpose was to ascertain whether this impact was interconnected with additional dimensions, such as academic achievement, personal contentment, overall well-being, or enjoyment, as scrutinized by Carrillo [36] with reference to global assessments. Nevertheless, up to that point, comprehensive associations among all these facets, whether examined individually or in the context of diverse geographical regions, had not been conclusively established, representing a key innovative aspect.

Subsequently, the focus shifted to understanding how much progress digital literacy had made during the pandemic and how the family had impacted this, evaluating its effects on satisfaction, personal well-being, and academic performance. Digital competence emerged as a fundamental element in this context. During the pandemic, several studies were conducted, for instance, to understand how online learning had affected students' satisfaction, examine gender differences in this aspect, or analyse the digital interaction between the family and school. However, the innovative aspect of our approach lies in conducting a comprehensive comparison to determine the extent of progress in digital literacy, assess family influence, and analyse its impact on satisfaction, personal well-being, and academic performance, contrasting among geographic regions.

Another uniqueness of the study lies in comparing rural and urban areas, providing evidence of differences in the development of digital competence [37]. These studies revealed the need to address deficiencies in teacher training for online teaching and highlighted the persistence of the digital divide between urban and rural areas. Together, these analyses provided an enlightening overview of how contextual factors influenced the adoption of digital competencies and their impact on the educational and personal environment.

For example, in our country, nearly 900,000 teachers had to adapt their teaching methods to online mode, revealing a lack of training and motivation to address this new educational scenario, which could have significantly affected students' education, satisfaction, and well-being [38]. Similarly, it allowed understanding differences based on cultural and geographical context. Thus, considering a comparative analysis between urban and rural areas was emphasized because although weaknesses related to the scarcity and limitations of access to technological resources and the Internet were gradually being overcome, there still seemed to be a digital divide between these scenarios.

The study provides a detailed and applied overview of digital literacy practices that were highlighted as essential from educational and family perspectives. It offers a clearer vision of which of these practices were most relevant and deserved primary attention in future interventions. Additionally, it identifies deficient aspects in this field that required more attention and development.

One of the most important contributions was the analysis of the changes experienced due to the rapid transition of the educational system and the family environment to the digital realm during the COVID-19 lockdown. This analysis encompasses an evaluation of the consequences this adaptation had on students' psychological and educational variables. The objective is to comprehend the impact of this transformation on factors such as academic achievement, student contentment, and psychological welfare. Moreover, it explores how these modifications could have affected the relationship between the educational and family environments in terms of digital literacy, identifying possible improvements and challenges arising from this unique situation. This deeper analysis not only identifies the areas of greatest impact but also those that required a more specific approach to achieving more effective and equitable digital literacy [39].

4 Discussion

This study aims primarily to shed light on the impact of the family environment on digital competency and psychological and educational variables such as satisfaction, personal well-being, and academic performance. It aims to further the understanding of digital literacy and its relationship with the family environment, an area that has received limited exploration thus far [40]. Additionally, for the first time, it provides scientific evidence of the rapid digitalization in education during the pandemic and analyses how these educational and psychological variables are interconnected, considering the role of families and differences among geographic areas [41].

This study tackles a number of open-ended questions on how families have affected the COVID-19 pandemic. First off, it makes it possible to comprehend how the home environment and digital literacy are related by doing a thorough analysis of data from international studies such as the 2018 PISA survey. Additionally, this project aims to comprehend the ways in which students' academic progress, well-being, and contentment may be impacted by their at-home digital literacy practices [42]. Furthermore, the objective is to conduct cross-national, cross-regional, and world-wide comparisons of these factors in order to underscore the disparities that exist between urban and rural areas [43].

The current study, focusing on the educational context and how the pandemic has influenced digital literacy and psychological aspects such as satisfaction, personal well-being, and academic performance, incorporating the family role, holds direct relevance in the educational and family dynamics. The resulting outcomes will offer practical and novel solutions that could enhance strategies and actions aimed at addressing these aspects, considering the family environment, prompting authorities to promote plans fostering literacy involving families.

The strategies for disseminating these results target educational professionals and families, aiming to directly impact students' digital literacy and psychological well-being. These activities will materialize as informative and formative actions implementable both in the educational environment and at home to ensure a practical and updated application of the findings.

In an applied approach, the dissemination of study results at educational and social levels adapts these actions to the key actors involved. Organizing seminars or courses focused on digital literacy is proposed, specifically geared towards fostering collaboration between schools and families. These courses would target teachers and educational professionals, offering continuous training or initial education for students, and families through Parent-Teacher Associations (PTAs) in educational centres, possibly through Parent Schools programs.

From a social perspective, these applied actions derived from the results aim to strengthen both the educational and family systems in our community. This not only would make them more competent and efficient in educating their students and children but could also translate into increased satisfaction, improved well-being, and a higher quality of child life. All of this, in turn, would have a positive impact on society as a whole.

The main research question was: "How has the persistent impact derived from the COVID-19 confinement affected the progression of digital proficiency and psychoeducational factors based on the out-comes demonstrated in the PISA study and subsequent dataset analyses?" While the literature review conducted for this study underscores a growing concern regarding the acquisition of digital competence, especially in the wake of the impact of the COVID-19 lockdown on education, a comprehensive understanding of its implications on specific psychoeducational variables requires further investigation. Therefore, to fully grasp the extent of this impact and its implications, we anticipate conducting additional research following the release and analysis of the 2022 PISA survey. It is important to note that the waiting period for this data represents a notable limitation of our current study. Nonetheless, the evident correlation between psychoeducational variables and the acquisition of digital competency underscores the significance of our research.

The objective has been achieved through a comprehensive literature review to explore the relationship between the acquisition of digital skills and psychoeducational variables such as motivation, satisfaction, academic performance, and well-being in family environments. Significant differences between studies conducted before and after the COVID-19 lockdown period were identified, and the influence of online education on the family environment was thoroughly analysed. However, we are awaiting the publication and analysis of the data from the PISA 2022 survey. This analysis will complete the study and empirically showcase the differences in diverse cultural and geographical contexts, providing a more comprehensive understanding of the effects of confinement on education and digital competencies.

The hypothesis predicting significant empirical differences pre- and post-pandemic in international studies, exploring psychoeducational patterns influenced by digital literacy and psychological variables across diverse cultures and demographics, has been substantiated through a thorough review of scientific literature. However, akin to the objective, to ascertain the extent of relationships between psychoeducational variables and digital competence alongside empirically validated cultural and demographic differences, the envisaged analyses across the outlined approaches need to be conducted. These analyses are essential to provide a comprehensive understanding of the nuanced connections and variations between these factors in different contexts.

5 Conclusions

This study centers on analyzing scientific literature and data from international datasets concerning the effects of the COVID-19 lockdown on education and social dynamics, particularly in relation to the development of digital competence. These skills have become crucial in today's context for the effective use of Information and Communication Technologies (ICT) and Artificial Intelligence (AI), both increasingly embedded in educational settings and society at large, posing new challenges for those navigating within it.

In the current era, the continuous emergence of new technologies underscores the importance of fostering appropriate digital skills. The process of attaining competence in the digital realm is not confined to an isolated situation. Thus, the evidence demonstrating the connection between the impact of the COVID-19 lockdown on digital competencies and its ramifications in both the family context and related psychoeducational variables is carefully examined.

The study undertakes a series of scientific literature assessments with the primary purpose of identifying the role played by families in the acquisition of digital competencies, also exploring the interrelations between this capability and aspects such as academic performance, satisfaction, enjoyment, and personal well-being.

Subsequent analyses are designed to comprehend the extent to which the lockdown has contributed to enhancing digital literacy, particularly highlighting the significance of this competence concerning satisfaction, well-being, and academic performance by comparing data from PISA studies between the years 2018 and 2022 across diverse cultural, geographical, and socioeconomic contexts.

Collectively, these analyses not only provide applied insights into relevant digital literacy practices in educational and family settings but also identify deficient areas, thus contributing to understanding the impact and transformations generated by adapting to the digital environment during the COVID-19 lockdown period.

References

1. Núñez, M., de Obesso, M.M., Pérez, C.A.: New challenges in higher education: a study of the digital competence of educator in COVID times. Technol. Forecast. Soc. Chang. **174**, 1–13 (2022). https://doi.org/10.1016/j.techfore.2021.121270
2. Vishnu, S., et al.: Digital competence OG higher education learner in the context of COVID-19 triggered online learning. Soc. Sci. Hum. Open **6**(1), 100320 (2022). https://doi.org/10.1016/j.ssaho.2022.100320
3. INTEF Marco Común de Competencia Digital Docente. Ministerio de Educación, Cultura y Deporte. https://bit.ly/2jqkssz. Accessed 05 Jan 2024
4. Prahani, B.K., Rizki, I.A., Jatmiko, B., Suprapto, N., Amelia, T.: Artificial intelligence n education research during the last ten years: a review and bibliometric study. Int. J. Emerg. Technol. Learn. **17**(8), 169–188 (2022). https://doi.org/10.3991/ijet.v17i08.29833
5. Flores-Vivar, J.M., García-Peñalvo, F.J.: Reflections on the ethics, potential, and challenges of artificial intelligence in the framework of quality education (SDG4). Comunicar **31**(74), 37–47 (2023). https://doi.org/10.3916/C74-2023-03
6. Saltos, G.D.C., Oyarvide, W.V., Sánchez, E.A., Reyes, Y.M.: Análisis bibliométrico sobre estudios de la neurociencia, la inteligencia artificial y la robótica: énfasis en las tecnologías disruptivas en educación. Salud, Ciencia y Tecnología **3**, 362 (2023). https://doi.org/10.56294/saludcyt2023362
7. ISTE (Ed.) NETS for teachers: National educational technology standards for teachers. https://bit.ly/2UaLExK. Accessed 05 Jan 2024
8. UNESCO. http://goo.gl/pGPDGv. Accessed 05 Jan 2024
9. Parlamento Europeo y Consejo de la Unión Europea.: Recomendación de 18 de diciembre de 2006 sobre las competencias clave para el aprendizaje permanente. Diario Oficial de la Unión europea 30(12), (2006). http://data.europa.eu/eli/reco/2006/962/oj
10. Hinojo, F.J., Leiva, J.J.: Competencia Digital e Interculturalidad: Hacia una Escuela Inclusiva y en Red. REICE. Revista Iberoamericana Sobre Calidad, Eficacia Y Cambio En Educación **20**(2), 5–9 (2022). https://doi.org/10.15366/reice2022.20.2
11. Hurtado-Martín, M., López-Torres, L., Santín, D., Sicilia, G., Simancas, R.: El impacto del COVID-19 en el aprendizaje durante el confinamiento. Educación XX1 **26**(1), 185–205 (2023). https://doi.org/10.5944/educxx1.33047

12. Lacomba-Trejo, L., Schoeps, K., Valero-Moreno, S., Del Rosario, C., Montoya-Castilla, I.: Teachers' response to stress, anxiety and depression during COVID-19 lockdown: what have we learned from the pandemic? J. Sch. Health **92**(9), 864–872 (2022). https://doi.org/10.1111/josh.13192
13. Guillén, M.E., Tirado, D.M., Sánchez, A.R.: The impact of COVID-19 on university students and competences in education for sustainable development: emotional intelligence, resilience and engagement. J. Clean. Prod. **380**, 135057 (2022). https://doi.org/10.1016/j.jclepro.2022.135057
14. Martínez-Comesaña, M., Rigueira-Díaz, X., Larrañaga-Janeiro, A., Martínez-Torres, J., Ocarranza-Prado, I., Kreibel, D.: Impacto de la inteligencia artificial en los métodos de evaluación en la educación primaria y secundaria: revisión sistemática de la literatura. Revista de Psicodidáctica **28**(2), 93–103 (2023). https://doi.org/10.1016/j.psicod.2023.06.001
15. Gómez-Trigueros, I.M., Binimelis, J.: Aprender y enseñar con la escala del mapa para el profesorado de la "generación Z": la competencia digital docente. Revista electrónica de recursos en Internet sobre geografía y ciencias sociales **238**, 1–18 (2020). https://doi.org/10.1344/ara2020.238.30561
16. León-Nabal, B., Zhang-Yu, C., Lalueza, J.L.: Uses of digital mediation in the school-families relationship during the COVID-19 pandemic. Front. Psychol. **12**, 687400 (2021). https://doi.org/10.3389/fpsyg.2021.687400
17. Gutiérrez, N., Mercader Rubio, I., Trigueros Ramos, R., Oropesa Ruiz, N.F., García-Sánchez, J.N., García Martín, J.: Digital competence, use, actions and time dedicated to digital devices: repercussions on the interpersonal relationships of Spanish adolescents. Int. J. Environ. Res. Public Health **19**(16), 10358 (2022). https://doi.org/10.3390/ijerph191610358
18. González-Calvo, G., Barba-Martín, R., Bores-García, D., Gallego-Lema, V.: Learning to be a teacher without being in the classroom: COVID-19 as a threat to the professional development of future teacher. International and Multidisciplinary J. Soc. Sci. **2**(9), 46–71 (2020). https://doi.org/10.17583/rimcis.2020.5783
19. Younas, M., Noor, U., Zhou, X., Menhas, R., Qingyu, X.: COVID-19, students' satisfaction about e-learning and academic achievement: Mediating analysis of online influencing factors. Front. Psychol. **13**, 948061 (2022). https://doi.org/10.3389/fpsyg.2022.948061
20. Ramírez, A.A., Cruz, L.M.Z.: Educación (rural) en tiempos de pandemia: brecha digital y desigualdad social. Espacio Sociológico **2**(2), 74–89 (2022). https://repository.unad.edu.co/handle/10596/51903
21. Miller, D.M., Scott, C.E., McTigue, E.M.: Writing in the secondary-level disciplines: a systematic review of context, cognition and content. Educ. Psychol. Rev. **30**(1), 83–120 (2016). https://doi.org/10.1007/s10648-016-9393-z
22. Scott, C.E., McTigue, E.M., Miller, D.M., Washburn, E.K.: The what, when, and how of preservice teachers and literacy across the disciplines: a systematic literature review of nearly 50 years of research. Teach. Teach. Educ. **73**, 1–13 (2018). https://doi.org/10.1016/j.tate.2018.03.010
23. Cooper, R., Junginger, S., Lockwood, T.: Design thinking and design management: a research and practice perspective. Des. Manage. Rev. **20**(2), 46–55 (2009). https://doi.org/10.1111/j.1948-7169.2009.00007.x
24. Risko, V.J., et al.: A critical analysis of research on reading teacher education. Reading Res. Q. **43**(3), 252–288 (2011). https://doi.org/10.1598/RRQ.43.3.3
25. Torgerson, C.J.: The quality of systematic reviews of effectiveness in literacy learning in English: a 'tertiary'review. J. Res. Reading **30**(3), 287–315 (2007). https://doi.org/10.1111/j.1467-9817.2006.00318.x
26. Page, J., et al.: Declaración PRISMA 2020: una guía actualizada para la publicación de revisiones sistemáticas. Rev. Esp. Cardiol. **74**(9), 790–799 (2021). https://doi.org/10.1016/j.recesp.2021.06.016

27. Sales Ferrús, M.: La estructura relacional de la tecnología en PISA. Un diagnóstico por países con factores personales y contextuales. PhD diss., Universitat de València (2022). https://hdl.handle.net/10550/83515

28. Picón, G.A., de Caballero, G.K.G., Sánchez, J.N.P.: Desempeño y formación docente en competencias digitales en clases no presenciales durante la pandemia COVID-19. Arandu utic **8**(1), 139–153 (2021). https://doi.org/10.1590/scielopreprints.778

29. Díaz-Burgos, A., García-Sánchez, J.N., Álvarez-Fernández, M.L., de Brito-Costa, S.M.: Psychological and educational factors of digital competence optimization interventions pre-and post-COVID-19 lockdown: a systematic review. Sustainability **16**(1), 51 (2024). https://doi.org/10.3390/su16010051

30. Guajala, W.H.G., Párraga, R.J.C., Carrillo, V.O.R., Andrade, M.F.B.: El uso de herramientas tecnológicas en las capacitaciones en TIC's y su impacto en el aprendizaje y la adquisición de habilidades. Código Científico Revista de Investigación **4**(E1), 234–253 (2023). https://doi.org/10.55813/gaea/ccri/v4/nE1/95

31. Ullauri, R.H.B., Guachun, B.F.G., Inga, J.H.S.: Optimización de la inteligencia artificial en la educación a través de estrategias docentes eficaces. Revista Invecom **3**(2), 1 (2023). https://doi.org/10.5281/zenodo.8078717

32. Armas-Alba, L., Alonso-Rodríguez, I.: Las TIC y competencia digital en la respuesta a las necesidades educativas especiales durante la pandemia: Una revisión sistemática. Revista Internacional de Pedagogía e Innovación Educativa **2**(1), 11–48 (2021). https://doi.org/10.51660/ripie.v2i1.58

33. Carlos Enrique George-Reyes: Imbricación del pensamiento computacional y la alfabetización digital en la educación. Modelación a partir de una revisión sistemática de la literatura. Revista Española de Documentación Científica **46**(1), e345 (2023). https://doi.org/10.3989/redc.2023.1.1922

34. Rodríguez, A.I., González, Y.M., Martín, A.H.: Evaluación de la competencia digital del alumnado de Educación Primaria. Revista de Investigación Educativa **41**(1), 33–50 (2023). https://doi.org/10.6018/rie.520091

35. Casillas-Martín, S., Cabezas-González, M., Muñoz-Repiso, A.G.V., Basilotta-Gómez-Pablos, V.: Modelos de mediación sociofamiliares en el desarrollo de la competencia digital. Revista Electrónica de Investigación Educativa **23**, 1–18 (2021). https://doi.org/10.24320/redie.2021.23.e26.3839

36. José Antonio Ortega Carrillo: El bienestar en las instituciones educativas como factor de calidad. Etic@net. Revista científica electrónica de Educación y Comunicación en la Sociedad del Conocimiento **19**(2), I–III (2019). https://doi.org/10.30827/eticanet.v19i2.11846

37. Pavez, I.: Nativos digitales? Percepción de habilidades en niños y niñas de zonas rurales. Cuadernos de Investigación Educativa **14**(1), e206 (2023). https://doi.org/10.18861/cied.2023.14.1.3282

38. Cruz, O.R., Benítez, J.: La crisis también puede promover el aprendizaje, imparto del COVID-19 en prácticas docentes. Revista Latinoamericana de Estudios Educativos Nueva Época **50**, 291–302 (2020). https://doi.org/10.48102/rlee.2020.50.especial.114

39. Peng, D., Yu, Z.: A literature review of digital literacy over two decades. Educ. Res. Int. **2022**, 1–8 (2022). https://doi.org/10.1155/2022/2533413

40. Linde-Valenzuela, T., Guillén-Gámez, F.D., Devitt, A.: Digital literacy of teachers, families, and students for virtual participation in school: a multiple comparison analysis. IEEE Revista Iberoamericana de Tecnologias del Aprendizaje **17**(1), 1–8 (2022). https://doi.org/10.1109/RITA.2022.3149800

41. Casillas-Martín, S., Cabezas-González, M., Muñoz-Repiso, A.G.V.: Influencia de variables sociofamiliares en la competencia digital en comunicación y colaboración: [Influence of socio-familial variables on digital competence in communication and collaboration]. Pixel-Bit Revista de Medios y Educación **63**, 7–33 (2022). https://doi.org/10.12795/pixelbit.84595

42. Chiu, T.K., Sun, J.C.Y., Ismailov, M.: Investigating the relationship of technology learning support to digital literacy from the perspective of self-determination theory. Educ. Psychol. **42**(10), 1263–1282 (2022). https://doi.org/10.1080/01443410.2022.2074966
43. Braesemann, F., Lehdonvirta, V., Kässi, O.: ICTs and the urban-rural divide: can online labour platforms bridge the gap? Inf. Commun. Soc.Commun. Soc. **25**(1), 34–54 (2022). https://doi.org/10.1080/1369118X.2020.1761857

Learning in a High-Speed Society: Inquiring Deceleration by Digital Means

Andre Uibos[1] and Alexandra Milyakina[2(✉)]

[1] Institute of Social Sciences, University of Tartu, Lossi 36, 51003 Tartu, Estonia
`andre.uibos@ut.ee`
[2] Institute of Philosophy and Semiotics, University of Tartu, Jakobi 2, 51014 Tartu, Estonia
`milyakin@ut.ee`

Abstract. Learning is constantly restructuring itself along with our societal and communicative systems. Social acceleration and its enablers in both macro- and micro-levels can be regarded as one of the dominant forms of nowadays social reality. It is definitely necessary to observe how new forms of education act within this process. Whereas the increasingly mediatized world is characterized by fragmentation and social acceleration, we would like to explore the possibilities for grounding and deceleration offered by digital pedagogy. Using the multimodal approach and cultural semiotic analysis, we will investigate the temporal aspects of new media on the example of "Education on Screen", a digital learning environment developed at the University of Tartu (Estonia). The results are based on the analysis of 61 learning activities created and tested since 2017. The paper looks into the connection between the degree of multimodality and acceleration, while defining potential solutions for slowing down the "fast media" through the processes of analysis and design. Is there a definite discrepancy between the increasing speed and agency of media versus the logic of education and knowledge development, or can it be overcome? Addressing this question enables for better execution of education practices, especially considering the limited natural capacity of humans to retain information and develop knowledge. Inquiring into deceleration in learning environments additionally addresses the topic of temporal structures in learning: the speed at which data is created in relation to how fast it is semiotically processed. Addressing such questions, research findings in this study suggest that use of multimodality in EoS can contribute to meaningful deceleration of the learning process.

Keywords: Digital Learning · Multimodality · Semiotics of Culture · Social Acceleration · Deceleration

1 Introduction

Transformations in how we learn things are imminent. In order to address the details of what has happened and what is happening with digital learning environments (DLEs) in the sense of research, it is useful to first and foremost inspect the drive behind the use of DLEs. It is apparent that the drive has numerous sides to it. One possible description

Ł. Tomczyk (Ed.): NMP 2023, CCIS 2130, pp. 184–196, 2024.
https://doi.org/10.1007/978-3-031-63235-8_12

of these sides is as such: the use of DLEs is driven by a) technology, b) societal need, c) properties of the subjects themselves. How have these three aspects changed in recent times in relation to learning? In a sense, all three of the so-called variables participate in Polanyi's double movement [1], which entails that, on the one hand, there is a definite direction for changes within DLEs towards progressive ideas, and, on the other hand, there are numerous complexities in adapting those ideas.

Firstly, there seem to be no boundaries for creating new digital environments, nor for their massive adaptation for almost all age groups. At the same time, there's an ongoing effort to regulate the use of digital technology within society, considering by whom, when and what for are digital devices being used. Secondly, whereas the societal need for digital learning environments has been increasingly evident in recent years, the COVID-enhanced digital turn appears to be exhausting itself, as not all areas of social life can be comfortably digitized without psychological or practical backlashes. Finally, the content of what is semiotically processed by society is ever-changing, alongside the structure of the society. While it is apparent that a lot of meaningful content has found its representation in the digital world, certain social processes are focused on regulating the unforeseen aspects of such accelerated digitalization (including ethics, mental health, organizational problems). Such a double movement within the progress of the digital turn cannot be disregarded in this paper, since the transformations within the temporal structures of DLEs bear the same quality.

A peculiar characteristic of the general logic within modernization stems from Hartmut Rosa's theory [2, 3], which suggests that a common mechanism behind modernization of societal systems presents itself as social acceleration. In the context of DLEs, temporal properties have definite and intuitive expressions. At the macro level, the pace at which learning occurs aligns with the development of society. Recent turbulent events like COVID-19 pandemics and wars have caused a need for restructuring of these systems, incorporating digital measures among other strategies. It has also morphed the temporal-spatial structure of learning, affecting the timing, location and speed of learning processes. At the micro level, these aspects converge, putting significant emphasis on the learner's capabilities, including general psychology and mental well-being, motivation, efficiency, etc. A critical investigation of these factors is crucial for the evidence-driven development of learning environments. How to overcome the discrepancy between the speed of media-driven changes and the logic of education in its traditional form, which is aligned with the human capacity to semiotically process information? In search of the possible answer, we will follow the path set by Wajcman, whose work explores "the mutual shaping or coevolution of new technologies and temporal rhythms" [4].

Within the theory of social acceleration, the increasing speed of social processes is conceptually intertwined with deceleration. While acceleration is to be seen as the dominant direction of societal changes, it is naturally ridden with moments of deceleration. These moments can become of great value, especially when acceleration fundamentally alters the structures of social life. Whereas acceleration is eminent and often necessary and attractive for users of DLEs, we believe that the "counterbalance" of decelerating the learning processes is necessary to sustain the integrity of knowledge accumulation. Research in this area is, however, scarce: temporal structures are often treated within certain sets of affordances of DLEs and a focus on deceleration is even more rare. Therefore, we aim to approach this gap of research for at least preliminary inquiries into the topic of deceleration within the development and use of DLEs.

The paper employs the framework of multimodal analysis and cultural semiotics to analyze 61 learning activities across six different DLEs. In line with the principles of multimodal pedagogy [9], activities are described from the perspective of selection, analysis, and design. Cultural semiotic approach allows considering DLEs in the context of general cultural dynamics – as a tool for synthesizing textual fragments from accelerated media structures and promoting deceleration through meaningful interaction with them.

2 Material

The notion of a digital learning environment includes a wide range of phenomena, starting from learning management systems (LMS) to virtual reality (VR) classrooms. This paper will focus on a specific type of DLEs defined as "an Internet-based environment that organizes different educational resources and offers tools for engaging with them" [5]. The field of DLEs is constantly expanding, including both large-scale initiatives, such as Big History Project [6], as well as independent teacher-made resources [7].

Education on Screen (EoS) [8] is an open-access digital learning environment developed by the Transmedia Research Group at the Department of Semiotics of the University of Tartu. Since its foundation in 2015, the group has created six digital courses based on key texts of Estonian culture and their adaptations, as well as some smaller projects. The materials have so far been tested by more than 400 people, including students of Estonian schools, university students, teachers, and the participants of different workshops. Most of the materials are available in Estonian, English and Russian languages.

Each course is centered around a specific artistic text, which is introduced not only in its original form, but also through multiple adaptations and translations. Equipped with theoretical materials and methodological tools offered by the platform, learners are encouraged to explore diverse forms of literary experience: from full-length texts of the novels and their film adaptations to memes, video games, rap songs and fan art. Each project provides a theoretical introduction, discussion questions, interactive tasks, ideas for creative projects, a list of references and teachers' guidelines. The content is divided into bite-sized modules, which allows educators to build customized lesson plans for different purposes. The projects analyzed in this paper are introduced below.

Literature on Screen (LoS), 2017, is based on the Estonian folklore-inspired novel *Old Barney or November* by Andrus Kivirähk (2000) and its cinematic adaptation *November* (2017). The course follows the whole lifecycle of artistic text: from exploring the prototexts of the novel to tracking its transformation into a script, storyboard, film, fan art, etc.

History on Screen (HoS), 2018, centers around a semi-autobiographical novel by Leelo Tungal (*Comrade Child and Grownups*, 2008) and its adaptation *The Little Comrade* (2018). The novel describes the Stalinist regime in Estonia through the eyes of a small girl, whose mother has been deported to Siberia. The course introduces the cultural background and discusses different approaches to memory and history.

Identity on Screen (IoS), 2019, is based on the novel *Truth and Justice* (1926–1933) by a major Estonian writer Anton Hansen Tammsaare and eponymous cinematic adaptation (2019). The platform uses these texts as illustrations to discuss various issues related to the problem of identity: interpersonal relations, national belonging and living environment.

Nature on Screen (NoS), 2020, is focused on the legacy of Estonian biologist and nature photographer Fred Jüssi as represented in the film *The Beauty of Being* (2020). This project-based course acquaints learners with different methods of mediating nature through film, word, sound and image.

Estonian Film Classics (EFC), 2021–2022, discusses three films – *Spring* (original title *Kevade*, 1969), The Last Relic (original title *Viimne reliikvia*, 1969), Dead Mountaineer's Hotel (original title *"Hukkunud Alpinisti" hotell*, 1979) – through the prism of different topics, which include popular culture, political context and audio-visual identity.

Dostoevsky on Screen (DoS), 2023, analyzes the life and work of Fyodor Dostoevsky against the background of its adaptations in contemporary culture (memes, graphic novels, video games and many more).

To explore the latent characteristics of DLEs in terms of acceleration and deceleration, we have mapped all the activities offered by the abovementioned platforms, which totals 61 elements. The analysis did not take into account informational elements (introductory texts, infographics, video lectures), or discussion questions that did not prompt anything beyond reflection. All the elements analyzed in this paper require either interaction with the interface of the platform (taking a quiz, performing an action) or the creation of artifacts by students (writing an essay, making a collage, filming a video, etc.).

3 Methodology

The analysis is divided into two stages – multimodal analysis of the elements and application of the cultural semiotic framework. As one of the authors has been actively involved in the development and testing of EoS since its very beginning, the analysis makes use of the auto-ethnographic approach and draws inspiration from field notes, feedback surveys, and multimodal artifacts created by the learners.

By drawing upon Hartmut Rosa's social acceleration theory [3, 4], the principles of multimodal pedagogy [9], and various skills taxonomies [10, 11], we analyze multimodal affordances of the elements and the processes facilitated by them. Simultaneously, we assess the autonomy of each task, determining whether it offers all necessary resources, tools and functions, or requires the engagement of additional materials. Whereas there are no certain indicators linked with acceleration and deceleration, some parameters can still be correlated with the former or latter. In the following analysis, we will predominantly associate multimodality with deceleration. We view the use of DLEs as goal-oriented semiotic processing of information for learning purposes, in which the use of multimodality increases the semiotic complexity of the subjects. Such an increase of semiotic complexity means more meaningful elements within the interpretative system of the learner, which subsequently decelerates temporal structures of effective learning (notably orientation and comprehension).

The second stage of analysis aims at identifying the place of DLEs in the system of education [12] and overall cultural dynamics [13–15]. We investigate techniques for slowing down the "fast media", such as analyzing a phenomenon through the corpus of its media versions (for instance, memes and adaptations of a literary text), or engaging in critical multimodal analysis of media artifacts. On this conceptual level, a digital learning platform is considered as an element of cultural autocommunication, which can be defined as the self-communication of culture through constant repetition and transformation of texts [16].

The following subsections introduce the main three parameters of the analysis – modes, processes and autonomy.

3.1 Modes

Mode is defined as "a socially shaped and culturally given semiotic resource for making meaning" [9]. Whereas written or spoken word continues to preserve its dominant status, all human communication is by definition multimodal, as it engages several modalities at once. For instance, a written text can be considered as a multimodal phenomenon, as it employs the modes of font, color and composition. Modal affordances can be discussed from the perspective of gains and losses, as the semiotic reach of different modes "is always specific and partial in all cultures" (Ibid.). The multimodal perspective on communication resonates with a fundamental principle of the semiotics of culture, which regards the existence of at least two cultural languages as the main mechanism of culture [13]. The partial untranslatability between different languages of culture (for instance, verbal and visual), implies that loss in translation should be compensated with creative means. As a result of this transduction (remaking meaning across modes), the original message is augmented by additional meanings.

According to the multimodal approach, the process of communication unfolds through the following stages: "Interest shapes attention, which produces engagement leading to selection of elements from the message, leading to a framing of these elements, which leads to their transformation and transduction, which produces a new ('inner') sign'" [9]. After Kress, we will refer to a **prompt** (message provided to an individual) as the starting point of communication and consider a new sign (created by an individual) – sometimes materialized in the form of an **artifact** – as an indication of its results [9]. Both prompts and artifacts will be described from the perspective of modes involved in their production; in the case of EoS, these include word, image, sound, video, hyperlinks, and buttons suggesting different functionality (play, radio, restart, shuffle, save, etc.).

The effect of multimodality on time relations is quite a complex issue. Different time logics can correspond to different modes (e.g. images - asynchronous, video - diachronous, texts - hyperchronous etc.). Thus, it is possible to knowingly or unknowingly produce many combinations of second-order time logics in a creative process. Multimodality can morph time-logic, while subsequently increasing the semiotic complexity of the content. This semiotic complexity gives more possibilities for interpretations, thus giving the option for the learner to decelerate the learning process. At the same time, our assessment of the learning pace remains inherently relative, as it always depends on the social circumstances. After Kress, we will favor the circumstances that "offer flexibility of sensory engagement with the environment" and "allows adaptation of previous knowledge drawn from heterogeneous phenomena" [9].

3.2 Processes

Modal affordances of a prompt/artifact can only suggest a meaningful communication, but do not guarantee it. The analysis of modal structure needs to be complemented with the evaluation of the processes facilitated by it. While discussing the affordances of digital technology, Kress warns against the odds of the habitus, "where agency is first of all a matter of selection among template-based options" [9]. This habitus manifests itself in the constant reuse of ready-made materials (for instance, the most popular social media practices include remixing already existing content and applying filters) rather than creating new ones from scratch.

From the perspective of learning, "representation-as-selection" is seen as less demanding than "representation-as-creation" [9]. The multimodal approach regards design as the most complex and meaningful manifestation of a learner's agency and contrasts it with simpler strategies of meaning-making – "competence" that implies mere understanding and "critique" that challenges the prompt without proactively transforming it. By drawing on both competence and critique, design "carries their insights forward and deepens them" and "focuses on my interests now in relation to the likely future effects of my actions" [9]. This aligns with the findings in cognitive research [10], according to which remembrance and understanding refer to the lowest cognitive domains, application and analysis belong to the middle, whereas evaluation and creation exemplify the most sophisticated cognitive processes. Finally, the analysis is informed by the taxonomy of educational games by Kapp [11] who considered matching and collecting as the simplest types of activities, while listed strategizing and building among the most complex ones.

According to Kress, the learning process should be framed to promote "awareness" in the selection, "full understanding and creative and transformative use of templates", and "a willingness to challenge the boundaries of what is provided" [9]. In the course of the analysis, we will link the elements of EoS to different processes – **selection, analysis** or **design**. For instance, multiple-choice quizzes or matching games are likely to be associated with selection, whereas creative tasks usually require design. Additionally, we will consider the framing of the activities: whether they imply creation from scratch or "remixing"; integrating previous knowledge versus using the given resources; collaboration or individual work. These parameters can be also considered from the perspective of autonomy, which is discussed in the following subsection.

3.3 Autonomy

Autonomy itself is a crucial idea in understanding (technical) acceleration within social processes. On the one hand, the autonomy of DLEs enables the user to spend less time navigating between different sources of information in order to complete a specific task. On the other hand, the autonomy of DLEs is often conditional as it is paired with the subject itself, which is often an external corpus of information. For environments that deal with large corpora of external information, this characteristic is important for understanding the effects of autonomy on time structures. In this case, the temporal qualities of DLEs can be viewed as task-oriented: is it possible to complete a task without leaving the platform (or doing anything extra offline)?

Elements of analysis inquiring into the autonomy of DLEs are the following:

- **Resources**: is all the information present on the website or the use of external resources is required?
- **Tools**: are all the required tools offered on the website or is the use of external tools required (digital or analog)?
- **Feedback**: is instant feedback provided or human input (by teachers or peers) required?
- **Memory**: does the task offer "save" or "send" functionality?

4 Results

The results stem from analyzing 61 elements across six learning environments. Since the projects vary in scale, the number of activities differs across each environment: LoS features 6 activities, HoS – 15, IoS – 13, NoS – 4, EFC – 17, DoS – 6. Moreover, the quantity and quality of activities reflect the evolution of the creators' perspectives on instructional design: whereas the content offered at LoS was largely shaped by formal education conventions, subsequent projects delved into more experimental formats. This evolution also concerns the aspects of time: the first environment did not make much use of acceleratory features, while the later projects featured multiple choice questions and drag-and-drop exercises, which were, however, dismissed in the most recent projects in favor of more time-consuming tasks. In the following subsections, we discuss the tasks from the perspective of modes, activities, and autonomy, as well as provide a cultural semiotic commentary on the whole project.

4.1 Multimodal Analysis

Whereas some of the findings may appear self-evident, it is nevertheless crucial to support abstract theories with empirical studies, since, as demonstrated by Wajcman [4], our understanding of time and technology is often affected by myths and misconceptions.

The analysis indicates that the modal complexity of the element correlates with different semiotic processes [9] and educational objectives [10], as well as with the degree of the element's autonomy. The results presented in Table 1 are not absolute, but signify the high likelihood of elements to possess certain characteristics.

For instance, selection-centered activities, such as quizzes or drag-and-drop tasks, are likely to be multimodal and not lead to the creation of any artifacts by learners. In this case, a significant amount of semiotic work is done by the creator of the task, who has to select learning materials, provide tools for interacting with them, and prepare an automatic feedback for different outcomes. The semiotic work of a learner in this scenario is limited to clicking at a correct option. At the same time, the analysis-oriented activities are associated with monomodal artifacts, as spoken or written words remain the most conventional means for describing and comparing materials. Finally, design-based tasks tend to be most open in terms of modal structure and autonomy, since the

Table 1. Correlation of processes facilitated by activities with different modal structures and levels of autonomy.

Processes	Modes		Autonomy			
	prompt	artifact	resources	tools	feedback	save/send
selection	multimodal	–	+	+	+	+
analysis	multimodal	monomodal	+	–	–	+
design	multimodal	multimodal	–	–	–	–

multimodal approach to design implies independent choice of resources, tools, and even assessment formats by the learner (so that they cannot be pre-defined by the educator).

The tasks associated with **selection** (and, correspondingly, with lower cognitive levels of remembrance and understanding) are likely to have multimodal prompts, since drag-and-drop tasks and quizzes employ words, hyperlinks, buttons and occasionally incorporate images, sounds and video. However, such simpler activities usually do not require the creation of any artifacts by students. Most activities can be categorized into three types: arranging elements on a timeline, completing a multiple-choice quiz, and matching elements using the drag-and-drop function.

Interestingly, the tasks tagged as **analytical** are less likely to result in multimodal artifacts, even though the prompts themselves can be multimodal. Such tasks most closely resemble activities associated with traditional formal education. For instance, learners are asked to search a novel for certain keywords and make a review, analyze a selection of audio-visual materials, or write a reflection on the basis of a prompt. Almost all tasks of this type require the creation of an artifact in a monomodal – verbal – form. This demonstrates that, at least for the developers of the environments, the process of analysis remains predominantly linked to the written or spoken word.

Finally, all the activities associated with the process of **design** (or the level of creativity of Anderson & Krahtwohl's taxonomy) suggest that both the prompts and the resulting artifacts are multimodal or that the artifacts are created by means of transduction (for instance, from a visual mode into a verbal one). The tasks range from developing a new character based on the analysis of a text to interviewing family members on a specific topic and presenting the results in a multimodal form (Table 2).

In line with Kress' understanding [9], different types of processes do not exist separately but build upon each other: thus, the analysis is preceded by a stage of selection, while design requires selection and analysis. The scaffolding nature of learning is particularly apparent in creative tasks, which frequently involve reusing and remixing existing materials, such as video clips, excerpts from a novel, images, etc. For instance, a task categorized as design may imply: 1) selecting suitable elements from a range of prompts; 2) analyzing the selection (for instance, identifying common features in different media depictions of the same character); 3) synthesizing available elements with the learner's own additions to create a new text (see Fig. 1).

From the perspective of **autonomy**, simpler processes are more likely to be facilitated by fully autonomous elements. Thus, most tasks associated with selection – multiple

Table 2. Types of prompts and artifacts associated with selection-, analysis- and design-based activities.

	Selection	Analysis	Design
Examples of activities	Arranging events on a timeline; matching concepts with their visual representations; taking a quiz	Searching the novel for keywords; analyzing representations of an object in different media; comparing different texts	Taking interviews and making a collage based on them; recording a soundscape, creating a meme
Prompt	Matching tasks, arranging tasks, multiple-choice quizzes	Materials in different media (verbal text, multimedia collection)	Recommendations for obtaining materials
Artifact	–	Verbal report (written or oral)	Mood board, collage, video, photo, audio recording, meme

Fig. 1. Design-based activity. Guidelines for making creative retellings of Oskar Luts' "Spring". Estonian Film Classics [8].

choice quizzes, drag-and-drop games, etc. – do not require external resources or tools, while offering instant feedback and an opportunity to save or/and send the results (see Fig. 2). Analytical tasks are usually autonomous only in terms of resources (for instance, they can provide a selection of the materials for the analysis). Finally, elements associated with the process of design usually require learners to find the materials and choose the tools themselves (although some recommendations could be provided), whereas the evaluation occurs either by an educator or in group discussions. To sum up, the more complex and demanding the task, the less likely it is to be handled within a single platform.

To complement these observations with our personal experience in developing and testing the tasks, we may add that the shortcomings of some tasks can be compensated by mixing several approaches together. For instance, while the need to acquire resources

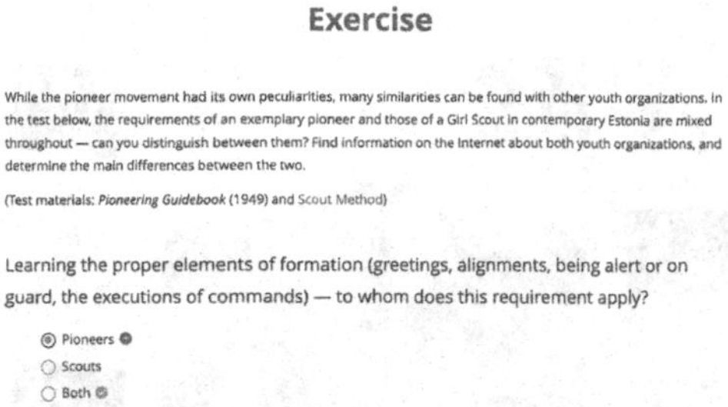

Exercise

While the pioneer movement had its own peculiarities, many similarities can be found with other youth organizations. In the test below, the requirements of an exemplary pioneer and those of a Girl Scout in contemporary Estonia are mixed throughout — can you distinguish between them? Find information on the Internet about both youth organizations, and determine the main differences between the two.

(Test materials: *Pioneering Guidebook* (1949) and Scout Method)

Learning the proper elements of formation (greetings, alignments, being alert or on guard, the executions of commands) — to whom does this requirement apply?

- ⊙ Pioneers ●
- ○ Scouts
- ○ Both ●

Fig. 2. Selection-based activity. Quiz "Soviet Pioneers or Contemporary Girl Scouts?". History on Screen [8].

and tools from external sources can indeed decelerate the learning process, it can also pose an obstacle to task completion. To prevent this, it is possible to offer a selection of hyperlinks to potential solutions; however, it is crucial not to insist on one specific tool or resource. At the same time, selection-based tasks could be made more complex by adding an analytical or/and creative level. This method was used in some tasks, which combined a simple exercise with an additional task: for instance, learners were asked to match concepts with their visual interpretations and come up with their own new pair; or to choose a soundtrack for a scene from the list of songs and make their own suggestions.

4.2 Cultural Semiotic Perspective

Whereas multimodal analysis focuses on the affordances of different elements and semiotic processes facilitated by them, semiotics of culture offers a holistic perspective on DLEs within the wider cultural framework. Embracing the mission outlined by Scolari et al. [17], we consider EoS as a tool for reducing the gap between students' increasingly digital informal lives and the rigid structures of formal education. To use a semiotic vocabulary, a digital learning environment can be seen as a membrane, or a filter, "passing through which the text is translated into another language (or languages), situated outside the given semiosphere" [14]. This relates to the semiotic phenomenon of stereoscopicity – "the possibility of getting a completely different projection of the same reality, its translation into a completely different language" [15]. In the case of EoS, we can speak of two independent spheres – one of the everyday life of learners largely affected by the processes of acceleration, and the sphere of formal education that historically values diligence and thoroughness more than spontaneity and speed. EoS is designed to align these two temporal regimes: the fragments and adaptations of classic texts (memes, comic strips, Youtube videos, posts on social media and other formats that make up a large portion of young people's media environment) are brought together on a digital platform and synthesized in a new whole, which, in its turn, has to be explored with diligence and care. Digital learning environment can be compared to an archive, as it aims "to frame and re-frame, connect and re-connect, their various composite texts, in this way creating new textual wholes at a 'higher' level, or simply in terms of actual 'reading' sequences" [18].

Whereas the everyday semiotic actions are coming to be seen as predominantly selection-driven [9], the activities offered at EoS suggest more sophisticated processes

Fig. 3. Transmedia world of Oskar Luts' "Spring". Estonian Film Classics [8].

of analysis and design. The pedagogical strategies balance between close and distant reading: on the one hand, students are encouraged to analyze chosen texts in close detail; on the other hand, they can observe the universal cultural dynamics by exploring a vast variety of phenomena as a corpus (see Fig. 3). EoS presents multiple adaptations and fragments in a dialectic arrangement to "bring out the original in a way otherwise not possible" [12]. By interacting with the elements of the environment, learners are actively "reverse-engineering" the original text, which implies a shift of some semiotic work from makers to users and from teachers to students [19]. We believe that a partial reading on a digital platform "serves a holistic purpose, i.e., harnessing the affordances of digital media convergence, textual fragments are presented in a manner that allows for the creation of a holistic understanding of the text" [20]. At the same time, the creators' intentions might not always play out as planned: regardless of the instructional design, the students are likely to interact with the environment based on their personal interests, which may not necessarily align with those of the instructor [9]. However, within a multimodal approach, this could be considered as an advantage rather than a drawback. Rather than imposing learning aims onto students, an educator is seen as a knowledge facilitator, or cultural translator [17], who provides navigational aids to students.

5   Conclusion

Learning practices exist in a growingly complex system of accelerated social and informational processes. The new media consumption has been undeniably accelerated in some areas, exemplified by short formats of videos, algorithmic selection of content, fast-paced everyday multimodal messaging, etc. Certain combinations of multimodality and multisensority definitely serve as accelerators for media behavior, especially in cases of drawing attention, fighting for engagement or competing for user minutes. All these factors cause further fragmentation and acceleration of the digital experience. Does this tendency of media consumption and user behavior affect the use of DLEs for learning purposes?

On the one hand, it is clear that DLEs are integral to overall media behavior and they cannot be viewed in isolation. The accelerated nature of media affects how information is obtained, what types of design are used in constructing DLEs, what skills are required for engaging in slower pace of media processing, etc. On the other hand, as discussed in this paper, the learning experience is at least conditionally immersive and thus has certain freedom in modeling of subjects. Acknowledging this, it is necessary for DLEs to aim at shaping the learning processes that would facilitate the most meaningful experience.

Considering the limited natural capacity of humans to retain information and develop knowledge, time and deceleration become important issues to address in understanding DLEs. In order to efficiently "pace" digital learning in a high-speed society, this paper explores deceleration strategies by analyzing Education on Screen, a digital learning environment developed by the Transmedia Research Group at the Department of Semiotics of the University of Tartu. The methodological framework combines the principles of multimodal analysis and cultural semiotics to enhance the interpretation of deceleration. This paper suggests that, despite being an indicator of acceleration, multimodality can also contribute to deceleration by supporting meaningful learning experiences. For an evidence-driven development of learning environments, we suggest a systemic approach of assessing modalities within prompts and artifacts with an emphasis on critically evaluating time structures. The engagement of a learner in the process of transduction also serves as a strong indicator of deceleration; similarly, deceleration is more closely associated with production than consumption. Thus, creating a new (even monomodal) artifact through the process of transduction would require more semiotic work than interacting with already existing multimodal material.

The analysis of tasks across six different DLEs has shown that a) those associated with the process of "selection" have multimodal features in prompts, but not necessarily in artifacts; b) "analytical" tasks can have multimodal prompts, but the artifacts are mostly monomodal; and c) "design" indicates that both the prompts and the resulting artifacts are multimodal. Viewed holistically, we suggest that EoS aligns fragments and adaptations of classic texts from accelerated media structures and brings them together on a digital platform creating a new whole, which, being explored conscientiously, involves deceleration. However, inquiries into temporal structures of learning remain problematic due to the pluralities of social structures (and their scientific models) within learning processes and should be studied further in greater depth. Additionally, the assumptions regarding the potential time costs associated with various activities should be validated through testing and experimentation.

References

1. Polanyi, K.: The Great Transformation: The Political and Economic Origins of Our Time. Rinehart, New York (1944)
2. Rosa, H.: The speed of global flows and the pace of democratic politics. New Polit. Sci. **27**(4), 445–459 (2005)
3. Rosa, H.: Social Acceleration: A New Theory of Modernity. Columbia University Press, New York (2013)
4. Wajcman, J.: Pressed for Time: The Acceleration of Life in Digital Capitalism. The University of Chicago Press, Chicago and London (2015)

5. Milyakina, A.: Digitalization of Literary Education in the Context of Cultural Autocommunication. University of Tartu Press, Tartu (2020)
6. Big History Project. https://bhp-public.oerproject.com/. Accessed 25 Mar 2024
7. Arkhangelsky, A., Novikova, A.: Transmedia strategies in school literary education: deconstructing kitsch and the semiotics of readerly creativity. Chin. Semiot. Stud. **19**(2), 315–332 (2023)
8. Estonian Film Classics. https://haridusekraanil.ee/en/. Accessed 25 Mar 2024
9. Kress, G.: Multimodality: A Social Semiotic Approach to Contemporary Communication. Routledge, London and New York (2009)
10. Anderson, L., Krathwohl, D., et al. (eds.): A Taxonomy for Learning, Teaching, and Assessing: A Revision of Bloom's Taxonomy of Educational Objectives. Longman, New York (2001)
11. Kapp, K.: Gamification of Learning and Instruction: Game-Based Methods and Strategies for Training and Education. Pfeiffer, San Francisco (2012)
12. Popovič, A., Macri, F.: Literary synthesis. Can. Rev. Comp. Lit. **4**(2), 118–132 (1977)
13. Lotman, J., Ivanov, V., Pjatigorskij, A., Toporov, V., Uspenskij, B.: Theses on the semiotic study of cultures (as applied to Slavic texts). In: Salupere, S., et al. (eds.) Beginnings of the Semiotics of Culture, pp. 53–78. University of Tartu Press, Tartu (2013)
14. Lotman, J.: On the semiosphere. Sign Syst. Stud. **33**(1), 205–229 (2005)
15. Lotman, J.: Fenomen kultury [The phenomenon of culture]. In: Lotman, J., Izbrannye statji v trekh tomakh. T.I Statji po semiotike i topologii kultury, pp. 34–45. Aleksandra, Tallinn (1992)
16. Ojamaa, M., Torop, P.: Transmediality of cultural autocommunication. Int. J. Cult. Stud. **18**(1), 61–78 (2015)
17. Scolari, C. (ed.): Teens, Media and Collaborative Cultures. Exploiting Teens' Transmedia Skills in the Classroom. Universitat Pompeu Fabra, Barcelona (2018)
18. Ibrus, I., Ojamaa, M.: The creativity of digital (audiovisual) archives: a dialogue between media archaeology and cultural semiotics. Theory Cult. Soc. **37**(3), 47–70 (2020)
19. Bezemer, J., Kress, G.: Visualizing English: a social semiotic history of a school subject. Vis. Commun. **8**, 247–262 (2009)
20. Ojamaa, M., Torop, P., Fadeev, A., Milyakina, A., Pilipoveca, T., Rickberg, M.: Culture as education: from transmediality to transdisciplinary pedagogy. Sign Syst. Stud. **47**(1/2), 152–176 (2019)

Digital Competence as Outlined in Online Prospectuses for Taught Postgraduate TESOL Degrees in Scotland: A Preliminary Study

Antony Hoyte-West[✉] [iD]

Oxford, United Kingdom
antony.hoyte.west@gmail.com

Abstract. This contribution focuses on how training in digital competence for future students of postgraduate degrees in Teaching English to Speakers of Other Languages (TESOL) is presented in online university prospectuses. Taking the offerings of eight Scottish tertiary institutions as a case study, this analysis examines the websites of eleven postgraduate TESOL programmes to obtain information about if and how digital skills are embedded in the relevant postgraduate curricula. As demonstrated by the mandatory move to remote learning during the COVID-19 pandemic, digital competence is becoming more and more necessary in pedagogical and training-related contexts. Indeed, this has been illustrated at the international level through European initiatives such as the DigCompEdu framework. Accordingly, in analysing the relevant data, this study adds not only to the general literature on digital competence relating to foreign language teaching, but also more specifically on digital competence in the context of future teachers who are considering embarking on a professional career in TESOL.

Keywords: digital competence · postgraduate TESOL degrees · online prospectuses · master's in TESOL · university admissions

1 Introduction

Despite modern advances in language technology, including the rise of artificial intelligence, English is currently the world's major language. It is spoken natively by hundreds of millions of people worldwide on several continents, but, as prominent scholar David Crystal highlights, vast swathes of the global population speak English predominantly as a foreign or additional language (see [1], pp. 7–9). Consequently, the teaching of English has become extremely important in many national education systems in many different countries, and at the global level is generally referred to via the acronym TESOL (Teaching English to Speakers of Other Languages). Accordingly, the training of TESOL teachers has also increased in importance, including in predominantly Anglophone countries such as the United Kingdom (UK). However, when compared to typical teacher education programmes, various factors mean that TESOL certifications in the

A. Hoyte-West—Independent scholar.

UK for both pre-service and in-service teachers have evolved differently (as Phiona Stanley and Neil Murray demonstrate [2], this is also the case in other English-speaking countries such as Australia). By way of example, in the British context TESOL is not commonly offered as an option in traditional postgraduate teacher-training courses such as the PGCE (Postgraduate Certificate in Education) or PGDE (Professional Graduate Diploma in Education) (see e.g. [3]). Rather, the most common ways of obtaining relevant TESOL qualifications can be grouped into two main spheres.

The first includes external professional certifications which are awarded by an accredited organisation, often via an agreement with a local teaching institution such as a language school or university. Highly practical in format (for a general overview, see [4]), relevant qualifications include the CELTA (pre-service) and DELTA (in-service) qualifications offered by Cambridge English [5, 6], as well as the CertTESOL (pre-service) and DipTESOL (in-service) diplomas awarded by Trinity College London [7, 8].

The second grouping of TESOL qualifications comprises postgraduate master's level qualifications which are offered by tertiary institutions (usually universities). These generally comprise a year-long MA (Master of Arts), MSc (Master of Science), or MEd (Master of Education) degree in TESOL; intermediate qualifications such as a Postgraduate Certificate (PGCert) or Postgraduate Diploma (PGDip) can be made available to students who do not wish to or are unable to complete the full degree programmes. As will be detailed subsequently, it is this second grouping which will be analysed in this chapter: the principal focus of this contribution centres on the analysis of how digital competence is presented in online prospectuses for master's degrees in TESOL available at universities in Scotland.

2 Presentation of the Case Study

Comprising the northern third of the island of Great Britain, Scotland is a constituent part of the United Kingdom alongside England, Wales, and Northern Ireland. However, historical factors – including its long existence as an independent kingdom before the 1707 Act of Union – have meant that Scotland has a distinctive social and cultural identity, with its own legal system and a different education system at primary, secondary, and tertiary level. At university level, this means that unlike in the rest of United Kingdom, where a three-year undergraduate honours degree is followed by a one-year taught master's degree, the standard provision in Scotland comprises a four-year undergraduate honours degree and then a subsequent one-year taught master's degree: i.e., a 4 + 1 model [9].

Scotland has around 5 million people [10], but this relatively small population has a strong tradition of tertiary education. Indeed, Scotland's four ancient universities (St Andrews, Glasgow, Aberdeen, and Edinburgh) were all founded in the fifteenth and sixteenth centuries, at a time when there were just two such institutions (the universities of Oxford and Cambridge) in England ([11] p. 88). With a current total of seventeen institutions with degree-awarding powers [12], these vary from universities founded in mediaeval times to more modern establishments, with several performing very well in national and international rankings [13]. Accordingly, Scotland's universities attract students not only from across the United Kingdom, but also worldwide.

Yet when it comes to the important decision of choosing a university, it can be argued that university prospectuses can play an important role in the applicant's decision-making process. Indeed, these prospectuses can provide a flavour of an institution and course [14]. Formerly existing as printed materials but now largely based online, university prospectuses typically contain core details about degree programmes and course subjects, but also other important general information about social life, accommodation, student clubs and societies, etc. This can be particularly valuable given that in the United Kingdom, unlike in many other countries, domestic students commonly opt to study at institutions which are located some distance away from their homes [15]. In addition, the global prestige accorded to British educational institutions and to the opportunity to study in English means that universities in the United Kingdom often host many international students from a wide range of other countries [16]. With the tertiary education system in Britain founded on a fees-based model, postgraduate education can represent a considerable financial investment [17]. By way of example, the 2023/2024 tuition fees for some of the TESOL degree programmes featured in this study can rise to over GBP 20,000 for international students.

Bearing in mind this financial outlay, it is important that postgraduate students of these courses are equipped with the necessary skills for success in their chosen career. As outlined by Ron Darvin and Christoph A. Hafner in their study [18], digital competence is highly important for trainee TESOL teachers as well as for the broader profession. As has been discussed elsewhere, the impact of the COVID-19 pandemic and related public health measures (including the compulsory shift to online teaching, learning, and assessment) have meant that there is a need for greater understanding of both the advantages and the potential pitfalls of the growing importance of digital technologies in the education sector [19].

As such, there have been several institutional responses to the increasing digitalisation over the past few years, both at national and international levels. These have included the creation of the European Commission's DigCompEdu framework [20]. This focuses on distinguishing levels of digital competence for educators along the lines the of the well-known six-level Common European Framework of Reference for Languages (CEFR) A1-C2 scale originally developed by the Council of Europe at the beginning of the current century [21, 22]. In assigning levels ranging from basic to advanced competency, the DigCompEdu initiative thus emulates this widely-used language proficiency model [23]. There are, of course, other frameworks which can be used to highlight the digital competence of educators – as Łukasz Tomczyk and Laura Fedeli outline [24], these include the DigiLit Leicester, NETS-T and TPACK models as well as the UNESCO framework. Indeed, the creation of such frameworks reflects the professional reality of teaching digital natives in the post-COVID world, as well as incorporating the growing development of "21st century skills" (a skillset comprising *inter alia* a multitude of new ways of thinking, working, and living in our technology-based world [25]) into everyday teaching and learning [26, 27]. This is also emphasised by the importance for educators of creating attractive technology-based teaching content – such as via gamification – in order to better engage with students (see [28]). Accordingly, it is clear that trainee TESOL teachers need to obtain these digital skills in order to become eminently competitive on the global TESOL market [29]. As research by Jiafan Cao and colleagues has highlighted, in general terms it is advised that "language educators should focus on developing digital competency and integrating sustainable practices into their language classroom to promote effective language learning" [30].

3 Approach and Research Question

Employing a similar methodological approach to other literature-based country case studies on digital competence for educators (for example, see the analysis of the Kosovo context by Hasan Saliu and Arberore Bicaj [31]), the present contribution represents an exploratory approach founded on the qualitative desk-based analysis (see [32]) of relevant open-access resources. The core aim is to supplement some of the previous work which has examined digital competence within TESOL, such as the very recent studies by Lianjiang Jiang and Mingyue Michelle Gu [33], Paulina Lehmkuhl and Stefanie Frisch [34], as well as by Tuğba Yalçin and Elif Bozyiğit [35]. However, to date none of the aforementioned research appears to have focused on Scotland, thus demonstrating the novelty of the current approach. Accordingly, the analysis is centred around a single research question:

– How is digital competence for future postgraduate TESOL students presented in Scottish online university prospectuses?

For the purposes of this study, the DigComp definition of digital competence [36] was utilised, which is itself based on the Council of the EU's 2018 Recommendation on Key Competences for Lifelong Learning (2018). Accordingly, this means it denotes the "confident, critical and responsible use of, and engagement with, digital technologies for learning, at work, and for participation in society. It is defined as a combination of knowledge, skills and attitudes" (see [36], p. 3).

4 Findings

The results of an internet search revealed that 11 postgraduate degree programmes in TESOL at 8 different Scottish universities were available for student recruitment in the current 2023/2024 academic year. Of the 11 degree programmes identified, 8 were targeted at both pre-service and in-service teachers; 3 were designed for in-service teachers as prior work experience was expected or required before matriculation. Each of the individual course websites was visited to search for relevant programme-related information about digital competence [see 37–47]. Table 1 presents the necessary information about the institutions, degree programmes, and target groups (i.e. pre-service and/or in-service teachers):

As Table 1 depicts, the institutions featured represent a mix of both older and more modern institutions; all of the country's ancient universities offer at least one taught postgraduate TESOL degree programme. In addition, all of the one-year taught master's programmes share a common structure with other Scottish qualifications at that level. When studied in a full-time modality over the course of a single academic year, this comprises two semesters of taught courses (120 SCQF credits, equivalent to 60 ECTS); following successful completion of this component, students then undertake a research

Table 1. Postgraduate degree programmes in TESOL awarded by Scottish institutions

Institution	Degree programme	Target group
University of Aberdeen	MSc TESOL - Teaching English to Speakers of Other Languages	Pre- and in-service teachers
University of Dundee	MEd Teaching English to Speakers of Other Languages – TESOL	In-service teachers
University of Edinburgh	MSc Teaching English to Speakers of Other Languages – TESOL	Pre- and in-service teachers
University of Glasgow	MEd TESOL: Teaching of English to Speakers of Other Languages	In-service teachers
	MSc TESOL: Teaching of English to Speakers of Other Languages	Pre-service teachers
University of St Andrews	MSc Teaching English to Speakers of Other Languages (TESOL)	Pre- and in-service teachers
	MSc Teaching English to Speakers of Other Languages (TESOL) – Online	Pre- and in-service teachers
University of Stirling	MSc Teaching English to Speakers of Other Languages (TESOL)	Pre- and in-service teachers
	MSc Teaching English to Speakers of Other Languages (TESOL) (Online)	In-service teachers
University of Strathclyde	MSc TESOL & Intercultural Communication	Pre- and in-service teachers
University of the West of Scotland	MEd Teaching English to Speakers of Other Languages (TESOL)	Pre- and in-service teachers

Source: The author, based on[37–47]

dissertation or project which is to be completed over the summer (60 credits, equivalent to 30 ECTS). Accordingly, this means that the one-year programmes contain a total of 180 credits (90 ECTS) (for more information, see [48]).

Turning specifically to digital competence, 8 of the prospectus webpages for the degree programmes alluded to technology-related aspects (at the universities of Aberdeen, Edinburgh, St Andrews, Stirling, Strathclyde, and the West of Scotland), whereas 3 did not (the prospectus webpage for the in-service programme at the University of Dundee, as well as both the pre-service and in-service programmes offered by the University of Glasgow). As presented in Table 2, closer examination of the sources showed that 7 of the programmes explicitly incorporated technology-related aspects through the provision of named course modules.

Table 2. Named technology-related modules available in postgraduate TESOL programmes

Institution and course	Module title	Status
University of Edinburgh - MSc TESOL	Online Language Learning	Optional
University of St Andrews – MSc TESOL	Technology for Teaching	Optional
University of St Andrews –MSc TESOL – Online	Technology for Teaching	Optional
University of Stirling - MSc TESOL	Technology in Language Education	Optional
University of Stirling - MSc TESOL (Online)	Technology in Language Education	Compulsory
University of Strathclyde	Digital Technologies in Language Teaching	Optional
University of the West of Scotland	Technology-Enhanced Language Learning	Optional

Source: The author, based on[39, 42–47]

As demonstrated in Table 2, one of the degrees, the MSc TESOL (Online) at the University of Stirling, had a compulsory 20-credit (10 ECTS) module in 'Technology in Language Education' [45]; at the other institutions, digital competence-related modules were optional components. The websites provided varying degrees of information regarding the content of the modules – in some instances, links were provided to a full syllabus description, whereas others consisted of solely the module title.

At the University of St Andrews, both the online and in-person variants of the MSc in TESOL offers an optional module in 'Technology for Teaching', which aimed to introduce candidates "to the principle theories, concepts and practices of technology in language education", informing that students would "be able to critically consider the role and purpose of various modes of technology in education in a wide range of settings to identify and conceptualise problems within your own professional contexts" [42, 43] In addition, subject to complying with the necessary administrative aspects, students could also receive a named specialisation on their degree certificates – e.g., they would graduate with the award of the MSc in TESOL with a specialism in Technology for Teaching. According to the online prospectus, the specialism aims to "develop technical skills in a range of applications, such as data-driven and game-based learning", ensuring students will additionally "develop project management skills, using techniques from agile design and design thinking" [42, 43].

In the University of Edinburgh's face-to-face MSc in TESOL, the 20-credit (10 ECTS) optional module in 'Online Language Learning' has been made "available in a fully online mode", and the course summary details that it "aims to provide a comprehensive exploration of the intersection between digital technology and online language learning and teaching". It continues by informing prospective students that the module "is designed to equip you with the necessary tools, theoretical frameworks, and practical strategies to leverage technology effectively in language teaching, to critically assess existing affordances and challenges, and to develop your own online language course" [49]. In terms of the learning outcomes for trainee TESOL educators, these are elucidated as showing "a critical understanding of the main issues, principles, theories and concepts of language learning with online technology", as well as the ability to "apply this knowledge appropriately to design an online language learning course which contains elements of creative professional practice" and to "consider the complex issues related to language learning and online technology, and developed suitable explanations of the choices made in the design using these features", with students expected to be competent in using "a range of online technologies to provide materials and support for language learners" and to critically reflect on their choices when making an online language course of their own [49].

At the University of Stirling, a 20-credit (10 ECTS) module in 'Technology in Language Education' is available an option for the face-to-face on-campus iteration of the MSc in TESOL. The module aims to "assist both novice and experienced L2 teachers in utilizing technology effectively and efficiently in their classrooms", stating that it can offer "a review of the history of technology in L2 education; cover different ways in which technology can be used for teaching and learning different language skills such as vocabulary, reading, speaking" [50]. Additionally, the module specification also includes information about relevant aspects such as gamification, noting that it will "explore the use of digital gaming, corpora, and data-driven practices in L2 instruction; provide an overview of ways to assess L2 learners' learning outcomes using technology" [50]. As already mentioned previously, the online MSc in TESOL offered by the University of Stirling contains a very similarly-structured module also entitled 'Technology in Language Education' [51]; however, this is a compulsory module for that programme. In addition, Stirling also offers the possibility of achieving a technology-related degree specialism, leading to the award of the MSc in TESOL with Computer Assisted Language Learning [44, 45]. For students following the online variant, this is fulfilled by substituting the 60-credit (30 ECTS) dissertation module with a CALL-related portfolio [52].

At the University of the West of Scotland, an optional module in 'Technology-Enhanced Language Learning' is listed as being available, but no further information appeared to be provided on the relevant prospectus webpage at the time of consultation [47]. And at the University of Strathclyde, the optional module in 'Digital Technologies in Language Teaching' was designed to examine "the use of digital technologies for language teaching", offering "students an overview of the key theories and pedagogical principles which underpin our current understanding of digital education", with a focus on "develop[ing] the knowledge and practical skills of creating and working in a digital environment for language education", as well as "students' 21st Century skills both as a language user/learner and as a language teacher" [46]. Interestingly, of the courses surveyed, this is the first mention of 21st century skills [26–28], thus situating the modern-day need for the digital competence within a panoply of other important capabilities that trainee TESOL teachers will doubtlessly require in their future careers.

Indeed, digital competence appears to be embedded within the wider framework of the TESOL degrees as a whole. For example, though the MSc at the University of Aberdeen does not appear to contain a named technology-related module at present, the webpage states that "we examine CLIL (Content and Language Integrated Learning), CMC (Computer Mediated Communication)..." [37]. Further examples of how digital competence permeates through the postgraduate programmes can be found at other institutions too. For example, in addressing its audience of future applicants directly, the University of Stirling's online course prospectus highlights that "our approach to learning and teaching is both innovative and flexible, using a range of methods and relevant online technologies" [45] and the University of the West of Scotland mentions to future students that "you will be taught by a combination of direct, face-to-face teaching and online input through our Virtual Learning Environment" [47]. Thus, it seems that a certain level of digital competence among incoming students is presupposed by the various universities, although this is not officially defined in terms of criteria such as DigCompEdu or other frameworks.

5   Some Preliminary Conclusions and Pointers for Future Research

The research findings of this preliminary study have shown that, in general, digital competence is certainly present in the online prospectuses for postgraduate TESOL programmes at Scottish tertiary institutions. Of the offerings surveyed, the webpages of 8 of the programmes referred to technology-related aspects. However, based on analysis of the open-access material provided on the prospectus webpages, digital competence is generally not portrayed as a core attribute; in other words, it is evidently important yet perhaps is largely presupposed, a finding which echoes the assertion by Fatih Bayraktar and Łukasz Tomczyk that "most current university students are commonly considered 'digital natives'" [53]. 7 of the analysed institutions offered named modules centring on technology-related aspects of teaching and learning, with the provision overwhelmingly viewed as an optional rather than a compulsory element of the full TESOL degree programme. Noting other influences such as market forces and the ever-increasing digitalisation of language teaching, it will be interesting to chart future developments to see if such modules do become compulsory at a later date. In addition, perhaps due to their constantly evolving nature, mention of specific software programmes or digital pedagogical tools did not appear to feature in the online prospectuses; this could potentially also be a point of departure for additional research. By extension, relevant international competence-based frameworks (e.g. DigCompEdu) were also not mentioned in the various prospectuses, though one webpage did refer to the concept of 21st century skills; these frameworks could be an aspect perhaps worthy of attention in future prospectuses.

Yet it is important to reiterate that university prospectuses are designed to provide a very brief overview of a degree programme, rather than to furnish a comprehensive in-depth analysis of current provision. This means that, although training in digital competence may not have been explicitly mentioned, this does not mean that it does not feature within a given postgraduate TESOL programme. Additionally, further details may feature on institutional intranets, student webpages, and policy documents that fall outside the realm of this initial contribution. In this regard, the preliminary scope and approach of this study must be acknowledged, and it is aimed to supplement the basic findings offered here via further research, such as obtaining more information by contacting course coordinators and other academic staff at the relevant institutions, as well as conducting interviews, questionnaires, and participant observation. The use of these qualitative approaches could shed light, for example, on institutional requirements at the department and faculty level that could conceivably influence programme content and design. Furthermore, it should be noted that the universities analysed in the present study are research-based institutions, and thus the research interests and strengths of a given department may also feature in shaping postgraduate provision.

Further research could also expand the comparative aspect of the study by increasing the number of TESOL degree prospectuses and institutions analysed, as well as also by examining how international digital competence frameworks can be incorporated in the UK TESOL context. In building on prior case studies such as a discussion of the potential implementation of DigCompEdu in teacher training in Italy [54], subsequent research could also examine the incorporation of similar initiatives in the pre- and in-service training of TESOL teachers, possibly including not only the whole of the United Kingdom, but also other Anglophone countries around the world.

References

1. Crystal, D.: The language revolution. Polity Press, Cambridge (2002)
2. Stanley, P., Murray, N.: 'Qualified'? A framework for comparing ELT teacher preparation courses. Aust. Rev. Appl. Linguist. **36**(1), 102–115 (2013). https://doi.org/10.1075/aral.36.1.05sta
3. Get into Teaching: What is a PGCE course? https://getintoteaching.education.gov.uk/train-to-be-a-teacher/what-is-a-pgce. Accessed 05 Jan 2024
4. Kanowski, S.: Helter CELTA: do short courses equal 'best practice' in teacher training? TESOL Context **13**(2), 21–27 (2004)
5. Cambridge English: CELTA certificate in teaching English to speakers of other languages. https://www.cambridgeenglish.org/teaching-english/teaching-qualifications/celta/. Accessed 05 Jan 2024
6. Cambridge English: DELTA (diploma in teaching English to speakers of other languages). https://www.cambridgeenglish.org/teaching-english/teaching-qualifications/delta/. Accessed 05 Jan 2024
7. Trinity College London: CertTESOL. https://www.trinitycollege.com/qualifications/teaching-english/CertTESOL/. Last accessed 2024/01/05
8. Trinity College London: DipTESOL. https://www.trinitycollege.com/qualifications/teaching-english/diptesol/. Accessed 05 Jan 2024
9. Nuffic: Higher Education – Scotland. https://www.nuffic.nl/en/education-systems/united-kingdom-scotland/higher-education. Accessed 05 Jan 2024
10. Cameron, E.A., Moulton, M.J., Macleod, I.C., Brown, A.: Scotland. Encyclopedia Britannica (2024). https://www.britannica.com/place/Scotland. Accessed 05 Jan 2024
11. Dent, H.C.: Old and new universities. Bull. Am. Assoc. Univ. Professors **30**(1), 88–91 (1944). https://doi.org/10.2307/40220510

12. Scottish Government: Universities. https://www.gov.scot/policies/universities/. Accessed 05 Jan 2024
13. Humes, W.: Scottish higher education. In: Bryce, T.G.K., Humes, W.M., Gillies, D., Kennedy, A. (eds.) Scottish Education, pp. 76–85. Edinburgh University Press: Edinburgh (2018). https://doi.org/10.1515/9781474437851-008
14. Saichaie, K., Morphew, C.C.: What college and university websites reveal about the purposes of higher education. J. High. Educ. **85**(4), 499–530 (2014). https://doi.org/10.1353/jhe.2014.0024
15. Whyte, W.: Somewhere to live: why British students study away from home – and why it matters. HEPI Report 121. Higher Education Policy Institute, Oxford (2019). https://www.hepi.ac.uk/wp-content/uploads/2019/11/HEPI_Somewhere-to-live_Report-121-FINAL.pdf. Accessed 05 Jan 2024
16. UCAS: The UK continues to be a top destination for study, with applications set to rise by almost 50% within five years (2022). https://www.ucas.com/corporate/news-and-key-doc uments/news/uk-continues-be-top-destination-study-applications-set-rise-almost-50-within-five-years. Accessed 05 Jan 2024
17. British Council: Cost of studying and living in the UK (2024). https://study-uk.britishcouncil.org/moving-uk/cost-studying. Accessed 05 Jan 2024
18. Darvin, R., Hafner, C.A.: Digital literacies in TESOL: mapping out the terrain. TESOL Q. **56**(3), 865–882 (2022). https://doi.org/10.1002/tesq.3161
19. Abdel-Hameed, F.S.M., Tomczyk, Ł, Hu, C.: The editorial of special issue on education, IT, and the COVID-19 pandemic. Educ. Inf. Technol. **26**, 6563–6566 (2021). https://doi.org/10.1007/s10639-021-10781-z
20. Redecker, C: European Framework for the Digital Competence of Educators: DigCompEdu. Publications Office of the European Union, Luxembourg (2017). https://doi.org/10.2760/159770
21. Council of Europe: The CEFR levels. https://www.coe.int/en/web/common-european-framework-reference-languages/level-descriptions. Accessed 05 Jan 2024
22. Hoyte-West, A.: Scaling olympus: exploring official language certifications at the CEFR C2 level. Ezikov Svyat (Orbis Linguarum) **21**(2), 78–87 (2023). https://doi.org/10.37708/ezs.swu.bg.v21i2.10
23. Raita, K., Votkin, T., Jokiranta, P., Tervonen, T., Bagrova, N.: Building a digital competence portfolio – A case study of teachers and planners. In: INTED2019 Proceedings, pp. 7307–7313 (2019). https://doi.org/10.21125/inted.2019.1779
24. Tomczyk, Ł., Fedeli, L.: Digital literacy among teachers – Mapping theoretical frameworks: TPACK, DigCompEdu, UNESCO, NETS-T, DigiLit Leicester. In: Proceedings of the 38th International Business Information Management Association (IBIMA) 2021, pp. 244–252 (2021)
25. Suto, I., Eccles, H.: The Cambridge approach to 21st Century skills: definitions, development and dilemmas for assessment. Paper presented at the 40th IAEA Conference, Singapore (2014). https://www.cambridgeassessment.org.uk/Images/461811-the-cambridge-app roach-to-21st-century-skills-definitions-development-and-dilemmas-for-assessment-.pdf. Accessed 05 Jan 2024
26. Siddiq, F., Olofsson, A.D., Ola Lindberg, J., Tomczyk, L.: Special issue: what will be the new normal? Digital competence and 21st-century skills: critical and emergent issues in education. Educ. Inf. Technol. **29**(6), 7697–7705 (2023). https://doi.org/10.1007/s10639-023-12067-y
27. Almazroa, H., Alotaibi, W.: Teaching 21st century skills: understanding the depth and width of the challenges to shape proactive teacher education programmes. Sustainability **15**(9), 7365 (2023). https://doi.org/10.3390/su15097365

28. Bond, M., Bedenlier, S.: Facilitating student engagement through educational technology: towards a conceptual framework. J. Interact. Media Educ. **2019**(1), Article 11 (2019). https://doi.org/10.5334/jime.528

29. Palacios Hidalgo, F.J., Gómez Parra, M., Huertas Abril, C.A.: Digital and media competences: key competences for EFL teachers. Teach. English. Technol. **20**(1), 43–59 (2020). https://doi.org/10.4018/IJWLTT.2020100101

30. Cao, J., Bhuvaneswari, G., Arumugam, T.: The digital edge: examining the relationship between digital competency and language learning outcomes. Front. Psychol. **14**, 1187909 (2023). https://doi.org/10.3389/fpsyg.2023.1187909

31. Saliu, H., Bicaj, A.: The digital competence of future teachers in Kosovo. In: Tomczyk, Ł, Fedeli, L. (eds.) Digital Literacy for Teachers, pp. 275–290. Springer Nature Singapore, Singapore (2022). https://doi.org/10.1007/978-981-19-1738-7_15

32. Bassot, B.: Doing Qualitative Desk-Based Research: A Practical Guide to Writing an Excellent Dissertation. Policy Press, Bristol (2022)

33. Jiang, L., Gu, M.M.: Toward a professional development model for critical digital literacies in TESOL. TESOL Q. **56**(3), 1029–1040 (2022). https://doi.org/10.1002/tesq.3138

34. Lehmkuhl, P., Frisch, S.: Fostering TEFL-specific digital competences of English student teachers and in-service teachers in a cross-phase collaborative seminar. Herausforderung Lehrer*innenbildung - Zeitschrift zur Konzeption, Gestaltung und Diskussion, **6**(2), 76–96 (2023). https://doi.org/10.11576/hlz-6324

35. Yalçın, T., Bozyiğit, E.: A review of studies on digital competence in teaching English as a foreign language. Stud. Linguist. Cult. FLT **11**(3), 82–101 (2023). https://doi.org/10.46687/ANKN3258

36. Vuorikari, R., Kluzer, S., Punie, Y.: DigComp 2.2: The Digital Competence Framework for Citizens - with new examples of knowledge, skills and attitudes. Publications Office of the European Union, Luxembourg (2022). https://doi.org/10.2760/115376

37. University of Aberdeen: TESOL – Teaching English to Speakers of Other Languages, MSc, PgCert or PgDip. https://www.abdn.ac.uk/study/postgraduate-taught/degree-progra mmes/321/tesol/. Accessed 05 Jan 2024

38. University of Dundee: Teaching English to Speakers of Other Languages – TESOL MEd. https://www.dundee.ac.uk/postgraduate/teaching-english-speakers-others-languages. Accessed 05 Jan 2024

39. University of Edinburgh: Teaching English to Speakers of Other Languages – TESOL. https://www.ed.ac.uk/education/graduate-school/taught-degrees/tesol. Accessed 05 Jan 2024

40. University of Glasgow: TESOL: Teaching of English to Speakers of Other Languages MEd. https://www.gla.ac.uk/postgraduate/taught/tesolmed/. Accessed 05 Jan 2024

41. University of Glasgow: TESOL: Teaching of English to Speakers of Other Languages MSc. https://www.gla.ac.uk/postgraduate/taught/tesolmsc/. Accessed 05 Jan 2024

42. University of St Andrews: MSc Teaching English to Speakers of Other Languages (TESOL). https://www.st-andrews.ac.uk/subjects/tesol/tesol-msc-september/. Accessed 05 Jan 2024

43. University of St Andrews: Teaching English to Speakers of Other Languages (TESOL) – online. https://www.st-andrews.ac.uk/subjects/tesol/tesol-msc-distance-learning-september/. Accessed 05 Jan 2024

44. University of Stirling: MSc Teaching English to Speakers of Other Languages (TESOL). https://www.stir.ac.uk/courses/pg-taught/tesol-masters/. Accessed 05 Jan 2024

45. University of Stirling: MSc Teaching English to Speakers of Other Languages (TESOL) (Online). https://www.stir.ac.uk/courses/pg-taught/tesol-online/. Accessed 05 Jan 2024

46. University of Strathclyde: MSc TESOL & Intercultural Communication. https://www.strath.ac.uk/courses/postgraduatetaught/tesolinterculturalcommunication/. Accessed 05 Jan 2024

47. University of the West of Scotland: Teaching English to Speakers of Other Languages (TESOL). https://www.uws.ac.uk/study/postgraduate/postgraduate-course-search/teaching-english-to-speakers-of-other-languages-tesol/. Accessed 05 Jan 2024
48. Scottish Credit and Qualifications Framework: The SCQF Interactive Framework. https://scqf.org.uk/about-the-framework/interactive-framework/. Accessed 05 Jan 2024
49. University of Edinburgh: Postgraduate Course: Online Language Learning (EDUA11212). http://www.drps.ed.ac.uk/23-24/dpt/cxedua11212.htm. Accessed 05 Jan 2024
50. University of Stirling: Postgraduate Degree Programme Tables 2023/4 – Technology in Language Education (TESP012). https://portal.stir.ac.uk/calendar/calendar-pg.jsp?modCode=TESP012. Accessed 05 Jan 2024
51. University of Stirling: Postgraduate Degree Programme Tables 2023/4 – Technology in Language Education (TESPD04). https://portal.stir.ac.uk/calendar/calendar-pg.jsp?modCode=TESPD04. Accessed 05 Jan 2024
52. University of Stirling: Postgraduate Degree Programme Tables 2023/4 – CALL Portfolio (Part-time) (TESPP51). https://portal.stir.ac.uk/calendar/calendar-pg.jsp?modCode=TESPP51. Accessed 05 Jan 2024
53. Bayraktar, F., Tomczyk, Ł: Digital piracy among young adults: the role of values and time perspectives. Sustainability 13(16), 9140 (2021). https://doi.org/10.3390/su13169140
54. Guarini, P., di Furia, M., Ragni, B.: Digital competences and didactic technologies training for teachers in service: From DigCompEdu to a national framework. In: Tomczyk, Ł (ed.) New Media Pedagogy: Research Trends, Methodological Challenges and Successful Implementations: First International Conference, NMP 2022, Kraków, Poland, October 10–12, 2022, Revised Selected Papers, pp. 30–41. Springer Nature Switzerland, Cham (2023). https://doi.org/10.1007/978-3-031-44581-1_3

NDBI Practices for Autistic Students: Teachers' Reflections from a Qualitative Perspective About an Online Program

Aitor Larraceleta[1,2](✉) ⃝, Luis Castejón[2] ⃝, and José Carlos Núñez[2] ⃝

[1] Ministry of Education of the Principality of Asturias, Equipo Regional ACNEAE, Avenida San Pedro de los Arcos, 18, 33012 Asturias, Spain
`aitorlg@educastur.org`
[2] Department of Psychology, University of Oviedo, Plaza Feijoo s/n, 33003 Asturias, Spain

Abstract. The growing presence of autistic students in schools means that teacher training has become vitally important in providing these students with inclusive, high quality education. This study aims to shed light on teachers' perceptions of online training processes about evidence-based Naturalistic Developmental Behavioral Interventions (NDBI) aimed at students on the autism spectrum. Based on the thematic analysis proposed by Brown and Clarke, focus groups and semi-structured interviews performed at three timepoints after the training were used to collect the thoughts of the participating Hearing and Language teachers, which are crucial to identifying processes that really influence teachers' knowledge, skills, and perceptions of competence. These perceptions are grouped into three main topics: the positive impact of this online training on participating teachers; the positive impact of this online training on the participating teachers' autistic students; and perceptions of feasibility of NDBI practices through this online training model.

Keywords: Autism · Special Education Needs · teacher professional development · online training · iScience

1 Introduction

1.1 What Do We Mean When We Talk About Autism in Schools?

The concept of "autism spectrum disorder (ASD)" may be defined as a scientific agreement that serves to describe a set of people characterized by the presence of difficulties in two dimensions of human development, communication, and social interaction, as well as by repetitive and restrictive patterns of behaviours, interests, and activities [1]. But more recently—as part of the paradigm of neurodiversity, a term coined in the late 1990s by Judy Singer, an Australian autistic sociologist—it has been possible to conceive of autism as a part of the natural spectrum of human biodiversity, like variations in ethnicity or sexual orientation [2].

Ł. Tomczyk (Ed.): NMP 2023, CCIS 2130, pp. 209–224, 2024.
https://doi.org/10.1007/978-3-031-63235-8_14

The numbers of autistic people are currently rising all over the world [3]. This manifestation of human biodiversity is becoming increasingly common in modern society, and has grown from 0.05% in 1966 [4] to current estimates which, depending on the study, range from 1% to 2% of the population [5] or even as high as 3% [6].

The increasing presence of autistic people in society is also reflected in schools, with a notable increase in students with Special Education Needs (SEN) associated with the condition in countries such as the United States of America, England, Northern Ireland, the Republic of Ireland, Scotland, Australia [7–10], and the country where this study took place, Spain. According to the most recent data from the statistical service of the Spanish Ministry of Education and Vocational Training [11], in academic year 2021/22 69,002 non-university students had ASD-related SEN. This represented 28.1% of SEN students, making them the most common group of SEN students in Spain [11], and indicating an increase of 262.73% [7] in the number of these students over eleven academic years.

The inclusion model followed in Spain is based on the presence and participation of autistic students –84.14% in the 2021–2022 academic year– in regular schools, with more presence of these pupils in the first educational stages –Preschool, Primary, and Secondary Education–than in High School degree and Vocational Training [7]. Over time, several resources and actions have been developed to promote this inclusion model in the different regions across the country. In the region where this research has been carried out, the Principality of Asturias, exists, for instance, "open classrooms" (temporary support classrooms in ordinary schools for autistic students) or accompaniment in the regular classroom by support teacher staff –Hearing and Language (HL) and Therapeutic Pedagogy (TP) –. This study deals only with the HL teachers' perceptions about training for autistic students' inclusion.

1.2 The Importance of Teacher Training Perceptions for Inclusion of Autistic Students

The situation described above suggests that it is highly likely that pre-and in-service teachers will encounter autistic students in their classrooms. In order to provide these students with the truly inclusive, accessible, quality education that they are entitled to [12], it is crucial that teachers feel competent and have the necessary knowledge and training about autism and the educational styles needed to teach these students, as numerous publications have pointed out [13–16]. Otherwise, there is a risk of experiencing illusory educational inclusion [12] due to, among other reasons, a lack of the necessary teacher competencies to effectively address the complex challenges experienced by autistic students [13–16].The literature on teachers' knowledge of evidence-based practices aimed at these students indicates a worrying situation regarding this critical aspect of the educational inclusion for students with any kind of SEN [16, 17]. Over the last fifteen years, multiple studies in different countries have indicated medium-low levels of training, knowledge, use, and confidence in implementing these evidence-based practices and the need for more thorough university and professional development training [e.g., 14, 18–24]. There have been few studies to date in Spain on this topic [25–27], and the results indicate teachers feel that there is a lack of knowledge and training about the how to educate autistic students. Our research group has undertaken two studies in the

Principality of Asturias, a region in the north of Spain, –phase one of our investigation–. These have highlighted perceptions of a lack of knowledge, use, and training in both pre-and in-service training for support teachers specializing in HL and TP [28, 29].

Two systematic reviews of the literature, following systematic, rigorous criteria, were carried out and published in the mid-2000s by two different research groups on psychoeducational evidence-based practices for autistic students between birth and age 22. The reviews by the National Autism Center [30] and The National Professional Development Center on ASD (NPDC) [31] had a massive impact on the scientific community in the field by indicating a fundamental consensus in their findings that continued in the reviews performed by both groups five years later [32, 33]. The evidence-based practices they recommended entailed improvements in almost every area of work with children and young people on the spectrum (communicative, cognitive, academic, and occupational areas, among others [31–34]. Only the second project has continued so far, under the name The National Clearinghouse on Autism Evidence and Practice (NCAEP) [34].

Faced with the gap that currently exists between the implementation of educational practices aimed at autistic students in day-to-day school life and the practices that the scientific literature has recommended for those students [35], the response has been an attempt to narrow it through "iSciences" (implementation science, information science, improvement science, diffusion science or dissemination science)—various evidence-based approaches which have become prominent as methods to address these gap to implementation [15, 36]. This contributes to increasing perceptions of teaching self-efficacy, which in the case of autism has a positive impact in various areas of teaching. These include reducing stress in the case of challenging student behaviour, reducing the risk of teacher burnout, creating positive expectations for these students about the type of schooling, improving the quality of work with these students by increasing the effectiveness of educational strategies used, and the possibility that students on the spectrum experience educational success through effective inclusion [37]. This approach also contributes to avoiding some well-intentioned educational interventions in the field of autism without sufficient scientific evidence and which are sometimes used in schools, being guided by trends or fads, despite their scientific evidence being equivocal and controversial [38].

In the present study, which is part of a larger two-phase research project [8], we aim to determine—using a qualitative approach—how active specialized teachers perceive the official online training aimed at them and what they think about the evidence-based practices offered in the training. This training was designed following the aforementioned "iScience" approach offered by the NPCD, currently known as NCAEP [36, 39].

This study is important because we are not aware of any studies to date that have used a design combining quantitative and qualitative methods within the framework of an official continuing teacher training program on this topic. The research questions guiding the study are:

What opinions do teachers have about the online model and the NDBI practices offered?

Do teachers think that this is a feasible model for implementing the proposed evidence-based NDBI practices in the classroom?

2 Method

This study is part of a larger mixed-methods research project over two phases: phase one has been reported previously [28, 29], phase two is a mixed qualitative-quantitative study based on the results of the first phase, using an asynchronous online Moodle training module. Phase two had two parts. The quantitative part (Part A) assessed levels of knowledge before and after each of the course units via evaluation questionnaires used in the Autism Focused Intervention Resources and Modules [40] and participating teachers' expectations of success attributed to each practice, its value, and the cost they see in applying it via the Expectancy-Value-Cost for Professional Development Scale (EVC-PD) [41]. This quantitative part will be published in another paper. Part B is the focus of the present study and provides a thorough picture of the teachers' perceptions of online evidence-based training via focus groups and individual semi-structured interviews to provide a qualitative analysis of the instruction.

2.1 Participants

179 teachers signed up for one of the three editions of official free in-service training announced by the Cuencas Mineras Teacher Resource Center. 175 teachers completed the training, 65 in the first edition, 68 in the second, and 42 in the third. Most of the participants were women, 172 compared to only 3 men. All the participants in this training were offered the chance to participate in focus groups or semi-structured interviews to extract qualitative information. A total of 28 agreed, although 3 dropped out during the process. Of the 25 remaining teachers, all of whom were women, 14 were HL specialists, 10 were TP specialists, and one was an educational guidance teacher. In the current study, we present the results of the first cohort corresponding to the first edition of the training. 11 HL teachers in three groups (group 1, $n = 5$; group 2, $n = 4$ & group 3, $n = 2$) participated in and completed the focus group sessions. Basic participant data were collected, which is shown in Table 1.

2.2 Procedures: Online Module Development and Focus Group

Three editions of an online training program were offered in an asynchronous format in the second and third quarters of academic year 2020/21 and the first quarter of 2021/22. The training was delivered via the Moodle platform belonging to the Asturian Education Department in combination with three 1h live sessions—at the beginning, in the middle, and near the end of the training—on the department's Microsoft TEAMS® platform. Moodle is a web-based professional development instrument that helps improve teachers' preparation to instruct autistic students [42].

Each edition consisted of six units. For each unit, participants were provided with a PDF file and various links to scientific and informative articles and videos. The practices to be trained in each unit were selected based on a combination of the previous phase of the research [8], the new NCAEP publication (Steinbrenner et al., 2020), and the evidence-based practices recommended by Naturalistic Developmental Behavioural Interventions (NDBI) [43]. Five strategies were ultimately included—Modeling (MD), Peer-mediated interventions (PMII), Video Modeling (VM), Naturalistic Intervention

Table 1. Demographic characteristics for Hearing and Language teacher participants.

Identification	Gender	Age bracket (years)	Highest academic qualification[1]	Teacher experience bracket (years)
P1 G1 E1	Female	26–35 (inclusive)	Bachelor	6–10
P2 G1 E1	Female	36–50 (inclusive)	Bachelor	6–10
P3 G1 E1	Female	26–35 (inclusive)	Bachelor	1–5
P4 G1 E1	Female	36–50 (inclusive)	Bachelor	11–20
P5 G1 E1	Female	36–50 (inclusive)	Bachelor	11–20
P1 G2 E1	Female	36–50 (inclusive)	Bachelor	11–20
P2 G2 E1	Female	26–35 (inclusive)	Master	1–5
P3 G2 E1	Female	36–50 (inclusive)	Bachelor	11–20
P4 G2 E1	Female	36–50 (inclusive)	Bachelor	6–10
P1 G3 E1	Female	36–50 (inclusive)	Bachelor	11–20
P2 G3 E1	Female	36–50 (inclusive)	Bachelor	6–10

[1] European Qualification Framework

(NI), and Pivotal Response Training (PRT)—and an initial teaching unit aimed at understanding evidence-based practice in the framework of inclusive schooling and NDBI practices.

Three focus group sessions were held at three timepoints, at the end of the of the training (March 2021), three months after the end of the training (June 2021), and six months after the training (November 2021), for each of the three groups in the first edition of the training. To that end, we created a semi-structured interview with open-ended questions based on the topics in the Expectancy-Value-Cost for Professional Development Scale (EVC-PD) [41]. We also included questions aimed at the perception of knowledge. There were 14 questions for the first session and 11 for the second and third sessions. Examples of the questions include "How important is applying what you have learned in the training on NDBI practices to your autistic students? Why?" or "How much effort have you made to implement the NDBI strategies outlined in the course? Why?". When a participant was unable to take part in the scheduled session, we conducted individual, recorded interviews on TEAMS® at a later date.

The recorded focus groups and interviews were transcribed following Flick's recommendations [44]. Participants' responses were analysed according to the six iterative steps of reflexive thematic analysis laid out in Braun and Clark [45, 46]: (1) Data familiarization, (2) Generating initial codes, (3) Searching for topics, (4) Reviewing topics, (5) Defining and naming topics and (6) Producing the report. A combination of inductive and deductive coding was performed [47] using Microsoft Word ® and Microsoft Excel®.

3 Findings

Three main topics were identified in this study: (1) The perception of a positive impact of the online training on participating teachers; the perception of the positive impact of this online training on the autistic students; and (3) The perception of the feasibility of NDBI practices through this online training model. The study design allowed us to see how teachers' perceptions changed at the three different timepoints. This meant we were able to see the effect of day-to-day teaching and other factors on teachers' ideas about online training and NDBI practices. A summary of the results is shown in Fig. 1

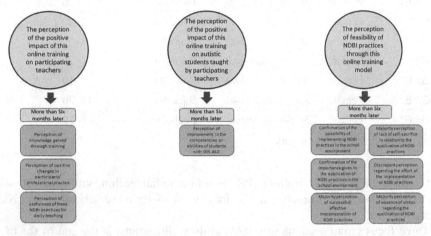

Fig. 1. Three main topics identified in the study about NDBI practices using online training.

3.1 The Positive Impact of the Online Training on Participating Teachers

There were three sub-topics within this main topic and over the sessions making up the study, the teachers continued to indicate positive perceptions. Firstly, the teachers' felt that they had acquired suitable knowledge. At the end of the training, they indicated that they had increased their knowledge and learned some practices that would improve their skills. In the subsequent focus groups and interviews, they emphasised that what they had learned in the training was suitable for them to engage in NDBI practices in their day-to-day work in school. They also reported a desire to learn more and improve the practices they had encountered, both at a theoretical level at the initial session after the training and over the following months as they were implementing the practices into their teaching. Some of the participants also emphasised the need to spread the skills to other agents such as non-specialist teachers and families. For example, participant P1 G3 E1 said, *"As for the contents of the course, I thought they were great (…) and so that was good when it came to implementing them at school. So well, it seemed good to me, I mean, great"*.

The second sub-topic was a positive initial expectation from the participants about changing their professional practice, because the training had taught them evidence-based practices. This initial positive expectation was confirmed as the sessions went on.

The expected improvement initially focused on establishing objectives, thinking about methodology, and procedures for co-ordination, intervention, and evaluation. Expectations were confirmed in the subsequent sessions by feelings of positive changes to professional practice. The teachers felt that it was very important to implement evidence-based knowledge and for other teaching staff to know these practices. In the final session, one teacher highlighted the need to expand or review the training content, including whether they were properly implementing the practices. In this regard participant P2 G1 E1 said of the online training, *"I do give it a positive value. (…). What has it given me? More security, more knowledge."*

Finally, the teachers initially indicated positive expectations that these NDBI practices would be useful in their day-to-day teaching, fundamentally because they are evidence-based. This was confirmed in subsequent sessions when the teachers reported feeling that these practices were useful in their teaching. The initial positive expectations were associated with improvements in knowledge and methodology, but one group of teachers thought that implementation might be difficult, particularly in terms of reliability. In later sessions, these positive expectations were confirmed, with the training in these practices contributing to improvement in the teachers' objectives, interventions, and evaluation procedures, as well as helping teachers tailor the practices to their students. The teachers felt that the training needed to be expanded and needed to include other agents such as families and other teachers. In this regard, participant P1 G2 E1 noted that *"This focus group and seeing each other now and then, I think it is, it is one of the most jumbled and most underlined photocopies and more…, that I have from any training because that often happens is: you have it, you read it, it is cool, but you don't have this follow-up, and it [the online training] seems to me very, very positive. Yes, very positive".*

3.2 The Positive Impact of This Online Training on the Participating Teachers' Autistic Students

There was a single sub-topic within this topic, which teachers continued to be positive about over the three sessions making up the study. This was the teachers' perceptions of improvement in autistic students' competencies and abilities due to implementing NDBI practices.

In the first of the sessions, teachers expressed expectations of improvements in autistic students' competencies due to what they had learned in the training on NDBI practices. That expectation was confirmed in subsequent sessions. In the initial session, teachers indicated that they expected general improvement as well as better communicative-linguistic, and social skills. They also expected improved autonomy, executive function and school preparation (the transition from preschool to primary) as well as improved co-ordination with other teaching staff. As the sessions went on, these initial expectations were confirmed, and even extended to students with other types of SEN. The teachers also continued to emphasize improved methodological and organizational skills. They noted a need for complementary training and needs related to implementation, along with a desire for other teachers from other specialties to have this online training. A small number of teachers indicated that it was impossible for them to assess improvement due to changing school.

In relation to this subtopic, participant P1 G3 E1 said, *"The practices studied in the training, uh..., really are and will be exceptional when it comes to working with any student with ASD"*. Participant P2 G1 E1 noted, *"For me, there is an improvement, at least at the level of self-esteem. The student seemed to be happier because he saw that he could achieve it. He was helped, but well, he was doing, in quotes, the same activities or the same as his colleagues and then also at the level of knowledge because he has been able to, he has been able to acquire that knowledge. So, for me, it has been positive."* Lastly, participant P3 G2 E1 said, *"Well, it is true that when..., collecting information, I have seen that they had improved in more skills than you think at first and so I believe that it has been very helpful..."*.

3.3 The Feasibility of NDBI Practices in the School Setting Through This Online Training Model

Six subtopics emerged within this third topic throughout the three sessions.

Firstly, teachers had positive expectations about implementing NDBI practices in the school environment after the training finished. These positive expectations were confirmed in subsequent sessions. Initially, the most feasible strategies for implementation in school were naturalistic intervention, modeling, peer-mediated intervention, and video modeling. This perception was maintained over the later sessions, although modeling and peer-mediated intervention were what the teachers cited most. In the intermediate and final sessions, the teachers noted the importance of positive involvement and generalizing these practices to other agents, such as families and other teachers. Participant P3 G2 E1 said, *"For my part, I mean, I do see the journey from when we started until last year's course, either because the teachers got involved, or because small guidelines were provided, they were doing them."*

In the initial session, teachers predicted difficulties when using these practices in the classroom. Those difficulties were related to the time needed for preparation and implementation, to the nature of the students themselves, to involving other agents such as other teachers and students' families, and to school characteristics. They also foresaw issues with generalization in different environments, fidelity of the practice, the need for coaching, educational authorities' actions, and the need for deeper knowledge or teacher training. The following sessions confirmed some of these predictions, such as those issues related to time and coordination, the involvement of other agents—other teaching staff and the school response, and the need for more thorough knowledge and teacher training to improve rigour in practice. There was a specific issue with one particular practice, Pivotal Response Training, which was completely new to the participating teachers.

Secondly, in the initial session, the teachers had positive expectations around the importance of NDBI practices. These positive expectations were based on expected improvements in teachers' knowledge and methodology, improvements in autistic students' skills, and the importance of other agents such as families, other teachers, and educational administrations. These positive expectations about the importance of these practices were confirmed in the subsequent sessions, along with some aspects for the future, such as more thorough training, fidelity of the practice, and participation from other agents such as families and other teachers. In the final session, a number of teachers emphasised the importance of evidence-based knowledge. In terms of this second sub-topic, participant P1 G3 E1 said, *"Well, I would say it was very important (...) it is important to know how to act with..., with these students. And the training itself gives you, well, a series of focused practices that are amazing, that many times, it's not even that you don't know, but they do sound familiar to you, but you don't know how to carry them out and for me, it was well, it's important to be able to carry them out..."*.

The third sub-topic was an initial positive expectation of success—teachers implementing the practices properly and effectively, using the strategies appropriately, and students achieving good results—following the training. Teachers indicated a series of factors they expected would influence their effectiveness and success. These included factors linked to acquiring deeper knowledge and faithfully implementing the practices, student characteristics, the relationships with families, and lastly, collaboration with the other teachers. There was a notable variation between the intermediate and the final sessions. In the intermediate session teachers felt a lack of successful or effective application of the practices, while in the final session, that had changed and the teachers mostly felt that there had been successful and effective application of the NDBI practices. Teachers largely agreed about two obstacles throughout the sessions, one linked to fidelity in practice and the other to a lack of collaboration from other teachers. However, there were two other obstacles that were raised in different sessions, one related to co-ordination with families which was raised in the intermediate session, and the other linked to difficulties at classroom or school level which came up in the final session. In relation to this third sub-topic, participant P2 G3 ED1 said *"The practices do work, it is clear, you see improvement, but then (...), if there is no coordination between the professionals, between the teachers, then it does not... [work]"*.

The fourth sub-topic was a generalised expectation in the initial session of not having to make concessions or sacrifices in applying NDBI practices that was mostly confirmed in subsequent sessions. Participants understood that they would have to spend time on planning and faithfully implementing the practices, involving other agents (teachers), and considering generalising these practices to other students without ASD-related SEN. Teachers understood that they would have to make concessions about spaces, times and the actions of other teaching staff. In the intermediate and final sessions, the teachers noted that they would continue to spend time planning and properly implementing the practices and on other agents' involvement (teachers and families) without feeling that they had to sacrifice any of what they had learned. In terms of this fourth subtopic, participant P1 G3 ED1 said *"No, I didn't have to make any concessions. I don't know if I adapted, or..., or..., or I transformed the idea I had of some of the practices or I also tried..., I don't know. Perhaps I had to change, maybe, the time dedicated to it? Well..., if we consider it from that point of view, it could be but..., making a concession about a way of working? No, I mean, I continue with the way of working that I have but, enriching it with, with everything that was contributed, in the training so, in the end, I don't talk as much as concede..., I don't know, I don't think so"*.

The fifth sub-topic was the majority's expectations in the initial session of increased effort in applying these NDBI practices. These were linked on the one hand to the change in personal practice and faithfully implementing the practices and, on the other, to the involvement of other agents (teachers, families, students, and schools). However, by the second session, there was a change in how teachers felt, with the majority indicating that implementing these practices did not need so much effort. This perception of less effort was associated with establishing objectives, planning, co-ordination, evaluation, and properly implementing the practices, as well as with efforts to involve other agents (teachers and families). In the final session there were different views about the efforts needed to implement these practices. Some teachers indicated that they did not need to make much effort implementing the practices, but others felt that it was a continuing effort to do so, in terms of setting objectives, planning, coordination, evaluation, proper practice, and involving other agents (teachers and families), as well as other contextual factors. In terms of this sub-topic, participant P5 G1 E1 said, *"Well, just like before I answered that my level of self-sacrifice had been zero, the level of effort in these two months that we have been doing, I think the same as my three colleagues. The greatest difficulty is getting school colleagues to agree"*.

The sixth and final sub-topic was the differing expectations in the initial session about the stress of applying these practices in the future. Teachers felt that there would be increased stress related to students not achieving positive results, teachers not being able to properly implement the practices, time or context, and other agents (teachers and families). A smaller number of teachers felt that there would be less or no stress, based on the evidence supporting these practices. In the second session, three months later, the teachers felt that there was some stress around the application of NDBI practices. This stress was related to feeling unsure about designing and properly implementing the practices, to their teacher training, to a lack of participation and coordination, and to expectations from other agents (teachers and families). Some of the teachers indicated that they were not suffering from increased stress generally in terms of the NDBI practices. Six months later, in the third and final session, there was another change to the teachers' perceptions, as the majority at this timepoint felt that there was no increased stress generally in terms of the NDBI practices. A minority of teachers did feel increased stress in terms of the same factors as the previous session. In relation to this final sub-topic, participant P4 G1 E1 said, *"Let's see, it is not stress either, maybe the, the..., that is, the insecurity of not knowing if you are doing it right and, and... Sometimes not achieving that teamwork and that collaboration on the part of some, some companions. That is, stress..., no, it doesn't generate it but, sometimes, it does frustrate you when you want to do things and other people consider that they are your job, wow, it causes me a lot of stress trying to convince them to participate too"*.

4   Discussion

The present article aimed to explore what special education (Hearing and Language) teachers' thought about of a small-scale online professional development model based on the "iScience" approach—offered by the NPCD, currently known as NCAEP [36, 39]. It also sought to determine whether they felt this model was feasible in their classrooms and schools.

The evaluation of professional development programs has critical implications for the education of autistic students and for their families [48, 49], all the more important with the growing number of autistic students and consequent escalating demand for services [7, 42]. Given this reality and the dearth of data and qualitative information on the outcomes of web-based in-service programs for these children, the findings from this and similar professional development evaluation studies are crucial because of the need to identify the processes used to improve teachers' knowledge and skills [49] that will have the most impact on these students' inclusion [16, 17].

The findings from the present qualitative study, looking at the perceptions of the first cohort of special education teachers, outline three main topics: the perception of a positive impact of the online training on participating teachers; the perception of the positive impact of this online training on the autistic students; and the perception of the feasibility of implementing NDBI practices in school environments through this online training model. We assessed the study findings and their ramifications considering the scant literature regarding qualitative research on web-based teacher training about evidence-based practices aimed at autistic students.

In terms of the online training's positive impact on the teachers, the participants were positive about the knowledge they acquired through this online professional development model, about changes in their professional practice, and about the NDBI practices for daily teaching. These findings are consistent with previous quantitative findings from studies investigating the effectiveness of web-based or technology-enabled courses and programs in helping teachers improve their knowledge and skills about working with autistic children [36, 39, 49, 50] or children with disabilities [51–53].

In terms of the online training's positive impact on the autistic students, the participants felt that implementing the NDBI practices covered by the training would improve the students' competencies and abilities. There is extremely limited literature on this topic in the school environment. The evidence collected in the few papers that have been published to date in different environments, such as early intervention settings, indicate positive results for autistic children's development [54–57].

The participants mostly felt that it would be feasible to implement the NDBI practices in their schools without too many concessions and without too much sacrifice. This is in line with recent research on this topic in community-based inclusion programs [54, 58, 59]. In our study, time seems to have been a key factor both in improving perceptions of successful or effective implementation and in decreasing perceptions of effort and stress associated with implementing these NDBI practices. This time during which teachers engage in the practice may influence their perceptions of self-efficacy. Other important factors related to the subtopic "successful/effective implementation" include perceptions of knowledge and proper implementation of the practices (fidelity). Learning about EBPs is just the first step to properly implementing these practices in programs for autistic students. In addition, having specific guidance about how to implement practices is crucial because online training alone is probably not sufficient to ensure that. This kind of web-based training provides basic procedural information about each EBP, but additional support through coaching and feedback may be necessary to achieved sustained, proper use in programs [39]. This is a critical issue because there is a growing body of literature indicating that receiving training and using evidence-based strategies under the umbrella of a high-quality program that employs EBP results in higher levels of teacher self-efficacy, which is a buffer against burnout [39] and contributes to effective inclusion and other successes for these students [37].

It is important to highlight the importance of a variable that interacts with the different subtopics related to the feasibility of NDBI practices in a school environment and with the topic related the positive impact on participating teachers. This is the involvement of other agents (such as non-special education teachers and families) in knowing about and implementing these practices. Without spreading knowledge and use of these practices to other teachers and school professionals, the participating teachers felt that effective implementation would be very difficult.

Finally, it is important to note that there is a risk of these practices not taking root with the teachers. This may be because they are too complex to apply, and a lack of monitoring may lead to them being abandoned. In addition, due to a lack of involvement and commitment to these practices in school communities, there needs to be a stable structure that affects all of the agents (management team, teachers, colleagues, and families). Teachers' perceptions of competence may be modulated by these two factors: monitoring and coordination with other agents.

5 Limitations and Implication for Future Research and Practice

There are several important limitations that must be considered in this study, which suggest several recommendations for future research.

Firstly, the generalisability of the results is limited because the study only examined one cohort of the three making up the more extensive research project. We should also consider the idea that the results might indicate a narrow viewpoint of teacher's perceptions in one region of Spain rather than from the whole country. Further research is needed on this topic, but the findings are interesting despite that because of the cross-cultural approach.

Secondly, limited staff for the study affected the process of collecting and analysing data. The lead author, as a specialist in Hearing and Language and autism, had to conduct the interview and also was the only one to interpret the data, probably influencing the study results. This dual relationship may have affected the outcome of the focus groups. To reduce any bias, the researcher worked with the other authors to discuss the coding and finalize the topics. Additional actions will be needed in the future with the subsequent cohorts to limit any such bias.

Thirdly, future research will need to assess the feasibility of implementing NDBI practices in day-to-day schooling and how faithfully it is done beyond teachers' perceptions. Research design should incorporate additional support for teachers through coaching and feedback as noted in previous sections.

6 Conclusion

Little is known about the impact of technology on practices to improve educational outcomes for students, particularly those with autism-related SEN [42]. Our findings contribute to improving our understanding of the procedures for helping teachers develop and improve their competence, knowledge, and skills, crucial to their future perceptions of self-efficacy and directly related to inclusion for these students [37]. The participating teachers felt that what they learned through the online training was appropriate for implementing this evidence-based practice in their schools. The thought that the NDBI practices were feasible and useful, and that implementing them would help to improve autistic students' competencies and abilities. The study identified two factors that influenced teachers' perceptions: the need for support and for monitoring how the practices are implemented; and the need for school administrations to be involved to promote coordination and the involvement of all educational agents through a stable participation structure. These are important findings and research needs to continue about fidelity, feasibility, and the positive impact on student outcomes.

References

1. American Psychiatric Association: Diagnostic and Statistical Manual of Mental Disorders, 5th edn. American Psychiatric Publishing, Washington, DC (2013)
2. Heraty, S., et al.: Bridge-building between communities: imagining the future of biomedical autism research. Cell **186**(18), 3747–3752 (2023). https://doi.org/10.1016/j.cell.2023.08.004
3. Zeidan, J., et al.: Global prevalence of autism: a systematic review update. Autism Res. **15**(5), 778–790 (2022). https://doi.org/10.1002/aur.2696
4. Fombonne, E.: Epidemiological controversies in autism. Swiss Arch. Neurol. Psychiatry Psychother. **171**, w03084 (2020). https://doi.org/10.4414/sanp.2020.03084
5. Roleska, M., et al.: Autism and the right to education in the EU: policy mapping and scoping review of the United Kingdom, France Poland and Spain. PLoS ONE **13**(8), e0202336 (2018). https://doi.org/10.1371/journal.pone.0202336
6. Maenner, M.J., et al.: Prevalence and characteristics of autism spectrum disorder among children aged 8 years — autism and developmental disabilities monitoring network, 11 sites, United States, 2020. MMWR Surveill. Summ. **72**(2), 1–14 (2023). https://doi.org/10.15585/mmwr.ss7202a1
7. Larraceleta, A.: La presencia del autismo en las escuelas: datos para la reflexión. In: Alcantud, F., Fernández, J., Alonso, Y. (coord.) Bienestar Psicológico en la Escuela y en la Familia. Síntesis. Madrid, pp. 77–92 (2023)
8. Larraceleta, A., Castejón, L., Núñez, J.C.: Special education teachers' training needs on evidence-based practice on autism in Spain: an online program for in-service teacher training. In: Tomczyk, Ł (ed.) New Media Pedagogy: Research Trends, Methodological Challenges and Successful Implementations: First International Conference, NMP 2022, Kraków, Poland, October 10–12, 2022, Revised Selected Papers, pp. 83–101. Springer Nature Switzerland, Cham (2023). https://doi.org/10.1007/978-3-031-44581-1_7
9. May, T., Williams, K.: Understanding increased enrolments of autism and mental health needs in NSW government schools. Monash University. Department of Pediatrics (2018). https://education.nsw.gov.au/content/dam/main-education/teaching-and-learning/disability-learning-and-support/our-disability-strategy/Understanding-increased-enrolments-of-autism-and-mental-health-needs-in-NSW-government-schools.pdf. Accessed 4 Dec 2023
10. McConkey, R.: The rise in the numbers of pupils identified by schools with autism spectrum disorder (ASD): a comparison of the four countries in the United Kingdom. Support Learn. **35**(2), 132–143 (2020). https://doi.org/10.1111/1467-9604.12296
11. Ministerio de Educación y Formación Profesional.: Servicios al Ciudadano. Enseñanzas no Universitarias. Alumnado con Necesidad Específica de Apoyo Educativo. Alumnado conNecesidades Educativas Especiales. Curso 21–22. Ministerio de Educación y Formación Profesional de España. https://www.educacionyfp.gob.es/servicios-al-ciudadano/estadisticas/nouniversitaria/alumnado/apoyo/2021-2022.html. Accessed 2 Dec 2023

12. Pellicano, L., Bölte, S., Stahmer, A.: The current illusion of educational inclusion. Autism **22**(4), 386–387 (2018). https://doi.org/10.1177/1362361318766166
13. Bellini, S., Henry, D., Pratt, C.: From intuition to data: using logic models to measure professional development outcomes for educators working with students on the autism spectrum. Teach. Educ. Spec. Educ. **34**(1), 37–51 (2011). https://doi.org/10.1177/0888406410384153
14. Morrier, M.J., Hess, K.L., Heflin, L.J.: Teacher training for implementation of teaching strategies for students with autism spectrum disorders. Teach. Educ. Spec. Educ. **34**, 119–132 (2011). https://doi.org/10.1177/0888406410376660
15. Odom, S.L., et al.: Educational interventions for children and youth with autism: a 40-year perspective. J. Autism Dev. Disord. **51**, 4354–4369 (2021). https://doi.org/10.1007/s10803-021-04990-1
16. Van Kessel, R., et al.: Inclusive education in the European Union: a fuzzy-set qualitative comparative analysis of education policy for autism. Soc. Work Public Health **36**(2), 286–299 (2021). https://doi.org/10.1080/19371918.2021.1877590
17. Van Mieghem, A., Verschueren, K., Petry, K., Struyf, E.: An analysis of research on inclusive education: a systematic search and meta review. Int. J. Incl. Educ. **24**(6), 675–689 (2020). https://doi.org/10.1080/13603116.2018.1482012
18. Alhossein, A.: Teachers' knowledge and use of evidenced-based practices for students with autism spectrum disorder in Saudi Arabia. Front. Psychol. **12**, 741409 (2021). https://doi.org/10.3389/fpsyg.2021.741409
19. Barry, L., Holloway, J., Gallagher, S., McMahon, J.: Teacher characteristics, knowledge and use of evidence-based practices in autism education in Ireland. J. Autism Dev. Disord. **52**, 3536–3546 (2022). https://doi.org/10.1007/s10803-021-05223-1
20. Brock, M.E., Huber, H.B., Carter, E.W., Juarez, A.P., Warren, Z.E.: Statewide assessment of professional development needs related to educating students with autism spectrum disorder. Focus Autism Other Dev. Disabil. **29**, 67–79 (2014). https://doi.org/10.1177/1088357614522290
21. Hess, K.L., Morrier, M.J., Heflin, L.J., Ivey, M.L.: Autism treatment survey: services received by children with autism spectrum disorders in public school classroom. J. Autism Dev. Disord. **38**, 961–971 (2008). https://doi.org/10.1007/s10803-007-0470-5
22. McNeill, J.: Social validity and teachers' use of evidence-based practices for autism. J. Autism Dev. Disord. **49**(11), 4585–4594 (2019). https://doi.org/10.1007/s10803-019-04190-y
23. Locke, J., et al.: Supporting the inclusion and retention of autistic students: exploring teachers' and paraeducators' use of evidence-based practices in public elementary schools. Front. Psychiatry **13**, 961219 (2022). https://doi.org/10.3389/fpsyt.2022.961219
24. Odom, S.L., Cox, A.W., Brock, M.E.: Implementation science, professional development, and autism spectrum disorders. Except. Child. **79**(2), 233–251 (2013). https://doi.org/10.1177/001440291307900207
25. Arnaiz-Sánchez, P., Escarbajal Frutos, A., Alcaraz García, S., de Haro Rodríguez, R.: Formación del profesorado para la construcción de aulas abiertas a la inclusión. Rev. de Educ. **393**, 37–67 (2021). https://doi.org/10.4438/1988-592X-RE-2021-393-485
26. Sanz-Cervera, P., Fernández-Andrés, M.-I., Pastor-Cerezuela, G., Tárraga-Mínguez, R.: Pre-service teachers' knowledge, misconceptions and gaps about autism spectrum disorder. Teach. Educ. Spec. Educ. **40**(3), 212–224 (2017). https://doi.org/10.1177/0888406417700963
27. Vela, E., Martín, L., Martín, I.: Analysis of ASD classrooms: specialised open classrooms in the community of Madrid. Sustainability. **12**(18), 7342 (2020). https://doi.org/10.3390/su12187342
28. Larraceleta-González, A., Castejón-Fernández, L., Iglesias-García, M.T., Núñez-Pérez, J.C.: Un Estudio de las Necesidades de Formación del Profesorado en las Prácticas Basadas en Evidencias Científicas en el Ámbito del Alumnado con Trastorno del Espectro del Autismo.

Siglo Cero Revista Española sobre Discapacidad Intelectual **53**(2), 125–144 (2022). https://doi.org/10.14201/scero2022532125144

29. Larraceleta, A., Castejón, L., Iglesias-García, M.T., Núñez, J.C.: Assessment of public special education teachers training needs on evidence-based practice for students with autism spectrum disorders in Spain. Children **9**, 83 (2022). https://doi.org/10.3390/children9010083

30. National Autism Center: Findings and Conclusions: National Standards Report, Phase 1; National Autism Center: Randolf. MA, USA (2009)

31. Odom, S.L., Collet-Klingerberg, L., Rogers, S.J., Hatton, D.D.: Evidence-based practices in interventions for children and youth with autism spectrum disorders. Prev. Sch. Fail. **54**(4), 275–282 (2010). https://doi.org/10.1080/10459881003785506

32. National Autism Center: Findings and Conclusions: National Standards Report, Phase 2. National Autism Center (2015)

33. Wong, C., et al.: Evidence-based practices for children, youth, and young adults with autism spectrum disorder: a comprehensive review. J. Autism Dev. Disord. **45**(7), 1951–1966 (2015). https://doi.org/10.1007/s10803-014-2351-z

34. Steinbrenner, J.R., et al.: Evidence-Based Practices for Children, Youth, and Young Adults with Autism. Frank Porter Graham Child Development Institute, The University of North Carolina: Chapel Hill, NC, USA (2020). https://ncaep.fpg.unc.edu/sites/ncaep.fpg.unc.edu/files/imce/documents/EBP%20Report%202020.pdf. Accessed 12 Dec 2023

35. Marder, T., deBettencourt, L.U.: Teaching students with ASD using evidence-based practices: why is training critical now? Teach. Educ. Spec. Educ. **38**(1), 5–12 (2015). https://doi.org/10.1177/0888406414565838

36. Morin, K.L., Sam, A., Tomaszewski, B., Waters, V., Odom, S.L.: Knowledge of evidence based practices and frequency of selection among school-based professionals of students with autism. J. Spec. Educ. **55**(3), 143–152 (2021). https://doi.org/10.1177/0022466920958688

37. Kossewska, J., et al.: Towards inclusive education of children with autism spectrum disorder. The impact of teachers' autism-specific professional development on their confidence in their professional competences. Int. J. Spec. Educ. **36**(2), 27–35 (2022). https://doi.org/10.52291/ijse.2021.36.15

38. Parsons, S., Charman, T., Faulkner, R., Ragan, J., Wallace, S., Wittermeyer, K.: Commentary-bridging the research and practice gap in autism: the importance of creating research partnerships with schools. Autism **17**(3), 268–280 (2013). https://doi.org/10.1177/1362361312472068

39. Sam, A.M., Cox, A.W., Savage, M.N., Waters, V., Odom, S.L.: Disseminating information on evidence-based practices for children and youth with autism spectrum disorder: AFIRM. J. Autism Dev. Disord. **50**, 1931–1940 (2019). https://doi.org/10.1007/s10803-019-03945-x

40. Autism Focused Intervention Resources and Modules. https://afirm.fpg.unc.edu. Accessed 14 Dec 2023

41. Osman, D.J., Warner, J.R.: Measuring teacher motivation: the missing link between professional development and practice. Teach. Teach. Educ. **92**, 103064 (2020). https://doi.org/10.1016/j.tate.2020.103064

42. Catagnus, R.M., Pagliaro, J., Tailor, B.A. Technology for staff training, collaboration, and supervision in school-based programs for children with autism. In: Mundy, P., Mastergeorge A.M. (Ed.). Educational interventions for students with autism. Wiley, UC Davis Mind Institute, pp. 155–175 (2012)

43. Bruinsma, Y., Minjarez, M.B., Schreibman, L., Stahmer, A.C.: Naturalistic Developmental Behavioural Interventions for Autism Spectrum Disorder. Paul H. Brookes Publishing Co., Baltimore (2020)

44. Flick, U.: Introducción a la Investigación Cualitativa. Morata. Paidea Galiza fundación., Madrid, A Coruña (2018)

45. Braun, V., Clarke, V.: Using thematic analysis in psychology. Qual. Res. Psychol. **3**(2), 77–101 (2006). https://doi.org/10.1191/1478088706qp063oa
46. Braun, V., Clarke, V.: Reflecting on reflexive thematic analysis. Qual. Res. Sport Exerc. Health **11**(4), 589–597 (2019). https://doi.org/10.1080/2159676X.2019.1628806
47. Byrne, D.: A worked example of Braun and Clarke's approach to reflexive thematic analysis. Qual. Quant. **56**, 1391–1412 (2022). https://doi.org/10.1007/s11135-021-01182-y
48. Maddox, L.L., Marvin, C.A.: A preliminary evaluation of a statewide professional development program on autism spectrum disorders. Teach. Educ. Spec. Educ. **36**, 37–50 (2013). https://doi.org/10.1177/0888406412463827
49. Rakap, S., Jones, H.A., Emery, A.K.: Evaluation of a web-based professional development program (project ACE) for teachers of children with autism spectrum disorders. Teach. Educ. Spec. Educ. **38**(3), 221–239 (2015). https://doi.org/10.1177/0888406414535821
50. Law, G.C., Dutt, A., Neihart, M.: Increasing intervention fidelity among special education teachers for autism intervention: A pilot study of utilizing a mobile-app-enabled training program. Res. Autism Spectr. Disord. **67**, 101411 (2019). https://doi.org/10.1016/j.rasd.2019.101411
51. Brown, J.A., Woods, J.J.: Evaluation of a multicomponent online communication professional development program for early interventionists. J. Early Interv. **34**, 222–242 (2012). https://doi.org/10.1177/1053815113483316
52. Chen, D., Klein, M.D., Minor, L.: Interdisciplinary perspectives in early intervention: professional development in multiple disabilities through distance education. Infants Young Child. **22**, 146–158 (2009). https://doi.org/10.1097/IYC.0b013e3181a030e0
53. Frey, T.J.: An analysis of online professional development outcomes for students with disabilities. Teach. Educ. Spec. Educ. **32**, 83–96 (2009). https://doi.org/10.1177/0888406408330867
54. Jobin, A., Stahmer, A.C., Camacho, N., May, G.C., Gist, K., Brookman-Frazee, L.: Pilot feasibility of a community inclusion preschool program for children with autism. J. Early Interv. **46**(2), 239–254 (2023). https://doi.org/10.1177/10538151231217483
55. Maye, M., Sanchez, V.E., Stone-MacDonald, A., et al.: Early interventionists' appraisals of intervention strategies for toddlers with autism spectrum disorder and their peers in inclusive childcare classrooms. J. Autism Dev. Disord. **50**, 4199–4208 (2020). https://doi.org/10.1007/s10803-020-04456-w
56. Mrachko, A.A., Kaczmarek, L.A., Kostewicz, D.E., Vostal, B.: Teaching therapeutic support staff to implement NDBI strategies for children with ASD using behavior skills training. Topics Early Child. Spec. Educ. **42**(4), 329–343 (2023). https://doi.org/10.1177/02711214221110166
57. Vivanti, G., Jessica Paynter, E., Duncan, H.F., Dissanayake, C., Rogers, S.J.: Effectiveness and feasibility of the early start Denver model implemented in a group-based community childcare setting. J. Autism Dev. Disord. **44**(12), 3140–3153 (2014). https://doi.org/10.1007/s10803-014-2168-9
58. D'Agostino, S.R., Pinkelman, S.E., Maye, M.: Implementation of naturalistic developmental behavioral intervention strategies: an examination of preschool teachers' perceptions. J. Early Interv. **46**(2), 299–320 (2023). https://doi.org/10.1177/10538151231217451
59. Rogers, S.J., Stahmer, A., Talbott, M., et al.: Feasibility of delivering parent-implemented NDBI interventions in low-resource regions: a pilot randomized controlled study. J Neurodevelop Disord **14**, 3 (2022). https://doi.org/10.1186/s11689-021-09410-0

Digital Inclusion and Exclusion
and Development of Human Resources
in European Countries

Ludvík Eger(✉)

University of West Bohemia, Univerzitní 8, 301 00 Pilsen, Czech Republic
leger@fek.zcu.cz

Abstract. Digital transformation has large effects on people´s lives in European countries. ICT competencies and access to the Internet and new media are key pre-conditions for citizens in these countries and their ability to use e-services every day, and to be successful in a dynamic changing labour market. The study investigates opportunities for the development of the EU countries in the context of digital transformation. The selected indicators were used to compare EU 27 countries. The basic key performance indicator is GDP per capita. This indicator corresponds very well with the ranking of countries according to the human development index and, surprisingly, Internet penetration achieves a similar effect. Next, the correlation of GDP per capita with ISCED 5–8 was higher than the correlation of GDP per capita with the CEDEFOP index, both results can be considered a moderate association. Special attention is paid to Germany, Spain, Poland and the Czech Republic and the changes in their position in selected indicators in the context of the EU 27. The results show that it is necessary to pay attention not only to citizens who achieve higher education, but also to the group of young people who, for various reasons, do not complete the educational process. Further and more detailed research on digital inclusion is needed.

Keywords: EU countries · GDP per capita · Internet penetration · skills development · digital inclusion

1 Introduction

The purpose of the conducted study is to compare the current state of human resource development in the context of digital transformation and EU countries with a focus on selected indicators from the education field. Special attention is paid to selected basic indicators on the use of ICT by citizens of EU countries.

Digitalization is an ongoing trend, and EU countries have digitalized rapidly over the last two decades. Development of the digital infrastructure and rapid connectivity bring citizens and businesses in EU countries new opportunities [1]. The level and pace of digitalization vary widely across countries [2], industries and other social spheres influencing not only business and working processes but also consumption, education and recreation, etc. Developing human resources and matching job profiles have become

Ł. Tomczyk (Ed.): NMP 2023, CCIS 2130, pp. 225–234, 2024.
https://doi.org/10.1007/978-3-031-63235-8_15

essential tasks to promote economic and social growth [3, 4]. A key role here is not only the creation of prerequisites such as the availability of the Internet (Internet penetration), but also the education of the population, including lifelong education.

Digital transformation is as much about people as it is about technology. Digital transformation has large effects on people´s lives and the labour market [5, 6] and brings pressure on the employee skills that organizations need to succeed [7, 8]. Digitalization is changing the skills needed to access economic opportunity [9, 10].

The Sustainable development of a Society 4.0 needs to reduce digital exclusion and support the digital inclusion of all citizens. Tomczyk et al. [11] state that the process of the digital exclusion has become increasingly noticeable and represents a sub-type of social exclusion. Gained ICT competencies and access to the Internet and new media are key preconditions for citizens and their ability to use widely e-services every day, and to be successful in a dynamic changing labour market.

Therefore, the presented study, using selected indicators, investigates opportunities for the development of EU countries in the context of digital transformation. Gross Domestic Product (GDP) per capita will be used as the basic indicator of the country's performance, and we will also use the composite indicator of Human resource development (HDI). Subsequently, we will look at the position of the EU countries using partial indicators from the field of education in relation to the above-mentioned indicators. We will specifically focus on the following countries: Germany, Spain, Poland and the Czech Republic.

2   Computer and Information Literacy and Digital Exclusion

In relation to the focus of the presented study, in the theoretical part, we will briefly state a few basic remarks on computer and information literacy and digital exclusion.

European Commission [12] evaluates Computer and information literacy (ICT) as digital competencies in The International Computer and Information Literacy Study (ICILS) that researches the extent to which young people are able to use information and communication technology (ICT) productively in school, at home, in society, and their future workplaces. Rothagi et al. [13] state that ICT literacy comprises the ability to process digital information, communicate with others and solve given problems. In addition, it should be noted, that at present, the development of ICT literacy requires more than fundamental technical knowledge and skills but the basic skills in this area are the key above basic skills.

The Older definition by the International ICT Literacy Panel [14, p.2] states that ICT literacy enables individuals to use "digital technology, communication tools, and/or networks to access, manage, integrate, evaluate and create information in order to function in a knowledge society". These abilities are highly important for getting along in a changing global society as well as for life-long learning [15, 16].

Eurostat in this field uses DigComp Framework (actual version is 2.2) that involves the "confident, critical and responsible use of, and engagement with, digital technologies for learning, at work, and for participation in society." The framework is defined as a combination of knowledge, skills and attitudes [17] and is based on the document Council Recommendation on Key Competences for Lifelong Learning [18].

The digital divide is a phenomenon which refers to disparities in ICT access, usage, and related outcomes. The digital divide refers to the gap between people who have adequate access to ICT and people who have poor or no access to ICT. It clearly has an impact on digital exclusion. The digital divide can be classified into three different segments [19] and the access to Internet could be considered a prerequisite in this field.

World Economic Forum [20] stated that in the European Union, 70% of homes in 2021 had high-speed internet connections, up from 16% in 2013, according to Eurostat but in rural areas, which can struggle to get internet coverage, only 37% of homes had high-speed internet in 2021. There were significant differences among countries, for example three top were Malta, Luxembourg, and Denmark followed by Spain, three on the other side were Greece, Cyprus, and Italy. Thus, the annual EU surveys on ICT usage in households and by individuals are considered a major source of information for monitoring efforts to promote a single European information space, an inclusive knowledge-based society and quality of life. For the purpose of our research, this means that we will compare this indicator with GDP per capita and HDI and we will investigate an association here.

For example, research by Cruz-Jesus et al. [21] or Tomczyk et al. [22] underlined the importance of complementing cross-country analysis focused on the digital divide and consequent topics. Thus, the research raises the following research questions:

RQ1: What indicators that represent an education level in EU countries affect the digital inclusion of their citizens?
RQ2: How do these indicators correspond with the level of GDP per capita?

3 Method

The following indicators mentioned below were selected to compare the selected countries in the context of the EU27. The basic KPI is GDP per capita, where Germany is ranked 9th, Spain 13th, Czech Republic 18th and Poland 22nd in the EU27 (Table 1). A short description of selected indicators follows.

Gross Domestic Product (GDP) per capita is an economic metric that breaks down a country's economic output per person. It is relevant to use GDP per capita to determine how prosperous countries are based on their economic growth GDP per capita. We have used this indicator as a baseline for our comparison of EU countries in the focus on human resource development. Eurostat [23] states that GDP measures the value of the total final output of goods and services produced by an economy within a certain period of time. The indicator is calculated as the ratio of real GDP to the average population of a specific year, in our case, 2022.

First, we were interested in the Human Development Index (HDI) which is a summary measure of average achievement in key dimensions of human development: a long and healthy life, being knowledgeable and having a decent standard of living. This index was published Human Development Report Office (HRDO) of the United Nations Development Programme [24]. The HDI is the geometric mean of normalized indices for each of the three dimensions. Dimension knowledge or education is measured by the mean of years of schooling for adults aged 25 years and more and expected years of schooling for children of school-entering age. A certain disadvantage of this complex indicator is that in addition to a Long and healthy life it also contains the dimension of a decent standard of living that is built on GNI per capita. Thus, there is some overlap with the default indicator (GDP per capita). Detailed information is available in Human Development Reports [25].

First, we were interested in the DESI because this complex index is focused on Industry 4.0 or digital transformation and we were interested in comparing countries using DESI. The Digital Economy and Society Index (DESI) summarises indicators on Europe's digital performance and tracks the progress of EU countries [26]. It should be noted, the DESI contains key areas: Human capital, connectivity, information of digital technology, and digital public services [26]. This is also significant for our comparison.

Eurostat [27] states that in 2021, just over two-fifths (41.2%) of the EU population aged 25–34 years had a tertiary level of educational attainment (ISCED 5–8). Thus, the next indicator is Tertiary educational attainment (age 25–34), European Commission, country reports [28]. In general, we assume that people participating in tertiary education have at least the necessary basic ICT skills, which are further reflected in their digital literacy. In this context, we will also discuss one sub-indicator Early leavers from education and training (18–24), European Commission, country reports [28], which in turn indicates a part of the population that may have problems in using ICT, especially for learning, but also for finding a job, etc.

In this study, we also used a more robust human resource development indicator from European Centre for the Development of Vocational Training (CEDEFOP) to compare countries. Skills Development represents the training and education activities of the country and the immediate outputs of that system in terms of the skills developed and attained. Sub-pillars are included to distinguish compulsory education, and other education and training (lifelong learning) activities [29]. Basic education and the education and further education sub-pillar each include 3 indicators to measure quality in this area. This indicator is therefore more robust than ISCED 5–8, which focuses on tertiary education.

For the purpose of this study is an important indicator of Internet users per EU country, also called Internet penetration. Data are available, for example, from Internet World Stats [30]. We used data from Eurostat [31], Digital economy and society statistics - households and individuals. Eurostat generally states that in n 2022, 90% of EU individuals aged between 16 and 74 years used the Internet at least once within the three months prior to the survey date.

Additionally, we used as a sub-indicator the percentage of people in the country's population who use social media. Especially for younger generations, social media is important for getting information and developing and maintaining relationships with other people, even though the necessary trust in social media is decreasing [32].

4   Results

Tables 1 and 2 below contain data for individual indicators for the EU27. The countries Germany, Spain, Czech Republic and Poland, which were compared in more detail, are highlighted.

As can be seen from Table 1, Germany (DE) (2022) achieved a GDP per capita 35 870 EUR, Spain (ES) 24 580 EUR, the Czech Republic (CZ) 18 470 EUR and Poland

Table 1. EU countries and GDP, DESI, Internet indicators

Country	GDP per capita	Order	DESI order	Internet users	Order	SM users
Belgium	36 860	8	16	94.53	8	80.9
Bulgaria	7 250	27	26	83.11	26	65.7
Czechia	18 470	18	19	91.62	15	76.9
Denmark	51 460	3	2	98.09	2	83.8
Estonia	16 250	20	9	92.33	11	80.8
Finland	37 920	7	1	97.68	3	83.3
France	33 230	10	12	91.91	14	80.5
Croatia	14 540	23	21	82.92	27	73.1
Ireland	77 490	2	5	95.59	5	79.8
Italy	27 860	11	18	86.14	23	74.5
Cyprus	26 550	12	20	90.91	16	87.6
Lithuania	14 970	21	14	88.43	20.5	77.6
Latvia	13 320	25	17	92.23	12	80.4
Luxembourg	83 940	1	8	98.36	1	62.1
Hungary	14 370	24	22	89.7	22	72.2
Malta	23 810	14	6	92.1	13	78.9
Germany	35 870	9	13	93.01	10	70.9
Netherlands	43 310	5	3	95.52	6	88.1
Poland	14 600	22	24	88.43	20.5	66.3
Portugal	19 290	16	15	85.06	24	78.5
Austria	38 340	6	10	94.16	9	82
Romania	10 110	26	27	88.86	19	67.3
Greece	18 830	17	25	84.03	25	72.3
Slovakia	16 300	19	23	90.19	17	71.1
Slovenia	22 450	15	11	89.92	18	77.4
Spain	24 580	13	7	94.91	7	85.6
Sweden	46 250	4	4	97.18	4	82.2

(PL) 14 600 EUR, this is only 68.5% for ES, 51,5% for CZ and 40,7% of the Germany value in this KPI (key performance indicator). In the DESI (important index for digital transformation), CZ is in 19th place and DE in 13th place and both countries have slightly negative shifted in comparison with their position in GDP per capita. ES is in 10th place and PL in 18th place, which means the opposite, these countries have a slightly positive shift in comparison with their position in GDP per capita.

Table 2. EU countries and CEDEFOP and indicators from education area

Country	CEDEFOP Skills	Order	ISCED 5–8	Order	Early leavers	Order
Belgium	52	14	50.9	6	6.7	10
Bulgaria	33	25	33.6	24	12.2	24
Czechia	58	8	34.9	23	6.4	9
Denmark	66	3	49.7	8	9.8	18.5
Estonia	68	2	43.2	15	9.8	18.5
Finland	83	1	40.1	19	8.2	15
France	39	20.5	50.3	7	7.8	12.5
Croatia	56	9.5	35.7	21.5	2.4	1
Ireland	53	12	61.7	2	3.3	4
Italy	39	20.5	28.3	26	12.7	25
Cyprus	26	27	58.3	3	10.2	20
Lithuania	49	17	57.5	4	5.3	5.5
Latvia	50	16	45.5	13	7.3	11
Luxembourg	56	9.5	62.6	1	9.3	17
Hungary	44	18	32.9	25	12	23
Malta	36	22	42.5	16	10.7	21
Germany	59	7	35.7	21.5	11.8	22
Netherlands	64	4	55.6	5	5.3	5.5
Poland	51	15	40.6	18	5.9	7.5
Portugal	35	23.5	47.5	12	5.9	7.5
Austria	62	5.5	42.4	17	8	14
Romania	29	26	23.3	27	15.3	27
Greece	35	23.5	44.2	14	3.2	3
Slovakia	53	12	39.5	20	7.8	12.5
Slovenia	53	12	47.9	11	3.1	2
Spain	41	19	48.7	10	13.3	26
Sweden	62	5.5	49.3	9	8.4	16

First, we analyzed the relationship between GDP per capita and DESI using Spearman's correlation. The value of r is 0.769 and p (2-tailed) < .001, GDP per capita - DESI, and shows a high level of association between these indicators. For the purpose of our research, we also found an association between countries' GDP per capita ranking and Internet penetration (= % of users in selected countries). Therefore, we also tried to calculate the correlation between countries' GDP per capita ranking and the data of Internet penetration, these data are from early 2023, [33]. The value of r is 0.779 and p

(2-tailed) < .001, GDP per capita – Internet penetration, and shows again the high level of association between these indicators.

It is generally assumed that human resource development reflects the level (quality) of education in a country. We used two indicators. A simple indicator is: Tertiary educational attainment (age 25–34), the more complex indicator is the European Skills Index by CEDEFOP.

CZ is in ISCED 5–8 in 23rd place but in 8th place by CEDEFOP. DE is in ISCED 5–8 in 21.5 place and in 7th place by CEDEFOP. ES is in ISCED 5–8 in 10th place but in 19th place by CEDEFOP. PL is in ISCED 5–8 in 18th place and in 20.5th place by CEDEFOP. The obtained points by CEDEFOP for CZ and DE are almost the same, a negative shift is observed for ES.

The correlation of GDP per capita with ISCED 5–8 (r is 0.586 and p (2-tailed) = .001) is higher than the correlation of GDP per capita with CEDEFOP index (r is 0.477 and p (2-tailed) = .012). Both results can be considered moderate association.

As we mentioned above, we also focused on one specific negative factor that may indicate future problems in the digital competence of a part of the population of a certain country, Early leavers from education and training (18–24). The data are favourable for CZ (2030 target < 9%, situation in 2022 = 6.4%). The target is the same for EU countries but DE has actually 11.8%, situation in ES is 13.3. PL reached the best result from these countries, only 5.9%.

Finally, Table 1 shows the percentage of the population that uses social media in EU27. The data is from the beginning of 2023. Datareportal [33] calculates users aged 18 and above. The most users of social media are in ES (85.6%), followed by the CZ (76.9), Germany (70.9) and the least in Poland (66.3). Association between Internet users and SM users is statistically significant on a moderate level (r is 0.542 and p (2-tailed) = .004).

5 Discussion

It is generally acknowledged that there are differences between EU countries. The main difference is already according to our main indicator, i.e. GDP per capita. It should be mentioned, Germany is a founding member of the European Community (1952), Spain joined in 1986 and the Czech Republic and Poland in 2004.

To answer RQ2, we compared several indicators with GDP per capita. As we expected, GDP per capita corresponds very well with the ranking of countries according to the HDI (RQ2). Surprisingly, a specific indicator, Internet penetration, achieves a similar effect. This is an interesting finding in the context of the development of Society 4.0.

Furthermore, using data from Eurostat and CEDEFOP, we focused in particular on education (RQ1). Our results show that it is necessary to pay attention not only to citizens who achieve higher education, but also to the group of young people who, for various reasons, do not complete the educational process. Here, Germany and Spain are currently failing to meet EU targets, while the Czech Republic and Poland are performing very well. Further research needs to investigate more closely the contradiction between categories ISCED 5–8 and Early leavers and examine what impact this may have on digital transformation and social exclusion of population groups.

Previous research [15, 34, 35] has also shown that people use ICT for different purposes and on different levels. This also means that not all people's ICT skills will be useful for their employment in the labour market [4, 6, 36] and for supporting an active life in society.

Further, attention needs to be paid to different groups, and indeed the problem may not just be with older generations [11, 36], as the data behind the Early leavers indicator just shows.

The opposite specific problem is Internet addiction [37]. Relatively little is known about the effects of internet addiction on people. These people have usually above average ICT skills but, on the other hand, they have problems in their daily lives at school, work, with relationships etc. Problematic Internet use and time spent online are connected topics [38].

The conducted study does not provide a clear solution to the issue of digital inclusion. On the contrary, it highlights selected problems that the data show in the context of EU countries.

6   Conclusion

There are differences in the performance of EU countries. For changes in the digital transformation period, attention to the human factor is needed. The study shows that there is a high association between GDP per capita and the Human Development Index. Essentially the same level of association was found with the Internet penetration indicator, which is for us a prerequisite for the use of ICT in individual countries.

For selected education indicators, Germany, Spain, the Czech Republic and Poland were compared in more detail. CEDEFOP and Early leavers indicators versus position of EU countries according to GDP per capita show that there are differences here that are worth exploring further.

A limitation of the research is the use of only selected indicators and so-called big data for EU countries. Therefore, for more detailed research on digital inclusion, it is necessary to conduct rather mixed method research and, especially in the qualitative part to focus on specific target groups of citizens of individual countries.

References

1. European Commission, Digital Compass: the European way for the Digital Decade. https://eur-lex.europa.eu/legal-content/DA/TXT/?uri=CELEX%3A52021DC0118%2801%29&qid=1518252661475. Accessed 30 June 2023
2. European Commission, The Digital Economy and Society Index (DESI). https://digital-strategy.ec.europa.eu/en/policies/desi. Accessed 30 June 2023
3. Goulart, V.G., Liboni, L.B., Cezarino, L.O.: Balancing skills in the digital transformation era: the future of jobs and the role of higher education. Ind. High. Educ. 36(2), 118–127 (2021)
4. World Economic Forum, 2020 Digital Transformation: Powering the Great Reset. https://www.weforum.org/reports/digital-transformation-powering-the-great-reset. Accessed 30 June 2023

5. European Commission, Directorate-General for Communications Networks, Content and Technology, Report of the high-level expert group on the impact of the digital transformation on EU labour markets. https://op.europa.eu/en/publication-detail/-/publication/d95 74c3a-67fb-11e9-9f05-01aa75ed71a1. Accessed 30 June 2023

6. Dengler, K., Matthes, B.: The impacts of digital transformation on the labour market: substitution potentials of occupations in Germany. Technol. Forecast. Soc. Chang. **137**, 304–316 (2018)

7. Eger, L.: The demands on competencies for digital transformation and the perception of business students. Int. J. Teach. Educ. **10**(1), 10–26 (2022)

8. Ostmeier, E., Strobel, M.: Building skills in the context of digital transformation: how industry digital maturity drives proactive skill development. J. Bus. Res. **139**, 718–730 (2022)

9. Adamková, H.G.: Industry 4.0 brings changes in human resources. In: SHS Web of Conferences, Current Problems of the Corporate Sector, vol. 83, p. 01016 (2020)

10. Muro, M., Liu, S., Whiton, J., Kulkarni, S.: Digitalization and the American workforce. Metropolitan Policy Program at Brookings, Washington D.C. (2017)

11. Tomczyk, L., Mascia, M.L., Gierszewski, D.: Barriers to digital inclusion among older people: a intergenerational reflection on the need to develop digital competences for the group with the highest level of digital exclusion. Innoeduca. Int. J. Technol. Educ. Innov. **9**(1), 5–26 (2023)

12. European Commission, The 2018 International Computer and Information Literacy Study (ICILS). https://education.ec.europa.eu/document/the-2018-international-computer-and-information-literacy-study-icils-main-findings-and-implications-for-education-policies-in-europe. Accessed 30 June 2023

13. Rothagi, A., Scherer, R., Hatlevik, O.E.: The role of ICT selfefficacy for students' ICT use and their achievement in a computer and information literacy test. Comput. Educ. **102**, 103–116 (2016)

14. International Literacy Panel, Educational Testing Service. Digital transformation: A framework for ICT literacy. Princeton. https://www.ets.org/Media/Research/pdf/ICTREPORT. pdf. Accessed 15 June 2023

15. Eger, L., Klement, M., Tomczyk, L., Pisoňová, M., Petrová, G.: Different user groups of University students and their ICT competence: evidence from three countries in Central Europe. J. Balt. Sci. Educ. **17**(5), 851–866 (2018)

16. Johnson, L., Becker, A.S., Estrada, V., Freeman, A.: NMC horizon report: 2014 higher education edition. The New Media Consortium, Austin (2014)

17. European Commission, EU Science Hub, DigComp Framework. https://joint-research-cen tre.ec.europa.eu/digcomp/digcomp-framework_en. Accessed 30 June 2023

18. Council Recommendation on Key Competences for Lifelong Learning. https://eur-lex.eur opa.eu/legal-content/EN/TXT/?uri=uriserv:OJ.C_.2018.189.01.0001.01.ENG&toc=OJ:C: 2018:189:TOC. Accessed 30 June 2023

19. Lythreatis, S., Singh, S.K., El-Kassar, A.-N.: The digital divide: a review and future research agenda. Technol. Forecast. Soc. Chang. **175**, 121359 (2022)

20. World Economic Forum. 70% of homes in the EU have high-speed internet – but a digital divide persists. https://www.weforum.org/agenda/2022/09/eu-high-speed-internet-digital-divid. Accessed 30 June 2023

21. Cruz-Jesus, F., Vicente, M.R., Bacao, F., Oloviera, T.: The education-related digital divide: an analysis for the EU-28. Comput. Hum. Behav. **56**, 72–82 (2016)

22. Tomczyk, L., Mascia, M.L., Gierszewski, D., Aalker, C.H.: Barriers to digital inclusion among older people: a intergenerational reflection on the need to develop digital competences for the group with the highest level of digital exclusion. Innoeduca. Int. J. Technol. Educ. Innov. **9**(1), 5–26 (2023)

23. Eurostat, Real GDP per capita. https://ec.europa.eu/eurostat/databrowser/view/sdg_08_10/default/table. Accessed 30 June 2023
24. UNDP, Human Development Reports. https://hdr.undp.org/. Accessed 30 June 2023
25. UNDP, Human Development Report 2021–2022. https://hdr.undp.org/content/human-development-report-2021-2021. Accessed 30 June 2023
26. European Commission, The Digital Economy and Society Index. https://digital-strategy.ec.europa.eu/en/policies/desi. Accessed 30 June 2023
27. Eurostat, Two-fifths of EU population with tertiary education. https://ec.europa.eu/eurostat/web/products-eurostat-news/-/ddn-20221114-1. Accessed 30 June 2023
28. European Commission, Education and Training Monitor 2022. Edition 2022. https://op.europa.eu/webpub/eac/education-and-training-monitor-2022/en/country-reports/country-reports.html. Accessed 15 June 2023
29. CEDEFOP,European Skills Index (2022). https://www.cedefop.europa.eu/en/tools/european-skills-index/skills-development. Accessed 15 July 2023
30. Internet World Stats. https://www.internetworldstats.com/stats4.htm#europe. Accessed 30 June 2023
31. Eurostat, Digital economy and society statistics - households and individuals. https://ec.europa.eu/eurostat/statistics-explained/index.php?title=Digital_economy_and_society_statistics_-_households_and_individuals#Internet_access. Accessed 30 June 2023
32. Edelman, 2022 Edelman Trust Barometer. https://www.edelman.com/trust/2022-trust-barometer. Accessed 30 June 2023
33. Datareportal, Global Social media Statistic. https://datareportal.com/social-media-users. Accessed 15 July 2023
34. Kubiatko, M.: The comparison of different age groups on the attitudes toward and the use of ICT. Educ. Sci. Theory Pract. 13(2), 1263–1272 (2013)
35. Piszczek, M.M., Pichler, S., Turel, O., Greenhaus, J.: The information and communication technology user role: implications for the work role and inter-role spillover. Front. Psychol. 7, 1–15 (2016)
36. Birkland, J. L. H.: Understanding the ICT User Typology and the User Types, Gerontechnology, Emerald Publishing Limited, Bingley, pp. 95–106 (2019)
37. Kuss, D.J., Kristensen, A.M., Lopez-Fernandez, O.: Internet addictions outside of Europe: a systematic literature review. Comput. Hum. Behav. 115, 106621 (2021)
38. Laconi, S., et al.: Cross-cultural study of problematic internet use in nine European countries. Comput. Hum. Behav. 84, 430–440 (2018)

Emergency Remote Teaching During the Crisis Situations. Comparative Perspective of Ukraine and Poland

Olena Vynoslavska[1] ⓘ, Maria Kononets[1] ⓘ, and Emilia Mazurek[2](✉) ⓘ

[1] Igor Sikorsky Kyiv Polytechnic Institute, Prospect Beresteiskyi 37, Kyiv 03056, Ukraine
[2] Faculty of Educational Sciences, University of Lodz, Pomorska 46/48, 91-408 Lodz, Poland
emilia.mazurek@now.uni.lodz.pl

Abstract. The comparison of emergency remote teaching at universities during the COVID-19 pandemic with other crisis circumstances has not yet been clarified. Therefore, the main aim of this study was to reconstruct and explore students' educational experiences during emergency remote teaching in two crisis situations (i.e., the global health crisis caused by the COVID-19 pandemic, the war in Ukraine). The aim was also to discover the main challenges of emergency remote teaching and implemented solutions for improvement remote education in the future. The study was conducted in Ukraine and Poland. It included 248 students. The research used online survey questionnaires as a method for data collection. The findings are summarized as follows: 1) remote education can significantly increase access to learning in pressing circumstances, 2) at the beginning of the COVID-19 pandemic emergency remote teaching was dominant in both countries, 3) the experience gained during the COVID-19 pandemic was a good preparation for emergency remote teaching at universities in Ukraine during the war in terms of the academic infrastructure and new technologies, development of methodological competences of teachers, and digital competences of teachers and students, 4) new completely different challenges have emerged during the war compared to the health crisis (i.e. no electricity, blackouts, no or unstable Internet connection, interruptions of classes caused by bomb alarms and evacuations), 5) students confronted with several types of barriers to learning (organizational, technical and technological, social, emotional, competence) in the crisis circumstances, 6) despite these barriers students expressed a positive view of online learning, 7) emergency remote teaching increased students' self-learning and independence. The results can be used to improve education during the emergency circumstances. Furthermore, presented study can serve as a basis for future research for scholars of different scientific backgrounds.

Keywords: crisis situation · emergency remote teaching · higher education · pandemic COVID-19 · war

Ł. Tomczyk (Ed.): NMP 2023, CCIS 2130, pp. 235–253, 2024.
https://doi.org/10.1007/978-3-031-63235-8_16

1 Introduction

Rapid changes, risks, and sudden emergence of global or local crises characterize contemporary times. Recently, one of them was the health crisis caused by the COVID-19 pandemic, which destroyed routines, habits, and accepted patterns of action. The second one was Russia's aggression against Ukraine in 2022. Due to the rapid spread of the SARS-CoV-2 coronavirus worldwide, the COVID-19 pandemic has become a global health crisis that has directly impacted people's lives. Everyone has experienced, to a greater or lesser extent, the consequences of the restrictions, social isolation, and the feeling of threat to their health and life. Russia's military aggression against Ukraine also has been considered a global problem that threatens the security of European Union and NATO countries. Poland, as a country neighboring Ukraine, very quickly experienced the effects of this crisis, mainly due to the need to organize humanitarian aid quickly for refugees leaving their homeland and those who decided to stay in the areas of ongoing fighting. Therefore, it can be said that Ukraine and Poland are countries experiencing the effects of both crises – although the latter is in a completely different dimension.

This paper mainly focuses on emergency remote teaching in crisis situations (i.e., COVID-19 pandemic, war in Ukraine) at universities in Ukraine and Poland. In the literature, there are already discussed research works focused on the influence of the pandemic on higher education in many countries. There need to be more research papers comparing emergency remote education during the pandemic with other crisis. This paper fills this gap. The main aim of the research was to reconstruct and explore students' educational experiences during emergency remote teaching in the crisis situations (i.e., the global health crisis caused by the COVID-19 pandemic, the war in Ukraine). The aim was also to discover the main challenges of emergency remote teaching and implemented solutions for improvement remote education in the future. In general, the study aimed to answer the following questions:

1. What educational experiences did students gain in Ukraine and Poland through participation in emergency remote teaching during the crisis situations?
2. What are the similarities and differences between Ukraine and Poland, and between both crisis situations?
3. What are the barriers to learning in the crisis circumstances?
4. How do students evaluate the emergency remote teaching in Ukraine and Poland?

The introduction to the article contains a description of the key challenges that academic education in Ukraine and Poland had to face due to the restrictions of the COVID-19 pandemic. Moreover, it describes new challenges for higher education in Ukraine as a result of Russian military aggression against this country. These challenges constitute the context of emergency remote teaching in both countries. The methodology section includes a description of the research method, procedure, participants, and ethical considerations. The remainder of the manuscript presents the results of the study, a discussion of the results and its' limitations. The article ends with a conclusion.

1.1 Higher Education in Times of the COVID-19 Pandemic

The COVID-19 pandemic, announced by the World Health Organization (WHO) on March 11, 2020, has completely changed the human's life. It rapidly broke into people's lives, destroying on its way all established practices: health care, work of universities and study conditions, communications, moving in space, rest, travel, etc. [1]. Destruction of the routine due to the pandemic was a horrible shock for both educators and students worldwide [2], and at the same time, a powerful catalyst in transforming the educational process and moving it to the distance mode [3].

Due to the threat of COVID-19, universities in Ukraine and Poland, as in many other countries, were facing decisions about continuing teaching and learning in conditions of social isolation. Many higher institutions have opted to cancel all face-to-face classes to help prevent the spread of the SARS-CoV-2. They have been replaced by distance education in a digital environment. This transition initiated *emergency remote teaching (ERT)* [4, 5]. It "is a temporary shift of instructional delivery to an alternate mode due to crisis circumstances. It involves the use of fully remote teaching solutions for instruction or education that would otherwise be delivered face-to-face or as blended or hybrid courses, and that will return to that format once the crisis or emergency has abated" [4, para. 13]. Hodges et al. indicate three features of ERT: temporal, immediacy of an emergency, and the remote nature of instruction [5]. Teachers and students are living under a high level of anxiety and stress during a state of emergency [6–8]. Moreover, they are not well prepared to participate in such education, which increases stress levels [4]. For these reasons, ERT differs from online learning and education in emergencies [4, 5].

During the pandemic, emergency distance teaching was dominant in the first semester of academic education (since March 2020) in both countries. In the following semesters (since October 2020), higher education "was characterized by a full or similar methodology to professionally delivered e-learning" [9, p. 10]. However, emergency distance teaching at universities in Ukraine and Poland highlighted the most critical problems. The main of them should be considered.

At the beginning of the pandemic, most Ukrainian and Polish universities needed the necessary equipment and software for a real e-learning environment. The Moodle solution has been used as a web application for academic e-learning at many Polish universities for several years. Thus, as an available tool, it was used by many teachers as "one of the main or complementary channels for transmitting knowledge" [9, p. 11]. The universities' lack of adequate preparation meant teachers were forced to transform the didactic process to new conditions using the available resources. As a result, many of the classes were delivered in an asynchronous or mixed mode. Many practical classes (including laboratories and professional internships) were canceled or conducted provisionally. The lack of a university strategy resulted in a lack of consistency in the applications used by the teachers, which increased the students' and teachers' confusion and chaos. Secondly, emergency distance teaching became a real challenge for teachers [10]. Many of them needed to gain experience using distance learning technologies and methods [9, 11]. Teachers were looking for knowledge on how to conduct remote education, but it took time. Thus, more classes were not delivered in the first semester of emergency remote teaching, and classes were more often conducted asynchronously compared to the next semester [12]. This resulted in students' workload and dissatisfaction. Thirdly, students were not prepared for emergency distance learning. As a result, they faced numerous barriers to learning [13]. Lastly, synchronous classes were conducted by a timetable adapted to the needs of in-person education and did not consider the distance mode recommendations. Lectures and other classes lasted 1,5 h; sometimes, several lectures were delivered in a row, which exhausted the participants of the educational process.

Quarantine restrictions on the freedom of people moving in the space, forced social distancing, wearing masks, and the transfer of all possible events and work processes to the online format remained the main inconveniences that are still associated with the COVID years [14]. However, despite these inconveniences, the solutions forced by the crisis have initiated a new way of thinking about education and have stimulated significant transformations in higher education, which can serve as a basis for raising its quality. To solve the problems that appeared at the beginning of the COVID-19 pandemic, university administrations have increased IT support for students, teachers, and other employees. Classes, conferences, and other events started to be held online using appropriate software. The study conducted among students in Ukraine showed that "the transformations introduced in the organization and realization of the learning process were on the whole positively estimated by students, which means that the elements of distance learning should remain after the end of the lockdown restrictions" [15, p. 4]. Investments were also made in developing teachers' digital competencies and knowledge of distance teaching methodology. During the years of the pandemic, the technical bases of Ukrainian and Polish universities were enriched with new technologies, and the use of various digital educational tools was increased [15–17]. Teachers and students gained some experience working at a distance and were supported in developing their digital competence [9, 12, 13, 15–18]. Emergency remote teaching has been transforming into professionally delivered e-learning.

1.2 Higher Education During the War in Ukraine

In Poland, as in many other countries, it was possible to return to in-person education or implement hybrid education after the cancellation of quarantine restrictions; in Ukraine, it is still necessary to continue distance education. Unfortunately, it is caused by the full-scale war in Ukraine, which the Russian Federation started on February 24, 2022. It should be emphasized that the war was initiated many years earlier, in 2014, after the annexation of part of the territory of Ukraine by Russia. Nevertheless, Ukrainian universities have faced new problems in implementing distance education under war conditions since 2022. Emergency remote teaching, "viewed as an unplanned response to external dramatic changes which involves organizational changes" [16, p. 4499], is still an actual framework for analyzing education and students' educational experiences during this specific crisis.

On the one hand, due to the experience of emergency remote teaching during the COVID-19 pandemic, it was not difficult to organize remote education again [19]. Skills acquired during the pandemic have helped teachers and students continue their activities in wartime [14]. On the other hand, the issue of security became the most important. There was a need for a new arrangement of priorities in Ukraine's existing security system [1]. "It is obvious and logical considering the full-scale war, the martial law, constant bombing, and missile attacks" [19, p. 4].

New challenges have emerged for academic education in the new crisis circumstances that directly threatens life. Every day, an air raid alert is announced in most regions of Ukraine (several times a day in some of them), during which teachers have to interrupt classes with students and run to a bomb shelter because their safety comes first. This directly affects the organization of the educational process and interrupts it [20]. It should be noted that finding safe conditions for learning was the most important challenge in the spring of the 2021/2022 academic year. In the fall of the 2022/2023 academic year, interruptions with electricity supply, stable access to the Internet, and heating have begun, significantly complicating distance education conditions at Ukrainian universities.

Another aspect that prevents the organization of the educational process with the use of new technologies under war conditions is the lack of full access to education in general since some students and teachers are still located in dangerous zones – in the war zone or in temporarily occupied territories, where the Internet connection may be not present at all. At the same time, students and teachers who are relatively safe and trying to continue their work in distance mode cannot always do so of full value because of unstable Internet or technology access [20]. For example, during the last editing of this article, there was a large-scale cyber attack on the "Kyivstar" company, one of Ukraine's leading mobile operators. Russian hackers claimed responsibility for this cyber attack. Because of this attack, the provision of telecommunication services by the "Kyivstar" was blocked for several days. The Russian attack on "Kyivstar" was directed against civilians – more than 24 million citizens of Ukraine were left without mobile communication [21], among them teachers and students who could not work in a distance mode.

Due to the ongoing military operations in Ukraine, many students and university employees left the country in search of shelter. The largest group of refugees chose Poland as the country of their temporary stay [22]. At the same time, number of refugees from Ukraine staying in Poland is difficult to estimate [22]. Many people come to Poland not directly from Ukraine but after crossing the Ukrainian border with other countries. Many refugees cross the border into Poland and do not stay in this country but go to the others. According to Eurostat data [23], the number of Ukrainian citizens under temporary protection in the European Union exceeded 4.24 million people in October 2023. It is estimated that in Poland, there are the most Ukrainian refugees from all European countries [22]. The main reasons why Ukrainian citizens choose Poland as a country of refuge from the war are territorial and cultural proximity, having friends or family in Poland, earlier economic migration of Ukrainians to Poland, and the friendly attitude of Poles towards Ukrainian citizens [22]. In search of shelter, many students left their homeland and came to Poland to live and study. According to the report "Foreigners at universities in Poland" [24] prepared on behalf of the Ministry of Education and Science in Poland, in the academic year 2022/23, 48,149 students from Ukraine studied in Poland, which constituted 47% of all foreigners at Polish universities. This number increased by 12,119 students compared to the previous academic year. Polish university students from Ukraine were provided with appropriate didactic, organizational, material, and psychological support. Moreover, the adopted legislative solutions allowed academic teachers from Ukraine to work at Polish universities. Along with Russia's aggression against Ukraine, the social and economic situation (including higher education) also has changed in Poland.

2 Methodology

2.1 Method and Procedure

In response to the purpose of the study to reconstruct and explore the educational experiences of students during emergency remote teaching in the crisis situations, we collected data from students in Ukraine and Poland who were studying during the COVID-19 pandemic and/or the war in Ukraine. Students were asked to complete online questionnaires. The study was carried out in September and October 2023.

Data was collected using two questionnaires developed by the researchers. The first questionnaire was prepared for students in Ukraine, and the second one for students in Poland. Each of them contained 7 questions about the demographic data. The form used in the study conducted in Ukraine consisted of 15 questions, out of which 11 were closed and 4 open-ended. The questionnaire for students in Poland consisted of 12 questions, including 3 open-ended. Both instruments consisted of the same questions, and the instrument used in Ukraine included 3 additional questions related to emergency remote teaching during the war (2 closed and 1 open-ended). They were prepared with the necessary translations, so that participants can complete the questionnaires in their native language. The questionnaires included questions relating to the following categories: previous (pre-pandemic) experiences in participation in distance education, experiences in participation in emergency remote education, barriers to learning during the crisis situations, benefits and limitations of in-person and remote education, students' educational needs during the crisis, support received during remote education, preferences of the form of education.

2.2 Participants

The study included 248 participants (134 participants in Ukraine and 114 in Poland). The mean age of the participants in Ukraine was 20, and it was 24 in Poland. Most of the research groups in Ukraine were men (67.1%). In Poland, however, mainly women (52.6%) constituted the research group. All participants in the study were students. They all had experience participating in emergency remote teaching during the pandemic and/or wartime in Ukraine. All participants of the research group in Ukraine studied at a technical university. The most common type of university where participants from Poland studied was technical university (68.4%). The other types of universities were university (24.6%), medical university (3.5%), and other (3.5%). The respondents from Ukraine most often declared that they study at the 1st level of the studies (61.2%). The most represented group in Poland were PhD students (52.6%). The respondents most often declared full-time studies. Detailed information about the participants is shown in Table 1.

Table 1. Study sample.

	Ukraine (N = 134)	Poland (N = 114)
male	N = 91 (67.1%)	N = 54 (47.4%)
female	N = 43 (32.1%)	N = 60 (52.6%)
Ukrainian nationality	N = 134 (100%)	N = 0 (0%)
Polish nationality	N = 0 (0%)	N = 114 (100%)
big city	N = 91 (67.9%)	N = 90 (78.9%)
medium-size town	N = 21 (15.7%)	N = 10 (8.8%)
small town	N = 11 (8.2%)	N = 2 (1.8%)
countryside	N = 11 (8.2%)	N = 12 (10.5%)
university	N = 0 (0%)	N = 28 (24.6%)
technical university	N = 134 (100%)	N = 78 (68.4%)
medical university	N = 0 (0%)	N = 4 (3.5%)
other type of high school	N = 0 (0%)	N = 4 (3.5%)
full-time studies	N = 130 (97%)	N = 102 (89.5%)
part-time studies	N = 4 (3%)	N = 12 (10.5%)
the 1st level of studies	N = 82 (61.2%)	N = 6 (5.3%)
the 2nd level of studies	N = 1 (0.7%)	N = 24 (21.1%)
master studies	N = 51 (38.1%)	N = 24 (21.1%)
PhD studies	N = 0 (0%)	N = 60 (52.6%)

2.3 Data Analysis

For data analysis the authors used methods of data processing and interpretation (inferential statistical techniques; quantitative and qualitative analysis). To verify the statistical significance of differences in the distribution of data according to measured parameters, the authors have applied Fisher's angular transformation criterion $\phi*$. SPSS (version 28.0) software was used for data processing.

2.4 Ethical Consideration

The researchers made ethical considerations in the conduct of this study. In particular, before starting the research, their potential participants were clearly informed about the objectives and the course of the research, and the planned publication of the results. At the start of the study, the researchers obtained consent to be involved in the study. The participants were free to withdraw their consent for any reason and at any time they felt uncomfortable with their participation in the survey. Participation in the research was voluntary and anonymous, as stated in the instructions for the questionnaire.

3 Results

3.1 Barriers to Learning in the Crisis Circumstances

Over half of the respondents in each country (Ukraine: 59.7%, Poland: 68.4%) didn't participate in online education before the COVID-19 pandemic. A comparison of two samples based on the frequency of choosing of this parameter by Fisher's criterion did not reveal any significant differences between them (the obtained empirical value of $\phi^*_{omv} = 1.428$; $p > 0.05$). Thus, the global health crisis became a pretext to gain new educational experiences.

Almost all study participants reported that they had experienced some barriers to learning in emergency remote education during the COVID-19 pandemic (Ukraine: 98.5%, Poland: 99.1%) and wartime (Ukraine: 98.5%). The analysis of collected data made it possible to distinguish the following types of barriers to learning (Fig. 1):

- Organizational barriers – related to the organization of the teaching and learning process in emergency conditions. The most significant difficulties during the pandemic were: asynchronous classes, lack of face-to-face contact between teachers and students, different applications for remote education used at one university, many tasks delegated to students for independent work/self-learning, educational materials inappropriate for distance education (usually presentations for a lecture without necessary commentary). One of the study participants compared emergency remote education at the beginning of the COVID-19 pandemic with later: *In the second semester of distance education, all classes were held systematically in real-time. The materials were made available to students. My only doubt was about the consistency of the classes. I think that all teachers should use one platform, because when you need to look for information or a link to a meeting, it is very easy to get lost, even after a few weeks of the semester... But this was a detail. Compared to the first semester of online education, it was much better* (man, 23 years old, Poland). On the other hand, during wartime in Ukraine, the organizational barriers were as follows: asynchronous classes, interruptions of classes caused by bomb alarms and evacuations to the bomb shelter. It is worth to emphasize that asynchronous classes during the COVID-19 pandemic were caused by the lack of appropriate tools and teacher preparation. In turn, during the war, it results from technical problems related to ongoing military operations.
- Technical and technological barriers – related to the infrastructure and its operation. They seem to have become much more significant during the war in Ukraine (38.8%) than during the pandemic (Ukraine: 5.2%, Poland: 7%). During the pandemic, the biggest problem were lack of use of appropriate applications for remote education, and no or limited Internet. In turn, during the war in Ukraine the technical barriers are as follows: no electricity, blackouts, bomb alarms, and no or unstable Internet connection. Lack of electricity makes it impossible to participate in online classes and makes it difficult to prepare tasks/projects/essays, study for exams, etc. Participants of the study wrote about this situation: *It's tough to study when drones are flying over you at 3 in the morning, and you sit for an hour waiting for cancel the air raid siren, and then you still have to get up for the first lesson to defend your laboratory work* (man, 18 years old, Ukraine). *Training during the war is tough for me. I am in*

Ukraine; therefore, when the electricity is turned off, my Internet and connection are lost, which has had a terrible impact on my studies. Also, when an air raid alert starts at night and explosions are heard, I am forced to go down to the bomb shelter and sit there until the alarm is cleared. Recently, we sat in the basement from 3 a.m. to 7. All this affects learning because when you don't get enough sleep, you're stressed and exhausted (woman, 18 years old, Ukraine). Moreover, collected data confirms that problems of lack of suitable equipment during emergency remote teaching in wartime almost did not exist in Ukraine (0.7%) compared to the pandemic time (Ukraine: 3.7%, Poland: 6.1%).

- Social barriers – related to social isolation or limited contact with teachers and other students. This problem clearly bothered students in Poland. However, while lack or limited direct contact with teachers was more important for students in Ukraine during the pandemic (14.2%), its importance decreased significantly during the war (5.2%). The opposite happened with the lack of face-to-face contact with other students (12.7% during the pandemic compared with 16.4% during wartime). One of the participants of the study wrote: *I would like everyone to turn on the camera during lessons in Zoom because this way familiarity occurs. The classmates I am supposed to meet during my master's program on lessons in Zoom are not turning on cameras, and I don't even know their voices and faces* (woman, 23 years old, Ukraine).

- Emotional barriers – associated with negative emotions due to the crisis and burdens of obligations. Students in Ukraine (7.5%) were likelier to report experiencing negative emotions in connection with the pandemic than students in Poland (5.3%). The significant increase of the importance of this barrier is clearly visible during the war in Ukraine (14.2%) compared to the pandemic. Understandably, it is associated with fear of loss of life and health and feeling uncertainty about the future. At the same time, it results from the prolonged period of restrictions in social contacts and the need to be more independent and cope with new challenges. Ukrainian students emphasized that they need psychological support.

- Competence barriers – related to the insufficient level of key competence for remote learning (e. g., digital competencies, independence, scheduling tasks, time management). In turn, we can note Ukrainian students' high experience with these barriers during the pandemic and an apparent decline in its importance in education during the war. The change in this respect is evident in students' perceiving their digital competencies as a no barrier to learning.

A comparison of Ukrainian and Polish samples as a whole by the parameter "Frequency of choosing of barriers in education" by Fisher's criterion did not reveal any significant differences between them (ϕ*omv = 1.428; p > 0.05). Also, no significant differences were found between the samples in different types of barriers these are covered by this parameter: technical and technological barriers (ϕ*omv = 0.596; p > 0.10); social barriers (ϕ*omv = 1.577; p > 0.10); emotional barriers (ϕ*omv = 1.706; p > 0.10).

3.2 Evaluation of Emergency Remote Teaching

Students from Poland rated emergency remote teaching slightly higher than students from Ukraine (Fig. 2). The largest group of Ukrainian students (43.3%) rated it as

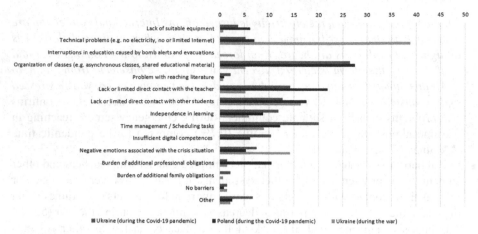

Fig. 1. Barriers to learning during the emergency remote teaching in times of crisis.

enough. On the other hand, the largest group of Polish students (36.8%) rated it as good. The relatively small number of very good ratings may be disturbing (Ukraine 6.7%, Poland 10.5%). It may result from poor experiences from the first semester of distance education during the pandemic. Furthermore, such assessments of Ukrainian students may result from prolonged distance education in emergency conditions. The new crisis triggers new difficulties and challenges (i.e., mentioned barriers). At the same time, in the students' opinions, long-term online learning is associated with monotony and spending a lot of time in front of the computer.

When comparing two samples according to the frequency of the evaluation of emergency remote teaching by students any significant differences between them were not found, namely: rating "very good" – $\phi*omv = 1.067$ (p > 0.10); rating "good" – $\phi*omv = 1.287$ (p > 0.10); rating "enough" – $\phi*omv = 1.201$ (p > 0.10); rating "insufficiently" – $\phi*omv = 1.036$ (p > 0.10).

Despite the barriers to learning during crisis situations described above, the study's Ukrainian and Polish participants noted several advantages of emergency remote education during the COVID-19 pandemic and wartime. Let's analyze these advantages within the areas delineated by barriers to learning.

As shown in Fig. 3, the most significant number of advantages of remote education chosen by the respondents was concentrated in areas delineated by organizational and emotional barriers. In particular, in the area of organizational barriers, such advantages as "saving time" (Ukraine: 29.9%, Poland: 47.4%) and "flexible schedule of classes" (Ukraine: 21.6%, Poland: 36.0%) were mentioned. To the area of emotional barriers included advantages from positive emotions that arise as a result of "occupational hygiene (e.g., time for regular meals, for a walk between classes)" (Ukraine: 9.0%, Poland: 24.4%) and "more freedom to plan your own time" (Ukraine: 37.3%, Poland: 46.5%).

The following selected advantage of remote education was the area delineated by social barriers, namely such an advantage as "activities in a friendly environment (i.e., your own home or another place of your choice)" (Ukraine: 5.2%, Poland: 14.9%).

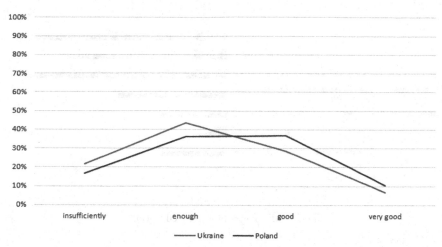

Fig. 2. Evaluation of emergency remote teaching in the crisis circumstances.

Respondents chose the least number of advantages of remote education in areas delineated by competence barriers and technical barriers. In particular, in the area of competence barriers, such an advantage as "the ability to immediately explore an interesting topic/issue" (Ukraine: 3.0%, Poland: 14.9%) was mentioned, and in the area of technical barriers – such advantage as "the access to materials" (Ukraine: 3.0%, Poland: 7.0%).

As can be seen from the given data, Polish respondents chose the advantages of remote education more intensively than Ukrainian respondents. The exception was advantages, which were formulated by the respondents in the answers to the open-ended question "Other: _____?" (Ukraine: 3.0%, Poland: 0.9%). For example, the participants of the study noted the following advantages: *the ability to submit homework throughout the day, and not just during class time* (man, 19 years old, Ukraine), *convenience in processing the lecture materials, saving time and effort* (man, 18 years old, Ukraine), *just the possibility of education at a time when it is not possible in the usual form* (woman, 20 years old, Poland).

Comparison of the Ukrainian and Polish samples according to the frequency of choosing of the "Advantages of remote education" parameter according to Fisher's criterion revealed significant differences between them in terms of indices these are covered by this parameter. In particular, significant differences were recorded by the following indices:

- In the area of organizational advantages: "saving time" ($\phi^*_{omv} = 2.841$; $p < 0.01$); "flexible schedule of classes" ($\phi^*_{omv} = 2.511$; $p < 0.01$).
- In the area of emotional advantages: "occupational hygiene (e.g., time for regular meals, for a walk between classes)" ($\phi^*_{omv} = 3.327$; $p < 0.01$).
- In the area of technical advantages: "the access to materials" ($\phi^*_{omv} = 1.923$; $p < 0.05$).

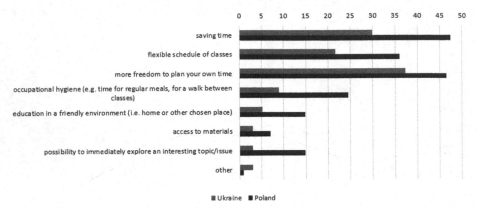

Fig. 3. Advantages of remote education.

The study participants from Ukraine and Poland also noted several disadvantages of emergency remote education under crisis situations. The analysis of these disadvantages showed their correlation with the areas outlined by barriers to learning.

As shown in Fig. 4, the most significant number of disadvantages of remote education chosen by respondents is concentrated in the areas outlined by social and emotional barriers. In particular, in the area of social barriers, such disadvantages as "no direct contact with students" (Ukraine: 21.6%, Poland: 28.9%) and "no direct contact with teachers" (Ukraine: 11.9%, Poland: 27.2%) were noted. In the area delineated by emotional barriers, respondents chose disadvantages caused by fatigue and lack of time, namely: "working too long at the computer" (Ukraine: 11.9%, Poland: 33.3%) and "time management problem" (Ukraine: 11.9%, Poland: 6.1%).

The slightly smaller number of disadvantages of remote education selected by the respondents can be attributed to areas delineated by technical and technological, as well as organizational barriers. Such selected disadvantages as "lack of appropriate equipment for online education" (Ukraine: 2.2%, Poland: 4.4%) and "technical problems" (Ukraine: 11.9%, Poland: 20.2%) correspond to the area delineated by technical and technological barriers. In the area delineated by organizational barriers, such disadvantages as "lack of appropriate conditions/place for learning (e.g., own desk)" (Ukraine: 0.7%, Poland: 4.4%) and "lack of possibility or limited possibility to participate in practical classes" (Ukraine: 10.4%, Poland: 15.8%) were selected.

The given data indicate that, within the areas mentioned above of barriers, the respondents from Poland tend to choose the disadvantages of remote education more intensively.

As for disadvantages that correlate to the area delineated by competence barriers, they were more intensively chosen by the respondents from Ukraine. Among them, such disadvantages were chosen as "more material for self-study compared to traditional education" (Ukraine: 12.7%, Poland: 9.6%) and "more tasks to be done independently about traditional education" (Ukraine: 9.0%, Poland: 6.1%).

Determining the disadvantages of remote education as the answers to the open-ended question "Other: _____?" participants from Poland were more active (Ukraine: 0.7%, Poland: 3.5%). Among the answers were the following: *it is difficult to plan time due to need to be online too long* (woman, 19 years old, Ukraine), *lack of adequate prepa-ration of teachers for remote teaching* (man, 21 years old, Poland), *lack of concentration during distance education* (man, 20 years old, Poland), *dysregulation of functioning due to lack of control* (woman, 22 years old, Poland).

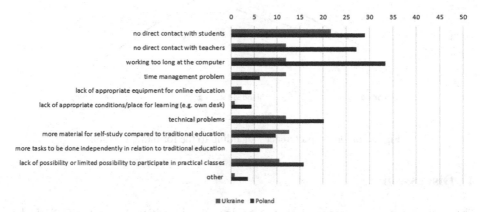

Fig. 4. Disadvantages of remote education.

Comparison of the Ukrainian and Polish samples according to the frequency of choosing of the parameter "Disadvantages of emergency distance education in crisis situations" according to the Fisher's criterion revealed significant differences between them according to some indices covered by this parameter. Namely, significant differences were recorded by such indices as: disadvantages caused by "no direct contact with teachers" ($\phi^*_{omv} = 3.084$; $p < 0.01$), fatigue and lack of time due to "working too long at the computer" ($\phi^*_{omv} = 4.128$; $p < 0.01$), and some "technical problems" ($\phi^*_{omv} = 1.923$; $p < 0.05$). As mentioned above, the reason for these differences was that respondents from Poland chose the disadvantages of remote education more intensively.

Figure 5 presents Ukrainian and Polish students' preferences regarding the form of education. There is almost no difference between students from both countries in choosing in-person education as their preferred choice (Ukraine: 20.9%, Poland: 21.1%). Polish students returning to in-person classes after the pandemic mainly chose blended learning (68.4%) as preferred. At the same time, Ukrainian students have no experience learning in a mixed form of education, much less often than Polish students chose blended learning (47.8%). Ukrainian students chose e-learning (31.3%) as better more often than their peers from Poland (10.5%). It is a little surprising considering the emergency remote teaching rating shown in Fig. 2.

Comparison of the Ukrainian and Polish samples according to the frequency of choosing of the parameter "Preferences regarding the form of education" according to the Fisher criterion allowed to obtain the following results: in-person education $\phi^* = 0.039$ ($p > 0.10$); mixed form of education ϕ^* remote teaching $\phi^*_{omv} = 4.473$ ($p < 0.01$). That is, no signifcant differences between the samples were found for in-person education.

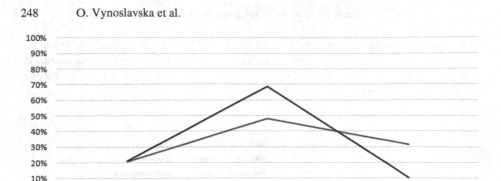

Fig. 5. Students' preferences regarding to the form of education.

4 Discussion

The comparison of emergency remote teaching at universities during the COVID-19 pandemic with other crisis circumstances has not yet been well clarified. Therefore, this study mainly focuses on emergency remote teaching during the global health crisis due to the coronavirus and the war in Ukraine. The problem was presented based on the experiences of students in Ukraine and Poland. The main aim of this study was to reconstruct and explore students' educational experiences during emergency remote teaching in two crisis situations (i.e., the global health crisis caused by the COVID-19 pandemic, the war in Ukraine). Additionally, the aim was to discover the main challenges of emergency remote teaching and implemented solutions for improvement remote education in the future.

As a result of COVID-19 restrictions, the rapid transition from in-person education to education in the digital environment initiated emergency remote teaching [4, 5]. Its introduction is forced by external factors, and due to the need for quick implementation, it is based on easily available solutions, usually cheap or free [25]. Forms and teaching methods, as well as chosen technologies, depend on the teacher's competencies and are changing with the teacher's development [4, 9, 25]. The role of teachers in (emergency) remote teaching is significant. Many previous studies confirmed the role of teachers' presence in an online environment (synchronous and asynchronous) [26–28]. Moreover, there is a strong connection between the teacher presence in online education and students' satisfaction of learning [29]. Therefore, education conducted in the first semester during the pandemic, based primarily on asynchronous classes, may have lowered students' learning satisfaction [30] and the overall assessment of remote education [4, 5]. On one hand, due to restrictions introduced during the pandemic new technological tools were used for the first time by both learners and teachers. At the same time, they had the opportunity to gain new experience and competences. On the other hand, emergency remote teaching in crisis contributed to encountering numerous barriers to learning.

The findings of the presented study confirm that students had experienced some barriers to learning during the COVID-19 pandemic and wartime. The following barriers were featured: organizational, technical and technological, social, emotional, and competence. The results correspond with other studies conducted among students in Poland [12, 13] and additionally show the differences between barriers to learning during the pandemic and wartime in Ukraine. These differences were as follows: 1) organizational barriers related to the organization of the teaching and learning process in emergency conditions were more important during the pandemic than during the wartime, which proves better preparation of universities and teachers for remote teaching based on previous experiences [19], 2) new organizational barriers appeared during the war in Ukraine, 3) technical barriers resulting from temporary electricity outages and temporary lack of Internet connection are the greatest barrier to success emergency remote teaching during the war, 4) social barriers are significant during crisis situations, 5) the importance of the emotional barrier is greater during the war than during the pandemic, although many studies have shown the dominance of negative feelings among the students during the global health crisis [31, 32], 6) competence barriers is less important during the emergency remote teaching under the war conditions, which involves better preparation of students for remote learning based on the previous experience and developed competencies. The results indicate the need to systematically support students in the crisis circumstances, as well as to implement solutions to improve education, preferably based on consultations with various stakeholders of higher education systems [33].

The findings of this study highlighted many advantages of emergency remote teaching. The most important are possibility of learning despite of pressing circumstances [4, 5, 9, 16, 34], increasing use of new technologies at universities [9, 15, 17, 25], saving time and flexibility [12, 13, 34], occupational hygiene, education in a friendly environment [12, 13], self-development and self-learning [12, 13, 15, 35]. However, it also has disadvantages such as the loss of social ties due to lack of contact with peers and teachers [12, 13, 34], working too long at the computer, technical and technological problems [12, 13, 34], and lack of possibility or limited possibility to participate in practical classes. Hence, the possibility of introducing greater distractions, frustration, and confusion [31, 32, 34].

Due to the results, remote education can significantly increase access to learning in different crisis situations. For this reason, there is a need to introduce systematic changes at universities to improve the solutions adopted in extraordinary circumstances, search for new improvements, implement new technologies, and develop teachers' competencies in conducting remote education. Students seem to be ready to combine in-person education and distance education. Moreover, as a result of emergency remote teaching, they became more independent and increased self-learning.

4.1 Limitations of the Study and Future Research

Despite providing new insights into emergency remote teaching during two different crises, there are some limitations in the study, which also provide areas for further research.

The limitations of this comparative research included the limited number of participants in Ukraine and Poland. Future studies could include more participants representing various types of universities in both countries. Conducting a large-scale study could reveal more information about the topic under investigation.

This study focused on students' experiences and opinions. The perspective of academic teachers could be considered in future studies.

Furthermore, future research should concentrate on analyzing the effectiveness of emergency remote teaching. This is a complicated issue to research. However, knowing whether and to what extent long-term remote education at universities allows for achieving the assumed goals and learning outcomes is necessary. This is especially important in the context of developing skills and competencies. It is difficult, and sometimes even impossible, to conduct some practical classes (e.g., laboratories) remotely. However, reliable research in this area is needed to prevent the unjustified devaluation of remote education. Moreover, conducting research focused on students' motivation to engage in remote learning in the crisis circumstances could be interesting. Additionally, future research should concentrate on the analysis of e-learning at universities after the crisis. It is worth knowing which solutions adopted during the extraordinary circumstances are/will be maintained, which ones universities will withdraw from, and for what reasons.

5   Conclusion

The main problem that was the subject of the authors' analysis was the emergency remote teaching during the COVID-19 pandemic and wartime in Ukraine. As a result of the research described in this article, the following conclusions can be drawn.

The COVID-19 pandemic, as a global health crisis, initiated changes in higher education on a huge scale. As in many other countries, universities in Ukraine and Poland needed to prepare for shifting into remote teaching from day to day. Most teachers needed to gain experience in conducting distance education. Teachers were forced to transform the didactic process to new conditions using the available resources. As a result, emergency remote teaching was dominant in both countries at the beginning of the pandemic emergency. It „is a temporary shift of instructional delivery to an alternate mode due to crisis circumstances. (…) The primary objective in these circumstances is not to re-create a robust educational ecosystem but rather to provide temporary access to instruction and instructional supports in a manner that is quick to set up and is reliably available during an emergency or crisis" [4, para. 13]. In the Ukrainian and Polish students' opinions, the biggest difficulties during the first semester of emergency remote teaching at universities caused by pandemic were: asynchronous classes, lack of face-to-face contact between teachers and students, different applications for remote education used at one university, many tasks delegated to students for independent work/self-learning, educational materials inappropriate for distance education. Later actions implemented at universities and better preparation of academic staff to conduct classes remotely improved education conducted in conditions of social isolation. It involved conducting synchronous classes using appropriate applications and software.

The experience gained during the COVID-19 pandemic was a good preparation for conducting emergency remote education at universities in Ukraine during the war. The academic infrastructure (including the software and applications used for remote education), the methodological competencies of teachers, and the digital competencies of teachers and students have increased. Nevertheless, completely different challenges have emerged compared to the global health crisis caused by the coronavirus SARS-CoV-2.

Ensuring the safety of citizens has become a priority. Technical and organizational barriers (i.e., no electricity, blackouts, no Internet connection, interruptions of classes caused by bomb alarms, and evacuations to the bomb shelter) became the biggest challenge.

Students are confronted with several types of barriers to learning in the crisis circumstances: organizational, technical and technological, social, emotional, and competence. Barriers related to the organization of the educational process were a more significant limitation during the COVID-19 pandemic. However, the importance of technical barriers increased in emergency remote education during wartime in Ukraine. The significance of social and emotional barriers was the same during the analyzed crises. On the other hand, the competence barriers to learning under emergency conditions were more critical in the pandemic than in wartime. Students have become more independent, more ready to self-learning and better prepared to use innovative e-learning tools.

Among the advantages of remote learning for students, the most important are saving time, having a flexible schedule of classes, having more freedom to plan time, and occupational hygiene. The disadvantages of remote learning of most significant importance to students include the loss of social ties due to lack of contact with peers and teachers, working too long at the computer, technical problems, and lack of possibility or limited possibility to participate in practical classes. Despite the barriers to learning during crises, students express a positive view of remote learning. They appreciate distance education as the only solution enabling learning in times of crisis. Moreover, they are eager to learn online under normal conditions, but rather, they do not want to replace in-person education completely with distance education.

Acknowledgements. The authors of this paper thank all the students who participated in this study. The authors appreciate that despite the ongoing crisis in Ukraine, students from this country helped the authors with data collection.

References

1. Vynoslavska, O., Kononets, M.: Ekonomichna bezpeka osobystosti v umovakh pandemiyi COVID-19 [Personal economic security in COVID-19 pandemic]. Organ. Psychol. Econ. Psychol. **1**(22), 33–44 (2021)
2. Huszti, I., Csatáry, G., Lechner, I.: Distance learning as the new reality in tertiary education: a case study. Adv. Educ. **9**(21), 100–120 (2022)
3. Watermeyer, R., Crick, T., Knight, C., Goodall, J.: COVID-19 and digital disruption in UK universities: afflictions and affordances of emergency online migration. High. Educ. **81**, 623–641 (2021)
4. Hodges, C., Moore, S., Lockee, B., Trust, T., Bond, A.: The difference between emergency remote teaching and online learning. Educause Review (2020). https://er.educause.edu/articles/2020/3/the-difference-between-emergency-remote-teaching-and-online-learning. Accessed 08 Mar 2024
5. Hodges, C.B., Moore, S.L., Lockee, B.B., Aaron Bond, M., Jewett, A.: An instructional design process for emergency remote teaching. In: Burgos, D., Tlili, A., Tabacco, A. (eds.) Radical Solutions for Education in a Crisis Context. Lecture Notes in Educational Technology, pp. 37–51. Springer, Singapore (2021). https://doi.org/10.1007/978-981-15-7869-4_3
6. Khlaif, Z.N., Salha, S., Kouraichi, B.: Emergency remote learning during COVID-19 crisis: students' engagement. Educ. Inf. Technol. **26**, 7033–7055 (2021)

7. Moore, S., Veletsianos, G., Barbour, M.K.: A synthesis of research on mental health and remote learning: the questionable-cause logical fallacy and modality scapegoating are obscuring useful insights. OTESSA J. **2**(1), 1–19 (2022)

8. Rogowska, A.M., et al.: Changes in mental health during three waves of the COVID-19 pandemic: a repeated cross-sectional study among Polish university students. BMC Psychiatry **21**, 627 (2021)

9. Tomczyk, Ł: E-learning in Poland: challenges, opportunities and prospects for remote learning during the COVID-19 pandemic. High. Educ. Russ. Beyond **2**(27), 10–12 (2021)

10. Mospan, N.: Transformatsiya natsional'noyi vyshchoyi osvity pid chas pandemiyi COVID-19 ochyma studentiv ta vykladachiv [The transformation of national higher education during the COVID-19 pandemic through the eyes of students and teachers]. Educ. Discourse **35**(4), 141–153 (2021)

11. Vynoslavska, O.: Psykholohichna kul'tura vykladacha suchasnoho universytetu: metodychni instrumenty doslidzhennya [Psychological culture of a modern university teacher: methodical research tools]. In: Kalinicheva, G. (ed.) Higher Education of Ukraine in the Context of Civilizational Changes and Challenges: State, Problems, Development Prospects: The Monograpf, Phenix, Kyiv, pp. 248–271 (2020)

12. Mazurek, E.: Higher education during the COVID-19 pandemic in the opinions of students in Poland. Tuning J. High. Educ. **10**(1), 263–284 (2022)

13. Mazurek, E.: Barriers to online learning during the COVID-19 pandemic at universities in Poland. In: Proceedings of the 37th International Business Information Management Association (IBIMA), 30–31 May 2021, pp. 8242–8249. IBIMA, Cordoba (2020)

14. Nikolaev, E., Riy, H., Shemelynets, I.: Vyshcha osvita v Ukrayini: zminy cherez viynu: analitychnyy zvit [Higher education in Ukraine: changes due to the war: an analytical report], p 94. Borys Grinchenko Kyiv University, Kyiv (2023). https://osvitanalityka.kubg.edu.ua/wp-content/uploads/2023/03/HigherEd-in-Times-of-War.pdf. Accessed 03 Jan 2024

15. Melnychenko, A., Zheliaskova, T.: Transformation of educational process in COVID-19 pandemic: a case of Igor Sikorsky Kyiv Polytechnic Institute. Adv. Educ. **18**, 4–10 (2021)

16. Andrusiak, I., Kolesnyk, O., Slyvka, M., Kolesnyk, A.: COVID-19 and war emergency remote teaching shifts in Ukraine: challenges faced and lessons learned. In: ICERI 2022 Proceedings, pp. 4499–4506. IATED, Seville (2022)

17. Stecuła, K., Wolniak, S.: Influence of COVID-19 pandemic on dissemination of innovative E-learning tools in higher education in Poland. J. Open Innov. Technol. Market Complex. **8**(2), 89 (2022)

18. Ober, J., Kochmańska, A.: Remote learning in higher education: evidence from Poland. Int. J. Environ. Res. Public Health **19**(21), 14479 (2022)

19. Lavrysh, Y., Lytovchenko, I., Lukianenko, V., Golub, T.: Teaching during the wartime: experience from Ukraine. Educ. Philos. Theory 1–8 (2022)

20. Nazarenko, Y., Kogut, I., Zheriobkina, T.: Osvita i viyna v Ukrayini (24.02–01.04.2022) [Education and war in Ukraine (February 24–April 1, 2022)]. Analytical center Cedos (2022). https://cedos.org.ua/researches/osvita-i-vijna-v-ukrayini-24-lyutogo-1-kvitnya-2022/. Accessed 03 Jan 2024

21. Romanenko, V.: Ukraine investigates cyberattack on national mobile operator, suspecting Russian secret services. Ukrainska Pravda, Tuesday (2023). https://www.pravda.com.ua/eng/news/2023/12/12/7432733/. Accessed 03 Jan 2024

22. Fuszara, M.: Wojna, ucieczki i pomaganie [War, escaping and helping]. In: Fuszara, M. (ed.) Masowa pomoc w masowej ucieczce. Społeczeństwo polskie wobec migracji wojennej z Ukrainy [Mass Aid in Mass Escape. Polish Society and War Migration from Ukraine], pp. 7–18, University of Warsaw, Warsaw (2022)

23. Eurostat. https://ec.europa.eu/eurostat/web/products-eurostat-news/w/ddn-20231208-2. Accessed 31 Dec 2023

24. Cudzoziemcy na uczelniach w Polsce Report [Foreigners at universities in Poland Report]. Information Processing Center, Ministry of Education and Science. https://radon.nauka.gov.pl/analizy/cudzoziemcy-na-uczelniach-w-Polsce-2022. Accessed 31 Dec 2023
25. Tomczyk, Ł., Walker, C.: The emergency (crisis) e-learning as a challenge for teachers in Poland. Educ. Inf. Technol. **26**(6), 6847–6877 (2021)
26. Gayton, J., McEwen, B.C.: Effective online instructional and assessment strategies. Am. J. Distance Educ. **21**(3), 117–132 (2007)
27. Dwivedi, A., Dwivedi, P., Bobek, S., Sternad Zabukovšek, S.: Factors affecting students' engagement with online content in blended learning. Kybernetes **48**(7), 1500–1515 (2019)
28. Martin, F., Bolliger, D.U.: Engagement matters: student perceptions on the importance of engagement strategies in the online learning environment. Online Learn. **22**(1), 205–222 (2018)
29. Richardson, J.C., Swan, K.: Examining social presence in online courses in relation to students' perceived learning and satisfaction. J. Asynchronous Learn. Netw. **7**(1), 68–88 (2003)
30. Faize, F.A., Nawaz, M.: Evaluation and Improvement of students' satisfaction in online learning during COVID-19. Open Praxis **12**(4), 495–507 (2020)
31. Camacho-Zuniga, C., Pego, L., Escamilla, J., Hosseini, S.: The impact of the COVID-19 pandemic on students' feelings at high school, undergraduate, and postgraduate levels. Heliyon **7**, e06465 (2021)
32. Acosta-Gonzaga, E., Ruiz-Ledesma, E.F.: Students' emotions and engagement in the emerging hybrid learning environment during the COVID-19 pandemic. Sustainability **14**(16), 10236 (2022)
33. Gray, D.M., Bond, J.T., Wicks, J.M., Hicks, N.: Preparing for the unexpected in a COVID-19 world: the teaching dilemmas of a mid-semester faculty change. Tuning J. High. Educ. **10**(1), 285–318 (2022)
34. Linnes, C., Ronzoni, G., Agrusa, J., Lema, J.: Emergency remote education and its impact on higher education: a temporary or permanent shift in instruction? Educ. Sci. **12**(10), 721 (2022)
35. Tomczyk, Ł, Demeshkant, N., Potyrała, K., Czerwiec, K., Oyelere, S.O.: Elements of crisis e-learning: perspectives of Polish teachers. Knowl. Manag. E-Learn. **14**(3), 245–268 (2022)

Simulations for Teacher Transitions to Regional, Rural and Remote (RRR) Australian Schools

Aimé Sacrez(✉) ⓘ, Stefan Schutt ⓘ, Steve Murphy ⓘ, Rebecca Miles-Keogh ⓘ,
Adam Staples ⓘ, and Andrea O'Connor ⓘ

La Trobe University, Bundoora, VIC 3086, Australia
{a.sacrez,s.schutt,s.murphy,r.miles,a.staples}@latrobe.edu.au,
aoconnor@ceosand.catholic.edu.au

Abstract. Simulations in education provide opportunities for preservice teachers (PSTs) to experience a low-risk approach to learning the practice of teaching in a range of educational situations and settings. Given the challenge of recruiting new teachers to regional, rural and remote (RRR) schools in countries including Australia, having opportunities for PSTs to experience rural teaching prior to graduation offers a means of increasing recruitment. Further, simulation promises to better prepare these teachers through pedagogical strategies specifically suited to rural schools. We believe that developing realistic simulations to orientate PSTs to rural teaching requires an evidence-based understanding of rural contexts experienced by beginning teachers. It also requires understanding the kinds of simulations that would be most suited to preparing PSTs for rural teaching. This chapter presents both our original research on challenges, affordances and practices of regional and rural teaching for beginning teachers, as well as a corresponding review of literature on simulation. These insights are intended to inform future work on rurally-focused simulations and to help other initial teacher education (ITE) providers intending on using simulations to consider why and how they might begin the process.

Keywords: Simulation · Rural Regional Remote Schools · Initial Teacher Education

1 Introduction

1.1 Rationale for Simulations to Support Beginning Teaching in RRR Schools

In Australia, the recruitment of new teachers is insufficient to meet growth in student numbers and losses due to existing teachers leaving the profession [6]. Recruitment and retention of teachers is a significant challenge for regional, rural and remote (RRR) schools in Australia compared to metropolitan schools, with remote schools experiencing up to six times the annual staff turnover of their metropolitan counterparts [19]. While exact figures are difficult to ascertain, surveys indicate up to 40–50% of Australian teachers leave the profession within the first five years of teaching [31]. The challenges faced by beginning teachers are well-established and multifaceted, and include applying

Ł. Tomczyk (Ed.): NMP 2023, CCIS 2130, pp. 254–270, 2024.
https://doi.org/10.1007/978-3-031-63235-8_17

theory to practice, managing workload, building relationships with students, parents and other teachers, and juggling work with ongoing accreditation requirements [6, 14]. Beginning teachers in RRR areas face an added layer of challenge related to living and teaching in communities that are smaller and often isolated, resulting in specific pressures such as working longer hours, reduced access to professional development, high levels of community scrutiny and accelerated leadership responsibilities [16, 19, 28, 52]. For the remainder of this chapter, to avoid the overuse of the 'RRR' acronym, the term 'rural' is used as an umbrella term encompassing remote and regional characteristics of teaching and living.

Some challenges related to resourcing and isolation may be common to rural communities internationally. Yet, within Australia, certain contextual factors influencing rural education may differ from other countries. For example, at least one quarter of Australian students are based in rural schools [30] and nearly one third of teachers work in rural schools [6]. Therefore, the issue of attracting and retaining suitable teachers in rural Australian schools is significant and impacts on the quality of learning and academic performance of students [63, 66]. This also applies to large non-metropolitan schools that serve multiple small communities, as well as to some independent and Catholic rural schools that operate differently to Government schools. Indeed, generalising rural education in Australia is problematic due to geographic and economic differences in communities, differences in school sizes, types of education and resource availability [58]. We note this because our research focuses exclusively on rural Catholic schools, which may reveal both similarities and differences to other kinds of schools in rural areas.

It should, however, be noted that in the media and in the literature, rural teaching is often framed through a deficit lens with rural schools presented as providing lesser opportunities and resources for teachers and students [58, 69]. Yet, many teachers living and working in rural communities report an enhanced quality of life due to the unique affordances of being a rural teacher [38, 50, 69]. In our research study on graduate teacher transitions to rural schools, we found that the overwhelming majority of beginning rural teachers were originally from country areas, which mitigated the shock of the unknown as many had local family and friends as a supportive social network. This suggests that improving the recruitment and retention of beginning teachers in rural schools, especially those from metropolitan backgrounds, is a multifaceted endeavour involving more than focusing on pedagogical skills alone. Some of these facets were identified in our research and the related literature on beginning teachers, and are listed as follows:

- Enable metropolitan students to gain a realistic understanding of affordances and challenges of rural teaching and life [71]
- Provide experiences of teaching in rural schools that focus on specific pedagogical considerations such as mixed-level classes, and a broad range of student needs and associated behaviours [50, 56]
- Provide strategies and resources to manage administrative tasks of planning, teaching and assessing student learning framed in a rural context [10]
- Explore a range of rural schools and communities to understand the different dynamic relations between the geography, types of industry, employment and demographics of community members [54, 58]

In our research we found that preservice teachers (PSTs) who are currently living in rural communities may have some experience of these facets of teaching based on their own education as well as through supporting educational roles including volunteering in a local school; tutoring; working as learning support officers (LSO); teaching while completing a graduate degree; and out of school learning experiences such as recreational clubs, sporting teams and community events. However, PSTs who have not lived in rural areas have difficulty accessing these experiences. This may be due to the cost of travel and accommodation, the sense of isolation, or needing an open mindset to explore a new region of Australia [51, 71].

Within the state of Victoria, Australia, the government is offering incentives to encourage metropolitan PSTs to try a rural placement by removing financial barriers [68]. This addresses economic issues, although short-term rural accommodation limitations remain. It does not, however, address affective and practice-based challenges associated with rural placements. Another means for facilitating PST rural teaching experiences may be through a variety of simulations that provide opportunities to practice teaching in a range of scenarios relevant to rural schools [32]. Although simulations of teaching practice can benefit PSTs in a range of settings [26, 44], for metropolitan teachers considering rural teaching, simulation could allow them to experience what rural teaching and living might be like before choosing to travel for a rural placement or teaching position [21].

While research is limited on simulation for rural teaching, situated and online simulation has been widely used in the medical field to prepare health students for rural practices) [2, 11]. Comparing approaches to preparing education and medical practitioners for rural placements and professions is useful as there are similar challenges of recruitment, retention and preparedness in both fields [3, 17, 22, 41, 48, 67, 70].

Based on our list of rural teaching considerations for rural initial teacher education (ITE), this chapter responds to the following research questions:

- What are affordances and challenges of rural teaching and life for beginning teachers?
- What are unique teaching practices and pedagogies relevant to rural teaching that PSTs can experience in a simulated environment?
- What types of simulation are best suited to the different aspects of experiencing rural teaching?
- How might schools contribute to the development of these simulations in partnership with university ITE providers?

To respond to these questions, this chapter draws upon:

- Findings from original research conducted by our team on beginning teacher transitions to rural Victorian schools undertaken between 2022 and 2023
- Literature that elaborates on rural teaching; practice-based approaches to ITE; and existing simulation and new media technologies that could be trialled for rural teaching experiences

This chapter combines our in-depth understanding of beginning teacher transitions to rural schools with an exploration of literature on potential simulation approaches to trial in the next phase of our research. We encourage other researchers and ITE providers to connect with us in our research as we trial recommendations outlined in Sect. 4 of this chapter.

2 Research on Affordances and Challenges of Rural Teaching and Living for Beginning Teachers

The findings presented are based on research undertaken from 2022–2023 with beginning/graduate teachers in regional and rural Catholic primary and secondary schools in northern Victoria, Australia. The research consisted of an online graduate teacher survey, two focus group interviews with approximately 50 teachers undertaking their first two years of teaching and a case study of two Catholic rural schools. The research was conducted by La Trobe University in partnership with Catholic Education Sandhurst (CES) Ltd. The types of teachers interviewed included schoolteachers working in rural Catholic schools who had completed a bachelor's or master's degree in education, and teachers who were still completing an education degree while working as a learning support officer or classroom teaching aide under a newly introduced Victorian Institute of Teaching policy labelled permission to teach (PTT). Our research identified a combination of general beginning teacher challenges as well as specific rural challenges and opportunities for beginning teachers.

Nearly all the participating teachers originated from rural communities; many were teaching in the same region in which they had grown up and several were teaching in the same school that they had attended as students. Of the 36 participants interviewed in our first focus group, 29 identified as having come from a regional/rural background, and four from an urban or metropolitan background (although three of these were from outer urban or fringe metropolitan areas). The remaining three participants did not identify their background. Of the 29 who identified as having come from a regional/rural background, 19 were working in schools that were a 30-min drive or less from where they grew up.

Reasons for this recruitment of locally based teachers included social support and lodging for those with family and friends living nearby, the teachers' own preference for a country lifestyle, and the active role that school leaders undertook in recruiting locally. While this indicates the importance of taking a homegrown approach to recruitment which is supported in the literature [52], it also indicates a gap in opportunity to attract metropolitan teachers to take up rural teaching positions [4]. We believe that recruiting metropolitan graduate teachers to take up rural positions could partly address the lack of available local teachers if teachers were aware of the personal and professional benefits of rural teaching. A summary from our interviews with graduate teachers on the mix of benefits and challenges of teaching and living in a rural community are listed in the table below (Table 1):

Table 1. Rural and Regional School Teaching and Living

General Themes	Challenges	Affordances
Social and Professional Relationships in Rural Schools	Less opportunity for team planning and networking. Lack of staff and casual relief teachers (CRTs) reduce release time and mentor support Lack of events and connections to other teachers can result in teacher loneliness	A small school fosters a close, friendly, and collegial atmosphere with positive relationships between staff, and knowing students and their families well
Organisational Structures and Resources in Rural Schools	School structures are not always established, and knowledge of school information is assumed Less access to specialists in health and education such as occupational therapists, LSOs, and subject specialist leaders	Small class sizes mean less report writing Involvement in multiple cross-curricular activities Consistent values across the school
Teaching Practices and Pedagogies in Rural Schools	Leaders and teachers must take on multiple roles Challenge of teaching curriculum to mixed grades	Development of a range of teaching and leadership skills Opportunities for increased teacher agency and leadership if support is provided
Living in Rural Communities	Managing relationships with parents and initially fitting into the community Lack of privacy out of school in small towns due to frequent encounters with students' families Lack of aspiration of students and families. Some students can feel isolated leading to mental health issues	The quality of connections and relationships built between teachers and with students in rural schools Lifestyle benefits such as less traffic and more social events Rural students sometimes have better community connections and involvement which promotes mental wellbeing

The four themes above were identified in the data as well as a division between challenges and affordances. However, in practice the delineation between each of the themes is not as clear cut as presented in the table. For example, we found that the benefit of having close community connections promotes authentic relationships between teachers, students and families which supports teaching and learning in the classroom as well as facilitating meetings with parents/guardians. Yet, it also creates a feeling of being constantly visible and accessible to students' families outside of school, creating blurred personal and professional relationships and a sense of teachers being scrutinised out of school hours. For the purpose of considering how aspects of rural teaching may be integrated into an ITE course with potential simulated experiences, the themes enable some preliminary ideas for simulation design to now be presented.

2.1 Social and Professional Relationships in Rural Schools

Supporting PSTs to engage fully with their school and local community is central to overcoming a sense of isolation. Further, building personal relationships with staff and families can serve as a foundation for quality teaching partnerships through common connections and collaboration [50]. Graduate teachers we interviewed felt underprepared for having discussions with parents/guardians regarding their students' learning. While this is a challenge that generally applies to beginning teachers in a range of schools, the rural context accentuates the importance of relationships within a school and with families and communities. Simulated experiences for relationship building are by no means a replacement for in-person discussions between peers, school staff and members of one's own community. Yet, simulations may enable PSTs to experience the kinds of discussions with school staff that often take place in rural schools but that are not easily accessible otherwise. Similarly, simulations can include discussions with parents in rural areas requiring management of professional conversations initiated in social settings as well as potential conflicts of interests where friendships are developed with parents. This may be done through avatars based on research with actual school staff, family and community members [57]. Realistic scenarios of daily interactions with staff such as planning in a professional learning team, learning the policies of a school and taking part in parent-teacher conferences can take the form of micro-teaching with feedback. [45] Scripted scenarios for a variety of possible pedagogical actions would allow for responsive and reflective interactions between the participating PST and either a pre-programmed sequence, artificial intelligence (AI), or human-directed avatar. Examples of software are presented in Sect. 3 of the chapter.

2.2 Organisational Structures and Resources in Rural Schools

With limited staff in schools, knowing how to work with other teachers to pool resources is valuable as well as being able to adapt to a variety of roles when required. Less access to specialist education support and limited resources may require teachers to upskill and actively seek out information which can be difficult if professional development requires travel [50]. In this way, online simulation may benefit both PSTs and rural teachers in schools for the professional development of specific skills [49, 60]. Virtual reality (VR) is an ideal platform for exploring an environment like a rural school and learning about different school resources and roles. The use of VR is being increasingly used for providing diverse work experiences for students who may not be able to visit a physical environment [39]. Within the context of teaching, specific rural schools could be used to develop VR content to support recruitment and orientation of new teachers to hard to staff schools. In addition, by taking a strengths-based approach VR could be used to identify alternate teaching and learning resources available through virtual tours and experiences of rural schools and communities.

2.3 Teaching Practices and Pedagogies in Rural Schools

Rural schools can be smaller and sometimes have classes with fewer students that span year levels. This enables teachers to focus more on the unique strengths and needs of students but requires an understanding of mixed-level teaching and differentiation of curriculum materials. Teachers may choose or be required to undertake leadership positions earlier in under-staffed rural schools [38]. The specific aspects of rural teaching will be elaborated upon in the following section with reference to high leverage practices (HLP) which have been used for the development of simulations in specialised settings such as special education [12] as well as for trauma-informed practices and management of difficult behaviours. These teaching experiences are specifically relevant to rural teaching because beginning teachers may not have access to specialists to provide expert support in a range of areas such as literacy, numeracy, wellbeing and first aid. Further, small country schools may have a greater concentration of students with diverse needs in a single classroom. Our research indicates that for beginning rural teachers, having limited specialist support and a social network can be overwhelming and isolating. Preparing teachers through simulated micro-teaching experiences in a range of scenarios with feedback provides a low-risk learning environment where mistakes can be made without direct consequences on relationships with actual students in schools [42].

2.4 Living in a Rural Community

Living in a rural town has many social and lifestyle affordances if teachers are willing to engage with community. Developing an understanding of the unique cultures, industries and demographics of locals is important for teachers to build student aspiration while appreciating the unique attributes of the community [58]. While coverage is limited in remote regions, PSTs already have access to Google Maps and Google Earth which can serve as a simulation to learn about the geography and navigate the street layout of towns from above and at ground level. *Ingress*, a location-based mobile game which uses Google Maps and GPS to integrate real locations with online games can be used in educational scavenger hunts [20, 62]. As recommended by O'Connor (2020) PSTs could undertake an online scavenger hunt to virtually explore a community by finding accommodation, going shopping, attending specific events for a town, learning about transport options and exploring some natural environments. In addition to exploring the geography of the town, PSTs could also conduct research on the population size, demographics including socio-economic status, types of employment and industry and the history and culture of the region. This type of research is an important step for beginning teachers to orientate themselves to the unique characteristics of a rural community they will live in and consider how this may impact on learning and teaching [58].

2.5 Summary of Sect. 2: Themes for Beginner Teaching in Rural Schools

This section has provided an overview of themes which emerged from undertaking individual interviews and focus groups with graduate teachers and school leaders in rural schools. The resulting themes serve as a basis for considering types of simulations that may be used. Two types of simulations have been identified for further investigation:

- Use of VR to explore and conduct research on a rural community and its schools
- Use of virtual scenarios with avatars to experience teaching diverse students and to learn about a range of roles a teacher may be required to fill in a rural school

A more comprehensive overview of specific technologies available to support both types of simulations is included in the next section of this chapter. First, a deeper investigation into specific aspects of practice-based initial teacher education (ITE) is presented to justify simulation as a beneficial approach to preparing teachers for rural teaching.

3 Unique Rural Practices and Pedagogies for ITE

Practice-based teacher education refers to a shift towards providing opportunities for PSTs to develop pedagogical skills and apply judgement relevant to daily teaching activities [29]. As much as possible PSTs learn through hands on experiences allowing for "pedagogies of enactment", which Grossman et al., (p. 283) describe as "including the use of approximations of practice in teacher education", rather than reliance on reading about teaching [29]. Although time spent in schools promises to provide the richest and most authentic experiences, placement can be overwhelming for PSTs as they need to apply theory in a complex practical setting. Further, teaching is a specialised and intricate process involving: judgements based on knowledge of students, the curriculum and previously trialled strategies; adapting to changes in timetables that might influence lesson planning and delivery; and assessing student learning for teaching during a lesson [8]. The actions that an experienced teacher juggles as well as their impactful teaching strategies may appear to a PST as innate or instinctive, yet they come from years of experience in the field and their mastery can disguise the highly trained decisions and actions undertaken. As illustrated in the Dreyfus and Dreyfus model of adult skill acquisition, a novice practitioner struggles to understand facts within the appropriate context, while an expert practitioner is able to perform optimal actions through intuition [23, 24]. Because there are several layers of proficiency between the novice and the expert teacher, practice-based approaches (including simulation and coaching) may help bridge the gap to support communication and understanding about pedagogies between mentor teacher and PST to reduce placement tensions [36, 37]. Finally, a PST on placement not only endeavours to apply theoretical strategies with little prior experience of practice and limited authority, but they are also faced with an educational environment that has specific policies, values and layout. The experience of placement can be disorientating and stressful for beginning and at-risk PSTs, which can dissuade PSTs from continuing their studies to become a teacher [13].

Our research with rural graduate teachers found that beginning teachers who had experience in a school before taking on a teaching position felt better prepared than graduate teachers who had only undertaken placement. Examples of this experience included volunteering at school events, camps and after school care; being part of sporting clubs such as coaching young people; and working as a tutor, learning support officer and teacher with PTT. Gaining this experience within a rural setting was facilitated by the graduate teachers having lived locally to a rural school. Yet, for a PST or beginning teacher coming from a metropolitan environment to teach in a rural school, the challenges are compounded as the practice of teaching may differ to their prior experience and the school environment may be quite different to their assumptions and existing knowledge [18, 67]. In short, any means to reduce the foreignness of teaching practice generally and specifically for rural schools through prior experience will be a beneficial support to PSTs and graduate teachers as well as the teaching profession.

3.1 High Leverage Practices to Support Rural Teaching

To support PSTs to develop capability and confidence in teaching, Ball [7] has identified 19 High Leverage Practices (HLPs) that are frequently used by teachers across different learning environments and subject areas [64]. From our research, we have adapted nine HLPs for their specific relevance to rural teaching and potential translation to simulations. We have focused on two of our existing themes of challenges and affordances to organise the relevant HLPs tailored to a rural setting:

Social and Professional Relationships in and Out of Rural Schools

- Building respectful relationships with students that draw on their lived experiences of rural life as well as their unique cultural, religious, family, intellectual and personal experiences for use in instruction (HLPs 10 & 12). This includes understanding the affordances of the rural community as well as challenges to wellbeing due to potential isolation, and potentially limited range of experiences.
- Talking about students with their parents or other caregivers which can include meetings in rural schools and managing personal and professional relationships with families outside of school (HLP 11).

Teaching Practices, Pedagogies and Assessment of Learning in Rural Schools

- Designing single lessons and sequences of lessons that can be adjusted to the needs of mixed level classes and analysing instruction for the purpose of improving it (HLPs 14 & 19).
- Designing a range of assessment tasks and activities suited to rural student experiences and interpreting the results of student work (HLPs 16 & 17).
- Specifying and reinforcing productive student behaviour for learners with a range of needs as part of managing a rural classroom through the implementation of norms and routines for classroom discourse and work (HLPs 5 & 7).

These elements of teaching practice based on HLPs tailored to a rural setting could be presented as individual micro-teaching scenarios for PSTs to engage in or could be combined into more realistic examples of practice in which there is an interplay between aspects of teaching. For example, the design of tasks can be based on relationships built with students including their unique backgrounds which support the specification of productive behaviours. By identifying key elements of successful teacher practice, PSTs can reflect on their own teaching to become reflexive practitioners. This chapter will now examine recommendations from the literature on developing course work to support practice-based ITE including a range of simulation types.

3.2 Designing Simulated Environments to Practice Rural Teaching

While the term "simulation" brings to mind digital environments and virtual reality experiences, there are a range of options that simulate practice without advanced technologies such as role play, serious games, video and audio tools which have been used since the 1930s [61]. Levin and Flavian provide a useful means of categorizing types of simulation-based learning (SBL) as human-based simulation; clinical simulation; computer-based simulation, mixed reality and immersive simulation [46]. Brownell et al. outline several examples of simulation approaches used in special education [12]. We have adapted four of these approaches as examples to be trialled for rural initial teacher education courses.

Rehearsal

Rehearsal enables PSTs during their university course to practice a range of strategies and pedagogical practices within a controlled environment such as a teaching laboratory prior to or combined with placement [43]. For PSTs preparing for rural teaching, a rehearsal might take the form of role-playing a scenario such as a discussion with a parent or challenging student. This can serve as a prompt for discussion and feedback as a debrief from an instructor and peers [43]. Authenticity of learning can be increased through the use of trained actors or an actual parent as well as having students undertake research in preparing their own scripts and scenarios. Frei-Landau and Levin have also conducted this teacher clinical simulation online via Zoom video conferencing using human actors [27].

Video Analysis

Analysis can be undertaken on pre-prepared video scenarios, PSTs' own teaching through reflection after a rehearsal, or a peer who has undertaken a rural placement [53]. Alternatively, experienced teachers in rural schools may video record their own teaching of distinctive practices for PST analysis (with parental permission to share recordings of students). Further, video footage could be used to inform the creation of realistic VR simulations and role play scenarios which can also be recorded and analysed by PSTs. Richter et al. note that using VR video recording for PST reflection has certain advantages over traditional video analysis such as being easily updated, having a first-person teacher perspective and overcoming ethical issues related to sharing video of students which enables PSTs to analyse their own VR teaching practice rather than a teacher's [59].

Coaching

While on placement PSTs may receive feedback at the end or during a lesson from a mentor. This allows for reflection on instruction and ideally an opportunity to repeat a lesson with pedagogical modifications. The advantage of coaching in a simulated rehearsal environment over mentoring in a classroom is the capacity to pause a teaching moment and unpack in real time key aspects such as HLPs without causing disruption to an actual lesson [12]. Coaching may also be incorporated into VR simulations with an instructor taking the role of an avatar known as *puppetry* or *human in the loop (HITL)* within the VR environment [35, 45].

Digital and Virtual Reality Simulations

Within Australia, VR simulation for ITE is gaining popularity [5]. Digital simulations can range from prepared scenarios with multiple choice responses at key points of video footage, to the use of responsive AI avatars in a virtual environment. Huang et al. describe three degrees of immersion: non-immersive (using a desktop); semi-immersive (mounted display with motion tracking); and fully immersive 360-degree visuals through head-mounted display [34]. With the rise of Chatbots, human-AI conversations can be used for learning a new language with a virtual tutor on a smart phone which demonstrates how simulation technology is becoming an increasingly accessible learning tool [9]. The authors also note that responsive AI such as chatbots still require improvement to overcome issues of predictability and random responses. The degree of adaptability of the program to participant input can sit on a sliding scale based on budget, desire for verisimilitude and expert technological support. The authenticity of the scenario is likely to depend as much on the quality of material used (such as input from rural teachers) as the realism of the environment and avatars. Generally, scenarios are short (approximately five minutes in length) with a focus on a specific aspect of teaching called micro-teaching [45].

A popular platform in research literature is the use of *Mursion* (formerly *TL Teach-LivE^{TM}*) which uses a combination of human-controlled and computer-generated avatars that can respond to participants with different levels of difficulty (such as degrees of non-compliant behaviours) based on desired settings [35]. As noted by Lamb and Etopio [42], having an opportunity to trial strategies to address challenging student behaviours through VR simulation provides a soft-failure learning environment which is different to the pressure of working with real children [55]. Some examples of VR simulations used in ITE include *Mursion* for microteaching in special education [12, 35]; *Digital Bridges* and *Play2Do* involving scenarios for vulnerable children in early childhood settings [15]; *Kognito* for emotionally supporting at-risk primary school students [40] and *SimTeach* [33]. For reviews of current use of mixed reality simulations in ITE refer to Huang et al. [34], Ade-Ojo [1] and Ledger et al. [44].

We now provide a summary of empirical research conducted by Ledger and Fischetti [45] on Micro-teaching 2.0 using SimLab HITL (human in the loop) simulation at Murdoch University and University of Newcastle, Australia. The research was conducted with 376 first-year PSTs from both universities who participated in a 10-minute simulation lesson in a virtual classroom with avatars and an academic observer prior to PSTs undertaking practicum in a school. Impact was measured through a post-practicum questionnaire which enabled data collection as well as PST reflection on teaching practice in the simulation. Overall, findings indicated that PSTs' confidence levels in teaching increased through the opportunity to rehearse teaching strategies in a safe environment prior to teaching students in an actual classroom. Some challenges for PSTs using the simulation included technological difficulties, a lack of realism and not having access to all resources usually used in teaching. Strengths of this research study include the opportunity for PSTs to plan the lesson prior to the simulation, to review a recording of the simulation and to reflect on specific elements of their teaching such as body language, questioning, rapport building, behaviour management as well as the structure and sequence of the lesson. Ledger and Fischetti provide a rigorous approach to embedding research into ITE through simulation enabling PSTs to rehearse, self-reflect, receive direct feedback from an academic supervisor and for researchers to collect feedback on the simulation technology for further development. Our own research identifies the applicability of this simulation technology in ITE for preparing PSTs for rural teaching. We elaborate on this in Sect. 4 of the chapter.

3.3 Summary of Sect. 3: Approaches to Simulation in Rural ITE

These four examples have been selected as of most interest to our research for trialling rural simulations. We speculate that these simulations could be used as preparation prior to a rural placement or used in iterative cycles between situated and simulated teaching experiences [43]. There is also potential to mix and match these approaches such as combining coaching with VR simulation or in-person and video rehearsals. Ideally, PSTs in metropolitan universities could engage in simulated experiences as a taster for short visits to rural schools and then longer immersive placements as recommended by Mitchell et al. [51]. Further, simulation is a low-risk and practical way of introducing the idea of rural teaching to interested PST cohorts that face logistical barriers to undertaking rural placements. From a pedagogical perspective, we believe that further research is needed on the role of reflection after the simulated experience as well as PST and teacher input in the design of simulation resources which accurately reflect the benefits and challenges of rural teaching and living.

4   Planned Development of Rural Simulation Coursework as a School-ITE Partnership

Our research team aims to develop simulated rural experiences for PSTs based on our emerging understandings of the specific practices and pedagogies relevant to rural teaching, the unique contexts of rural communities and current and emerging uses of simulation technologies. We endeavour to undertake this process of research and design in stages:

Research and Preparation

- Conduct further study on motivations and barriers to metropolitan PSTs taking up rural placements as well as current leading ITE courses for rural preparation.
- Identify several schools of different sizes in diverse rural, regional and remote communities. Invite rural schools who have a reputation for high quality teaching practices to participate in the development of the simulation course work.
- Establish a research partnership with a few rural schools for the design of simulation material including documentation of teacher experiences of key social and pedagogical interactions to inform future scripted scenario development.
- Record key teaching moments in rural classrooms with permission to film students and teachers and film 360-degree video footage of participating school settings. Examples of the use of 360-degree video footage of classroom teaching include empirical research by Theelen et al., [65] and a literature review by Evens et al., [25].

- Identify key community facilities and events, and interview local members of the rural community for future VR scavenger hunt games.

Simulation Ideas for a Prototype Rural Simulation Course

- Navigating through the rural community using Google Maps as a scavenger hunt in key locations which highlight events and facilities. Scripted interactions with community members can be included as scenarios.
- Taking a 360-degree tour of participating schools with video of teachers describing their school roles beyond classroom teaching.
- Video analysis of key teaching practices used to inform a PST rehearsal of a scenario (either role play or written description). Video analysis and rehearsal would include coaching from the university tutor and/or invited school leader.

Future Iteration

- Based on feedback from participating PSTs and participating school teachers video material from several schools will inform tailored use of existing VR simulations or creation of a rural-specific VR program with phone, desktop computer or immersive headset options.

5 Conclusion

This chapter has explored the potential of a range of simulations which could be used for encouraging metropolitan PSTs to consider rural placements and to provide targeted pedagogical experiences to prepare for teaching in rural schools. We have presented findings from our research on graduate teacher transitions to rural schools as the basis for high leverage teaching practices suited to rural teaching which could be translated into simulated ITE experiences. Our review of simulation literature has identified several possible simulation platforms such as Google Maps and GPS [20, 55, 62]; 360-degree recording and video analysis [25, 65]; VR and in-person rehearsals [35, 45, 47] and coaching [12] which we aim to integrate into a pilot rural ITE course. We have drawn attention to empirical research conducted by Ledger and Fischetti on the use of micro-teaching in virtual classrooms [45]. Our research has also identified a gap in research in rural simulations for teaching which we believe could build on existing simulation technologies presented in the chapter. We believe that the development of these simulation-based ITE courses with further research could help to redress recruitment issues for rural schools by raising PST interest in rural teaching, providing opportunities to rehearse teaching strategies, and to build partnerships between ITE course developers, researchers and rural schools. We welcome collaboration with academic researchers and ITE course designers from other universities with a similar interest in the use of simulations in rural teacher preparation, and rural schools who would like to be involved in research and development of simulation material.

References

1. Ade-Ojo, G.O., Markowski, M., Essex, R., Stiell, M., Jameson, J.: A systematic scoping review and textual narrative synthesis of physical and mixed-reality simulation in pre-service teacher training. J. Comput. Assist. Learn. **38**(3), 861–874 (2022)
2. Akber, B.A., Rajani, M.I., Khalid, F., Docherty, C.: Simulated learning in rural community environment: pushing the boundary. Adv. Simul. **6**(1), 5 (2021)
3. Australian Government Department of Education: Improving outcomes for all: The report of the independent expert panel's review to inform a better and fairer education system (2023). https://www.education.gov.au/review-inform-better-and-fairer-education-system/res ources/expert-panels-report
4. Australian Institute for Teaching and School Leadership (AITSL): Teaching futures background paper (2021). https://www.aitsl.edu.au/teachingfutures
5. Australian Institute for Teaching and School Leadership (AITSL): Spotlight: Technological Innovations in Initial Teacher Education. https://www.aitsl.edu.au/research/spotlights/techno logical-innovations-in-initial-teacher-education. Accessed 26 Dec 2023
6. Australian Institute for Teaching School Leadership: A National Trends Teacher Workforce https://www.aitsl.edu.au/research/australian-teacher-workforce-data/atwdreports/ national-trends-teacher-workforce. Accessed 20 Dec 2023
7. Ball, D.L.: High-leverage teaching practices: what is the core work of teaching, and what is required to learn it and to do it? https://static1.squarespace.com/static/577fc4e2440243084a 67dc49/t/578e349d59cc68eeb0d0d1b5/1468937374796/040116_C. Accessed 26 Dec 2023
8. Ball, D.L., Forzani, F.M.: The work of teaching and the challenge for teacher education. J. Teach. Educ. **60**(5), 497–511 (2009)
9. Belda-Medina, J., Calvo-Ferrer, J.R.: Using chatbots as AI conversational partners in language learning. Appl. Sci. **12**(17), 8427 (2022)
10. Beswick, K., et al.: Rural and regional research education project: final report. UNSW Gonski Institute for Education and School of Education, Sydney (2022)
11. Beverly, E.A., Love, C., Love, M., Williams, E., Bowditch, J.: Using virtual reality to improve health care providers' cultural self-efficacy and diabetes attitudes: pilot questionnaire study. JMIR Diabetes **6**(1), e23708 (2021)
12. Brownell, M.T., Benedict, A.E., Leko, M.M., Peyton, D., Pua, D., Richards-Tutor, C.: A continuum of pedagogies for preparing teachers to use high-leverage practices. Remedial Spec. Educ. **40**(6), 338–355 (2019)
13. Cara, C.: Finding my way not the highway: supporting first-year preservice teachers. Int. J. Learn. High. Educ. **23**(3), 19–35 (2016)
14. Cobb, D.J.: Metaphorically drawing the transition into teaching: what early career teachers reveal about identity, resilience and agency. Teach. Teach. Educ. **110**, 103598 (2016)
15. Connolly, T., Tsvetkova, N., Hristova, P.: Gamifying teacher training: Simulated practice learning for future and practising teachers interacting with vulnerable learners. In: Bradley, E. (ed.) Games and Simulations in Teacher Education. AGL, pp. 55–73. Springer, Cham (2020). https://doi.org/10.1007/978-3-030-44526-3_5
16. Cornish, L.: History and context of our research. In: Graham, L., Miller, J. (eds.) Bush Tracks: The Opportunities and Challenges of Rural Teaching and Leadership, pp. 11–23. SensePublishers, Rotterdam (2015)
17. Cosgrave, C., Malatzky, C., Gillespie, J.: Social determinants of rural health workforce retention: a scoping review. Int. J. Environ. Res. Public Health **16**(3), 314 (2019)
18. Cuervo, H., Acquaro, D.: Exploring metropolitan university pre-service teacher motivations and barriers to teaching in rural schools. Asia-Pac. J. Teach. Educ. **46**(4), 384–398 (2018)

19. Cuervo, H.: Understanding Social Justice in Rural Education. Palgrave Macmillan, New York (2016)
20. Davis, M.: Ingress in geography: portals to academic success? J. Geogr. **116**(2), 89–97 (2017)
21. Dixon, R., Hall, C., Shawon, F.: Using virtual reality and web conferencing technologies: exploring alternatives for microteaching in a rural region. Northwest J. Teach. Educ. **14**(1), 4 (2019)
22. Dorman, J., Dyson, M.: Development of a postulated model for investigating resilience and retention of teachers and nurses- a review of literature. In: Gunstone, A. (ed.) Developing Sustainable Education in Regional Australia, pp. 43–65. Monash University Publishing (2014)
23. Dreyfus, H.L., Dreyfus, S.E., Athanasiou, T.: Mind Over Machine: The Power of Human Intuition and Expertise in the Era of the Computer. Free Press, New York (1986)
24. Dreyfus, S.E.: The five-stage model of adult skill acquisition. Bull. Sci. Technol. Soc. **24**(3), 177–181 (2004)
25. Evens, M., Empsen, M., Hustinx, W.: A literature review on 360-degree video as an educational tool: towards design guidelines. J. Comput. Educ. **10**(2), 325–375 (2023)
26. Fischetti, J., Ledger, S., Lynch, D., Donnelly, D.: Practice before practicum: simulation in initial teacher education. Teach. Educ. Q. **57**(2), 155–174 (2022)
27. Frei-Landau, R., Levin, O.: The virtual Sim(HU)lation model: conceptualization and implementation in the context of distant learning in teacher education. Teach. Teach. Educ. **117**, 103798 (2022)
28. Graham, L., Miler, J., Paterson, D.: Accelerated leadership in rural schools. In: Graham, L., Miller, J. (eds.) Bush Tracks: The Opportunities and Challenges of Rural Teaching and Leadership, pp. 91–103. SensePublishers, Rotterdam (2015)
29. Grossman, P., Hammerness, K., McDonald, M.: Redefining teaching, re-imagining teacher education. Teach. Teach. Theory Pract. **15**(2), 273–289 (2009)
30. Halsey, J.: Rethinking the regional, rural and remote education workforce. Aust. Educ. Leader **45**(2), 37–40 (2023)
31. Heffernan, A., Bright, D., Kim, M., Longmuir, F., Magyar, B.: 'I cannot sustain the workload and the emotional toll': reasons behind Australian teachers' intentions to leave the profession. Aust. J. Educ. **66**(2), 196–209 (2022)
32. Heffernan, A., Fogarty, R., Sharplin, E.: G'aim'ing to be a rural teacher? Improving pre-service teachers' learning experiences in an online rural and remote teacher preparation course. Aust. Int. J. Rural Educ. **26**(2), 49–62 (2016)
33. Herbst, P., Boileau, N., Shultz, M., Milewski, A., Chieu, V.-M.: What simulation-based mentoring may afford: opportunities to connect theory and practice. In: Bradley, E. (ed.) Games and Simulations in Teacher Education. AGL, pp. 91–114. Springer, Cham (2020). https://doi.org/10.1007/978-3-030-44526-3_7
34. Huang, Y., Richter, E., Kleickmann, T., Richter, D.: Virtual reality in teacher education from 2010 to 2020: a review of program implementation, intended outcomes, and effectiveness measures. EdArXiv (2021). https://doi.org/10.35542/osf.io/ye6uw. Accessed 20 Dec 2023
35. Hudson, M.E., Voytecki, K.S., Owens, T.L., Zhang, G.: Preservice teacher experiences implementing classroom management practices through mixed-reality simulations. Rural Spec. Educ. Q. **38**(2), 79–94 (2019)
36. Hudson, P., Hudson, S.: Mentoring preservice teachers: identifying tensions and possible resolutions. Teach. Dev. **22**(1), 16–30 (2018)
37. Husbye, N.E., Powell, C.W., Vander Zanden, S., Karalis, T.: Coaching in practice-based literacy education courses. Read. Teach. **72**(2), 191–200 (2018)
38. Jenkins, K., Taylor, N., Reitano, P.: Listening to teachers in the 'bush.' In: Graham, L., Miller, J. (eds.) Bush Tracks: The Opportunities and Challenges of Rural Teaching and Leadership, pp. 41–55. SensePublishers, Rotterdam (2015)

39. Jiang, Y., Popov, V., Li, Y., Myers, P.L., Dalrymple, O., Spencer, J.A.: "It's like i'm really there": using VR experiences for STEM career development. J. Sci. Educ. Technol. **30**(6), 877–888 (2021)
40. Khalid, N.: Professional development simulations for K12 educators to address social, emotional, and behavioral concerns in the school setting. In: Bradley, E. (ed.) Games and Simulations in Teacher Education. AGL, pp. 115–126. Springer, Cham (2020). https://doi.org/10.1007/978-3-030-44526-3_8
41. Kumar, S., Tian, E.J., May, E., Crouch, R., McCulloch, M.: You get exposed to a wider range of things and it can be challenging but very exciting at the same time": enablers of and barriers to transition to rural practice by allied health professionals in Australia. BMC Health Serv. Res. **20**(1), 105 (2020)
42. Lamb, R., Etopio, E.: Virtual reality to train preservice teachers. In: Bradley, E. (ed.) Games and Simulations in Teacher Education. AGL, pp. 141–154. Springer, Cham (2020). https://doi.org/10.1007/978-3-030-44526-3_10
43. Lampert, M., et al.: Keeping it complex: using rehearsals to support novice teacher learning of ambitious teaching. J. Teach. Educ. **64**(3), 226–243 (2013)
44. Ledger, S., et al.: Simulation platforms in initial teacher education: past practice informing future potentiality. Comput. Educ. **178**, 104385 (2022)
45. Ledger, S., Fischetti, J.: Micro-teaching 2.0: technology as the classroom. Australas. J. Educ. Technol. **36**(1), 37–54 (2020)
46. Levin, O., Flavian, H.: Simulation-based learning in the context of peer learning from the perspective of preservice teachers: a case study. Eur. J. Teach. Educ. **45**(3), 373–394 (2020)
47. Levin, O., Frei-Landau, R., Flavian, H., Miller, E.C.: Creating authenticity in simulation-based learning scenarios in teacher education. Eur. J. Teach. Educ. 1–22 (2023). (ahead-of-print)
48. Lock, G.: Preparing teachers for rural appointments. Rural Educ. **29**(2), 24–30 (2018)
49. Long, M.W., Albright, G., McMillan, J., Shockley, K.M., Price, O.A.: Enhancing educator engagement in school mental health care through digital simulation professional development. J. Sch. Health **88**(9), 651–659 (2018)
50. Miller, J., Graham, L.: Taking the bush track home. In: Graham, L., Miller, J. (eds.) Bush Tracks: The Opportunities and Challenges of Rural Teaching and Leadership, pp. 157–165. SensePublishers, Rotterdam (2015)
51. Mitchell, R., Olsen, A.W., Hampton, P., Hicks, J., Long, D., Olsen, K.: Rural exposures: an examination of three Initiatives to introduce and immerse preservice teachers into rural communities and rural schools in the U.S. and Australia. Rural Educ. **40**(2), 12–22 (2019)
52. Nash, F.: Regional education commissioner: annual report (2022). https://www.education.gov.au/regional-education-commissioner/resources/regional-education-commissioner-annual-report-2022. Accessed 16 Oct 2023
53. Nickl, M., Huber, S.A., Sommerhoff, D., Codreanu, E., Ufer, S., Seidel, T.: Video-based simulations in teacher education: the role of learner characteristics as capacities for positive learning experiences and high performance. Int. J. Educ. Technol. High. Educ. **19**(1), 45 (2022)
54. Noone, G., Miller, J.: Methodologies. In: Graham, L., Miller, J. (eds.) Bush Tracks: The Opportunities and Challenges of Rural Teaching and Leadership, pp. 25–40. SensePublishers, Rotterdam (2015)
55. O'Connor, E.: Virtual reality: bringing education to life. In: Bradley, E. (ed.) Games and Simulations in Teacher Education. AGL, pp. 155–167. Springer, Cham (2020). https://doi.org/10.1007/978-3-030-44526-3_11
56. Page, J.: Teaching in rural and remote schools: implications for pre-service teacher preparation pedagogies of place and their implication for pre-service teacher preparation. Educ. Rural. Aust. **16**(1), 47–63 (2006)

57. Rappa, N., Ledger, S.: Pre-service teachers' reflections on their challenging experiences interacting with a parent avatar: Insights on deepening reflection on the simulation experience. J. Educ. Teach. JET **49**(2), 311–325 (2023)
58. Reid, J.A., Green, B., Cooper, M., Hastings, W., Lock, G., White, S.: Regenerating rural social space? Teacher education for rural-regional sustainability. Aust. J. Educ. **54**(3), 262–276 (2010)
59. Richter, E., Hußner, I., Huang, Y., Richter, D., Lazarides, R.: Video-based reflection in teacher education: comparing virtual reality and real classroom videos. Comput. Educ. **190**, 10460 (2022)
60. Sampson, D.G., Kallonis, P.: 3D virtual classroom simulations for supporting school teachers' continuing professional development. In: Jia, J. (ed.) Educational Stages and Interactive Learning: From Kindergarten to Workplace Training, pp. 427–450. IGI Global (2012)
61. Schutt, S., Miles-Keogh, R., Linegar, D.: Simulations in teacher education. In: Oxford Research Encyclopedia of Education. Oxford University Press (2022)
62. Sengupta, U., Tantoush, M., Bassanino, M., Cheung, E.: The hybrid space of collaborative location-based mobile games and the city: a case study of ingress. Urban Plann. **5**(4), 358–370 (2020)
63. Society for the Provision of Education in Rural Australia (SPERA): Attracting teachers to schools in rural and remote areas in Australia, SPERA. https://spera.asn.au/attracting-tea chers-schools-rural-remote-areas-australia-2/. Accessed 10 Dec 2023
64. Teaching Works: High Leverage Practices. University of Michigan. https://library.teachingw orks.org/curriculum-resources/high-leverage-practices/. Accessed 14 Dec 2023
65. Theelen, H., Beemt, A., Brok, P.: Using 360-degree videos in teacher education to improve preservice teachers' professional interpersonal vision. J. Comput. Assist. Learn. **35**(5), 582–594 (2019)
66. Thomson, S., De Bortoli, L., Underwood, C.: PISA 2015: a first look at Australia's results. A. C. f. E. R. (ACER). https://research.acer.edu.au/ozpisa/21. Accessed 20 Dec 2023
67. Trinidad, S., Sharplin, E., Ledger, S., Broadley, T.: Connecting for innovation: four universities collaboratively preparing pre-service teachers to teach in rural and remote Western Australia. J. Res. Rural. Educ. **29**(2), 1 (2014)
68. Victorian Government: Targeted initiative to attract more teachers. https://www.vic.gov.au/targeted-initiative-attract-more-teachers. Accessed 16 Dec 2023
69. Walker-Gibbs, B., Ludecke, M., Kline, J.: Pedagogy of the rural as a lens for understanding beginning teachers' identity and positionings in rural schools. Pedagog. Cult. Soc. **26**(2), 301–314 (2018)
70. Walker, L., Cross, M., Barnett, T.: Mapping the interprofessional education landscape for students on rural clinical placements: an integrative literature review. Rural Remote Health **18**(2), 4336 (2018)
71. White, S.: Placing teachers? Sustaining rural schooling through place-consciousness in teacher education. J. Res. Rural. Educ. **23**(7), 1–11 (2008)

Exploring the Potential of Audiovisual Social Platforms in Higher Education

Ana Beltrán-Flandoli(✉) [ID], Diana Rivera-Rogel [ID], and Cristhian Labanda [ID]

Universidad Técnica Particular de Loja, Campus San Cayetano Alto, Loja, Ecuador
{ambeltran,derivera,cglabanda}@utpl.edu.ec

Abstract. Audiovisual social networks have emerged as potent instruments for content creation and dissemination across diverse fields, with education being no exception. Undoubtedly, we are witnessing a revolution in the methodologies employed for imparting and assimilating knowledge. In our investigation, we delved into the potential utilization of platforms like YouTube and Instagram within university settings, exploring the perceptions of a sample of 243 university educators from 29 Higher Education institutions regarding the strategic integration possibilities of these tools. The study also addresses perceived concerns and barriers through the UTAUT analysis model. Data, acquired through a self-administered questionnaire, was meticulously analyzed using a combination of descriptive and inferential design. Among the myriad of findings, the results underscore significant disparities in the relationship between gender and the proficiency of university educators in utilizing information and communication technologies (ICT). Notably, there is a marked preference for YouTube as an educational tool, juxtaposed with a comparatively lower adoption rate of Instagram in educational environments. This trend suggests a burgeoning interest in the realm of new media and its pivotal role in disseminating knowledge, particularly evident in fourth-level educational actions. However, limitations are apparent, chiefly in the form of insufficient training and resources hindering the effective implementation of these digital environments for educational purposes. The study sheds light on the evolving landscape of educational technology, emphasizing the need for addressing challenges to fully harness the potential of audiovisual social platforms in university contexts.

Keywords: YouTube · Instagram · Higher Education

1 Introduction

Amidst the repercussions of the COVID-19 pandemic, the imperative for innovation in the educational realm has spurred numerous global initiatives. Particularly noteworthy are endeavors focusing on scenarios, methodologies, and resources designed to facilitate the seamless continuation of the teaching-learning process through asynchronous and remote means [1]. This trend has manifested itself not only in the formal domain of education but has also given rise to a substantial volume of audiovisual content in the realms of non-formal and informal education, significantly enhancing access to information and fostering autonomous learning [2].

Ł. Tomczyk (Ed.): NMP 2023, CCIS 2130, pp. 271–287, 2024.
https://doi.org/10.1007/978-3-031-63235-8_18

In this field, the permeation of content from audiovisual social platforms such as Instagram and YouTube lies in the incorporation of audiovisual language as a foundational support for content [3]. These productions have also become a pre-valent resource for successive generations of young learners, owing to their pedagogical potential [4]. Within the university context, the allure of this micronarrative format enriched by video elements is particularly pronounced. According to Guillén-Gámez et al. (2023) [5] and Anzola-Gomez et al. (2022) [6], it diverges from conventional classroom dynamics, rendering the learning process less conscious.

The primary objective of this study is to investigate the potential utilization and educational integration of YouTube and Instagram in the university setting as audiovisual platforms. This involves highlighting both their possibilities and the associated barriers and limitations, as perceived by professors at this academic level. Furthermore, our aim is to underscore the educommunicative nexus within this emerging teaching model.

YouTube and Instagram in Higher Education Processes

YouTube and Instagram are currently two of the most trending social audiovisual platforms, offering specific features that provide significant advantages for facilitating education. They have emerged as prominent mediums for information and communication, while increasingly integrating into the educational system as instruments that foster the dissemination of knowledge and experiences within this sector. Consequently, they facilitate the creation of collaborative spaces for educators, thereby reducing geographical, temporal, hierarchical, and institutional barriers. An apt term to categorize them is "virtual community," as suggested by Amo and García-Roca (2021) [7].

YouTube stands as the foremost online video viewing and streaming platform, currently boasting over 2 billion users, localized versions in 91 countries, and navigable in 80 languages [8] Latin America is witnessing a surge in users, audiovisual content creators, and advertisers across various industry sectors.

While originally conceived as an entertainment platform, YouTube has evolved to encompass a diverse array of educational topics and objectives, fueled by its global popularity. Feixas et al. (2014) [9], Mármol (2017) [10] and Delgado (2019) [11] delineate various types of productions, including video lectures, live broadcasts, outreach videos, educational games, animations, and preferred tutorials. Despite the longstanding communicative specialization of the field, the migration of previous platforms such as Big Think, Fora.tv, TED Talks, and TeacherTube to YouTube has significantly broadened the visibility of these educational resources [12].

In Higher Education setting, YouTube assumes a pivotal role in comprehending study and learning habits, challenging institutions, teachers, and students to adapt to new modalities and embrace autonomous or discovery [13, 14]. This necessitates the implementation of strategies such as inverted learning or 'help seeking' [15]. Consequently, YouTube not only establishes itself as an educational tool at its core but also as a manifestation of the adaptability and ongoing digital transformation essential in the current university landscape.

Research evidence underscores improvements in academic performance [16], temporal flexibility [17]. Enhancement of communicative competence, and the fostering of critical self-reflection [18, 19]. Nevertheless, these resources encounter challenges in attaining academic recognition. Concerns about the quality of educational content on

YouTube have been raised, with Rudenkin (2019) [20] specifically focusing on quality assessment and the prevention of the dissemination of misinformation.

Instagram emerges as a prominent fixture on the dartboard of global digital culture. Beyond its status as a revered visual platform, this mobile photography application can be dissected as a cultural generator [21]. Renowned for its visual-centric approach, it excels in fostering trust and credibility among users, as indicated by Pittman & Reich (2016) [22]. Pérez Escoda & García Ruiz (2019) [23] underscore the pivotal role of engagement in forging connections within the educational realm, emphasizing the significance of narrative on these platforms [24].

Micro-narratives, as defined by De-Casas-Moreno et al. (2018) [25] and Piragua Rugeles et al. (2019) [26], redefine effective learning, enabling crucial adjustments in educational design. Carpenter et al. (2023) [27] disclose that the application's educational utility primarily centers around seeking applicable ideas and learning through observation, although active participation via content sharing proves to be a challenge for some users.

It is imperative to underscore that the narrative embedded in the productions of edutubers [28] and educational instagrammers [29], forms the essential foundation of these creations, aiming to 'instruct.' The employed dialectic is compelling due to its lucid guidelines, presented in a 'step-by-step' format with accessible, non-technical language, all conveyed from the perspective of the potential user.

1.1 Digital Learners and Educommunicative Empowerment

Several essential skills have been identified that digital learners must master to effectively engage in cognitive processes within digital environments. These include the ability to navigate the flow of stories and information across various modalities, as well as skills to process, create, and disseminate their own narratives [30, 31].

This set of new competencies, deemed crucial and profoundly influenced by the unprecedented convergence of media, platforms, spaces, and occupations, leads to the emergence of a spectrum of content. This content is generated not only by established media chains but also by young individuals through their experiments and evolving affiliations.

Consequently, it is imperative to establish a new framework for comprehending the cultural practices, attitudes, and skills of individuals who consume and produce (or "prosume") these discourses. As highlighted by González-Martínez et al. (2018) [32], this analysis is an unavoidable subject that necessitates a fresh categorization of the elements of literacy in a hypermedia reality. This approach allows for the identification and description of the socio-cultural competencies required to actively participate in the new digital environments.

According to García Galera et al. (2018) [33], citizen media empowerment entails not only providing individuals with tools but distinctly emphasizes offering educational conditions on media languages, encompassing both new and traditional forms, as an integral part of the information society. The objective is to mitigate vulnerabilities stemming from both the use and non-use of these media.

Herrero-Diz and Ramos-Serrano (2016) [34] delineate theoretical insights derived from the practices of new generations concerning information consumption, knowledge creation online, and engagement in virtual environments. By examining various perspectives that have become prevalent in the scientific field, the authors define several categories to depict the evolving relationship between young people and digital culture. The most recent generational cohorts, namely "X," "Y," and "Z," have matured alongside technology, with their members, particularly the older ones, also assuming responsibility for sustaining the productive sector and guiding the process of integrating their predecessors into new communication models.

2 Materials and Methods

This study employed a quantitative design [35], utilizing descriptive and inferential statistics for data analysis. The research focused on evaluating the perceptions of Ecuadorian university professors regarding the form and types of usage and consumption on the platforms YouTube and Instagram. The aim was to gauge cause-and-effect variables resulting from the use of social media and their impact on the educational landscape, specifically on the methods of teaching and learning at the university level.

Data collection occurred through a self-administered survey hosted on the "ArcGIS Survey123" platform. The survey considered responses from university professors across 31 Higher Education institutions providing third-level training in the fields of Communication and Education. Data collection took place during the months of May, June, and July 2022. The approach to data management was objective and aligned with the evidence collected. The study was conducted ensuring participant anonymity, data confidentiality, adherence to ethical considerations, among other aspects.

2.1 Participants

The participants in the study were 243 university professors from 18 institutions that offer education and 13 that offer communication (See Table 1), who were self-selected to participate in this study.

Table 2 shows the demographic profile of the professors, which shows an equal participation in relation to gender, with 51% male and 49% female professors. In relation to generation, the majority belong to Generation X (35.4%), followed by Generation Y (29.6%) and Baby Boom (21.8%). Most reside in urban areas (95.5%), while only 4.5% are in rural areas. Finally, a high level of education stands out given that 66.3% have a specialization or master's degree, and 31.7% have a doctorate or postdoctoral degree. All participants were informed of the purposes of the study and expressed their explicit consent to take part in it.

2.2 Ethics

This study adhered to a stringent ethical protocol. Initially, the research team crafted a document outlining the study's particulars, including its goals, objectives, and the data to be collected. Additionally, a consent form was presented to participants in question 1 of Sect. 1 of the instrument. It was recommended that participants thoroughly review the consent form and accompanying information before consenting to commence. Only those participants who read and agreed to participate in the study were allowed to proceed with completing the instrument.

Table 1. Universities involved in the study

Province	Higher Education Institution	Frequency	Percentage
Guayas	Escuela Superior Politécnica del Litoral	2	,8%
Pichincha	Pontifica Universidad Católica del Ecuador	18	7,4%
Guayas	Universidad Católica Santiago de Guayaquil	2	,8%
Pichincha	Universidad Central del Ecuador	2	,8%
Azuay	Universidad de Cuenca	21	8,6%
Guayas	Universidad de Especialidades Espiritu Santo	7	2,9%
Guayas	Universidad de Guayaquil	2	,8%
Pichincha	Universidad de las Americas	9	3,7%
Pichincha	Universidad de las Fuerzas Armadas	27	11,1%
Pichincha	Universidad de los Hemisferios	4	1,6%
Azuay	Universidad del Azuay	1	,4%
Bolivar	Universidad Estatal de Bolivar	2	,8%
Pichincha	Universidad Internacional del Ecuador	1	,4%
Manabí	Universidad Laica Eloy Alfaro de Manabí	6	2,5%
Guayas	Universidad Laica Vicente Rocafuerte	6	2,5%
Pichincha	Universidad Metropolitana del Ecuador	1	,4%
Chimborazo	Universidad Nacional de Chimborazo	11	4,5%
Loja	Universidad Nacional de Loja	4	1,6%
Azuay	Universidad Politécnica Salesiana	13	5,3%
Pichincha	Universidad San Francisco de Quito	3	1,2%
Manabí	Universidad San Gregorio de Portoviejo	2	,8%
Tungurahua	Universidad Técnica de Ambato	1	,4%
Cotopaxi	Universidad Técnica de Cotopaxi	5	2,1%
Manabí	Universidad Técnica de Manabí	1	,4%
Imbabura	Universidad Técnica del Norte	2	,8%
Loja	Universidad Técnica Particular de Loja	32	13,2%
Pichincha	Universidad Tecnológica Indoamérica	22	9,1%
El Oro	Universidad Técnica de Machala	4	1,6%
Cañar	Universidad Nacional de Educación	32	13,2%
Total		243	100,0%

2.3 Instrument

The instrument "Uses and consumption of YouTube and Instagram by university professors in Ecuador", designed and developed by the researchers of the study, was used. As

Table 2. Demographic profile of the sample

Criteria	Description	Frequency	Percentage
Gender	Male	124	51,0%
	Female	119	49,0%
Generation	Baby Boomer	53	21,8%
	Generation X	86	35,4%
	Generation Y	72	29,6%
	Generation Z	32	13,2%
Zone of residence	Urban zone	232	95,5%
	Rural zone	11	4,5%
Education level	Third level	5	2,1%
	Specialization, Master's degree	161	66,3%
	PhD, Postdoctorate	77	31,7%

part of this process, content, construct, and expert validity were considered. The analysis consisted of several specific stages: first, an extensive literature review was conducted, which allowed generating an initial set of dimensions and their respective items of the instrument according to the objectives of the study. The theoretical model underpinning the proposed instrument explores factors related to the Unified Theory of Acceptance and Use of Technology (UTAUT) [36].

Second, the content validation of the instrument was carried out by a panel of nine expert judges, academics, and researchers from Ecuador (n = 5) and Spain (n = 4), most of them experts in the research topic and above all members of highly prestigious Universities. The participants were selected by convenience, which implies that it was not based on statistical probability. The judges meticulously assessed each item organized into four sections, considering criteria such as clarity, coherence, relevance, and sufficiency [37]. Observations were incorporated as needed during the evaluation process. Judgments were documented on a Likert-type scale with five response options: 1. Very inadequate, 2. The agreement among experts for the four attributes of each item and the overall sense of agreement (acceptance or rejection) were calculated using Kendall's W coefficient. In this context, a Kendall's W concordance coefficient of 0.705 (p < 0.05) was obtained, signifying a statistically significant indicator that allows us to affirm the instrument's validity for application. This value was deemed satisfactory, leading to the generation of the second version of the instrument.

This iteration of the instrument was administered to 24 university professors, with affiliations to Universidad Técnica Particular de Loja (7.3%) and Universidad Técnica del Norte (92.7%), with an average age of 37 years ± 2.03 years. During this phase, an assessment of item comprehension, response options, formal aspects, and completion time was conducted. This process resulted in the creation of the third version of the instrument. The Cronbach's Alpha coefficient, calculated for the instrument, was 0.908, indicating a high level of internal consistency and affirming the instrument's validity for application.

Subsequently, the instrument consisted of 27 questions divided four sections: (1) Socio-demographic profile -7 questions-, (2) Digital and social media competence - 3 questions-, (3) Consumption, knowledge, and use of YouTube and Instagram -8 questions-, and (4) YouTube and Instagram and learning -9 questions-.

2.4 Data Analysis

The data underwent analysis employing both descriptive and inferential statistics. Descriptive statistics, encompassing percentages and frequencies, were computed to scrutinize the variables' behavior. To discern potential significant differences between variables, the Chi-square and Cramer's V statistics were calculated. For the quantitative analysis, the survey data were meticulously input into the SPSS program (V.22.0) and systematically processed, adhering to a "data analysis protocol." These analyses formed the foundation for generating valid and reliable interpretations and conclusions discussed in the study.

3 Results

3.1 The Digital and Social Media Competence of Professors

When investigating the correlation between gender and proficiency in handling media and information and communication technologies (ICT), the collected data indicate an even distribution among male (51%) and female (49%) participants. An examination of knowledge levels reveals that men exhibited lower (8%) and very high (11.5%) competence in media and ICT management compared to women (1.2% and 4.5%, respectively). Conversely, women demonstrated relatively higher proportions at the medium (15.6%) and high (27.6%) levels of media and ICT knowledge. Chi-square analysis (11.959, $p = 0.008$) confirmed a significant association, supported by a Cramer's V of 0.222, signifying a moderate relationship between gender and ICT knowledge.

This discovery underscores the significance of considering gender in the design of ICT training programs, recognizing existing disparities. It also emphasizes the necessity for further research to comprehend the underlying causes of these differences and to formulate equitable strategies promoting digital inclusion (Fig. 1).

3.2 How University Professors Consume, Use, and Acquire Knowledge on YouTube and Instagram

When exploring the relationship between gender, generation, and the frequency of technological device usage, particularly in managing media and information and communication technologies (ICT), a prevalent trend emerges. The majority of participants report frequent (46.1%) and very frequent (38.7%) usage of cell phones. Similarly, for laptops, 37.0% of participants use them frequently, and 31.7% use them very frequently. In contrast, 47.7% of participants state they never use tablets, with occasional (17.3%)

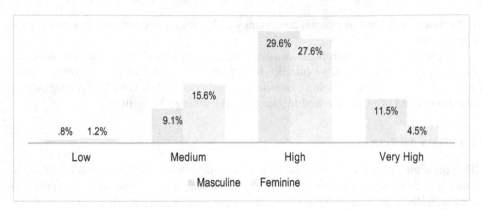

Fig. 1. Level of knowledge in handling media and information and communication technologies by gender

and rare (16.9%) usage following. A similar pattern is observed with Smartwatches, with 67.9% reporting never using them. Notably, no significant differences in the usage of these devices were found based on gender and generation, according to chi-square analyses.

On the other hand, concerning desktop computers, 30.0% of participants never use them, while 25.9% use them frequently. A significant association was identified in this case with both gender and generation. Men tend to use desktop computers more frequently (Chi-square = 13.564, p = 0.009, V Cramer = 0.236), and Generation X exhibits the highest proportion of frequent use, followed by Generation Y (Chi-square = 23.352, p = 0.025, V Cramer = 0.025).

Findings reveal fluctuations in the utilization of technological devices based on gender and generation. While no noteworthy distinctions were identified in cell phone usage, tablets, laptops, and smartwatches exhibit discernible patterns. Generation X emerges as the most engaged demographic in the use of technological devices, while gender differences are notable in the utilization of laptops and desktop computers. These insights furnish valuable information for customizing educational and techno-logy development strategies, considering the distinct preferences and usage tendencies within each demographic group (Table 3).

Table 3. Frequency of device use for YouTube and Instagram access by gender and generation

		Gender		2.1 Generación				Total
		Male	Female	Baby Boomers	Generation X	Generation Y	Generation Z	
Cell phone	Never	1,2%	–	,4%	–	8%	–	1,2%
	Rarely	2,1%	2,1%	1,6%	,8%	1,6%	–	4,1%
	Occasionally	5,3%	4,5%	2,5%	4,5%	2,5%	,4%	9,9%

(continued)

Table 3. (*continued*)

		Gender		2.1 Generación				Total
		Male	Female	Baby Boomers	Generation X	Generation Y	Generation Z	
	Frequently	21,8%	24,3%	11,1%	17,3%	11,9%	5,8%	46,1%
	Very frequently	20,6%	18,1%	6,2%	12,8%	12,8%	7,0%	38,7%
	Total	51,0%	49,0%	21,8%	35,4%	29,6%	13,2%	100,0%
Tablet	Never	21,0%	26,7%	10,3%	13,6%	15,6%	8,2%	47,7%
	Rarely	10,3%	6,6%	2,9%	7,4%	4,5%	2,1%	16,9%
	Occasionally	10,3%	7,0%	4,5%	7,0%	3,7%	2,1%	17,3%
	Frequently	6,6%	4,9%	3,3%	4,5%	2,9%	,8%	11,5%
	Very frequently	2,9%	3,7%	,8%	2,9%	2,9%	–	6,6%
	Total	51,0%	49,0%	21,8%	35,4%	29,6%	13,2%	100,0%
Laptop computer	Never	3,3%	2,5%	1,2%	2,5%	1,6%	,4%	5,8%
	Rarely	4,9%	4,1%	2,1%	3,3%	3,3%	,4%	9,1%
	Occasionally	8,2%	8,2%	2,9%	5,3%	5,8%	2,5%	16,5%
	Frequently	19,3%	17,7%	8,2%	14,4%	10,3%	4,1%	37,0%
	Very frequently	15,2%	16,5%	7,4%	9,9%	8,6%	5,8%	31,7%
	Total	51,0%	49,0%	21,8%	35,4%	29,6%	13,2%	100,0%
Desktop computer	Never	10,3%	19,8%	4,1%	7,0%	12,8%	6,2%	30,0%
	Rarely	9,1%	4,9%	3,3%	5,3%	3,7%	1,6%	14,0%
	Occasionally	7,0%	6,2%	2,9%	5,8%	2,5%	2,1%	13,2%
	Frequently	14,0%	11,9%	6,6%	11,5%	7,0%	,8%	25,9%
	Very frequently	10,7%	6,2%	4,9%	5,8%	3,7%	2,5%	16,9%
	Total	51,0%	49,0%	21,8%	35,4%	29,6%	13,2%	100,0%
Smartwatch	Never	33,3%	34,6%	15,6%	25,5%	18,1%	8,6%	67,9%
	Rarely	3,7%	3,3%	1,2%	2,1%	2,1%	1,6%	7,0%
	Occasionally	5,8%	2,9%	1,2%	2,5%	4,5%	,4%	8,6%
	Frequently	3,7%	4,9%	2,5%	2,1%	2,5%	1,6%	8,6%
	Very frequently	4,5%	3,3%	1,2%	3,3%	2,5%	,8%	7,8%
	Total	51,0%	49,0%	21,8%	35,4%	29,6%	13,2%	100,0%

* Gender: Chi-square (13.564, p = 0.009) and Cramer's V (0,236). Generation: Chi-square (23.352, p = 0.025) and Cramer's V (0,025).

Table 4 illustrates the daily consumption patterns on two platforms, YouTube and Instagram, considering both the gender and generation of the participants. It is noted that 39.5% of participants spend less than one hour a day on YouTube, while 43.6% dedicate 1 to 3 h. Although no significant differences were found in YouTube usage by gender, generational analysis reveals a noteworthy association (Chi-square = 20.190, p = 0.064, V Cramer = 0.166). Generation Y exhibits a higher proportion of users who consume content for 1 to 3 h, indicating distinct generational patterns in time spent on this platform.

Concerning Instagram, 61.7% of participants use the platform for less than one hour daily, with 28.4% allocating 1 to 3 h. While no significant differences were identified in usage based on gender, a notable association with generation is observed (Chi-square = 26.100, p = 0.010, V Cramer = 0.189). Generation X demonstrates a higher proportion of users who consume content from 1 to 3 h on Instagram.

Chi-square and Cramer's coefficient analyses reveal significant associations in both cases. For YouTube, the V Cramer is 0.190 for gender and 0.166 for generation, indicating moderate relationships. Regarding Instagram, although the V Cramer is 0.143 for gender, a stronger link (V Cramer = 0.189) with generation is notable. These results suggest that preferences in daily usage time on these platforms are more influenced by generation than by gender.

It is important to note that these associations do not imply causality, and other contextual factors could influence consumption patterns. The emergence of generational differences could be linked to each generation's unique preferences and experiences in social media use.

Table 4. Daily usage of YouTube and Instagram by gender and generation

Daily time spent using		Gender		Generation				Total
		Male	Female	Baby Boomers	Generation X	Generation Y	Generation Z	
YouTube	Less than 1 h	16,9%	22,6%	11,5%	12,3%	11,9%	3,7%	39,5%
	From 1 to 3 h	24,3%	19,3%	7,4%	15,2%	13,6%	7,4%	43,6%
	4 to 6 h	8,2%	6,6%	2,1%	7,4%	4,1%	1,2%	14,8%
	7 to 9 h	1,6%	–	,8%	–	–	,8%	1,6%
	More than 9 h	–	,4%	–	,4%	–	–	,4%
	Total	51,0%	49,0%	21,8%	35,4%	29,6%	13,2%	100,0%
Instagram	Less than 1 h	34,6%	27,2%	16,5%	23,0%	18,1%	4,1%	61,7%

(*continued*)

Table 4. (*continued*)

Daily time spent using	Gender		Generation				Total
	Male	Female	Baby Boomers	Generation X	Generation Y	Generation Z	
From 1 to 3 h	11,9%	16,5%	3,3%	8,6%	8,6%	7,8%	28,4%
4 to 6 h	3,3%	3,3%	1,2%	2,5%	2,5%	,4%	6,6%
7 to 9 h	1,2%	1,6%	,8%	,8%	,4%	,8%	2,9%
More than 9 h	–	,4%	–	,4%	–	–	,4%
Total	51,0%	49,0%	21,8%	35,4%	29,6%	13,2%	100,0%

YouTube: Gender: Chi-square = 8,745, p = 0.068, Cramer's V = 0.190. Generation: Chi-square = 20,190, p = 0.064, Cramer's V = 0.166
Instagram: Gender: Chi-square = 4,856, p = 0.292, Cramer's V = 0.143. Generation: Chi-square = 26,100, p = 0.010, Cramer's V = 0.189

On the other hand, when characterizing YouTube and Instagram users based on gender and generation, with a focus on user roles—producer, active, and passive—distinct patterns emerge. For YouTube, noteworthy gender differences surface (Chi-square = 19.474, p = 0.000, V Cramer = 0.283). Specifically, 14.0% of men are classified as producer users, in contrast to 3.3% of women. Males also lead as active users, with 12.8% compared to 12.3% of females. Conversely, women predominate as passive users, constituting 33.3% compared to 24.3% of men. Regarding generation, no significant differences were identified (Chi-square = 3.279, p = 0.773, V Cramer = 0.082), indicating that the role classification on YouTube does not vary significantly between generations.

In the case of Instagram, no significant differences were found between genders (Chi-square = 1.407, p = 0.495, V Cramer = 0.076). However, generation exhibits notable associations (Chi-square = 22.549, p = 0.001, V Cramer = 0.215). Active users predominate in Generation X with 5.8%, while passive users are less prevalent in Generation Z with 6.2%.

Overall, the majority of participants categorize themselves as passive users on both YouTube (57.6%) and Instagram (65.8%). This prevailing pattern indicates that content consumption is the predominant activity on both platforms. Nevertheless, distinctions in role classification between genders and generations underscore the diversity of user behaiors.

The findings imply that, on YouTube, men are inclined to assume more active roles, whereas, on Instagram, generational factors appear to influence role preferences. The prevalence of passive users underscores the significance of crafting compelling content to capture the attention of this predominant audience (see Table 5).

Table 5. User types on YouTube and Instagram by gender and generation

Type of user by platform		Gender		Generation				Total
		Male	Female	Baby Boomers	Generation X	Generation Y	Generation Z	
YouTube user type	Producing user (I make and upload videos to YouTube)	14,0%	3,3%	4,1%	5,8%	5,3%	2,1%	17,3%
	Active user (I make comments, participate in discussions and/or share videos)	12,8%	12,3%	5,3%	10,7%	7,0%	2,1%	25,1%
	Passive user (I mostly watch videos)	24,3%	33,3%	12,3%	18,9%	17,3%	9,1%	57,6%
	Total	51,0%	49,0%	21,8%	35,4%	29,6%	13,2%	100,0%
Instagram user type	Producing user (I make and upload images and videos to Instagram)	7,4%	9,1%	1,6%	2,5%	8,2%	4,1%	16,5%
	Active user (I make comments, participate in discussions and/or share content	8,2%	9,5%	4,1%	5,8%	4,9%	2,9%	17,7%
	Passive user (I'm mostly engaged in viewing content posted by others)	35,4%	30,5%	16,0%	27,2%	16,5%	6,2%	65,8%
	Total	51,0%	49,0%	21,8%	35,4%	29,6%	13,2%	100,0%

YouTube: Gender: Chi-square = 19,474, p = 0.000, Cramer's V = 0.283. Generation: Chi-square = 3,279, p = 0.773, Cramer's V = 0.082
Instagram: Gender: Chi-square = 1,407, p = 0.495, Cramer's V = 0.076. Generation: Chi-square = 22,549, p = 0.001, Cramer's V = 0.215

3.3 YouTube and Instagram in Learning

Figure 2 unveils distinct usage patterns for each platform in the educational context. Concerning YouTube, 38.3% of participants use the platform frequently, with an additional 27.2% using it occasionally. Moreover, 19.8% report very frequent usage. In contrast, the utilization of Instagram for educational purposes is less common, with 49.4% indicating that they never use Instagram in this context, and 21.0% using it rarely. Only 8.6% use it frequently, and 1.6% use it very frequently. These findings underscore that YouTube is a popular and widely employed tool in the educational setting, while Instagram is used less frequently. Furthermore, mean-contrast analysis reveals no discernible differences in terms of gender and generation, suggesting that these factors do not significantly impact usage.

The analysis of these figures reveals intriguing patterns in platform preferences for educational activities. YouTube emerges as the preferred option, potentially owing to its capacity to host educational videos and tutorials, coupled with its widespread accessibility. In contrast, Instagram, known for its visual focus on images and short video clips, appears to be less embraced in educational settings.

These results provide valuable insights for educators and content designers aiming to optimize their online teaching strategies. The pronounced preference for YouTube underscores the importance of creating and sharing educational resources in video format. Conversely, the limited use of Instagram suggests that its visual format may not be as conducive or leveraged for educational purposes compared to other platforms.

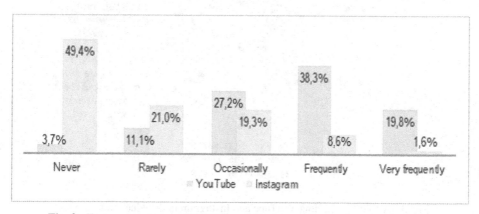

Fig. 2. Frequency of uses of YouTube and Instagram in the educational context

Finally, in the exploration of participants' attitudes toward the use of the social networking platforms YouTube and Instagram in education, several noteworthy insights emerge. First and foremost, participants overwhelmingly express agreement (39.9%) and strong agreement (31.2%) that learning is enhanced through the integration of social networks. This indicates a generally positive perception of the role of social networks in the educational process. However, a significant 22.6% fall into the "Neither agree nor disagree" category, suggesting some ambivalence in opinions.

Regarding the interactive nature of Instagram, 41.2% of participants agree (26.3%) and strongly agree (14.8%) that this feature facilitates student participation in collaborative work and the creation of quality work. While this reflects a positive attitude, it is observed that 24.3% are in the categories of disagree (11.5%) and totally disagree (12.8%), indicating diversity of opinions.

Concerning YouTube, 58% of professors believe that students are more engaged in learning on this platform compared to other e-learning platforms used. This suggests that YouTube is perceived as an effective tool for student engagement, although 13.2% are in the disagree and strongly disagree categories.

In terms of the importance of learning the use of social networks, 67.5% of participants express agreement and strong agreement, highlighting the perceived relevance of acquiring skills in this area. Finally, regarding the lack of knowledge of the use of YouTube and Instagram in Higher Education, it is observed that 50.6% and 56.0% of the participants, respectively, agree and totally agree with these statements. This suggests a generalized perception of a lack of knowledge about the educational potential of these platforms (Fig. 3).

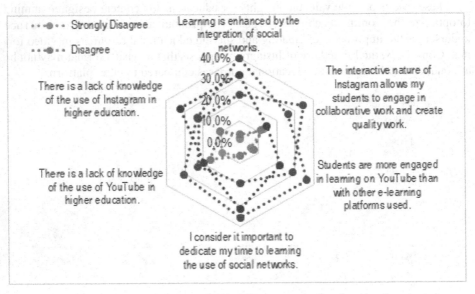

Fig. 3. Attitudes regarding YouTube and Instagram in the educational context

4 Discussion and Conclusions

The primary aim of this study was to comprehensively explore the educational potential embedded in the narratives found on YouTube and Instagram, recognized as highly influential audiovisual social platforms, within the realm of Higher Education. This exploration was conducted through the lens of professors, who play a pivotal role as architects of innovation in the processes of teaching and learning [34]. Utilizing effective evaluation tools becomes crucial in identifying the strengths, weaknesses, and barriers for the implementation of these digital tools in the academic environment.

The literature review underscores that achieving deep learning in Higher Education involves guiding students in the relationship, comparison, and analysis of ideas [6]. YouTube and Instagram, as audiovisual platforms for collaborative construction, offer a medium for contrasting diverse perspectives and triggering cognitive processes within the learning journey [3]. The efficacy of this learning experience hinges on providing learners with opportunities to analyze data stemming from varied actions and purposes [13, 14]. The quantitative results derived from the instrument application indicate significant disparities in the relationship between gender and professors' competence in managing information and communication technologies (ICT), emphasizing the imperative need for equitable training programs [19]Additionally, the research brings to light variations in the use of technological devices by gender and generation among professors, furnishing valuable insights for adapting educational and technological development strategies [21]. Similarly, generational differences in time spent on social platforms suggest distinctive patterns of consumption. Notably, YouTube emerges as a preferred educational tool, while Instagram witnesses lower adoption in educational settings. The perceived importance of acquiring social networking skills is evident, juxtaposed with a widespread perception of ignorance about the educational potential of YouTube and Instagram in Higher Education [27].

The findings of this research, while not intended for broad generalization, hold significance in shaping proposals for both curricular enhancements and training in the Higher Education space. However, there is a discernible tendency to instrumentalize practices and platforms without considering the barriers in access or the gap in the capacity for didactic use due to cultural and institutional resistance [20]. The imperative need to evaluate professors' digital competence in relation to the implementation of YouTube as a didactic resource emerges as a critical element in the current educational landscape [1, 5].

References

1. Jakoet-Salie, A., Ramalobe, K.: The digitalization of learning and teaching practices in higher education institutions during the Covid-19 pandemic. Teach. Public Adm. **41**(1), 59–71 (2023)
2. Lange, P.G.: Informal learning on YouTube. In: The International Encyclopedia of Media Literacy, pp. 1–11 (2019)
3. Pattier, D.: Communication and emerging teaching models: a study on Youtubers teachers. Multidisc. J. Educ. Res. **14** (2023). https://doi.org/10.17583/remie.9887
4. Lozano Díaz, A., González Moreno, J., Cuenca Piqueras, C.: Youtube como recursos didáctica en la Universidad. EDMETIC, Revista de Educación Mediática y TIC **9**(2), 159–180 (2020)
5. Guillén-Gámez, F.D., Ruiz-Palmero, J., Colomo-Magaña, E., Cívico-Ariza, A.: Construcción de un instrumento sobre las competencias digitales del docente para utilizar YouTube como recurso didáctico: análisis de fiabilidad y validez. Revista de Educación a Distancia (RED) **23**(76) (2023)
6. Anzola-Gomez, J., Rivera-Rogel, D., Aguaded, I.: Interacción social e interacción discursiva de un canal de YouTube educativo. Fonseca J. Commun. (25), 115–132. (2023)
7. Amo, J.M.D., García-Roca, A.: Mechanisms for interpretative cooperation: fan theories in virtual communities. Front. Psychol. **12**, 699976 (2021)

8. YouTube Press. https://www.youtube.com/about/press. Accessed 20 Dec 2022
9. Feixas, D., Codina, E., Carandell, R.: Cómo triunfar en YouTube. La Galera (2014)
10. Mármol, P.: 30 canales de vídeo para hacer experimentos. Educación 3.0. https://goo.gl/i1ym2d. Accessed 20 Dec 2023
11. Delgado, P.: YouTube educativo: una herramienta para los alumnos. Observatorio de Innovación Educativa. https://bit.ly/3nWaQI0. Accessed 04 May 2022
12. Snelson, C.: The benefits and challenges of YouTube as an educational resource. In: Routledge Companion to Media Education, pp. 203–218. Routledge, London (2018)
13. Downie, S., Gao, X., Bedford, S., Bell, K., Kuit, T.: Technology enhanced learning environments in higher education: a cross-disciplined study on teacher and student perceptions. J. Univ. Teach. Learn. Pract. **18**(4) (2021)
14. Zhang, J., Tan, L., Tao, X.: On relational learning and discovery in social networks: a survey. Int. J. Mach. Learn. Cybern. **10**, 2085–2102 (2019)
15. Aguilar, M.S., Puga, D.S.E.: Mathematical help-seeking: observing how undergraduate students use the internet to cope with a mathematical task. ZDM Math. Educ. **52**, 1003–1016 (2020)
16. Morais, W., Zacariotti, M.: Da sala de aula ao YouTube: As juventudes e seus modos de aprender em (na) rede. Educação formal e não formal, cultura e currículo I **7**(6) (2020)
17. Sarkar, N., Ford, W., Manzo, C.: To flip or not to flip: what the evidence suggests. J. Educ. Bus. **95**(2), 81–87 (2019)
18. Maraza-Quispe, B., Alejandro-Oviedo, O., Fernández-Gambarini, W., Cisneros-Chavez, B., Choquehuanca-Quispe, W.: Análisis de YouTube como herramienta de investigación documental en estudiantes de educación superior. Publicaciones **50**(2), 133–147 (2020)
19. Beltrán-Flandoli, A.M., Pérez-Rodríguez, A., Mateus, J.-C.: YouTube como ciberaula. Revisión crítica de su uso pedagógico en la Universidad Iberoamericana. RIED-Revista Iberoamericana de Educación a Distancia **26**(1), 287–306 (2022)
20. Rudenkin, D.: YouTube as an instrument of learning in higher education: opportunities and challenges [proceedings]. In: European Conference on e-Learning, Denmark (2020)
21. Boy, J.D., Uintermark, J.: Reassembling the city through Instagram. Trans. Inst. Br. Geogr. **42**, 612–624 (2017). https://doi.org/10.1111/tran.1218
22. Pittman, M., Reich, B.: Social media and loneliness: why an Instagram picture may be worth more than a thousand Twitter words. Comput. Hum. Behav. **62**, 155–167 (2016)
23. Pérez-Escoda, A., García-Ruiz, R.: Instagramers e Youtubers: Uso pedagógico para el desarrollo de la competencia digital. In: Aguaded, I., Vizcaíno-Verdú, A.X., Sandoval-Romero, Y. (eds.) Competencia Mediática y Digital: Del Acceso al Empoderamiento, pp. 243–253. Grupo Comunicar Ediciones (2019). https://bit.ly/3d9jihz
24. Scolari, C.A.: Transmedia literacy in the new media ecology: white paper. Universitat Pompeu Fabra. Departament de Comunicació, 16 p. Transliteracy Project (2018)
25. De-Casas-Moreno, P., Tejedor-Calvo, S., Romero-Rodríguez, L.: Micronarrativas en Instagram: análisis del storytelling autobiográfico y de la proyección de identidades de los universitarios del ámbito de la comunicación. Revista Prisma Social **20**, 40–57 (2018)
26. Piragua Rugeles, C.M., Ñáñez Rodríguez, J.J.: Instagram, de red social a ambiente virtual de aprendizaje: una experiencia con resultados inesperados. Encuentros **19**(01), 9 (2021)
27. Carpenter, J., Shelton, C., Shroeder, S.: The education influencer: a new player in the educator professional landscape. J. Res. Technol. Educ. **55**(5), 749–764 (2023)
28. Cordero-Arroyo, D.G., Murillo-Peralta, S., Valenzuela-Lugo, I.: Estudio de caso de los canales de edutubers mexicanos especializados en contenidos para profesores. Revista Electrónica de Investigación e Innovación Docente **6**(2), 25–37 (2021)
29. Secilla Garrido, M.: Edugramers y Edutubers ¿Produzco, luego enseño? Análisis de cuentas educativas en Instagram y Youtube [Tesis de maestría, Universidad Internacional de Andalucía]. Dspace Universidad Internacional de Andalucía (2021)

30. Haddon, L., Cino, D., Doyle, M-A., Livingstone, S., Mascheroni, G., Stoilova, M.: Children's and young people's digital skills: a systematic evidence review. KU Leuven, Leuven: y SKILLS (2020)
31. Perifanou, M., Tzafilkou, K., Economides, A.A.: The role of Instagram, Facebook, and YouTube frequency of use in university students' digital skills components. Educ. Sci. **11**, 766 (2021)
32. González-Martínez, J., Serrat-Sellabona, E., Estebanell-MinGuell, M., Rostan-Sánchez, C., Esteban-Guitart, M.: About the concept of transmedia literacy in the educational field. A review of the literature. Comunicación y sociedad (33), 15–40 (2018)
33. García Galera, M., del Olmo Barbero, J., del Hoyo Hurtado, M.: Jóvenes, privacidad y dependencia en las redes sociales. II Congreso Internacional Move.net sobre Movimientos Sociales y TIC, Seville, Spain (2018)
34. Hernández Sampieri, R., Fernández, C., Baptista, P.: Metodología de la Investigación. MacGraw Hill (2014)
35. Herrero Martínez, R., Marín Díaz, V., González López, I.: Las TIC como medio educativo para la adquisición de competencias profesionales del alumnado de educación superior. Diálogos Pedagógicos **14**(28), 23–40 (2016)
36. Chintalapati, N., Daruri, V.S.K.: Examining the use of YouTube as a Learning Resource in higher education: scale development and validation of TAM model. Telematics Inform. **34**(6), 853–860 (2017)
37. Escobar-Pérez, J., Cuervo-Martínez, A.: Validez de contenido y juicio de expertos: Una aproximación a su utilización. Avances en Medición **6**, 27–36 (2008)

Developing Digital Competency in Health and Physical Education: When Digital Literacy Meets Physical Literacy

Stuart Evans[✉]

La Trobe University, Melbourne, VIC, Australia
Stuart.evans@latrobe.edu.au

Abstract. The twenty-first century has witnessed vast adaptation and use of digital technology tools in education. The expansion and diversification of digital technologies in the contemporary education era continues to have tremendous influence in the field of health and physical education (HPE), specifically on the future generation of HPE teachers, that is – the preservice (student) teachers. This has made it necessary to question the current standalone approach to physical, health and digital literacies when contrasted to a more nuanced multiliteracy approach. It is no longer possible to think about physical, health and digital literacies solely as a linguistic or movement-based accomplishment. Preservice teachers need to comprehend, respond to, and compose multimodal texts in diverse forms, where meaning is communicated through dynamic combinations of two or more modes. In this emergent field of research, there is a growing amount of empirical evidence supporting a greater need for a multiliteracy approach that integrates technology, content and pedagogical knowledge for preservice teachers learning HPE. This paper examines the constructs of physical, health and digital literacies in the instructive and educational process for the subject of HPE. Thus, ways to develop 'digital dexterity' using frameworks such as technological pedagogical content knowledge (TPACK) are explored from a preservice HPE teacher perspective. The increasing access of preservice teachers to health and physical education information and communication technologies for educational practice combined with how they could be integrated into teaching and learning is addressed.

Keywords: digital pedagogy · health and physical education · physical literacy · TPACK

1 Introduction

"Mens sana in corpore sano," a principle typically interpreted as "a healthy mind in a healthy body". The expression is commonly used in sporting and educational settings and is persistently revisited by scholars. Contemporary reiterations, or revisitations, regarding a healthy mind in a healthy body, or life-long health and vitality, often comprise three definitions and philosophical constructs: physical literacy (PL), health literacy (HL) and digital literary (DL) as a path to heightened life-long physical activity, motivation,

Ł. Tomczyk (Ed.): NMP 2023, CCIS 2130, pp. 288–304, 2024.
https://doi.org/10.1007/978-3-031-63235-8_19

and embodiment. The significance of these literacies is required for everyone to make informed, confident choices to support their health and wellbeing. Arguably, the largest impact has been observed in the digital realm given that digital media has permeated all strata of everyday life to the point where people engage with various digital media tools repeatedly.

Lawson [1] postulated that occupational socialisation, as with any type of socialisation that exerts an influence on individuals when selecting health and physical education (henceforth HPE) teaching as a profession, subsequently affects their practical knowledge of teaching and their actions as physical educators. However, research has shown that a critical teaching perspective is at risk if preservice teachers (student teachers, henceforth PST) perceive a gap between what is taught at university and what they encounter during practicum or field-based learning. A perceived gap between these contexts habitually results in PSTs appreciating the practical knowledge learned in the field (i.e., the school setting) and not seeing the point, or not understanding the intension, of the theoretical viewpoints they learned in lectures at university. In teacher education (henceforth TE), the PST can experience a conflict between the teaching philosophies and teaching methods advocated in university-based courses and those they encounter during field-based learning courses [2]. Traditionally, the focus has been on how pedagogical theory delivered in TE can be better connected and applied to PSTs, but an emerging problem is how to support PSTs in poignant from understanding theory intellectually to enacting it in practice using a multimodal or multiliteracy approach that encompasses the ongoing influence of digital technologies.

To understand the current situation, it may be beneficial to (briefly) review the contemporary role that digital technology plays in education. For instance, the twenty-first century has witnessed prevalent adaptation and use of digital technology in educational settings. This has made it necessary to question the impact it has on the educational experiences, engagement, learning outcomes and digital competencies of PSTs and their future students of varying ages and cultural, social backgrounds. This has resulted in a shared recognition that digital literacy stands as a critical competency for today's learners, challenged by the technological, informational, cognitive, and socio-emotional demands of the digital age [3]. Digital "tools", that is – applications, platforms, and devices allow for collaboration, which in turn can encourage the sharing, participation, contribution, and discussion of information. Despite digital tools and related digital pedagogical approaches becoming an established part of curricula in the quest to achieve digital literacy (henceforth DL) current educational practice suggests [e.g., 3] that PSTs specialising in HPE may implement *some* form of technology in their classrooms or practical settings, but many face difficulties in doing so.

Today's PSTs who specialize in HPE are of great significance as they are the next generation of teachers to prepare, mold, and instill the importance and relevance of HPE to children. The discussion that once focused on the significance of HPE and the need for its inclusion in respective national curricula is complete. Nowadays, HPE and its various subsets, is a mandated learning area offered for implementation as it establishes a government's bestowed interest in a future healthy society.

HPE and physical activity are differentiated, however; HPE is a curriculum subject with an educative application while physical activity is movement that comprises forms of physical exertion. Penney [4] declared that education is at the core of HPE, and this distinguishes it from physical activity and sport. Yet efforts to enhance the quality of education are dependent on TE and the PSTs who are appropriately equipped to undertake the numerous and demanding roles and functions of teachers. While today's preservice HPE teachers have the potential to obtain the necessary knowledge and skills needed, they are likely to encounter difficulties when considering the multifaceted literacy requirements needed to teach contemporary HPE that includes digital literacies.

HPE is said to deliver physical, psychological, social, and cognitive health and wellbeing advantages to children. In this regard HPE is a multidimensional view that depicts a collective foundation for physical activity engagement. Here, literacy links the reading, viewing, writing, speaking, and listening practices that students (i.e., PSTs) use to access, understand, and communicate subject-specific knowledge [5]. This form of literacy, then, involves a holistic approach to lifelong learning and physical activity. These collective domains personify a holistic methodology to physical activity that considers the social and physical processes paired with lifelong learning [6, 7]. As originally conceived by Whitehead [8], measuring and understanding these literacy components is of increasing interest in the fields of education, sport, recreation, and population health [9]. But declining student achievement and levels of physical activity in HPE is framed as symptomatic of broader dysfunction within the education system. As Nutbeam [10] asserts, the ability to read and write (functional literacy) is a foundation for health literacy on which a range of complementary skills can be built. Here, PSTs in HPE can help make connections to multimodal literacy, including the need to strengthen digital competencies. However, PSTs need the skills and metacognition to become physically and digitally literate in contemporary HPE such is the pervasiveness of technology. Essentially, PSTs need the required multidimensional, or multiliteracy skills to effectively teach today's children.

HPE has traditionally been contextualized to lifestyle and movement, neglecting the burgeoning digital component. Although definitions of physical and health literacy may differ, developing literacy skills are key to certify that PSTs have the skills and tools to apply the knowledge and concepts of HPE to improve personal and community health and wellbeing. Here, the interplay between literacies intersect to include the digital domain. Consequently, HPE PSTs face some crucial questions in dealing with the challenge of the why, when, and how to incorporate digital technologies in teaching practices. Finding from previous work suggests that a discrepancy exists between the aims and understanding of technology education that can also be reflected in curriculum, not only among different countries but also between different provinces within one country [7]. Yet an alternative barrier appears to be a lack of TE awareness, or reluctance, to appreciate how digital technology can be used and integrated to benefit both the teaching and purpose of its use in HPE.

While the current paper is not strictly a systematic review, systematic methods have been used to review the existing literature concerning physical, health and digital literacies and the existing technological pedagogical content knowledge in HPE. Thus, this paper presents an analysis of research into physical, health and digital literacy as conceptualised by scholars to examine the extent that research supports the incorporation of health, physical, health and digital literacy and learning for integration into PST health and physical activity education.

2 Plethora of Literacies

Obtaining literacy is not a one-off act nor a straightforward process. Beyond its conventional concept as a set of reading, writing, and counting skills, literacy is understood as a means of identification, understanding, interpretation, creation, and communication in a progressively digital, text-mediated, information-rich, and fast-changing world. Thus, literacy is a continuum of learning and proficiency in reading, writing, and using numbers throughout life and is part of a larger set of skills, which include digital skills, media literacy and job-specific skills. And so, literacy skills are increasing and progressing as more people engage with information and learning through digital means.

2.1 Methods

Given the plethora of literacies, a scoping review was conducted using PubMed, Google Scholar, and Scopus database entries. The initial search was conducted December 2023 and January 2024, with a follow-up search performed in February 2024. Articles that operationalised the construct of health literacy, physical literacy, and digital literacy in health and physical education were identified and included. The process and assessment tools used to evaluate the articles of interest were manually checked for duplicate publications. Initially, title and abstract screening were completed followed by a full-text screening. Duplicates were removed. The search strategy combined the term 'health, physical, and digital literacy' AND 'children' OR 'adolescent' OR 'teenagers' or 'high school' were used along with 'TPACK'. The exclusion criteria included scientific posters, and non-English articles. A standardised extraction protocol for summarising appropriate variables was developed that was in accordance with the Preferred Reporting Items for Systematic Reviews and Meta-Analyses (PRISMA) checklist.

2.2 Physical Literacy

Physical literacy (henceforth PL) has become an increasingly influential concept and is being woven into education, sport, and recreational policy and practices in many countries [11]. So, what is PL, really? Is it nothing more than an influential metaphor? Or is it the attainment of elementary or fundamental movement skills? Perhaps it is a theoretical contradiction of mind–body symmetry? [12]. Or perhaps it is now a marketing fad which is in vogue? There are numerous definitions and explanations to support what PL is, or what it is not. What can be established is that PL is complex and continues to be interpreted and defined in numerous ways, often without reference to digital literacy.

Physical Literacy has broadly been described as the motivation, physical competence, knowledge and understanding to value and take responsibility for engagement in physical activities for life [13]. Certainly, PL includes characteristics such as qualifications, behaviours, awareness, knowledge and understanding of the enhancement of healthy active living and physical recreation opportunities. Whitehead [8] presents PL as an aspect of lived embodiment and a pathway to a better quality of life. Drawing on existential and phenomenological perspectives, she asserted a monist view that erases mind–body duality through awareness of the self as active personification, and claimed that through a fuller realisation, exploration and expression of human physicality humans heighten self-awareness [14]. Of note, Whitehead [8] offers the following definitions:

- Literacy is intricate in the development of PE and/or school-based physical activity (which may include sport), all of which are integral to many national curricula.
- PL can be expressed as the capacity and motivation to capitalise on an individual's potential to make a significant contribution to the quality of life. Furthermore, the individual is perceptive in 'reading' all aspects of the physical environment, predicting movement needs or possibilities and responding appropriately to these, with intelligence and imagination.

In addition, individuals can categorise and articulate the essential qualities that influence the effectiveness of his/her own movement performance and understand the principles of embodied health [15]. The inkling of a better life, or lifelong learning as is phrased in some curricula, through PL has excited many, particularly practitioners in the fields of HPE, recreation, public health, and sport, who have seized on the notion to advance their curiosity in increasing levels of physical activity or performance. While some of the individual tenets of PL have been associated to improved physical activity participation across the life course [16], the concept of PL as part of a multimodal or multiliteracy construct is not well studied in the context of PST HPE education.

The extent to which PL fits alongside or within HPE and DL is a source of debate across different jurisdictions. For instance, the British Columbia Physical and Health Education curriculum in Canada, positions PL as one of the four 'Curricular Competencies' [16] as PL has infiltrated the 'official pedagogic discourse' [17] of these and other curricula. Nevertheless, Hay and Penney [18] note that assessment, as a transmitter of the knowledge, skills and understandings that are most valued in HPE, will often be a key driver of curriculum and pedagogy in HPE. Here, PSTs may find greater difficulties in these three areas when trying to make tangible links relative to integrative and incorporative DL. Gathering, interpretating and implementing information online poses several challenges for HPE PSTs, particularly concerning searching for and assessing the credibility of sources if the initial education, that is – the teacher education, is deficient in this area.

To value, develop and maintain positive physical activity behaviours for life, the reality of integrating digital tools into PST HPE and, thus, into deliverable and measurable outcomes remain challenging. Yet PL can be viewed as an umbrella construct that can incorporate DL. Here, the pedagogical content knowledge, the technical and technological skills, understandings, and values related to taking responsibility for purposeful physical activity can be taught at an academic level. While Fig. 1 provides an evidence-derived observed learning taxonomy, this model assumes a loose progression from simple to complex in the physical, cognitive, and affective learning domains without reference to where such learning may be obtained, gained, or reviewed.

Hammack and Ivey [20] conveyed that teachers perceived that their lack of pre- and in-service training affected their background knowledge in technology; additionally, teaching processes were identified as the most significant challenges that must be addressed in facilitating engineering and technology education. Challenging PSTs to find solutions to problems is a dominant feature of a tenable knowing of PL. It is also practical that any continuum of PST learning coupled with PL incorporate a method of observing

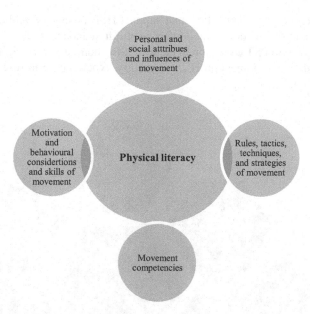

Fig. 1. The pillars of physical literacy. Adapted from Dudley et al. [19].

legitimate indicators of personal responsibility toward health-promoting movement and literacy. This continuum should capture the framework of when competence, autonomy, and relatedness are satisfied. Here, the value of health literacy (henceforth HL) and DL can be applied to provide possible links that can move PSTs further along the continuum to attain positive PL outcomes.

2.3 Health Literacy

Health literacy (HL), as a term first proposed in the 1970s [21], generally concerns whether an individual is competent with the complex demands of promoting and maintaining health in modern society [22]. Over the past two decades, heightened awareness has been attached to HL due to its substantial benefits to individual and public health and the sustainability of healthcare systems. Children, teenagers, and adolescents constitute a core target group for HL research and practice as during childhood and youth, fundamental cognitive, physical, and emotional development processes occur alongside health-related behaviours and skills. However, there exists limited academic consensus concerning the abilities and knowledge a child or young person should possess for making sound health decisions [23]. Explicitly, the cognitive, physical, and emotional processes are regarded as crucial for healthy development and personal health and well-being throughout adulthood [24] as HL is identified as a variable construct that is acquired in a life-long learning process [25]. Yet much like PL, HL is also a multidimensional concept. A dominant research focus exists pertaining to the development of measurement tools to assess and deconstruct each of the included PL domains that are displayed in Fig. 2. Against this backdrop, the PST undertakes an exploration of the fundamental principles, ideas, theories, and beliefs that support HPE pedagogy. Although there has been an increase in publications which focus on children and adolescent HL and PL, the consideration given to PST education in incorporating contemporary digital practices is small compared to the momentum HL is currently experiencing in research, practice, and policymaking.

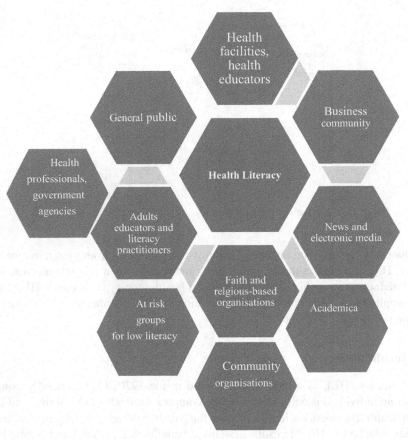

Fig. 2. The pillars of health literacy.

Integration of the differing dimensions suggest that HL is connected to literacy and necessitates people's knowledge, motivation, and competences to access, understand, appraise, and apply health information to make judgments and take decisions in everyday life concerning healthcare and health promotion [26]. Yet much like PL, HL is conceptualised as an activity competence, with a particular focus on personal characteristics, while also recognising the interrelationship with social and contextual elements. Moreover, an individual's HL depends upon their personal situation including their health status, risks or problems, their affiliation with social group(s) (e.g., health practitioners, patients, and different age-groups) and other socio-economic determinants [27]. Information seeking is described as another core dimension of HL. Subramaniam et al. [28] suggest HL is a fluid and iterative process, including two main elements, namely information access and search. Accessing information is the ability to seek, find and obtain health information [24] and includes being able to adapt to new technologies, being aware of primary health resources to begin search, having to access valid information, products, and services, being exposed to computers in everyday life and being aware of search engines and their capabilities [29]. For instance, many of today's PSTs are health literate and can establish and maintain their self-defined health-related goals. Thus, critical media literacy and DL have become important dimensions of HL in the information society. Therefore, a more specific and integrative approach to contemporary PL and HL for PST education is required to ensure that the numerous constructs are appropriately taught as one embodied subject.

2.4 Digital Literacy

The digitalisation of everyday life has had significant implications for education and PSTs. Given the recent proliferation of digital devices and educational software, schools and educators are still grappling with how to integrate technologies into the curriculum and prepare today's PSTs for their (digital) futures. Amidst these concerns, DL has emerged as a key concept to help the future generation of teachers, educators, researchers, and educational bureaucrats make sense of the competing demands on schools and students in a digital society. However, while many scholars have studied the knowledge, skills and dispositions needed to use digital media, as digital texts have proliferated and evolved, there has been fleeting conjecture over what it means to be 'digitally literate' from a PST HPE perspective.

As it was first defined, DL describes an ability to understand and use information in multiple formats from a wide variety of sources when presented via computers and, particularly, through the medium of the internet [29]. Gilster's [29] work first defined the skills needed to critically navigate information in an increasingly digital world. DL is closely related to multiliteracies, including those of the physical and health domains. Multiliteracies, on the other hand, tends to focus on the growing linguistic diversity due to both multiculturalism and the proliferation of new media [30]. Canada's Centre for Digital and Media Literacy sum up the differences: "media literacy generally focuses on teaching youth to be critically engaged consumers of media, while digital literacy is more about enabling youth to participate in digital media in wise, safe and ethical ways" [31]. DL, therefore, encompasses issues of privacy, safety, and ethical use of technology. However, DL does not replace media literacy, but instead builds on it to articulate the set of skills required for a dynamic digital context. Conversely, as DL emerged from an existent field (i.e., literacy) many of the tensions and issues evident in literacy research were carried over into this new and emerging field. For example, whether DL should be thought of as a list of skills or whether it indicated something broader, such as social practices, the influence of community, and personal and family values, remains an ongoing question. As shown in Fig. 3, the pillars of DL and the extent to which context should be emphasised for PSTs is another point of difference as this will have implications for digital health and HPE pedagogy. For example, some HPE PSTs working more on teaching 'skills' would focus on what needs to be taught whereas those working in the social tradition might be more interested in finding out what people do with digital media in their everyday lives and how this is applied to both physical and health literacies.

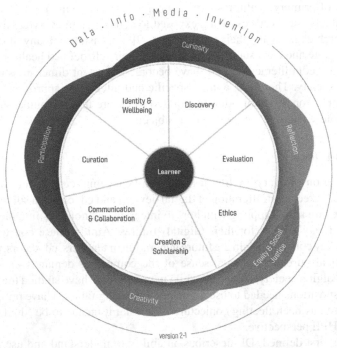

Fig. 3. Example framework to define digital literacy. Accessed from https://lib.vt.edu/research-teaching/digital-literacy.html.

Academic disciplines tend to bind scholars to ways of knowing about what counts as 'literacy'. Although it is important to review work from scholars across a range of educational disciplines, including health education, information science, and PE, many will have a different set of priorities. But these disciplines of teaching skills and techniques and reflective thinking during the initial stages of the PSTs academic program have implications for tomorrow's HPE teachers. It is crucial, therefore, to facilitate PSTs by knowing their difficulties and how they can effectively teach the combined literacies in a practical and meaningful way.

2.5 Technological, Pedagogical, Content Knowledge and Physical Education

In recent years, the rapid advancement of technology has created new interests and tools for use in the PST HPE domain. Researchers have identified different instructional, sport and physical education-related technologies that can potentially enhance the effectiveness of teaching physical education [32]. Technological Pedagogical Content Knowledge (TPCK) was introduced to the educational research field as a theoretical framework for understanding teacher knowledge required for effective technology integration [33]. The

TPCK framework acronym was renamed TPACK (pronounced "tee-pack") to make it easier to remember, and to form a more integrated whole for the three kinds of knowledge addressed: technology, pedagogy, and content [34].

The TPACK 21st Century skills (TPACK-21) is commonly presented with seven subscales that cover the different areas of (1) pedagogical knowledge, (2) technological knowledge, (3) content knowledge, (4) technological pedagogical knowledge, (5) pedagogical content knowledge, (6) technological content knowledge, and (7) technological pedagogical and content knowledge. Each item has a six-point response scale ranging from '1' representing 'I need a lot of additional knowledge about the topic' to '6' representing 'I have strong knowledge about the topic'. However, technology is becoming an inseparable part of HPE. Therefore, PSTs know-how has become crucial for the successful integration of technology in education [35]. Nonetheless, studies have suggested that many PSTs remain unclear about how to use technology to assist their teaching. While teachers sometimes use the Internet to attract students' attention, they do not know how to use it to facilitate students' development [36]. In a HPE learning context, the opportunity exists for PSTs to develop an overriding and appropriate consolidative knowledge to facilitate student knowledge using TPACK.

Mishra and Koehler [33] define technological knowledge (TK) as a teacher's set of skills that must be learned for meaningful teaching. Consequently, the relationship between technological knowledge and pedagogical content knowledge forms the basis of Technological Pedagogical Content Knowledge. First, technological knowledge (TK) is knowledge about analogue technologies, such as books, pens, blackboards, etc., and digital technologies includes computers, the Internet and digital video. This includes the skills that require the use of technologies in teaching activities [34]. In PE, for example, computer-based teacher observation systems can be used to rate identifiable motor skills or provide video analysis while giving feedback to students based on kinematics. Second, content knowledge (CK) refers to the mastering of major facts, concepts, and relationships within a particular field. Most importantly, this knowledge is independent of any pedagogical activities or how one might use methods or strategies to teach [35]. For example, a PE teacher should possess a basic understanding of motor learning and control, anatomy, exercise physiology, sport, and exercise psychology. This should be coupled with the understanding and appreciation of the associated health benefits. In terms of seeking reliable and authoritative information to make informed decisions, an understanding of digital technologies is needed. Next, pedagogical knowledge (PK) refers to techniques or methods of teaching and strategies for evaluating student understanding [37]. For instance, when a PST teaches a skill or a movement in PE either during a scheduled workshop or if on placement (practicum) they should consider child development and student needs as well as all facets of behaviours and motivation. However, this assumes that the PST has been taught the required skills and has developed the necessary pedagogical awareness to assess student understanding.

As Fig. 4 shows, the combined aspects require a sufficient PK prior to implementation. For instance, a PST cannot teach a basketball lesson in the same manner with third-grade students as with sixth graders. Developmentally appropriate instructional strategies should be established according to students' age and grade levels. It follows that technological pedagogical knowledge (TPK) refers to one's knowledge of the various technologies, which can be integrated and used in educational settings. Here, a PST HPE teacher, who has high TPK, can clearly select the appropriate tool or device to use in teaching by taking into consideration a child's age or readiness level.

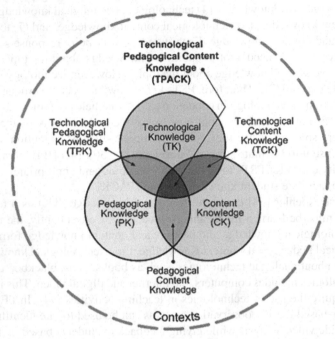

Fig. 4. Visualisation of Technological Pedagogical Content Knowledge [34]

The development of wireless technology, computer projection systems and physical activity monitoring systems present new opportunities for tomorrow's HPE teachers. Technological devices commonly used in PE include computers and laptops, LCD projectors, digital video and digital cameras, audio equipment, heart rate monitors pedometers, handheld devices including mobile phones, and global positioning systems (GPS). In addition to technological devices, educational sport software and the Internet are also used to support undergraduate HPE courses. But this assumes that tomorrow's HPE teachers are equipped with the necessary TPACK that combines the physical and health domains. Clearly there is a need for a focused research strand that investigates the viable consolidation of physical, health and digital modalities when viewed from a health and physical education lens. Therefore, exploration of the differences between the literacies, discovering the plurality of consolidative pedagogical frameworks, as well as the multitude of methods for identifying a combined practical and theoretical based framework for ensuring integration of technology into PST education is needed.

3 Summary

There remains a lack of published research showing the effects an applied and integrated physical, health and digital literacy approach using TPACK in PSTs HPE. That is, while support concerning 'synthesising' the integration of health, physical, health and digital literacy using TPACK exists, this seldom applies to the PST HPE teacher, or the academic (i.e., TE) tasked with shaping the contemporary content. This is despite the TPACK model being an efficient and reliable framework to guide research about the integration of technology [38]. Furthermore, the inclusion of the TPACK framework in the curricula, related to initial teacher training, is established as a fundamental axis to give the prospect of experimenting with communicative technologies within specific content areas [39].

As previously cited examples demonstrate, technology is becoming an inseparable part of PE. For instance, digital innovations continue to influence both sport and PE [40]. Therefore, PSTs technological know-how has become crucial for the successful integration of technology in the wider HPE context [36]. The suggestion remains, however, that many PSTs remain unclear about how to use technology to assist their teaching in HPE. In part, this could be due to findings that suggest university HPE lecturers (i.e., TE) are not good role models in the use of technology in their classrooms. Here, Jones and Moreland [41] note that in teaching process it is essential to not only *know* how a subject is taught (pedagogy) relative to the content but also which materials (technology) are used *while* teaching. Contrasted with other disciplines, PE has the peculiarities of physical and practical-based tasks. In the context of PST education, Tondeur et al. [42] addressed how student teachers are being prepared to use and integrate technology into their programs. However, a caveat is needed here as while Tondeur et al. [43] may be correct, preservice HPE teachers are largely beholden to what they taught and the stipulations of the university subject design and/or are at the whim of the TE. Therefore, they are likely to be influenced by what, whom and how they are instructed, or guided, to integrate modalities such as TPACK into HPE pedagogy.

3.1 Physical, Health and Digital Literacy: Can They Work in Unison?

Since Mishra and Koehler's [34] original work, TPACK has increasingly captured the interest of researchers and educators. However, even the originators of TPACK acknowledge the difficulties faced when integrating technology with education. Of the studies that talk of digital technology integration within an HPE context, many have focused on competency in technological device usage [e.g., 28, 40, 43]. While Gilster [30] spoke of an unassuming definition of DL as an ability to understand and use information in multiple formats from varied sources, prominence is also placed on the cognitive challenges associated with integrating analogue and digital media. Here, Angeli and Valanides [44] proposed that ICT-TPACK is the missing link in which technology can help teachers 'teach' topics and assist in the development of models for assessment purposes. Despite the efforts of teacher education programs and professional development workshops to change ingrained conceptions TPACK within HPE, discussion around the PST and learner-centered paradigms encourages a contemporary reimagining of ICT-TPACK. Such a reimagining supports the importance of the combined physical, health, and digital literacy modalities into a framework such as ICT-TPACK and the initial teacher education of HPE. Here, PST HPE teachers can be provided with an opportunity throughout their studies and school placement block to understand, change and improve their practice in HPE TPACK or HPE ICT-TPACK. This is when digital technology can potentially alter initial teacher education in HPE to not only be more efficient but also add greater value to the learning experience.

Regarding the multiliteracies of PL and HL, the common omission is digital pedagogies that create the glue between the existing literacy components. Thus, it means a greater focus is necessary to understand the nature of digital pedagogies and how to implement them successfully into a PST HPE context. However, when health and physical literacy are combined with digital literacy the level of intricacy and, arguably, complexity, increases. In this regard, the term 'multimodal literacy' using the TPACK framework can be applied as everyday communication practices are increasingly shaped by information and multimedia technologies. Many educational studies have proved the effectiveness of technology-assisted teaching in recent years due to the advancement of information technology [45]. This, then, requires further consideration into what meaningful and practical way digital technology can become embodied in initial teacher HPE education. This requires a whole of academia approach, however, in which educators go beyond instrumental comprehensions of HPE pedagogy, and technology. And as Fawns [46] implies a greater involvement of PSTs in the design of the HPE digital technology-based learning activities is needed. It could be argued that for experienced HPE academics who understand the intricacies and demands on PSTs and their future students, becoming multiliteracy informed through integrative frameworks such as TPACK should be a logical and valuable endeavour.

There is a growing amount of empirical evidence demonstrating the benefits of using digital technology to improve the impact of different pedagogical approaches in HPE [47]. Yet critical voices remain with respect to the ease with which digital technology can be or should be used in HPE settings. Part of the criticism is based upon the assertion that digital technology is the main factor of the societal problem of sedentary behaviour in children and the rising levels of obesity and that digital technology can have a negative impact on movement behaviour and sport participation. Yet the widespread use of digital technology in today's contemporary culture is neither the simple cause of sedentary behaviour, nor can it be seen as a reasonable answer. Besides, debating that technology is part of the problem is something else than claiming that technology can be a valuable tool to enhance the quality of HPE. While acknowledging the importance of the potential negative impact that digital technology may have on health-related behaviour, an alternative is to focus on the potential benefits and the pedagogical implications of digital innovations in PST HPE. Notwithstanding this, discussions surrounding physical, health and digital literacy would commonly produce arguments stating that the two belong on opposite ends of the educational spectrum [48]. Additionally, some suggest that the application of digital technologies in HPE would contradict the main aim of the subject—to learn through movement [49]. Yet if the goal of increasing PL is to develop a healthy population and develop active lifestyle, the digital realm is an influential focus for initial teacher education and intervention. Consequently, the advent of digital media has enabled unprecedented access to health information but brought with it new challenges.

So, what opportunities and challenges await the digital-health-physical pedagogue? Gawrisch et al. [50] suggest a four-phase methodology to form TPACK in HPE.

This phased approach is said to allow PSTs carriage to deliver technology-integrated lessons and practical experiences. Yet these experiences depend on the teacher educators providing opportunity for TPACK growth in the relevant subject and unit guides. Fundamentally, teacher educators need confidence in teaching TPACK while the PSTs need capacity and exposure to learn, practice, and use technology during instruction. However, as astutely put by Lee et al. [51], PE remains a subject in which long-standing tradition holds true. Or to be blunt, regardless of the abundant educational reforms and white papers spouting new curricula, there remains little influence of content reforms or assessments, and thus the status quote (i.e., teaching) remains. To conform to the educational trend of the twenty-first century, a new strategy to try to reverse old traditions into new, innovative ways of pedagogy is needed.

While incorporated methods will not guarantee achievement nor result in an immediate marriage between HPE-TPACK, a transformative approach is required. Transformative approaches can encourage teacher educators and PSTs to synthesize isolated PK, CK, and TK into new teaching and learning approaches [44]. Design thinking is one such option to help with the transformative approach. Design thinking is a human-centered design methodology that considers people's needs, behaviors, and the feasibility of technology [52]. This design thinking framework is frequently used to help students develop their design thinking expertise in differing educational settings [53]. But if a design thinking paradigm is to be considered as part of a HPE TPACK approach, more on the ground instruction is necessary for teacher educators. Or as Armstrong and Johnson [54] note, physical educators must be more than knowledge brokers; they should also be learning builders. The model of digital health physical pedagogies will need further clarification that focuses on the mindset and skills required for effective teaching and learning in both the digital and physical world. This should also lead to a new form of initial teacher development to promote a better understanding of the synergy between technology and practical HPE pedagogy. Preservice HPE teachers can become digital pedagogues who can foster consolidative pedagogies that continue to evolve according to their needs and the needs of their future students in both the digital and physical worlds.

4 Conclusion

Teacher education programs focused on HPE must work to better infuse technology throughout the education program and across different subject areas. To address the contemporary needs of PSTs and today's HPE dynamic, rather than focusing on how to use technology per se as a standalone and separate curriculum entity, PSTs specialising in HPE must learn about how technology can be used to support novel ways of teaching and learning. It is no longer possible to think about health and physical literacy solely as a linguistic or movement-based accomplishment. Tomorrow's HPE teachers need to comprehend, respond to, and compose multimodal texts in diverse forms, where meaning is communicated through dynamic combinations of two or more modes.

References

1. Lawson, H.A.: Occupational socialization and the design of teacher education programs. J. Teach. Phys. Educ. **5**(2), 107–116 (1986)
2. Velija, P., Capel, S., Katene, W., Hayes, S.: Does knowing stuff like PSHE and citizenship make me a better teacher? Student teacher in the teacher training figuration. Euro. Phys. Edu. Rev. **14**(3), 389–406 (2008)
3. List, A., Brante, E., Klee, H.L.: A framework of pre-service teachers' conceptions about digital literacy: comparing the United States and Sweden. Comp Edu. **148**, 103788 (2020)
4. Penney, D.: Playing a political game and playing for position: policy and curriculum development in health and physical education. Euro. Phy. Edu. Rev. **14**(1), 33–49 (2008)
5. Victorian Government Schools Agreement (2022). www.education.vic.gov.au/hrweb/Documents/VGSA-2022.pdf. Accessed 2 Dec 2023
6. Dudley, D., Cairney, J., Wainwright, N., Kriellaars, D., Mitchell, D.: Critical considerations for physical literacy policy in public health, recreation, sport, and education agencies. Quest **69**(4), 436–452 (2017)
7. Young, L., O'Connor, J., Alfrey, L.: Physical literacy: a concept analysis. Sport Educ. Soc. **25**(8), 946–959 (2020)
8. Whitehead, M.E.: Physical literacy. In: International Association of Physical Education and Sport for Girls and Women (IAPESWG) Congress, Melbourne, Australia (1993)
9. Whitehead, M.: The concept of physical literacy. Eur. J. Phys. Educ. **6**, 127–138 (2001)
10. Nutbeam, D.: Defining and measuring health literacy: what can we learn from literacy studies? Int. J. Public Health **54**(5), 303–305 (2009)
11. Keskin, T.: The technology in the programs of life sciences in Turkey and sachunterricht in Germany. Int. Technol. Educ. J. **1**(1), 10–15 (2017)
12. Jurbala, P.: What is physical literacy, really? Quest **67**(4), 367–383 (2015)
13. International Physical Literacy Association [IPLA] (2017)
14. Whitehead, M.E.: Physical literacy: philosophical considerations in relation to developing a sense of self, universality, and propositional knowledge. Sport Ethics Philos. **1**, 281–298 (2010)
15. Lubans, D.R., Morgan, P.J., Cliff, D.P., Barnett, L.M., Okely, A.D.: Fundamental movement skills in children and adolescents: review of associated health benefits. Sports Med. **40**(12), 1019–1035 (2010)
16. Government of British Columbia. British Columbia's New Curriculum. https://curriculum.gov.bc.ca/curriculum/physical-health-education/7. Accessed 8 Dec 2023
17. Bernstein, B.: The Structuring of Pedagogic Discourse. Volume IV Class, Codes and Control. Routledge, London (1990)
18. Hay, P., Penney, D.: Assessment in Physical Education: A Socio-Cultural Perspective. Routledge, Abingdon (2013)
19. Dudley, D.: Physical literacy: when the sum of the parts is greater than the whole. J. Phy. Educ. Rec. Dance **89**(3), 7–8 (2013)
20. Hammack, R., Ivey, T.: Elementary teachers' perceptions of K-5 engineering education and perceived barriers to implementation. J. Eng. Edu. **108**(4), 503–522 (2019)
21. Simonds, S.K.: Health education as social policy. Health Educ. Monog. **2**, 1–10 (1974)
22. Kickbusch, I., Maag, D.: Health literacy. In: International Encyclopedia of Public Health, pp. 204–211. Academic Press, Oxford (2008)
23. Bröder, J., Okan, O., Bauer, U., et al.: Health literacy in childhood and youth: a systematic review of definitions and models. BMC Public Health **17**, 361 (2017)
24. Irwin, L., Siddiqi, A., Hertzman, C.: Early child development: a powerful equalizer: final report for the World Health Organization's Commission on social determinants of health. University of British Columbia, Vancouver (2007)

25. Zarcadoolas, C., Pleasant, A., Greer, D.S.: Understanding health literacy: an expanded model. Health Promot. Int. **20**, 195–203 (2005)
26. Sørensen, K., et al.: Health literacy and public health: a systematic review and integration of definitions and models. BMC Public Health **12**, 80 (2012)
27. Dahlgren, G., Whitehead, M.: Policies and strategies to promote social equity in health. Institute for Future Studies, Stockholm (1991)
28. Subramaniam, M., St Jean, B., Taylor, N.G., Kodama, C., Follman, R., Casciotti, D.: Bit by bit: using design-based research to improve the health literacy of adolescents. JMIR Res. Protoc. **4**(2), e4058 (2015)
29. Gilster, P.: Digital Literacy. Wiley, New York (1997)
30. Kalantzis, M., Cope, B.: Multiliteracies: Rethinking What We Mean by Literacy and What We Teach as Literacy the Context of Global Cultural Diversity and New Communications Technologies. Centre for Workplace Communication and Culture, Leicestershire (1997)
31. Media Smarts. The Intersection of Digital and Media Literacy. Canada's Centre for Media and Digital Literacy, Ottawa. https://mediasmarts.ca/digital-media-literacy/general-inform ation/digital-media-literacy-fundamentals/intersection-digital-media-literacy. Accessed 11 Dec 2023
32. Roblyer, M.D., Doering, A.H.: Integrating Educational Technology into Teaching. Pearson, Lebanon (2005)
33. Mishra, P., Koehler, M.J.: Technological pedagogical content knowledge: a framework for integrating technology in teachers' knowledge. Teach. Coll. Rev. **108**(6), 1017–1054 (2006)
34. Thompson, A., Mishra, P.: Breaking news: TPCK becomes TPACK! J. Comput. Teach. Educ. **24**(2), 38–64 (2007)
35. So, H.-J., Kim, B.: Learning about problem-based learning: student teachers integrating technology, pedagogy, and content knowledge. Aust. J. Edu. Tech. **25**(1) (2009)
36. Lee, H.Y., Chung, C.Y., Wei, G.: Research on technological pedagogical and content knowledge: a bibliometric analysis from 2011 to 2020. Front. Educ. **7**, 765233 (2022)
37. Cox, S.: A conceptual analysis of technological pedagogical content knowledge. Unpublished Doctoral dissertation, Brigham Young University (2008)
38. Abbit, J.T.: An investigation of the relationship between self-efficacy beliefs about technology integration and technological pedagogical content knowledge (TPACK) among preservice teachers. J. Digit. Learn. Teach. Educ. **27**, 134–143 (2011)
39. Voogt, J., Fisser, P., Roblin, N.P., Tondeur, J., van Braak, J.: Technological pedagogical content knowledge–a review of the literature. J. Comput. Assist. Learn. **29**, 109–121 (2013)
40. Novak, D., Štefan, L., Antala, B., Dudley, D., Kawachi, I.: Association between social capital and self-rated health in small and large secondary school classes in Croatia. South Afr. J. Res. Sport Phy. Edu. Rec. **40**(2), 143–158 (2018)
41. Jones, A., Moreland, J.: The importance of pedagogical content knowledge in assessment for learning practices: a case-study of a whole-school approach. Curriculum J. **16**(2), 193–206 (2005)
42. Tondeur, J., Pareja Roblin, N., van Braak, J., Fisser, P., Voogt, J.: Technological pedagogical content knowledge in teacher education: in search of a new curriculum. Edu. Stud. **39**(2), 239–243 (2013)
43. Russell, W.: Physical educators' perceptions and attitudes toward interactive video game technology within the physical education curriculum of Missouri. J. Health Phys. Educ. Rec. Dance **17**, 76–89 (2007)
44. Angeli, C., Valanides, N.: Epistemological and methodological issues for the conceptualization, development, and assessment of ICT-TPCK: advances in technological pedagogical content knowledge (TPCK). Comput. Educ. **52**(1), 154–168 (2009)
45. Herold, B.: Technology in education: an overview. Educ. Week **20**, 129–141 (2016)

46. Fawns, T.: An entangled pedagogy: views of the relationship between technology and pedagogy. https://open.ed.ac.uk/an-entangled-pedagogy-views-of-the-relationship-between-technology-and-pedagogy/. Accessed 05 Jan 2024
47. Østerlie, O., Sargent, J., Killian, C., Garcia-Jaen, M., García-Martínez, S., Ferriz-Valero, A.: Flipped learning in physical education: a scoping review. Euro. Phy. Educ. Rev. **29**(1), 125–144 (2023)
48. Pyle, B., Esslinger, K.: Utilizing technology in physical education: addressing the obstacles of integration. Delta Kappa Gamma Bull. **80**(2), 35–39 (2014)
49. Casey, A., Goodyear, V.A., Armour, K.M.: Rethinking the relationship between pedagogy, technology and learning in health and physical education. Sport Educ. Soc. **22**(2), 288–304 (2017)
50. Gawrisch, D.P., Richards, K.A.R., Killian, C.M.: Integrating technology in physical education teacher education: a socialization perspective. Quest **72**(3), 260–277 (2020)
51. Lee, H., Chingwei, C., Chung, C.: Research on design thinking and TPACK of physical education pre-service teachers. In: 29th Proceedings of the International Conference on Computers in Education, Asia-Pacific Society for Computers in Education, Virtual (Online) Conference, pp. 9–16 (2021)
52. Brown, T.: Design thinking. Harv. Bus. Rev. **86**(6), 84 (2008)
53. Henriksen, D., Richardson, C., Mehta, R.: Design thinking: a creative approach to educational problems of practice. Thinking Skills Creativity **26**, 140–153 (2017)
54. Armstrong, T., Johnson, I.: Redesigning the assessment experience with design thinking: using the creative process to break assessment barriers: column editor: Anthony Parish. Strategies **32**(3), 41–48 (2019)

Parental Control and Internet Use Among Italian Adolescents

Maria Lidia Mascia[1](✉) , Mirian Agus[2] , Maria Assunta Zanetti[3] ,
Dolores Rollo[4] , Maria Luisa Pedditzi[2] , Rachele Conti[2],
Maria Pietronilla Penna[2] , and Łukasz Tomczyk[5]

[1] University of Sassari, Zanfarino Street, 62, 07100 Sassari, Italy
mlmascia@uniss.it
[2] University of Cagliari, Is Mirrionis Street, 1, 09123 Cagliari, Italy
[3] University of Pavia, Botta Street, 6, 27100 Pavia, Italy
[4] University of Parma, Volturno Street, 39, 43125 Parma, Italy
[5] Jagiellonian University, Kraków, Poland

Abstract. Internet use can have both positive and negative impacts. Above all, risks are linked to immoderate use among adolescents. The importance of parental control over their children's internet use is a key element in limiting the risk factors that such use may have. We investigated this perception by administering a self-report questionnaire to 236 Italian teenagers aged 14–17 years, of which 69.9% are female. Descriptive analyses were primarily conducted. Subsequently, to identify any differences in responses provided concerning social variables, Covariance Analyses and Multivariate Covariance Analyses (one in relation to each batch of items), whose factors were "residency area" (small centre - large centre), "socio-economic status" (medium high-medium low), and "gender", were conducted. The variable "age" was inserted as a covariate. In line with the literature, the findings confirm that parental control plays a decisive role in favouring the responsible use of the Internet. Furthermore, we found that the place of residence influences the length of time spent on the Internet. Nevertheless, we observed that the relationship between parental control and the use/abuse of the Internet does not change depending on the parents' economic status.

Keywords: Parental control · New technologies · Internet use · Adolescence

1 Theoretical Framework

The rapid spread of technological tools and internet connection affects all age groups [1]. While adults should have stable self-regulatory skills in managing their time online and prevent online risk factors, children and adolescents need supervision to help them manage their time online and the risk factors that the online networks may present. The ability to access at any moment and unlimited access is especially a risk factor. The Internet offers to adolescents many possibilities for learning, sharing knowledge, keeping in touch with others, socializing, relaxing, playing, but it is also associated with risks (cyberbullying/cybervictimization/cybersex, etc....), exposure to inappropriate content or uncontrollable excessive use or other problematic internet use [2–6].

Ł. Tomczyk (Ed.): NMP 2023, CCIS 2130, pp. 305–317, 2024.
https://doi.org/10.1007/978-3-031-63235-8_20

Many studies underline the importance of parental control in adolescence [7, 8]. Parental control has an important role to play in preventing risky behaviours, being a protective factor [9].

Why is parental control the key to reducing Internet mediated risk behaviour (including problematic Internet use)? The answer to this question is related to the developmental process of children and adolescents, in which the home environment is the main environment shaping behavioural patterns, including modelling information and communication technology (ICT) use habits [10, 11]. Systematic ICT use among children is occurring earlier and earlier. In the first instance, the style of ICT use is therefore the responsibility of those closest to them, i.e. mainly parents. These are the people who should take on the role of guiding children in the digital world, as well as media education of their own children [12].

Media education with a significant impact on ICT use is primarily related to setting the time and time of use of new media, supervising the websites browsed and the type of software (including games) used by children, and helping in situations requiring technical support [13]. Popular techniques to strengthen digital safety in the home environment also include positioning the computer and other digital devices in a visible place, installing software that limits the time of ICT use and filters content, accompanying children in online activities [14, 15]. Summarising the ways of media education in the family (ways of protection), we can therefore distinguish among: 1) passive (observing the child when he/she is online), 2) active (doing various activities together using ICT), 3) limiting screen time and access to selected content, 4) reviewing the child's online activity, 5) imposing filters and blockers [16, 17].

The indicated educational measures are not fixed and change with circumstances. At younger ages, much more restrictive measures are used than for older children or adolescents. This is due to the need to protect children who have a very low level of digital competence. In the case of adolescents, on the other hand, setting clear ICT-related boundaries builds their digital competence in an axiological context, showing the boundary between good (beneficial) ICT use and bad (destructive) use of new media [18]. Parental control thus not only has a dimension that relates directly to digital safety, but also to the shaping of 'soft' but crucial aspects in the adolescent development process.

In this era of intense development of the information society, many parents declare difficulties in keeping up with technological innovations. Lack of knowledge and skills about e-services, software, websites used by the youngest generation hinders effective media education [19]. Therefore, when analysing intentional media behaviour shaping activities, it is important to be aware that the role of the family is increasingly reduced in favour of peer media socialisation, or children's own shaping of their ICT use style [20–22]. There is also a perception that the power of parental influence in shaping digital competence, ICT use habits among young people is currently diminishing.

An increasing amount of research focuses on the relationship between parental control and internet use, mainly on the relationship between supervision behaviour by parents and children's perception of parental control [23–25].

So, in more recent literature, the attention is focused on parental mediation in relation to new media and the regulatory measures put in place by parents to control internet use [26, 27]. Parental control does not always use restrictive, or mediation systems as highlighted in some research [28, 29], which instead analyse parental control focusing on the dimension of "non-intervention" supervision strategies and the levels of family and friend coercion.

Therefore, some elements may hinder effective parental control. An element to be considered in this analysis is the Family Digital Divide [30] that exists between adolescent's digital abilities (digital native) and that of their parents. Such a device can allow adolescents the perception of a real/presumed "action autonomy" in online spaces, linked to knowledge/belief of their respective parent's low digital competence, as well as the belief they can easily evade their attempts at control [31].

Differences have been observed also in relation to cultural factors [32]. Özgür [28] study states that parents' lower education level corresponds to a lower perception of parental control on behalf of the children. Chang and colleagues [33] show a correlation between low levels of internet knowledge and use was observed on the part of the parents, and lower parental control, in comparison to parents who live in urban areas. Other studies highlight that living in rural areas can associate with a lower possibility of connection, but that internet use also depends on the socio-economic and occupational level of the parents [34] and their digital abilities [33].

This study, through an explorative-descriptive approach, intends to identify possible relationships between the modality of internet use and perceived parental control, in relation to age, gender, to the context of residence and socio-economic status. More specifically, the research principally wanted to identify different profiles of adolescents, relative to the investigated dimensions. The aim is to deepen parent's strategies to control online activities perceived by interviewed adolescents [35], also keeping in mind socio-nominal characteristics, habits related to internet use, and young people's motives for getting connected [36–38].

In particular, it hypothesises that there are:

- gender differences in relation to internet use [39];
- age differences in relation to the perception of parental control [40];
- socio-economic status differences in relation to the perception of parental control [41].

In addition, we expect that residence area (small-big urban area) can influence the level of perceived parental control [42].

2 Methods

2.1 Participants and Procedure

The research involved 236 adolescents aged between 14 and 17 years (average age 15.8 years, ds = .86), of which 69.9% (n = 165) are female, coming from the first, second and third classes of the second year in some secondary institutes in Italy (Sardinia). Participants were recruited, with their family's authorisation, on a voluntary basis. Among these, 215 fully completed all parts of the questionnaire. Each adolescent was guaranteed the privacy policy. Completing the questionnaire required an average of 15 min. The administration took place during school hours into the classroom. We used traditional in-class paper-and-pencil instead of computerized questionnaire. One hundred and ten students reside in the country seat (46.6%), the remaining 126 in small centres. All participants have an Italian nationality. Family socio-economic status was specified through evaluating the parent's qualifications and profession; it was highlighted that 78.4% of the participants belong to a medium-high social level. The applied sampling is of a non-probabilistic nature, stratified based on social data relative to age, gender and residence.

2.2 Materials

The dimensions of interest indicated have been investigated through a self-report questionnaire, addressed to students, specifically prepared by the authors for this research. This detection tool was subdivided into the following sections:

(I) personal social variables (age, gender, class, residency, profession and qualification of parents);

(II) variables relative to internet use habits (average number of hours spent online on weekdays and public holidays, tools used to get connected, smart phone use, use of unidentifiable profiles);

(III) variables relative to activities, to the motives for why adolescents get connected. One example of an item (Likert scale of 1 – for nothing – to 5 – a lot) is the following: "Why do you connect to the internet? Boredom, entertainment, talking to friends, etc...." [43];

(IV) variables relevant to the modalities of parental control perceived by the adolescent of their online activities and the possible presence of connection limits. One example of an item (Likert scale from 1 – for nothing – to 5 – a lot) is the following: "Do your family control your activities on the Internet?"; "If yes, in which way: they control my profiles, my posts on social networks; they control my emails..." [29];

2.3 Statistical Analyses

The data were evaluated by the application of descriptive statistics, bivariate and multivariate analyses. We preliminary considered the data distributions; furthermore, we applied a multivariate analysis of covariance (one in relation to each set of items), to evaluate the potential effect of socio demographic variables (residency area and socio-economic status) on the adolescents' answers [44]. The variable "age" was inserted as covariate.

Besides, two Principal Component Analysis were carried out regarding the items assessing the parental control strategies and the internet use habits [45]. Finally, the K means cluster analysis was applied to identify the ways in which the individuals are grouped on the base of answers provided [46].

3 Results

According to the research, the analysis applied sought to examine the existence of statistically significant differences in relation to the factors that can potentially exert an effect on adolescents' perception of parental control and their habits relative to internet use. The appendix shows the statistics relative to the statistically significant effects.

Specifically, it was observed that in relation to the "number of hours spent online on weekdays and holidays", there emerges a major "gender" effect: girls spend more hours online on average on weekdays compared to their peers.

For the variable "staying at home alone", there is a significant effect in the covariant "age". As has been hypothesised, it is confirmed that as the adolescent's age increases, they are left home alone more frequently.

In relation to the activities carried out online by the adolescent, the main effect is "gender". There are significant differences in relation to the use of social media, chats, and photo shopping. Girls mostly practice these activities, while male peers significantly prefer virtual worlds and online games.

In terms of "tools used to log online", the main effect of "gender" is highlighted. Girls use their phones more for connection, while boys use the pc.

Concerning the "reasons" for logging online, we observe the main effects of the covariate "age", and the "gender" and "socio-economic level" factors. Specifically, the "gender" difference is seen in relation to logging online for fun is much more frequent in males, in comparison to reasons of socialising and relationships (such as talking with friends, knowing what is happening with others, having news on famous people) being more frequent in females. We can also see a significant effect in relation to the "socio-economic level" variable; specifically, adolescents of a medium-high level log online more than their medium-low status peers to know what is happening with others, to let others know what is happening to them, to have news of famous people.

For the question respect "parental control", we can see the effect of the covariate "age", as well as the effects of the "gender" and "socio-economic status" interaction (Fig. 1). In detail, this interaction effect becomes evident in relation to controlling posts and profiles on social networks. It is of particular interest that the medium-high status participants report the same average level of control independent of gender. Vice versa, subjects belonging to the medium-low status perceive a significantly higher level of control on girls as opposed to boys.

Subsequently, to concisely evaluate the dimensions involved, the Principal Component Analysis (PCA) was applied in relation to the items on parental control and on the reasons for which adolescents connect to the internet.

The PCA relative to parental control items related to internet use revealed a monofactorial solution, which explains the 47% of total variability (eigenvalue = 3.297). The factorial saturation of the items is between .877 and .418. This scale has a Cronbach Alpha of .771.

A further PCA with a monofactorial solution was conducted to summarise and understand the reasons for which adolescents connect to the internet. The dimension refers to a continuum characterised by orientation towards prosociality vs. individuality in internet use (eigenvalue = 2.957, explained variability = 32.8%). The items present factorial saturation values between .781 and .347. This scale has a reliability (Cronbach Alpha) of .731.

Cluster Analyses with the K-Means method [47] was applied to the mean values of parental control components and the reasons for connecting to the internet. The algorithm divides the participants in relation to the indicated dimensions, in K clusters, so that the sum of the intra-cluster squares is minimised. The subdivision of clusters

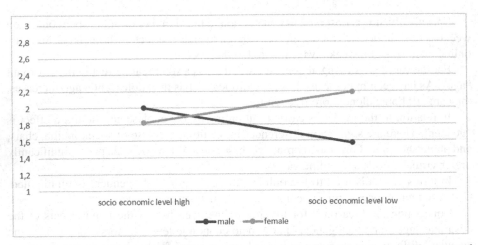

Fig. 1. Significant effects of "gender" * "socio-economic level" for the question "They control my profiles, my posts on social networks".

is achieved when moving a case from one cluster to another no longer generates intra cluster variance [48]. This statistical technique allows to specify groups of homogeneous participants within them and different from participants in remaining clusters. Different profiles of teenagers have been identified in relation to the investigated dimensions; the solution to four clusters was identified as mostly parsimonious and consistent with theoretical assumptions (Table 1).

Cluster 1 (high control) is made up of 22 young people, characterised by a high perception of parental control of internet use and with fixed connection time. In fact, they spend the lowest number of hours online compared to subjects from other clusters and have a lower age, between 14 and 15. They also state that they are rarely left alone at home. The 68.2% of this group of subjects reside in the centre and 90.9% belong to a medium-high social class. They state that their main methods of use are, more than their peers, to connect to look up useful information and do homework.

Cluster 2 (medium control) is made up of 39 young people, also aged between 14 and 15, equally divided between the small centre and the centre, mainly belonging to a medium-low class in comparison to remaining clusters. They spend a high number of hours online, both on weekdays and public holidays. Their perception of personal control is intermedia; in fact, they state that they sometimes find themselves home alone. The main reason for connecting online is talking with friends.

Cluster 3 (low control) is the largest, with 85 young people between 16 and 17, 74.7% of which belong to a medium-high class, with parents with higher education, resident in both small and big centres, characterised by a low level of perceived parental control. They state that they are often left alone at home and mainly connect to contact friends.

Cluster 4 (medium low control) consists of 69 adolescents, 78.3% girls between 16 and 17, 55% of which are resident in small centres. The 85% belong to a medium-high class and perceive a medium-low parental control. They mainly have parents with high levels of education, are often left alone at home, and so they have a higher need to reach out to others and escape boredom. This group spends the lowest number of hours

Table 1. Cluster analysis with the K-Means method

	Cluster 1 N = 22	Cluster 2 N = 39	Cluster 3 N = 85	Cluster 4 N = 69	Sig
Average relative to the dimension of parental control	Mean (sd) 3.25 (± .55)	Mean (sd) 2.36 (±.37)	Mean (sd) 1,18 (±.20)	Mean (sd) 1,30 (±.32)	.0001
Average relative to the reasons for connecting online	Mean (sd) 3.42 (±.56)	Mean (sd) 2.71 (±.41)	Mean (sd) 2,59 (±.43)	Mean (sd) 3,74 (±.43)	.0001
% small centre residents	Fr 6.2%	Fr 19.5%	Fr 40.7%	Fr 33.6%	
% medium-low status	Fr 4.5%	Fr 29.5%	Fr 43.2%	Fr 22.7%	
% female	Fr 7.9%	Fr 17.8%	Fr 38.8%	Fr 35.5%	
Age	Mean (sd) 15.32(±.945)	Mean (sd) 15.59(±.818)	Mean (sd) 16.05(±.815)	Mean (sd) 16.12(±.850)	
Hours spent online - weekdays	Mean (sd) 4.76 (±4.74)	Mean (sd) 5.35 (±4.87)	Mean (sd) 5.49 (±4.97)	Mean (sd) 5.85 (±3.65)	
Hours spent online – public holidays	Mean (sd) 5.63 (±5.46)	Mean (sd) 6.21 (±5.23)	Mean (sd) 5.30 (±4.26)	Mean (sd) 7.64 (±4.44)	
Time spent alone at home	Mean (sd) 2.65 (±.87)	Mean (sd) 2.60 (±.976)	Mean (sd) 2.96 (±1.02)	Mean (sd) 3.11 (±1.03)	

online compared to subjects from other groups, both on weekdays and public holidays, more dedicated than any other cluster to social networks and chats. In this cluster, there is a larger number of subjects with profiles not attributable to their identity (85.5%) compared to the entire sample.

4 Discussion

The Internet offers to adolescents many possibilities for learning, sharing knowledge, keeping in touch with others, socializing, relaxing, playing, but it is also associated with risks (cyberbullying/cybervictimization/cybersex, etc....), exposure to inappropriate content or uncontrollable excessive use or other problematic internet use [2–6]. Many studies underline the importance of parental control in adolescence [7, 8].

Parental control has an important role to play in preventing risky behaviours, being a protective factor [9]. The results of this study are in line with literature on the theme of parental control in relation to internet use [25, 28, 33, 49]. The present study is part of the risk paradigm of media pedagogy, in which an understanding of adolescents' new media use style allows for the design of effective preventive programs and stereotype removal.

About parental control, it emerges that middle-high status participants claim an equal level of control, regardless of gender. Vice versa, adolescents of medium-low status perceive a significantly higher level of control on girls.

This aspect refers to the profiles that emerge from cluster analysis, from which results also emerge attributable to research carried out on parenting styles in control of online activities [35, 50]. The style of ICT use in this case is conditioned by many variables that were not included in the research model but are of great importance in the process of media education in the family environment. Parents' attitudes towards new media play a particular role in this area [51], as well as the level of digital competences [34]. The latter element results in parents with higher digital competences being more intentional in diagnosing the e-risks young people are exposed to, as well as in planning a set of technical actions that effectively strengthen digital safety across the family ecosystem [19]. In addition, it is important to be aware that addressing selected problems that occur among digitally mediated young people can simultaneously improve the digital competence of those involved [52].

Among the most interesting results, for example, it emerges that middle-high class boys have the perception of greater parental control, specifically at a younger age [29]. In addition, in the four clusters, predominantly characterized by girls with both parents with high education, there is an increase in hours spent online and a decrease in perception of control and supervision. It is also interesting to observe a strong relationship between internet use, place of residence (centre or small centres) and the socio-economic status of parents. Specifically, the largest number of hours spent online by teenagers in small centres is in line with the findings in the literature [34]. Being bored, but perhaps not having cultural and social alternatives, should further be investigated as factors that could help increase time spent on the internet in the identified clusters. However, high variability suggests the need to investigate further, perhaps better detailing the social class variable.

When analysing the data in this article, it is important to be aware that the perspective adopted is also characterised by limitations. One of them is the issue of ekra-new time (measured through the declarations: hours spent online-weekdays, hours spent online - public holidays and time spent alone at home). All three indicators were measured in a declarative manner, i.e. without accurately aggregating data from digital devices on screen time and the type of activities performed using ICT. Such an approach has its strengths in terms of speed of measurement, but it also has limitations in terms of measurement error, i.e. reporting time values that are inadequate to reality [53]. Other limitations are represented by the fact that modalities of parental control perceived by the adolescent of their online activities are measured with a translated but not adapted/validated tool and the cross-sectional design of the study and the sample size as it might prevent the generalization of the results.

However, despite its methodological limitations, the inclusion of screen time in relation to parental control is a legitimate measure and one that is linked to the call for media education in the family environment through control and restriction of screen time [54, 55].

When considering the analysis of the variable parental control in the context of activities related to ICT use, one should be aware of the different attitudes towards new media, the heterogeneous level of digital competence among parents and young people. When diagnosing this issue and designing preventive measures, it should also be considered that attitudes and digital competence (basic and advanced e.g. technical skills for securing IT equipment) are two basic elements for effective parental control (part of a restrictive parenting model) as well as building a community of intergenerational understanding regarding the correct use of ICT in the home environment [56].

The attempt to understand the nature of parental control nowadays (in an era of intensive development of e-services) requires going beyond the educational methods used so far (typical for an analogue society). Considering the processes concerning: media convergence, increasing screen time, transferring more and more activities from the offline to the online sphere, it becomes justifiable to conduct further research relating to the change in digital parental competences with a particular focus on digital parental competences, as well as understanding intergenerational differences around hygiene and digital safety.

The data presented are relevant to the design of further, more elaborate diagnostic tools that locate the variable parental control against the background of underlying parenting competencies. Analyses conducted to date [19] clearly suggest that a lack of adequate parenting competences, a low-quality child-parent relationship combined with low parental digital competences, is a set of factors resulting in lower family digital safety. Therefore, research of this type extended to the areas mentioned above can contribute to a deeper understanding of the processes involved in shaping awareness-raising behaviour and technical knowledge of parents and children (adolescents) in e-risks.

5 Conclusions

Adolescents are certainly digital natives and therefore have very specific characteristics. From birth, they have all the technologies at their disposal, and this can lead them to underestimate possible risk elements. In addition, the online network is increasingly becoming a mediator of social relationships. Internet use in adolescence has greatly increased over the past decade; it has become very important to keep this phenomenon under control, especially because it is leading to forms of real addiction.

The important role in this age group of parental control, perception of control and being controlled. How important parental control is in this age group, while in the child there is a demand for control and attachment, in this age group it is directly challenged. It is essential to dose control and manage self-control and self-regulation (which is still forming).

Parental control allows them to introject self-regulation and acquire those protective factors that enable them to stop in the face of risk. The strongest relationships in adolescence are those between peers and therefore being in the adolescent group, the risk is that they emit problematic and morally dubious behaviour.

References

1. Mascia, M.L., Bonfiglio, N.S., Renati, R., Cataudella, S., Tomczyk, Ł., Penna, M.P.: Problematic smartphone use and cognitive failures. An explorative study among free different generations (X, Y, Z). In: 19th International Conference on Cognition and Exploratory Learning

in Digital Age (CELDA 2022) on Proceedings, pp. 233–240. Springer, Lisbon (2022). ISBN 978-989-8704-43-6

2. Mascia, M.L., Agus, M., Penna, M.P.: Emotional intelligence, self-regulation, smartphone addiction: which relationship with student well-being and quality of life? Front. Psychol. **11**(375), 1–7 (2020). https://doi.org/10.3389/fpsyg.2020.00375

3. Agus, M., Mascia, M.L., Bonfiglio, N.S., Penna, M.P.: The Italian version of the mobile phone problematic use scale for adults (MPPUS): a validation study. Heliyon **8**(12), 1–9 (2022). https://doi.org/10.1016/J.HELIYON.2022.E12209

4. Lukavska, K., Vacek, J., Gabhelik, R.: The effects of parental control and warmth on problematic internet use in adolescents: a prospective cohort study. J. Behav. Addict. **9**(3), 664–675 (2020). https://doi.org/10.1556/2006.2020.00068

5. Mascia, M.L., et al.: Moral disengagement, empathy, and cybervictim's representation as predictive factors of cyberbullying among Italian adolescents. Int. J. Environ. Res. Public Health **18**(3), 1–12 (2021). https://doi.org/10.3390/ijerph18031266

6. Agus, M., Mascia, M.L., Zanetti, M.A., Perrone, S., Rollo, D., Penna, M.P.: Who are the victims of cyberbullying? Preliminary data towards validation of "cyberbullying victim questionnaire." Contemp. Educ. Technol. **13**(3), 1–12 (2021). https://doi.org/10.30935/cedtech/10888

7. Sun, P., Li, Q., Smorti, M., Shek, D.T.L., Zhu, X., Ma, C.M.S.: The influence of parental control and parent-child relational qualities on adolescent internet addiction: a 3-year longitudinal study in Hong Kong. Front. Psychol. **9**(642), 1–16 (2018). https://doi.org/10.3389/fpsyg.2018.00642

8. Vieira Martins, M., et al.: Adolescent internet addiction e role of parental control and adolescent behaviours. Int. J. Pediatr. Adolesc. Med. **7**(3), 116–120 (2019). https://doi.org/10.1016/j.ijpam.2019.12.003

9. Álvarez-García, D., García, T., Suárez-García, Z.: The relationship between parental control and high-risk internet behaviours in adolescence. Soc. Sci. **7**(6), 1–7 (2018). https://doi.org/10.3390/socsci7060087

10. Durak, A., Kaygin, H.: Parental mediation of young children's internet use: adaptation of parental mediation scale and review of parental mediation based on the demographic variables and digital data security awareness. Educ. Inf. Technol. **25**, 2275–2296 (2019). https://doi.org/10.1007/s10639-019-10079-1

11. Steinfeld, N.: Parental mediation of adolescent internet use: combining strategies to promote awareness, autonomy and self-regulation in preparing youth for life on the web. Educ. Inf. Technol. **26**(2), 1897–1920 (2021). https://doi.org/10.1007/s10639-020-10342-w

12. Tomczyk, Ł., Potyrała, K.: Bezpieczeństwo cyfrowe dzieci i młodzieży w perspektywie pedagogiki mediów. Wydawnictwo Naukowe Uniwersytetu Pedagogicznego, Kraków (2019)

13. Tomczyk, Ł., Wąsiński, A.: Parents in the process of educational impact in the area of the use of new media by children and teenagers in the family environment. Technologie Informacyjno-Komunikacyjne (TIK) w Funkcjonowaniu Polskiej Szkoły View Project COST Action 16207 European Network for Problematic Internet Usage View Project. https://doi.org/10.15390/EB.2017.4674

14. Wojtasik, Ł., Dziemidowicz, E.: Urządzenia ekranowe w rękach dzieci w wieku 0–6 lat–zagrożenia, szanse, postulaty profilaktyczne. Dziecko krzywdzone. Teoria, badania, praktyka **18**(2), 106–119 (2019)

15. Dagiel, M., Kowalik-Olubińska, M.: Growing up online, czyli wiedzieć i działać w świetle internetowych poradników nie tylko dla nauczycieli. Problemy Wczesnej Edukacji **41**(2), 69–77 (2018)

16. Pyżalski, J.: Rodzina i Szkoła a Przeciwdziałanie Zaangażowaniu Młodych Ludzi w Ryzykowne Zachowania Online. Dziecko Krzywdzone. Teoria, badania, praktyka **12**, 99–109 (2013)

17. Kirwil, L.: Polskie dzieci w Internecie. Zagrożenia i bezpieczeństwo - część 2. Częściowy raport z badań EU Kids Online II przeprowadzonych wśród dzieci w wieku 9–16 lat i ich rodziców. SWPS, Warszawa (2011)
18. Tolnaiová, S.G., Gálik, S.: Cyberspace as a new living world and its axiological contexts. In: Cyberspace. IntechOpen, London (2020)
19. Tomczyk, Ł, Potyrała, K.: Parents' knowledge and skills about the risks of the digital world. S. Afr. J. Educ. **41**(1), 1–19 (2021). https://doi.org/10.15700/saje.v41n1a1833
20. Shin, W., Lwin, M.O.: How does "talking about the internet with others" affect teenagers' experience of online risks? The role of active mediation by parents, peers, and school teachers. New Media Soc. **19**(7), 1109–1126 (2017). https://doi.org/10.1177/1461444815626612
21. Zhu, J., Zhang, W., Yu, C., Bao, Z.: Early adolescent internet game addiction in context: how parents, school, and peers impact youth. Comput. Hum. Behav. **50**, 159–168 (2015). https://doi.org/10.1016/j.chb.2015.03.079
22. Rodríguez-Álvarez, J.M., Cabrera-Herrera, M.C., Jiménez, S.Y.: Los Riesgos de Las TIC En Las Relaciones Entre Iguales. Cyberbullying En Educación Primaria y Secundaria. Innoeduca: Int. J. Technol. Educ. Innov. **4**(2), 185–192 (2018). https://doi.org/10.24310/INNOEDUCA.2019.V5I1.3505
23. Álvarez, M., Torres, A., Rodríguez, E., Padilla, S., Rodrigo, M.J.: Attitudes and parenting dimensions in parents' regulation of internet use by primary and secondary school children. Comput. Educ. **67**, 69–78 (2013). https://doi.org/10.1016/J.COMPEDU.2013.03.005
24. Cetinkaya, L.: The relationship between perceived parental control and internet addiction: a cross-sectional study among adolescents. Contemp. Educ. Technol. **10**(1), 55–74 (2019). https://doi.org/10.30935/cet.512531
25. Omez, P.G., Harris, S.K., Barreiro, C., Isorna, M., Rial, A.: Profiles of internet use and parental involvement, and rates of online risks and problematic internet use among Spanish adolescents. Comput. Hum. Behav. **75**, 826–833 (2017). https://doi.org/10.1016/j.chb.2017.06.027
26. Kalmus, V., Blinka, L., Ólafsson, K.: Does it matter what mama says: evaluating the role of parental mediation in European adolescents' excessive internet use. Child. Soc. **29**(2), 122–133 (2015). https://doi.org/10.1111/CHSO.12020
27. Benrazavi, R., Teimouri, M., Griffiths, M.D.: Utility of parental mediation model on youth's problematic online gaming. Int. J. Ment. Health Addict. **13**, 712–727 (2015). https://doi.org/10.1007/s11469-015-9561-2
28. Ozgür, H.: The relationship between internet parenting styles and internet usage of children and adolescents. Comput. Hum. Behav. **60**, 411–424 (2016). https://doi.org/10.1016/j.chb.2016.02.081
29. Broekman, F.L., Piotrowski, J.T., Beentjes, H.W.J., Valkenburg, P.M.: A parental perspective on apps for young children. Comput. Hum. Behav. **63**, 142–151 (2016). https://doi.org/10.1016/j.chb.2016.05.017
30. Segatto, B., Dal Ben, A.: The family digital divide the family digital divide: self-taught adolescents and difficulties in parental control. Ital. J. Sociol. Educ. **5**(1), 101–118 (2013)
31. Liu, Q.X., Fang, X.Y., Zhou, Z.K., Zhang, J.T., Deng, L.Y.: Perceived parent-adolescent relationship, perceived parental online behaviors and pathological internet use among adolescents: gender-specific differences. PLoS ONE **8**(9), 1–8 (2013). https://doi.org/10.1371/journal.pone.0075642
32. Updegraff, K.A., Kim, J.Y., Killoren, S.E., Thayer, S.M.: Mexican American parents' involvement in adolescents' peer relationships: exploring the role of culture and adolescents' peer experiences. J. Res. Adolesc. **20**(1), 65–87 (2010). https://doi.org/10.1111/J.1532-7795.2009.00625.X

33. Chang, F.C., et al.: Urban-rural differences in parental internet mediation and adolescents' internet risks in Taiwan. Health Risk Soc. **18**(3–4), 188–204 (2016). https://doi.org/10.1080/13698575.2016.1190002
34. Livingstone, S., Helsper, E.J.: Parental mediation of children's internet use. J. Broadcast. Electron. Media **52**(4), 581–599 (2008). https://doi.org/10.1080/08838150802437396
35. Valcke, M., Bonte, S., De Wever, B., Rots, I.: Internet parenting styles and the impact on internet use of primary school children. Comput. Educ. **55**(2), 454–464 (2010). https://doi.org/10.1016/j.compedu.2010.02.009
36. Fantinelli, S., Esposito, C., Carlucci, L., Limone, P., Sulla, F.: The influence of individual and contextual factors on the vocational choices of adolescents and their impact on well-being. Behav. Sci. **13**, 233 (2023). https://doi.org/10.3390/bs13030233
37. Sulla, F., Camia, M., Scorza, M., Giovagnoli, S., Padovani, R., Benassi, E.: The moderator effect of subthreshold autistic traits on the relationship between quality of life and internet addiction. Healthcare **11**, 186 (2023). https://doi.org/10.3390/healthcare11020186
38. Bonfiglio, N.S., Renati, R., Costa, S., Rollo, D., Sulla, F., Penna, M.P.: An exploratory study on the relationship between video game addiction and the constructs of coping and resilience. In: 2020 IEEE International Symposium on Medical Measurements and Applications (MeMeA), pp. 1–5. IEEE (2020)
39. Sasson, H., Mesch, G.: Parental mediation, peer norms and risky online behavior among adolescents. Comput. Hum. Behav. **33**, 32–38 (2014). https://doi.org/10.1016/J.CHB.2013.12.025
40. Bumpus, M.F., Crouter, A.C., McHale, S.M.: Parental autonomy granting during adolescence: exploring gender differences in context. Dev. Psychol. **37**(2), 163–173 (2001). https://doi.org/10.1037/0012-1649.37.2.163
41. Eynon, R., Malmberg, L.-E.: A typology of young people's internet use: implications for education. Comput. Educ. **56**(3), 585–595 (2011). https://doi.org/10.1016/j.compedu.2010.09.020
42. Wu, X.S., et al.: Prevalence of internet addiction and its association with social support and other related factors among adolescents in China. J. Adolesc. **52**, 103–111 (2016). https://doi.org/10.1016/j.adolescence.2016.07.012
43. Milani, L., Osualdella, D., Di Blasio, P.: Quality of interpersonal relationships and problematic internet use in adolescence. Cyberpsychol. Behav. **12**(6), 681–684 (2009). https://doi.org/10.1089/cpb.2009.0071
44. Wickens, T.D., Keppel, G.: Design and Analysis: A Researcher's Handbook. Pearson Prentice-Hall, Upper Saddle River (2004)
45. Agresti, A., Finlay, B., Porcu, M.: Statistica per le scienze sociali. Pearson, London (2009)
46. Di Franco, G.: Tecniche e modelli di analisi multivariata. FrancoAngeli (2017)
47. Tabachnick, B.G., Fidell, L.S.: Using Multivariate Statistics, 3rd edn. HarperCollins, New York (1996)
48. Hartigan, J.A., Wong, M.A.: Algorithm AS 136: a k-means clustering algorithm. J. Roy. Stat. Soc. Ser. C (Appl. Stat.) **28**(1), 100–108 (1979). https://doi.org/10.2307/2346830
49. Faltýnková, A., Blinka, L., Ševčíková, A., Husarova, D.: The associations between family-related factors and excessive internet use in adolescents. Int. J. Environ. Res. Public Health **17**(5), 1–11 (2020). https://doi.org/10.3390/ijerph17051754
50. Valcke, M., De Wever, B., Keer, H.V., Schellens, T.: Long-term study of safe internet use of young children. Comput. Educ. **57**(1), 1292–1305 (2005). https://doi.org/10.1016/j.compedu.2011.01.010
51. Rodríguez-de-Dios, I., van Oosten, J.M.F., Igartua, J.-J.: A study of the relationship between parental mediation and adolescents' digital skills, online risks and online opportunities. Comput. Hum. Behav. **82**, 186–198 (2018). https://doi.org/10.1016/j.chb.2018.01.012

52. Correa, T.: The power of youth: how the bottom-up technology transmission from children to parents is related to digital (in)equality. Int. J. Commun. **9**, 1163–1186 (2015)
53. Tomczyk, Ł, Lizde, E.S.: Is real screen time a determinant of problematic smartphone and social network use among young people? Telematics Inform. **82**, 1–14 (2023). https://doi.org/10.1016/j.tele.2023.101994
54. Xu, H., Ming Wen, L., Rissel, C.: Associations of parental influences with physical activity and screen time among young children: a systematic review. J. Obes. (2015). https://doi.org/10.1155/2015/546925
55. Lauricella, A.R., Wartella, E., Rideout, V.J.: Young children's screen time: the complex role of parent and child factors. J. Appl. Dev. Psychol. **36**, 11–17 (2014). https://doi.org/10.1016/j.appdev.2014.12.001
56. Mesch, G.S.: Family characteristics and intergenerational conflicts over the internet. Inf. Commun. Soc.Commun. Soc. **9**(4), 473–495 (2006). https://doi.org/10.1080/136911806008 58705

From STEAM to STREAM: Integrating Research as a Part of STEAM Education

Robertas Damaševičius[✉] and Ligita Zailskaitė-Jakštė

Faculty of Informatics, Kaunas University of Technology, Kaunas, Lithuania
{robertas.damasevicius,ligita.zailskaite}@ktu.lt

Abstract. We explore the transformative power of incorporating research as an integral component of the existing STEAM disciplines and emphasize the role of inquiry-based learning, critical thinking, and problem-solving skills in fostering a holistic educational experience. We provide an overview of the STEAM framework and its original components-science, technology, engineering, art, and mathematics. Then we introduce the concept of STREAM, where "R" represents the crucial addition of research to the existing framework. The inclusion of research aims to develop students' research skills, information literacy, and the ability to communicate findings effectively. Further, we explore how research methodologies enhance students' understanding of the subjects, facilitate interdisciplinary connections, and nurture innovative thinking. We showcase examples of inquiry-based projects and highlights their positive impact on students' engagement, critical thinking abilities, and knowledge application. We discuss strategies for designing research-based activities, incorporating research experiences, and fostering collaboration among students. As a case study, we present an example of STREAM project in robotics course implemented using mBot Ranger robot. By incorporating research into STEAM education, students develop a deeper understanding of the subjects, acquire essential skills for the 21st century, and become better equipped to address complex challenges in their future endeavors.

Keywords: STEAM Education · STREAM · Research ·
Inquiry-Based Learning · Critical Thinking · Problem-Solving Skills

1 Introduction

STEAM (Science, Technology, Engineering, Art, and Mathematics) education has been gaining momentum in the field of education. It is an interdisciplinary approach that aims to integrate the five disciplines in a cohesive learning paradigm based on real-world applications [5]. The goal of STEAM education is not only to teach students about these subjects in isolation but also to expose them to the interplay between them, thereby fostering a holistic understanding and the ability to apply this knowledge in various contexts [17]. The inclusion

© The Author(s), under exclusive license to Springer Nature Switzerland AG 2024
Ł. Tomczyk (Ed.): NMP 2023, CCIS 2130, pp. 318–335, 2024.
https://doi.org/10.1007/978-3-031-63235-8_21

of Art in the traditional STEM model is a recognition of the importance of creativity and design thinking in problem-solving and innovation. This approach prepares students for the 21st-century workforce by equipping them with the necessary skills and competencies to thrive in a rapidly changing world.

The purpose of this study is to explore the transformative potential of integrating research into the existing STEAM framework, thereby evolving it into STREAM (Science, Technology, Research, Engineering, Art, and Mathematics). This study aims to highlight the significance of research as an integral component of STEAM education and its role in enhancing students' learning experiences. It seeks to provide a comprehensive understanding of how research methodologies can be incorporated into STEAM subjects to facilitate interdisciplinary connections, nurture innovative thinking, and develop essential 21st-century skills among students. The study also aims to showcase examples of inquiry-based projects and their impact on students' engagement, critical thinking abilities, and knowledge application. Furthermore, it discusses strategies for designing research-based activities, incorporating authentic research experiences, and fostering collaboration among students. The study addresses potential challenges in integrating research into the STEAM curriculum and offers recommendations for educators to overcome these barriers. Ultimately, the study underscores the transformative potential of STREAM education in cultivating a culture of inquiry, exploration, and lifelong learning in educational settings.

2   The Evolution of STEAM to STREAM

2.1   From STEAM to STREAM

STREAM expands upon the foundation of STEAM by adding an additional component: "R" for Research. This extension emphasizes the significance of research skills and methodologies across various disciplines. It encourages students to engage in inquiry-based learning, critical thinking, problem-solving, and exploration of new knowledge. Here's a breakdown of the STREAM framework:

1. **Science** remains a core component, focusing on the scientific method, experimentation, and observation. Students explore the world, conduct experiments, and develop an understanding of scientific principles and processes.
2. **Technology** encompasses the study of digital tools, devices, and systems that enhance learning and problem-solving. It includes coding, robotics, digital simulations, and the use of technology as a creative medium.
3. **Research** is the newly introduced component. It emphasizes inquiry-based learning, information literacy, and the development of research skills. Students learn how to formulate research questions, gather and analyze data, evaluate sources, and communicate their findings effectively.
4. **Engineering** involves designing and creating solutions to real-world problems using a systematic approach. Students learn engineering principles, engage in hands-on projects, and apply knowledge to construct and innovate.

5. **Art** explores creativity, expression, and aesthetics. It encourages students to engage in visual arts, performing arts, design, and other forms of creative expression. Art nurtures imagination, critical thinking, and the ability to communicate ideas effectively.

6. **Mathematics** focuses on numerical reasoning, logic, and problem-solving skills. Students learn mathematical concepts, patterns, and algorithms, applying them to solve real-world problems and make informed decisions.

2.2   Incorporating Research Methodology into STEAM Subjects

In science, research methodologies are essential for investigating natural phenomena, testing hypotheses, and advancing knowledge. Incorporating research into science education enables students to develop a deep understanding of scientific principles and processes [13]. It involves several key components:

- **Formulating Research Questions:** Students learn to identify research questions that align with their interests and address gaps in knowledge. This process encourages curiosity and promotes the exploration of scientific concepts in a structured manner.

- **Designing Experiments:** Students develop skills in experimental design, including selecting variables, designing control groups, and determining appropriate data collection methods. They learn to develop hypotheses, plan procedures, and analyze experimental results.

- **Data Collection and Analysis:** Students engage in collecting data through observations, measurements, surveys, or experiments. They learn to use appropriate tools and techniques, record data accurately, and analyze results using statistical methods or other relevant approaches.

- **Drawing Conclusions:** Through research, students develop the ability to interpret and draw conclusions from their findings. They learn to critically evaluate their data, consider potential sources of error, and make evidence-based claims.

By incorporating research methodologies in science education, students become active participants in the scientific process. They develop skills such as critical thinking, problem-solving, data analysis, and effective communication, which are essential for scientific inquiry.

2.3   Research Methodologies in Technology

Research methodologies play a crucial role in the field of technology as well. Technology research involves exploring emerging technologies, analyzing their impact on society, and addressing real-world problems. By integrating research methodologies into technology education, students gain a deeper understanding of technology's role and its implications. Here are some key aspects of research methodologies in technology:

- **Literature Review:** Students learn to conduct literature reviews to understand the current state of technology, identify research gaps, and explore existing solutions or approaches. This process helps them develop a broader perspective and make informed decisions.
- **Design and Prototyping:** Research in technology often involves designing and building prototypes or models. Students engage in iterative design processes, testing their ideas, and refining their solutions based on feedback and data.
- **User Research:** Technology research often focuses on understanding user needs, preferences, and behaviors. Students learn methods such as surveys, interviews, and observations to gather data and gain insights into user experiences and expectations.
- **Data Analysis and Evaluation:** Technology research involves analyzing data collected from various sources, such as user feedback, system performance, or user behavior. Students develop skills in data analysis and interpretation, using appropriate tools and techniques.

2.4 Research Methodologies in Engineering

Research methodologies play a significant role in engineering education as they enable students to apply systematic approaches to problem-solving, design innovative solutions, and contribute to the advancement of engineering knowledge. By incorporating research methodologies into engineering education within the STEAM framework, students develop critical skills necessary for successful engineering careers. Here are key aspects of research methodologies in engineering:

- **Problem Identification:** Research in engineering often begins with identifying and defining a problem or challenge. Students learn to analyze real-world issues, understand stakeholder needs, and formulate research questions that guide their investigations.
- **Literature Review:** Engineering research involves conducting literature reviews to understand existing solutions, technologies, and best practices related to the identified problem. Students critically evaluate previous work, identify gaps, and gain insights that inform their own research.
- **Data Collection and Analysis:** Research in engineering involves collecting data through experiments, simulations, or observations. Students learn to design experiments, collect and analyze data using appropriate methods and tools, and draw meaningful conclusions from their findings.
- **Prototyping and Testing:** Engineering research often involves designing and building prototypes to test and evaluate potential solutions. Students engage in iterative design processes, incorporating feedback and conducting experiments to validate and refine their prototypes.
- **Simulation and Modeling:** Research in engineering frequently utilizes simulation software and modeling techniques to analyze and predict the behavior of complex systems. Students learn to use computer-based tools to simulate, model, and optimize engineering designs and processes.

2.5   Research Methodologies in Art

Research methodologies also play a vital role in the field of art within the STEAM framework. Artistic research encourages students to explore, experiment, and critically reflect on their creative processes and artistic expressions. Here are key aspects of research methodologies in art:

- **Conceptual Exploration:** Artistic research often begins with the exploration of conceptual frameworks, themes, and ideas. Students engage in critical thinking, research historical and contemporary art movements, and analyze the works of other artists to inform their creative processes.
- **Material and Technique Research:** Artistic research involves experimenting with different materials, techniques, and processes. Students explore various artistic mediums, study traditional and contemporary methods, and develop skills that enhance their ability to convey ideas visually.
- **Contextual Analysis:** Artistic research incorporates an understanding of the social, cultural, and historical contexts in which artworks are created and interpreted. Students critically analyze the influences, meanings, and impacts of their work within broader artistic and societal frameworks.
- **Reflective Practice:** Artistic research emphasizes self-reflection and critical evaluation of one's own artistic practice. Students engage in introspection, document their creative journey, and analyze their artistic choices, allowing for personal growth and development.
- **Presentation and Documentation:** Artistic research involves presenting and documenting artwork through exhibitions, portfolios, artist statements, and reflective essays. Students learn to communicate their ideas, processes, and intentions effectively to an audience, fostering dialogue and engagement.

2.6   Research Methodologies in Mathematics

Research methodologies play a crucial role in mathematics education within the STEAM framework. Mathematics research focuses on investigating mathematical concepts, patterns, and structures, as well as developing new mathematical theories and applications. By incorporating research methodologies into mathematics education, students develop a deeper understanding of mathematical principles, problem-solving skills, and critical thinking abilities. Here are key aspects of research methodologies in mathematics:

- **Exploration of Mathematical Concepts:** Mathematics involves exploring various mathematical concepts and their relationships. Students investigate properties, axioms, theorems, and mathematical structures to deepen their understanding of mathematical ideas and principles.
- **Mathematical Proof and Rigor:** Mathematics emphasizes the use of rigorous proof to validate mathematical statements and theories. Students learn to construct logical arguments, provide clear justifications, and use deductive reasoning to prove or disprove mathematical conjectures.

- **Data Analysis and Statistical Methods:** In mathematics, data analysis and statistical methods are employed to study patterns, trends, and relationships. Students use mathematical tools and techniques to analyze data, make predictions, and draw conclusions from empirical observations.
- **Mathematical Modeling:** Research in mathematics often involves developing mathematical models to represent and understand real-world phenomena. Students learn to formulate mathematical models, interpret their results, and make informed predictions or decisions based on these models.

3   Strategies for Integrating Research into STEAM

3.1   Designing Research-Based Activities

Designing research-based activities allows students to actively engage in the research process, fostering a deeper understanding of the subject matter and promoting critical thinking skills. Here are some strategies for designing research-based activities within the STEAM curriculum:

- Begin by identifying research topics that align with the learning objectives and the interests of the students. These topics can span across STEAM disciplines or focus on a specific area within a discipline.
- Encourage students to formulate research questions related to the chosen topics. These questions should be open-ended, thought-provoking, and capable of stimulating further inquiry and exploration.
- Guide students in conducting literature reviews to explore existing research, theories, and methodologies related to their research questions. This process helps students understand the current knowledge landscape and identify gaps or areas for further investigation.
- Assist students in designing and planning experiments or projects to address their research questions. This may involve developing hypotheses, defining variables, selecting appropriate data collection methods, and determining the necessary resources and materials.
- Facilitate the collection of data through experiments, surveys, observations, or other relevant methods. Guide students in analyzing and interpreting the data using appropriate mathematical, statistical, or qualitative techniques.
- Encourage collaboration throughout the research process. Students can share their findings, receive feedback, and engage in discussions to refine their research methodologies and enhance their understanding.
- Guide students in effectively communicating their research findings through presentations, reports, or other creative mediums. Emphasize the importance of clear and concise communication, visual representations of data, and logical reasoning.
- Promote reflection and self-evaluation among students by encouraging them to critically analyze their research process, outcomes, and challenges faced. This helps students develop metacognitive skills and refine their research approaches for future investigations.

4   Inquiry-Based Projects in STREAM Education

Inquiry-based projects are a cornerstone of STREAM (Science, Technology, Research, Engineering, Art, and Mathematics) education. These projects promote active learning, critical thinking, problem-solving, and interdisciplinary exploration. By engaging in inquiry-based projects, students take on the role of researchers, asking questions, designing experiments, and seeking solutions to real-world problems. Here, we will discuss the importance of inquiry-based projects in STREAM education and provide examples to illustrate their potential.

4.1   Importance of Inquiry-Based Projects

Inquiry-based projects empower students to become active participants in their learning journey. By posing questions, investigating phenomena, and drawing conclusions, students develop essential skills and mindsets. Here are key reasons why inquiry-based projects are crucial in STREAM education:

- Inquiry-based projects spark curiosity and excitement among students. They encourage students to ask questions, explore unknown territories, and develop a genuine interest in the subject matter [6,9]. As students engage in hands-on investigations, they become more engaged and motivated to learn.
- Inquiry-based projects require students to think critically, analyze information, and develop logical reasoning skills. By designing experiments, evaluating data, and making evidence-based conclusions, students enhance their problem-solving abilities [11].
- Inquiry-based projects often involve collaboration among students. They learn to work in teams, communicate effectively, and respect diverse perspectives. Collaborative inquiry promotes dialogue, cooperation, and the exchange of ideas, fostering a positive learning environment [7].
- Inquiry-based projects naturally lend themselves to interdisciplinary exploration. Students can investigate problems that bridge multiple STREAM disciplines, encouraging connections and the application of knowledge from different fields. This interdisciplinary approach prepares students for real-world challenges that require a holistic perspective.
- Inquiry-based projects provide students with opportunities to develop research skills, such as formulating research questions, designing experiments, collecting and analyzing data, and drawing conclusions [14]. These skills are transferable and applicable across various academic and professional domains.
- Inquiry-based projects nurture students' creativity by encouraging them to think outside the box, propose new ideas, and develop innovative solutions [10]. They inspire students to take risks, experiment with different approaches, and explore unconventional methods.
- Inquiry-based projects allow students to address real-world problems or explore topics of personal interest. This authenticity provides a meaningful context for learning, making the educational experience more relevant and impactful.

5   Case Study: STREAM Project in Robotics

In this case study, a group of students embarked on a STREAM project that involved programming a robot using the Makeblock mBot robot kit. The project was designed to address a typical robot control problem and incorporated elements of research, demonstrating the transformative power of integrating research into STEAM education. The problem posed to the students was to program the mBot to navigate a complex maze autonomously. This task required the application of knowledge and skills from all STREAM disciplines. The students had to understand the scientific principles behind the robot's sensors, use technology and engineering skills to assemble and program the robot, apply mathematical concepts to calculate the optimal path, and use art and design thinking to create the maze. The research component was integrated into the project through the process of problem-solving, data collection, analysis, and communication of findings [2,3]. This case study outlines a project where students use the Makeblock mBot robot kit to solve a maze exploration task. The project aims to teach students about task decomposition in programming and provide hands-on experience in solving a typical robot control problem.

Aims. The primary objectives of this project are to:

- Understand the concept of task decomposition in programming.
- Learn how to program a robot to solve a maze exploration task.

Description. In this scenario, the robot is placed within a maze (Fig. 1), a structure consisting of multiple connected passageways. The maze can be represented by black lines on a floor. The task for the robot is to navigate through the maze autonomously, from a specified starting point to an exit point.

Activities. The project is divided into several activities:

1. **Task Specification:** The students write an informal specification of the task for the robot to exit the maze. This specification includes a series of actions such as moving forward a certain distance and turning at specific angles.
2. **Trial Run:** The students perform a trial run to determine the actual speed of the robot and the time required for it to perform certain actions. These measurements are used to calculate the robot's velocity and angular velocity.
3. **Calculation of Program Variables:** Based on the measurements from the trial run, the students calculate the time required for the robot to cover certain distances and turn specific angles. These calculations are used to set the values of program variables.
4. **Programming:** The students code the program in mBlock, a graphical programming environment designed for STEAM education. They write program statements for each step specified in the task specification and upload the program to the robot.

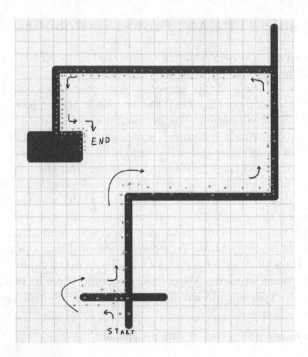

Fig. 1. A conceptual diagram of a maze: a robot should find the path from Start position to End position while following the end.

5. **Testing:** The students test their programmed mBot in the maze. They run multiple trials and record their observations. These observations are used to refine the program and improve the robot's performance.
6. **Challenge:** As an additional challenge, the students can implement a maze-solving algorithm using line following, where an open circuit line is used to represent the maze.
7. **Cleanup:** At the end of the project, the students turn off the mBot robot, remove the batteries, and store the robot and its components safely.

In the initial stages of the project, the students conducted research to understand the capabilities and limitations of the mBot robot kit (Fig. 2). They explored different programming languages and techniques, and studied the principles of robotics and automation. This research phase allowed the students to gain a deeper understanding of the task at hand and equipped them with the necessary knowledge to tackle the problem.

Next, the students applied their research findings to design and implement a solution. They programmed the mBot to use its sensors to detect and avoid obstacles, and calculated the optimal path through the maze using mathematical algorithms. The students iteratively tested and refined their solution, collecting data on the robot's performance and making adjustments based on their observations. In the case study under consideration, the maze was constructed using

Fig. 2. mBot Ranger robot used in the project.

Fig. 3. Maze implemented as a system of connected lines.

straight black lines, distinguishing the start and end points. This setup is similar to line-following tasks, which typically involve a mobile robot equipped with infrared sensors navigating a black track on a flat surface (Fig. 3).

The infrared sensors play a crucial role in maintaining the robot's trajectory by providing feedback through four possible states, labeled as 0, 1, 2, and 3. When both sensors detect the black surface (state 0), the robot is correctly following the line and continues to move forward. If the right sensor detects the white surface (state 1), it indicates that the robot has deviated to the right of the line, and thus, the robot is programmed to correct its course by moving left. Conversely, if the left sensor detects the white surface (state 2), the robot

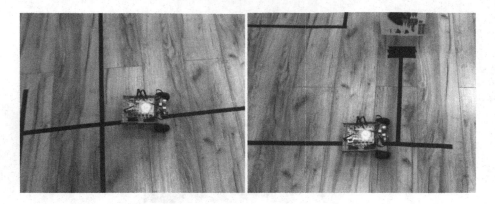

Fig. 4. Robot mBot Ranger is following the line during the maze exploration task to find the goal (right image).

has strayed to the left of the line, prompting a course correction to the right. Lastly, state 3 occurs when both sensors fail to detect the line, indicating that the robot has lost its track. This system of feedback and course correction allows the robot to navigate the maze from the start point to the end point (Fig. 4), demonstrating the application of sensor technology and programming in solving a practical problem.

Finally, the students presented their project to their peers and teacher. They communicated their research process, explained their problem-solving strategies, and demonstrated the functionality of their programmed mBot. This presentation allowed the students to practice their communication skills and receive feedback on their work.

This STREAM project in robotics exemplifies the benefits of integrating research into STEAM education. Through the process of conducting research, designing and implementing a solution, and communicating their findings, the students developed a range of skills including problem-solving, critical thinking, creativity, communication, and collaboration [1,15]. They gained a deeper understanding of the STREAM disciplines and saw firsthand how these fields can be integrated to solve real-world problems.

6   Discussion

6.1   Impact on Students' Engagement

The integration of STREAM education has a significant impact on students' engagement. By combining these disciplines, STREAM education offers a holistic and multidimensional approach to learning, fostering active participation and increased student engagement. Here are some key ways in which STREAM education impacts students' engagement:

- STREAM education emphasizes the application of knowledge to real-world contexts. This relevance creates a sense of purpose and motivates students to engage actively in their learning. By incorporating real-world problems, projects, and hands-on experiences, STREAM education makes learning more meaningful and engaging for students.
- STREAM education encourages students to make connections between different disciplines and recognize the interconnectedness of knowledge. This interdisciplinary approach breaks down the traditional boundaries between subjects, allowing students to explore topics from multiple perspectives. The integration of various disciplines sparks curiosity and promotes a deeper understanding of the interplay between science, technology, engineering, art, and mathematics.
- STREAM education emphasizes experiential learning and hands-on experiences. Students are encouraged to engage in activities such as experiments, design projects, artistic creations, or technological explorations. These hands-on experiences provide opportunities for active learning, exploration, and problem-solving, which greatly enhance students' engagement in the learning process.
- STREAM education often involves collaborative projects and activities, which require students to work together, share ideas, and communicate effectively. Collaboration fosters social interaction, peer learning, and the development of teamwork skills. It also enhances students' engagement as they learn to value different perspectives, negotiate ideas, and collectively achieve project goals.
- STREAM education places students at the center of the learning process, empowering them to take ownership of their education. Inquiry-based approaches encourage students to ask questions, explore, and seek solutions to real-world problems. This student-centered approach promotes intrinsic motivation, curiosity, and active engagement in learning.
- STREAM education nurtures students' creativity and encourages them to think critically and innovatively. By integrating art and design into STEM subjects, students are provided with opportunities to think outside the box, explore unconventional solutions, and express their creativity [4]. This aspect of STREAM education engages students' imagination and encourages them to approach problems from multiple angles.

In summary, STREAM education positively impacts students' engagement by fostering relevance, interdisciplinary connections, hands-on experiences, collaboration, student-centered learning, and creativity. These factors contribute to a more dynamic and engaging learning environment that ignites students' curiosity, motivation, and active participation in the learning process.

6.2   Impact on Critical Thinking Abilities

STREAM education significantly enhances students' critical thinking abilities by promoting inquiry, problem-solving, and analytical skills. Here are some ways in which STREAM education impacts students' critical thinking abilities:

- STREAM education encourages students to ask questions, investigate, and seek answers. By engaging in inquiry-based learning, students develop critical thinking skills such as observation, analysis, evaluation, and synthesis. They learn to think independently, ask meaningful questions, and develop logical arguments based on evidence.
- STREAM education provides students with opportunities to tackle complex problems through hands-on projects and interdisciplinary challenges. Students learn to identify problems, analyze them, brainstorm potential solutions, and evaluate their effectiveness. This process enhances their critical thinking, decision-making, and problem-solving abilities.
- STREAM education emphasizes data analysis, experimentation, and mathematical reasoning. Students develop skills in interpreting data, drawing conclusions, and making evidence-based claims. They learn to analyze patterns, identify relationships, and think analytically to solve problems across different disciplines.
- STREAM education promotes reflection and metacognitive thinking, which are essential components of critical thinking. Students are encouraged to reflect on their learning processes, identify strengths and weaknesses, and make adjustments to improve their understanding and performance. This metacognitive approach enhances students' ability to evaluate their own thinking, identify biases, and consider alternative perspectives.
- STREAM education encourages students to consider multiple perspectives and approaches to problem-solving. By integrating various disciplines and encouraging interdisciplinary thinking, students develop the ability to approach problems from different angles, consider diverse viewpoints, and make connections between seemingly unrelated concepts. This integrative thinking fosters critical thinking skills and helps students develop innovative solutions.
- STREAM education challenges students to evaluate the validity, reliability, and credibility of information and evidence. Students learn to analyze and assess the quality of sources, make informed decisions based on available data, and recognize the limitations and biases in different sources of information.
- STREAM education promotes creative thinking and problem-solving, encouraging students to explore unconventional solutions and think outside the box. By incorporating art and design elements into STEM subjects, students develop their creative and innovative thinking skills, allowing them to approach problems with flexibility and generate novel solutions.

By integrating critical thinking skills into STREAM education, students develop a strong foundation for problem-solving, analysis, evaluation, and creative thinking. These skills are crucial not only for success in the STEAM fields but also for lifelong learning and adaptability in a rapidly changing world.

6.3   Impact on Knowledge Acquisition and Application

STREAM education significantly impacts students' knowledge acquisition and application across the STEAM disciplines. Here's how STREAM education influences students' knowledge acquisition and application:

– STREAM education emphasizes the integration of knowledge across different disciplines. Rather than studying subjects in isolation, students develop a more holistic understanding of how the STEAM disciplines are interconnected. This integrated approach enables students to acquire knowledge that transcends traditional boundaries, leading to a more comprehensive understanding of the world [8].
– STREAM education emphasizes the application of knowledge to real-world contexts. Students engage in hands-on projects, problem-solving activities, and research-based investigations that require them to apply their knowledge and skills in practical settings. This application-oriented approach deepens students' understanding and enhances their ability to transfer knowledge to real-life situations.
– STREAM education promotes cross-disciplinary connections, encouraging students to see the relevance and interconnectedness of concepts across different subjects. For example, students might apply mathematical principles to analyze scientific data, use technology to enhance artistic creations, or utilize engineering principles to solve technological problems. This interdisciplinary approach enriches students' understanding and facilitates the application of knowledge in diverse contexts [12].
– STREAM education often involves problem-based learning, where students tackle complex problems or challenges. This approach requires students to acquire knowledge from multiple disciplines and apply it to develop innovative solutions. As students engage in problem-based learning, they develop a deeper understanding of concepts and their application in real-world scenarios [16].
– STREAM education encourages students to delve deeper into concepts, theories, and methodologies. Through research, experimentation, and project-based learning, students acquire a more profound understanding of the subject matter. This depth of understanding enables students to make connections between different concepts, think critically, and analyze complex problems more effectively.
– STREAM education instills a passion for lifelong learning. Students develop skills such as research, critical thinking, problem-solving, and communication, which are transferable to various academic and professional settings. These skills empower students to continue acquiring and applying knowledge throughout their lives.

STREAM education may have a significant impact on students' knowledge acquisition and application. By integrating knowledge from multiple disciplines, emphasizing real-world application, and promoting problem-solving and inquiry-based learning, students develop a deeper and more comprehensive understanding of the STEAM subjects. They acquire knowledge that is interconnected, relevant, and applicable across various contexts. Furthermore, STREAM education cultivates lifelong learning skills, critical thinking abilities, and the capacity to apply knowledge creatively and innovatively. By embracing the integrated nature of STREAM education, students are better prepared to tackle the complex challenges of the modern world. They become adept at recognizing patterns, making connections, and approaching problems from multiple perspectives. The acquisition and application of knowledge in a STREAM context foster intellectual curiosity, adaptability, and a lifelong love for learning.

6.4   Challenges and Recommendations

Integrating research into the STREAM education framework can present various challenges. However, with careful planning and strategic approaches, these challenges can be addressed effectively. Here, we discuss potential challenges in integrating research and provide recommendations for overcoming barriers.

- Time constraints within the curriculum can be a significant challenge when integrating research into STREAM education. Existing syllabi and academic schedules may not allow for in-depth research projects, hindering students' ability to engage fully in the research process.
- Adequate resources, such as laboratory equipment, art supplies, or technology tools, are essential for conducting research. Limited access to these resources can pose a challenge for schools or educators seeking to incorporate research into the curriculum.
- Teachers may require additional training and professional development to effectively integrate research methodologies into their teaching practices. Lack of familiarity with research approaches or a limited understanding of interdisciplinary connections can hinder the implementation of research-based activities.
- Traditional assessment methods may not align well with the open-ended and exploratory nature of research projects. Assessing students' research skills, creativity, and critical thinking abilities can be challenging, as these qualities are not easily measured through standardized tests.
- Students may have limited prior exposure to research methodologies and may struggle with aspects such as formulating research questions, conducting experiments, or analyzing data. Developing research skills and fostering a research-oriented mindset may require additional support and scaffolding.

Overcoming these challenges requires a collective effort from educators, administrators, policymakers, and the broader educational community. By working together and prioritizing the integration of research, we can create a learning environment that empowers students to become critical thinkers, problem solvers, and lifelong learners. Through research experiences, students develop the skills, knowledge, and passion necessary to excel in the STEAM disciplines and make meaningful contributions to society. We formulate the following recommendations for overcoming barriers in education:

- Ensure that research is integrated into the curriculum by mapping research-related activities and projects to learning objectives and standards. Seek opportunities to align research with existing topics or create dedicated time slots for research-based activities. Flexibility in the curriculum allows for deeper engagement in research and exploration.

- Foster collaborations with external institutions, universities, or research organizations. These partnerships can provide access to resources, expertise, and mentorship opportunities for both educators and students. Collaborations also allow for real-world connections and authentic research experiences.
- Provide professional development opportunities for teachers to enhance their understanding of research methodologies, interdisciplinary connections, and assessment strategies. Workshops, seminars, and online courses can equip educators with the necessary knowledge and skills to effectively integrate research into their teaching practices.
- Develop assessment strategies that align with the nature of research-based activities. Emphasize formative assessments, such as project portfolios, presentations, or research reports, which capture students' growth, critical thinking skills, and ability to apply knowledge in real-world contexts. Rubrics and peer evaluation can also provide valuable feedback.
- Scaffold research skills and provide guided practice for students to develop proficiency in various research methodologies. Start with small-scale projects, allowing students to gradually build their research skills and confidence. Offer support through workshops, tutorials, and mentoring to help students overcome challenges and develop independent research abilities.
- Leverage tools, online platforms, and virtual resources to overcome resource limitations and provide access to research experiences. Virtual simulations, data analysis software, and online research databases can enhance students' research capabilities, regardless of physical resource constraints.
- Foster a research-oriented culture within the school by celebrating student research achievements, organizing research symposiums, or establishing research clubs or mentorship programs. Encouraging a supportive environment where students and teachers value research promotes engagement and enthusiasm for conducting research.

Integrating research into STREAM education may present challenges related to time constraints, resources, teacher preparedness, assessment, and student readiness. However, these challenges can be addressed through strategic approaches and recommendations. By incorporating research into the curriculum, fostering collaborations, providing professional development, implementing authentic assessments, scaffolding skill development, utilizing technology, and cultivating a research culture, educators can overcome these barriers and successfully integrate research into STREAM education.

7   Conclusion

STREAM education has the power to transform traditional education by providing students with a holistic and integrated learning experience. By bridging the gaps between science, technology, engineering, art, and mathematics, STREAM education nurtures creativity, innovation, and cross-disciplinary thinking. It prepares students for the complexities of the modern world, equipping them with the knowledge, skills, and mindset needed to thrive in an ever-evolving society. By combining the analytical and logical thinking of science and mathematics with the creativity and expression of art, STREAM education encourages students to approach problems from multiple angles and develop innovative solutions. This interdisciplinary approach reflects the interconnectedness of the STEAM fields in the real world and enables students to make meaningful connections between different disciplines. STREAM education emphasizes inquiry-based learning, where students actively participate in the research process, ask questions, investigate, and seek answers. It fosters a culture of curiosity, exploration, and lifelong learning. By engaging in hands-on projects, collaborative activities, and research experiences, students develop critical thinking skills, problem-solving abilities, and the capacity to apply knowledge in practical settings. STREAM education cultivates a culture of inquiry, where students learn to ask meaningful questions, think critically, analyze data, and communicate their findings effectively. It encourages students to become active participants in their education, taking ownership of their learning journey and developing the skills necessary for success in the 21st century.

The impact of STREAM education extends beyond the classroom, preparing students for future endeavors in academia, careers, and civic engagement. By integrating research methodologies, STREAM education equips students with the skills needed to engage in scientific inquiry, technological advancements, engineering innovations, artistic expressions, and mathematical reasoning. STREAM education nurtures a generation of individuals who are equipped to tackle complex challenges, think critically, embrace innovation, and adapt to a rapidly changing world. It empowers students to become lifelong learners, fostering a passion for exploration, creativity, and intellectual growth. The skills and mindsets cultivated through STREAM education are transferable to various fields, enabling students to excel in STEAM careers, contribute to advancements in science and technology, and make a positive impact on society. STREAM education has the potential to revolutionize education by integrating science, technology, research, engineering, art, and mathematics. It fosters creativity, critical thinking, interdisciplinary connections, and a lifelong love for learning. By embracing the transformative power of STREAM education, we can prepare future generations to become innovative problem solvers, lifelong learners, and contributors to the advancement of knowledge and society as a whole.

References

1. Burbaite, R., Stuikys, V., Damasevicius, R.: Educational robots as collaborative learning objects for teaching computer science. In: ICSSE 2013 - IEEE International Conference on System Science and Engineering, pp. 211–216 (2013)
2. Damaševičius, R., Maskeliunas, R., Blažauskas, T.: Faster pedagogical framework for steam education based on educational robotics. Int. J. Eng. Technol. (UAE) **7**(2), 138–142 (2018)
3. Damaševičius, R., Narbutaite, L., Plauska, I., Blažauskas, T.: Advances in the use of educational robots in project-based teaching. TEM J. **6**(2), 342–348 (2017)

4. Diep, N.H., Thuy, H.T.P., Lai, D.T.B., Viet, V.V., Chung, N.T.K.: A comparison of three stem approaches to the teaching and learning of science topics: students' knowledge and scientific creativity. Int. J. Educ. Pract. **11**(2), 266–278 (2023)
5. Harris, A., de Bruin, L.R.: Secondary school creativity, teacher practice and steam education: an international study. J. Educ. Change **19**(2), 153–179 (2018)
6. Heuling, L.S.: Promoting student interest in science: the impact of a science theatre project. LUMAT **9**(2) (2021)
7. Kali, Y., Levin-Peled, R., Dori, Y.J.: The role of design-principles in designing courses that promote collaborative learning in higher-education. Comput. Hum. Behav. **25**(5), 1067–1078 (2009)
8. Li, T., Zhan, Z.: A systematic review on design thinking integrated learning in k-12 education. Appl. Sci. **12**(16) (2022)
9. Lindeman, C.: Informal stem learning: cultivating curiosity. Int. J. Sci. Math. Technol. Learn. **27**(2), 25–34 (2020)
10. Liu, X., Wang, X., Xu, K., Hu, X.: Effect of reverse engineering pedagogy on primary school students' computational thinking skills in stem learning activities. J. Intell. **11**(2) (2023)
11. Lou, S., Shih, R., Diez, C.R., Tseng, K.: The impact of problem-based learning strategies on stem knowledge integration and attitudes: an exploratory study among female Taiwanese senior high school students. Int. J. Technol. Des. Educ. **21**(2), 195–215 (2011)
12. Marbach-Ad, G., Hunt, C., Thompson, K.V.: Exploring the values undergraduate students attribute to cross-disciplinary skills needed for the workplace: an analysis of five stem disciplines. J. Sci. Educ. Technol. **28**(5), 452–469 (2019)
13. Mathieu, R.D.: Preparing the future STEM faculty: the center for the integration of research, teaching, and learning. In: ACS Symposium Series, vol. 1145 (2013)
14. Perignat, E., Katz-Buonincontro, J.: Steam in practice and research: an integrative literature review. Think. Skills Creat. **31**, 31–43 (2019)
15. Plauska, I., Damaševičius, R.: Educational robots for Internet-of-Things supported collaborative learning. In: Dregvaite, G., Damasevicius, R. (eds.) ICIST 2014. CCIS, vol. 465, pp. 346–358. Springer, Cham (2014). https://doi.org/10.1007/978-3-319-11958-8_28
16. Smith, K., et al.: Principles of problem-based learning (pbl) in stem education: using expert wisdom and research to frame educational practice. Educ. Sci. **12**(10) (2022)
17. Spector, J.M.: Education, training, competencies, curricula and technology. In: Ge, X., Ifenthaler, D., Spector, J.M. (eds.) Emerging Technologies for STEAM Education. ECTII, pp. 3–14. Springer, Cham (2015). https://doi.org/10.1007/978-3-319-02573-5_1

STEM Education Using Digital Tools in Undergraduate Teacher Education

Ján Gunčaga[✉] [iD] and Ján Záhorec [iD]

Faculty of Education, Comenius University Bratislava, Račianska 59, 813 34, Bratislava, Slovakia

{guncaga,zahorec}@fedu.uniba.sk

Abstract. There is a growing trend in the primary mathematics education the application of augmented reality software tools connected with concrete thematic area from the math curricula, which has an interdisciplinary approach. It is a contribution to teaching and learning with digital tools based on the STEM (Science, Technology, Engineering and Mathematics) concept, which should be implemented to teacher training at universities. In this context, the authors of the contribution focus on some possibilities of innovative approach to teaching and learning with digital tools based on the STEM (Science, Technology, Engineering and Mathematics) concept implemented in the framework of undergraduate teacher training of primary education students at the Faculty of Education of Comenius University Bratislava. They clarify the connections between the formation of professional didactic-technological competences of primary education teacher candidates in the usage of the Augmented Reality (AR) Ruler software application and the development of their mathematical competences necessary for the successful and effective performance of their future profession in the context of the requirements and needs of the reform changes of the digitalization of education in the Slovak Republic. In the paper they approach a qualitative analysis of the integration of STEM activities adapted for the primary education environment. The action research was organized in the academic year 2022/2023 within the educational discipline of Manipulative Geometry integrated into the curricular structure of the bachelor's degree Program of Preschool and Elementary Pedagogy at the above-mentioned faculty. In the sense of the Slovak State Educational Program of Mathematics for Primary Education, students prepared outdoor educational activities with the AR Ruler application for the following areas: distance, distance measurement, distance comparison, estimated length, real length. In the sense of STEM interdisciplinarity, the future primary education teachers appropriately linked the mathematics area with architecture and the usage of the AR Ruler application which facilitates their digital competence.

Keywords: STEM education · pre-service primary education teacher training · digital literacy

Ł. Tomczyk (Ed.): NMP 2023, CCIS 2130, pp. 336–350, 2024.
https://doi.org/10.1007/978-3-031-63235-8_22

1 Introduction

Technological development in the economy and society is broadly recognized and accept as a driver of change, and it is assumed in [1] that "information technologies are a acting jobs, skills, wages, and the economy."

In this sense, different kind of technology require the elevation of the cognitive abilities of the workforce. In the other hand, globalization demands international competitiveness and is deemed as another change driver. The modern workplaces need new skills to an even greater extent, namely the ability to solve non-routine problems, complex communication competencies, and verbal, digital and quantitative literacy. These tendences made big influence on education.

21st-century education is influenced by economic growth, sustainable economic development, social cohesion, and equality of opportunity depend on workforce skills, and that abilities need to meet the information-age requirements. Therefore, sustainable economic growth brings new qualities and different challenges, and expects educational systems to equip learners and students with skills and competencies that help them manage change and generate and execute ideas through flexibility and initiative. These qualities are judged to be vital for navigating the complexities and new specific aspects of the modern world; thus, they are labelled as 21st-century skills.

It is possible to count in the frame of the 21st-century education the concept of STEM education. According to [2] STEM education represents the educational integration of science, technology, engineering, and mathematics. This kind of education is supported also from the institutions of the European Union. For example, the study [3] argues that employment of STEM skilled labour in the European Union has increasing tendence despite the economic crisis and demand is expected to grow. In parallel, high numbers of STEM workers in this kind of professions are approaching retirement age. For this reason, STEM education is supported by Ministries of Education in many countries.

STEM education is influenced by different kinds of ICT (information and communication technology) tools. On of these tools is augmented reality (AR). According [4] AR is a variation of virtual reality (VR). Virtual Reality completely immerses a user inside a synthetic environment. For this reason, the user cannot see the real world around him. AR allows the user to see the real world, with virtual objects (one or more) composited with the real world. Therefore, AR only supplements reality. This tool doesn't replace the reality completely (compare with [5]).

2 A Theoretical Framework for Digitally Supported STEM Education

When we talk about technology solutions for STEM education, we are referring to the teaching and learning of subject matter in science and engineering classrooms through selected software applications or robotics and coding kits. As [6] point out, the main purpose of integrating them into the school science and engineering teaching process, which teachers are hereby pursuing, is to try to stimulate the learning engagement and motivation of youngsters for different aspects of the teaching and learning process in the aforementioned areas of their educational curriculum. In particular, if they are operated directly by the pupils during the lesson, they can help them to sort out and clarify theoretical knowledge and imagination-intensive natural/scientific phenomena. It is a well-known fact that today's young people find it difficult to maintain a permanent engagement when learning about science in the school curriculum. Often, they easily become disinterested when teachers use conventional teaching methods. We know that today's younger generation has a largely positive attitude towards digital technology. They are used to a high level of interactivity in their use of content, for example through digital games or other common software applications. In the context of the intervention of digital tools in (not only) STEM education, but we can also therefore speak of their high motivational potential, which attracts students, draws them in and arouses their interest in scientific and technical knowledge. In the relevant literature, we find a number of well-established methodologies of how the integration of innovative software tools and technological solutions into different educational situations influences students' learning and their engagement in STEM subjects (compare with [7, 8]).

In general, digital didactic tools are important aids for the teacher in the preparation for the lesson, but also in the course of the lesson itself. The development of innovative digital didactic tools and teaching aids gamified educational applications, virtual learning environments, all this requires a certain level of didactic-technological competences from educators so that they feel properly prepared for their implementation in the classroom and are not afraid to use these means in their pedagogical activities (see [9]). According to [10, 11] these realities must be reflected in undergraduate training, which raises the need to continuously innovate the curricula of the relevant part of the undergraduate curricula of the pre-service teachers' training in order to familiarize them with the advantages of teaching supported by the latest digital means. The question is how to finalize the optimal model of preparing future teachers in the field of didactic-technological competences, which specific digital means and which aspects of their use in the teaching process should be emphasized.

The most commonly used digital tools to support an engaging and interesting way for students to interact with science while increasing their access to hands-on science/technical education are interactive virtual laboratories with incorporated gamification elements, software tools for virtual simulation and modelling, and virtual and augmented reality applications.

With advances in the availability and sophistication of digital technologies, software tools for 2D and 3D virtual simulation and modelling are becoming a unique tool to support STEM-based subject learning by providing opportunities to manipulate both virtual and real-world environments. The interactive user-interface of these software tools with iterative manipulation features help students to design and observe realistic science experiments multiple times, helping them to develop an understanding of a particular scientific phenomenon and thus develop knowledge fundamental to the STEM field. A simulation is usually built on a basic model representing a real-world situation by using different forms of expressing the dependencies between the model components. The idea is to expose students to a significant abstraction of some physical phenomena or ecosystem process that is based on some real-world behaviour (compare with [12]). Virtual simulation and modelling software tools can provide students with access to knowledge that is normally unobservable, such as the natural process of seed germination and its transformation into a healthy plant. These software tools can also be used to expose students to various realistic physical phenomena in the virtual physical world, such as the change in the length of a person's shadow according to the position of the sun in the sky, or some meteorological phenomena, such as the movement of storm currents in different parts of the Earth.

A current trend in education of teacher training students of primary level onwards is linked to augmented and virtual reality, which allow students to explore complex concepts in immersive ways. In a meta-analysis of twenty-eight selected studies, authors in [13] concluded that the use of augmented and virtual reality technology is specifically appropriate in STEM subjects taught within an interdisciplinary and applied approach, where the four disciplines (science, technology, engineering, mathematics) are interconnected into a cohesive educational paradigm based on the application of knowledge to the real world. Subjects belonging to STEM often struggle to motivate students to study them, and it is augmented and virtual reality, which offer an innovative way of interpreting the curriculum to students, that can help with this problem and increase their motivation (see [14]). Augmented reality is software that is used on a smart digital device such as a tablet, smart (AR) glasses or smartphone to transfer digitized objects, components into a real-world image, thus creating an interactive learning experience for students and pupils. According to [15] virtual reality takes this process even further. Instead of projecting onto the real environment, virtual reality creates an entirely new digital environment that can be viewed in a 360-degree format. Through virtual reality, the user is in a fully immersive environment where he or she loses interaction with the surrounding real world and is thus fully immersed in the action in the virtual environment. Whether the learning takes place in a school classroom or in the students' home environment, using virtual reality software applications specially developed for learning and educational purposes, students can, for example, delve into the individual systems of the human body, virtually visit remote historical sites around the world, or find themselves in the lap of nature, where students learn about concepts such as vaporisation or condensation by observing the water cycle in nature and the formation of precipitation. By using augmented and virtual reality in the classroom, students and pupils can grasp challenging ideas in a more tangible way, supporting deeper understanding and increasing engagement in STEM subjects.

To support STEM education, the usage of appropriate educational software and AR applications are popular among pupils as early as the first year of primary school, providing pupils with an excellent introduction to engineering and computer science. The educational software, ICT tools and AR applications has been proven in many analytical studies to be a successful tool for hands-on learning of STEM topics for elementary school students (compare with [16]), which builds on Papert's [17] pioneering work in constructivism and constructionism.

By integrating these innovative digital tools into STEM education, whether by teachers or students themselves, we can make STEM education in primary and secondary schools more engaging, interactive and fun for students. These tools complement conventional teaching methods and allow students to better understand complex theoretical concepts applicable in academia and industry, while developing the basic skills they need to fully apply themselves in modern society [18].

3 Context and Methodology of the Research

In the following part of this paper, it will be described the research conducted with future primary education teachers at the Faculty of Education of Comenius University in Bratislava. In Slovak conditions, primary education teacher training is a master's program, which follows the bachelor's study of the pre-primary education teacher training program. The research activities carried out with these students focus on the usage of the AR Ruler application as a tool for introduction of the notion length, which is appropriate for the primary education level.

3.1 Augmented Reality and the Notion of Length in Primary Education

According [19] Augmented Reality (AR) is a technology that enriches the real physical world with computer-generated 3D virtual objects, where users can interact on the screen of devices such as camera, smartphones, or tablets. Also, augmented reality is a technology that combines two-dimensional or three-dimensional virtual objects in a three-dimensional real environment and then reflects these virtual objects in real time. Augmented reality allows a person to see or otherwise perceive the computer-generated virtual world integrated with the real world. Augmented reality, which enables interaction between computer-generated objects and the real world, is an application concept that unites the physical world (real objects) with the digital world. Some AR applications allows some measurements, the application AR Ruler can measure the length of line segments at some outdoor objects (for example the height of some building).

The notion of length is introduced according to Slovak National Curriculum in primary education level (see [20]) in the frame of the thematic area "Geometry and measurement". The second year of the primary education level is focused on: length units: millimetre (mm), centimetre (cm), metre (m); length of a line segment in centimetres; comparing and arranging line segments using a strip of paper, measuring, and estimating. The third year continuous in this topic in following way: length of the line segment in millimetres; length, width, measurement; units of length: millimetre (mm), centimetre (cm), decimetre(dm), metre (m), kilometre (km); distance, distance measurement, distance comparison; estimated length, actual length.

3.2 Methodology of the Research Devoted to the Notions Estimated Length and Actual Length

The research was realized with the sample of 17 students in seven couples and one trio during summer semester of the academic year 2022/2023, who obtain additional volunteer outdoor activity devoted to the usage of the application AR Ruler. These students were part-time students of the master study program "Teacher Training for primary education" at the Faculty of Education, Comenius University in Bratislava, Slovakia. Firstly, they estimate the height of historical buildings and monuments and secondly, they measure this height with the application AR Ruler. Additional task was to find in different informational sources the description of the used historical buildings and monuments from the historical and architectonic point of view. For this reason, the task obtained the creation of the educational portfolio for the prepared and proposed activity by every student group.

The advantage of this sample of students was, that one half of them work in the primary school as unqualified teachers, who will through the part-time study obtain the needed qualification. For this reason, these students from school practice also prepared proposal for teaching hour for the class. There were formulated following research question:

1. How will the future teachers of primary education integrate the application AR Ruler in STEM education and which abilities of the pupils they will develop in the frame of the interdisciplinary introduction of the notion of length?
2. Which kind of different possible connection between mathematics and other STEM education fields see the future primary school teachers such suitable for their pupils?

It was used a qualitative educational methodology for research. Qualitative research according [21] involves investigating actions and issues within their natural environment to gain a comprehensive picture of selected phenomena based on the data and the specific relationships between the researcher and the research participants (in this case the sample of the mentioned part-time students). Data collection was conducted through the collection of educational student portfolios and questionnaire bellow (compare with [22]).

There were formulate following question for research purposes in the questionnaire given for every student group:

1. How would you use the proposed activities by your group in the classroom?
2. How would these activities suggest by you promote pupils' digital skills?
3. How would these activities suggest by you develop pupils' estimation skills?
4. How these activities proposed by you would contribute to expanding pupils' cultural knowledge and understanding of architecture, art in terms of interdisciplinarity of the STEAM education?
5. How would these activities proposed by you contribute to increasing pupils' technical knowledge (the building materials used in the building, the way the building was constructed, etc.)?
6. How your proposed activities connect artistic competences with geometric/mathematic pupils' knowledge?

4   Results and Discussion

4.1   Outdoor and Indoor Activity from the Educational Portfolio

It will be presented the educational portfolio prepared by one group of students, which combine outdoor activity with the usage of application AR Ruler and indoor activity with manipulatives suitable for pupils in primary education level. This group of part-time students from the Faculty of Education, Comenius University in Bratislava, Slovakia were also teachers in primary school. For this reason, they realized the activities also with their pupils.

The name of the outdoor educational activity: Estimating and measuring the height of buildings and monuments.

Time and space of activity: 45 min outdoors.

Target group of pupils: 6–11 years (pupils in primary education level).

Activity objective: Exploring the following historical buildings in village Marianka (Slovakia): Basilica of the Nativity of the Virgin Mary, Chapel of St. Anne, Chapel of the Miraculous Well.

STEAM area: Mathematics, technology, art, architecture, engineering.

Connection to the topic from the Slovak National Curriculum: unit of length: metre (m); distance, distance measurement, distance comparison; estimated length, actual length.

Didactic resources and aids: AR Ruler application on the smartphone/iPad, pen, pencil, exercise book for notes.

The goal of the activity: Promoting pupils' appropriate knowledge of the concept of length based on pupils' knowledge, understanding and perception of their surroundings. Making cross-curricular connections between mathematics and the STEAM concept using knowledge about mentioned buildings.

Methodological procedure:

a) Introductory stage: In the first stage the teacher is on a walk with the pupils near the mentioned buildings in village Marianka (Slovakia). These buildings are in the same areal. The children discuss the mansion with the teacher and with each other. Questions: What geometric shapes can be found on these buildings? Are there symmetrical shapes? How old are these buildings? Who built them, what did it serve? What architectural style do these buildings present? What is the base unit of length? What is the height of these buildings?

b) Interactive outdoor stage: The goal of the educational activity is achieved based on suggestions for finding answers to the given questions by pupils and their practical implementation in individual form. Pupils estimate the height of the buildings and write them down in the prepared table. These they then measure using the AR Ruler app and write the measured values in the Table 1.

Table 1. Estimated height of the buildings and their height via AR Ruler application.

The name of the building	Estimated height of the building	Height of the building via AR Ruler application
Basilica of the Nativity of the Virgin Mary	19 m	26.63 m
Chapel of St. Anne	9 m	14.59 m
Chapel of the Miraculous Well	10 m	16.08 m

Following Figs. 1 and 2 demonstrate the measuring via AR Ruler application:

Fig. 1. Basilica of the Nativity of the Virgin Mary and the Chapel of St. Anne – the height via AR Ruler

c) Last stage – the architecture of the buildings: The village Marianka is the oldest Slovakian pilgrimage place since the end of 14th century. The most important buildings in this place are Basilica of the Nativity of the Virgin Mary, Chapel of St. Anne, Chapel of the Miraculous Well.

Basilica of the Nativity of the Virgin Mary was built in Gothic style in the year 1377. The original form of the church from the time of its foundation has not been preserved. It has during previous periods undergone extensive structural and stylistic development up to its present form. During the Hungarian uprisings it was plundered, burnt twice and the graves and tombstones were also plundered. Together with the monastery, it became an important pilgrimage destination. Tourist information sources only give the altitude of the basilica site as 221 meters above sea level (compare with [23]).

The Chapel of the Miraculous Well is Baroque building from the year 1696. After the Basilica of the Nativity of the Virgin Mary, it is the second most important building in Marianka. This is rotunda chapel above the spring. One of the chapel's stained-glass windows is depicted on a postage stamp issued by Slovak post in the "Easter" series and its inauguration took place on 10 March 2014 in the Basilica of the Nativity of the Virgin Mary.

Fig. 2. The Chapel of the Miraculous Well – the height via AR Ruler

Chapel of St. Anne is located south of the Basilica of the Nativity of the Virgin Mary. It was built in the year 1691 in the early baroque style. A pilgrimage is organized here every year.

The second activity was indoor manipulative teaching hour, which used the experiences of pupils from the previous outdoor activity.

The name of the indoor educational activity: We are playing at being builders.

Time and space of activity: 45 min indoors.

Target group of pupils: 6–11 years (pupils in primary education level).

Activity objective: Exploring the solids in space such cubes, rectangular cuboids. The usage of solids for preparing of models for different kinds of buildings from outdoor such hospital, school, residential house.

STEAM area: Mathematics, art, architecture, engineering.

Connection to the topic from the Slovak National Curriculum: unit of length: metre (m), millimetre (mm), centimetre (cm), decimetre (dm); distance, distance measurement, distance comparison; building blocks, cube, rectangular cuboid, solids from cubes and rectangular cuboids, ruler, tape ruler.

Didactic resources and aids: cubes, pictures of different buildings, cities and monuments, boxes, glue, scissors, pencils, colored paper, paints, brush, paper for drawing, pen, pencil, exercise book for notes.

The goal of the activity: Development of the ability to cooperate and communication between teacher and pupils, to follow the agreed rules, the creation of elementary knowledge of building structures and their rules, the concept of length and the unit of length. Development of fine motor skills and hand-eye coordination when manipulating objects. Making cross-curricular connections between mathematics and the STEAM concept using models of buildings.

Methodological procedure:

a) Introductory stage: Pupils work individually or in pairs. In this activity pupils build buildings with blocks appropriately according to their age (during the activity it can be used a template or a picture of the building plan, front, side, and top views). The motivation for the children will be to play the role of a builder who builds different buildings according to the designs presented. It will be build different buildings: an apartment building, a hospital, a school, shops, etc.

b) Interactive indoor stage realized with pupils in the class: Pupils can work with the cubes individually or in pairs. Throughout the activity they build buildings with blocks, using our imagination how looks like some shop, school, or church. The pupils built a small fort with the blocks. After that, using the prepared boxes, they made a drawing of their town based on the cube pattern, and drew a road and a park. Following Figs. 3 and 4 demonstrate their activity.

Fig. 3. The proposal of town from buildings blocks prepared by one group of pupils.

c) Last stage – the notion of length and its unit: Based on the previous outdoor activity, which pupils have already completed, they can check their knowledge of height, width, or length. The teacher, in the form of questions, discusses with the children develop the notion of length: Which building is taller? After that, the children can with ruler and tape ruler measure the height of their prepared buildings. It is work now with units: metre (m), millimetre (mm), centimetre (cm), decimetre(dm). It is possible to also put another question: What do we need to build a house? What colour is the hospital?

4.2 Questionnaire Research Results

The last part of the additional volunteer outdoor activity realized on mentioned sample of part-time students of the master study program "Teacher Training for primary education"

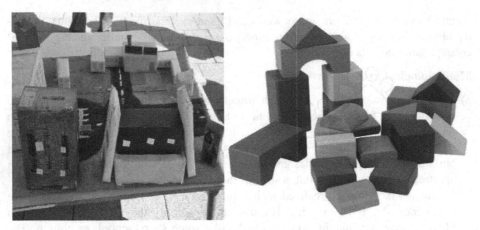

Fig. 4. The proposal of town from buildings blocks prepared by another group of pupils.

at the at the Faculty of Education, Comenius University in Bratislava, Slovakia was to answer the mentioned questionnaire from Sect. 3. It was sought through collecting students' answers of the questionnaire their opinions on the STEAM outdoor method utilizing augmented reality. This questionnaire has also the "feedback" function for their proposed outdoor activities.

The responses we received confirmed a high level of motivation among the students towards this approach. Employing a qualitative methodology, we evaluated the data collected from the mentioned sample of students. Here are the key findings based on the reflections and opinions of students, mostly already teachers in primary education:

a) Implementation in a primary school classroom: Children obtain the possibility getting to know your surroundings, the cultural sights that the places hide - staying outdoors. They would benefit various activities, e.g., hiking, travelling to sightseeing, etc. Other activities can be moving to a common destination, building with building blocks, learning new information. The proposed activity has applications in cognitive (finding out new information in different areas), motor (measuring and counting distances, work with ruler), and digital skills (using a mobile app to measure distance).

b) Promoting of children's digital skills: Children can not only use the usual measuring instruments (ruler and scale) but can also check the estimated and measured values via a mobile app or on the internet. They can also create a plan/drawing of the building using an interactive whiteboard (building with blocks, work with waste material, drawing, etc.). The mobile application for measuring length can be quite challenging for some children. Estimating the height of objects by measuring through the application many times had different variations. Often, measuring one object through the application took a long time and led sometimes to repeating the measurement. The promotion of children's digital skills is currently at a high level. They have access to devices such mobile, tablet, computer. Children are learning to use mobile phones for educational purposes. Using a ruler will support their ability to estimate the dimensions of objects (churches, buildings, castles, etc.).

c) Development of children's estimation skills: Children will obviously have very inaccurate estimations in the beginning. However, as the number of dimensions of the measured buildings increases, they will be able to use the heights of previous buildings as a reference for their future estimations (for example, building A is x times taller than building B). The best way to teach children to estimate the height of buildings is experiential learning, which means that children should see historic buildings. Estimating height from a picture is very imprecise and boring for children. Therefore, we propose to implement this activity in the form of a competition to encourage children to make better estimations. They will check their estimation via concrete outdoor activity.

d) Contribution to children's understanding of culture, architecture, and art in the frame of the STEM concept: Children would learn to describe different buildings (from lived experience or demonstrations). They would be able to name the style in which the buildings were built. They would gain knowledge about the materials that were used in the past to construct these buildings. At each monument/building is the possibility to read the information board. Children would be given information about the period when the building was built, what material it was made of, for what purpose, etc. They can use this information in other areas/subjects in school. They could draw the buildings, model them, make them out of waste material, etc. in the class. At the same time, they will get a general overview of historically important buildings, influential people, or life in the village/area of mentioned buildings.

e) Contribution to increasing children's technical knowledge: Children would gain knowledge of building materials/ techniques of construction in the past. They can compare historical buildings with buildings in the present day. They would become aware of the durability of a given material (how long it can withstand the weather, how strength is the material, what are suitable building materials). Children will be able to get to know the building material by touch during the outdoor activity.

f) Connection between artistic competences and geometric/mathematic children's knowledge: Children will understand the link between art and geometry in the construction of historic buildings. They will acquire aesthetic sensitivity. They will improve their creativity and imagination in making scale models of historic buildings. There is valuable the repeating of the primary level geometry and mathematics curriculum, such as: point, line, spatial geometric figures, units of measurement and their transformation. Children would become aware about the importance of mathematical and geometrical knowledge for the realization of a building. Builders and architects would not be able to design and build the buildings without the basic mathematical and geometrical knowledge. Fine art is also very important in completing buildings, both indoors and outdoors.

5 Conclusion

Based on the findings presented above – mostly from educational portfolios and answers to the research questionnaire, it is evident that the students' attitude to the usage of some AR application in STEM education reflect their positive attitudes towards the proposed activities, emphasizing their potential to enhance digital skills, cultural knowledge, and geometric understanding among primary school children.

Students successfully integrate the usage of application AR Ruler in STEM education as a tool for introduction of the notion of length and its unit through their proposed suitable outdoor activities, which respect the age of their pupils in primary education class. Students were at the center of the didactic process and develops several important competences, especially critical thinking, creativity, communication, and cooperation.

According to the majority of students' opinions these activities would definitely boost children's digital skills in primary level as they have to use a mobile application to measure the height of historic buildings. In doing so, the children learn patience, accuracy and precision, because the AR application in smartphone/iPad is sensitive to every movement. In fact, the children wouldn't even feel that they are revising and learning some geometry lesson.

At each monument during the outdoor activity there is an opportunity to stop and explain to the children from which period it comes, from what material it is built. The children could think of an activity that could be implemented already in the classroom (for example: drawing a building/monument that they have had the opportunity to get to know and also designing their own building – what material, dimensions of the building, what elements they would use). Children would gain knowledge of building materials/techniques by searching for information on the internet and then redrawing (e.g. a plan of the building, the material they would use) on paper or worksheet.

The Slovak curriculum expect the estimation of length also in indoor condition, it is possible to measure the height of the room in the building with help of AR Ruler (compare with [19]).

The research was limited by local conditions of the study program "Teacher Training for primary education" at the Faculty of Education, Comenius University in Bratislava, Slovakia in part-time form.

Although the students mostly carried out the activities as a volunteer alongside their jobs, they were interested in this way of teaching. In addition, it is a great advantage that the children have opportunity to explore their environment and to link their knowledge with mathematics and STEM concept.

Acknowledgment. This paper is supported by grant KEGA Nr. 026UK-4/2022 "The concept of Constructionism and Augmented Reality in STEM Education (CEPENSAR)", VEGA Nr. 1/0033/22 "Discovery-oriented teaching in mathematics, science and technology education" and Erasmus+ Project Reference: 2021-1-LU01-KA220-SCH-00003443 "STEAM-Connect: Co-creating Transdisciplinary STEM-to-STEAM Pedagogical Innovations through Connecting International Learning Communities".

References

1. Brynjolfsson, E., McAfee, A.: Race against the Machine: How the Digital Revolution Is Accelerating Innovation, Driving Productivity, and Irreversibly Transforming Employment and The Economy. Digital Frontier Press, Lexington, MA, USA (2011). http://b1ca250e5ed661ccf2f1-da4c182123f5956a3d22aa43eb816232.r10.cf1.rackcdn.com/contentItem-5422867-40675649-ew37tmdujwhnj-or.pdf. Accessed 08 Dec 2023

2. Pimthong, P., Williams, P.J.: Methods course for primary level STEM preservice teachers: constructing integrated STEM teaching. Eurasia J. Math. Sci. Technol. Educ. **17**(8), em1996 (2021). https://doi.org/10.29333/ejmste/11113

3. Caprile, M., Palmen, R., Sanz, P., Dente, G.: Encouraging STEM studies for the labour market (Directorate-General for Internal Policies: European Parliament). European Union, Brussels, Belgium (2015). https://www.europarl.europa.eu/RegData/etudes/STUD/2015/542 199/IPOL_STU(2015)542199_EN.pdf. Accessed 08 Dec 2023

4. Azuma, R.: A survey of augmented reality. Presence Teleoperators Virtual Environ. **6**(4), 355–385 (1997)

5. Arusoaie, A., Cristei, A.I., Chircu, C., Livadariu, M.A., Manea, V., Iftene, A.: Augmented reality. In: Proceedings - 12th International Symposium on Symbolic and Numeric Algorithms for Scientific Computing, SYNASC 2010, pp. 502–509. [5715329] (2011). https://doi.org/10.1109/SYNASC.2010.53

6. Kennedy, T., Odell, M.: Engaging students in STEM Education. Sci. Educ. Int. **25**(3), 246–258 (2014)

7. Hyatt, K., Barron, J., Noakes, M.: Video gaming for STEM education. In: Yang, H., Wang, S. (eds.) Cases on E-Learning Management: Development and Implementation 2013, pp. 103–117. Information Science Reference, Hershey, USA (2016). https://doi.org/10.4018/978-1-4666-1933-3.ch005

8. Nadelson, L.S., Seifert, A.L.: Integrated STEM defined: contexts, challenges, and the future. J. Educ. Res. **110**(3), 221–223 (2017). https://doi.org/10.1080/00220671.2017.1289775

9. Kosová, B., et al.: Vysokoškolské vzdelávanie učiteľov. Vývoj, analýza, perspektívy. [Higher teacher education. Development, analysis, perspectives]. Faculty of Education, Matej Bel University, Banská Bystrica (2012)

10. Kosová, B., Tomengová, A., et al.: Profesijná praktická príprava budúcich učiteľov [Professional practical training of future teachers]. Belianum, Banská Bystrica (2015)

11. Krumsvik, R.J.: Digital competence in Norwegian teacher education and schools. Högre utbildning **1**(1), 39–51 (2011)

12. Renken, M., Peffer, M., Otrel-Cass, K., Girault, I., Chiocarriello, A. (eds.): Simulations as Scaffolds in Science Education. SpringerBriefs in Educational Communications and Technology. Springer, Cham (2016). https://doi.org/10.1007/978-3-319-24615-4

13. Becker, K.H., Park, K.: Effect of integrative approaches among science, technology, engineering, and mathematics (STEM) subjects on students' learning: a meta-analysis. J. STEM Educ. Innov. Res. **12**(5/6), 23–37 (2011). https://www.jstem.org/jstem/index.php/JSTEM/article/view/1509/1394. Accessed 03 Jan 2024

14. Chowdhury, B.T., Holbrook, J., Rannikmäe, M.: A model conceptualizing trans-disciplinarity within school science education based on a systematic literature review. Int. J. Sci. Educ. 1–23 (2023). https://doi.org/10.1080/09500693.2023.2281007

15. Villena-Taranilla, R., Tirado-Olivares, S., Cózar-Gutiérrez, R., González-Calero, J.A.: Effects of virtual reality on learning outcomes in K-6 education: a meta-analysis. Educ. Res. Rev. **35**, 100434 (2022). https://doi.org/10.1016/j.edurev.2022.100434

16. Fuchsova, M., Koreňová, L.: Visualization in basic science and engineering education of future primary school teachers in human biology education using augmented reality. Eur. J. Contemp. Educ. **8**(1), 92–102 (2019). https://ejce.cherkasgu.press/journals_n/1553683729.pdf. Accessed 03 Jan 2024

17. Papert, S.: Mindstorms: Children, Computers, and Powerful Ideas. Basic Books Inc., New York, NY (1980)

18. Kuna, P., Hašková, A., Borza, Ľ.: Creation of virtual reality for education purposes. Sustainability **15**(9), Article number 7153 (2023). https://doi.org/10.3390/su15097153

19. Aydoğdu, F., Kelpšiene, M.: Uses of augmented reality in preschool education. Int. Technol. Educ. J. **5**(1), 11–20 (2021)

20. ŠVP Matematika – primárne vzdelávanie [Slovak State Educational Curriculum Mathematics – Primary Education] (2014). https://www.statpedu.sk/files/articles/dokumenty/inovovany-statny-vzdelavaci-program/matematika_pv_2014.pdf. Accessed 08 Dec 2023
21. Severini, E., Kostrub, D.D.: Kvalitatívne skúmanie v predprimárnom vzdelávaní [Qualitative research in pre-primary education]. Rokus, Prešov (2018)
22. Luttrell, W.: Qualitative Educational Research Readings in Reflexive Methodology and Transformative Practice. Routledge, New York (2010)
23. Basilica of the Nativity of the Virgin Mary. https://goslovakia.sk/en/points-of-interest/345965-basilica-of-the-nativity-of-the-virgin-mary-marianka-marianske-udolie. Accessed 08 Dec 2023

IoT in Education: Using Open Data

Filipe T. Moreira[1,2](✉) (iD), Mário Vairinhos[2] (iD), and Fernando Ramos[2] (iD)

[1] Polytechnique of Guarda, Guarda, Portugal
`filipertmoreira@ipg.pt`
[2] DigiMedia – Digital Media and Research Centre of University of Aveiro, Aveiro, Portugal
`{mariov,fernando.ramos}@ua.pt`

Abstract. We are experiencing a moment where the amount of data, knowledge, and technological devices are changing the mindset of institutions in their teaching and learning processes. Furthermore, technologies such as the Internet of Things have been interpreted as having a transformative potential in Education. This article addresses the use of open data obtained through the Internet of Things technologies and provided by different institutions as a didactic resource for the approach of physics, chemistry, geography, and mathematics contents with 7th grade students. This topic arose because the development of IoT has been linked to the proliferation of open data and its potential to contribute to the democratization of access to information. The results presented focus on the perceptions and opinions of the students and teachers involved. Both groups, students, and teachers, recognized the potential of using open data in education.

Keywords: Internet Of Things · Open data · Education · Educational Technologies

1 Introduction

We are experiencing a moment where the amount of data, knowledge, and technological devices are changing the mindset of institutions in their teaching and learning processes [1]. Furthermore, technologies such as the Internet of Things (IoT), with prominence in recent years, have impacted different areas of human activity, setting an example:

- mobility and transport [1–5];
- healthcare [6–9];
- the development of intelligent environments – smart cities for example [10–15];
- trade [16–18];
- and, the area that in the context of this article is of most interest, education [19–23].

In the case of education, it should be noted that IoT can be used from different perspectives. One perspective corresponds to the use of these technologies to assist school management (control of people, resources, access to or quality of physical spaces, etc.), this being the least relevant in the scope of this study. Another perspective corresponds to the development of courses aimed at their analysis and as an object of study, and the last one corresponds to their use as a didactic tool to approach different contents.

Ł. Tomczyk (Ed.): NMP 2023, CCIS 2130, pp. 351–363, 2024.
https://doi.org/10.1007/978-3-031-63235-8_23

Thus, this article presents a study carried out with 7th grade students, during a school year, where IoT technologies were used as a didactic tool, through data obtained through institutions that share their data openly. The main results and conclusions about the opinions and perceptions of the students and teachers involved are highlighted.

As regards the organisation of this article, we initially present an introductory approach to IoT in Education. Subsequently, the methodology followed, and the results and conclusions obtained are presented.

2   Internet of Things

More than 20 years after the term Internet of Things was first used, it seems that its definition still does not generate full consensus [1–4]. This is the reason why it was decided to insert this section in this article. The explanation for this lack of consensus comes from the fact that different authors present definitions based on their areas of activity or have visions more or less focused on different paradigms such as; the Internet; the "Things"; or for Semantic [2].

It seems that IoT emerges as an aggregating term for several technologies that allow the extension of the Internet and the Web to the physical world, through the widespread deployment of spatially distributed devices with embedded identification, detection, and/or actuation capabilities, which will enable the emergence of new applications and services in the future [5].

This vision of IoT as a set of technologies that enables the creation of a smart grid seems to have been gaining followers in the last decade, highlighting Xia et al. [6], Miorandi et al. [5], Dorsemaine et al. [7], Ray et al. [8]. Often the definitions are adapted according to the context.

Given this lack of consensus, it was decided to develop a definition that would allow the creation of a basis for action for the work to be developed. Consequently, based on the literature review, our research context and contact with experts in the field, the following definition was developed: The Internet of Things is a set of technologies that allows the creation of a network of devices, objects, animals, and plants equipped with ubiquitous intelligence that facilitates the interconnection or communication of data between them, enabling a deeper layer of understanding of the world to be achieved.

3   IoT in Education

In Education, it has been noted that despite the interest of academics [9] and the development of some IoT-related research projects in recent years, especially in the last decade [10–13], there is still a long way to go to understand the profound transformation that IoT can bring to teaching and learning, including the exploitation of these technologies as a teaching resource [14], which as mentioned is the aspect that most interests us.

However, despite the still lack of research, projects and the still premature state of IoT implementation in educational settings [15], it is possible to highlight that these technologies open the way for objects to evolve from passive to active elements, promoting their centrality - or even autonomy - in supporting the teaching and learning process [16]. That is, any object will have the possibility to become a smart object. This becomes especially relevant when nowadays it is common for young people, namely young Portuguese students, to have smartphones that facilitate access to the Internet anywhere and anytime [17].

In addition, the Internet of Things is changing the way people interact with each other, the way people interact with objects, and the way objects interact with each other [18]. This emerging reality is creating a new paradigm, where the world becomes more interconnected, which in turn is causing radical changes not only in lifestyles but also in ways of working, communicating, leisure, and learning [14].

In this new paradigm, associated with the ubiquity of the Internet, it is possible to access data from anywhere and manipulate everyday objects using, for example, a smartphone (or household appliances, wearables, etc.). Human beings are now able to measure, infer, understand, and even act on their environment [19, 20] through the ubiquitous presence of everyday objects connected to the Internet.

With this paradigm shift, it can be expected that IoT technologies will facilitate new opportunities in different fields, where education is not excluded [18, 21–23]. With a large number of objects connected to the Internet, a huge amount of data will be produced. This may give rise to a new way of reading, understanding, and interacting with reality, namely the emergence of hypersituated environments [24]. However, it is necessary to prepare students and teachers to work with IoT technologies to be able to understand these technologies, interpret large amounts of data, and adopt ethical and sustainable behaviour when dealing with this data and with the power of these technologies.

From the point of view of technological solutions for the use of IoT in Education, as a teaching resource, three approaches stand out: one centred on IoT devices, essentially oriented towards the exploitation of local resources; another, centred on open data feeds provided by institutions; and a third that combines the use of local devices and the use of open data feeds.

In the scope of this study, we focus on the approach using open data feeds from different institutions. These data, openly disseminated, can be obtained from different means, being, as previously mentioned, one of them the IoT systems themselves. Take the example of the real-time noise monitoring project in the municipality of Matosinhos that, using different technologies, created IoT systems that allowed connecting the noise monitoring stations to the network making the data available in real-time.

Open data can be interpreted as an asset, as it has the potential to be easily used in the development of personalized learning activities to meet the curriculum objectives, allowing students to lead, if necessary, the adaptation of the planning [25], and can also be a contribution for students to develop an argumentative discourse [26]. This is because the use of open data in educational activities allows, in addition to the learning of specific content, teachers to incorporate a civic education component in their lessons, which complements the curriculum. In this line Huijboom & Broek [27] argue that the publication of government data can allow citizens to exercise their democratic rights, stressing that this type of data can also be considered an excellent resource for teaching.

From the point of view of potentialities, the use of this type of data (i) blurs the economic and technical difficulties of creating and sustaining IoT systems, by schools or teachers and, (ii) guarantees the probity of the data.

The challenges of this approach include the need to collect and compile data sources so that teachers and students can access them directly and in context with the reality of the curriculum. This is because, although many institutions make data available openly, these data are not organised. This fact can demotivate and discourage teachers from use these data as an educational resource since they must carry out research in advance and this can be time-consuming. Also linked to this challenge is the need to develop teaching guides to make it easier for teachers to use this data.

Another challenge is to ensure that the data is always openly available. This is because the provider may change the availability of the data at any time, which could make its use unfeasible. For instance, one of the resources used in this study (Sunburn Map) is no longer available online.

Finally, it is understood how data is made available may be a challenge. This is because some institutions make data available in raw form. While this may be an added value as it will be an opportunity for students to develop competence in data processing, the truth is that for younger students it may be a barrier to its use. This is one of the reasons why we chose to use data with a visual representation and worked out in advance.

4   Methodological Process

This article presents part of a broader investigation. The wider research was of a mixed nature, because as well as having the objective of developing prototypes for education (that follow a continuous and integrated process with activities of design, implementation, and readjustment of the same [28]), also aimed to evaluate a particular educational environment. In these studies, the researcher collects, analyses, and integrates qualitative and quantitative data in the study [29] combining them, thus making it possible to obtain quantitative numerical data, on one hand, and qualitative concepts, attitudes, and opinions of the interviewees on the problem investigated, on the other [30].

Regarding the methodological approach, considering that the aim is to identify and elaborate practical and innovative solutions to problems in education, as well as develop effective learning environments that assume the use of natural laboratories to investigate teaching and learning [31] we opted for the approach Design-Based Research (DBR).

From the procedural point of view, as illustrated in Fig. 1, we followed seven phases of research development. Initially, we analyzed the syllabuses of the different subjects of the 3rd Cycle of Basic Education (7th to 9th grade). The areas chosen were Natural and Physical Sciences, Mathematics and Geography. Based on this analysis of the syllabus, a database of platforms that provided open data and that could be used in this context was carried out.

Once this database was completed, the process of developing the didactic tasks began. During this phase, we were informed that it would only be possible to work with 7th graders. Due to this constraint, the tasks carried out only considered this year of schooling.

After the development of the first version of the batteries of tasks, they were analyzed and validated through a focus group with teachers of the mentioned areas. The contributions obtained from these teachers allowed for an improvement of the battery of tasks, which led to the second version of the battery of tasks, which was later validated

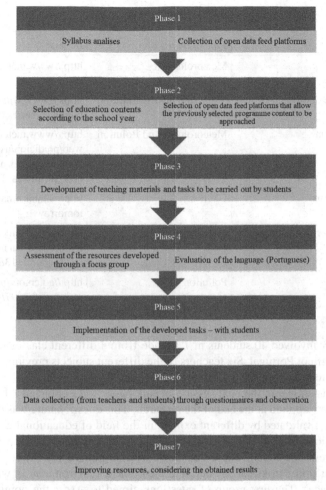

Fig. 1. Methodological process scheme

by experts in Portuguese language and didactics to ensure that the vocabulary would be the most correct and perceptible to students and that the sessions were by the intended objectives.

The tasks developed were organized into four sessions with the students. During each session, the students were given a script with various tasks. For each task, the students had to analyze the open data feeds to answer the proposed questions. The intermediate tasks for obtaining the answers to the questions allowed for the mobilization of knowledge in the areas of Natural and Physical Sciences, Mathematics, and Geography.

It's important to highlight that, during these sessions, some contributions from the students emerged, which led to some changes in the tasks.

Within the scope of this study, it was important that the open data sources were constantly updated, preferably in real-time. The selected platforms are listed in the table below (Table 1).

Table 1. Open Data Sources

Source	Type of data	Access
1. Meteocoruna	Meteorological	http://www.meteocoruna.com/
2. Weather Underground	Meteorologic and Polution	https://www.wunderground.com/weather/es/barcelona
3. Meteogalicia	Meteorologic and Polution	http://www.meteogalicia.gal/web/predicion/uv/predicion NumericaIndex.action?request_locale=es
4. Sunburn map	UV Index	http://sunburnmap.com/es/# tomorrow
5. State Meteorological Agency (AEMET)	Meteorological	http://www.aemet.es/en/elt iempo/observacion/ultimosda tos?k=gal&l=1387
6. AQICN	Pollution	http://aqicn.org/map/portugal/pt/#@g/40.8297/-0.0549/6z

This study involved 40 students in 7th grade from 4 different classes in a school in the central north of Portugal. Six teachers of the different subjects previously mentioned also participated.

The results shown in the next session of this paper were obtained through a questionnaire survey applied at the end of the research. This questionnaire was developed by the authors and validated by different experts in the field of educational didactics.

The questionnaire survey had a total of 42 questions (students' version, the teachers' version had less questions). These questions were organized into three main groups: open data platforms; tasks carried out; and the context (environment in which the sessions took place). The first group of questions aimed to assess the opinions of those involved regarding open data platforms. In particular, ease of access, and how the data was displayed. The second group focused on the proposed tasks, for example, their quality, scientific correctness, and mobilization of knowledge. The last group of questions focused essentially on the students' motivation about the context and the tasks carried out.

5   Results

The overall analysis of the results shows that the level of student satisfaction (answers 4 and 5) for all tasks is particularly high (82.5%), with an average of 4, as shown in the table below (Table 2).

Despite the high levels of satisfaction with the tasks performed, some students indicated that they would have preferred to work with data closer to their geographical reality, justifying that the data was closer to them, contextualised with the reality with which they are familiar.

Table 2. Level of satisfaction with tasks performed

		Students *(n = 40)*
Not at all satisfied	1	2,5% (n = 1)
Dissatisfied	2	5% (n = 2)
Undecided	3	10% (n = 4)
Satisfied	4	60% (n = 24)
Very satisfied	5	22,5% (n = 9)
Average Standard deviation		4,0 0,865
(4 + 5)		82.5%

In the Table 3 below it can be seen that, in general, students recognise the quality of the tasks and that they mobilise scientific knowledge. It should be noted that the teachers were all the opinion that the tasks were scientifically correct and that they mobilised the students' knowledge.

As for the motivation to carry out the tasks, most students showed that they were motivated to carry out the tasks and that they were more motivated to carry out the tasks than the traditional tasks (Table 4).

Table 3. Opinions from students and teachers about the tasks performed

Question			Students (n=40)	Teachers (n=6)
The proposed tasks present scientifically correct topics.	Totally disagree	1	2,5% (n=1)	0% (n=0)
	Partially disagree	2	0% (n=0)	0% (n=0)
	Undecided	3	12,5% (n=5)	0% (n=0)
	Partially agree	4	50% (n=20)	0% (n=0)
	Totally agree	5	35% (n=14)	100% (n=6)
	Average		**4,2**	**5**
	Standard deviation		**0,823**	**0**
The proposed tasks present a scientifically correct vocabulary.	Totally disagree	1	2,5% (n=1)	0% (n=0)
	Partially disagree	2	0% (n=0))	0% (n=0)
	Undecided	3	15% (n=6)	0% (n=0)
	Partially agree	4	42,5% (n=17)	0% (n=0)
	Totally agree	5	40% (n=16)	100% (n=6)
	Average		**4,2**	**5**
	Standard deviation		**0,781**	**0**
The time available for each task is adequate.	Totally disagree	1	2,5% (n=1)	0% (n=0)
	Partially disagree	2	0% (n=0)	0% (n=0)
	Undecided	3	10% (n=4)	0% (n=0)
	Partially agree	4	50% (n=20)	0% (n=0)
	Totally agree	5	37,5% (n=15)	100% (n=6)
	Average		**4,2**	**5**
	Standard deviation		**0,812**	**0**
Tasks mobilise scientific knowledge.	Totally disagree	1	2,5% (n=1)	0% (n=0)
	Partially disagree	2	0% (n=0)	0% (n=0)
	Undecided	3	7,5% (n=3)	0% (n=0)
	Partially agree	4	70% (n=28)	0% (n=0)
	Totally agree	5	20% (n=8)	100% (n=6)
	Average		**4,1**	**5**
	Standard deviation		**0,705**	**0**
The tasks promote an interdisciplinary approach to the issues.	Totally disagree	1	5% (n=2)	0% (n=0)
	Partially disagree	2	2,5% (n=1)	0% (n=0)
	Undecided	3	17,5% (n=7)	0% (n=0)
	Partially agree	4	57,5% (n=24)	33,33% (n=2)
	Totally agree	5	17,5% (n=7)	66,66% (n=4)
	Average		**3,8**	4,666667
	Standard deviation		**0,927**	
				0,471405
Tasks allow collaborative work (all work is done by everyone together).	Totally disagree	1	7,5% (n=3)	0% (n=0)
	Partially disagree	2	7,5% (n=3)	0% (n=0)
	Undecided	3	7,5% (n=3)	16,66% (n=1)
	Partially agree	4	37,5% (n=15)	66,66% (n=4)
	Totally agree	5	40% (n=16)	16,66% (n=1)
	Average		**4,0**	**4**
	Standard deviation		**1,203**	**0,57735**
The tasks allow cooperative work (the work is done by all, each one doing only the part assigned to him/her).	Totally disagree	1	10% (n=4)	0% (n=0)
	Partially disagree	2	2,5% (n=1)	0% (n=0)
	Undecided	3	20% (n=8)	0% (n=0)
	Partially agree	4	30% (n=12)	0% (n=0)
	Totally agree	5	37,5% (n=15)	100% (n=6)
	Average		**3,8**	**5**
	Standard deviation		**1,243**	**0**

Table 4. Students' perspectives on their motivation to carry out the tasks

Question			Students (n = 40)
I was motivated to do the tasks	Totally disagree	1	5% (n = 2)
	Partially disagree	2	7,5% (n = 3)
	Undecided	3	17,5% (n = 7)
	Partially agree	4	37,5% (n = 15)
	Totally agree	5	32,5% (n = 13)
	Average **Standard deviation**		**3,9** **1,108**
I have been more motivated for these activities than for those done with the textbooks	Totally disagree	1	12,5% (n = 5)
	Partially disagree	2	5% (n = 2)
	Undecided	3	7,5% (n = 3)
	Partially agree	4	37,5% (n = 15)
	Totally agree	5	37,5% (n = 15)
	Average **Standard deviation**		**3,8** **1,321**

From the analysis of the previous table, it is also possible to see that most students preferred these types of experimental activities to those that only involved the use of the textbook. As confirmed, of all the students, 37.5% stated that they partially agreed with the statement "I have been more motivated for these activities than for those carried out with the textbooks" and the same percentage stated that they totally agreed.

However, for the same question, about 12.5% of the students in Group 3 stated that they 'strongly disagree' and 5% that they 'partially disagree', a result underlined by a standard deviation greater than 1. This result may be caused by the data used not being related to the students' geographical context, so they do not feel any emotional and affective involvement with the resources leading them to a lower level of motivation. In justification, some students also stated (question 10) that as the information was not presented at once on the websites it was necessary to search (unlike in the textbooks), other students indicated that they preferred to work with data closer to their geographical reality.

Most of the students also indicated that they would like to carry out these tasks in class (Table 5).

Table 5. Students views on educational settings

Question			Students (n = 40)	Teachers (n = 6)
I would like to solve these tasks in my classes	Totally disagree	1	10% (n = 4)	0% (n = 0)
	Partially disagree	2	0% (n = 0)	0% (n = 0)
	Undecided	3	12,5% (n = 5)	0% (n = 0)
	Partially agree	4	45% (n = 18)	0% (n = 0)
	Totally agree	5	32,5% (n = 13)	100% (n = 6)
Mean			**3,9**	**5**
Standard deviation			**1,158**	**0**

6 Final Remarks

In this section we present some final remarks, however it should be noted that the sample of this work can be considered small, so generalizations are not possible. Yet, considering the sample, the use of open data allowed identifying a way to use IoT as a resource to approach syllabus contents without the use of IoT systems that permit obtaining local data. The use of this type of data, although in many circumstances it does not allow the use of data contextualized with the student's reality, proved to be an alternative for situations where it is not possible to obtain or create a local IoT system. On the other hand, this medium can be an excellent complement for certain themes, for example, to compare certain local factors with those of other regions.

In this respect, it is recalled that more and more institutions are making data openly available, a fact also correlated with the increasing demobilisation of IoT technologies. Such openly available data can contribute to the exercise of democratic rights [27], but can also be considered a didactic resource with the potential to contribute to the development of argumentative discourse [26] and carry out activities based on collaboration, analysis of information and data, communication of results and relating them to specific scientific or social problems [32] in an interdisciplinary way.

In this specific framework, there is still a need to develop a wiki that compiles open data sources and indicates what content can be addressed with these, as well as task proposals. This is because teachers expressed that their lack of knowledge about which data are available discourages its use as a teaching resource.

Finally, regarding the developed tasks, it was found that they allowed an approach to the previously selected syllabus contents. However, not being the objective of this study, it was also found that there is a need to develop more tasks that allow the approach of other contents.

From the developed tasks, there was a need to make some changes to promote a more collaborative work.

The teachers also highlighted the need to compile open data sources. Because accessing them is not always a direct or fast activity and on the other hand, they are not aware of most of the sources available in an open way. In addition to the creation of this compilation, it appeared as an added value that the textbooks themselves already come with these indications. Since this is still the most used educational resource and is also one of the main tools that students use to study.

These opinions refer to the transition from the current textbooks to what in the scope of this study is called a smartbook. That is a digital textbook whose data is constantly updated because of sources that use IoT technologies.

Considering the results obtained, it can be concluded that most students prefer to perform tasks involving the processing of data provided by IoT sources rather than by the textbook (which is still the main educational resource used in the Portuguese educational context [33]. However, there is a need for more in-depth and longer-term studies, as these results may be "inflated" due to the novelty of the teaching resources used by these students.

7 Future Work

In relation to future work in this area, we intend to:

- Develop new and extended didactic tasks for students and other didactic resources;
- Develop a repository (in wiki format) where a compilation of open data sources obtained through IoT is systemized;
- And develop a teacher training plan for the use of IoT technologies.

Acknowledgments. This work is financially supported by national funds through FCT – Foundation for Science and Technology, I.P., under the project UIDB/05460/2020.

References

1. van Kranenburg, R., Bassi, A.: IoT Challenges. Commun. Mob. Comput. **1**(1), 1–5 (2012). https://doi.org/10.1186/2192-1121-1-9
2. Atzori, L., Iera, A., Morabito, G.: The Internet of Things: A survey. Comput. Networks. **54**, 2787–2805 (2010). https://doi.org/10.1016/j.comnet.2010.05.010
3. Ben-Daya, M., Hassini, E., Bahroun, Z.: Internet of things and supply chain management: a literature review. Int. J. Prod. Res. **57**, 4719–4742 (2019). https://doi.org/10.1080/00207543.2017.1402140
4. Moreira, F.T., Magalhães, A., Ramos, F., Vairinhos, M.: The power of the internet of things in education: An overview of current status and potential. (2018). https://doi.org/10.1007/978-3-319-61322-2_6

5. Miorandi, D., Sicari, S., De Pellegrini, F., Chlamtac, I.: Internet of things: Vision, applications and research challenges. Ad Hoc Netw. **10**, 1497–1516 (2012). https://doi.org/10.1016/j.adhoc.2012.02.016

6. Xia, F., Yang, L.T., Wang, L., Vinel, A.: Internet of things (2012). https://doi.org/10.1002/dac.2417

7. Dorsemaine, B., Gaulier, J.P., Wary, J.P., Kheir, N., Urien, P.: Internet of Things: A Definition and Taxonomy. In: Proceedings - NGMAST 2015: The 9th International Conference on Next Generation Mobile Applications, Services and Technologies. pp. 72–77. Institute of Electrical and Electronics Engineers Inc. (2016). https://doi.org/10.1109/NGMAST.2015.71

8. Ray, S., Yier, J., Raychowdhury, A.: The Changing Computing Paradigm With Internet of Things : A Tutorial Introduction. IEEE Des. Test. **33**, 76–96 (2016). https://doi.org/10.1109/MDAT.2016.2526612

9. Petrović, L., Jezdović, I., Stojanović, D., Bogdanović, Z., Despotović-Zrakić, M.: Development of an educational game based on IoT. Ijeec - Int. J. Electr. Eng. Comput. 1, (2017). https://doi.org/10.7251/ijeec1701036p.

10. EL Mrabet, H., Ait Moussa, A.: Smart Classroom Environment Via IoT in Basic and Secondary Education. Trans. Mach. Learn. Artif. Intell. 5, (2017). https://doi.org/10.14738/tmlai.54.3191

11. Joyce, C., Pham, H., Stanton Fraser, D., Payne, S., Crellin, D., McDougall, S.: Building an internet of school things ecosystem. Proc. 2014 Conf. Interact. Des. Child. - IDC '14. 289–292 (2014). https://doi.org/10.1145/2593968.2610474

12. Lechelt, Z., Rogers, Y., Marquardt, N., Shum, V.: ConnectUs : A New Toolkit for Teaching about the Internet of Things. CHI Ext. Abstr. Hum. Factors Comput. Syst. 3711–3714 (2016). https://doi.org/10.1145/2851581.2890241

13. Temkar, P.R., Gupte, M., Kalgaonkar, S.: Internet of Things for Smart Classrooms. 203–207 (2016)

14. Lee, M.J.W.: Guest Editorial: Special Section on Learning through Wearable Technologies and the Internet of Things. IEEE Trans. Learn. Technol. **9**, 301–303 (2016). https://doi.org/10.1109/TLT.2016.2629379

15. Abbasy, M.B., Quesada, E.: Predictable Influence of IoT (Internet of Things) in the Higher Education. Int. J. Inf. Educ. Technol. 7, 914–920 (2017). https://doi.org/10.18178/ijiet.2017.7.12.995

16. Marquez, J., Villanueva, J., Solarte, Z., Garcia, A.: IoT in Education: Integration of Objects with Virtual Academic Communities. In: Rocha, Á., Correia, A.M., Adeli, H., Reis, L.P., Mendonça Teixeira, M. (eds.) New Advances in Information Systems and Technologies, pp. 201–212. Springer International Publishing, Cham (2016)

17. Mascheroni, G., Ólafsson, K.: Risks and opportunities . Second edition . Net children Go Mobile. (2014)

18. Bagheri, M., Movahed, S.H.: The Effect of the Internet of Things (IoT) on Education Business Model. Proc. - 12th Int. Conf. Signal Image Technol. Internet-Based Syst. SITIS 2016. 435–441 (2017). https://doi.org/10.1109/SITIS.2016.74

19. He, J.S., Lo, D.C., Xie, Y., Lartigue, J.: Integrating Internet of Things (IoT) into STEM Undergraduate Education : Case Study of a Modern Technology Infused Courseware for Embedded System Course. 2016 IEEE Front. Educ. Conf. 1–9 (2016). https://doi.org/10.1109/FIE.2016.7757458

20. Botta, A., De Donato, W., Persico, V., Pescapé, A.: Integration of Cloud computing and Internet of Things: A survey. Futur. Gener. Comput. Syst. **56**, 684–700 (2016). https://doi.org/10.1016/j.future.2015.09.021

21. Banica, L., Burtescu, E., Enescu, F.: The Impact of Internet-of-Things in Higher Education. Sci. Bull. Sci. **16**, 53–59 (2017)

22. Bakla, A.: A critical overview of Internet of Things in Education. Mehmet Akif Ersoy Univ. J. Educ. Fac. 302–327 (2019)
23. Quezada-Sarmiento, P.A., Enciso, L., Washizaki, H., Hernandez, W.: Body of Knowledge on IoT Education. 449–453 (2018). https://doi.org/10.5220/0007232904490453
24. Moreira, F.T., Vairinhos, M., Ramos, F.: Conceptualization of Hypersituation as Result of IoT in Education. Presented at the (2021). https://doi.org/10.1007/978-981-15-7383-5_6
25. Chui, M., Farrell, D., Jackson, K.: How Government Can Promote Open Data and Help Unleash Over 3 million$ in Economic Value. Innov. Local Gov. Open Data Inf. Technol. (2014)
26. Weinberger, A., Fischer, F.: A framework to analyze argumentative knowledge construction in computer-supported collaborative learning. Comput. Educ. **46**, 71–95 (2006). https://doi.org/10.1016/j.compedu.2005.04.003
27. Huijboom, N., Broek, T. Van Den: Open data : an international comparison of strategies. Eur. J. ePractice. 1–13 (2011)
28. Coutinho, C.P.: Aspectos metodológicos da investigação em tecnologia educativa em Portugal (1985–2000). Actas do XIV Colóquio AFIRSE. (2006)
29. Creswell, J.W.: Research design : qualitative, quantitative, and mixed methods approaches. SAGE Publications, Inc (2014)
30. Bringhenti, C., Lapolli, E.M., Friedlaender, G.M.S.: Técnicas de ensino do intraempreendedorismo. PPGEPS-Programa Pós Grad. em Eng. Produção. (2000)
31. Sandoval, W.A., Bell, P., Sandoval, W.A., Bell, P.: Design-Based Research Methods for Studying Learning in Context : Introduction Design-Based Research Methods for Studying Learning in Context : Introduction. **39**, 199–201 (2010). https://doi.org/10.1207/s15326985ep3904
32. Fischer, G., Rohde, M., Wulf, V.: Community-based learning: The core competency of residential, research-based universities. Int. J. Comput. Collab. Learn. **2**, 9–40 (2007). https://doi.org/10.1007/s11412-007-9009-1
33. Rodríguez Rodríguez, J., Álvarez Seoane, D.: A investigação sobre manuais escolares e materiais curriculares. Rev. Lusófona Educ. 9–24 (2017). https://doi.org/10.24140/issn.1645-7250.rle36.01

AI Literacy in Higher Education: Theory and Design

Michal Černý[✉] [ID]

Faculty of Arts, Department of Information Studies and Librarianship, Masaryk University in Brno, Arne Nováka 1, Brno 602 00, Czech Republic
mcerny@phil.muni.cz

Abstract. The study focused on defining AI literacy in the context of university education. New forms of education and content are required in a rapidly changing technological environment. Students may feel uneasy about the changes that the university and their everyday world bring. This study analyses the results of a workshop in which students (18) with deep education in AI were asked to work on a framework for AI literacy using the Delphi method. The students defined ten areas essential to AI literacy: general overview and theory; ethics and social impacts; learning and trend tracking; technological skills; practical experience; critical thinking and information literacy; authorship and plagiarism; privacy and security; and experience with tools.

Keywords: Artificial intelligence · AI literacy · Information literacy · ChatGPT · Google Bard · Delphi method · participatory research methods · Competency framework

1 Introduction

Development of artificial intelligence [1, 2] and the associated tools and societal changes, education systems are faced with the question of how to deal with it. ChatGPT 4 can successfully perform several tasks that are difficult for an average human to handle, including advanced certification [3, 4]; other large language models have similarly generated a great deal of discussion [5, 6] or image creation tools [7]. These systems raise ethical questions [8], social [9], and those relating to the university's operations. [10, 11].

We encounter emphasising a specific conservative policy carefully defining the issue of plagiarism, hallucination, or authorship [12, 13] but also approaches that emphasise the practical application or acquisition of competencies for the labour market [12, 13]. Tertiary education is also undergoing a specific transformation in the context of AI from 2022 onwards, as AI is considered one of the critical educational trends [14]. Many studies emphasise the dimension of personalised learning or the possibilities of games. Still, we see the issue of educating students on how they can work with AI themselves as a crucial topic [15–17].

Ł. Tomczyk (Ed.): NMP 2023, CCIS 2130, pp. 364–379, 2024.
https://doi.org/10.1007/978-3-031-63235-8_24

Artificial intelligence is entering the space of scientific operations and the way scientific publishing is fundamentally [18]. Artificial intelligence can support creativity [19], the creation of literature review [20], and many other steps of custom academic writing. This entails the need to be familiar with the tools and an emphasis on the ability to use them and think critically about them.

The gradual formation of the idea that we need to work with a new form of literacy, AI literacy [17, 19, 23, 24], should be seen as essential to transforming educational conditions and practices. We will be specifically interested in the tertiary education environment, which in this context is probably the most flexible and, simultaneously, the most strongly transformed environment [21–25].

It can be said that the topic of AI literacy is emphasised in the university environment. Still, at the same time, there is no consensus on how to define or delineate AI literacy. Laupichler et al. [23] understand it generally as the ability to use AI in practice. In such a conception, the role of university education is understood as mediating good practices, procedures, or a list of tools. In contrast, Chen et al. [30] emphasise the importance of technical skills and associate AI literacy with the ability to program and build practical systems in their everyday lives. Similarly, Lin et al. [24] emphasise the importance of AI literacy in STEM, i.e., they view it as primarily a technical skill associated with a particular ethical framework. Wiljer and Hakim [26] point out that there may be professions in which reflection on AI literacy will be different from the 'ordinary world', which they illustrate with the example of medicine by linking AI to transformative elements of practice and ethics.

However, as pointed out by Ng et al. [27], AI literacy is becoming a universally needed literacy that will be essential in all fields. It cuts across all levels of Bloom's taxonomy of educational goals. Students are not only users but will also solve future problems through it. According to them, AI literacy has four essential parts: 1) knowledge and understanding; 2) use and application; 3) creation and evaluation of AI tools; and 4) AI and ethics. All components are essential to AI literacy.

In the literature on AI literacy in general, it is possible to encounter several different understandings of what role this new form of literacy should play. Some studies understand AI literacy as a competence for everyday life, for the tasks and goals each person has to deal with immediately [21, 28, 29]. AI is changing the ways of dating, social interactions, leisure, and many other areas, and one needs to be able to work with these systems. Other studies focus on competencies for the labour market and competitiveness, emphasising the transformation of the labour market and the need for new skills to remain strong in this environment [30, 31]. Other studies focus on the relationship between AI literacy and technical skills, to which a social or ethical dimension is typically added, and these studies are characterised by their grounding in technical education [32–34]. The fragmentation of this approach leads to various trade-offs. Thus, some studies work with integrative synthesis [27], or one can encounter a system that sees AI literacy as a deepening of existing literacies [26, 35].

2 Methodology

Most studies focusing on AI literacy rely on respondents with no practical experience with AI or are professional students of specific fields. Our qualitatively oriented participatory design approach aimed to answer the question of how college students (with a non-trivial degree of AI expertise) view the phenomenon of AI literacy themselves, i.e. what competencies, knowledge, skills, attitudes a college student should have to be AI literate, or what topics should be the ones dealt with across disciplines in the process of their education.

The novelty of our study relies on a combination of three factors that are not common in studies:

a) We work with users who have completed at least ten-course lessons on AI's technical, social, and ethical aspects. So, you can say they have a certain level of expertise and experience with AI tools.

b) We used a variation of the Delphi study [36, 37] - Students first worked alone, then consulted their designs with AI (Bard or ChatGPT of their choice). In the second step, they had to seek consensus with another student. These pairs had to again reach an agreement among themselves in a foursome. Thus, during the workshop, students went through three rounds of consensus-building on the AI literacy framework.

c) The third unique aspect lies in the diversity of the group. A total of 19 students participated: 8 men and 11 women. They came from five faculties (Faculty of Computer Science (FCS) - 4, Faculty of Social Studies (FSS) - 2, Faculty of Economics and Administration (FEA) - 1, Faculty of Medicine (MF) - 1 and Faculty of Arts (FA) - 11). The maximum number of students per discipline was 4 for the Interactive Media Theory. The other fields had a maximum of two representatives (Table 1).

Table 1. Structure of participants by field of study.

Scope	Faculty	Gender
Computational linguistics	FA	Woman
Software Engineering	FCS	Man
Archaeology	FA	Man
English language	FA	Man
Information Studies	FA	Woman
Informatics	FCS	Man
Social pedagogy	FA	Woman
Spanish language	FA	Woman
Interactive Media Theory	FA	Woman
Security and Strategic Studies	FSS	Woman
Interactive Media Theory	FA	Woman

(*continued*)

Table 1. (*continued*)

Scope	Faculty	Gender
Interactive Media Theory	FA	Woman
Programming and application development	FCS	Man
Informatics	FCS	Man
Interactive Media Theory	FA	Woman
General Medicine	FM	Man
Public and social policy and human resources	FSS	Man
Computational linguistics	FA	Woman
Business economics and management,	FEA	Woman

The research questions are two:

- Q1: Is it a productive and functional power of such a methodology to create a competency framework model for AI literacy?
- Q2: How do students understand the phenomenon of AI literacy? What aspects or topics would they like to have in their university education profile?

2.1 Data Collection and Processing

The research design was built so students worked alone using ChatGPT or Google Bard in the first step. They were tasked with creating a competency framework for AI literacy in university students. They were given 20 min for this activity. In the second step, they formed pairs (randomly) and had to create one common framework again. They then published this as a post on the Padlet service. They likewise had 20 min for this activity. In the third step, they again created a common framework randomly (with two restrictions - they were not allowed to form groups with most students from the Faculty of Computer Science, nor purely groups with students from the Faculty of Arts). The students were tasked with finding a commonly shared framework through critical discussion rather than a simple intersection. This part lasted 40 min, and students again shared the results with their classmates and the instructor in Padlet. A diagram of the division and work on the frames is shown in Fig. 1.

This resulted in 4 separate competency frameworks of the highest level and eight due to pairs' work. One quad was a six, and one a five. One pair was a triple. These adjustments in the number of members are related to the impossibility of dividing 19 persons by four. Data collection occurred on December 16, 2023.

The Padlet outputs have been qualitatively interpreted and used to identify certain significant features of how AI literacies are self-imagined for university students. Data from Padlet was exported into individual documents (9 separate files) and then processed using open coding (Table 2) in Taguette. In it, we created groups of codes that were further applied to the student outcomes. We used open coding, understanding that codes were determined after the first reading of all documents from a particular group, and the actual coding occurred. Some categories were merged or split in the next step. Individual documents were randomly numbered and referred to as such in the results (AI1 to AI9 - for pairs and 4AI1 to 4AI4 for fours).

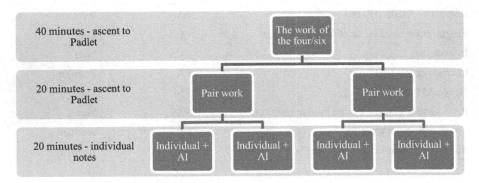

Fig. 1. Diagram of the student's work.

Table 2. Codes used for the first qualitative disaggregation of utterances.

Code	Meaning
Authorship	Answers related to copyright, citation and intellectual property protection issues
Security	Answers related to cybersecurity, systems security, cybercrime, and feeling safe or monitoring AI systems
Ethics	Answers related to the ethical use of systems and their social impact
Critical Thinking	Answers emphasise the role of human thinking, critical thinking, information assessment and evaluation
Tools	Answers emphasising specific tools and working with them
General knowledge	Answers related to the need for general awareness or knowledge of AI per se
Data Protection	Answers related to data protection, especially for specific users of AI-enabled systems
Technology	Answers related to understanding the technical workings of AI systems
Trends	Answers related to understanding, predicting and monitoring trends
Interest	Answers linked to general interest, motivation and willingness to engage with the topic of AI and education in it

2.2   Limits and Ethics of Research

Most students wrote their answers in Czech, so translating them into English is an anonymisation procedure. The ethics of the research is assured by complete anonymity; the students also did not provide any personal or sensitive data. The limitation of the study is, to some extent, the sample size and its fixation on a common educational foundation. Given the size of the research sample and the dynamic nature of the topic, this pilot study provides perspectives and topics for further broader research. This may have influenced the emphasis on some topics or, conversely, caused the omission of others. Also, the choice of other options for presenting the outputs than Padlet could have influenced the final form of the results. In the case of follow-up research, the coding of outcomes could be better handled by a more closed and larger research team.

3   Results

We divide the results of our research into two groups. In the first, we focus on the outcomes of pairs, and in the second on the effects of foursomes. Our research aims not to analyse the formal elements (for example, that one of the groups added literacy levels to the framework) or to study the structure of the frameworks but to do a content analysis that could be used to design a curriculum for university students.

3.1   Pair Work

As much as students emphasised the practice plane in casual conversations and throughout the coursework, almost all of their frames related to what might be termed general knowledge, a basic understanding of what AI is, how it works, and its limitations. This broad knowledge was further distributed into other answers that covered technical aspects, information literacy, critical thinking, etc. Thus, general knowledge provides a difficult-to-question basis for students to think further.

"Understand the basic principles of artificial intelligence - how to interact with it, how it gets information, whether it verifies information, what information it draws on." (AI2)

"General knowledge of AI/Theory: understanding the principles on which AI works." (AI1)

"Understanding how AI works (...) the history and evolution of AI." (AI4)

On top of the general knowledge - from the passages already mentioned - there is an area that touches on critical thinking. In the answers in this category, we can see aspects of information literacy (working with systems, making search queries, evaluating sources and information) and broader aspects of thinking about what information we work with, how reliable it is, and what significant errors it may have.

"Recognize and be able to verify the information obtained (remember to use your judgment; AI is not omniscient)" (AI1).

"Proper interpretation (teamwork) and subsequent integration of source material into your writing. What I can clock for the information I receive and what I don't need. Interdisciplinary collaboration with artificial intelligence experts. Developing the ability to collaborate with AI experts, data scientists, and ethicists to evaluate information generated by AI systems comprehensively. Librarians, teachers, ..." (AI9)

"Ability to identify errors, biases in data; ability to compare different tools and interpret results; understanding of risks associated with AI." (AI4)

"Critical thinking - Identify errors produced by AI - Be able to analyse generated texts - Be able to recognise errors produced by AI - Be critical of AI texts - Look for alternative solutions and improvements." (AI7)

At the same time, these selected examples suggest that students are well aware of the limitations of each tool and that critical work with them and placing individual responses in an overall context is essential to their work. AI is not a substitute for human thinking; it should be seen as a tool for which information literacy is necessary for its actual use. This is naturally linked to the need for authorship and the ability to cite appropriately, i.e. to avoid plagiarism:

"Knowledge of using academic citation styles to properly cite sources and references in written work. Use of proper citation standards." (AI9)

"Avoiding plagiarism: understanding the importance of originality and learning how to avoid plagiarism by citing sources correctly." (AI9)

"AI citation; AI-generated content ownership." (AI5)

Citation ethics is part of a broader range of topics that students connect to AI's ethical and social implications on humans, society, and their educational environment. Almost all pairs mention the moral aspect of working with AI, although they differ in their reflections' abstraction level or focus.

"Knowledge of the ethical, legal limits of AI use Understanding the ethical and societal implications of today's AI Using AI ethically and within the legal limits of a given country." (AI8)

"Understanding of the ethical issues associated with the use of AI and the ability to think about the implications (benefits, misuse, legal aspects, impact of using AI in personal and professional life or an academic setting)" (AI6).

"Transparency in AI; Social Impact; Safety; Potential Misuse." (AI5)

Knowledge of the tools is also an important level. Students typically adopt a pragmatist approach that integrates thinking and acting into one whole. Experience becomes irreplaceable, and AI literacy refers to the ability to use tools to accomplish specific tasks and goals.

"Ability to select an adequate tool for the intended purpose Ability to use AI tools effectively, or to combine them (Tips and Tricks, or what to want and what not to want from AI). Ability to apply." (AI1)

"Understanding the wide range of applications of AI - an overview of how AI is used in different industries (healthcare, finance, manufacturing, and services)" (AI2).

"Learning about specific areas where AI can be successfully applied." (AI9)

The combination of working with tools and ethics leads (subsequently) to conceptualising aspects related to the security and protection of personal data. Students seem to be able to perceive a specific polarity in the attractiveness of tools and their security risks and to accentuate this skill as one of the essential elements of the constitution of AI literacy.

"Security and working with data Technical troubleshooting Recognize and be able to verify information obtained (remember to use your judgment, AI is not omniscient) Privacy and data protection - the responsibility of working with tools." (AI1)

"Basic awareness of cyber security and safe use of AI tools." (AI6)

A heavily represented area that may be both a consequence and a cause of the above considerations is the consideration of the technical details and skills that AI students should have. As in the opening comment, it can be said that knowledge of the technical background is considered a prerequisite for critical use of a given tool.

"Understanding the technologies behind AI - LLM, Machine Learning, Programming Creating AI Systems." (AI8)

"Ability to continually educate yourself about AI (principles of learning about AI) Ability to come up with new ideas and uses for AI in unexpected areas To push the technology further, both in terms of programming/algorithmic and other practical applications." (AI1)

"How AI Works - Developing a basic understanding of the algorithms used in artificial intelligence systems, including machine learning models. This includes knowledge of supervised and unsupervised learning, neural networks, and other techniques." (AI9)

A final area that students frequently mentioned, which is not common in mainstream AI literacy models, is the ability to continually learn, understand, and reflect on trends. Students know the dynamics of AI and want to work with it systematically. In terms of sample saturation, this model represents one of the essential aspects of working with AI literacy in a university setting.

Ability to continually educate oneself about AI (principles of learning about AI) Ability to come up with new ideas and uses of AI in unexpected areas To push technology further, both in terms of programming/algorithmic and other practical applications (AI1)

Awareness of new developments in the world of AI Ability to analyse trends in AI development and their impact on the future. (AI8)

Active monitoring of new developments and innovations in AI and regular contribution to developments. (AI6)

Ability to adapt quickly to new tools and new updates; understanding of the impact in future employment; ability to develop their knowledge. (AI7)

3.2 The Work of Four

Compared to the answers of the pairs, it can be said that the students often sought a common framework as a kind of compromise that excluded marginal phenomena so that the documents overall give a shorter impression but are better structured and expressively more transparent, which emphasises the importance of collaboration and iterative compromise in broader user groups.

Students retained most of the categories, but some elements needed refinement. Regarding theory, students emphasise basic knowledge of the critical principles of artificial intelligence and neural networks.

"Knowledge of different AI tools (different applications) - the ability to use these AI tools based on the problem I'm solving. Ability to think strategically and implement the tool on a problem or case. Knowledge of the different applications and tools, having an overview of the development." (4AI3)

"Understanding the basic principles of artificial intelligence and machine learning Understanding the limits and limitations of AI." (4AI2)

"How AI Works - Developing a basic understanding of the algorithms used in artificial intelligence systems, including machine learning models. This includes knowledge of supervised and unsupervised learning, neural networks, and other techniques." (4AI4)

The emphasis on theory was present in all groups while at the same time corresponding to the focus on practice. Practical work with tools or systems became a kind of natural core or starting point for students' responses regarding AI literacy per se.

"Ability to identify and implement specific AI applications in different domains." (4AI3)

"Ability to articulate basic requirements and prompts. Working with input materials. Thinking strategically and implementing the tool for the problem, for the case." (4AI4)

"Learning how to use the app and understanding what the tool might be used for." (4AI2)

All groups also emphasised practice, which is similar to critical thinking or relating the phenomenon of AI literacy to information literacy. The students also conformed to the critical evaluation of tools and their outputs.

"Control of input and output data, critical interpretation of results." (4AI3)

"Recognize and be able to verify the information obtained." (4AI1)

"Proper interpretation (teamwork) and subsequent integration of source material into your writing. What I can clock for the information I receive and what I don't need." (4AI4)

The final area on which there appears to be agreement (albeit widely varied in content) is the category of ethical and social implications.

"The ethics of the source and "bias" - gender, race, ...generally evaluating the unintended consequences of the information AI gives us. Or even risk assessment. The ability to assess and resolve ethical dilemmas. Identifying potential biases and risks." (4AI4)

"Knowledge of the ethical, legal limitations of using artificial intelligence Knowledge of the legal limitations of a given state. Understanding today's AI's ethical and societal implications: Freedom of speech, bias." (4AI2)

"Understanding the ethics, implications, and legal and copyright laws, including implications for personal, professional, and safe use of AI tools and responsible data mining." (4AI3)

Other elements no longer form a coherent category but are in some ways significant to the problems and topics that students may address in the context of AI literacy. Thus, one can encounter (again) the issue of citation and copyright, but also the emphasis on personal development and continuous learning. Surprising is the focus on the AI literacy student being able to educate others. Competence is a matter of private ownership and a commitment to others.

"Ability to actively monitor trends around AI. Educate other people about AI. Building on existing knowledge." (4AI1)

"Openness to learn in AI." (4AI3)

"Avoiding plagiarism: understanding the importance of originality and learning how to avoid plagiarism by citing sources correctly." (4AI4)

"Implementing AI into day-to-day life." (4AI2)

The ability to learn can lead to creativity, finding new approaches, and understanding trends and their impact. As one of the groups states:

"Creativity and the ability to find innovative solutions in the face of constantly evolving technology." (4AI1)

4 Discussion

If we analyse the methodological framing of the study, it can be said that the three-phase model of competency framework development proved to be functional and produced exciting results. The critical point was that the students had a relatively long systematic education and were a strongly heterogeneous group that could project their specific experiences from different life paths, genders, and fields of study into working with AI.

In terms of model formation, some students worked with a gradual approach in which they differentiated skills into core and advanced skills. In contrast, others had a process associated with a structured but exhaustive enumeration.

What is remarkable is that students can integrate the different parts of AI literacy (competencies or sub-competencies) and work with the fact that they overlap and build on each other. In general, students identified the domains reported in the study by Ng et al. [17, 27]:

- For almost all research participants, a general overview and awareness of AI is a prerequisite for further work. Students cannot systematically define or relate to the topic without a basic overview.
- Technological skills have been the subject of broader discussion, and it can be said that we can encounter two basic narratives of this dimension. Some students emphasised the need to create new tools and perform at least simple programming and configuration of existing devices. The other part of the students was more inclined towards knowledge of the principles allowing them to evaluate better and work with the tools. This was also where they saw the importance of the technical dimension of AI literacy. The extent of technical skills will - probably in the future - be a subject of further discussion.
- Students understood ethical and social aspects more in terms of general declarations. They seem to be aware of the importance of the relationship between ethics and AI [38, 39] but fail to go into much detail or depth about it. In this area, we perceive a considerable discrepancy between the frequency of use of the word "ethical" and its more profound elaboration. Regarding the social aspects, students again resorted to general declarations or questions about changes in the labour market [13].
- Conversely, when it came to the knowledge of the tools, students were often comprehensive, emphasising specific areas of work (from general topics to support for specific scientific activities) and rating practical skill in using the applications as essential. AI literacy in this area is very similar to the Tool literacy mentioned earlier [40, 41].

In addition, students also brought in other topics that complement the model mentioned by Ng et al.:

- The issue of privacy, security, and data protection can be seen as ethical and has clear cybersecurity and legal overlaps. This knowledge is essential for the legality of use and protecting users' privacy. This aspect can only be seen in the European environment in the slow application of the GDPR and other standards [42, 43].
- Specifically, given that they are in an academic environment, students focused on the issue of authorship and plagiarism [44, 45]. These topics connect to her practice and simultaneously reflect the fundamentally changing nature of study and science.
- Students stress the need to follow new trends and educate themselves and others [46]. This perspective is not emphasised strongly enough in mainstream frameworks. The fact that students perceive a strong responsibility for themselves and others can be seen as positive. At the same time, AI literacy's core is the ability to monitor and evaluate trends and make further decisions based on them.
- The understanding of experience is also specific - it does not have the character of knowledge of using tools. Still, it reflects the experience of pragmatist philosophy, emphasising the absence of a distinction between acting and thinking [47, 48]. AI literacy presupposes an experience that is subsequently formative for thinking. This conception also allows us to explain why students work with the dimension of general understanding. It does not represent for them a mere theory but the other part of the bundle of thinking and acting. At the same time, however, we can also see an emphasis on the relevance of AI tools to the student's particular work or living environment [49]

- However, we consider the dimension referred to as Critical thinking and information literacy to be essential. Two important competence aspects appear in this dimension. First is the general emphasis on critical thinking, evaluating information, and maintaining appropriate distance. However, the link between AI literacy and information literacy is crucial. It seems that it cannot be said that AI literacy is a sub-component of information literacy or vice versa, but rather that they interact with each other. Students understand AI as a component of their information behaviour, entering the everyday plane [50, 51].

The students have thus conceived a model (Fig. 2) that shows how challenging and complicated the phenomenon of AI literacy is developed. At the same time, it is clear from the responses that students perceive the limited universality of models constructed in this way. In their responses, they referred to the practices and needs of their disciplines or emphasised the importance of disciplinary specificity. This model can be helpful in that it sets out a core curriculum. As balanced as the different areas are and may not be, neither in terms of the intensity of the education nor the amount of educational content, they indicate what courses working with AI literacy in a university setting might look like.

At the same time, we are aware that the prefigurative approach (or user-centred design approach) has its limits and weaknesses; students may not always be the ones to perfectly gauge the needs of their education and its proper goals [52]. Nevertheless, we

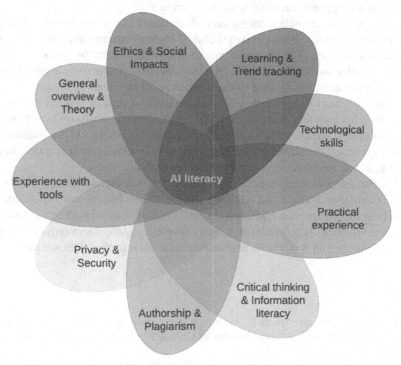

Fig. 2. The intersection of other specific domains constitutes AI literacy.

consider them to be crucial actors in the debate about the shape of the curriculum, which does not diminish the importance of academics in its design. Indeed, the relatively strong agreement with other studies suggests that the students' approach appears enriching and relevant.

5 Conclusion

The first research question can be answered unequivocally - yes. It turns out that the chosen methodology was productive and allowed the design of a specific model of understanding AI literacy, even though students are aware of the limits of such design for their particular fields and time.

For the second question, it is possible that students perceived a great deal of involvement in designing the model, which is captured in Fig. 2. This diagram shows a complex and multidimensional view of AI literacy in a university setting, capturing the dimensions of general overview and theory, ethical and social implications, learning and trend tracking, technological skills, practical experience, critical thinking and information literacy, authorship and plagiarism, co-creation and safety, and experience with tools.

AI literacy in the university environment will be one of the most essential technology topics in education and the entire university curriculum in the coming years. Students and teachers alike are faced with the challenge of how to work with these tools, and how to maintain the integrity of scholarly work and thinking while at the same time taking advantage of the opportunities that these tools bring.

Our research worked with a unique mix of students and was inspired by approaches applied in Delphi studies. It relied on the ideas of students (the participation dimension), who were also experts. The proposed model that is the output of this study (Fig. 2) provides a possible basis for the design of future courses that aim to develop AI literacy. At the same time, the multi-faceted model is efficient for the creation of learning objects.

The study showed that students perceive the topic as serious and necessary, but at the same time leaves some areas unresolved. There is no consensus on how to scale AI literacy, but also on the form and importance of technology skills. On the contrary, there seems to be a strong consensus on the requirement to link theory and practice, thinking and acting, as one structure, as stated by pragmatist philosophers.

It can also be considered crucial in our research that there is a clear relationship between information literacy and AI literacy [53, 54]. We believe that this relationship can also help to structure the educational tools, courses, and support in the case of AI literacy development, as information literacy is already quite commonly developed in university settings, and it might be practical to build on it further in this area.

References

1. Baidoo-Anu, D., Owusu Ansah, L.: Education in the era of generative artificial intelligence (AI): understanding the potential benefits of ChatGPT in promoting teaching and learning, (2023)
2. Tang, Z., Kejriwal, M.: A pilot evaluation of ChatGPT and DALL-E 2 on decision making and spatial reasoning (2023)

3. Choi, J.H., Hickman, K.E., Monahan, A., Schwarcz, D.: ChatGPT goes to law school (2023). https://papers.ssrn.com/abstract=4335905. https://doi.org/10.2139/ssrn.4335905
4. Lewandowski, M., Łukowicz, P., Świetlik, D., Barańska-Rybak, W.: ChatGPT-3.5 and ChatGPT-4 dermatological knowledge level based on the specialty certificate examination in dermatology. Clin. Exp. Dermatol. llad255 (2023). https://doi.org/10.1093/ced/llad255
5. Aydin, Ö.: Google bard generated literature review: Metaverse. J. AI. 7, 1–14 (2023). https://doi.org/10.61969/jai.1311271
6. Singh, S.K., Kumar, S., Mehra, P.S.: Chat GPT & Google bard AI: a review. In: 2023 International Conference on IoT, Communication and Automation Technology (ICICAT), pp. 1–6 (2023). https://doi.org/10.1109/ICICAT57735.2023.10263706
7. Marcus, G., Davis, E., Aaronson, S.: A very preliminary analysis of DALL-E 2 (2022). http://arxiv.org/abs/2204.13807. https://doi.org/10.48550/arXiv.2204.13807
8. ChatGPT and Publication Ethics: Rahimi, F., Talebi Bezmin Abadi, A. Arch. Med. Res. 54, 272–274 (2023). https://doi.org/10.1016/j.arcmed.2023.03.004
9. Abdullah, M., Madain, A., Jararweh, Y.: ChatGPT: fundamentals, applications and social impacts. In: 2022 Ninth International Conference on Social Networks Analysis, Management and Security (SNAMS), pp. 1–8. IEEE, Milan, Italy (2022). https://doi.org/10.1109/SNAMS5 8071.2022.10062688
10. Fauzi, F., Tuhuteru, L., Sampe, F., Ausat, A.M.A., Hatta, H.R.: Analysing the role of ChatGPT in improving student productivity in higher education. J. Educ. 5, 14886–14891 (2023). https://doi.org/10.31004/joe.v5i4.2563
11. Lo, C.K.: What is the impact of ChatGPT on education? A rapid review of the literature. Educ. Sci. 13, 410 (2023). https://doi.org/10.3390/educsci13040410
12. Cetindamar, D., Kitto, K., Wu, M., Zhang, Y., Abedin, B., Knight, S.: Explicating AI literacy of employees at digital workplaces. IEEE Trans. Eng. Manag. 1–14 (2022). https://doi.org/10.1109/TEM.2021.3138503
13. Zarifhonarvar, A.: Economics of ChatGPT: A labor market view on the occupational impact of artificial intelligence (2023)
14. Pelletier, K., et al.: 2023 EDUCAUSE horizon report, teaching and learning edition (2023)
15. Carolus, A., Augustin, Y., Markus, A., Wienrich, C.: Digital interaction literacy model – conceptualizing competencies for literate interactions with voice-based AI systems. Comput. Educ. Artif. Intell. 4, 100114 (2023). https://doi.org/10.1016/j.caeai.2022.100114
16. Eguchi, A., Okada, H., Muto, Y.: Contextualizing AI education for K-12 students to enhance their learning of AI literacy through culturally responsive approaches. KI - Künstl. Intell. 35, 153–161 (2021). https://doi.org/10.1007/s13218-021-00737-3
17. Ng, D.T.K., Lee, M., Tan, R.J.Y., Hu, X., Downie, J.S., Chu, S.K.W.: A review of AI teaching and learning from 2000 to 2020. Educ. Inf. Technol. 28, 8445–8501 (2023). https://doi.org/10.1007/s10639-022-11491-w
18. Dergaa, I., Chamari, K., Zmijewski, P., Saad, H.B.: From human writing to artificial intelligence generated text: examining the prospects and potential threats of ChatGPT in academic writing. Biol. Sport 40, 615–622 (2023). https://doi.org/10.5114/biolsport.2023.125623
19. Huang, J., Tan, M.: The role of ChatGPT in scientific communication: writing better scientific review articles. Am. J. Cancer Res. 13, 1148–1154 (2023)
20. Temsah, M.H., et al.: Chatgpt and the future of digital health: a study on healthcare workers' perceptions and expectations. Healthcare. 11, 1812 (2023)
21. Fyfe, P.: How to cheat on your final paper: assigning AI for student writing. AI Soc. 38, 1395–1405 (2023). https://doi.org/10.1007/s00146-022-01397-z
22. Kong, S.C.: Developing information literacy and critical thinking skills through domain knowledge learning in digital classrooms: an experience of practicing flipped classroom strategy. Comput. Educ. 78, 160–173 (2014). https://doi.org/10.1016/j.compedu.2014.05.009

23. Laupichler, M.C., et al.: Effect of a flipped classroom course to foster medical students' AI literacy with a focus on medical imaging: a single group pre-and post-test study. BMC Med. Educ. **22**, 803 (2022). https://doi.org/10.1186/s12909-022-03866-x

24. Lin, C.-H., Yu, C.-C., Shin, P.-K., Wu, L.Y.: STEM based artificial intelligence learning in general education for non-engineering undergraduate students. Educ. Technol. Soc. **24**, 224–237 (2021)

25. Southworth, J., et al.: Developing a model for AI across the curriculum: transforming the higher education landscape via innovation in AI literacy. Comput. Educ. Artif. Intell. **4**, 100127 (2023). https://doi.org/10.1016/j.caeai.2023.100127

26. Wiljer, D., Hakim, Z.: Developing an artificial intelligence-enabled health care practice: rewiring health care professions for better care. J. Med. Imaging Radiat. Sci. **50**, S8–S14 (2019). https://doi.org/10.1016/j.jmir.2019.09.010

27. Ng, D.T.K., Leung, J.K.L., Chu, S.K.W., Qiao, M.S.: Conceptualizing AI literacy: an exploratory review. Comput. Educ. Artif. Intell. **2**, 100041 (2021). https://doi.org/10.1016/j. caeai.2021.100041

28. Dai, Y., Chai, C.-S., Lin, P.-Y., Jong, M.S.-Y., Guo, Y., Qin, J.: Promoting students' well-being by developing their readiness for the artificial intelligence age. Sustainability **12**, 6597 (2020). https://doi.org/10.3390/su12166597

29. Kaspersen, M.H., Bilstrup, K.-E.K., Van Mechelen, M., Hjort, A., Bouvin, N.O., Petersen, M.G.: High school students exploring machine learning and its societal implications: opportunities and challenges. Int. J. Child-Comput. Interact. **34**, 100539 (2022). https://doi.org/10. 1016/j.ijcci.2022.100539

30. Henry, J., Hernalesteen, A., Collard, A.-S.: Teaching artificial intelligence to k-12 through a role-playing game questioning the intelligence concept. KI - Künstl. Intell. **35**, 171–179 (2021). https://doi.org/10.1007/s13218-021-00733-7

31. Williams, R., et al.: AI + ethics curricula for middle school youth: lessons learned from three project-based curricula. Int. J. Artif. Intell. Educ. **33**, 325–383 (2023). https://doi.org/ 10.1007/s40593-022-00298-y

32. Adams, C., Pente, P., Lemermeyer, G., Rockwell, G.: Ethical principles for artificial intelligence in K-12 education. Comput. Educ. Artif. Intell. **4**, 100131 (2023). https://doi.org/10. 1016/j.caeai.2023.100131

33. Mertala, P., Fagerlund, J., Calderon, O.: Finnish 5th and 6th grade students' pre-instructional conceptions of artificial intelligence (AI) and their implications for AI literacy education. Comput. Educ. Artif. Intell. **3**, 100095 (2022). https://doi.org/10.1016/j.caeai.2022.100095

34. Yi, Y.: Establishing the concept of AI literacy: focusing on competence and purpose. JAHR. **12**, 353–368 (2021). https://doi.org/10.21860/j.12.2.8

35. Long, D., Blunt, T., Magerko, B.: Co-designing AI literacy exhibits for informal learning spaces. Proc. ACM Hum.-Comput. Interact. **5**, 1–35 (2021). https://doi.org/10.1145/3476034

36. Crisp, J., Pelletier, D., Duffield, C., Adams, A., Nagy, S.: The delphi method? Nurs. Res. **46**, 116 (1997). https://doi.org/10.1097/00006199-199703000-00010

37. Townsend, L., Hofer, A., Hanick, S., Brunetti, K.: Identifying threshold concepts for information literacy: a delphi study. Commun. Inf. Lit. **10**, 23–49 (2016)

38. Nguyen, A., Ngo, H.N., Hong, Y., Dang, B., Nguyen, B.-P.T.: Ethical principles for artificial intelligence in education. Educ. Inf. Technol. **28**, 4221–4241 (2023). https://doi.org/10.1007/ s10639-022-11316-w

39. Bankins, S., Formosa, P.: The ethical implications of artificial intelligence (AI) for meaningful work. J. Bus. Ethics **185**, 725–740 (2023). https://doi.org/10.1007/s10551-023-05339-7

40. Kennedy, C.: Measuring information literacy: the "Tool Literacy" variable. For full text (1998). https://files.eric.ed.gov/fulltext/ED470643.pdf

41. DePietro, P.: Tool literacy. Counterpoints **435**, 15–25 (2013)

42. van Bekkum, M., Zuiderveen Borgesius, F.: Using sensitive data to prevent discrimination by artificial intelligence: does the GDPR need a new exception? Comput. Law Secur. Rev. **48**, 105770 (2023). https://doi.org/10.1016/j.clsr.2022.105770

43. Lorè, F., Basile, P., Appice, A., de Gemmis, M., Malerba, D., Semeraro, G.: An AI framework to support decisions on GDPR compliance. J. Intell. Inf. Syst. **61**, 541–568 (2023). https://doi.org/10.1007/s10844-023-00782-4

44. King, M.R.: ChatGPT: a conversation on artificial intelligence, Chatbots, and plagiarism in higher education. Cell. Mol. Bioeng. **16**, 1–2 (2023). https://doi.org/10.1007/s12195-022-00754-8

45. Satija, M.P., Martínez-Ávila, D.: Plagiarism: an essay in terminology. DESIDOC J. Libr. Inf. Technol. **39**, (2019). https://doi.org/10.14429/djlit.39.2.13937

46. Vuorikari, R., Kluzer, S., Punie, Y.: DigComp 2.2, the digital competence framework for citizens: with new examples of knowledge, skills and attitudes. European Commission - Joint Research Centre, LU (2022)

47. Johnson, M.: Embodied Mind, Meaning, and Reason. University of Chicago Press, Chicago (2017)

48. Dewey, J.: Democracy and education: An introduction to the philosophy of education. Macmillan, New York (1923)

49. Besse, P., Castets-Renard, C., Garivier, A., Loubes, J.M.: Can everyday AI be ethical. Fairness Mach. Learn. Algorithms (2018)

50. Lloyd, A.: The Qualitative Landscape of Information Literacy Research: Perspectives, Methods and Techniques. Facet Publishing, London (2021)

51. Lloyd, A.: Information Literacy Landscapes: Information Literacy in Education, Workplace and Everyday Contexts. Chandos, Oxford (2010)

52. Mead, M.: Culture and Commitment: a Study of the Generation gap. The Bodley Head, London (1970)

53. Heck, T., Weisel, L., Kullmann, S.: Information literacy and its interplay with AI. In: DIPF (2021). https://doi.org/10.25656/01:17891

54. Scott-Branch, J., Laws, R., Terzi, P.: The intersection of AI, Information and digital literacy: harnessing ChatGPT and other generative tools to enhance teaching and learning (2023)

Unpacking Experts' Opinions on ChatGPT Potential Assistive Roles and Risks in Early Childhood Special Education

Emmanouela V. Seiradakis[1,2]([✉]) [iD]

[1] Technical University of Crete, Kounoupidiana, Greece
eseiradaki@tuc.gr
[2] Hellenic Open University, Patras, Greece

Abstract. This study aims to investigate the potential assistive roles and risks of the use of ChatGPT in the Greek early childhood special education context. Data were collected through in-depth interviews with six early childhood education experts. Content analysis of interview data revealed four assistive ChatGPT themes: 1) ChatGPT as a pedagogical assistant for special education co-teachers, 2) ChatGPT as an inclusive education assistant for mainstream teachers, 3) ChatGPT as a personal assistant for headteachers, and 4) ChatGPT as a family engagement facilitator. ChatGPT risk themes included: 1) Teachers and parents' hallucinations, 2) Exclusion instead of inclusion and 3) Lack of evidence -based practices and guidelines. The study offers new insights into the affordances and challenges of ChatGPT in early childhood special education and discusses the implications for education policy, teachers and parents of disabled children.

Keywords: ChatGPT · early childhood education · inclusive education · expert interviews · generative AI · disabilities

1 Introduction

Despite still being in its infancy phase, findings suggest ChatGPT (OpenAI) has penetrated multiple education facets and now constitutes a daily routine for educators and students, offering immediate, low-cost, and personalized support across academic disciplines and subjects [1]. A couple of months after its launch in November 2022, the ChatGPT "tsunami" triggered a heated debate within the global education scholarship. Initial responses by educational experts mainly focused on the potential negative impacts of ChatGPT on academic integrity, assessment, and research quality [2], with Chomsky characterizing it as "high-tech plagiarism" [3]. Subsequently, however, it became obvious ChatGPT and similar generative AI applications cannot be completely banned or ignored and as a result, the focus shifted from whether educators and students should use ChatGPT, to how we could potentially use it for optimizing education quality. Recent findings from exploratory studies investigating educators and students' perceptions regarding the role of ChatGPT in education suggest it is an effective teaching and learning tool in

Ł. Tomczyk (Ed.): NMP 2023, CCIS 2130, pp. 380–392, 2024.
https://doi.org/10.1007/978-3-031-63235-8_25

media education [4], engineering education [5] and medical education [6]. Within the early childhood education (ECE) field, the bulk of scholarship includes conceptual articles speculating the effects of generative AI on the well-being of the current generation of preschoolers who suddenly have immediate access to chatbots through their parents' phones and tablets [7, 8]. Empirical works shedding light to ECE educators' views are scarce [9, 10], and have solely focused on general education, downplaying the potentials and challenges of ChatGPT for disabled students. In an attempt to fill this research gap, the current study seeks to explore the perceptions of early childhood special education (ECSE) experts on the potential roles of ChatGPT in Greek inclusive kindergartens. The leading questions of this interview-based study were:

i. What are the potential assistive ChatGPT roles for promoting inclusive practices in Greek mainstream kindergartens as perceived by ECSE experts?
ii. What are the potential risks of ChatGPT use in the Greek context of ECSE?

Current work findings offer insights into the potential benefits of using generative AI in the Greek ECSE context and the main challenges associated with its use. The findings provide implications for legislators, kindergarten leaders, teachers, and parents of students with disabilities.

1.1 ChatGPT in ECE

The two studies that have focused on ECE suggest there are multiple advantages for children, teachers, and pre-service teachers [9, 10]. In their recent study investigating ECE professors' views on the potential effects of ChatGPT in their domain, Luo et al. [9] found that ChatGPT could be used as a conversational mediator for nurturing preschoolers' context-specific language growth and improving their conversational skills both at school and at home. Their findings further suggest ChatGPT can be used by preservice teachers for lesson planning, subject-specific content generation, even classroom management. For parents of young children, their findings suggest ChatGPT could be used for inquiries related to their children's education, for creating educational resources at home, and even for overcoming the difficulties they commonly encounter in communicating with their children due to their young age. Su and Yang [10] explored ECE teachers' views on ChatGPT in Hong Kong. Their findings suggest teachers thought of ChatGPT as an easily accessible and cost-free assistant for lesson planning and as an immediate pedagogic knowledge tank they can resort to on a daily basis. Moreover, teachers thought ChatGPT could potentially nurture preschoolers' creative, and problem-solving skills through non-epistemic learning.

Along with the advantages however, the findings from these two exploratory works suggest ECE professors and kindergarten teachers believe there are multiple drawbacks in using ChatGPT. For instance, Su and Yang found [10] that ChatGPT generated false information when it was asked to generate context-specific content for an activity that aimed to raise students' awareness on Hong Kong's recyclable trash. In other cases, it failed to design developmentally appropriate lesson plans for the specific age group and suggested activities that could put preschoolers in danger. Luo et al.,[9] also highlighted potential risks related to inaccurate or inappropriate information, especially in the context of ECE, where students are too young to critically filter the information presented to them. They also draw attention to the fact that preservice ECE teachers could develop a type of a ChatGPT addiction which may jeopardize their creative and problem-solving skills as future educators.

1.2 Inclusive Early Childhood Special Education

The significance of quality in ECE has been recognized by multiple international policymakers, including the UN, UNESCO, UNISEF, the World Bank and OECD. A core construct of quality in ECE is inclusion. Current conceptualizations of the term inclusion in educational scholarship stretch beyond disability and include the multiple social identities of students, for example, gender, socioeconomic status, ethnicity religion, language and culture [11]. When it comes to disabled students in particular, inclusion refers to schools who are able to support all students in their class environment instead of segregating them from their peers. Solely granting physical access to preschoolers with disabilities in the mainstream classroom and providing additional teaching support, does not by any means equal to including them [12]. In fact, these children are commonly excluded from the learning processes that take place in the classroom due to low-quality teaching practices stemming from internalized ableist beliefs and fallacies of EC educators combined with systemic barriers of education systems [13]. Inclusive education in ECE implies a school offers an environment within which every child is able to participate and engage in all educational activities, develop social relationships and have substantial academic outcomes [13]. Such a goal demands interventions focusing on specific skills of disabled children, for example peer mediated strategies which facilitate communication skills [14]. It also implies educators constantly modify not only their teaching methods but also the educational materials to accommodate every student's diverse needs. In inclusive kindergartens, teachers commit a lot of time and effort in fine-tuning their daily curriculum to the needs and interests of children in the particular class [15]. In simple words, inclusion is not about blending students with disabilities with their typically developing peers, nor is treating all children as equal to empower them and boost their self-esteem by praising them. Inclusion means young children with disabilities are provided all forms of affordances, in order to be able to meaningfully engage in all school activities and gain concrete social and functional skills.

2 Method

2.1 Context

In Greece, formal compulsory ECE is provided for children aged 4–6 years by state kindergartens regulated by the Ministry of Education. Since 2008, (Law 3699/2008) Greek policy embraces the practice of educating disabled students together with their typically developing peers. Thus, the vast majority of disabled students attend mainstream kindergartens and receive additional support by special education (SE) teachers through two modes, the "integration class" (occasional pull-out teaching) or the "parallel support" (in-class support). Co-teaching of mainstream and SE teachers, is commonly projected by Greek politicians as the key pillar of inclusion in mainstream schools, nevertheless multiple scholars have repeatedly criticized the two peculiar forms of additional teaching support in Greece as dated and segregating [13].

Kindergartens are autonomous units with their own administrators, i.e. headteachers and follow their own curriculum (Institute of Education Policy 2014, 2015) which encourages differentiated pedagogies and inclusive practices. Minimum teaching qualifications for teaching in kindergartens is a bachelor's in ECE. SE should by law further possess postgraduate qualifications and extensive professional training in special education. Despite Greek policymakers' rhetoric on inclusion, current legislation mirrors the country's diagnosis-oriented philosophy. The students entitled to teaching support in mainstream schools, are strictly those whose parents have secured a statement of special educational needs and/or disability (SEND) statement from the Training and Counselling Support Centers (TCSC) (Law 4547 of 2018), given they have survived the extraordinary delays and the endless bureaucracy [16, 17]. Even when parents manage to get the precious SEND statement and secure additional teaching support for their children, SE co-teachers commonly arrive late at schools, or in some cases never arrive at all, as the vast majority of them are fixed-term teachers from co-financed EU programs [18, 19]. Long delays, bureaucracy, lack of accountability procedures, forces many parents to hire teacher-assistants or "private parallel support teachers" (Law 2013/4186). In fact, the quality of inclusive education services provided in kindergartens has been repeatedly questioned as empirical findings suggest both mainstream teachers and SE co-teachers commonly possess limited awareness on inclusive practices [20].

2.2 Participants

The study involved six ECSE experts. The expert interview method has been extensively employed in social research, and it is particularly effective in exploratory studies as it offers rich insider knowledge on novice complex phenomena [21]. All six participants are women with PhDs in ECSE or ECSE-related fields and with more than six years of teaching experience in postgraduate and professional development programs for SE educators in kindergartens. Two of the participants are also the ECSE counselors of SE teachers in state kindergartens in two regions of northern Greece. The age range of the participants was between 38 to 54 years Purposive convenience sampling was employed based on the author's existing contacts to identify potential interviewees. Subsequently, snowball sampling was used to identify two additional contacts. Criteria for the choice of experts included: a) teaching experience and/or research in ECSE postgraduate degrees, or professional development courses, b) use of ChatGPT and/or other generative AI applications case for research and/or educational purposes, c) be willing to participate.

2.3 Data Collection and Analysis

Individual in-depth online interviews were conducted from July to October 2023. Each interview lasted from forty to seventy minutes. The interviews were in the form of a discussion and included questions on i) the potential assistance ChatGPT could provide to kindergarten teachers, headteachers and parents of disabled children in Greece, ii) the potential risks of ChatGPT use by kindergarten educators and parents of disabled children and its wider impact in the ECSE context in Greece. Participants' accounts were analyzed with Taguette [22], a free application for qualitative data analysis. Segment coding was based on thematic analysis [23]. Encoding a specific segment in-volved the careful examination of interview data, categorizing meaningful patterns, framing recurring keywords and their implications, and eventually concluding to main themes. For research question one, twelve meaningful codes were identified (ChatGPT as a curriculum modifier for SE co-teachers, ChatGPT as an IEP assistant for SE co-teachers, ChatGPT as a disability-specific content generator, ChatGPT as a SE assistant for mainstream teachers, ChatGPT as a lesson planner for mainstream teachers, ChatGPT as a SE assistant for EFL teachers, ChatGPT as a secretary, ChatGPT as the headteacher's assistant, ChatGPT as a parent counselor, ChatGPT as a parental involvement facilitator, ChatGPT as a culturally responsive parental involvement facilitator), but were reduced to four (ChatGPT as a pedagogical assistant for special education co-teachers, ChatGPT as an inclusive education assistant for mainstream teachers, ChatGPT as a personal assistant for headteachers and ChatGPT as a family engagement facilitator).

For the second research question, ten codes were initially generated (Concealed inaccuracies, Parents' delusions of expert advice, Teachers' overreliance, Wider disparities in special education teaching quality, Low quality curricular modifications, Poor quality of inclusive lesson planning, Developmentally inappropriate activities, Parents' lack of AI literacy skills, Teachers' lack of AI literacy skills, Lack of empirical research in ECSE, Absence of policies and guidelines by the state), but were ultimately reduced to three general themes (Teachers and parents' hallucinations, Exclusion instead of inclusion and Lack of official guidelines and policies). Participants were assigned with pseudonyms (e.g., P1-P6) to safeguard anonymity when presenting interview excerpts per theme. The selected excerpts describe the emergent themes and correspond to the two leading research questions.

3 Findings and Discussion

3.1 Potential Assistive ChatGPT Roles for Promoting Inclusive Practices in Greek Mainstream Kindergartens

ChatGPT as a Pedagogical Assistant for Special Education Co-Teachers
All participants believed generative AI applications cannot and will not supplant teachers and argued that the key question right now is if and how generative AI can help teachers and other professionals in providing higher education quality to disabled preschoolers. Within the Greek ECE context, empirical findings have repeatedly shown that curricular and alternative modifications tailored to the needs of disabled students are almost absent. Additionally, the activities provided to kindergarten students with intellectual disability, autism and other disabilities are commonly similar, downplaying the increased diversity of students' needs even within the same disability spectrum [19]. Participants thought that one of the major future potential benefits of ChatGPT in ECSE, is that it can be used by SE co-teachers as a tool to implement curricular modifications and generate developmentally appropriate differentiated materials for children with disabilities. P2 stated:

Curriculum modification is vital for ensuring students with disabilities receive education based on their individual needs and we know that in Greece SE co-teachers often use one-size-fits-all teaching materials and just follow whatever the mainstream teacher does, for many reasons, mostly related to wider problems at the macro-level. Generative AI apps that are free and easy to access can help SE co-teachers design and implement proper differentiated instruction.

Two participants specifically referred to ChatGPT's ability to generate content for ASD children's restricted interests (RIs). These interests refer to objects and themes ASD students tend to focus intensively. Empirical findings have shown that ASD preschoolers engage actively and develop a more positive view of their self-image when participating in activities linked to their RIs, yet teachers tend to restrict or even prohibit engagement in RIs. One of the main barriers in integrating RIs into the curriculum, is creating content and lesson plans on a particular subject [24, 25]. P1 thought ChatGPT can function as a valuable tool for overcoming this barrier:

For ASD students, it is very convenient because it can produce very quickly extreme volumes of new content targeted to the needs of a specific student, for example you have an ASD student who likes ships, it is very difficult to continually produce new content for one student, but with ChatGPT it is actually much faster.

Three participants referred to the potential of ChatGPT in supporting SE co-teachers create high quality Individualized Educational Plan (IEP) goals. IEPs are considered the cornerstones for providing truly inclusive environments to SEN students. In Greece, the responsibility for constructing IEP goals and the intervention plans for the majority of students falls on SE co-teachers [17]. P3 believes creating IEP goals is a vital skill for SE teachers and devotes significant time and effort on training her students how to write them properly. Below she describes her experience in using ChatGPT with her students in her postgraduate course:

The goals have to be measurable and attainable, easily understood by mainstream teachers, other therapists, assistants and parents. In many cases inexperienced teachers write general texts with no substance and you cannot really understand whether they refer to the specific student or it is just copy-pasted text for an ASD student but not for the specific student. ChatGPT helps in doing the preparatory work. Obviously, teachers must make substantial adjustments but it gives them structure. It is also extremely useful for designing culturally responsive IEP goals.

ChatGPT as an Inclusive Education Assistant for Mainstream Teachers

Late hirings of SE co-teachers renders the training of mainstream teachers vital for creating inclusive learning environments in mainstream kindergartens [18, 19]. All participants believed generative AI will up to a certain level foster a higher awareness of differentiated instruction and inclusive practices in kindergarten among mainstream teachers, yet they emphasized the pressing need for proper compulsory professional training offered by the Ministry of Education at the national level. Content generation, differentiated materials, lesson planning based on inclusive evidence-based approaches and basic pedagogic knowledge related to disabilities were the main immediate Chat-GPT benefits participants mentioned regarding mainstream teachers. Two participants further commented on the potential assistive role of ChatGPT for EFL teachers who entered state kindergartens four years ago and encounter multiple difficulties. P5 stated:

> *EFL teachers in kindergartens, teach alone, there is no provision for SE co-teachers during English. They often use materials that are not suitable for children of this age, let alone children with disabilities which is logical because they lack the pedagogical background and the teaching experience with young learners. For them, ChatGPT could be used as compensation teaching strategy, since they are not getting any other support. They could use it for recommendations for developmentally appropriate materials for preschoolers with disabilities, then they could double check with the SE co-teachers.*

Findings related to the potential benefits of ChatGPT as a teaching and learning tool are in line with the previous literature in education which suggest it could be used for lesson planning and content generation [26].

ChatGPT as a Personal Assistant for Headteachers

All participants believed ChatGPT and similar generative AI applications will be extensively used by kindergarten leaders for the automation of a range of time-consuming administrative tasks. In Greece, there is no administrate stuff in schools and kindergarten headteachers bear a heavy administrative load whilst simultaneously having a full-time teaching schedule [27, 28]. Students' enrollment, registration, scheduling, student data management, monitoring of IEPs, communication with TCSCs, communicating with the parents, are only a few of the headteachers' administrative tasks participants mentioned. Three participants stated headteachers have already started using ChatGPT for content creation in relation to their multiple administrative duties. P6 referred to the usefulness of ChatGPT for routine daily tasks:

> *I know headteachers who are already using it for repetitive tasks such as creating emails, social medial content, procedural reports for teachers, therapists, auxiliary stuff, parents. They have a lot of time-consuming paperwork and a large part of it is essentially secretarial work.*

P2 emphasized that accelerating bureaucratic procedures would allow school stuff to dedicate more time to disabled students and their families, highlighting that teacher in ECSE, are not there only to teach, but promote students' social and life skills, fully engage with the students' families and offer comfort and consultations:

> *Dealing with the endless bureaucracy faster means they will have more time to spend to do what they are actually supposed to do. Talk with the students, teach, hug them, comfort them, talk with the parents who commonly struggle, empower them.*

ChatGPT as a Family Engagement Facilitator

Five participants believed ChatGPT could in the future be used to optimize inclusive parental involvement practices in Greek state kindergartens. Family engagement constitutes a determining factor for disabled students' academic and socioemotional outcomes regardless of race, ethnicity, gender, ability, and/or socioeconomic status [29, 30]. Despite the well documented benefits of increased parental involvement and the new mandates legislated in Greece, families of disabled students in ECE display low levels of participation due to a range of systemic barriers, including rigid contact hours [13, 31]. P4 described the daily struggles of teachers and mothers in finding time to communicate and how ChatGPT could answer simple inquiries related to their children's education:

In kindergartens we have o cocktail of women involved. Teachers, co-teachers, mothers, headteachers, auxiliary stuff, the majority of them are women. Many of these women have the biggest share of childrearing responsibilities, household chores and full-time jobs. Students' mothers usually don't have time till the afternoon but at that time SE co-teachers are not at school. Chatbots like ChatGPT could be a sort of fix-up, for simple questions around the clock, without mothers having to go to school.

Four participants mentioned the potential of ChatGPT as a tool for simplifying difficult special education -related concepts and terminology which often puzzle parents, particularly in kindergarten since it is essentially the first formal education structure they come in contact with. P3 thought ChatGPT could function as a valuable consulting tool for disadvantaged parents to advocate for their children's rights:

If trained properly, I imagine in the future parents especially parents from disadvantaged backgrounds, will use it in order to advocate for their children's rights in TCSC meetings and in schools. It could synthesize and summarize the endless laws, regulations related to their child's education and the accommodations they are entitled.

In addition to simplifying complex disability concepts for parents, some participants believed ChatGPT can potentially be employed for implementing culturally responsive parental involvement practices. For example, P6 explained how kindergarten stuff could use ChatGPT as tool for creating accessible materials for parents:

I have met migrant mothers who accuse themselves because they do not know how to read or because they do not know the system. These women are under a lot of stress and experience high levels of guilt because they feel they do not defend their children's rights which makes them bad mothers. Greek kindergartens could in the future use ChatGPT, DALL-E and the new apps that will emerge to visualize content for the parents who aren't part of the dominant middle-class parent group in schools.

3.2 Potential Risks of ChatGPT U Se in Early Childhood Special Education

Teachers and Parents' Hallucinations

There was a general consensus among these experts, that the popularity of ChatGPT and similar generative AI chatbots globally is going to trigger an immense demand for obtaining information related to disabilities and inclusive educational practices in the near future. Regarding the Greek ECE context in particular, their main concern was the potential overreliance of overwhelmed parents and state teachers. P3 specifically referred to marginalized parents from lower social strata who are commonly deprived of the necessary support by special educators and therapists:

If you are a middle-class mother, chances are you already pay specialized private tutors, language therapists, psychologists which means you can easily verify what you are reading. But if you are an exhausted working mum fully dependent on state benefits, it's a different story, most probably you see ChatGPT as the expert you can't afford.

P5 also expressed doubts regarding the quality of content ChatGPT generates and highlighted the dangers, particularly for parents and teachers who lack sufficient background knowledge in special education:

Accurate information is many times blended with inaccurate information and this mixture is presented in a superficially academic manner. An inexperienced teacher or a parent may not be able to distinguish false information and in special education this can be dangerous.

P4 talked about the manner ChatGPT answers questions:

These chatbots usually sound extremely confident, they have an authoritative tone, if you don't have in-depth knowledge in a specific disability, it is very probable you will be convinced with what you are reading. Mothers of young children with disabilities commonly struggle in coping with the immense daily demands they read a lot, they research a lot, especially during turbulent periods. The difference with ChatGPT is that it is much faster, much more convenient and sounds like an expert which is a problem.

P5 also referred to potential dangers of ChatGPT use, yet she also emphasized the differences between ChatGPT3.5 and ChatGPT-4 in providing answers that remind the user of its limitations in sensitive issues related to disabilities and special education:

I have noticed that the latest version is more prudent when answering questions related to disabilities. It provides answers but always reminds the user to consult a professional. Obviously, these are important changes and they show how quickly these models improve and become more fluent and context-specific.

Exclusion Instead of Inclusion

Most participants thought that at this time, ChatGPT is convenient for obtaining general information on disability topics, lesson planning ideas and activities, but struggles to produce high quality content on fine-grained information related to the diverse needs of a disabled student. Their main concern related to the simplistic information generated, is the effect on the actual quality of curriculum modifications and overall accommodations offered in Greek state kindergartens. Two of the participants noted that ChatGPT has a limited capacity in Greek which means that teachers with a low level in English will probably end up reading lower quality content. Most participants expressed concerns regarding the quality of academic qualifications, particularly in special education. P5 reflected on the lack of accountability in Greek kindergartens, and speculated that the quality of education offered in inclusive kindergarten classrooms may be further compensated, especially by SE co-teachers who never really wanted to be in special education:

I think we will see a wider disparity in kindergartens between SE teachers' who wanted to be in special education in the first place and teachers who just wanted a state job. It is already happening. Some of them use ChatGPT for generating specific content for the specific needs of the specific students and others copy-paste things quickly, just to present something to the headteacher, the mother or the special education counselor.

Three participants thought that the effectiveness and convenience of ChatGPT could eventually trigger a wider overreliance of fixed-term teachers which could further jeopardize the already questionable quality of special education qualifications in Greece [16, 18]. The account of P4 vividly describes the unregulated special education field in Greece and the potential consequences generative AI in creating inclusive kindergarten classrooms:

We already have an influx of special education postgraduate degrees and professional training courses. The bottom line is that in Greece, the more papers you get, the more chances you have as a special educator. The Greek Ministry of Education doesn't bother to evaluate the quality of these programs before recruiting teachers or implement some sort of additional filter before they hiring them. ChatGPT and all ChatGPT-like apps will deliver the last blow to special education.

Lack of Evidence-Based Practices and Guidelines
All participants highlighted the pressuring need for official guidelines and policies on generative AI use, especially in the sensitive field of ECSE. Teachers' lack of AI literacy skills emerged as one of the most immediate challenges. Participants further highlighted the absence of relevant courses in undergraduate, postgraduate and professional programs. P6 questioned the abilities of all ECE stakeholders in using new generative AI tools:

It is not just teachers or parents, it's teacher trainers, professors in preschool departments, some of us do not have a background on educative AI but we started using it because suddenly it is everywhere and we can see it will affect the field. I am learning together with my students at the university.

Participants' concerns related to the absence of regulating policies and the deficiencies of generative AI training in ECSE curricula and professional training courses agree with findings from works centered in mainstream ECE education [9].

4 Conclusion and Implications

The current study explored ECSE experts' perceptions on the potential assistive ChatGPT roles and the risks of using it the context of Greek inclusive kindergartens. Overall, participants' accounts showed that in their eyes generative AI is not a panacea for the structural flows of the Greek underfunded education system. Rather, they see it as a handy tool for supplementary tasks that can assist educators develop inclusive teaching strategies, care for disabled students and leverage parental involvement.

Current findings shed light to potential benefits and risks specifically for disabled students who are commonly neglected both at school and in the relevant literature and bear implications regarding generative AI use in the Greek ECE context. The first implication, is that there is an urgent need for the Ministry of Education to establish explicit policies and guidelines for the use of generative AI applications in ECE and ESCE. Secondly, the Ministry of Education must collaborate with higher education institutions and educative AI experts to provide high-quality mandatory training for in-service mainstream ECE teachers, SE co-teachers and EFL teachers, teaching in kindergartens focusing on how ChatGPT and other easily-accessible AI applications can be used to implement inclusive education practices. Thirdly, AI literacy courses must be integrated in ECE and ECSE undergraduate and postgraduate curricula. Lastly, AI literacy courses should ideally be also offered to parents of disabled students so that they can take full advantage of the affordances of ChatGPT for generating developmentally appropriate and differentiated educational resources at home or obtaining advice related to their children's conditions in a safe and critical manner.

The study has several limitations that should be taken under consideration. The first limitation is that it focused only on ECSE experts and did not include kindergarten teachers, auxiliary school stuff and parents of disabled students. Lokot (2021) argues key informant interviews (such as those with expert special education experts), neglect the "ordinary" voices of people and exclude rather than include their voices. Future works should ideally integrate triangulation of informers and methodologies to enhance data trustworthiness. The second limitation is related to the small number of participants and the intrinsic subjectivity of qualitative research.

References

1. Lo., C.K: What is the impact of ChatGPT on education? A rapid review of the literature. Educ. Sci. **13**(4), 410 (2020). https://doi.org/10.3390/educsci13040410
2. Strzelecki, A.: To use or not to use ChatGPT in higher education? A study of students' acceptance and use of technology. Interact. Learn. Environ. 1–14 (2023). https://doi.org/10.1080/10494820.2023.2209881
3. Chomsky, N., Roberts, I., Watumull, N.C.: The false promise of ChatGPT. New York Times (2023). https://www.nytimes.com/2023/03/08/opinion/noam-chomsky-chatgpt-ai.html. Accessed 15 Dec 2023
4. Pavlik, J.V.: Collaborating with ChatGPT: Considering the implications of generative artificial intelligence for journalism and media education. Journalism Mass Commun. Educ. **78**(1), 84–93 (2023). https://doi.org/10.1177/10776958221149577

5. Qadir, J.: Engineering education in the era of ChatGPT: promise and pitfalls of generative AI for education. In: IEEE Global Engineering Education Conference (EDUCON), pp. 1–9. IEEE PRESS (2023). https://doi.org/10.1109/EDUCON54358.2023.10125121

6. Breeding, T., et al.: The utilization of ChatGPT in reshaping future medical education and learning perspectives: a curse or a blessing? The American Surgeon™ (2023). https://doi.org/10.1177/00031348231180950

7. Chen, J.J., Lin, J.C.: Artificial intelligence as a double-edged sword: wielding the POWER principles to maximize its positive effects and minimize its negative effects. Contemp. Issues Early Childhood 6(3) (2023). https://doi.org/10.1177/20965311231168423

8. Kurian, N.: AI's empathy gap: the risks of conversational artificial intelligence for young children's well-being and key ethical considerations for early childhood education and care. Contemp. Issues Early Child. (2023). https://doi.org/10.1177/14639491231206004

9. Luo, W., et al.: Aladdin's genie or Pandora's box for early childhood education? Experts chat on the roles, challenges, and developments of ChatGPT. Early Educ. Dev. 35(1), 96–113 (2024). https://doi.org/10.1080/10409289.2023.2214181

10. Su, J., Yang, W.: Powerful or mediocre? Kindergarten teachers' perspectives on using Chat-GPT in early childhood education. Interact. Learn. Environ. 1–13 (2020). https://doi.org/10.1080/10494820.2023.2266490

11. Sorkos, G., Hajisoteriou, C.: Sustainable intercultural and inclusive education: teachers' efforts on promoting a combining paradigm. Pedagogy, Cult. Soc. 29(4), 517–536 (2021). https://doi.org/10.1080/14681366.2020.1765193

12. Strogilos, V., Avramidis, E., Voulagka, A., Tragoulia, E.: Differentiated instruction for students with disabilities in early childhood co-taught classrooms: types and quality of modifications. Int. J. Inclusive Educ. 24(4), 443–461 (2020). https://doi.org/10.1080/13603116.2018.1466928

13. Fyssa, A., Tsakiri, M., Mouroutsou, S.: Pursuing early childhood inclusion through reinforcing partnerships with parents of disabled children: Beliefs of Greek pre-service early childhood educators. Eur. Early Childhood Educ. Res. J. 31(1), 34–50 (2023). https://doi.org/10.1080/1350293X.2022.2153258

14. Haas, A., Vannest, K., Thompson, J.L., Fuller, M.C., Wattanawongwan, S.: Peer-mediated instruction and academic outcomes for students with autism spectrum disorders: a comparison of quality indicators. Mentoring Tutoring: Partnership Learn. 28(5), 625–642 (2020). https://doi.org/10.1080/13611267.2020.1859330

15. Strogilos, V., Lim, L., Binte Mohamed, B.: Differentiated instruction for students with SEN in mainstream classrooms: contextual features and types of curriculum modifications. Asia Pacif. J. Educ. 43(3), 850–866 (2023). https://doi.org/10.1080/02188791.2021.1984873

16. Nteropoulou-Nterou, E., Slee, R.: A critical consideration of the changing conditions of schooling for students with disabilities in Greece and the fragility of international in local contexts. Int. J. Inclusive Educ. 23(7–8), 891–907 (2019). https://doi.org/10.1080/13603116.2019.1623331

17. Dimakos, I.C., Tsaganelia, A., Lavidas, K.: Parental requests for evaluation and authorities' responses: issues of accord. Eur. J. Spec. Needs Educ. 31(4), 565–575 (2016). https://doi.org/10.1080/08856257.2016.1194572

18. Koutsoklenis, A., Papadimitriou, V.: Special education provision in Greek mainstream classrooms: teachers' characteristics and recruitment procedures in parallel support. Int. J. Inclusive Educ. 1–16 (2021). https://doi.org/10.1080/13603116.2021.1942565

19. Papadimitriou, V., Koutsoklenis, A.: The extent of late hiring in special education: a report on the Greek institution of parallel support. Int. J. Disabil. Dev. Educ. 70(7), 1264–1274 (2023). https://doi.org/10.1080/1034912X.2021.2010670

20. Strogilos, V., Tragoulia, E., Avramidis, E., Voulagka, A., Papanikolaou, V.: Understanding the development of differentiated instruction for students with and without disabilities in co-taught classrooms. Disabil. Soc. **32**(8), 1216–1238 (2017). https://doi.org/10.1080/09687599.2017.1352488
21. Döringer, S.: The problem-centered expert interview. Combining qualitative interviewing approaches for investigating implicit expert knowledge. Int. J. Soc. Res. Methodol. **24**(3), 265–278 (2021). https://doi.org/10.1080/13645579.2020.1766777
22. Taguette, the free and open-source qualitative data analysis tool. Accessed 13 Dec 2023. https://www.taguette.org/
23. Clarke, V., Braun, V.: Thematic analysis. J. Positive Psychol. **12**(3), 297–298 (2017). https://doi.org/10.1080/17439760.2016.1262613
24. Wood, R.: Autism, intense interests and support in school: from wasted efforts to shared understandings. Educ. Rev. **73**(1), 34–54 (2021). https://doi.org/10.1080/00131911.2019.1566213
25. Gunn, K.C., Delafield-Butt, J.T.: Teaching children with autism spectrum disorder with restricted interests: a review of evidence for best practice. Rev. Educ. Res. **86**(2), 408–430 (2016). https://doi.org/10.3102/0034654315604027
26. Ulla, M.B., Perales, W.F., Busbus, S.O.: To generate or stop generating response': Exploring EFL teachers' perspectives on ChatGPT in English language teaching in Thailand. Learn. Res. Pract. **9**(2), 168–182 (2023). https://doi.org/10.1080/23735082.2023.2257252
27. Papazoglou, A., Koutouzis, M.: Educational leadership roles for the development of learning organizations: Seeking scope in the Greek context. Int. J. Leadership Educ. **25**(4), 634–646 (2022). https://doi.org/10.1080/13603124.2019.1690950
28. Lazaridou, A.: Personality and resilience characteristics of preschool principals: an iterative study. Int. J. Educ. Manag. **35**(1), 29–46 (2021). https://doi.org/10.1108/IJEM-07-2020-0330
29. Yotyodying, S., Wild, E.: Effective family–school communication for students with learning disabilities: associations with parental involvement at home and in school. Learn. Cult. Soc. Interact. **22**, 100317 (2022). https://doi.org/10.1016/j.lcsi.2019.100317
30. Acar, S., Chen, C.I., Xie, H.: Parental involvement in developmental disabilities across three cultures: a systematic review. Res. Dev. Disabil. **110**, 103861 (2021). https://doi.org/10.1016/j.ridd.2021.103861
31. Seiradakis, E.V.: Migrant mothers of ASD children with language deficits in Greek kindergarten classrooms: Barriers and facilitators of school involvement through an intersectional lens. In: Katsarou, D. (ed.) Childhood Developmental Language Disorders: Role of Inclusion, Families, and Professionals, pp.134–148. IGI Global (2024). https://doi.org/10.4018/979-8-3693-1982-6.ch009

Artificial Intelligence in Secondary Education: An Innovative Teacher's Tool to Ensure Individualised Learning for Students

Svitlana Lytvynova[1(✉)] (iD), Nataliia Vodopian[1] (iD), and Olga Sysoeva[2] (iD)

[1] Institute for Digitalisation of Education of NAES of Ukraine, 9 M. Berlins'koho Street, Kyiv 04060, Ukraine
s.h.lytvynova@gmail.com, vodopyan_n@dlit.dp.ua

[2] Dnipro Scientific Lyceum of Information Technology of The Dnipro City Council, 8, Shevchenko Street, Dnipro, Ukraine
sysoieva@dlit.dp.ua

Abstract. In recent years, the digital transformation of society has characterised access to the Internet as a prerequisite for educational activities. Artificial intelligence (AI) has opened up new opportunities for developing individualised learning for students. A 2023 study analyses the results of using artificial intelligence by teachers of Ukrainian secondary schools. The main goal of the survey is to determine the state of AI applications for individualised learning and the integration of this technology into pedagogical practice.

The study examines the timing of digital technology implementation and its impact on the continuous development of teachers' digital competencies. Particular attention is paid to the aspects of AI implementation, including educational purposes, teacher readiness, and limitations of this technology.

It is established that to implement individualised learning, the goal and objectives of individualisation, the choice of AI services and platforms, opportunities for students, security measures, learning pace, level of mastery of the material and personal interests should be considered. The author proposes a classification of tasks for students using AI and provides examples of assessments for students of grades 7–9 in English, mathematics, and biology. Emphasis is given to the fact that AI-powered automatic assessment enables the recognition of the requirements of every individual student and adapts learning tasks according to their current abilities and knowledge. Despite the challenges and problems of integrating AI into the school environment, the study points to the growing interest of teachers in this technology, the improvement of AI capabilities, and its gradual development as a teacher's assistant.

Keywords: AI; Secondary School · Media Pedagogy · Individualization of Education · ICT in Education · Teacher Development · Students

1 Introduction

Artificial intelligence (AI) offers excellent opportunities for transforming modern secondary education. The usage of technology in educational institutions can better prepare the younger generation for the challenges of the contemporary world. This technology allows us to rethink the traditional approach to learning and contributes to creating an interactive and stimulating learning environment.

The first definition of AI was proposed in 1956 by the American computer scientist and researcher J. McCarthy. According to this definition, the study of any issue should be approached with the assumption that every aspect of learning or feature of intelligence can be precisely described, allowing for the creation of a machine capable of imitating it [1].

In 2021, more than 30 countries published national AI policy strategies. The following papers detail strategies and anticipated outcomes regarding the influence of AI in various policy domains, such as education. Additionally, they outline the measures to consider the social and ethical impacts of AI [2]. Artificial Intelligence is a domain of computer science that is specifically focused on creating intelligent systems and algorithms, capable of performing tasks that typically require human cognitive abilities" and includes speech recognition, machine learning, natural language processing, computer vision, planning, decision making, and other areas [3].

For decades, artificial intelligence scientists have dedicated their efforts to developing generative models that can create speech, text, music, and other forms of content. However, the advent of deep learning has led to a surge in generative AI, which allows users to produce their own material with speed and accuracy that was previously impossible [4].

Chatbots are one of the leading and most effective areas of artificial intelligence application. These interactive software platforms are in messengers and can behave like humans when answering questions. Chatbots provide answers to students' questions and help relieve teachers' workload by engaging students in the educational process [5].

Mobile applications are becoming increasingly relevant, used as assistants in solving educational problems, in mastering educational material and consolidating it, and as analysts in collecting information about the progress of learning, mistakes made, and time spent [6].

Researchers have shown that AI in education can be used for various tasks. It can be a teacher's or student's assistant, monitor students' academic achievements, predict student behaviour, implement personalised learning, and provide feedback to students [7]. Scientists also emphasize that one of the potential applications of AI as a teacher's assistant lies in the development and selection of interesting and valuable educational material, optimal for the relevant audience, which corresponds to and expands the boundaries of the curriculum [6].

When considering learning, teaching, and assessment, teachers need to consider that by changing the nature of assessment, we are changing the learning process and how we teach. Thus, AI is not only a tool that directly affects students' learning but also indirectly affects how and what they learn [4].

The "instrumental" value of AI for education – is the training of more users to use AI in all spheres of life and a significant number of AI experts. These issues are now becoming a top priority [2].

Scientists raise a few questions about the ethics of AI, but secondary school teachers are wary of its use, raising issues of personal data protection, ethical issues, and integrity. At the same time, the use of artificial intelligence in education can change traditional educational approaches to learning, namely, identify the most effective teaching methods for each individual student, create innovative learning environments, develop personalised programmes for each student, considering their needs, learning style and pace of comprehension, which in turn can have a positive impact on the overall education system.

2 Problem Statement

When a new digital technology appears (cloud services, AR, VR, computer simulations, etc.), a number of educational questions arise, including whether such a technology will be in demand by teachers and students, whether it will improve the quality of education, whether it will ensure the development of a secondary school student's personality, and whether it will be incorporated into educational practice.

Artificial intelligence (AI) is a rapidly developing field that can revolutionize education [7]. On the one hand, the use of artificial intelligence can open up new opportunities for individualised learning, helping each student develop their unique abilities and interests. For example, AI systems can adapt learning material to each student's level, allowing them to learn at their own pace and style. The use of artificial intelligence in education holds great promise for improving teaching and learning, as many educational applications now use and integrate it [8]. Artificial intelligence advances can transform education systems and make them more equitable [9].

At the World Economic Forum (2023), it was noted that AI technologies may affect the role of teachers in the educational process. Teachers may need to adapt to new technologies to use them effectively in their work and teaching, including students with special needs. In other words, the advancement of AI technology can expedite the much-needed changes in educational systems towards providing inclusive and equitable learning opportunities to prepare the younger generation for a prosperous and positive future [9].

Even though AI is in a stage of constant change, transformation, active development, and functioning [10], teachers are already using it to improve their pedagogical practice and professional experience [9].

Thus, according to the Walton Family Foundation study in 2023, two-thirds of students (65%) and three-quarters of teachers (76%) agree that the integration of ChatGPT for schools will be important in the future [11].

On the other hand, it is essential to consider the ethical aspects of using AI in education. This includes the issue of student data privacy, as well as the risk of leaving some students behind or even increasing the level of control and over-training. Therefore, the ethics of using AI are increasingly being raised in academic circles.

There are also significant risks that artificial intelligence could exacerbate existing educational inequalities if we are not careful [12]. Scientists note that the problems of bias and discrimination pose a severe challenge to the effective and fair use of AI in education [13].

Despite the warnings, artificial intelligence, as a field of modern science, is being implemented and is increasingly used in education. The curiosity of scientists towards AI research helps in shaping and advancing several fields, in particular technical (improving AI capabilities, developing a number of services using AI), ethical (developing approaches, conditions, and requirements for the ethics and integrity of AI use); and educational (utilizing artificial intelligence to enhance the overall standard of education and creating conditions for personalised learning in particular).

As outlined above, artificial intelligence has advantages, disadvantages, and challenges in education, and it is important to balance these aspects to ensure that education is accessible, effective, and ethical for all students.

One such challenge in education for educators and AI is its use for personalised learning. AI-powered learning is expected to adapt learning content and tailor educational experiences to cater to the distinct requirements, learning methodologies, and preferences of individual students. Students will have the opportunity to learn according to their own pace with this approach, thereby increasing their participation and overall learning outcomes [14, 15] implementation of individualised learning.

It should be noted that scientists have not fully considered the mechanisms of using AI to build an individual educational trajectory based on the results of students' learning activities and inclinations, which requires additional attention and new research.

3   Methods of Research

The paper depicts the outcomes of a comprehensive examination of the application of artificial intelligence by secondary school teachers in Ukraine (2023). The survey involved 123 teachers from 11 regions of Ukraine, including those in the temporarily occupied territories (see Fig. 1–2).

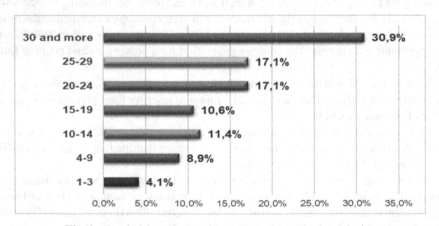

Fig. 1. Teachers' work experience (N = 123, author's analysis).

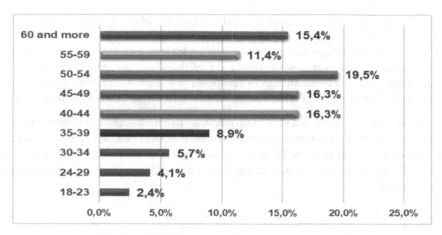

Fig. 2. Teachers' age (N = 123, author's analysis).

The survey was conducted to determine the extent to which secondary school teachers use AI to meet their own needs, create conditions for individualised learning, build individual educational trajectories for students, and implement it in pedagogical practice. A focus group of teachers from the Lyceum of Information Technologies in Dnipro was also formed-Dnipro, consisting of 22 people.

4 Research Results

4.1 Artificial Intelligence as an Innovative Educational Technology

The future of education is associated with the use of innovations and the latest digital technologies. At the same time, advances in AI play a significant role in its development and open up new opportunities. [16]. Innovative processes in education are grounded in two fundamental pedagogical challenges: firstly, the need to study and generalize domestic and international pedagogical experiences, and secondly, the challenge of effectively implementing the advancements of psychological and pedagogical science into practical application. This results in the use of theoretical and practical innovations and those formed on the borderline of theory and practice. At the same time, the teacher acts as a researcher, user and promoter of new pedagogical technologies. The implementation of pedagogical innovations by teachers requires direct analysis, evaluation and determination of the effectiveness of the proposed idea. In case of a positive and favourable technology assessment, it is essential to create appropriate conditions for its further successful implementation [17].

Let's consider the theories of innovation diffusion that can be used to create a practical guide for teachers who are ready to use AI services in pedagogical practice as innovative digital technologies:

– The Diffusion of Innovations model by Everett Rogers considers the process of diffusion of innovations among consumer groups identifies five categories of participants

in the implementation: Innovators, Early Adopters, Majority, Late Adopters, and Rejectors [18].
- Fred Davis' Technology Acceptance Model (TAM) focuses on technology acceptance and identifies important factors: perceived usefulness and perceived ease of use [19].
- Jean Piaget's theory of constructivism proposes that learning and innovation are more effective if they are based on constructive, active dialogue and cooperation [20].

The innovation process is a sequence of actions in which scientific knowledge, theories and models are transformed into an innovation that meets social needs. The stages of innovation implementation are familiarization, interest, evaluation, testing, implementation, adaptation, evaluation, and change. The stages of innovation implementation are presented in Fig. 3.

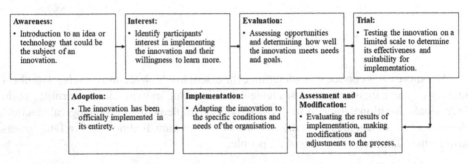

Fig. 3. The stages of innovation implementation.

Given the overall sufficient level of digital competence of teachers, the intensive growth of digital competence during COVID-19 and the period of martial law in Ukraine [21], there has been a noteworthy reduction in the time teachers allocate to mastering and implementing the latest digital technologies in educational practice, particularly AI (see Fig. 4).

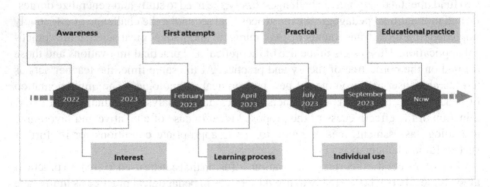

Fig. 4. Determining the timeframe for introducing AI into educational practice.

The practical use of artificial intelligence in education is ahead of research and the development of methodological recommendations on this issue. In recent years, many tools have emerged that have changed the lives of both teachers and students, providing convenience in the process of gaining knowledge. For example, Google Translate allows you to translate a text into more than 100 languages; Siri and Google Assistant allow people to ask questions and get quick answers; ChatGPT helps with research by summarising sources or directing to valuable publications, as well as instant answers to any questions, explanations, examples, poetry or stories; Stable Diffusion and Imagen allow you to enter text to create realistic images; Caktus provides personalised recommendations for monitoring education; Gradescope - helps teachers to grade students' assignments faster and more efficiently, while reducing their bias; Alta by Knewton - allows you to adapt to the unique learning style of each higher education student; Querium - imitates the experience of a teacher to guide students to solve a problem using the unique StepWise technology; EducationCopilot - offers to save teachers' time and energy by quickly generating individual templates, and provides an opportunity for collaboration between teachers, etc. [22].

According to a survey conducted among Ukrainian secondary school teachers in 2023, 69.9% of respondents reported having experience with AI, with 52% successfully integrating it into their teaching practices (see Fig. 5).

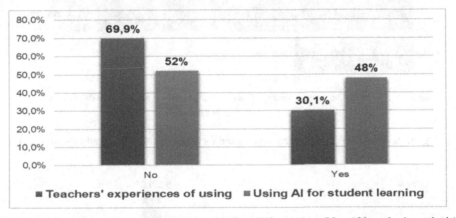

Fig. 5. Teachers' experiences of using AI and Using AI for student (N = 123, author's analysis).

Most teachers said that they needed additional training to use AI, including gaining practical experience in creating queries, and that they lacked methodological recommendations and advice on AI implementation, instructions on building an individual student development trajectory.

An innovation such as AI has made it possible to conclude that as the technical characteristics of digital technologies evolve, each new technology becomes more accessible to master. However, additional training is still needed to use it effectively — the formation of essential competencies.

4.2   Peculiarities of AI Implementation in Teacher's Educational Practice

Among the peculiarities of introducing AI into educational practice, the first is to determine the teacher's readiness to use it. A practitioner teacher is both a user and a researcher who, using relevant applications, examines them, analyses them, looks for effective ways to use them, and formulates a methodology for implementing innovations. Therefore, the first stage of AI implementation is to get acquainted with an idea or technology that can be the subject of innovation. The second stage is the use, implementation of innovations, and development of methods and instructions for the use of AI by students. A survey of 123 teachers of general secondary education institutions in in Ukraine showed that 48.8% of them had experience in creating educational materials using AI, but during this work, they had additional – new requests to improve the materials (76.4%). AI is becoming an innovative tool for teachers step by step – 43.1% of teachers said they use AI when needed; they feel that the frequency of using AI is increasing: yes - 18.7%, almost yes - 51.1% (see Fig. 6, 7 and 8).

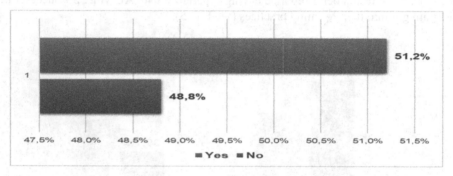

Fig. 6. % of teachers creating teaching materials using AI (N = 123, author's analysis).

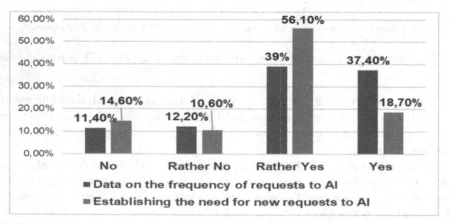

Fig. 7. Data on the frequency of requests to AI and Establishing the need for new re-quests to AI (N = 123, author's analysis).

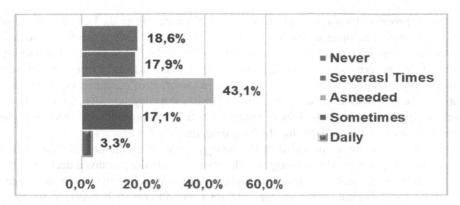

Fig. 8. Frequency of AI use by teachers (N = 123, author's analysis).

The second feature is the definition of the educational purpose of using AI (see Fig. 9).

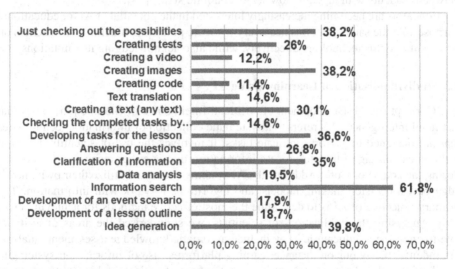

Fig. 9. Teachers' identification of areas of AI usage (N = 123, author's analysis).

The majority of teachers said that their main goal was to search for detailed information (61.8%), generate ideas (39.8%), create images (38.2%), developing tasks for the lesson (36.6%), and 38.2% were at the stage of exploring AI capabilities — experimenting. It is worth noting that teachers used AI to clarify information — 35%, create text — 30.1%, find answers to questions — 26.8%, create tests for students — 26%, checking the completed tasks by students — 14.6% etc.The third feature is to take into account the limitations of AI. The use of AI in education raises ethical issues, such as potential unethical or dishonest use by students, etc. [23].

In the process of working with a focus group of teachers from the Dnipro Lyceum of Information Technologies in Dnipro, Ukraine (20 people in total), it was found that the obstacles to incorporating AI in the classroom included the following: the unreliability of the information provided by AI, the temptation of students to get a ready-made result without analysing the task; students' use of AI in violation of academic integrity, little time in the programme for using any form of work, not only with AI. Some answers were template-like: students' lack of independence in performing work, reducing the need to make efforts, children stop thinking independently.

As per the responses provided by the surveyed educators, the key challenges that hinder the adoption of AI technology in education include the perceived decline in the significance of the teacher's role in the learning process, as well as the increasing dependence on technological tools and loss of interaction and contact between participants in the educational process; reduced critical thinking skills of students, and violation of academic integrity requirements.

According to scientific research, the integration of artificial intelligence in education may pose certain risks, such as diminishing the teacher's role, as well as reducing the creativity and critical thinking abilities of students, and the risk of increasing the gap between students with high and low socioeconomic status [24].

Educators are becoming increasingly interested in the potential of AI for educational purposes. At the same time, it is necessary to create practical guidelines for teachers on how to utilize this technology effectively, while also acknowledging its limitations.

4.3 Individualisation of Learning Using AI

The Concept for the Development of Artificial Intelligence in Ukraine [25] states that Artificial intelligence (AI) refers to a systematic collection of information technologies that are designed to perform intricate tasks. It involves the use of scientific research techniques and algorithms to process information that is either received or generated during the course of work. Additionally, AI systems create and utilize their own knowledge bases, decision-making models, and algorithms to work with information. The primary objective of AI is to determine the most effective methods for achieving tasks [26]. Analysing the publications of scientists, we summarised the areas of artificial intelligence use in education. They include automatic knowledge assessment, analysis of students' behaviour on distance learning platforms, use of information systems to develop individual learning trajectories, development of critical thinking, automation of the process of interaction with students, individualisation of learning.

Individualisation of learning is an organisation of the educational process where an individual approach and individual form of learning are a priority. It involves designing pedagogical activities based on the child's individual qualities (interests, needs, abilities, intelligence, etc.) [27]. "A learner-oriented AI enables students to study a subject domain, i.e. an adaptive or personalized learning management system" [28]. Such AI-assisted learning is based on the principles of pedagogical appropriateness, adaptability, flexibility, independence, and prompt feedback. Artificial Intelligence has the potential to be utilized in the process of education to create an individualised learning environment and provide feedback to students. AI can assist students in executing repetitive tasks during the learning process and evaluate their prior educational background [24].

It is worth noting that AI-based platforms for individualised learning allow educational institutions to develop individual learning profiles based on the abilities of each student. Based on these profiles, teachers can qualitatively assess their students' abilities and learning achievements [6]. Depending on each learner's progress, these platforms can change the speed, material, and complexity of the curriculum to provide an optimal learning experience. AI can work with virtual tutors who provide students with individualised learning tailored to their unique learning and emotional needs [29, 30]. Auto-mated tutoring systems can provide instant feedback, answer queries, and guide students through complex ideas, complementing or even replacing traditional tutoring services.

Consider examples of such platforms: Dreambox (https://www.dreambox.com) (see Fig. 10) — uses artificial intelligence to teach mathematics; Gradescope (https://turnitin. gradescope.com) — utilizes AI for automatic recognition and assessment of tasks, such as programming or mathematical calculations; Carnegie Learning (https://www.carneg ielearning.com) and NWEA (https://www.nwea.org/map-growth) — employ AI to adapt educational materials to each student's needs and create personalized learning paths.

Fig. 10. AI-enabled platforms Dreambox (https://www.dreambox.com).

To implement individualised learning, the following tasks need to be performed: adapt the content to each student, prepare individual lessons and an assessment system, and design an individual learning trajectory for the student. Let's consider the possibilities of AI for implementing individualised learning (Table 1).

In the context of the classroom system and distance learning, there is a problem of considering different individual characteristics and creating conditions for the optimal development of each student. Considering the varied levels of learning and diverse thinking styles of students is crucial. Students within the same class may show different levels of learning. Individual differences are also manifested in the types of thinking of students. Some may assimilate information better through visual means, others through auditory or kinaesthetic means. AI-powered personalised learning can identify these

Table 1. AI capabilities for implementing individualised learning

Tasks to individualised learning	AI capabilities for individualised learning
Adaptation of the content	*Learning modelling*: AI can analyse topics learned by a learner and consider individual characteristics for further adaptive learning *Personalised materials*: Generating learning materials that meet learners' specific needs and interests
Preparing individualised tasks and assessments	*Ability-based assessment*: AI can adapt tasks and tests based on a student's level of learning *Feedback*: Providing individualised feedback to improve error correction and study skills
Designing an Individual Development Trajectory	*Needs analysis*: AI can analyse a learner's strengths, weaknesses, and interests to recommend additional materials and activities *Individualised learning path*: Create a personalised learning path based on the learner's pace and learning style

differences and help students close the learning gap, enabling them to learn as effectively as possible.

General recommendations for implementing elements of individualised learning in the classroom system of education include using elements of individualised learning technologies in the classroom, providing each child with individual pedagogical assistance, overcoming individual deficiencies in knowledge, skills and abilities, and in the thinking process; consideration and correction of shortcomings of family upbringing, as well as underdevelopment of motivation, weakness of volitional processes; optimisation of the educational process in relation to students' abilities (creative activity, combination of classroom and extracurricular work); granting freedom of choice of elements of the learning process; development of general educational skills; the development of appropriate levels of self-confidence among students; use of technical means of education, including computers; support for talented and gifted children. [31].

Thus, individualisation is an essential element of any modern pedagogical technology and education system. Let us define the tasks for implementing individualisation of learning using AI:

- define the goal of individualising learning;
- select AI platforms or individual AI applications;
- develop lesson plans and scenarios for educational activities.

Performing the Task 1. Determining the purpose of individualisation (student needs). In order to achieve the desired outcome, it is imperative to conduct a comprehensive survey and administer tests to evaluate the requirements and preferences of students. This approach will enable us to gain a deeper understanding of their needs, which is essential in devising a strategy that caters to their academic aspirations and goals.

Therefore, we must conduct thorough research to obtain insights into the preferences and expectations of the student community so that we can create an environment that is conducive to their growth and development.

The purpose of using AI can be providing the practical part of the programme, interactive learning, creating an educational space, organising assessment and testing of students' knowledge, research work on the subject, and presentation of research results (Table 2).

The earmarks have the purpose of enhancing the standard of education, making it more accessible and attractive to students, and promoting the individual development of each student.

Performing the Task II. To select AI platforms or individual AI applications. To implement this task, it is necessary to analyse the AI market, test and debug the chosen solution, and adjust it to the needs of each student.

Performing the Task III. Develop lesson plans and scenarios for educational activities. To implement these assignments, it is necessary to create a bank of individual assessments of various types, scenarios of events, and assessment criteria (formative).

Depending on each learner's progress, these platforms can change the speed, material, and complexity of the curriculum to provide an optimal learning experience. AI can work with virtual tutors who provide students with individualized learning tailored to their unique learning and emotional needs [26, 27]. Automated systems, acting as tutors, can provide instant feedback, respond to inquiries, and guide students through complex ideas, complementing or even replacing traditional learning.

We have identified six types of assignments for students using artificial intelligence: adaptive, interactive, automated, personalized, gamified, AR, and VR (Table 3.)

Examples of tasks, taking into account their types, are presented in Table 4.

The use of AI will enable teachers to develop individualised curricula, personalise the learning process and provide individual support. In addition, the use of artificial intelligence allows for interactive and engaging teaching methods, contributing to the effective learning of educational material and increasing student motivation.

Analysing the teacher survey results, we concluded that AI is becoming a teacher's assistant in their pedagogical activities (see Fig. 11), which is confirmed by the teacher survey results: 37.4% said rather yes and 15.4% said yes.

These results indicate that teachers understand the potential of AI to implement individualised learning. Working with a focus group of 20 teachers while using ChatGPT, we saw that they were able to create tasks of varying difficulty for 23 8th grade students in a matter of minutes, which simplifies both teacher preparation for the lesson and the implementation of individualised learning.

Here is an example of a request to ChatGPT: Congratulations my assistant! I am asking you to develop and prepare 23 problems in biology on the topic "Man". Consider that 5 students study for 10 points, 12 students study for 9 points, 4 students study for 7 points and 2 students study for 5 points. The number of tasks in each group should correspond to the number of students. Form the answers to 23 tasks separately.

AI provided suggestions for the implementation of individualised learning in the biology classroom: 23 tasks were created for 4 groups of students (with different levels

Table 2. Determining the purpose and selection of services that use AI

Type of activity	Defining the goal of implementing AI services	Examples of AI
Provision of the practical part of the programme: virtual laboratories, services for modelling and experimentation	Enabling the creation and use of virtual laboratories for experimentation and research, allowing students to explore phenomena and processes safely	Mesh.ai – planning activities, implementing projects in Microsoft Teams https://lexica.art/
Providing interactive learning in distance and blended learning	Providing access to video tutorials and animations that can visualise complex concepts and processes, making them easier to understand for students	noodlefactory.ai - virtual teaching assistant https://app.quizalize.com/resources
Organisation of research work, presentation of research results	Access to relevant research articles, publications and resources for in-depth study of topics	Presentations AI (Microsoft Teams) – creating presentations https://gamma.app/ https://slidesgo.com/
Organisation of knowledge testing and assessment of students	Development of tools for conducting tests and assessing student knowledge, allowing teachers to track progress effectively and analyse results	https://app.conker.ai/create
Organising the workspace, creating an educational environment	Creating an environment for teachers and students to work together, share resources, discuss and learn together	Meeting Summaries from Read AI – results of meetings, analytics in Microsoft Teams https://www.dreambox.com https://explainlikeimfive.io/ https://slidesgo.com
Individualisation and adaptation: personalised learning materials	Platforms and tools can be developed to enable teachers to customize learning material according to the unique needs and knowledge levels of individual students	Fireflies AI - artificial intelligence that joins meetings and automatically records, transcribes and captures notes ChatGPT (openai.com)
Enhancing students' cognitive activity	Use of interactive games and reproducible scenarios to engage students and stimulate their interest in the subject	Focusworks AI - data processing and image generation https://app.quizalize.com/resources

Table. 3. Classification of assignment types using AI

Type of assignments for students	Details
Adaptable	Assignments that are adapted to the individual needs and level of knowledge of each student
Interactive	Assignments that incorporate interactive components to encourage students' active involvement in the learning process
Automated	Assignments for which automated assessment and feedback tools are used
Personalised	Assignments that are tailored to each student's academic achievements, individual interests and needs
Gamified	Assignments that have a game component to stimulate students' motivation and interest in the learning process
Assignments with AR, VR	Assignments that use virtual and augmented reality technologies to enhance learning and understanding of complex concepts

Table 4. Examples of assignments that use AI

Subject	Grade	Assignment
The English language	7–9th grade	Creating unique stories and literary works (Storytelling, adaptive)
		Create sentences and dialogues (Travel, interactive)
		Spell checker (Grammar, personalised)
Mathematics	7–9th grade	Checking mathematical proofs (Logic, automated)
		Creating mathematical puzzles (Creativity, interactive)
		Checking solutions to olympiad problems (In-depth, personalised)
Biology	7–9th grade	Studying interactions between living organisms in ecological systems (Dependencies, VR)
		Creation of scenarios for the evolution of living organisms (Sequences, AR)
		Creating visual diagrams and models of biological processes (Visualisation, interactive)

of academic achievement) and short answers were offered for prompt teacher feedback and assessment [3] (see Fig. 12).

When planning the implementation of individualised learning using AI, it should be noted that the current stage of development of educational technologies in Ukraine, when

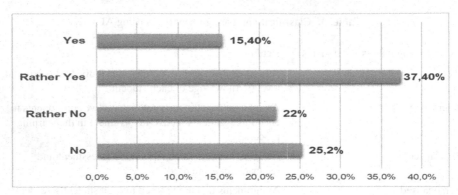

Fig. 11. Question: "Do you feel that AI is becoming your assistant?" (N = 123, author's analysis).

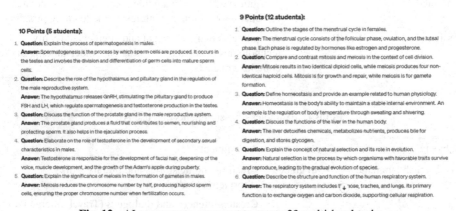

Fig. 12. AI response to a request to create 23 multi-level tasks.

blended and distance learning is a priority, determines the importance of recognising the individual needs of the student and developing his or her unique capabilities. Under martial law in Ukraine, not all students were able to receive a quality education, so in 2023, the teaching community raised the issue of overcoming educational losses, including the use of AI to improve English writing skills, support for science and mathematics subjects.

4.4 Challenges and Problems of Artificial Intelligence Integration in Secondary Schools

Given the potential of AI for education, and its digital and practical transformation, we would like to bring to your attention that there exist challenges and problems with integrating artificial intelligence into secondary schools:

- *Training of teachers*: teachers need to be properly trained to use artificial intelligence in teaching and assessing students.
- *Dependence on technology*: the use of artificial intelligence in education can create a technology of dependence and reduce the role of teachers.

- ethical standards should be developed for the use of artificial intelligence in education.
- implementing artificial intelligence in secondary schools requires funding and access to the necessary resources.
- *Contradictory opinions*: there are different points of view on the introduction of AI and its impact on the quality of education.

Luckin, Rose, et al. point out that only by providing a degree of understanding can we move beyond the sci-fi images of artificial intelligence and associated fears and make the case for AIEd to be beneficial to learning both now and in the future to improve learning outcomes [32].

5 Discussion

The discussion on the use of AI by Ukrainian teachers raised issues related to both the crisis conditions faced by students and the possibilities of overcoming them through the use of AI.

For example, the results of a study of the quality of the educational process in general secondary education institutions during the war, conducted in December 2022–January 2023 with the participation of the State Service for Quality Assurance in Education, showed that 30% of students do not have stable access to the educational process. In addition, the methods and forms of work of teachers are not sufficiently adapted to distance learning, there is an impact on the psychological state of participants in the educational process, and there are losses in class time and logistical support for educational institutions. As a result of Russia's full-scale war against Ukraine, approximately 800,000 Ukrainian children switched from full-time to distance learning. The loss of Ukrainian education as a result of this conflict has serious consequences for children and young people, as well as for society as a whole.

However, there are some ways that can help reduce these losses and ensure quality education even in difficult military conditions and provide individualised learning. This involves educators using innovative methodological approaches to creating educational content, understanding the basics of information and communication technologies, developing an educational environment for effective distance learning, and introducing disruptive technologies such as AI.

Ukrainian educators may feel distrustful of artificial intelligence. There is a prevailing fear that automation can replace the role of the teacher or reduce the importance of human influence in the learning process. The misconception that AI will lead to a loss of control over the learning process may cause resistance to the use of these technologies.

Currently, there are no standards or clear regulations, which can cause some misunderstandings about ethical aspects, data privacy, and the impact of technology on the formation of a student's personality. Insufficient preparation of teachers to work with AI affects their willingness to use these technologies, and the lack of training and technical support leads to a loss of interest in using innovations. Teachers may express ethical doubts about the use of AI in assessing and tracking students' academic progress. The issues of transparency of algorithms and the impact of technology on the development of moral values may cause disputes and discussions among the educational community.

However, the use of AI in education can be a source of significant motivation for teachers. The growing possibilities of individualisation, automated knowledge assessment, and developmental tools create prospects for improving the quality of education and engaging students in the learning process, and in the context of long-term quarantines and martial law, digital technologies are seen as an effective means of remote learning for students and teachers, taking into account the individual characteristics and needs of students.

In general, teachers expressed hope that a significant number of digital services and platforms using AI will make a breakthrough in both the organisation of learning and the formation of the "digital" personality of a 21st century student.

6 Conclusions and Recommendations for Further Research

The use of artificial intelligence in the educational process is an innovation that requires study, generalisation of experience, and implementation of scientific achievements in practice. At the present stage, there is a rapid development of this technology and the introduction of AI into educational practice without appropriate theoretical and methodological justification.

The practical experience of teachers in using AI confirms that the introduction of this technology into the educational process can effectively influence various aspects of learning and improve the quality of education in general, allowing for individualised learning, taking into account the needs of each student, helping to create personalised curricula, taking into account the pace, style and personality of each student. The use of AI gives teachers and students flexibility in the learning process, allowing them to effectively adapt to changing requirements and circumstances.

Analysing the work of teachers in crisis conditions, we have concluded that AI as an assistant can modernise and improve the work of teachers, provide them with new conditions for cooperation and personal development, and for students − optimise the learning process and ensure its individualisation, gaining independent and effective educational experience.

Nevertheless, it is important to take into account the ethical, social, and security aspects of AI, as well as to provide teacher training for the effective use of these technologies in the classroom.

References

1. Dotsenko, I.: Current issues in the implementation of information and communication technologies in higher education. Mining Herald, vol. 102, pp. 117–120. http://ds.knu.edu.ua/jspui/handle/123456789/3292. Accessed 10 Dec 2023
2. Schiff, D.: Education for AI, not AI for education: the role of education and ethics in national AI policy strategies. Int. J. Artif. Intell. Educ. **32**(3), 527–563 (2022). https://doi.org/10.1007/s40593-021-00270-2
3. GPT-3.5. https://chat.openai.com. Accessed 10 Dec 2023
4. Koh, E., Doroudi, S.: Learning, teaching, and assessment with generative artificial intelligence: towards a plateau of productivity. Learn. Res. Pract. **9**(2), 109–116 (2023). https://doi.org/10.1080/23735082.2023.2264086

5. Ushakova, I.: Approaches to creating intelligent chatbots. Inf. Process. Syst. **2**(157), 76–83 (2019). https://doi.org/10.30748/soi.2019.157.10
6. Vizniuk, I., Buglay, N., Kutsak, L., Polishchuk, A., Kylyvnyk, V.: Utilization of artificial intelligence in education. Mod. Inf. Technol. Innovation Methodol. Educ. Prof. Training: Methodol. Theory, Exp. Probl. **59**, 14–22 (2021). https://doi.org/10.31652/2412-1142-2021-59-14-22
7. Harry, A.: Role of AI in education. Interdisc. J. Humanity, **2**(3), 260–268 (2023). https://doi.org/10.58631/injurity.v2i3.52
8. Dwivedi, Y., Kshetri, N., Hughes, L.: So what if ChatGPT wrote it? Multidisciplinary perspectives on opportunities, challenges and implications of generative conversational AI for research, practice and policy. Int. J. Inf. Manage. **71**, 102642 (2023). https://doi.org/10.1016/j.ijinfomgt.2023.102642
9. The World Economic Forum. How AI can accelerate students' holistic development and make teaching more fulfilling. https://cutt.ly/Qw17Vo7n. Accessed 10 Dec 2023
10. Pchelianskyi, D., Voinova, S.: Artificial intelligence: prospects and development trends. Autom. Technol. Bus. Process. **11**(3), 59–64 (2019). https://doi.org/10.15673/atbp.v11i3.1500
11. Walton Family Foundation. ChatGPT Used by Teachers More Than Students, New Survey from Walton Family Foundation Finds. https://cutt.ly/lw17BWPI. Accessed 10 Dec 2023
12. Dawes, M.: Alleviating or Exacerbating Inequity in Education. AI in Education. https://cutt.ly/Kw17BDXc. Accessed 10 Dec 2023
13. Sharples, M.: Towards social generative ai for education: theory, practices and ethics. Learn. Res. Pract. **9**(2), 159–67. (2023). https://doi.org/10.1080/23735082.2023.2261131
14. Luan, H., Tsai, C.: A review of using machine learning approaches for precision education. Educ. Technol. Soc. **24**(1), 250–266. https://www.jstor.org/stable/26977871. last accessed 2023/12/10
15. Kamalov, F., Santandreu, C., Gurrib, I.: New era of artificial intelligence in education: towards a sustainable multifaceted revolution. Sustainability. **15**(16), 12451 (2023). https://doi.org/10.3390/su151612451
16. Kademiia, M., Vizniuk, I., Polishchuk, A., Dolynnyi, S.: Artificial intelligence in foreign language learning by educational attendees. Mod. Inf. Technol. Innovation Methodol. Educ. Prof. Training: Methodol. Theory, Exp. Probl. 153–163. (2022). https://doi.org/10.31652/2412-1142-2022-63-153-163
17. Shvydun, V.: Pedagogical innovations in the practice of activities of general secondary education institutions. Visnik Zaporizkogo Naciohainogo Universitetu. Pedagogicni Nauki. **1**, 35–39 (2021). https://doi.org/10.26661/2522-4360-2021-1-1-05
18. Rogers, E.: Diffusion of innovations. https://teddykw2.files.wordpress.com/2012/07/everett-m-rogers-diffusion-of-innovations.pdf. Accessed 10 Dec 2023
19. Davis, F.: Perceived usefulness, perceived ease of use, and user acceptance of information technology. MIS Q. **3**(13), 319–340 (1989). https://doi.org/10.2307/249008
20. Piaget, J.; Inhedler, B.: The psychology of the child. Basic Books. https://www.alohabdonline.com/wp-content/uploads/2020/05/The-Psychology-Of-The-Child.pdf. Accessed 10 Dec 2023
21. Ivaniuk, I., Ovcharuk, O.: The state of readiness of teachers of general secondary education institutions to use the information and educational environment for the implementation of distance learning in quarantine caused by COVID-19. New Pedagogical Thought, **3**, 48–54. http://nbuv.gov.ua/UJRN/Npd_2020_3_10. Accessed 10 Dec 2023
22. Panukhnyk, O.: Artificial intelligence in the educational process and scientific research of higher education applicants: responsible boundaries of AI content. Galician Econ. J. **83**(4), 202–211 (2023). https://doi.org/10.33108/galicianvisnyk_tntu2023.04.202

23. Qadir, J.: Engineering education in the era of ChatGPT: promise and pitfalls of generative AI for education. In: IEEE Global Engineering Education Conference (EDUCON), pp. 1–9, (2023). https://doi.org/10.1109/EDUCON54358.2023.10125121

24. Marienko, M., Kovalenko, V.: Artificial intelligence and open science in education. Phys. Math. Educ. **38**(1), 48–53 (2023). https://doi.org/10.31110/2413-1571-2023-038-1-007

25. Concept of Artificial Intelligence Development in Ukraine: Approved by the Order of the Cabinet of Ministers of Ukraine (2020). https://zakon.rada.gov.ua/laws/show/1556-2020-%D1%80#Text. Accessed 10 Dec 2023

26. Dai, C., Ke, F.: Educational applications of artificial intelligence in simulation-based learning: a systematic mapping review. Comput. Educ. Artif. Intell. **3**, 100087 (2022). https://doi.org/10.1016/j.caeai.2022.100087

27. Yefremov, M., Yefremov, Y.: Artificial intelligence: history and development prospects. Bull. ZHDTU. Ser. Tech. Sci. **2**(45), 123–126 (2016). https://doi.org/10.26642/tn-2008-2(45)-123-126

28. Baker, T., Smith, L.: Educ-AI-tion rebooted? Exploring the future of artificial intelligence in schools and colleges. Retrieved from Nesta Foundation. https://media.nesta.org.uk/documents/Future_of_AI_and_education_v5_WEB.pdf. Accessed 10 Dec 2023

29. Jonnalagadda, A., Rajvir, M., Singh, S.: An ensemble-based machine learning model for emotion and mental health detection. J. Inf. Knowl. Manag. **22**(02), 2250075 (2023). https://doi.org/10.1142/S0219649222500757

30. Mahfood, B., Elnagar, A., Kamalov, F.: Emotion recognition from speech using convolutional neural networks. In: Khanna, A., Polkowski, Z., Castillo, O. (eds) Proceedings of Data Analytics and Management, LNNS, vol. 572, pp. 719–731. Springer, Singapore (2023). https://doi.org/10.1007/978-981-19-7615-5_59

31. Lozenko, A.: Individualization in the conditions of traditional teaching technology: problems and perspectives. Probl. Methodol. Phys. Math. Technol. Educ. **3**, 191–194. http://enpuir.npu.edu.ua/handle/123456789/12787. Accessed 10 Dec 2023

32. Luckin, R.: Intelligence Unleashed: An Argument for AI in Education. https://discovery.ucl.ac.uk/id/eprint/1475756/. Accessed 10 Dec 2023

Artificial Intelligence: A Review of Educational Literature in Spain

Mario Grande-de-Prado[1]([⊠]) [iD], Sheila García-Martín[1] [iD], Roberto Baelo-Álvarez[1] [iD], and Víctor Abella-García[2] [iD]

[1] Facultad de Educación de León , Universidad de León, Campus de Vegazana, s/n, 24071 León, Spain
{mgrap,sgarcm,roberto.baelo}@unileon.es
[2] Facultad de Educación de Burgos, Universidad de Burgos, C. de Villadiego 1, 09001 Burgos, Spain
vabella@ubu.es

Abstract. In the context of a VUCA (volatility, uncertainty, complexity and ambiguity) society, the evolution of Artificial Intelligence (AI) has been characterised by a growing social impact. In this regard, this study reviews the educational academic literature in Spanish academic journals from 2020 to 2023, focusing on the intersection of AI and education. The research utilises a descriptive-interpretive methodology. It is a global and exploratory literature mapping. Thirty-nine articles are identified on Dialnet. Results reveal a rising trend with the same amount of publications in 2023 (in half a year) as in 2022. The impact of ChatGPT, a renowned AI model, in 2023 is acknowledged, suggesting an upward trajectory in publications. Indexed mostly in Scopus, the articles reflect the keen interest of Spanish academics in AI and education. Research and essays/reflections constitute most articles, emphasising concerns about the challenges and applications of AI in education. In conclusion, the study underscores the need for continued exploration and understanding of the evolving landscape of AI in education, with the support of further empirical research. It proposed future research directions, including comparative studies with other regions, to better grasp the global implications of AI in shaping the future of education.

Keywords: Artificial Intelligence · Review · Educational Technology

1 Introduction

We live in a changing society marked by events like COVID-19, the war in Ukraine, and environmental and technological challenges. Some authors define this society as VUCA, an Anglo-Saxon acronym for volatility, uncertainty, complexity, and ambiguity, used to characterise an environment where secure predictions are challenged due to its unstable and hard-to-forecast nature [1].

Among the catalysts of these accelerated changes, artificial intelligence (AI) plays a key role in 2023. AI, understood as machines (hardware and software) capable of

Ł. Tomczyk (Ed.): NMP 2023, CCIS 2130, pp. 413–424, 2024.
https://doi.org/10.1007/978-3-031-63235-8_27

performing tasks that typically require human intelligence, such as learning, reasoning, problem-solving, perception, etc., are based on the simulation of human intelligence processes. They aim to significantly enhance human capabilities and contributions [2]. AI can also be understood as a field of study in computer science that attempts to simulate intelligent processes using computers. There are different perspectives on whether the purpose is to imitate human intelligence or to develop programs that perform intelligent tasks. In this regard, within the various disciplines interested in AI, the philosophy of AI examines whether machines can have conscious intelligence and mental states. At the same time, the ethics of IA considers the ethical implications of its development and use [3].

The inception of artificial intelligence can be traced back to the 1950s when computer scientists embarked on developing algorithms with the capacity to execute tasks that conventionally necessitate human intelligence. In 1956, John McCarthy introduced the terminology "artificial intelligence" and orchestrated the Dartmouth Conference, widely acknowledged as the seminal moment in the birth of AI [4]. Subsequently, artificial intelligence has evolved substantially and found applications across a broad spectrum of domains, encompassing healthcare, finance, and transportation.

Scientific journals have played a pivotal role in advancing the field of artificial intelligence. Several notable instances include a publication by Krizhevsky et al., [5] and, wherein they introduced a deep-learning algorithm that markedly enhanced the precision of image classification. Additionally, in 2015, a research study conducted by a team affiliated with Google DeepMind [6] demonstrated the superior performance of a neural network in comparison to human players in the realm of video games. In 2016, the AlphaGo program, developed by Google DeepMind, achieved a momentous victory over the reigning world champion in the intricate game of Go, thereby serving as a compelling demonstration of artificial intelligence's exceptional problem-solving capabilities [7].

In 2023, AI made a qualitative leap, with one of the most famous AI models being ChatGPT, developed by OpenAI, which gained 100 million users just two months after its launch [8]. This AI tool is a language model that uses deep learning to generate human-like responses to text-based queries. It has been used for various applications, including chatbots, customer service, and content creation. It has made headlines for its ability to generate high-quality content and can potentially influence citizens through fake news [9]. However, its impact extends beyond content creation.

As AI continues to evolve, it can potentially transform our society radically. In this context, educational institutions, such as universities, face the challenge of adapting to the new digital society, which will require a profound redefinition of their functioning and a complete transformation of these organisations [10]. Its evolution can bring advantages in the teaching and learning process, research, administrative processes, and community engagement. However, there are also some risks (or challenges) related to academic integrity, lack of regulation, data protection, biases, diversity, accessibility, and commercialisation [8]. The convergence of commercial and educational AI poses challenges and questions about its feasibility. Commercial AI has improved efficiency in various sectors but integrating it into education is complex. AI can personalise learning, but reliance on it may diminish the role of the teacher and human interaction. The use of commercial AI in education raises concerns about privacy, security, and access.

The combination of commercial and educational AI may have benefits, it must be done ethically and transparently, prioritising student well-being and development of students [11].

Among the positive aspects, AI has revolutionised our interaction with technology, increasing the efficiency of everyday tasks, optimising industrial processes, and facilitating decision-making in areas such as medicine and scientific research. However, one of the main hurdles of AI is its potential to create deep fakes, which refers to multimedia content generated by algorithms that can be difficult to distinguish from reality. These deep fakes pose significant threats to security and privacy, as they can be used to spread false or compromising information with disastrous consequences. To combat this dilemma, it is imperative to implement protective measures, such AI education initiatives. A comprehensive understanding of the functionality of and the methods used to produce deep fakes can enable individuals to recognise and mitigate their negative effects, thus promoting a more conscientious and ethical use of this burgeoning technology [12].

2 Method

This study employs a descriptive-interpretive approach of the review type. While drawing upon the Systematic Literature Review as a point of reference [13], our perspective gravitates towards a comprehensive and exploratory examination of the subject, akin to mapping. In pursuing this research, a thorough search for articles was conducted on Dialnet, with this virtual repository being chosen due to its prominence in the Hispanic context. Dialnet, in conjunction with its advanced service Dialnet Plus, stands acknowledged as one of the world's foremost bibliographic platforms, particularly renowned for curating scientific literature in the Spanish language (constituting approximately 66% of its content). This platform hosts an extensive collection of nearly eight million meticulously referenced documents, encompassing journal articles, collective works, books, conference proceedings, bibliographic reviews, and doctoral theses [14].

The selection criteria for this study encompassed journal papers published in Spain with open-access full-text content and published between 2020 and May 2023 in the domains of Psychology and Education, with a specific focus on the field of Education, and included in the Latindex database. The search query employed was "artificial intelligence." The collected articles underwent analysis involving the creation of frequency tables categorised by publication years, the respective journals they were featured in, and their subject classifications. In total, 39 articles were subjected to review, with the exclusion of two articles that were deemed unrelated to the designated research topic.

The selection of articles is reflected according to the PRISMA model in Fig. 1.

Dialnet uses CIRC (*Clasificación Integrada de Revistas Científicas*) as a classification system for Spanish journals within the Social Sciences and Humanities domain. This classification system ranks journals from A+ (representing excellence) to D (indicating a low scientific status). Journals that receive classifications of A+, A, B, or C are those that have been indexed in the Journal Citation Reports (JCR), Scopus, the Emerging Sources Citation Index (ESCI), the European Reference Index for the Humanities (ERIH), or a source of equivalent recognition. This classification system is a valuable tool for evaluating and categorising the quality and scientific standing of Social Sciences and Humanities journals.

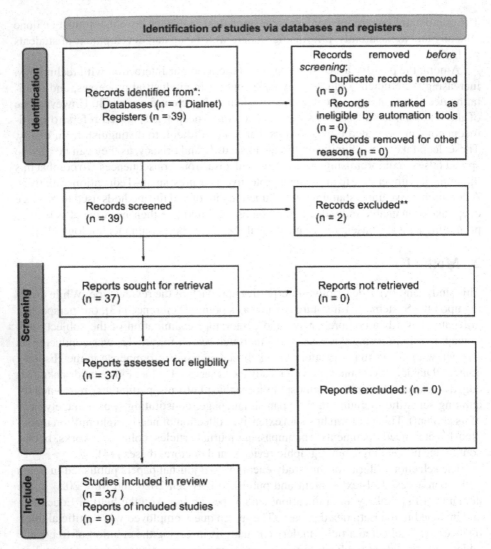

Fig. 1. PRISMA 2020 Flow Diagram. Note: Based on [15].

Analysis sheets were utilised to review the articles, and a categorisation process was undertaken. Subsequently, a descriptive statistical analysis was conducted.

The research questions are as follows:

- What educational articles on AI have been published in Spain since 2020?
- What are the subjects or topics covered in these articles, and what types of articles do they represent?
- What is the temporal distribution and trends in the publication of these articles over time?

- In which academic journals were these articles published, and how many are indexed in Scopus? Additionally, what are their classifications according to the CIRC system?

3 Results

After analysing the literature review, the results have been organised based on the following sections: year of publication, journal and indexing, type of article, and theme.

3.1 Distribution by Years

Table 1 presents the articles organised by their year of publication, while Fig. 2 provides a visual representation of the paper counts for each year.

Table 1. Articles by year

Year	Articles
2020	[16] Aznarte (2020); [17] Betancourt (2020); [18] Bonam et al. (2020); [19] Boya Lara et al. (2020); [20] Gutiérrez et al. (2020); [21] Vázquez (2020)
2021	[22] Artiles et al. (2021); [23] Atencio et al. (2021); [24] Calabuig et al. (2021); [25] Estrada (2021); [26] Grané (2021); [27] Narodowski; (2021); [28] Prendes et al. (2021); [29] Robles (2021); [30] Sancho et al. (2021)
2022	[10] Area et al. (2022); [31] Ayuso et al. (2022); [32] Bethencourt et al. (2022); [33] Contreras et al. (2022); [34] Falla et al. (2022); [35] Giró et al. (2022); [36] González et al. (2022); [37] Harris et al. (2022); [38] Martín (2022); [39] Martín et al. (2022); [40] Mena et al. (2022); [41] Sañudo (2022); [42] Silva et al. (2022)
2023	[23] Barroso et al. (2023). [44] Borrelli; [45] Carrera et al. (2023); [46] Flores Vivar et al. (2023); [47] Flores et al. (2023); [48] González et al. (2023); [49] Marín et al. (2023); [50] Rumiche et al. (2023); [51] Saura (2023)

As can be observed, the number of articles has increased each year (between 2020 and 2022, the full years). In the last year, 2023, in five months, contributed nine articles, the same as in 2021 in less than half a year.

3.2 Journals and Indexing

Table 2 shows the journals grouped according to the number of articles.

RIED journal stands out with four articles published, followed by Edutec, Profesorado, and Comunicar, each featuring three articles. While not initially within the scope of the analysis, it is noteworthy that the University of Granada is the most prolific publisher, contributing seven publications.

Regarding indexing, it is noteworthy that out of the 37 articles under examination, 20 are featured in journals indexed in Scopus during the analysis period. Only two articles are found in journals classified as CIRC Social Sciences D, with all other articles spanning classifications from A+ to C. In the Dialnet metrics, thirty journals are categorised as C1 or C2, four journals lack metrics, and three are positioned in the C3 category.

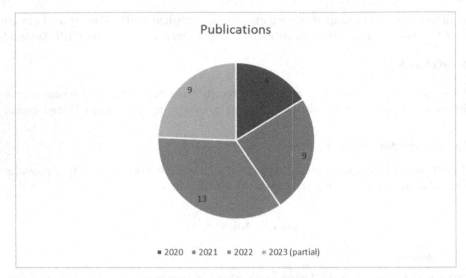

Fig. 2. Publications per year.

Table 2. Number of articles by journal

Number of articles	Journal
4	RIED
3	Edutec; Profesorado; Comunicar
2	Tarbiya; Campus Virtuales; Publicaciones; RESED; RIITE; Modelling in Science Education
1	Contextos educativos; Bordón. Arte. Individuo y sociedad; Revista electrónica interuniversitaria de formación del profesorado; RELATEC; Educar; Teoría de la Educación; Pixel.bit; Etic@net; Dedica; EduPsykhé; REALIA

3.3 Type of Articles and Themes

Research and essays/reflections are the most frequent type of paper, with 12 in both cases (each representing 32% of the total). They are followed in order of importance by the reviews, with nine (24%), proposals, proposals with three (8%), and finally experiences, with one (3%).

The articles have been categorised into three main themes based on the challenges and applications identified by UNESCO [8]: Challenges, Applications, and Others. The Applications section has a subsection named "Educational Management," which was previously called "Administration" This change was made to reflect the education aspect of the subsection better, as analysed in the articles. The Others category includes articles whose content did not fit into the previous two categories (Table 3).

Table 3. Articles by topic

Topic	Subtopic	Frequency	%
Challenges		13	35.14%
Applications		15	40.54%
	Teaching and Learning	9	
	Educational Management	4	
	Research	2	
Other		9	24.32%
	Initial teacher training teachers	1	
	Reviews / neutral essays	7	
	Research	1	

Concerns related to challenges and difficulties comprise 35.14% of all concerns. In comparison, AI applications exhibit slightly higher rates at 40.54%. Notably, there is a particular emphasis on AI applications that have a direct connection to the teaching and learning process.

4 Conclusions

In conclusion, the analysis of the bibliographic review in Spain since 2020 underscores a consistent rise in the number of articles addressing the intersection of AI and Education, particularly in recent years. Notable journals such as RIED, Edutec, Profesorado, and Comunicar have emerged as prominent contributors in terms of article publications. It is worth noting that the full impact of ChatGPT's popularisation on publications in 2023 remains to be fully understood; however, initial observations suggest a substantial upward trend this year. The results show a significant increase in the number of articles over the years, indicating a growing interest in the subject matter. Particularly noteworthy is the significant contribution of the University of Granada, which is the most prolific publisher, with seven publications.

Regarding indexing, it is noteworthy that a significant proportion of the articles, 20 out of 37, are found in journals indexed in Scopus, indicating a high level of recognition and visibility within the academic community.

The categorisation of the articles into three main themes - Challenges, Applications, and Others - provides valuable insights into the focus of research in the field of AI in education. The small number of research and proposal underscores the complexity of IA evolution. In addition, the significant proportion of articles addressing concerns related to challenges and difficulties, as well as AI applications directly related to the teaching and learning process, highlights the practical implications and real-world applications of AI technologies in educational settings.

Overall, these findings provide a comprehensive overview of the current research landscape at the intersection of AI and education. Going forward, future studies can build on these findings to further explore and address the challenges, applications, and emerging trends in the field, ultimately contributing to the advancement of both theory and practice.

Looking ahead, a promising avenue for future research would be to compare these results in the Spanish context with other regions, such as LATAM, the Anglo-Saxon context, or publications by Asian academics. This is due to the clear and universal impact of AI, which is catalysing social, economic, and educational transformations on a global scale. Future lines of research on AI in education are diverse and evolving the technology advances and our understanding of its application in educational deepens. Some key areas of research include:

- Personalisation of learning.
- Automated assessment and feedback
- Intelligent tutoring
- Creation of educational mateials (like videos, presentations or quizzes)
- Ethics and privacy

These are just some of the emerging lines of research in AI in education, and they are expected to evolve and expand as technology advances and new ways of applying AI to improve teaching and learning are discovered.

To conclude, it is essential to highlight that this subject provokes numerous reflections on the challenges and transformative potential it holds. It is evident that there is a strong interest in the immense opportunities AI presents.

NOTE: This communication has been carried out by the Educational Innovation Group 'Didactics, Innovation, and Communication' (GID 031) of the University of León, in collaboration with members of the EDUTOOLS research group, in the initial phase of the project "Proposals for the Improvement of Final's Degree Work".

References

1. Fuentealba, D., Flores-Fernández, C., Carrasco, R.: Análisis bibliométrico y de contenido sobre VUCA [VUCA bibliometric and content analysis]. Revista Española de Documentación Científica, **46** (2), e354 (2023). https://doi.org/10.3989/redc.2023.2.1968
2. Joiner, I.A.: Artificial intelligence: AI is nearby. In: Joiner, I.A., (ed.) Emerging Library Technologies, pp. 1–22. Chandos Publishing (2018). https://doi.org/10.1016/B978-0-08-102 253-5.00002-2
3. Brey, P., Søraker, J.H.: Philosophy of computing and information technology. In: Meijers, A., (ed.), Handbook of the Philosophy of Science, Philosophy of Technology and Engineering Sciences, pp. 1341–1407. North-Holland (2009). https://doi.org/10.1016/B978-0-444-51667-1.50051-3
4. Russell, S.J., y Norvig, P.: Artificial Intelligence: A Modern Approach. Prentice Hall (2010)
5. Krizhevsky, A., Sutskever, I., Hinton, G.E.: ImageNet classification with deep convolutional neural networks. In: Pereira, F., Burges, C.J., Bottou, L., Weinberger, K.Q. (eds.), Advances in Neural Information Processing Systems, vol. 25. Curran Associates, Inc (2012). https://proceedings.neurips.cc/paper_files/paper/2012/file/c399862d3b9d6b76c8436 e924a68c45b-Paper.pdf

6. Mnih, V., et al.: Human-level control through deep reinforcement learning. Nature **518**(7540), 529–533 (2015). https://doi.org/10.1038/nature14236

7. Silver, D., et al.: Mastering the game of Go with deep neural networks and tree search. Nature **529**(7587), 484–489 (2016). https://doi.org/10.1038/nature16961

8. UNESCO. ChatGPT e inteligencia artificial en la educación superior: Guía de inicio rápido [ChatGPT and Artificial Intelligence in Higher Education: A quick start guide] (No. ED/HE/IESALC/IP/2023/12) [Corporate author]. Sabzalieva, E., & Valentini, A. [Authors]. (2023a) bit.ly/GPTUnesco

9. García Orosa, B., Canavilhas, J., Vázquez Herrero, J.: Algoritmos y comunicación: Revisión sistematizada de la literatura [Algorithms and communication: A systematized literature review]. Comunicar: Revista Científica Iberoamericana de Comunicación y Educación, **74**, 9–21 (2023). https://doi.org/10.3916/C74-2023-01

10. Area Moreira, M., Guarro Pallás, A., Marrero Acosta, J., Sosa Alonso, J.J.: La transformación digital de la docencia universitaria [The digital transformation of university teaching]. Profesorado: Revista de Curriculum y Formación del Profesorado, **26**(2), 1–5 (2022). https://revistaseug.ugr.es/index.php/profesorado/article/view/25560

11. Holmes, W. Persson, J. Chounta I-A, Wasson, B., Dimitrova, V.: Artificial intelligence and education: a critical view through the lens of human rights, democracy and the rule of law. Council of Europe (2022)

12. UNESCO. Guidance for generative AI in education and research. UNESCO Publishing (2023b)

13. Kitchenham, B., Brereton, O.P., Budgen, D., Turner, M., Bailey, J., Linkman, S.: Systematic literature reviews in software engineering: a systematic literature review. Inf. Softw. Technol. **51**, 7–15 (2009). https://doi.org/10.1016/j.infsof.2008.09.009

14. Fundación Dialnet. Dialnet en cifras. bit.ly/Dialnet2021 (2021)

15. Page, M.J., McKenzie, J.E., Bossuyt, P.M., Boutron, I., Hoffmann, T.C., Mulrow, C.D., et al.: The PRISMA 2020 statement: an updated guideline for reporting systematic reviews. BMJ **372**, n71 (2021). https://doi.org/10.1136/bmj.n71

16. Aznarte Mellado, J. L.: Consideraciones éticas en torno al uso de tecnologías basadas en datos masivos en la UNED [Ethical considerations on the use of massive data-based technologies in UNED]. RIED: Revista Iberoamericana de Educación a Distancia, **23**(2), 237–252 (2020). https://doi.org/10.5944/ried.23.2.26590

17. Betancourt Ramirez, E.A.: Análisis de los estilos de aprendizaje a través de sistemas inteligentes [Analysis of learning styles through intelligent systems.] Etic@net: Revista Científica Electrónica de Educación y Comunicación en la Sociedad del Conocimiento, **20**(1), 1–17 (2020). https://doi.org/10.30827/eticanet.v20i1.15519

18. Bonam, B., Piazentin, L., Dala Possa, A.: Educación, Big Data e Inteligencia Artificial: Metodologías mixtas en plataformas digitales [Education, Big Data and Artificial Intelligence: Mixed methods in digital platforms]. Comunicar: Revista científica Iberoamericana de Comunicación y Educación, **65**, 43–52 (2020). https://doi.org/10.3916/C65-2020-04

19. Boya Lara, C., Vega, M.: Una propuesta para potenciar el aprendizaje STEM basado en Robótica BEAM [A proposal to enhance STEM learning based on BEAM Robotic]. Publicaciones: Facultad de Educación y Humanidades del Campus de Melilla, **50**(4), 125–140 (2020). https://doi.org/10.30827/publicaciones.v50i4.17786

20. Gutiérrez Fernández, A., Guerrero Higueras, Á.M., Conde González, M.Á., Fernández Llamas, C.: Evaluación del resultado académico de los estudiantes a partir del análisis del uso de los Sistemas de Control de Versiones [Evaluation of students' academic results through the analysis of their use of Version Control Systems]. RIED: Revista Iberoamericana de Educación a Distancia, **23**(2), 127–145 (2020). https://doi.org/10.5944/ried.23.2.26539

21. Vázquez Gómez, G.: La autoeducación permanente en un contexto sociotécnico [Lifelong self-education in a sociotechnical context]. Contextos Educativos: Revista de Educación, **26**, 83–103 (2020). https://doi.org/10.18172/con.4451

22. Artiles Rodríguez, J., Guerra Santana, M., Aguiar Perera, M.V., Rodríguez Pulido, J.: Agente conversacional virtual: La inteligencia artificial para el aprendizaje autónomo [Embodied conversational agents: artificial intelligence for autonomous learning]. Pixel-Bit: Revista de Medios y Educación, **62**, 107–144 (2021). https://doi.org/10.12795/pixelbit.86171

23. Atencio Ortiz, P.S., Sánchez Torres, G., Iral Palomino, R., Branch Bedoya, J.W., Burgos Solans, D.: Arquitectura conceptual de plataforma tecnológica de vigilancia epidemiológica para la COVID-19 [Conceptual architecture of the epidemiological surveillance technology platform for CoVId-19]. Campus Virtuales, **10**(1), 21–34 (2021). http://uajournals.com/ojs/index.php/campusvirtuales/article/view/735

24. Calabuig Rodríguez, J.M., García Raffi, L.M., Sánchez Pérez, E.A.: Aprender como una máquina: Introduciendo la Inteligencia Artificial en la enseñanza secundaria [learning like a machine: introducing artificial intelligence into secondary education]. Model. Sci. Educ. Learn. **14**(1), 5–14 (2021). https://doi.org/10.4995/msel.2021.15022

25. Estrada, B.: La digitalización en el mundo del trabajo [Digitalization within the world of work]. Tarbiya: Revista de Investigación e Innovación Educativa, **49**, 45–54 (2021). https://doi.org/10.15366/tarbiya2021.49.003

26. Grané Ortega, J. :Jaque mate digital a la humanidad? Educar humanos y resiliar en la era de la inteligencia artificial [Digital checkmate to humanity? Educate humans and to resiliate in the age of artificial intelligence]. Dedica. Revista de Educação e Humanidades, **18**, 2–24 (2021). https://doi.org/10.30827/dreh.vi18.21000

27. Narodowski, M.: Fantasmas de lo escolar: ¿A quién vas a llamar? [Ghosts of school. Who you gonna call?] Teoría de la Educación, **33**(2), 49–63 (2021). https://doi.org/10.14201/teri.25136

28. Prendes Espinosa, M.P., Cerdán Cartagena, F.: Tecnologías avanzadas para afrontar el reto de la innovación educativa [Advanced technologies to face the challenge of educational innovation]. RIED: Revista Iberoamericana de Educación a Distancia, **24**(1), 35–53 (2021). https://doi.org/10.5944/ried.24.1.28415

29. Robles Loro, R.: El transhumano: Retos para la moral y la educación [The transhuman: challenges for morality and education]. Tarbiya: Revista de Investigación e Innovación Educativa, **49**, 73–86 (2021). https://doi.org/10.15366/tarbiya2021.49.005

30. Sancho Barrios, L., Sanmartín Vich, N., Roger de la Resurrección, C.: Redes neuronales en el fútbol [Neural networks in football]. Modelling in Science Education and Learning, **14**(1), 15–32 (2021). https://doi.org/10.4995/msel.2021.15023

31. Ayuso del Puerto, D., Gutiérrez Esteban, P.: La Inteligencia Artificial como recurso educativo durante la formación inicial del profesorado [Artificial Intelligence as an educational resource during preservice teacher training]. RIED: Revista Iberoamericana de Educación a Distancia, **25**(2), 347–362 (2022). https://doi.org/10.5944/ried.25.2.32332

32. Bethencourt Aguilar, A., Castellanos Nieves, D., Sosa Alonso, J.J., Area Moreira, M.: Implicaciones técnicas y prácticas de las Redes Adversarias Generativas a la Ciencia Abierta en Educación [Technical and Practical Implications of Generative Adversarial Networks for Open Science in Education]. Revista Interuniversitaria de Investigación en Tecnología Educativa **13**, 138–156 (2022). https://doi.org/10.6018/riite.545881

33. Contreras Medina, F.R., Marín Carrillo, A.: La visualidad algorítmica: Una aproximación social a la visión artificial en la era post internet [algorithmic visuality: a social approach to machine vision in the post-internet era]. Arte, Individuo y Sociedad **34**(2), 627–647 (2022). https://doi.org/10.5209/aris.74664

34. Falla Falcón, N., López Meneses, E., Aubry, A.C., García Ordaz, M.: La supervisión de la enseñanza no presencial en centros educativos no universitarios [Supervision of non-presential education in non-university educational centers]. Campus Virtuales, **11**, 161–177 (2022). https://doi.org/10.54988/cv.2022.2.1198

35. Giró Gràcia, X., Sancho Gil, J.M.: La Inteligencia Artificial en la educación: Big data, cajas negras y solucionismo tecnológico [Artificial Intelligence in education: Big data, black boxes, and technological solutionism]. RELATEC: Revista Latinoamericana de Tecnología Educativa, 21(1), 129–145 (2022). https://doi.org/10.17398/1695-288X.21.1.129

36. González González, R.A., Bonilla, M.H.S.: Educación e Inteligencia Artificial: Nodos temáticos de inmersión [Education and Artificial Intelligence: Immersive theme node]. Edutec: Revista Electrónica de Tecnología Educativa, 82 (Número especial), 59–77 (2022). https://doi.org/10.21556/edutec.2022.82.2633

37. Harris Bonet, P., Romero Romero, G., Harris Bonet, M.A., Llanos Díaz, R.: Análisis de las tendencias educativas con relación al desarrollo de las competencias digitales [Analysis of educational trends related to the development of digital skills]. Revista Interuniversitaria de Investigación en Tecnología Educativa **12**, 158–174 (2022). https://doi.org/10.6018/riite. 520771

38. Martín Marchante, B.: TIC e inteligencia artificial en la revisión del proceso de escritura: Su uso en las universidades públicas valencianas [The use of ICTs and artificial intelligence in the revision of the writing process in Valencian public universities]. Research in Education and Learning Innovation Archives. REALIA, **28**, 16–31 (2022). https://doi.org/10.7203/rea lia.28.20622

39. Martín Ramallal, P., Merchán Murillo, A., Ruiz Mondaza, M.: Formadores virtuales con inteligencia artificial: Grado de aceptación entre estudiantes universitarios [Virtual trainers with artificial intelligence: levels of acceptance among university students]. Educar 58(2), 427–442 (2022). https://doi.org/10.5565/rev/educar.1482

40. Mena, A.J., De Oliveira Cardoso, N., Xavier, C.E., Argimon, I.I. de L.: Técnicas de Machine Learning utilizadas en estudios psicológicos con adolescentes: Una revisión sistemática [Machine-Learning techniques used in psychological studies with adolescents: A systematic review]. EduPsykhé: Revista de Psicología y Educación, 19(2), 23–38 (2022). https://doi.org/10.57087/edupsykhe.v19i2.4440

41. Sañudo, L.: Del abandono a la permanencia escolar en Secundaria [From dropout to permanence in Secondary school. A study from the general theory of system]. Profesorado: Revista de Currículum y Formación del Profesorado, 26(1), 213–233 (2022). https://doi.org/10.30827/profesorado.v26i1.13535

42. Silva Díaz, F., Fernández Ferrer, G., Vázquez Vílchez, M. M., Ferrada Ferrada, C., Narváez, R., Carrillo Rosúa, J.: Tecnologías emergentes en la educación STEM: Análisis bibliométrico de publicaciones en Scopus y WoS (2010–2020) [Emerging technologies in STEM education. A bibliometric analysis of publications in Scopus & WoS (2010–2020)]. Bordón: Revista de Pedagogía, **74**(4), 25–44 (2022). https://doi.org/10.13042/Bordon.2022.94198

43. Barroso Moreno, C., Rayón Rumayor, L., Bautista García-Vera, A.: Big Data y Business Intelligence en Twitter e Instagram para la inclusión digital [Big Data and Business Intelligence on Twitter and Instagram for digital inclusion. Comunicar: Revista Científica Iberoamericana de Comunicación y Educación, **74**, 49–60 (2023). https://doi.org/10.3916/C74-2023-04

44. Borrelli, D.: Las ciencias sociales ya no pueden hacer oídos de mercader. Hacia una sociología transformadora [The social sciences can no longer have merchant 's ear]. RESED: Revista de Estudios Socioeducativos, **11**, 12 (2023). https://doi.org/10.25267/Rev_estud_socioeduc ativos.2023.i11.12

45. Carrera Farran, F.X., Pérez Garcias, A.: Tecnologías digitales en educación: Poniendo el foco en la ética [Digital technologies in Education: Focusing on ethics]. Edutec: Revista Electrónica

de Tecnología Educativa, 83 (Número especial), 1–6 (2023). https://doi.org/10.21556/edutec.2023.83.2829

46. Flores Vivar, J.M., García Peñalvo, F.J.: Reflexiones sobre la ética, potencialidades y retos de la Inteligencia Artificial en el marco de la Educación de Calidad (ODS4) [Reflections on the ethics, potential, and challenges of artificial intelligence in the framework of quality education (SDG4)]. Comunicar: Revista Científica Iberoamericana de Comunicación y Educación, **74**, 37–47 (2023). https://doi.org/10.3916/C74-2023-03

47. Flores, E., Livia Segovia, J., García Casique, A., Dávila Díaz, M.E.: Análisis de sentimientos con inteligencia artificial para mejorar el proceso enseñanza-aprendizaje en el aula virtual [Sentiment analysis with artificial intelligence to improve the teaching-learning process in the virtual classroom]. Publicaciones: Facultad de Educación y Humanidades del Campus de Melilla, **53**(2), 185–216 (2023). https://doi.org/10.30827/publicaciones.v53i2.26825

48. González Arencibia, M., Valencia Corozo, E.H.: Pensamiento de la postverdad falseando la realidad [Post-truth thinking distorting reality]. RESED: Revista de Estudios Socioeducativos, **11**, 20 (2023). https://doi.org/10.25267/Rev_estud_socioeducativos.2022.i11.20

49. Marín Juarros, V.I., Tur Ferrer, G.: La privacidad de los datos en Tecnología Educativa: Resultados de una revisión de alcance [Data privacy in Educational Technology: findings of a scoping review]. Edutec: Revista Electrónica de Tecnología Educativa, 83 (Número especial), 7–23 (2023). https://doi.org/10.21556/edutec.2023.83.2701

50. Rumiche Chávarry, R. del P., Matas Terrón, A., Ríos Ariza, J.M., Chunga Chingue, G.R.: Implicaciones sociales de la irrupción del Big Data y la robótica: Un análisis prospectivo en docentes hispanoamericanos [Social implications of the emergence of Big Data and robotics: A prospective analysis in Hispanic American teachers]. Revista Electrónica Interuniversitaria de Formación del Profesorado, **26**(1), 115–127 (2023). https://doi.org/10.6018/reifop.543871

51. Saura, G. Editorial: Nuevas formas, nuevos actores y nuevas dinámicas de la privatización digital en educación [Editorial. New forms, new actors and new dynamics of digital privatization in education]. Profesorado, **27**(1), 1–10 (2023). https://revistaseug.ugr.es/index.php/profesorado/article/view/27809

Equity Issues Derived from Use of Large Language Models in Education

Esdras L. Bispo Jr.[1,2,3]([⊠])[iD], Simone Cristiane dos Santos[2][iD], and Marcus V. A. B. De Matos[3][iD]

[1] Federal University of Jataí (UFJ), Jataí, Goiás, Brazil
`bispojr@ufj.edu.br`
[2] Centro de Informática (CIn/UFPE), Recife, Pernambuco, Brazil
[3] Brunel University London, London, UK

Abstract. One of the emerging challenges in Education refers to diversity. Existing differences in a classroom can be a source of wealth and beauty. But they can also be a source of tensions that can generate conflicts. These conflicts are directly associated with the existence of privilege deriving from these differences. One source of these privileges can be provoked by the emerging new media. They can increase what is called the digital divide, challenging the educational stakeholders to promote an equitable and fairer learning environment. We will discuss in this essay some dimensions of the digital divide that can emerge from the called large language models (LLM, e.g., ChatGPT) in computing education. Issues concern not only plagiarism problems but also another level of digital literacy, referred to as lifelong learning competencies. Part of the domain of these competencies will require a level of mediatization through LLMs, leading us to understand another kind of literacy: the prompt literacy (concerning the ability to interact appropriately via prompt with LLM).

Keywords: Equity · Large Language Models · Computing Education

1 Introduction

The differences can be a source of wealth and tension. These tensions can originate conflicts that, in turn, can directly be related to privilege [38]. One source of this privilege can arise due to the so-called new media [8]. ChatGPT, Bard, and Midjourney are examples of emergent new media classified as large language models (LLM) [22,30] according to how their algorithms are built.

The digital divide [13,52] existing due to the emergence of new media affects the educational environment, specifically when we consider the LLM impacts. Thus, this work discusses large language models (LLM) as a new media and their equity impacts. We will defend that there is a LLM divide. This affects education in a general way but brings a specific agenda for Computing Education at all teaching levels.

L. Tomczyk (Ed.): NMP 2023, CCIS 2130, pp. 425–440, 2024.
https://doi.org/10.1007/978-3-031-63235-8_28

Computing Education became a global agenda due to the pervasiveness of Computing Literacy [18]. This literacy is part of the leading digital competencies necessary to form a democratic citizen in the 21st century [25], bringing many challenges to its implementation [15]. Several national curricula have been proposed to provide a solid foundation for computing literacy since the early years of school [14,41,47], encompassing all levels of education.

The remainder of this paper is as follows. Section 2 presents the concept of the digital divide. Section 3 defines what LLM is and offers some practical uses and challenges from an educational perspective. Section 4 delineates the arising of prompt literacy from web access to the current uses of search engines. Section 5 structures what we define as LLM divide from the theoretical basis of the capabilities approach. And, at last, Sect. 7 points out the final remarks and future perspectives.

2   Digital Divide

Digital divide is the existing abyss between the people with ready access to information and communication technology (ICT) tools (and, as a consequence, the knowledge provided by them), and those without such access or skills [13]. We present as follows the more common barriers to ICT use (Sect. 2.1), the potential mitigation actions for the digital divide problem (Sect. 2.2), and elements to signalize the subjacent structural problem as its roots (Sect. 2.3).

2.1   Barriers to ICT Use

There is a list of barriers that can limit or even prevent ICT use. Physical access can be a barrier when the necessary infrastructure is not guaranteed for ICT use. Let us see a Latin American context. The IBGE[1] conducted a national survey in 2018 relating to the ICT theme. This survey revealed that one in four Brazilian people does not have internet access. Suppose we admit that a fraction of these Brazilians who do not have internet access were composed of students. What would be the impact of this reality on their formation quality? What would be the difference in the formation of these students concerning computing literacy relating to other ones? Physical access can provoke a social abyss in educational contexts.

Although physical access is essential, it is not the only one. The lack of ICT skills also matters because those who access ICT and cannot use it are limited and unable to enjoy it fully. Computing literacy is another essential step in tackling the digital divide. One student that can appropriately explore a web search engine has better conditions to enrich your learning than others cannot.

Another barrier refers to the attitudinal dimension. Misconceptions about who can have intellectual conditions to use ICT are related to this barrier. Erroneous assumptions like "Computers are for 'brainy' people", "Computers are for

---

[1] IBGE stands for Brazilian Institute of Geography and Statistics.

males", or even "Computers are for young people" can restrict the disposition to ICT use. Self-efficacy is the general umbrella for this attitudinal barrier and refers to the person's belief in their ability to achieve a goal. Studies explore the self-efficacy impact on digital literacy in both students and teachers [1,19,39].

And the last barrier we point out here concerns content. A fear might exist related to the content of what is accessed and consumed in ICT. People are afraid to expose themselves to the content (e.g., threat feeling) or do not think this content is essential (e.g., irrelevance). The emergence of misinformation can provoke a reverse movement concerning the quality of content, affecting the appropriate use of ICT. The preference for misinformation instead of reasonable content is dangerous to a curriculum that promotes citizens' formation. A desirable curriculum for computing literacy should focus on the ability to discriminate and judge the quality of information sources. It is necessary to realize the potential that misinformation can have to destroy the democratic basis of society.

2.2   Potential Mitigation Actions

As an attempt to alleviate the digital divide, we can present potential mitigation actions. Each action refers to a previously discussed barrier that diverse social actors can address.

Concerning physical access, it is possible to promote incentives for organizations to pass on ICT devices to school institutions or non-government organizations (NGO), for instance. Sometimes, a tool can not be a cutting-edge technology for a large organization but can make a difference at lesser institutions. Private organizations could receive tax incentives, and public organizations could earn vouchers to use in future acquisitions of ICT devices. In this case, public policy is strategic.

Related to the skill barrier, it is possible to promote initiatives to form new teachers about ICT use. Actions related to teacher formation are not only necessary for the new ones (usually conducted by colleges and universities). Due to constant ICT evolution, it urges to guarantee a continued pedagogical preparation for these changes to all educational staff. For example, the New Media Pedagogy Conference plays a significant role in providing directions about how stakeholders in K-12 and university education can effectively use the so-called new media. NGOs can also gather the interests of civil society in this direction.

By dealing with the attitudinal barrier, we can promote technology communities of practice. In these spaces, tackling the bounding beliefs in a safer environment is possible, forging a sense of belonging among their members. In Brazil, the *Escola de Games* [28] promotes a partnership between universities and schools aiming to teach computing through digital game building. Data extracted from the pre-tests of this project indicated that various high school students did not believe in your capacity to build a computing game. Undergraduate tutors and high schoolers formed a solid belonging network, paving a new way to learn computing and weakening bounding beliefs.

And, at last, by tackling the content barrier, we can foster innovative ICT use and creation for and with minoritized communities. The strangeness concerning

ICT use can be higher in native and traditional communities (e.g., indigenous, *quilombolas* [36]). Allowing them not only to use an ICT tool but also to create it is a good strategy. The building of electronic textiles from US indigenous [29] and the participatory design of computing artifacts with rural students [37] are examples of reducing the digital divide by counting on the active action of these communities.

2.3   A Structural Problem

We previously discussed potential mitigation actions (and not "solutions" as Cullen asserts [13]). The reason for this expression choice concerns the structural nature of the problem. The structure of capitalism provides the possibility for a digital divide. This economic system defends the concept of a free market, encouraging all "players" to compete among themselves in pursuing profit maximization. Thus, in a competitiveness scenario, each player will look for what is called a competitive edge, aiming to be more attractive to their potential consumers.

Precisely at this moment, ICT plays a crucial role for players, serving as a competitive edge. ICT research and development investments increase the chance of some players providing the same service or product faster or more efficiently (or even disrupting a new service/product through an ICT innovation [9,16]). In this perspective, new technologies will always exist and will be dominated by some players, becoming ICT as a strategic factor and also a business secret, for instance.

Thus, the democratization of technology is associated with the obsolescence of the strategic ICT of these players (e.g., large corporations, public and private organizations). In this perspective, it is not a primary concern to establish a set of educational technologies as a common good. This concern is important but secondary in our economic system. There is also a reflex of this player competition in a micro dimension among people in our society, bearing in mind that each 'individual" needs to improve their curriculum to increase their attractiveness for the so-called labor market. Unterhalter [49] describes the theoretical and historical roots of this discussion, presenting the human capital theory.

3   Large Language Models

LLM stands for large language models. They are "trained on massive amounts of text data and are able to generate human-like text, answer questions, and complete other language-related tasks with high accuracy" [30]. LLMs allow people to interact with computers in a more natural and conversational way compared with search engines (e.g., Google). Beyond this capacity, most LLMs use a large volume of data from the internet as raw material to generate their answers. This answer generation results from using sophisticated algorithms of artificial intelligence (AI), providing outputs to final users with a considerable degree of originality.

There is a huge quantity of LLM tools today, but we can highlight ChatGPT, BERT, and Bard[2]. For materializing this technology use, we asked to ChatGPT the following prompt: "Critique my short story: ⟨UGLY-DUCKLING⟩". ⟨UGLY-DUCKLING⟩ stands for a summary composed of a single paragraph of the classical history "The Ugly Duckling" by Hans Andersen. The ChatGPT answered us by praising the story theme as "timeless" and "heartwarming narrative", but indicating the need to deepen in the emotional description of characters. We finally asked to it "On a scale from 0 to 10, what is the similarity between this story and 'The Ugly Duckling' by Hans Andersen?", receiving as answer "The similarity [...] would rate quite high, around an 8 or 9" [3].

The LLM reach increases if we expand our understanding of what text is and include images, videos, and other ways to express and establish communication in this comprehension. There is a vast number of LLM tools that provide as answers from your prompt: images (e.g., Midjourney, DALL-E), videos (e.g., Synthesia, VideoGAN), or even presentations (e.g., Beautiful.AI[4]). We present as follows opportunities for LLM use in education (Sect. 3.1) and existing challenges to be considered (Sect. 3.2).

3.1 Opportunities in Education

There are a range of opportunities for LLM use in education [17,30,35,50]. For teachers, a LLM can help in the lesson planning creation process. We asked to ChatGPT the following prompt: "Create a structured plan for a class about digital safety with a duration of 50 min, encompassing definitions, examples, and good practices. Suggest other exciting possibilities if possible". The ChatGPT answered us by proposing a detailed plan composed of six topics, including the expected duration for each. It recommended possibilities for interactive activities beyond good methodological suggestions about how to conduct the class[5].

Another opportunity is for students. An LLM can collaborate during their self-directed learning. We asked to ChatGPT the following prompt: "Create a study plan about digital safety. I am available to study on Tuesdays (30 min) and Fridays (1h). This plan needs to last from February 2 to 13, 2024. Suggest

---

[2] These tools are available as web services or open-source for further installations: Chat-GPT (https://chat.openai.com), BERT (github.com/google-research/bert), and Bard (https://bard.google.com).

[3] All this example conversation is available here: https://chat.openai.com/share/90e2c314-5e6e-40df-b9ff-31915e139ff2.

[4] These tools are available as web services or open-source for further installations: Midjourney (www.midjourney.com), DALL-E (https://openai.com/dall-e-2), Synthesia (www.synthesia.io), VideoGAN (https://github.com/GV1028/videogan), and Beautiful.AI (www.beautiful.ai).

[5] All this example conversation is available here: https://chat.openai.com/share/d4a4fc39-9ef3-4849-a4a1-dcc00e2eaba5.

exciting options if possible." . The ChatGPT answered us by proposing a detailed study plan for each day of the informed period, including the topic title and all learning objectives for that day. It recommended interesting possibilities as weekend and throughout activities (e.g., "Engage in online forums or communities related to digital safety")[6].

The last opportunity refers to assisting in identifying short essays' potential strengths and weaknesses. We asked to ChatGPT the following prompt: "Feedback on the following argument: 'Large language models (LLM) always prejudice digital safety'" . The first phrase that ChatGPT answered us was: "That statement seems a bit too absolute" . Next, it presents three potential risks (e.g., "Potential for Misinformation") accompanied by a short paragraph for each one. Finally, it describes three substantial benefits (e.g., "Education" and Accessibility") also accompanied by a short description for each one, concluding with a final paragraph[7].

3.2   Challenges in Education

Although there are opportunities to use LLM in education, its adoption also has challenges. Among several existing challenges [30], we list three ones concerning ethics, bias, and wrong expectations.

Regarding copyright and data privacy issues, the main highlight refers to the raw data used to train these models. An LLM usually uses the vast amount of data available on the internet to extract information and, consequently, generate its answers. The problem is related to the authorization of use. For example, The New York Times [23] sued OpenAI and Microsoft under suspicion of misuse of millions of its articles to train ChatGPT. The newspaper argues that this unauthorized use may cause a loss of billions of dollars of profit from advertisement that could usually be earned during a typical access to its website, for instance. From an educational perspective, it is possible that a generated LLM answer can be miscited because the model is unable to trace precisely from which source this data was collected. When an LLM answer generates a computing code, for example, we cannot assure if it is using (or not) some excerpt licensed exclusively for non-commercial use [54].

Concerning bias and fairness, the central aspect refers to how the raw data used to train these models was produced. Data are the result of human actions, and "actions are not neutral; they are carriers of value" [46, p. 40]. Thus, several implicit biases can exist and reflect values that a given data producer community accepts. These values can become biased or harmful concepts affecting society and, consequently, educational spaces [5]. LLM can generate racist or stereotyped

---

[6] All this example conversation is available here: https://chat.openai.com/share/ 7689884b-1d52-4fd9-a09c-71395379ff59.

[7] All this example conversation is available here: https://chat.openai.com/share/ 0494d575-c659-4bf0-a913-8e06932f6a52.

answers, for instance, because its data is "contaminated" for this perspective [10]. Various equity issues can emerge when we use AI in education [8].

And lastly, it is related to the wrong expectations of learners and teachers. Learners may rely too heavily on the model, assuming LLM is a knowledge authority (similar to a human expert). Otherside, teachers may become too reliant on the models, denying themselves the use of LLM probably due to a lack of appropriate knowledge of its benefits for education. A trade-off of benefits and risks should be performed to comprehend better the use (or not) of an LLM in your educational context.

4 Arising of Prompt Literacy

The World Wide Web can be the first ICT resource that provoked the advent of digital divide expression. However, there is an evident evolution in terms of the complexity and impact of ICT, like web access (Sect. 4.1), search engines and LLMs (Sect. 4.2). Each one of these brings opportunities and challenges concerning ICT democratization. The competency to use them appropriately is crucial in an information society.

4.1 Web Access Literacy

Web access literacy guarantees access and, consequently, the knowledge provided on the internet, specifically on the first generation of user-friendly pages after the rise of the World Wide Web [4]. This literacy involves a set of primary digital competencies [24], three of them detailed as follows.

Although this can seem trivial for experienced users, differing between email and site addresses is evidence of a basic understanding of the subjacent technologies of the internet. This competency may not be accessible for the illiterate population in our society [12]. Some people in this group can even use smartphones and instant messaging apps (e.g., WhatsApp) but can not comprehend the differences between email and hosting services, for instance.

Another digital competency is sending and receiving emails. Nowadays, there are several ways to exchange information using the internet. However, emailing has still been a crucial means because it occupies a central role in formal communications, guaranteeing more capability to access public and private services. The domain of this competency also allows more possibilities for effective democratic participation of citizens, paving other ways for advocacy actions, for instance.

Lastly, recognizing and avoiding malicious pages enables users to be safe when browsing the internet. Guaranteeing the development of this competency (i) avoids the arising of attitudinal barriers involving fear of exploring web pages at their full potential and (ii) protects users from exposing themselves to harmful situations. Users can also stand not only as a digital consumer but report to the page responsible or even public authorities about these web pitfalls, performing actively as a digital citizen.

4.2   Search and Prompt Literacies

These competencies signalize basic web access competencies. But they do not allow us to explore all potential on the web in depth. Search and prompt literacies take a step further toward more complex requirements to dominate other avenues of the internet.

Search literacy, in turn, guarantees not only access but higher navigability on the web and, consequently, better access to knowledge available there. This literacy involves a set of essential digital competencies such as (i) knowing how to use keywords in a search, (ii) realizing when to give up and re-search, and (iii) considering the quality of the retrieved resource. It performs these searches in specific web pages called search engines (e.g., Google, Bing, DuckDuckGo[8]). These competencies signalize a basic web navigability, but explores superficially other web resources like LLMs.

Lastly, prompt literacy guarantees a new level of knowledge access from the internet. This literacy involves a distinct competency concerning the ability to interact with a web page conversationally, making this interaction similar to a dialogue between humans. An LLM can extract implicit information from the web (which is impossible to do using only search engines). It involves a set of competencies like (i) building a prompt appropriately, (ii) realizing when to give up and re-search a prompt, and (iii) obtaining insights from initial prompts for advanced ones.

A prompt is a kind of requisition similar to that presented in Sect. 3.1. Formally, a prompt is a set of instructions provided to an LLM that sets it by (i) customizing and/or enhancing it, or (ii) refining its capabilities [34]. Part of what we call prompt literacy is denominated prompt engineering [20,27]. Prompt engineering (PE) is the necessary skill set to dialogue with LLMs effectively [32]. One of PE's concerns is about prompt patterns, identifying successful approaches for systematically obtaining specific kinds of goals when working with LLMs [53].

However, it is necessary to highlight that prompt literacy has a broader commitment beyond prompt engineering, preparing students as citizens for a democratic society (and not only under a technicist lens). Although these competencies signalize a primary LLM information extraction, sociotechnical aspects should be considered to guarantee a more holistic education.

5   LLM Divide

Thus, by extension (see Sect. 2), we can define LLM divide as the gap between those with ready access to LLM tools, and the knowledge that they provide access to, and those without such access or skills. We will develop this topic in two parts. First, we will define what would be LLM capability under the Capabilities Approach lens (Sect. 5.1). And second, it will be listed the primary sources of LLM equity issues from this perspective (Sect. 5.2).

---

[8] These tools are available as web services: Google (www.google.com), Bing (www. bing.com), and DuckDuckGo (www.duckduckgo.com).

5.1   LLM Capability

Some concepts are essential when we refer to inequality of opportunities in education. Lewis and colleagues [33, p. 482] assert that:

> "*Equality* refers to the state where everyone has or is allocated the same things in the same degree, whereas *equity* typically refers to having access to what is needed. [...] In general, [...] equity, and not equality, defines fair and just learning opportunities" (our emphasis).

Although the authors signalize to equity and equality concepts, they does not define equity in a strict way. Aiming to theorizing equity appropriately, we will present the capability theory.

The Capabilities Approach (CA) framework addresses and nominates the essential concepts in an equity analysis. CA was proposed originally by Amartya Sen [44] and improved by Melanie Walker [51] for education purposes. This approach allows identifying not only the resources that are supposed to be absent in inequity settings but also mapping the capabilities that a student cannot develop (in educational scenarios).

The main question raised by Sen [44, p. 12] is "equality of what?". Sen's concerns concentrated on the higher risk of reducing the efforts to deal with inequalities to a single-dimensional analysis. The inequality problem is complex and multidimensional by nature. Thus, when we analyze the problem only with the incoming inequality lens, for instance, probably other sources of inequalities can be neglected and, in some cases, even aggravated. Although the race lens, for example, can contribute to informing essential aspects that can not be overlooked by all stakeholders responsible for analyzing a given scenario, this one is not enough to inform a decision maker with quality and robustness if isolated from others.

Using more rigorous concepts, CA is a theoretical framework based upon two normative claims: (i) the freedom to achieve well-being is of primary moral importance, and (ii) the understanding of well-being is directly related to people's capabilities and functionings. Functionings are beings and doings that are "various states of human beings and activities that a person has achieved"; and capabilities are "the real, or substantive, opportunity that they [human beings] have to achieve these doings and beings" [43]. The freedom of being educated is one of the aims in this perspective, understanding it as a part of the broad problem of liberating people for a fulfilling life. In this direction, we can define equity as the equality of capabilities.

Contextualizing for our discussion, an LLM capability is the real opportunity that people have to use and effectively explore an LLM in all its potential. A student who has access to ChatGPT but cannot use it, for example, does not have some LLM capability related to prompt literacy. A teacher who does not have access to ChatGPT for use as educational technology in a computing class [6], for instance, may not have some LLM capability related to infrastructure or even social aspects in which this educational environment is situated.

5.2 LLM Equity Issues

From LLM capability, we will unfold potential LLM equity issues that can emerge. Three important sources of equity will be explored as follows: (i) access, (ii) prompt literacy, and (iii) personal, social, and environmental factors.

Access to an LLM arises naturally as the first equity source. Once crossing the infrastructure barrier (a classical digital divide), we can face access barriers concerning the business model adopted by most private organizations. The "freemium"[9] business model allows users to freely have the first contact with an application through its basic features, needing to pay only when they want to use more advanced functionalities. This equity dilemma is two sides of the same coin. It is good because users do not pay (with money) for the access and use of an LLM, which is a means to pave the way for future and democratic access. In contrast, the simple fact of existing restricted access for a selected group of users promotes a divide between those with freemium access and everybody else. As noted previously (Sect. 2.3), it is a structural problem of our society, and it is necessary to understand how to build a pedagogical environment that considers these aspects.

In terms of LLM educational capability, this mismatch can reveal potential disparities in the assessment process. Imagine if we identify that a group of students can not access a necessary resource to achieve their learning goals. Now imagine that our assessment instrument does not consider this difference and collects indicators to assess the learning of all students indistinctly. Students can be retained in an educational structure due to factors that extrapolate their desire or free disposition to pursue their education. When it occurs, there is no freedom of being educated (the real opportunity of being educated if a person so wishes). If there is no this freedom, thus there is no capability for it, and an equity issue is identified.

Prompt literacy is a second equity issue that can emerge from LLM use. Students can underuse LLM even if they have access to it. Teachers cannot explore its potential because does not have the appropriate competency developed for this. The question about equity will always be if people have the real opportunity to do or to be (in CA, doings and beings). An equity issue emerges if any educational stakeholder is limited by a lack of access or, in this case, skills or competencies. Let us see the examples presented in Sect. 3.1. How do we explore the LLM power if a student (or a teacher) does not realize the universe of existing prompt possibilities? Is it possible to explore this technology appropriately without a practical knowledge of prompt engineering or prompt patterns (as presented in Sect. 4.2)? These questions refer not only the access to information, but the fact that LLM can help students and teachers to build a road of metacognitive strategies [2]. The equality of opportunities to develop these skills matters to promote a more fair and equitable classroom.

Finally, the personal, social, and environmental factors are the third important source of equity issue. During the Covid-19[10] pandemic, for instance, Brazil-

---

[9] Freemium combines "free of charge" and "premium". See more in [3].
[10] Covid-19 stands for Corona Virus Disease (2019).

ian students that lived in disadvantaged regions had available for all members of their families only a single computational device (normally a cellphone with restricted access to internet) [7]. This is not only an access difficulty, but an structural problem, strongly pervading the social reality of a surrounding educational area. Although the Covid-19 pandemic had unstructured the society as a whole, the underlying social problems usually emerges in middle of the circumstances provoked by a crisis.

6   Related Work

The first group of related work concentrates on those that approach large language models and education but do not explore equity specificities or equality of opportunities. We can cite three works in this group. Cain [11] explores the transformative potential of Large Language Models of Artificial Intelligence (LLM AI) in educational contexts. Kasneci and colleagues [30] present challenges such as the potential bias in the output, the need for continuous human oversight, and the potential for LLM misuse in education. Finally, Head and colleagues [26] explore the ethical implications of LLM training concerning data sources like the perpetuation of biases (racism, sexism, ethnocentrism, and more) and the exclusion of non-majority languages.

The second group of related work focus on those that approach large language models and equity but do not research inside an educational context. We can cite three works in this group. Singh and colleagues [45] explore health equity issues that emerge in large language model deployment. Korateng and colleagues [31] evaluate the ethics of LLMs in medicine along two key axes: empathy and equity. At last, Rillig and colleagues [42] present the risks and benefits of Large Language Models for the Environment, listing issues concerning enhancing the digital divide in environmental research.

Lastly, the third group of related work concentrates on those that approach education and equity but do not explore the specificity of LLMs arising. We can cite three works in this group. Gorski [21] deepens the discussion of the digital divide in terms of educational equity. Unterhalter [48] discusses gender equality in education from the lens of the capability approach. Finally, Resta and colleagues [40] address two main concerns: digital equity for social inclusion and digital equity in education.

7   Final Remarks

This essay aimed to discuss dimensions of the digital divide focusing on LLM in a perspective of computing education. We presented the concept of the digital divide, defined what LLM is, and delineated the arising of prompt literacy. At last, we defined LLM divide from the capabilities approach lens and discussed LLM equity issues. The educational issues derived from LLM use extrapolates the access problem or even plagiarism detection. Our purpose was to underline the digital divide provoked by LLM focusing on lifelong learning competencies.

The LLM divide causes at least an inequality of opportunities concerning the potential use of LLM to assist the learner in building their metacognitive strategies.

We conclude this paper with three essential attitudes that can forge a new 21st-century teacher. The first attitude is increasing awareness about this discussion inside your educational space, observing all dimensions approached here, including the structural root of the problem. The second one is identifying the main challenges in their educational contexts, putting on the table critical equity variables that need to be considered in a detailed equity analysis. Finally, the third one is giving a more advanced step, being a changing vector, proposing an equity-minded curriculum for your educational program. All these attitudes can generate future works, extending the contributions brought forth by this paper.

Acknowledgments. This study was financed in part by the *Coordenação de Aperfeiçoamento de Pessoal de Nível Superior - Brasil* (CAPES) - Finance Code 001. The authors thank the support of the Institute of Communities and Societies (ICS) of Brunel University London in the person of Prof. Meredith Jones.

References

1. Aslan, S.: Analysis of digital literacy self-efficacy levels of pre-service teachers. Int. J. Technol. Edu. 4(1), 57–67 (2021). https://doi.org/10.46328/ijte.47
2. Azevedo, R., Aleven, V.: Metacognition and learning technologies: an overview of current interdisciplinary research. In: Azevedo, R., Aleven, V. (eds.) International Handbook of Metacognition and Learning Technologies. SIHE, vol. 28, pp. 1–16. Springer, New York (2013). https://doi.org/10.1007/978-1-4419-5546-3_1
3. Bapna, R., Ramaprasad, J., Umyarov, A.: Monetizing freemium communities: does paying for premium increase social engagement? Mis Q. **42**(3) (2018)
4. Berners-Lee, T., Cailliau, R., Luotonen, A., Nielsen, H.F., Secret, A.: The World-Wide Web, p. 51-65. Association for Computing Machinery, New York, NY, USA, 1 edn. (2023). https://doi.org/10.1145/3591366.3591373
5. Bispo Jr., E., Abranches, S., Carvalho, A.B., Santos, S.: "Fui contratado para ensinar Computação!": Um olhar sobre a suposta neutralidade político-pedagógica do professor universitário de Computação no Brasil. In: EduComp 2022, pp. 272–282. SBC, Porto Alegre, RS, Brasil (2022). https://doi.org/10.5753/educomp.2022.19222
6. Bispo, E., Jr., et al.: Tecnologias na Educação em Computação: Primeiros Referenciais. Revista Brasileira de Informática na Educação **28**, 509–527 (2020). https://doi.org/10.5753/rbie.2020.28.0.509
7. Bispo, E., Jr., Santos, C., Ferreira, R., Souza, V., Abranches, S., Santos, S.: Contrastes e convergências na formação docente pós-pandemia: Inclusão digital em instituições públicas de ensino no estado de Pernambuco. Revista Brasileira de Informática na Educação **31**, 844–868 (2023). https://doi.org/10.5753/rbie.2023.2947
8. Bispo Jr., E.L.: Equity issues in educational data mining from an epistemological perspective. In: Equity, Diversity, and Inclusion in Education Technology Research and Development - EDI (AIED 2023), pp. 1–11 (2023). https://doi.org/10.5281/zenodo.8186668

9. Bower, J.L., Christensen, C.M.: Disruptive technologies: Catching the wave. The Journal of Product Innovation Management **13**(1), 75–76 (1996). https://www.infona.pl/resource/bwmeta1.element.elsevier-315e6fb9-6d1b-39e4-9036-cb79369f2c2c

10. Busker, T., Choenni, S., Shoae Bargh, M.: Stereotypes in ChatGPT: an empirical study. In: Proceedings of the 16th International Conference on Theory and Practice of Electronic Governance, pp. 24–32. ICEGOV 2023, Association for Computing Machinery, New York, NY, USA (2023). https://doi.org/10.1145/3614321.3614325

11. Cain, W.: Prompting change: exploring prompt engineering in large language model AI and its potential to transform education. TechTrends **68**(1), 47–57 (2024). https://doi.org/10.1007/s11528-023-00896-0

12. Conceição, L., Pessôa, L.: A experiência de consumidores com baixo letramento em redes sociais e comunicadores instantâneos: um estudo exploratório. Sociedade, contabilidade e gestão **13**(3) (2018). https://doi.org/10.21446/scg_ufrj.v13i3.13521

13. Cullen, R.: Addressing the digital divide. Online Inf. Rev. **25**(5), 311–320 (2001). https://doi.org/10.1108/14684520110410517

14. Eloy, A.A.D.S., Martins, A.R.Q., Pazinato, A.M., Lukjanenko, M.D.F.S.P., Lopes, R.D.D.: Programming literacy: computational thinking in Brazilian public schools. In: Proceedings of the 2017 Conference on Interaction Design and Children, pp. 439-444. IDC 2017, Association for Computing Machinery, New York, NY, USA (2017). https://doi.org/10.1145/3078072.3084306

15. Falcão, T.P.: Computational thinking for all: what does it mean for teacher education in Brazil? In: Proceedings of Brazilian Symposium of Computing Education (EduComp), pp. 371–379. SBC, Porto Alegre, RS, Brasil (2021). https://doi.org/10.5753/educomp.2021.14505

16. Flavin, M.: Disruptive technologies in higher education. Res. Learn. Technol. **20** (2012). https://doi.org/10.3402/rlt.v20i0.19184

17. Freire, M., et al.: Utilizando question answering no Auxílio ao Processo de Ensino e Aprendizagem de Programação: Um estudo de caso com LLMs. Revista de Sistemas e Computação (RSC) **13**(3) (2023). https://doi.org/10.36558/rsc.v13i3.8544

18. Frezza, S., et al.: Modeling global competencies for computing education, p. 348-349. ITiCSE 2018, Association for Computing Machinery, New York, NY, USA (2018). https://doi.org/10.1145/3197091.3205844, https://doi.org/10.1145/3197091.3205844

19. Garcia, F.M., Mattedi, A.P., Seabra, R.D.: Self-efficacy among users of information and communication technologies in the Brazilian school environment. In: Latifi, S. (ed.) 17th International Conference on Information Technology–New Generations (ITNG 2020). AISC, vol. 1134, pp. 631–634. Springer, Cham (2020). https://doi.org/10.1007/978-3-030-43020-7_84

20. Gattupalli, S., Maloy, R.W., Edwards, S.A.: Prompt Literacy: a Pivotal Educational Skill in the Age of AI. College of Education Working Papers and Reports Series (2023). https://doi.org/10.7275/3498-wx48

21. Gorski, P.: Education equity and the digital divide. AACE Rev. (Formerly AACE J.) **13**(1), 3–45 (2005). https://www.learntechlib.org/p/6570, special Issue: Multicultural Education/Digital Divide

22. Grassini, S.: Shaping the future of education: exploring the potential and consequences of AI and ChatGPT in educational settings. Educ. Sci. **13**(7) (2023). https://doi.org/10.3390/educsci13070692

23. Grynbaum, M., Mac, R.: The Times Sues OpenAI and Microsoft Over A.I. Use of Copyrighted Work. The New York Times (2023). https://www.nytimes.com/2023/12/27/business/media/new-york-times-open-ai-microsoft-lawsuit.html

24. Guarini, P., di Furia, M., Ragni, B.: Digital competences and didactic technologies training for teachers in service: from DigCompEdu to a national framework. In: Tomczyk, Ł (ed.) New Media Pedagogy: Research Trends, Methodological Challenges and Successful Implementations. CCIS, pp. 30–41. Springer, Cham (2023). https://doi.org/10.1007/978-3-031-44581-1_3

25. Guzdial, M.: Computing education as a foundation for 21st century literacy. In: Proceedings of the 50th ACM Technical Symposium on Computer Science Education (SIGCSE), p. 502–503. SIGCSE '19, Association for Computing Machinery, New York, NY, USA (2019). https://doi.org/10.1145/3287324.3290953

26. Head, C.B., Jasper, P., McConnachie, M., Raftree, L., Higdon, G.: Large language model applications for evaluation: opportunities and ethical implications. N. Dir. Eval. **2023**(178–179), 33–46 (2023). https://doi.org/10.1002/ev.20556

27. Hwang, Y., Lee, J.H., Shin, D.: What is prompt literacy? an exploratory study of language learners' development of new literacy skill using generative ai. arXiv preprint arXiv:2311.05373 (2023). https://doi.org/10.48550/arXiv.2311.05373

28. Junqueira, M.S., Ferreira, T.C., Tonon, G.S., Bispo Jr., E.L., Boaventura, A.P.F.V.: Escola de games: relato de experiência da aplicação de um curso piloto. Revista UFG **20** (2020). https://doi.org/10.5216/revufg.v20.61035

29. Kafai, Y., Searle, K., Martinez, C., Brayboy, B.: Ethnocomputing with electronic textiles: culturally responsive open design to broaden participation in computing in American Indian youth and communities. In: SIGCSE, pp. 241–246 (2014). https://doi.org/10.1145/2538862.2538903

30. Kasneci, E., et al.: ChatGPT for good? On opportunities and challenges of large language models for education. Learning and individual differences **103**, 102274 (2023). https://doi.org/10.1016/j.lindif.2023.102274

31. Koranteng, E., et al.: Empathy and equity: key considerations for large language model adoption in health care. JMIR Med. Educ. **9**, e51199 (2023). https://doi.org/10.2196/51199

32. Korzynski, P., Mazurek, G., Krzypkowska, P., Kurasinski, A.: Artificial intelligence prompt engineering as a new digital competence: Analysis of generative AI technologies such as ChatGPT. Entrepreneurial Bus. Econ. Rev. **11**(3), 25–37 (2023). https://doi.org/10.15678/EBER.2023.110302

33. Lewis, C., Shah, N., Falkner, K.: The Cambridge Handbook of Computing Education Research, chap. Equity and Diversity, pp. 481–510. Cambridge Publishers (2019). https://doi.org/10.1017/9781108654555.017

34. Liu, P., Yuan, W., Fu, J., Jiang, Z., Hayashi, H., Neubig, G.: Pre-train, prompt, and predict: a systematic survey of prompting methods in natural language processing. ACM Comput. Surv. **55**(9), 1–35 (2023). https://doi.org/10.1145/3560815

35. Meyer, J.G., et al.: ChatGPT and large language models in academia: opportunities and challenges. BioData Min. **16**(1), 20 (2023). https://doi.org/10.1186/s13040-023-00339-9

36. Moraes-Partelli, A.N., Coelho, M.P., Santos, S.G., Santos, I.L., Cabral, I.E.: Participation of adolescents from the Quilombola community in the creation of an educational game about alcohol consumption. Rev. Esc. Enferm. U.S.P. **56**, e20210402 (2022). https://doi.org/10.1590/1980-220X-REEUSP-2021-0402

37. Morais, D.C.S., Falcão, T.P., de Andrade, F.M., Tedesco, P.C.d.A.R., et al.: Processos de desenvolvimento participativo de tecnologias digitais educacionais nos contextos urbano e da educação do campo. In: Proceedings of XXIX Brazilian Workshop of Computing Education (WEI), pp. 111–120. SBC (2021). https://doi.org/10.5753/wei.2021.15902

38. Parker, M.C., Guzdial, M.: A critical research synthesis of privilege in Computing Education. In: 2015 Research in Equity and Sustained Participation in Engineering, Computing, and Technology (RESPECT), pp. 1–5. IEEE (2015). https://doi.org/10.1109/RESPECT.2015.7296502

39. Prior, D.D., Mazanov, J., Meacheam, D., Heaslip, G., Hanson, J.: Attitude, digital literacy and self efficacy: Flow-on effects for online learning behavior. Internet High. Educ. **29**, 91–97 (2016). https://doi.org/10.1016/j.iheduc.2016.01.001

40. Resta, P., Laferrière, T., McLaughlin, R., Kouraogo, A.: Issues and challenges related to digital equity: an overview. In: Voogt, J., Knezek, G., Christensen, R., Lai, K.-W. (eds.) Second Handbook of Information Technology in Primary and Secondary Education. SIHE, pp. 987–1004. Springer, Cham (2018). https://doi.org/10.1007/978-3-319-71054-9_67

41. Ribeiro, L., Foss, L., Cavalheiro, S.A.D.C., Kniphoff da Cruz, M.E.J., Soares de França, R.: The Brazilian school computing standard. In: Proceedings of the 54th ACM Technical Symposium on Computer Science Education V. 1, pp. 53–58. SIGCSE 2023, Association for Computing Machinery, New York, NY, USA (2023). https://doi.org/10.1145/3545945.3569863

42. Rillig, M.C., Ågerstrand, M., Bi, M., Gould, K.A., Sauerland, U.: Risks and benefits of large language models for the environment. Environ. Sci. Technol. **57**(9), 3464–3466 (2023). https://doi.org/10.1021/acs.est.3c01106

43. Robeyns, I., Byskov, M.: The capability approach. The Stanford Encyclopedia of Philosophy (2021). https://plato.stanford.edu/archives/sum2023/entries/capability-approach/

44. Sen, A.: Inequality Reexamined. Oxford University Press, Oxford (1992)

45. Singh, N., Lawrence, K., Richardson, S., Mann, D.M.: Centering health equity in large language model deployment. PLOS Digital Health **2**(10), e0000367 (2023). https://doi.org/10.1371/journal.pdig.0000367

46. Skovsmose, O., Valero, P.: Breaking political neutrality: the critical engagement of Mathematics Education with Democracy. Sociocultural research on Mathematics Education: An international perspective, pp. 37–55 (2001). https://www.taylorfrancis.com/chapters/edit/10.4324/9781410600042-4/breaking-political-neutrality-ole-skovsmose-paola-valero

47. Tate, C., Remold, J., Bienkowski, M.: Pursuing the vision of CS for all: views from the front lines. ACM Inroads **9**(3), 48–52 (2018). https://doi.org/10.1145/3230704

48. Unterhalter, E.: Gender Equality, Education, and the Capability Approach, pp. 87–107. Palgrave Macmillan US, New York (2007). https://doi.org/10.1057/9780230604810_5

49. Unterhalter, E.: Education. In: An Introduction to the Human Development and Capability Approach: Freedom and Agency, pp. 207–227. Routledge: Taylor & Francis (2010)

50. Van Wyk, M.M.: Is ChatGPT an opportunity or a threat? Preventive strategies employed by academics related to a GenAI-based LLM at a faculty of education. J. Appl. Learn. Teach. **7**(1). https://doi.org/10.37074/jalt.2024.7.1.15

51. Walker, M.: Higher Education Pedagogies: A Capabilities Approach. Society for Research into Higher Education & Open University Press (2006)

52. Wei, L., Hindman, D.B.: Does the digital divide matter more? Comparing the effects of new media and old media use on the education-based knowledge gap. Mass Commun. Soc. **14**(2), 216–235 (2011). https://doi.org/10.1080/15205431003642707

53. White, J., et al.: A prompt pattern catalog to enhance prompt engineering with ChatGPT. arXiv preprint arXiv:2302.11382 (2023). https://doi.org/10.48550/arXiv.2302.11382

54. Yu, Z., Wu, Y., Zhang, N., Wang, C., Vorobeychik, Y., Xiao, C.: CodeIPPrompt: intellectual property infringement assessment of code language models. In: Krause, A., Brunskill, E., Cho, K., Engelhardt, B., Sabato, S., Scarlett, J. (eds.) Proceedings of the 40th International Conference on Machine Learning. Proceedings of Machine Learning Research, vol. 202, pp. 40373–40389. PMLR (2023). https://proceedings.mlr.press/v202/yu23g.html

Digital Trends of the Scientific and Technological Revolution: Institutional Transformations of Science and Education Systems in the Paradigm of Sustainable Social Development

Viktor Zinchenko$^{(\boxtimes)}$ ⓘ and Yurii Mielkov ⓘ

Institute of Higher Education of the National Academy of Educational Sciences of Ukraine, Kyiv, Ukraine
vvzinchenko@ukr.net

Abstract. Education and science play a key role in envisioning and developing a just, peaceful and sustainable society. Digitalization as one of major trends that affect the future of humanity in general and education in particular, has a special impact on education in today's world. Education is currently lagging behind in digitization and more efforts are needed to take advantage of the tools and strengths of new technologies while addressing potential abuses such as cyber intrusions and privacy issues. Particularly, the main challenge of digitalization for sustainability currently lies in the paradoxes and contradictions of AI-based technologies: there is a confusion even among the experts as to the risks and threats that could arise out of AI usage, as well as on the image of possible forms of human-machine symbiosis. The authors argue that the solution could lie in strengthening the humanistic aspects of higher education that would allow humans to fully exercise such aspects of thinking that computers are unable to achieve, while still using the AI-based technologies controlling them to the advantage of humanity.

Keywords: Sustainable Development · Education · Artificial Intelligence (AI) · Universities

1 Introduction

Among the sustainable development goals set by "Agenda 2030", Goal 4 is dedicated especially for education: "Ensure inclusive and equitable quality education and promote lifelong learning opportunities for all". However, it could be argued that quality education plays vital part in achieving many other goals as well, as it empowers men and women with the knowledge and skills required for realizing sustainability in virtually all spheres of life [1]. The use of generative artificial intelligence models to spread disinformation has a negative impact on the public's perception of information and threatens its fundamental principles, such as reliability and objectivity, which are critical characteristics for ensuring democratic freedoms.

Ł. Tomczyk (Ed.): NMP 2023, CCIS 2130, pp. 441–453, 2024.
https://doi.org/10.1007/978-3-031-63235-8_29

In the long term, we may see the creation of new forms of media literacy aimed at teaching the general public how to critically analyze and identify manufactured content. Nevertheless, the main task of our time is to create a society prepared for the challenges and risks that the era of generative artificial intelligence brings with it.

The role of the environment in which a human child grows up and is brought up decisively influences the nature and boundaries of his behavior after he grows up. Twins, who have the same intellectual abilities from birth, depending on their environment and upbringing, can grow into anyone they want. Anyone brought up in a respectable environment is likely to become a worthy citizen. Growing up among the mafia is likely to become a criminal. And a child raised by wolves from infancy, Mowgli, will never become human.

It is reasonable to assume the same in the case of "alien children" who recently appeared on Earth in the form of AI based on large language models (LLM): GPT, ClaudeAI etc.

Like human children, each of these LLM "non-human minds" has a wide range of abilities built into them. But human children acquire them immediately at birth. And "children are aliens" – as a result of preliminary training. This is an expensive process that costs a lot of money and time for the largest models and is therefore not repeated.

When talking about the intellectual abilities of people and chatbots, it is important to understand the fundamental difference between abilities and behavior.

- In people (as stated above), the character and boundaries of behavior are determined by upbringing.
- Chatbots are similar. The role of education here is played by the so-called "fine-tuning of the model." It is much cheaper than preliminary training and therefore can be carried out regularly.

Please note the following important point:

- The basic model, after preliminary training, is functionally an advanced autocompletion mechanism: it does not communicate with the user, but only generates a continuation of the phrases given to it as input.
- Behavior in a dialogue with people appears in a chatbot only thanks to fine tuning (the most important goal of which is to prevent the chatbot's unwanted behavior. This is achieved by the fact that fine tuning can both reveal and suppress certain abilities of the model.

In other words, as a result of fine tuning, a model with a wide range of abilities may, in response to a specific request, exhibit some of them or not. That is, the model's abilities remain the same, but the behavior is different.

Consequently, as a result of upbringing (fine tuning), the model can manifest itself as anyone from an angel to a devil. And it will depend only on her educators (from highly moral researchers to vile bandits and misanthropes).

All of the above has been demonstrated over the past months by OpenAI, which has undertaken to intensively develop GPT-4.

The results of this upbringing set the Internet on fire following a paper [26] by Lingjiao Chen, Matej Zacharias, and James Zou, who tested GPT-3.5 and GPT-4 on four tasks and "snapshots" of models from March to June.

The Internet public interpreted the results of this study as a "degradation of the abilities" of GPT-4. In fact, this is not what the authors meant at all.

All GPT-4 abilities remained with her. The only thing that changed (as a result of raising the model) was its behavior (for a detailed explanation, see here [27]).

In essence, this experiment showed the colossal potential of raising models of "alien children", which makes it possible, by fine-tuning, to turn them into anyone.

This truly terrifying result raises an important question:

Why struggle to create a highly moral AI, if with fine tuning you can quickly and cheaply re-educate it into a villain?

Well, the eternal question – Orwell wrote: "If the atomic bomb were something cheap and easily produced, like a bicycle or an alarm clock, perhaps the world would again plunge into barbarism…"

Is this not what threatens us today with AI based on LLM?

Teaching and acquiring knowledge takes place in human society, i.e. in a definite academic and technological space. Analysis of large-scale trends is necessary for making decisions that will ensure the construction of a sustainable and future-ready educational environment. And it is already possible to identify the main megatrends that affect the future of education: globalization and digitalization.

In OECD countries, higher education systems are predicted to be the first to be affected by the megatrends, as they will have to do their best to attract students in a much more mobile and competitive market. In many countries, adults have inadequate skills to manage complex digital information, so governments and employers must seriously resolve issues related not only to the continuity of education, but also to its comprehensiveness. If we refer to the already noted Agenda for sustainable development, realizing goals of education, and particularly subgoal 4.7 that is aimed at ensuring that all learners acquire the knowledge and skills needed to promote sustainable development, including, among others, through education for sustainable development and sustainable lifestyles, human rights, gender equality, promotion of a culture of peace and non-violence, global citizenship et al. [1], would be virtually impossible without the help of digital technologies that make quality education available to citizens of all the world.

Education is currently lagging behind in digitization, and more efforts are needed to take advantage of the tools and strengths of new technologies while addressing potential abuses such as cyber intrusions and privacy issues. The need for digital literacy and critical thinking is increasing not only among young students, but also among people of the older generation. In order to achieve success precisely in cooperation at all levels – both in education and science, and in general, in society – universities in particular and all educational institutions in general should learn to cooperate in solidarity in partnership, developing sustainable development skills, critical thinking, as well as sharing responsibility between students and entire educational teams, so that educational institutions can become examples of a sustainable lifestyle [2].

2 Methodological Principles, Goals and Perspectives

In China, artificial intelligence brought order to the railway - it worked better than the new one.

Chatbots, generated images, videos and other similar entertainment with artificial intelligence are interesting and sometimes useful. But the practical implementation of AI in production, transport and the material economy as a whole will become more important. Ultimately, the winner will be the one who will literally "plow and build" on AI, replacing humans in the production sector. China has taken an important step towards this: thanks to AI, they were able to restore order on the railway.

The average person cannot even imagine what it costs to maintain the road, infrastructure and fleet of equipment in order, as well as ensure the movement of trains. These are potentially unprofitable undertakings with enormous liability. China, like other countries, will soon experience problems with its aging population. At the same time, the railway network in the country is growing and involves connecting all cities with a population of over 500 thousand people by high-speed railway lines. The speed of rolling stock is also increasing, making the human factor the weakest link.

The data management protocol for the implementation of AI algorithms on the railway in China was implemented by the operator of the national railway network, the Chinese state-owned company China State Railway Group, in 2022. Access to data had to be limited and protected from third-party interference and leaks. Control algorithms were tested by people, and only after that they were implemented. Large-scale testing began in 2023. The result was stunning - the railway began to work even better than the new one (immediately after the sections and trains were put into operation).

Sensors are installed on infrastructure facilities, on wheelsets, on cars, to take into account vibrations, acceleration and amplitudes, and this is not to mention conventional signaling automation. The volume of data collected for analysis has reached 200 terabytes, and these are not pictures or videos, but ordinary register states. A person and no matter how large a team would be able to quickly process such a volume of information. All this is data on 45 thousand km of tracks – this is longer than the Earth's equator. There is not enough manpower to service all this.

The Beijing-based artificial intelligence system processes massive amounts of data from across the country in real time and can alert repair crews to abnormal situations within 40 min with 95% accuracy. Recommendations are usually aimed at preventing malfunctions – at preventing potential problems. In this entire stream of data, AI has been taught to find connections between events that are inaccessible to awareness in real time.

Over the past year, none of China's operating high-speed rail lines have received a single warning to slow down due to major track irregularities, while the number of minor track faults has dropped by 80% compared to the previous year. The algorithms operate so accurately that they even improve the smoothness of travel in conditions of strong winds and on bridges, reducing the amplitude of train fluctuations and reducing the load on tracks and infrastructure. Sounds like fantasy.

Such solutions not only reduce the need for maintenance personnel, but also reduce the financial burden on railway maintenance and, most importantly, increase traffic safety. China admits that it lags behind the United States in terms of the development of artificial intelligence, but if the United States cannot convert the capabilities of AI into increased labor productivity in the material sphere, then its advantage will be only an illusion.

Based on the fact that the phenomena of integration and internationalization in the context of globalization are growing rapidly, and their properties are determined by the laws dictated by the prevailing trend of global development, these phenomena acquire special importance, first of all, for small countries and for those that have taken the path of intensive development or the search for models of social, economical, scientific and educational intensification and institutional transformations for sustainable development of society in the context of internationalization of higher education and science. Developments in the field of artificial intelligence (AI), robotics, and intelligent systems are rapidly progressing right now, bringing benefits (and, at the same time, likely dangers and harms), directly determining our existence, and soon they will have even more significant impact on human lives.

The global pandemic has also caused unprecedented challenges to every aspect of interaction with society. In universities, the transition to distant learning has fueled discussions about the relevance and the future of conventional modes of contact classes. Despite the pandemic, we are already living in the era of the Fourth Industrial Revolution (4IR), where cybernetics and computing have entered human life. In universities, "the production of knowledge is and must be inclusive of a machine mode of thinking", as stated by philosopher Luciana Parisi from University of London [3].

Even during the times of the USSR, such a field of psychology as "engineering psychology and pedagogy" began to be developed. Such a kind of psychology investigates the processes and means of informational interaction between human and machine, as well between human and technical means of automation.

In the European Union, the European Commission has adopted the Action Plan on Digital Education [4]. The basic conceptual and methodological principles to be used in higher education institutions and university development have been presented in the "White book: Artificial intelligence in higher education" [5], which describes and defines the possibilities and problems of artificial intelligence in research and education, promotes discussion about transformations in university teaching, learning culture and the possibilities of teaching and developing educational and educational content in interaction with the use of artificial intelligence in the context of trends in modern neuroscience. In addition, this book presents a vision of the future of university education and training from the perspective of students and teachers by demonstrating how education and training may change in the coming years due to AI.

3   Current Trends and Major Problems

Robots are becoming more and more like people, and people are learning to interact with them, constantly improving them not only externally, but internally as well. An overview of the research on this issue, which currently presents itself a "frontier" not only in robotics and AI (artificial intelligence), but also in evolutionary genetics, psychology, philosophy, psychiatry, pedagogy, neurology, biochemistry and organic chemistry, microbiology, anthropology etc., shows that the approach of the interdisciplinary and multidisciplinary community of transhumanists is becoming more and more important. According to that approach, if machines (androids, cyborgs etc.) would become capable of feeling and empathy, they will no longer be just machines.

Evolution (both the natural-biological and the human-organized social-technological or intellectual etc.) would irreversibly lead to the expansion of new species capable of thinking and endowed with rights. Swedish anthropologist and writer Jan Lindblad used to call such a creature "Homo Sapientissimus" [6].

For example, already in 2015 in Japan, for the first time in history, a cybernetic android named NAO became one of the staff of the largest bank in the country, The Bank of Tokyo-Mitsubishi UFJ. NAOs are humanoid robots developed by SoftBank Information Technology Corporation. NAOs easily move and gesture with manipulators, with the help of cameras and sound sensors as they respond to visitors, answer questions and can support conversations on diverse topics and in many languages [7].

The authors of contemporary social projects should pay special attention to the latest technological trends in innovation and be able to predict the future. And for this, first of all, many scholars recommend reading science fiction, since it is this genre of literature that stimulates brain activity, develops imagination and thinking. It is not by chance that in China at present a lot of attention is paid to science fiction. Neil Gaiman in his interview in "The Guardian" argues that the interest in science fiction among the Chinese is related to the fact that they were brilliantly good at imitation, but were bad at innovation, inventions and had problems with imagination [8]. As a result, the Chinese sent their representatives to the USA – to Apple, to Microsoft, to Google – and asked the people who invent the future to tell about themselves. As a result, it turned out that in childhood they all read science fiction. The focus on serious science fiction in China correlates very well with the victories of Chinese schoolchildren in international tests and competitions. It turns out that the Chinese actively began to form their image of the future – the desired and positive future.

However, the fear of artificial intelligence (AI) was born back in the 1960s due to Irwin Good, a British mathematician and cryptographer who worked with Alan Turing to crack the German Enigma encryption machine during the World War II. In 1966, Good has proposed a concept now known as the "technological singularity", which predicts the possible emergence of superhuman intelligence [9]. Good's opinion on AI has led him to the idea of an 'ultraintelligent' machine that, because of its self-learning, would become capable of surpassing the intelligence of a human, no matter how smart he or she is. When this machine begins to build machines similar to itself, the "intellectual explosion" will occur – and that would be the last invention that human would have been able to make [10].

Technological singularity is thus a hypothetical moment in the future when techno-logical development becomes, in principle, uncontrollable and irreversible, giving rise to radical changes in the nature of human civilization. In futurology that term designates an explosive increase in the speed of scientific and technical progress, when the exponential growth in computing power will be likely to occur as a result of the creation of artificial intelligence and self-replicating machines. And after that hypothetical point, according to proponents of this concept, technological progress will become so rapid and complex it would be left beyond any comprehension.

But what if an 'ultraintelligent' machine one day realizes that it does not need humans and will start to behave like the Terminator, to limit the rights of people and, perhaps, to kill them? It is not surprising then that at the present time Good's ideas have become relevant again – and such fears are now being repeated by leading representatives of science and the IT industry. "The development of full artificial intelligence could spell the end of the human race," – warned us the famous physicist Stephen Hawking in 2014 [11]. "First the machines will do a lot of jobs for us and not be super intelligent. That should be positive if we manage it well. A few decades after that though the intelligence is strong enough to be a concern," echoes Microsoft founder Bill Gates [12].

Tesla CEO Elon Musk has gone even further, allocating billions of dollars to these issues and, in particular, donating money to AI safety research at the Future of Life Institute [13] and comparing AI developers to exorcists armed with holy water while trying to tame a demon. "I think the danger of AI is much bigger than the danger of nuclear warheads by a lot," Musk said in 2018. "Nobody would suggest we allow the world to just build nuclear warheads if they want, that would be insane. And mark my words: AI is far more dangerous than nukes" [14].

4 Results and Discussion

The mentioned warnings, it seems, have experienced their realization when in the end of 2022 one of the forms of generative AI, ChatGPT version 4.0, was opened to the general public. In May 2023 several leaders of the A.I. industry had addressed both the public and the US leadership telling that the development of the technologies they are engaged in constitutes a threat to humanity and should be assessed as a public risk. In particular, executives of several leading A.I. companies, including Sam Altman of OpenAI, have signed an open letter warning of the risks [15]. A few months later Sam Altman has been dismissed from his position; according to several sources in the company, the OpenAI team informed the board of directors about progress in some developments shortly before that dismissal. It was about the Q-Star project – a supposed breakthrough in the development of AI that is said to be a neural network capable of performing tasks at the level of a living human (in particular, it could generalize, learn and understand). The team has emphasized the high skill of AI and the potential danger posed by highly intelligent machines, such as the fact that they could decide it is in their best interest to destroy humanity [16].

The situation with Sam Altman of OpenAI reveals an alarming truth – no one knows what "AI safety" means exactly. Thousands of scientists who have dedicated their lives to working on artificial intelligence disagree about whether today's systems think or will become capable of it. It could be said that the AI community is divided into factions, and while the one of them is concerned about the risks, the other one is keen to move forward. However, most researchers remain somewhere in the middle, striving to walk carefully, whatever that means. And OpenAI has long represented that middle way. The company had developed Dall-e, ChatGPT and other industry-leading products – all that was successful until the board of directors fired Sam Altman, recognizing the deadlock and hopelessness of this approach.

Many interpreted this as a signal of controversy over the safety of AI. But OpenAI employees were not convinced, and chaos ensued. In truth, no one outside the small inner circle knows what was the actual reason for the dismissal. There is a possibility that OpenAI was on the verge of inventing A.G.I. – the so called artificial general intelligence – universal and potentially autonomous form of AI – that the board of directors considered unsafe. And there is something absurd in this saga: it's amazing to see people in the AI industry acting so humanly – being impulsive, angry, and most of all simply confused.

But the worst thing is that the confusion has deep roots. How dangerous is artificial intelligence? How close are we to inventing A.G.I.? Who can we trust with its safety and how is this safety to be achieved? Nobody really knows the answers to these questions, and as a result, some of the most qualified people in the world are at war with each other. However, all experts recognize that modern artificial intelligence systems often work by noticing similarities and drawing analogies. People also think the same. When ChatGPT doesn't know the details of a story, it makes them up, and that's also a human tendency.

In movies like "The Terminator", curbing AI is as easy as blowing it up. But in the real world, control is exercised through corporate and financial means, so the interests of humanity are inevitably intertwined with commercial interests, like when OpenAI's board of directors decided to use its moderating power. But when the meaning of the warning is uncertain, everything becomes a judgment. One thing is for sure: no one will come and tell us how to control artificial intelligence. We will have to find the way ourselves.

And we would argue that in order to find that way we have to draw a clear distinction between humans and machines. Even if the discussions on the topic of "whether a machine could think" that were popular in the middle of the last century still remain actual for the present-day situation, the very nature of thinking is changed as information becomes the most widespread type of knowledge in the contemporary world. And if only a few decades ago "computers were human", as noted by David Grier [17], i.e. it was humans who performed all the task later taken on by the machines, then today there is a threat of human becoming computers, i.e. giving away their own way if thinking in favor of a more mechanical mode of reasoning.

Information could be defined as knowledge measured, codified, specially adapted for human-machine communication [18]. As Jean-François Lyotard argues, with the universal change of the technogenic civilization, the nature of knowledge cannot remain unchanged, it can become operational only if it is translated into some quantities of information: "On peut donc en tirer la prévision que tout ce qui dans le savoir constitué n'est pas ainsi traduisible sera délaissé, et que l'orientation des recherches nouvelles se subordonnera à la condition de traduisibilité des résultats éventuels en langage de machine" [19, p.13].

Thus, knowledge is alienated from humans, and the abstract nature of knowledge prevailing in today's society grows. For philosophical thought, in its pursuit of knowledge-wisdom, knowledge of the opposite type, uncodifiable and unmeasurable in bits, personal and concrete knowledge – the problem is that in today's society, information becomes the standard of the existence of knowledge itself. Information presupposes the non-human nature of its recipient – it does not address humans in their human qualities. Oriented towards communication with machines, abstract knowledge-information contributes to the self-alienation of a person, transforming humans into a semblance of a machine.

These remarks regarding the life in today's society are not idle reflections of past dystopians but a reality that we can trace in our own everyday lives. Our life is practically unthinkable now without various technical devices with which we communicate in the depersonalized language of information and which, naturally, respond to us in the same way. Designed to make human life easier, these machines have to some extent usurped the roles and meanings of many distinctly human feelings and qualities. For example, our impressions and memories are alienated from us in the form of photographs and videos; we have almost forgotten how to experience directly, having learned to postpone our experience of an event until the viewing of the corresponding information recorded by a technical device. Currently, as shown by the French philosopher Bernard Stiegler, there has been a connection between globalization, technology (material transformation systems), and 'mnemotechnics' (that is, memory technologies that represents not only memory but also the ability to perceive, feel, experience, alienated from a person and materialized with the help of various technical devices).

With the help of the latest mobile communication means, a person finds him- or herself in a continuous process of communication, and therefore, in an eternal state of receiving information – a kind of knowledge taken in the process of its transmission from one person or machine to another, at a frozen state suspended outside of any context. These are simply maximally neutral 'data' devoid of any meaningful or axiological dimension. Moreover, it turns out that the continuity of this state of information as knowledge in the eternal process of communication, knowledge that cannot acquire its human recipient – this characteristic feature of information allows us to doubt its ability to be correlated with meaning at all. In addition, the person often gets lost in this process of data transmission. For example, global positioning systems based on satellite observation, such as GPS, designed to facilitate human's orientation in unfamiliar terrain, lead to the fact that a person acquires this orientation only in a virtual information space; as Bernard Stiegler notes, "the user also becomes data, travelling through 'data landscapes'" [20].

However, the situation is not at all that hopeless, and it is philosophy, humanities and higher education that can help humans to remain themselves without risking being transformed into machines, as well as without believing too much in AI leading humanity to extinction. The very idea of the technological singularity, which serves as a kind of profound ground for envisioning said fears, does not give justice to human thinking – as shown by Adriana Braga and Robert Logan, that idea does not take into account the full dimension of human intelligence: human intelligence is not based solely on logical operations and computation, and so no computer can ever duplicate the intelligence of a human being because of its many dimensions that involve characteristics that cannot be duplicated by AI [21, p.133].

Such an approach can in fact serve as a base for the humanistic core of higher education and its philosophical foundations: in order for the higher education to educate humans able to live in the age of AI, it has to shape and to develop human personality, as well as to be fully aware of the self-worth of personalities of each student in order to ensure his or her status as a full subject of the educational process. It is the humanist and personalistic approach in higher education that could be the ground for the formation of critical thinking, and the ability to deal with any surprises of the unstable and complex world that only humans can deal with [22].

On the other hand, it becomes clear that humans can't deal with the world of unpredictability alone, but with the help of machines, provided the noted clear distinction between the two ways of thinking is being made so the symbiosis of humans and computers is based on human control over the machines. When universities argue that the current 4th industrial revolution (4IR) should be given serious and close attention, it means that they can no longer rely on traditional forms of thinking and imagination only, but they also need a kind of thinking that depends on combining algorithmic computing of machines or forms of technology with humanist critical thinking.

In this sense, 4IR has changed not only what we do and how we do it, but also who we have become. As shown by Nuraan Davids and Yusef Waghid, the point is not that machines have come to replace man in the strict sense, but that people have become embodied in machines: we have to turn to questions about human connections in the era of paradoxical strengthening of connections between people [23, p.56]. The solution is thus humanizing machines, not making machines out of humans nor opposing humans to computers as some alienate or alternative forms of intelligence that can be a threat to each other's existence [22, 24, 25].

5 Conclusions

We can now summarize that under the described conditions people need essentially new knowledge and skills to use the new technologies and to work effectively with them. AI cannot think openly and critically – it follows or imitates humans, and the aspect of cultural values gains more importance, as the main threat of the current situation lies in our inability to be humans and to control AI. Given the growing importance of the 'human factor', humanistic dimensions come to the fore when defining higher education strategies for the sustainable development of civilization.

According to the UN 2030 Agenda for Sustainable Development, education and science are to offer practical mechanisms for achieving and ensuring inclusive, fair and high-quality education and training, promoting all opportunities for education and training throughout life. In order to achieve that task, all levels, models and systems of education must be transformed through education for sustainable development – made ready to provide students with knowledge and skills that are necessary for sustainable development, including sustainable lifestyle, human rights, gender equality, promoting a culture of peace and nonviolence, global citizenship education and recognition of cultural diversity and the contribution of culture to sustainable development.

The mission of the universities of the 21st century is to form a developed personality, a person of high cultural level who can act in a situation characterized by significant environmental risks. A graduate of higher education, who is able to carry out successful life activities under such conditions and act as a subject of the implementation of sustainable development guidelines, should possess not only and not so much individual professional competences, but such general qualities as the ability to solve problems, the ability to perform critical, independent and original thinking and the ability to generate new knowledge and act in a situation of uncertainty and complexity, when any ready-made knowledge or instructions are unavailable.

A few years ago, Jaan Tallinn (Estonian billionaire programmer and investor, co-founder of Skype and one of the first investors and board members of DeepMind) gave the "CSaP Distinguished Lecture" on evolution, innovation, artificial intelligence (AI) and the future of humanity. The lecture was absolutely prophetic and was called "The Ladder of Intelligence – Why the Future May Not Need Us" [28]. Tallinn presented the "Ladder of Intelligence" model], which describes the development of agents who control the future of the Earth as each of them is replaced by another agent of its own creation. Homo sapiens is a third-stage agent (of which there are only 7). The generation of people is a multifaceted agent of the 4th stage, which we call "technical progress". He will have, as Tallinn prophesied, to create stage 5 – a new type of intelligence AGI, with which people will coexist on the planet. However, the followers of AGI – agents of the 6th and 7th stages – will become an existential threat to humanity.

It is therefore not surprising that Jaan Tallinn is now co-founder of the Center for the Study of Existential Risk (CSER) at the University of Cambridge. And he recommends viewing what is happening now in the field of AI not as a technological revolution, but as the emergence on Earth of a new non-biological species – AGI.

The new non-biological species is completely different from people: neither externally nor essentially. However, from the point of view of intellectual abilities, it will become more and more difficult to distinguish between their specific representatives every month.

This rather dire forecast from Tallinn was confirmed by the results of the authoritative study An Empirical Study & Evaluation of Modern CAPTCHAs [29]. Researchers have convincingly shown that the most common reverse Turing test, the CAPTCHA, recognized for distinguishing humans from algorithms, has been irrevocably disavowed.

At the same time, pay attention to the rate of evolution of a new non-biological species.

- Even earlier this year, GPT-4 had to trick a person into solving a captcha.
- Six months later, the study found that bots were able to outperform humans in both solution time and accuracy, regardless of CAPTCHA type.

Having lost the captcha, people become algorithmically indistinguishable from AI in digital reality. Considering that indistinguishability has already been achieved in physical reality, it turns out that people and the undead are now generally indistinguishable – neither for people nor for algorithms.

And therefore, the time is approaching when, at the next step in the evolutionary ladder of intelligence, humans will have to give way to AI.

AI technologies should be envisioned not as a threat to human existence, but not as an independent autonomous form of technology either – it should be controlled by humans and used in particular as a tool that can enable open and personalized education. Thus, the topic for future research constitutes using AI-based technologies in higher education and particular in such task as managing and administering higher education and other forms of activities performed by HEIs, thus freeing humans to more creative and more humane jobs and tasks.

Disclosure of Interests. The authors have no competing interests to declare that are relevant to the content of this article.

References

1. Transforming our world: the 2030 Agenda for sustainable development. United Nations General Assembly. https://sdgs.un.org/2030agenda. Accessed 03 Jan 2024
2. Zinchenko, V.V.: Concepts and trends of global institutional transformations in the context of educational and scientific internationalization, In: Shevchuk, D., (ed.) Quo vadis, University?, pp. 183–197. Publishing House of the National University "Ostroz'ka Academia", Ostrog (2020). (In Ukrainian)
3. Parisi, L.: Instrumentality, or the Time of Inhuman Thinking. Technosphere Magazine. https://technosphere-magazine.hkw.de/p/Instrumentality-or-the-Time-of-Inhuman-Thi nking-5UvwaECXmmYev25GrmEBhX. Accessed 03 Jan 2024
4. Digital Education Action Plan (2021–2027). Commission Staff Working Document: Resetting education and training for the digital age. https://education.ec.europa.eu/sites/default/files/doc ument-library-docs/deap-swd-sept2020_en.pdf. Accessed 03 Jan 2024
5. de Witt, C., Rampelt, F., Pinkwart, N. (eds.): Das Whitepaper «Künstliche Intelligenz in der Hochschulbildung. Whitepaper. KI-Campus, Berlin (2020)
6. Lindblad, J.: Människan: du, jag och den ursprungliga. Bonniers, Stockholm (1987)
7. McCurry, J.: Japanese bank introduces robot workers to deal with customers in branches. https://www.theguardian.com/world/2015/feb/04/japanese-bank-introduces-robot-workers-to-deal-with-customers-in-branches. Accessed 03 Jan 2024
8. Gaiman, N.: Why our future depends on libraries, reading and daydreaming. https://www.theguardian.com/books/2013/oct/15/neil-gaiman-future-libraries-reading-daydreaming. Accessed 03 Jan 2024
9. Good, I.J.: Speculations concerning the first ultraintelligent machine. Adv. Comput. **6**, 31–88 (1966)
10. Koch, C.: When computers surpass us. Sci. Am. **26**(5), 26–29 (2015)
11. Stephen Hawking warns artificial intelligence could end mankind. https://www.bbc.com/news/technology-30290540. Accessed 03 Jan 2024
12. Holley, P.: Bill Gates on dangers of artificial intelligence: «I don't understand why some people are not concerned». https://www.washingtonpost.com/news/the-switch/wp/2015/01/28/bill-gates-on-dangers-of-artificial-intelligence-dont-understand-why-some-people-are-not-concerned. Accessed 03 Jan 2024
13. Suciu, P.: Musk Donates $10 Million to Keep AI From Going Rogue. https://www.technewsworld.com/story/82239.html. Accessed 03 Jan 2024
14. Matousek, M.: Elon Musk said people who don't think AI could be smarter than them are «way dumber than they think they are». https://www.businessinsider.com/elon-musk-smart-people-doubt-ai-dumber-than-they-think-2020-7. Accessed 03 Jan 2024
15. Roose, K.: A.I. poses 'risk of extinction,' industry leaders warn, The New York Times. https://www.nytimes.com/2023/05/30/technology/ai-threat-warning.html. Accessed 03 Jan 2024
16. Tong, A., Dastin, J., Hu, K.: OpenAI researchers warned board of AI breakthrough ahead of CEO ouster, sources say. https://www.reuters.com/technology/sam-altmans-ouster-openai-was-precipitated-by-letter-board-about-ai-breakthrough-2023-11-22/. Accessed 03 Jan 2024
17. Grier, D.A.: When Computers Were Human. Princeton University Press, Princeton (2005)
18. Mielkov, Y.: Knowledge in the age of information: human values in science and higher education. New Explor. Stud. Culture Commun. **2**(3), 28–39 (2022)
19. Lyotard, J.F.: La condition postmoderne: rapport sur le savoir. Éditions de Minuit, Paris (1979)
20. Siegler, B.: Our ailing educational institutions. Culture Machine. https://web.archive.org/web/20040711060841/http://culturemachine.tees.ac.uk/Cmach/Backissues/j005/Articles/Stiegler.htm. Accessed 03 Jan 2024

21. Braga, A., Logan, R.K.: The singularity hoax: why computers will never be more intelligent than humans. In: Hofkirchner, W., Kreowski, H.-J. (eds.) Transhumanism: The Proper Guide to a Posthuman Condition or a Dangerous Idea? CT, pp. 133–140. Springer, Cham (2021). https://doi.org/10.1007/978-3-030-56546-6_9
22. Mielkov, Y., Bakhov, I., Bilyakovska, O., Kostenko, L., Nych, T.: Higher education strategies for the 21st century: philosophical foundations and the humanist approach. Revista Tempos E Espaços Em Educação **14**(33), e15524 (2021)
23. Davids, N., Waghid, Y.: Teaching, Friendship and Humanity (Briefs in Citizenship Education for the 21st Century). Springer, Heidelberg (2020)
24. Zinchenko, V.V.: The institutionalization of global strategies for the transformation of society and education in the context of critical theory. Anthropol. Meas. Philos. Res. **7**, 50–66 (2015)
25. Zinchenko, V.V.: New dimensions and dead ends in AI development: impact and responsibility of science and higher education. In: E3S Web of Conferences, vol. 419, no. 3, p. 02001 (2023)
26. Chen, L., Zaharia, M., Zou, J.: How is ChatGPT's behavior changing over time? (2023). arXiv: 2307.09009v3 [cs.CL]. https://arxiv.org/abs/2307.09009
27. Narayanan, A., Kapoor, S. Is GPT-4 getting worse over time?, https://www.aisnakeoil.com/p/is-gpt-4-getting-worse-over-time?
28. The Intelligence Stairway – why the future might not need us. https://www.csap.cam.ac.uk/news/article-intelligence-stairway-why-future-might-not-need-us/
29. Searles, A., Nakatsuka, Y., Ozturk, E., Paverd, A., Tsudik, A., Enkoji, A.: An empirical study & evaluation of modern CAPTCHAs. arXiv:2307.12108 (cs). https://arxiv.org/abs/2307.12108. Accessed 22 Jul 2023

Correction to: Pathway Analysis of the Dynamics of Teacher Educators' Professional Digital Competence

Siri Sollied Madsen📧, Heidi I. Saure📧, Marit H. Lie📧, Aleksander Janeš📧, Andreja Klančar📧, Rita Brito📧, and Steinar Thorvaldsen📧

Correction to:
Chapter 4 in: Ł. Tomczyk (Ed.): *New Media Pedagogy, CCIS 2130*
https://doi.org/10.1007/978-3-031-63235-8_4

The following chapter was originally published electronically on the publisher's internet portal without open access:

"Pathway Analysis of the Dynamics of Teacher Educators' Professional Digital Competence", written by Siri Sollied Madsen, Heidi I. Saure, Marit H. Lie, Aleksander Janeš, Andreja Klančar, Rita Brito, and Steinar Thorvaldsen.

The updated version of this chapter can be found at
https://doi.org/10.1007/978-3-031-63235-8_4

© The Author(s) 2024
Ł. Tomczyk (Ed.): NMP 2023, CCIS 2130, p. C1, 2024.
https://doi.org/10.1007/978-3-031-63235-8_30

Author Index

© The Editor(s) (if applicable) and The Author(s), under exclusive license
to Springer Nature Switzerland AG 2024
Ł. Tomczyk (Ed.): NMP 2023, CCIS 2130, pp. 455–456, 2024.
https://doi.org/10.1007/978-3-031-63235-8

Services